Weimar

PHILOSOPHY, SOCIAL THEORY, AND THE RULE OF LAW

General Editors
Andrew Arato, Seyla Benhabib, Ferenc Fehér, William Forbath,
Agnes Heller, Arthur J. Jacobson, and Michel Rosenfeld

Weimar

A Jurisprudence of Crisis

Arthur J. Jacobson

AND

Bernhard Schlink

EDITORS

TRANSLATED BY

Belinda Cooper

WITH

Peter C. Caldwell, Stephen Cloyd, David Dyzenhaus,
Stephan Hemetsberger, Arthur J. Jacobson, and Bernhard Schlink

UNIVERSITY OF CALIFORNIA PRESS
Berkeley   Los Angeles   London

University of California Press
Berkeley and Los Angeles, California

University of California Press, Ltd.
London, England

Library of Congress Cataloging-in-Publication Data

Weimar : a jurisprudence of crisis / edited by Arthur J. Jacobson and Bernhard Schlink;
translated by Belinda Cooper with Peter C. Caldwell . . . [et al.].

    p.   cm. — (Philosophy, social theory, and the rule of law ; 8)
Includes bibliographical references and index.
ISBN 0-520-22059-5 (cloth : alk. paper)
    1. Constitutional history—Germany—Sources. 2. Constitutional law—
Germany—Philosophy—History—Sources. 3. State, The—History—Sources.
4. Germany—Politics and government—1918–1933—Sources. I. Jacobson,
Arthur J. II. Schlink, Bernhard. III. Series.
KK4710. W45 2000
342.43′029′09042—dc21   00-037772

Manufactured in the United States of America

09 08 07 06 05 04 03 02 01 00

10 9 8 7 6 5 4 3 2 1

For Peninah Petruck

CONTENTS

PREFACE

We began work on the Weimar jurisprudence of crisis almost ten years ago, soon after the fall of the Berlin Wall. Our hope was that the Weimar debates would provide a unique vantage from which to survey states throughout the world struggling to embrace political democracy and a liberal legal culture. Weimar offers a dark but useful paradigm for states in which constitutionalism and the rule of law must confront lasting and entrenched anti-democratic and anti-liberal forces. Nations in which the state precedes the constitution face significantly different and perhaps more difficult paths toward constitutional government than nations, such as the United States, in which the constitution precedes the state.

We have been lucky in our collaborators, especially our lead translator, Belinda Cooper, who helped wrestle some extremely difficult texts into English. Our contributing editors gave generously of their knowledge and patience. Our colleagues, Michel Rosenfeld, Paul Shupack, and Charles Yablon, provided critical assistance at crucial moments in our work on the introduction. Susanne Leiterer's assistance on the technical apparatus was painstaking and invaluable.

We owe special thanks to the former dean of the Benjamin N. Cardozo School of Law, Frank Macchiarola, for his support and for helping to provide precious time together in New York to work on the project. The Charney Program in International Law and the International Law Program, both of the Benjamin N. Cardozo School of Law, helped finance the translations.

Dorothea Muenchberg of the Humboldt University Faculty of Law Secretariat shouldered the immense burden of coordination with precision and kindness.

Edward Dimendberg, formerly of the University of California Press, was our persistent and encouraging editor. His enthusiasm for Weimar helped sustain many years of collaboration.

TRANSLATION AND APPARATUS

Translation is always choice, and translation of texts in legal theory faces double the ordinary difficulty of choosing. The translator faces the usual task of rendering German thoughts that all too often do not "think" in English, when differences in cultural tradition and linguistic habits propel thinking in different directions. But the translator of legal theory must also make available the words, ideas, and themes of a legal system and theory that map the world in ways that are not easily comprehensible to those steeped in the common law tradition. Unlike most specialized fields of knowledge, law and legal theory have languages and sets of principles and understandings that are not wholly universal. A theorem by Carl Friedrich Gauss on the algebra of groups, once translated, can be thoroughly grasped by any adequately trained mathematician. But the translation of an essay in *Staatsrechtslehre* by Triepel or Thoma, Kelsen or Schmitt, can be fully understood only if it makes the relevant portions of German law and legal theory transparent to readers in a different tradition.

In editing the translations in this volume, we have tried as far as possible to make the ideas and spirit of the works transparent to the educated reader of English. When direct and plain translations of the German words accomplish this purpose, we have used them, despite some awkwardness in the music. Often enough, however, direct and plain translation successfully communicates the stylistic power and passion of the original German. When direct and plain translation is impossible, either because English does not think the German thought or because an institution of German law or legal theory does not exist in the same way in the common law tradition, then we have been forced to craft a suitably transparent English substitute. In so doing, we have avoided using lengthy notes describing German legal institutions. Rather, we have insisted on finding formulations that transparently convey the institutions in the text itself.

Besides transparency, our guiding principle has been consistency within texts, and from text to text. The *Rechtsstaat*, whether used by Heller or Schmitt, remains the "state based on the rule of law," even though Heller and Schmitt bring to it vastly different attitudes and meanings. It is precisely consistency that allows one to map variations in attitude that Weimar theorists had toward their common legal and theoretical heritage. At the same time, consistency must sometimes yield to a lack of congruence between German and English terms. For example, *Herrschaft* is almost always "domination," but *Majoritätsherrschaft* must be "majority rule," as "domination by a majority" would be too odd a departure from the standard English. We have usually chosen, nonetheless, to tolerate oddness in order to achieve the virtue of consistency.

In the same spirit of transparency and consistency we have updated the citations in the works of the Weimar theorists to conform to modern practice. We have also included citations to modern editions, unavailable during Weimar, so that readers may have broader access to the rich literature upon which Weimar theorists drew. To that end, the writers of the introductions have compiled the main works of the theorists and the significant scholarly commentary.

Unless otherwise indicated, the translator is Belinda Cooper. The general editors have reviewed each translation for consistency, accuracy, and style. The introductory essays by Peter C. Caldwell, Stephen Cloyd, and David Dyzenhaus, and parts of the general introduction, were originally written in English.

Constitutional Crisis

The German and the American Experience

Arthur J. Jacobson and Bernhard Schlink

German legal theory in the Weimar period focused on what in Germany is known as the "law of the state" [*Staatsrecht*]. Though Weimar had a rich private law culture, the distinctive contribution of its legal theorists was to the law of the state. For the law of the state was in crisis in Weimar. It was in crisis because the state was in crisis for all but a brief period from the inception of the Weimar Republic in 1919 until its demise in 1933.

That a crisis of the state should result in a crisis of the law framing and founding it is not self-evident; certainly the American experience is to the contrary. Crises of the American state have never led political elites to question the legitimacy of constitutional government.[1] Even the extraordinary struggles leading up to the Civil War did not cast doubt on the legitimacy of constitutional government itself. They were the ordinary, even if ultimately violent, struggles of constitutional interpretation, rather than a sustained search for a fundamentally different principle of political organization. Even secession was justified on the basis of fidelity to the constitutional document. The American Revolution established beyond practical challenge that government is conceivable only as constitutional government, "one whose powers have been adapted to the interests of its people and to the maintenance of individual liberty."[2] The American state is the creature of a constitution framed by the people through its representatives. It is inconceivable upon any other basis. The constitution precedes the state, logically and temporally. This is the traditional American understanding of the nature and source of the state's law and power.

The German state, by contrast, precedes the constitution. It does so historically—the state as object of the monarch's will and power was there before any constitution could frame or found it—and the course of history has guided legal thinking. Until the Federal Republic [*Bundesrepublik*] the constitution was understood not as founding and framing the state, but rather as shaping and limiting the inherently unlimited powers of an already existing political organization. The constitution derived its legitimacy from the state, not the state from the constitution. This understanding has shifted only in the Federal Republic, under the Basic Law of 1949 [*Grundgesetz*]. Only under the Basic Law has the term "law of the state," as the name for a field of law, legal learning, and teaching, gradually been replaced by the term "constitutional law" [*Verfassungsrecht*]. Nevertheless, the systematic textbooks on constitutional law from which students learn are still presented under the title "Law of the State," and the Association of Professors of Constitutional Law still bears the name "Association of German Teachers of the Law of the State" [*Vereinigung der Deutschen Staatsrechtslehrer*]. Moreover, the choice between calling the law governing the state *Staatsrecht* (the word the political right tends to prefer) and *Verfassungsrecht* (the left) still has powerful resonance in German politics. Germany has still not definitively and unambiguously—without residue from the past—foreclosed the possibility of a law of the state animated by other than constitutional principles.

In Germany, as a result, a crisis of the state can produce discourses to challenge and compete with constitutional discourse. Certainly it did when a German state founded on strictly constitutional principles was young, in the Weimar Republic. In the United States, it is precisely the most divisive political questions—the ones the political system cannot answer in strictly political terms through political mechanisms—that are framed as constitutional questions. Political crisis only strengthens constitutionalism. It has never put the idea of a constitution itself in jeopardy. Political crisis in Weimar, in contrast, was hardly constitution-affirming. But by threatening constitutionalism, political crisis made those Weimar theorists who defended it pursue a profound inquiry into the preconditions of constitutional government.

The work of the Weimar theorists had passionate urgency for another reason as well. German legal scholarship [*Rechtswissenschaft*] attempts to be at once theoretical and practical, to craft doctrine [*Dogmatik*] to reflect the state of legal theory and at the same time guide legal practice—be it the practice of courts, attorneys, administrators, or legislators. In the United States, judicial or doctrinal practice and the elaboration of theories in a field of law are more or less independent from each other. American judges just muddle through by a mix, characteristic of common law jurisdictions, of pragmatic reasoning, policy argument, sound common sense, and the mastery of an aesthetic of rules. Very few believe that direct reference to theory commends the soundness of decision.[3] As a result, lawyers and judges make almost no demands on legal theorists, and legal theorists—especially American legal realists and their successors in Critical Legal Studies—have responded in kind, attacking the very possibility of coherent doctrinal decision making. German judges cannot ignore theory. They make demands on theorists, and theorists, to earn their salt, must respond to the demands. Strains in doctrinal practice inevitably show up as strains in legal theory. When the law of the state was in crisis in Weimar, the theory of the law of the state had to be in crisis as well.

Of course, legal scholarship on the German model can have a more theoretical or a more practical bent, and legal philosophy, history, doctrine, and practice are not the same. Doctrine, to be sure, is always there as a switch yard guiding theoretical, philosophical, and historical legal knowledge into practical advice, putting practical problems into theoretical perspective; and scholarship concerning state law [*Staatsrechtswissenschaft*] is, in principle, as doctrinal as legal scholarship in general. Nevertheless, because state law scholarship developed in the late nineteenth and early twentieth centuries when there were no courts and no court practice dealing with state law, its theoretical side was stronger than those of other fields of law. This justifies translating *Staatsrechtwissenschaft* briefly as "theory of the law of the state" or "state law theory," when *Wissenschaft* ordinarily refers more broadly to a knowledge of practice as well as to theoretical knowledge.

Two events in this century have left a decisive mark on the theory of the law of the state in Germany: the "struggle over methods and aims" [*Methoden- und Richtungsstreit*] during the Weimar period, and the introduction of far-reaching judicial control by the Federal Constitutional Court [*Bundesverfassungsgericht*] in the Federal Republic. The decisive significance of the second event is obvious: The theory of the law of the state plays theoretical and practical orientations, methods, and themes in different keys, when faced (or not) with a constitutional court and court practice. The significance of the struggle over methods and aims is not as obvious. Some of its problems and consequences have indeed been settled by the establishment of a constitutional jurisdiction. But because it was caused by a crisis of the state and developed into a jurisprudence of crisis, whenever the state and the law of the state are threatened or even touched by crisis, interest in the Weimar struggle reemerges.

Weimar is the only period in German history before the Federal Republic, apart from a few months in 1848, when theorizing about the law of the state took place in a democratic political context. Thus the Weimar debates about the law of the state play a role today in Germany reminiscent of the role of *The Federalist* in the United States: They are an essential source for thinking about the foundation of a German democratic state and, like the *The Federalist,* have universal significance as well.

I

When a theory struggles for new methods, then the old ones have become fragile. When it strives to determine anew the direction it ought to follow, then the direction followed so far has lost its clarity and orienting power. The theory is in crisis.

The struggle over methods and aims in the Weimar Republic was conducted in the consciousness, and under the rubric, of crisis. Along with Kaufmann, Schmitt, Smend, and Heller, state law theorists who had turned against the theoretical tradition handed down from the Empire spoke of crisis. However, even those who continued the imperial tradition and maintained a dominant position in the spectrum of theoretical opinion were conscious that the situation was one of change and rupture. Their consciousness assumed less a fighting, than a resigned expression. Anschütz, the most prominent traditionalist, saw old views returning in the new currents— views he had considered, until then, outstripped and vanquished. "All at once, I must consider myself now very old-fashioned, where I had earlier intended to represent progress. The world is changing."[4]

That the crisis in state law theory was connected with changes in state and society brought about by the First World War was generally known. Yet, views on how this connection should be understood differed. Only seldom were the real factors underlying the changes studied—the social condition and economic and political opportunities of the bourgeoisie, working class, and aristocracy before, during, and after the world war; the respective power and roles of the military; and the bureaucracy. Nor was the significance of these factors for the situation of the state, its constitution and theory, realistically [*wirklichkeitswissenschaftlich*] analyzed. An idealist viewpoint spread, in which the experience of ideals and values was more important than reality. "The experiences that our nation [*Volk*], and we along with it, have had in war, in collapse, in revolution, and under the Versailles Treaty, domestically and in foreign policy, have shaken us violently awake and led to immense self-reflection. These experiences have forced us to subject our thinking on law and the state to fresh examination."[5] These words of Kaufmann's demonstrate in two ways the connection between transformations in state and society and the crisis of state law theory: The transformations themselves are less interesting than the experiences they occasioned, and more interesting than the experiences is the process of self-reflection and reexamination in the theory of the law of the state that the experiences awakened.

But the law of the state is too political for political changes to claim recognition in theory only if comprehended and analyzed correctly. The realist or idealist, normative and positivist, or anti-normative and anti-positivist theoretical tendencies of state law theory were themselves reactions to and recognitions of the political changes—various attempts to grasp and master them. State law theory in the Empire had already been geared to this political situation—to the specific, precarious balance of power that the bourgeoisie, the monarch, and the aristocracy had found in the Empire. After the collapse of this balance of power, a new constellation of power had to be found. What positions the bourgeoisie could assert and the working class achieve; whether, for example, the working class could be integrated into the bourgeois social and economic order of the Weimar Republic, or whether civil war was ultimately unavoidable and ought to be prepared for; how the strength of the German Reich was to be regained in foreign affairs, and how the necessary internal unity for this was to be engendered; whether the state and constitutional order would lay out a framework and establish rules for impending conflicts over power and distribution or would become merely a plaything in those conflicts—these fundamental political questions of the changing Weimar situation were condensed into the struggle over methods and aims in the law of the state. How, from a methodological standpoint, the relationship between the crisis in state law theory and changes in state and society was to be viewed, was itself an element in the struggle over correct answers to these basic political questions.

The Empire's balance of power and its condensation at the time in state law theory—the starting point for the Weimar struggle over methods and aims—were the result of the defeat of the bourgeois revolution of 1848–49 and the military successes of the Prussian monarchy in 1866 and 1870–71. After that, the German bourgeoisie could no longer hope for quick achievement of its demands through its own strength. The monarchy was responsible for fulfilling its demand for unity with the creation of the German Empire and its demand for democracy with the institution of the Reichstag as the Empire's parliament. But the demands were indeed only half fulfilled, or even deflected and reversed. According to the constitution, the unity of the German Reich was derived not from the unity of the people, but from a league [Bund] of monarchs, and the Reichstag not only was faced with a government dependent on the monarch, a monarchic administration, and a monarchic military but also had to share lawmaking with the monarchic Bundesrat, a council of delegates from the mostly monarchic German states. True, laws could not be made without the Reichstag and contrary to its wishes. True, the second half of the Empire saw tendencies toward parliamentarization that increasingly led to the chancellor's de facto dependency on the Reichstag. Overall, however, the Reichstag's potential for action and influence, its responsibility and readiness to take responsibility, remained small. Furthermore, the bourgeoisie was less and less ready to act as an opposition during the second half of the Empire for fear of an increasingly strong working class, organized in the Social Democratic movement. In the mid-nineteenth century, the bourgeoisie had united all progressive and revolutionary energies. By the end of the century, it had to count on becoming the victim of revolutionary change instead of being its bearer.

In the Empire, state law theory was a bourgeois theory, a theory of bourgeois jurists mirroring the situation of the bourgeoisie and its transformations. In the contest between Paul Laband—who limited state law theory to the deployment of legal concepts and constructions and to the interpretation of positive, statutory law, vigorously screening out political and philosophical content[6]—and Otto von Gierke—who understood state and law as an organism and attempted to penetrate this organism legally, politically, and philosophically[7]—Laband emerged victorious. But this did not reflect a victory of the conservative and monarchist over the progressive and democratic principle, as is occasionally represented. The concept of an organism can accompany a demand that state action derive from society and from the life and activity of the people rather than from the will of the monarch, as well as authoritarian ideas that dictate to each person a rigid, confined place in the structure of the whole, and both shimmer throughout von Gierke's work. On the other side, a purely legal, positivist way of thinking focusing merely on the technical consistency of law leaves no room for conservative and monarchic legitimation and mystification. Thus Laband saw the monarch as a function only, the relationship of civil servants and officers to the monarch as one of function, not loyalty, the German Reich as a legal person, not as a league of princes. The positivist theory of the law of the state viewed state institutions above all from the viewpoint of limits. The lawmaking power of the Reichstag was limited by the Bundesrat, but, at the same time, the power of the monarchic administration to interfere with the freedom and property of citizens was limited by the requirement of statutory authorization. Thus positivist theory protected the freedom both of individual citizen and bourgeois economy against the monarchic state. It was, to this extent, individualist and liberal. It took the balance among the bourgeoisie and monarch and aristocracy fashioned in 1871 as a given while denuding it, on the one hand, of its elegant, traditional, and monarchic facade and, on the other, renouncing every democratic, parliamentary perspective. Thus it acquired a progressive quality for conservative forces and a conservative quality for progressive forces. Like political acceptance of the balance, it could go hand in hand with resignation over the failure of the original bourgeois demands, with apolitical saturation, or with fear of revolutionary change in the political status quo brought about by the proletariat. When toward the end of the Empire the constitutional balance was experienced as endangered by the constant growth of the Social Democratic electorate, the foolishness of the personal rule of Wilhelm II and, during the world war, the uncontrolled and uncontrollable primacy of the military, doubt was also cast upon the positivist theory of the law of the state. Groundwork for critique of the positivist concept, while fully developed in the Weimar Republic, was laid and occasionally even expressed in the late Empire.

Critique was, for one thing, anti-normative and anti-formalist. In the Empire, positivist theory had been attuned to the constitutional balance, without reflecting its attunement. It acted as though the concepts and constructions it developed, with which it interpreted and deployed positive law, had nothing to do with political conditions—as though it stood by itself. It regulated the interpretation and deployment of norms for the law of the state more according to the command that concepts and constructions be formally and technically consistent than according to a correct understanding of political substance, of political constellations and conflicts governed by norms. What, critique reproached, could a theory of the law of the state handled in such a manner contribute to mastering the political changes brought about by the world war? Nothing? The state and the law of the state were in upheaval, and the theory of the law of the state could say nothing about it—was forced to be silent?

Critique during the Weimar Republic was, for another thing, anti-liberal and anti-individualist. For the positivist theory of the law of the state, the freedom of the individual had been not a political freedom of participation, but an apolitical freedom, not a freedom *in* the state, but *from* the state. What, critique again reproached, could this individualism and liberalism contribute to mastering the upheavals that were taking place? Was not responsibility for the state more necessary now than freedom from it, adaptation to the community more important than the preservation of individualist distance? Liberal ideas seemed to have value only for a social class that was

> not itself in possession of state power, but that aspires to protect itself with the help of liberal institutions against the state and its bearers of domination. Consequently, while these ideas were necessary for the German bourgeoisie during the Empire, they lost all meaning for its champions the moment the bourgeoisie itself seized state power. In this new situation, liberal ideas and arrangements even threatened to become a weapon against the bourgeoisie—a weapon in the hands of the proletariat, which could protect itself against abuse of power with the help of liberal precautions and achieve participation in ruling with the help of the parliamentary system.[8]

This quotation is from an analysis of the crisis of state law theory written in 1931, at the height of the crisis of the Weimar Republic. The analysis saw the political system as already failed, its social and economic foundations as already destroyed. It saw "political society transformed . . . in a battle of social opponents for state power" and state law theory ensnared in that battle. In fact, state law theory at the end of the Weimar Republic was as much a theory in crisis as it was at the beginning. The short history of the Weimar Republic[9] is above all a history of its crises, and the short history of the doctrinal and theoretical elaboration of the law of the state in the Weimar Republic is no less so.

Certainly one must not neglect or fail to mention that changes in the doctrinal and theoretical elaboration of the law of the state were also encouraged by changes in the law of the state and constitutional law. Even without its crises, the Weimar Republic presented state law theory with new challenges. The constitution of the Empire had contained only laws of organization; the Weimar Constitution [*Weimarer Reichsverfassung*] also contained basic rights. In its laws of organization, the constitution of the Empire had left state power in the hands of a monarchic executive, granting the Reichstag only limited shares; the Weimar Constitution developed a complicated interplay among the Reichstag, the president of the Reich [*Reichspräsident*] and the government of the Reich [*Reichsregierung*]. The constitution of the Empire had not known any sort of constitutional jurisdiction; the Weimar Constitution assigned the Federal Supreme Court [*Reichsgericht*] as the court for disputes over the law of the state [*Staatsgerichtshof*], at least the beginnings of a constitutional jurisdiction. State law theory consequently had more fields to cultivate and faced more practical problems, from giving political advice to representing clients in court. The upshot of this was, among other things, the replacement of systematic textbooks on the law of the state, committed above all to a theoretical perspective, by constitutional commentaries serving practical needs. The fact that the Weimar Constitution came mainly from the pen of a scholar of state law theory is another obvious expression of the different relations between the theory and the practice of the law of the state. Bismarck had written the constitution of the Empire.

II

The Weimar Constitution was the result of the German defeat in the First World War. Defeat had spelled the end of the institution of the Kaiser and single-state dynasties and brought about a revolution in which a parliamentary and democratic future was by no means self-evident; on the contrary, elements on the left strove for a soviet republic on the model of Soviet Russia. In this situation, the Council of People's Delegates [*Rat der Volksbeauftragten*] under Friedrich Ebert, formed on 9 November 1918 in Berlin by representatives of the German Social Democratic Party [*Sozialdemokratische Partei Deutschlands,* SPD] and the Independent German Social Democratic Party [*Unabhängige Sozialdemokratische Partei Deutschlands,* USPD] that had split off from it, decided in favor of the rapid convocation of a constituent National Assembly.[10] This was elected in January 1919 and, because of the uncertain situation in Berlin, met in Weimar in February 1919. Meanwhile, important precedents for the future system had already been established. Constitution-making by a National Assembly meant rejection of the revolutionary establishment of a soviet republic. The provisional loyalty of troops returning from the front, which Ebert had assured in an agreement with General Groener in November 1918, meant the exclusion of a conservative or reactionary revolution. Trade unions and employers had concluded a sort of truce in the Stinnes-Legin Pact of November 1918, in which they came to an understanding about their mutual recognition as partners in the negotiation of industrywide terms and conditions of employment and had agreed to the introduction of an eight-hour day—the Weimar Constitution took this up in its provisions on economic councils [*Wirtschaftsräte*], paying a small tribute to the revolutionary soviet model.

Elections to the National Assembly brought a clear majority for the "Weimar Coalition" of the SPD, the Catholic Center Party [*Zentrum*], and the German Democratic Party [*Deutsche Demokratische Partei*, DDP], which also formed the first federal government. In February 1919, the National Assembly chose Ebert as president for a transitional period. In June 1919, it voted, of necessity, for the Versailles Treaty; the debates on ratifying the treaty were a major burden on constitutional deliberations and led ministers belonging to the DDP, who refused to be a part of ratification, to leave the government. But the votes of the SPD and Center assured the Constitution a sufficient majority. It was signed by the president on 11 August 1919 and proclaimed on 14 August. The National Assembly had deliberated on the basis of a draft constitution discussed with the governments of the individual states [*Länder*] of the new republic and prepared in the Reich Office of Internal Affairs [*Reichsamt des Inneren*] under the direction of Hugo Preuss.[11]

In contrast to the Constitution of the Empire of 1871, which in its preamble had derived its legitimacy from the monarchs and governments of the individual states, the Weimar Constitution referred to the German people in its totality. In Article 1, it declared the German Reich a republic in which all state power emanated from the people. Nevertheless, the relation between the Reich and individual states retained central significance, just as in the constitution of the Empire. Like the Empire, the Weimar Republic was a federal state. There was no fundamental reworking of federalism, as Preuss had wanted. In particular, there would be no breakup of Prussia, which, despite the loss of Memel and the provinces of Posen and West Prussia as a result of the Versailles Treaty, still comprised three-fifths of the territory and population of the Reich. Coordination between Prussia and the Reich, achieved under the Kaiser by the personal union of Prussian king and German Kaiser, and also regularly of the Prussian minister-president and the Reich chancellor, would become a handicap for the Weimar Republic under democratic conditions, in which different parliamentary majorities could emerge in Prussia and the Reich.[12]

In most areas, the Weimar Constitution gave the Reich at least concurrent legislative authority, meaning that the Länder could enact laws only until the Reich itself took legislative action. The Reich obtained comprehensive authority to impose taxes and other levies; this led to the constitution's regulation of finance in a unitary direction. In contrast to the constitution of the Empire, under which the Reich was dependent on contributions from the Länder, the Länder were now, conversely, dependent on the Reich's concession of a share in tax revenues. In 1919, a fundamental reform of finance was undertaken in which the Reich organized its own tax administration.

If a state failed to fulfill its constitutional and statutory obligations, the president had at his disposal an enforcement power in Article 48 (1), which included the use of armed force. Ebert used this power in the early 1920s against the governments created in Thuringia and Saxony by the SPD and the German Communist Party [*Kommunistischen Partei Deutschlands*, KPD]. In 1932, in the "coup against Prussia" [*Preußenschlag*], the government of Franz von Papen under President Hindenburg based its dismissal of the Social Democratic government of Otto Braun in Prussia on this provision.

The Länder were represented in the Reich by the Reichsrat. As in the imperial Bundesrat, its members were emissaries of the Land governments, bound to obey their instructions. The number of votes cast by each Land was guided by population without corresponding exactly to it; Prussian ascendancy was prevented by the requirement that no Land have more than two-fifths of the votes in the Reichsrat. In contrast to the imperial Bundesrat, the Reichsrat possessed only a suspensive veto over statutes enacted by the Reichstag; here, too, the republic took a unitary track. The Reichsrat could, however, still participate in the issuance of general administrative regulations. The power of the Reich to issue these regulations was important, because the Reich had as a rule no administration of its own but depended on Länder administrations to carry out its laws.

The central organ of the Reich was the Reichstag. It was directly elected on the basis of general suffrage, which included women, and according to the principle of proportional voting. In accordance with the principles of the parliamentary system, the chancellor and ministers of the Reich required the confidence of the Reichstag (Article 54). The president was also directly elected by the people, to a term of seven years. According to the idea of the authors of the Constitution, the president ought to play an active political role, to be a counterweight to the Reichstag and to guarantee continuity in the face of its changing majorities. He was supreme commander of the military, appointed Reich officials and officers, and under Article 48 (2), the infamous "dictatorship article," had the authority to take appropriate measures—including use of the military and suspension of basic rights—in the event of an important disturbance of public security and order.

The power of the president to appoint and dismiss the chancellor and ministers (Article 53) was in a certain tension with the fact that the chancellor and ministers required the confidence of the Reichstag to hold office. As a rule, the government had to have the confidence of both the president and the Reichstag, which it had in the 1920s, despite all the government crises. When, toward the end of the Weimar Republic, accord between the president and the Reichstag could no longer be reached, the result was a series of "president's cabinets," relying not on the confidence of the Reichstag but on that of the president. The president also had the right to subject decisions of the Reichstag to popular plebiscite, as well as to dissolve the Reichstag—only once, however, for the same reason and with the proviso that new elections be held within sixty days at the latest. Both rights were rooted in the idea that the president was to ensure that the will of the Reichstag reflected the will of the people; the Weimar Constitution distrusted the Reichstag more than it did the president. But it also constantly bound the president back to the Reichstag. Thus he was required to repeal dictatorial measures in Article 48 at the request of the Reichstag. Further, the Weimar Constitution gave the president scarce recourse against a stable parliamentary majority. To be sure, the salient characteristic of the party system in the Weimar Republic was precisely its inability to produce stable parliamentary majorities. Under these conditions, the position of the president was stronger than suited the ideas of equilibrium held by the Constitution's authors; the combination of the right to appoint and dismiss the chancellor, the right to dissolve the Reichstag, and the emergency powers in Article 48 represented a considerable agglomeration of power in the office of the president, which he could use to full effect precisely against a Reichstag weakened by party splintering. Thus the president was accurately described by the historian Friedrich Meinecke as an *Ersatzkaiser*.

The National Assembly debated most heatedly the second major part of the Constitution, titled "Basic Rights and Duties of the Germans." It included the classical freedoms such as freedom of speech and conscience and freedom of association and assembly, the classical property guaranty, as well as a wealth of basic social rights, such as the right of every German to earn a living through work. Myriad compromises found their way into the basic-rights section of the Constitution. Thus the traditional close relationship between church and state was loosened but not severed; the church retained its status as a corporate body constituted by public law and its right to collect taxes. The National Assembly similarly opted for "communal schools," that is, schools in which students of various denominations learned together; however, religiously affiliated denominational schools by and large remained the norm. With its many compromises, the section of the Constitution devoted to basic rights and duties itself reflected the many conflicts troubling the republic. Its interpretation was one of the fields upon which the struggle over methods and aims was conducted. The question whether and to what extent the basic rights, especially the principle of equality, ought to bind the legislature was especially in contention.

The fact that the short history of the Weimar Republic was above all a history of its crises was not primarily the fault of the Constitution.[13] The republic had to deal with the consequences of the war: transforming a wartime into a peacetime economy, demobilizing millions of soldiers, stopping the galloping inflation, paying high reparations, and enduring the occupation of the Ruhr by the French and Belgians; and all this in an overheated postrevolutionary climate in which strikes and unrest were daily events, along with putsch attempts on the right, especially the Kapp Putsch of 1920, and uprisings on the left, such as the communist uprisings in the Ruhr in 1920 and in Saxony and Thuringia in 1923. Not until the mid-1920s did a temporary stability set in.

The reason that this situation (which would have been a burden on any political system) made unrealizable demands on the political system of the Weimar Republic lay above all in the party structure inherited from the Empire. No Reichstag in the Weimar Republic saw a regular end to its term; all were dissolved prematurely because of government crises. This was not primarily the responsibility of the electoral system. It is true that the system of proportional voting introduced in 1919 favored a splintering of parties. However, majority voting with runoffs, which was practiced in the Empire, had not led to a less splintered party landscape. More crucial was the character of the parties themselves. With the founding of the republic, many new parties had been formed in addition to the SPD and Center, both of which continued. However, all were successors to parties that had already existed under the Kaiser. The USPD and KPD had split from the left wing of the SPD; the national-conservatives of the bourgeois camp had formed into the German National People's Party [*Deutsche Nationale Volkspartei,* DNVP], the right-wing liberals into Gustav Stresemann's German People's Party [*Deutsche Volkspartei,* DVP], and the left-liberals into the DDP. As already in the Empire, the Center and SPD, and to a smaller extent the bourgeois parties, had their roots in tightly bound social milieus that were separate from each other. The parties were communities of conviction and struggle; represented regional, social, and religious interests; and were scarcely capable of pragmatic give-and-take, compromise, and coalition.[14] Accustomed to the constitutional opposition in the Empire between parliament and government and to irresponsible opposition rather than to the assumption of responsibility *for* government, they found it hard to form governments and often faced their own ministers with mistrust, forcing them to vote against government proposals in the Reichstag. This legacy of the Empire was one of the many "historical handicaps on German parliamentarism."[15]

By the Reichstag elections of July 1920, the parties of the Weimar coalition had lost their majority. The DDP in particular, but also the SPD and Center, lost a considerable number of votes. The winners of the election were the parties that had rejected the Weimar Constitution and the Versailles Treaty: the DNVP, DVP, and USPD. So the Weimar Republic soon sought refuge in the president. Ebert himself used the emergency powers under Article 48 (2) in many ways.[16] States of emergency were decreed and the

Reichswehr deployed against domestic unrest. A right of the president to institute emergency decrees for restoring public security and order was also based on Article 48 (2), and immediate economic measures were taken on the same basis, especially to stabilize the currency and economy in the "year of crisis 1923." These extraordinary measures were supplemented in the early twenties with five "enabling laws" [*Ermächtigungsgesetze*] that transferred extensive legislative powers to the government. All this took place under the aegis of the Reichstag. But it demonstrated how easily Parliament's weakness could turn the president into the key figure in times of crisis.

Following the "year of crisis 1923," in which the Reich ended the fight for the Ruhr; survived the conflicts with Saxony, Thuringia, and Bavaria; and stopped the inflation, a short period of relative stability ensued. Stresemann succeeded, as foreign minister, in leading the Reich out of its isolation in foreign affairs and in improving its economic position. The Dawes Plan of 1924 placed reparations on a more realistic footing and made possible an influx of credit from abroad. However, this also made Germany heavily dependent on the economic condition of the creditor nations, as the Great Depression would prove. The fact that inflation had destroyed the economic existence of broad sectors of the German middle class and had deeply shaken them remained a severe burden on the Weimar Republic even during the period of stability. Identification with the political system of the Weimar Republic continued to diminish, and this accelerated the demise of the liberal parties, the DDP and DVP.[17] The difficulty of forming governments also persisted in the period of stability.[18] The election of Hindenburg—the general field marshal and now elderly hero of the First World War—as president following Ebert's death in 1925 demonstrated a deep yearning for the lost stability of the prewar period.

The Great Depression ended the years of stabilization.[19] There were already 3.5 million unemployed at the beginning of 1930. In March 1930, the grand coalition of the SPD, DDP, Center, DVP, and Bavarian People's Party that had been governing since 1928 broke apart. The SPD and the DVP, which was beholden to big business, could not agree on economic and social measures for overcoming the crisis. Thus the parties gave up control. The governments that followed were formed by the president as "president's cabinets" without consulting the parties or assuring parliamentary support. Under the government of Heinrich Brüning, a member of Parliament from the Center, the ministries were still filled with members of Parliament, afterwards only with experts without party affiliation. Lacking parliamentary backing, the governments were entirely dependent on the president, who gave them the opportunity, through Article 48 (2), of putting their economic and social programs into practice. To be sure, the Reichstag could demand that these measures be lifted, but the president could respond by dissolving Parliament. This in fact happened in July 1930. New elections in September 1930 failed to strengthen the parties of the Center, as the Brüning government had hoped. Instead, votes for the Nazi Party—the National Socialist German Workers Party [*Nationalsozialistische Deutsche Arbeiter Partei*, NSDAP]—rose to 18.3 percent and their seats from 12 to 107, while the KPD also gained. To avoid a vote of no confidence by the Reichstag, the Brüning government depended on the tolerance of the SPD, still the strongest party. The SPD granted its tolerance and enabled the Brüning government in the two years following to attempt to master the economic and financial crisis with extensive emergency decrees. But the economic crisis worsened apace; in 1932 there were over six million unemployed. The Reichstag met less and less frequently; in 1932 it passed only five laws, while at the same time fifty-nine emergency decrees were issued.

The conservative circles around the president, who was reelected in April 1932, called for a more clearly right-wing course. In May 1932, Hindenburg dismissed Brüning and appointed Franz von Papen as chancellor. His cabinet had no chance of getting the Reichstag's tolerance. Once again, the Reichstag was dissolved. Further, on 20 July 1932, in the "coup against Prussia," the Social Democratic-led Prussian government, the last weak bastion of forces faithful to the Republic,[20] was removed on the basis of Article 48. The Reichstag elections of July 1932 represented the final breakthrough of the NSDAP, which became the strongest party with 37.7 percent of the votes and held, along with the KPD, over half of the Reichstag seats. The newly elected Reichstag held a vote of no confidence in Papen in September 1932. Another dissolution of the Reichstag led to renewed voting in November 1932, in which the NSDAP, while receiving only 33.1 percent of the vote—thus losing votes—retained its position as the strongest party. The Papen cabinet was finished, to be replaced by the government of General Kurt von Schleicher of the Reichswehr Ministry. Through a social program, Schleicher hoped to bypass the party system and to find extraparty support from the military and the unions. But this proved an illusion. Hindenburg was unprepared to dissolve Parliament again, perhaps accompanied by an unconstitutional postponement of elections and the establishment of a dictatorship backed by the president and by prohibition of the NSDAP and the KPD. His adviser, Papen, suggested a different solution. Hitler would become chancellor but would be so "hemmed in" [*eingerahmt*] by Papen himself and ministers from the DNVP that the NSDAP would be unable to pursue any extremist policies. On 30 January 1933, Hindenburg appointed Hitler the last chancellor of the Weimar Republic. Papen's cabal proved to be a fatal error in judgment. The last president's cabinet of the Weimar Republic was rapidly transformed into a National Socialist dictatorship.

III

The answers suggested in the theory of the law of the state to the crises of the Weimar Republic and at the same time to its own crisis were manifold. Politically, they can be arrayed in a spectrum from left to right, from the Social Democrat Hermann Heller to the future National Socialist Carl Schmitt. Methodologically, they can be arrayed in a spectrum that reached from Gerhard Anschütz's positivism to Rudolf Smend's idealist, and Heller's realist, anti-positivism. However, it is also possible to distinguish between positions more focused on organization and procedure and those more concerned with substance; here Hans Kelsen, Smend, and Heller are related and, on the other side, Erich Kaufmann and Schmitt. Distinguished according to the nationalism of their positions, Anschütz, Kaufmann, and Schmitt join ranks on one side and, on the other again, Kelsen, Smend, and Heller. The differences overlap. Thus prominent positivists such as Kelsen, Anschütz, and Richard Thoma were among the defenders of the Weimar Republic; but among positivist-influenced practitioners in the judiciary and the administration, there were enough who executed the laws of the Weimar Republic with political reservations and those of the Third Reich with concurrence. In addition, the anti-positivists Hugo Preuss and Heller were also among the advocates of the Weimar Republic. Methodologically, the idealist and realist dispositions of Smend and Heller are farther apart than the similarity of their rejection of Kelsen's positivism would suggest. In the conflict over the constitutionality of the "coup against Prussia" before the *Staatsgerichtshof,* Anschütz and Heller were on Prussia's side, while Schmitt was on the side of the Reich. There is no simple pattern into which the discussions of state law theory can be fit.

Grasping the chronological progression of the discussion is an obvious way of proceeding. Thus the first edition of Kelsen's *On the Essence and Value of Democracy* was published in 1920, and Anschütz's lecture, *Three Guiding Principles of the Weimar Constitution,* delivered in 1922, was published in the "year of crisis 1923." Preuss's *The Significance of the Democratic Republic for t he Idea of Justice,* Schmitt's *The Status Quo and the Peace* and *The Rule of Law,* Triepel's *Law of the State and Politics,* Smend's *Constitution and Constitutional Law,* Heller's *Political Democracy and Social Homogeneity,* and Kelsen's *Legal Formalism and the Pure Theory of Law* were all published during the period of relative stability between 1924 and 1928. Thoma's *The Reich as a Democracy,* Schmitt's *State Ethics and the Pluralist State,* and Kaufmann's *On the Problem of the People's Will* all appeared in the final, crisis-laden years of the Weimar Republic. Heller's manuscripts on the theory of the state, written in these years, were published even later. But this chronological classification contributes little toward grasping the discussion of state law theory substantively. The authors who wrote the pieces reprinted here during the period of stability pursue convictions they had already begun to develop in the preceding years of crisis. Thus, for example, Preuss had already written *The People's State or the Inverted Authoritarian State* in 1919, Schmitt *Dictatorship* in 1919 and *Political Theology* in 1923, and Kaufmann had published his *Critique of Neo-Kantian Legal Philosophy* in 1921. Moreover, during the period of stability, consciousness of the preceding years of crisis was acute, just as the years of crisis that followed were experienced by contemporaries in connection with the period of stability, not as the *Götterdämmerung* of the Weimar Republic as it appears in retrospect today. The Weimar discussion does not break down into temporal segments; it was homogeneous and unbroken. November 1918 to January 1933 covered hardly more than fourteen years—not a long time.

Our collection opens with Kelsen, not because the first edition of his work *On the Essence and Value of Democracy* was published before all the other pieces, but because he links the Empire with Weimar in a particular way. Unlike Preuss, Triepel, Kaufmann, Smend, or Schmitt, who had already turned away from state law positivism in the Empire, Kelsen took it to an extreme. The positivism of Laband and Georg Jellinek in the Empire, as well as that of Anschütz and Thoma in Weimar, meant abstinence in regard to the inclusion of political and philosophical arguments in legal doctrine and restraint in the use of historical and sociological arguments. Even though the positivists mentioned above were familiar with the state as the object not only of state law theory but also of the social and historical sciences and moral and political philosophy, and even though (as the pieces by Anschütz and Thoma demonstrate) they also repeatedly treated the state from a historical or sociological, political or philosophical point of view, they tried to keep these various ways of viewing and treating apart, leaving legal doctrine free of the other arguments. They did not succeed consistently, however, and Kelsen's theory was that they had to fail. In Kelsen's view, their approach, which allowed for other ways of viewing and treating the state apart from the legal and thus aimed to view the state from several cognitive perspectives, ignored the fact that the state, as one cognitive object, could be viewed from only one cognitive perspective. The state could be recognized only from a standpoint committed to the "ought" category, not from one committed to causality as an "is" category, since the unity of the state was a unity of the state's legal order, a unity of "ought." Kelsen considered unity to be a hierarchical order [*Stufenbau*] of empowering and empowered law creation [*Rechtsetzung*], which legal doctrine could capture correctly only by precisely determining the will of the various law creators [*Rechtsetzer*] at the various steps of the hierarchy. Laband did in fact go far beyond this with his doctrinal concepts and constructs; his system of state law integrated the norms of positive law and at the same time reshaped these norms according to the needs of the system.

He could not do so, as Kelsen had already proved in his 1911 postdoctoral dissertation [*Habilitationsschrift*], without (albeit subconscious and unspecified) historical, political, and philosophical presumptions and options.

Even though Kelsen was opposed by the other participants in the Weimar debate and rejected by them, it was not possible for them to carry on without encountering his work. The concept of viewing and treating the state simultaneously in various ways, developed particularly by Jellinek in his distinction between the theory of the state as a legal and as a social entity—the "theory of the state's two-sidedness" [*Zwei-Seiten Lehre*]—had no further advocates in the Weimar debate. By taking the positivism of the Empire to its extreme, Kelsen also forced those who rejected positivism and urged going beyond it to an extreme. They all believed in a one-sided state and in a one-sided way of viewing and treating it—albeit in a form very different from Kelsen's. Even positivists such as Anschütz and Thoma no longer supported the positivism of the Empire, which Kelsen had shattered. Their positivism was no longer a legal positivism [*Rechtspositivismus*], but a statutory positivism [*Gesetzespositivismus*]. Statutory positivism as practiced by Anschütz and Thoma no longer put the needs of the system before the actual norms of positive law, as Laband's legal positivism had done, but made interpretation of these norms its focus. However, unlike the statutory positivist Kelsen, Anschütz and Thoma made free use of historical and political arguments in interpretation.

The contributions continued with Preuss, because, as father of the Weimar Constitution, he represented the beginnings of the Weimar Republic. He, too, linked the Empire with Weimar, and the constitution he drafted, with its neglect of parties, its distrust of the Reichstag, and its elevation of the president to an *Ersatzkaiser,* remained committed to the Empire. Given his position as critic and outsider to the imperial theory of the law of the state, one might have expected otherwise of him. But because this expectation was disappointed, because even a critic and outsider—not a professor in the dependent position of the public servant, but a financially independent member of the upper class; not a conservative German nationalist, but a left-wing Jewish liberal; not a mere theorist, but an active practitioner of municipal and Reich politics—could not completely free himself from the legal structures and experiences of the Empire. One gains a sense of the horizon within which the Weimar debate took place and within which it must be seen. Weimar democracy was not developed through exchange with the French, English, or American democratic traditions, but with an eye to its own past.

Anschütz and Thoma are linked methodologically as positivists, politically as republicans and democrats, and, through scholarly cooperation, as colleagues on the Heidelberg faculty and joint publishers of the *Handbook of the German Law of the State* [*Handbuch des deutschen Staatsrechts*]. Even if the scholarly and political, positivist and republican-democratic positions do not necessarily correlate, in Anschütz and Thoma they convincingly complement one another. Respecting statutory law meant respecting the popular representative body that legislated. Rejecting a teleological, integrationist, decisionist, or natural law interpretation and control of statutory law through scholarly and judicial elaboration also meant keeping the political process open and fluid and defending its possible progressive results against conservative judges and professors.

These were represented by Triepel and Kaufmann. Both had turned away from positivism, both sought new methodological paths, and both ended up focusing on justice and on a legislature bound and controlled by justice. Neither was sympathetic to the Weimar Republic, yet their critique and skepticism were more constructive than destructive. Kaufmann is in every respect the more philosophical and programmatic; his rejection of positivism was accompanied by a settlement of accounts with neo-Kantianism; he understood and presented his methodological ideas as a contribution to the development of an idealist methodology [*geisteswissenschaftliche Methode*] for state law theory; and his reference to justice developed into a natural law theory of institutions. Triepel was theoretically more modest; methodologically, he worked with the understanding that the interests reflected in norms are at least as important as what the norms express, and justice for him did not involve a theory of institutions but was the notion of doing the right thing in the right way, taken for granted by conservatives.

For Smend, Heller, and Schmitt, nothing was taken for granted. This is the link among them, for all their variety of methodological approaches, substantive results, and political positions. If positivism is accompanied, in a broad sense, by a certain trust in the world's positivity, its givenness, and reliability, and legal positivism by a corresponding trust in the givenness and reliability of law, then the true anti-positivists of the Weimar debate were Smend, Heller, and Schmitt. Integration, the key concept in Smend's theory of the state and constitution, is not a given, not something created in and of itself or signed and sealed by a social contract or constituted by a constitution once and for all; it is a process, constantly renewed, to be newly formed and experienced. The state "is there only in this process of constant renewal." It can therefore also succeed or fail, depending on whether the process— which Smend sought to grasp and describe in its various cultural and attitudinal, political and legal aspects—succeeds or fails. For Heller, too, state unity is something that must be established and maintained and that can fail. But where Smend relies on culture, values, and meaning, and their common spiritual experience to establish and maintain unity, Heller recognizes the importance of economic and social conditions, state organization and state procedure. Propagating a realist approach against Smend's idealist one, Heller confronts the state as a unity of culture, values, and meaning, with the state as a unity through action and decision [*Wirkungs-und Entscheidungseinheit*], where unity must be achieved through organization and procedure and enforced in decisions. It is not enough for Heller that the state's unity through action and decision is effective. For him, unity must be created and maintained—unlike Smend's integration, at least as it is commonly understood—not merely in being effective, but in conforming to ethical standards that should arise from and correlate with a society's ethical practices. Heller did not elaborate on how conformity would come to pass. Nevertheless, the possibility of achieving conformity linked his political activity as a Social Democrat and champion of the Weimar Republic with his scholarly work.

Schmitt does not see state unity as a given, either. However, he counts on decision making, the decision between friend and enemy, not on process—be it the process of experiencing culture, values, and meaning or that of state organizations and procedures. For Schmitt, the concept of the state presupposes the concept of the political; the criterion of the political is distinguishing friend from enemy; a nation is a state if it can distinguish between friend and enemy and thus decide on the type and form of its political existence. If it is not capable of doing this, it can survive neither in domestic nor in foreign policy, in neither civil nor external war. This position—which Schmitt developed in an essay (translated and published elsewhere and not included here) titled *The Concept of the Political* [*Der Begriff des Politischen*]—is called "decisionism." In the Third Reich, however, he abandoned decisionism and propagated a concrete theory of order and structure that was rooted in the decision of 1933—the Nazi's accession to power—and drew ordering and structuring consequences from it. Schmitt thereby classified his decisionism as part of the crisis of bourgeois society and state that he saw in the Weimar Republic but no longer in the Third Reich. Smend, too, developed his theory of integration as a theory of the "healthy sense of the life of the constitution," against the "chaos of the sickly constitutional state of the 1920s." It was Schmitt, however, who supplied a theory that not only emerged from the crisis but was coined expressly for it.

IV

Like philosophy, the theory of the law of the state is "its time, embodied in thought"; it remains in its time and cannot go beyond it. But like philosophy, the theory of the law of the state sometimes succeeds in leaving an insight of lasting validity. The prerequisite for this is that the times bring forth with particular intensity a recurring social theme and problem.

The crisis of the Weimar Republic had this particular intensity in three ways. First, it had both a foreign and a domestic policy dimension, bringing together the effects of defeat in an external war and the threat of civil war.

Second, it was a cultural crisis, marked by dissolution of a world of monarchy and aristocracy, officers and bureaucrats, and their replacement with an egalitarian world, as well as an economic crisis, marked by the inflation of the first years and later by the depression; the urban middle class was rocked by one as much as by the other. Third, the crisis put the state up for grabs—at first its territorial identity, by separatist efforts in the south and west, and later its institutional identity.

The Weimar Republic and its crisis lasted just long enough to be embodied in thought. Had the crisis slid into civil war in its early years or led to genuine, long-term stability, it would not have become a theme in and problem for state law theory nor would have remained so for long. If the "battle of social opponents for state power" does not last, state law theory cannot become enmeshed in it. A struggle over methods and aims requires a certain amount of time.

As varied as the distinctions are with which the positions in the Weimar debate can be captured and classified, one that is especially fruitful is a division based on the responses their authors found to the challenge of crisis. The positivists attempted to assert the state and constitutional order as a framework and guideline for the "battle of social opponents for state power." Some, particularly many positivist judges and administrators, did so as "republicans of convenience" [*Vernunftrepublikaner*], while in their hearts preserving monarchic tendencies and distancing themselves from the republican state; others did so by being apolitical and disinterested; still others who cared about the Weimar Republic—Anschütz and Thoma—did so with growing despair; and Kelsen remained true to the banner of individualism, liberalism, and parliamentarism, in sometimes stoic contempt for the actual "battle of social opponents," even while the ship was sinking. In contrast, among the new currents there were, on the one hand, various attempts to overcome the "battle of social opponents" by reclaiming unity. Kaufmann postulated unity as a national community of essence [*Wesensgemeinschaft*]; Smend saw it as the task and result of a spiritual integration process, mediated by shared experiences of culture, value, and meaning; and Heller, as the result of social homogeneity and organizational and institutional efforts. Schmitt, on the other hand, offered a vision that counted not on unity but on rupture. In this view, because not all can be linked in unity—because friend-enemy decisions and distinctions must be made both in foreign and domestic policy—it is only through these decisions and distinctions that unity can be achieved, a unity that shuts out the other and thus brings together those who are alike. This is a call to the bourgeoisie not to go down in defeat as a "chattering class" bickering in Parliament but to find the strength for distinction and decision. The appeal for decision could be directed as much to the left as to the bourgeois right, and the leftist theorist Otto Kirchheimer agreed with Schmitt that "the principal, irreparable error of this constitution lies in the fact that it has not itself decided."[21]

V

Like Weimar, the American state was in crisis from its inception,[22] and at varying levels of intensity almost continuously during the first ninety years of its existence. Unlike Weimar, however, crises of the American state served only to strengthen, not to challenge, fidelity to constitutional government. This was as true at the founding as in the aftermath of the Civil War. It was true as well in the crisis of the American state at the time of Weimar. Each crisis had its own specific causes and legal and political solutions. Each forced legal theorists to elaborate a new and different dimension of constitutional government. The challenge to the American state at the time of Weimar was curiously like the challenge to Weimar, and responses to the challenge in both states implicated legal theory. Nevertheless, differences in history, in political and legal culture, caused different expressions of incapacity in each state and propelled legal theory along very different tracks.

The first crisis of the American state, in the 1780s, focused on the question of unity. It was impelled primarily by social and economic causes, and its resolution required a new conception of sovereignty, alien to eighteenth-century political theory. The second crisis, which came to a head in the Civil War, was impelled by the conflict over slavery. It focused on two issues that resolution of the first crisis had left open: the nature of citizenship in a federal union and the right of states to secede unilaterally from the Union. Resolution of the second crisis created a new conception of citizenship, engraved in the Fourteenth Amendment. The third crisis, which lasted from the Progressive Era through the New Deal, challenged the capacity of government to act "in the interests of its people" while preserving the "maintenance of individual liberty." Resolution of the third crisis led to a transformation of the jurisprudence in which constitutional interpretation—indeed all legal interpretation—would be conducted.

The crisis of the American state at the founding took the form of a series of questions. What is union? Why must we have it? What political form should it take?[23] These questions were, at first, forced on revolutionary America by military necessity, and the answers at first—the behavior of the Continental Congress as sovereign in all but name[24]—were driven by this necessity. But military necessity would not last forever, and planning the frame of a postwar regime required allocating sovereignty between the central government and the governments of the thirteen former colonies, as well as defining the form each sovereign would take.

Defining the form of sovereignty for the colonies was largely accomplished during 1776. By resolution of 15 May (six weeks before the Declaration of Independence) Congress called on the colonies to suppress the Crown's authority and to exercise "all the powers of government . . . under the authority of the people of the colonies." The delegates of "the United States in Congress assembled" were clear from the start that all government in the United States—however it might work out in detail, whatever principles might animate it—would be under "the authority of the people." It would be constitutional government. By the end of 1776, eight colonies had adopted new constitutions (the two corporate colonies, Rhode Island and Connecticut, were already republics); only Georgia, New York, and Vermont (the latter was not recognized by other states until the 1780s) delayed until 1777.[25]

Congress accomplished an allocation of sovereignty in the Articles of Confederation, which it proposed for ratification by the now-constitutional governments of the states in 1778. Nothing was clearer in political theory at the time than that sovereignty could not be shared, that it had to be put either in a central government (in which case the states would be reduced to provinces) or in the states themselves (in which case the central government could at most be a confederation). Article II of the Articles of Confederation provides that "[e]ach State retains its sovereignty, freedom, and independence, and every power, jurisdiction, and right, which is not by this confederation expressly delegated to the United States in Congress assembled." Though embracing limitations on the states' "power, jurisdiction, and right," the formulation is clear that their "sovereignty, freedom, and independence" remain unlimited. Since the limitations imposed by the Articles of Confederation were indeed significant,[26] one might consider Article II's insistence that sovereignty was in the states a mere fiction, a way of accommodating a distribution of sovereignty between the central government and the states without compromising eighteenth-century political theory. Yet, despite the existence of substantial nationalist sentiment in the early 1780s,[27] the Confederation did lack crucial attributes of sovereignty as it was understood in the eighteenth century,[28] and it would be a mistake to underestimate the extent to which the notion of a unitary sovereign both expressed political valences and oriented them towards the states. The assembled Congress of the United States was, after all, an emergency committee of states united on the single project of winning independence from the Crown. When war ceased in 1781, so did the effective operation of Congress, and the general understanding that sovereignty reposed in the states had increasing practical effect.[29] "What is truly remarkable about the Confederation," writes Gordon Wood, "is the degree of union that was achieved."[30] But this union, as it turned out, was only a paper union, and by the middle eighties politicians and theorists had to return to the fundamental questions.

The turn in sentiment was remarkable. A scant six years after Congress first met under the Articles of Confederation, in 1781, the Philadelphia Convention began a process of overturning the Confederation's allocation of sovereignty not, as it turned out, in favor of a total reallocation of sovereignty from the states to the central government, but of a wholly new concept of sovereignty—a federal concept, dividing sovereignty between the states and the central government.[31] The argument for union was pragmatic. Revolutionaries who as representatives of popular sovereignty had assembled in committees and conventions to oppose the legislative tyranny of Parliament assembled once more against what they perceived to be the legislative tyrannies of the states.[32] Splitting sovereignty between the states and a central government would dampen the ability of faction to capture state government for the purpose of self-aggrandizing legislation.[33] The argument for union was also enhanced by an air of crisis that gripped the country starting around 1784. Historians have argued bitterly over the reality of the crisis,[34] but recent evidence suggests that the years 1784 through 1790 witnessed "in depth and duration . . . the most serious economic setback suffered by Americans since the earliest days of colonial settlement."[35] Contributing to the depression were many factors—instability of the currency, overextension of credit, loss of British subsidies, British trade prohibitions introduced by the North-Fox ministry in 1782, among others. Some factors had dangerous implications for social order: Toward the end of 1783 the Continental Army demobilized, sending into civilian life tens of thousands of soldiers, most of whom were poor, if not when they entered the Army, then after years of receiving little or no pay from Congress. Between 80,000 and 100,000 Loyalists, among the most educated and productive in a colonial society of 2.6 million in 1775, left during and at the end of the Revolution. Depression caused and coincided with a dramatic commodity deflation that hampered the ability of debtors to pay off debts and taxpayers to pay taxes.[36] Shays' Rebellion in Western Massachusetts between September 1786 and February 1787 was only the most pointed in an outbreak of back-country resistance to debt and tax collection.[37] It was proof to the nationalists, if any was needed, of the urgency of the convention they were to join in Philadelphia on 14 May 1787.[38]

But the efficient lineage of the Philadelphia Convention was neither social unrest nor economic depression, rather a series of conventions of various states to work out problems in common, ranging from regulating the economy to settling boundary disputes.[39] It was the opaque status of these conventions under the Articles and resulting ambiguities in the process of ratification of the Constitution that set the stage for the second crisis of American constitutional government in the events leading up to the Civil War.

The conventions started during the period of the Continental Congress and continued during Confederation. The Mount Vernon Conference of 1785 between Maryland and Virginia set a pattern that would eventually lead the states to Philadelphia. The conference took a first step away from the Articles, by recommending an action that states had unanimously bound themselves not to take: The legislatures of both states ratified the compact without submitting it to Congress as required in Article VI. And the conference led irrepressibly to further steps in the evolution of national action. Ratifying the compact, the Virginia legislature authorized a meeting with other states at Annapolis in 1786 to discuss "such commercial regulations [as] may be necessary to their common interest and their permanent harmony."[40] Annapolis, in turn, unanimously adopted an "Address of the Annapolis Convention" calling on states to appoint commissioners to meet at Philadelphia to devise amendments to the Articles "and to report such an Act for that purpose to the United States in Congress assembled, as when agreed to, by them, and afterwards confirmed by the Legislatures of every State will effectually provide the same."[41] Congress responded to the call from Annapolis on 21 February 1787 with a resolution expressing "the opinion of Congress" that delegates assemble in Philadelphia "for the sole and express purpose of revising the Articles of Confederation and reporting to Congress and the several legislatures such alterations and provisions therein as shall when agreed to in Congress and confirmed by the states render the federal constitution adequate to the exigencies of Government and the preservation of the Union."[42] As matters turned out, the document proposed for ratification was a new constitution, not amendments to the Articles. It was nonetheless reported to Congress, which by the unanimous vote of twelve states present on 28 September transmitted it, not for the approval of state legislatures, which could hardly be expected to support a dramatic shift of power to the central government, but "to the several Legislatures in Order to be submitted to a convention of Delegates chosen in each state by the people thereof."[43] The Philadelphia Convention thus exceeded the call of Congress and in any case sidestepped the method of amendment required in Article XIII of the Articles.[44]

However difficult and indirect the process by which the United States got its Constitution, the political class in the United States responded to the exigencies of the moment, in rebellion and war during the 1770s and in the economic, social, and especially moral crisis of the 1780s. The response of the 1770s, bound as it was by the theory of unitary sovereignty, was inadequate for tolerating the coexistence of a deeply entrenched state establishment with a continent-wide economy and the political vision of those who had fought against England as a nation and won. Only the theory of dual sovereignty developed in the late eighties was up to the task.

The second crisis of the American state—over the nature of citizenship in a federal union and the right of states to unilateral secession—began within the framework established by resolution of the first. The achievement of the first crisis—dual sovereignty and the foundation of its basic institutions—left many questions to be answered in political and legal struggle over succeeding generations: What commerce can states regulate once Congress has exercised its power to regulate interstate commerce?[45] Can a state levy a tax upon the salary of an officer of the United States,[46] or upon a bank chartered by the United States?[47] Can the United States tax the salary of an officer of a state?[48] These and a host of other questions could be, and were, resolved within the constitutional order set by the Framers. Even issues concerning the structure of the order itself could be resolved this way, though fraught with resistance and peril. Thus in 1816, in *Martin v. Hunter's Lessee*,[49] the Supreme Court of the United States faced a defiant Virginia Court of Appeals, which upon appeal refused to obey the Supreme Court's mandate on the ground that Congress had no power under the Constitution to give the Supreme Court appellate jurisdiction over state court decisions.[50] The Supreme Court held that Congress did have the power but, in order to avoid conflict, directed the second mandate to the trial court in which the suit had originally been instituted.[51] The sustained conflict over nullification, in which state legislatures asserted the power to declare acts of Congress unconstitutional and, in John Calhoun's view, inoperative within the state,[52] came closer to a question that could not be resolved in the ordinary way, challenging as it did the very nature of union. Nullification, however, danced close to the edge, not over. It did not drive states to challenge the fundamental legitimacy of the constitutional order;[53] the political dynamics of nullification prevented that. The acts states sought to nullify either were capable of political adjustment, like a tariff, in which case nullification was simply another weapon in the ordinary clash of interests or, like the Alien and Sedition Acts, offended fundamental and widely held principles, in which case nullification triggered general and overwhelming disgust with the legislation. In neither case was nullification the scene of intense and unresolvable confrontation sufficient to challenge the legitimacy of the order.

Only two questions could not be answered within the order set by the Framers. First, can a state unilaterally secede from the union, or must secession, to be effective, be accompanied by the concurrence of other states in some constitutionally sanctioned procedure? Second, to which branch of the dual sovereign, the states or the federal government, do citizens owe their primary loyalty? And from this last question flows a series of others: Which branch of the dual sovereign has final say over citizenship? Are there two forms of citizenship, state and federal, or only one? If only one, which? If not just one, is it possible to be a citizen of a state but not of the United States? A citizen of the United States but not the citizen of a state?

These questions had been elided in the founding.[54] Unlike the Articles of Confederation, the Constitution makes no mention of sovereignty. Unlike the Articles, it says nothing about "perpetual union" (Article XIII). It makes elaborate provision for the admission of new states by Congress (Article IV, Section 3), but not for secession. It says little about citizenship, other than implicit acknowledgment of the existence of state citizenship (in two clauses: Article III, Section 2; Article IV, Section 2) and federal citizenship (in Congress's power "[t]o establish an uniform Rule of Naturalization," Article I, Section 8).

Citizenship and secession were one question really: the source of the authority of the Constitution itself. For if the Constitution obtains its authority from the states, then the states are the branch of the dual sovereign to which citizens owe undivided loyalty. Their loyalty to the federal government is derivative from the states' decision to ratify the Constitution. No event of national citizenship severed or compromised the bond of loyalty between states and citizens. No new spring of citizenship drowned out the old. Moreover, as there would be no national citizenship binding the citizens of a state directly to the union over the heads of state government, a state could reverse its decision to join the union without the consent or participation of other states. If, on the other hand, the Constitution gets its authority from the people assembled in convention—whether the people as a whole in Philadelphia or the people of each state in conventions called by state legislatures to ratify the work of Philadelphia—then citizens owe their primary loyalty to the federal government, and not to the states. Then the people assembled in convention for the purpose of creating the new national government replace the states as the source of citizenship and the goal towards which its affections bend. Then secession requires an expression of assent by the citizens of the nation as a whole.

The Constitution is plain enough that the source of its authority is the people assembled in convention. It is "WE the People of the United States" that ordains and establishes the Constitution. It is "the Conventions of nine States" that ratifies it, not state legislatures. Nevertheless, the silence of the Constitution on sovereignty, the nature of citizenship in a dual sovereignty, and secession provided sufficient ambiguity to permit those who were so inclined to argue that the source of the Constitution's authority was the states. This ambiguity was expressed as well in the process of ratification. The formulation in Congress's resolution to the states, transmitting the Constitution "to the several Legislatures in Order to be submitted to a convention of Delegates chosen in each state by the people thereof," finessed the question.[55] When the citizen's loyalty would be put to the test—a conflict squarely posing the issue of citizenship, a state claiming the power of unilateral secession—the question could be finessed no more.

Precisely these events occurred in the Supreme Court's 1857 decision in *Dred Scott v. Sandford*[56] and in its aftermath leading up to the "secession winter" of 1860–61. Although the immediate issues it addressed were narrower,

Dred Scott amounted to an attempt to resolve the issue of citizenship in a dual sovereignty. And the particular resolution the Court found gave comfort to those who would assert the claim of unilateral secession three years later in the wake of events the decision encouraged or impelled.

In his opinion for the Court,[57] Chief Justice Roger Taney conceives of state and federal citizenship as coordinate. Each branch retains the power, fettered by the Constitution only, to choose its citizens, to specify their rights and obligations.[58] The states get this power directly as sovereigns antedating the formation of the federal government. The only constraint is that whatever they decide about citizenship and citizens has effect only within their borders. But, says Taney, states can make anyone a citizen of the state, even aliens. Presumably (though Taney is silent on the subject) they can even make "negro slaves" or their descendants citizens, even when, as the Court holds, the Constitution forbids including them as citizens of the United States. The federal government, by contrast, gets this power only indirectly, by implication, since nowhere does the Constitution (as it stood in 1791) define or discuss citizenship of the United States, only the power of Congress to make a uniform rule of naturalization.

Taney's model of coordinate citizenship as he developed it in *Dred Scott* probably goes as far as it is possible to go within the constitutional order set by the Framers in answering the questions of citizenship in a dual sovereign, and Taney's model does answer most of the questions. It says that each branch of the dual sovereign makes citizens, that each makes them independently of the other, and that it is possible to be a citizen of one branch only. But the model says nothing about primary loyalty, and without a position on primary loyalty a position on secession is impossible. The Framers had met every challenge to dual sovereignty posed by eighteenth-century political theory but this, and Taney, sticking close to their structure, failed as well.

Nor did the immediate issues in *Dred Scott* push Taney beyond the Framers' structure, assuming he would have been willing or able to go: Did the Constitution mean to include "negro slaves" or their descendants as citizens of the United States? Did the Constitution permit the Missouri Compromise of 1820, which forbade slavery north of the latitude 36° 30' north in the Louisiana Territory? Either the Framers intended to include "negro slaves" and their descendants as citizens of the United States or they did not. Either they contemplated congressional control over the citizenship of states that would be formed out of the territories or they did not. Taney answered both questions in the negative. Though controversial, his answers were plausible within the doctrine of coordinate citizenship, which was a plausible model of the state of the Framers' understanding of citizenship.

Taney and a majority of justices on the Court believed that resolution of these issues—especially the constitutionality of congressional control over slavery in the territories—would defuse the political crisis that had been brewing since the repeal of the Missouri Compromise in the Kansas-Nebraska Act of 1854.[59] Instead, it produced a firestorm of controversy. No political issue was more important than the fight between slavery and freedom for control of the territories, hence the future character of the Union. The political system had struggled with this issue since before the founding, and the thought that it was resolvable by an appeal to the constitutional order of the Framers was simply wrong. *Dred Scott*'s unsuccessful attempt to wrestle the politics of slavery into legal form may not have been the fuel powering events to secession, but it certainly was a lit match.[60]

The Constitution had run out. The constitutional order of the Framers failed to contain the furor over slavery. "The nation's weakness in the secession winter," note Harold Hyman and William Wiecek, "and lawyers' inability to direct events into pacific channels, had caused a depression of spirit among leading spokesmen of the profession."[61] The secession winter witnessed the gravest crisis in American constitutional government. It was the moment when even supporters of the Constitution lost "constitutional faith,"[62] the moment when the American republic came closest to Weimar.

Far from disproving the thesis that crisis has always strengthened American constitutionalism, the Civil War is its most compelling example. War brought not further disillusion, but reconstruction of a belief in constitutional government. The reason ironically lay in the war itself: the Constitution responded to the demands war made on it with a flowering of methods yet with little damage to the fundamental structure.[63] The American habit of vigorous and widespread public engagement in constitutional discourse fully recovered by 1862, and law rapidly resumed the position of respect it had enjoyed in the first half-century of the Republic.[64]

Events readily disposed of the holdings in *Dred Scott*. In June 1862 Congress prohibited slavery in the territories, and by December 1865 twenty-seven states (including eleven reconstructed states of thirteen seceding) had ratified the Thirteenth Amendment, abolishing the condition that had provided the basis in *Dred Scott* for excluding "negro slaves" and their descendants from national citizenship.[65] Events also effectively answered the broader questions that were perplexing the Republic about dual sovereignty. The surrender at Appomattox established that states do not have the power of unilateral secession and that citizens owe primary loyalty to the nation. But the conclusion of war and the ratification of the Thirteenth Amendment left Taney's doctrine of coordinate citizenship substantially intact, since the doctrine had said nothing about primary loyalty in the first place. Despite the opinion of some that Appomattox and Gettysburg killed off both slavery and state sovereignty,[66] reality was far more complex and difficult.

Making "negro slaves" into citizens of the nation had no obvious or immediate impact on their status as citizens of states.[67] Emancipation by itself
failed to guarantee former slaves the freedoms enjoyed by other citizens.
Even if the Thirteenth Amendment could be construed to require states
to make emancipated slaves citizens, there was substantial disagreement
whether it would require states to make them equal citizens. There was substantial agreement that the enforcement clause of the Thirteenth Amendment allowed Congress to ensure that whatever inequalities did exist
not re-create the incidents of slavery—that was how the enforcement
clause had been sold to Southern Democrats who were considering the
Thirteenth Amendment for ratification[68]—but little agreement about
which disabilities, beyond a core, could be considered incidents of slavery.
And the "Black Codes" of 1865 did visit a host of disabilities upon emancipated slaves. On 19 April 1866, over President Andrew Johnson's veto, Congress enacted the first of several Civil Rights Acts, removing some of these
disabilities through the enforcement power of the Thirteenth Amendment.[69] However, even supporters of the substance of the legislation, like
Representative John Bingham, believed that Congress lacked the power to
reach as deeply as it had into the police power of the states to determine the
powers and disabilities of their citizens.[70] As a result, on 30 April the Joint
Committee on Reconstruction proposed what in 1868 became the Fourteenth Amendment.

The Fourteenth Amendment put an end to the possibility that emancipated slaves could be citizens of the nation but not of a state, or citizens of
a state burdened by unequal disabilities. The amendment accomplished
this revolution in two momentous steps: It first overturned Taney's doctrine
of coordinate citizenship, replacing it with a doctrine of unified citizenship
instead. The first clause of Section 1 creates a national citizenship open to
"[a]ll persons born or naturalized in the United States" and makes them
"citizens . . . of the State wherein they reside." Taken with the surrender at
Appomattox, the amendment effectively resolves the dilemma that dual
sovereignty presented to the eighteenth-century conception of citizenship.
Henceforth all citizens of the nation were to be citizens of states, and citizens of states, citizens of the nation. The Fourteenth Amendment clarifies
what the Thirteenth left obscure: Emancipated slaves, by virtue of their citizenship in the nation, are "citizens . . . of the State wherein they reside."
By itself, however, unified citizenship could not stop states from using state
citizenship as an instrument for creating two classes of citizens. After all, the
Fourteenth Amendment does not abolish state citizenship;[71] it simply unifies
the criteria of membership, and, without more, states could have claimed
that the power to create unequal classes of citizens remained undisturbed.
Hence the second step, which follows immediately upon the first in the text

of the amendment: "No State shall make or enforce any law which shall abridge the privileges or immunities of citizens of the United States; nor shall any State deprive any person of life, liberty, or property, without due process of law; nor deny to any person within its jurisdiction equal protection of the laws." At the least, the prohibition against states making or enforcing laws that abridge the privileges or immunities of citizens of the United States stops states from burdening emancipated slaves as a class with unequal disabilities and supplies a clear retrospective justification for the first Civil Rights Act. The doctrine of unified citizenship, coupled with the Equal Protection Clause, created a powerful, flexible instrument for tracking down the incidents of slavery, expansively and dynamically construed, to follow wherever in the future these incidents might lead, even beyond the provisions of the first Civil Rights Act.[72]

Just as resolution of the first crisis of American constitutional governance in the 1780s required transformation in the understanding of sovereignty, resolution of the crisis of the 1860s invoked a new conception of citizenship. The unified citizen of the Fourteenth Amendment has a relationship to the sovereign different from that of any citizen before. Citizenship had always meant the right to participate in the political community or membership in the collectivity constituting the sovereign. The unified citizen, in contrast, has rights *against* the political community, or the right to be free from disabilities that the collectivity constituting the sovereign might otherwise impose. The Fourteenth Amendment dissociates citizenship from sovereignty altogether. It resolves the dilemma of citizenship in a dual sovereign this way: It sets citizenship as a limitation on sovereignty—a principle of antisovereignty, an independent, competing source of powers and disabilities. Far from conceding that eighteenth-century political theory had been right all along—that dual sovereignty is impossible—unified citizenship takes the revolution in political thinking one step further, revising the very place of sovereignty in constitutional governance.

The Fourteenth Amendment also harbored an important ambiguity, and this ambiguity could not be wholly resolved within the new constitutional order set by its drafters. The question was whether the Equal Protection Clause applies only to emancipated slaves as a class or, more broadly, to other classes. If more broadly, then states are prohibited from dividing citizens into classes, not just from making one of them slaves. Then the prohibited class divisions and prohibited reasons for making the divisions would presumably be determined by the same dynamic approach the Fourteenth Amendment uses to track incidents of slavery. If, however, the Equal Protection Clause applies only to emancipated slaves, then states may do whatever their exercise of the police power leads them to do, so long as they do not re-create the incidents of slavery, dynamically construed. And there are a host of intermediate positions, almost all taken by one court or another, one commentator or another, since adoption of the Fourteenth Amendment. It was clear that the framers of the Fourteenth Amendment intended a dynamic approach to eliminating the vestiges of slavery. But did they also intend a dynamic approach to eliminating unequal burdens in general? Could the dynamic approach be restricted to "negro slaves" and their descendants, or were all citizens—the unified citizens of the Fourteenth Amendment—to be its beneficiaries as well?

The Supreme Court's initial resolution of this ambiguity, in the *Slaughter-House Cases* of 1873, was that the Equal Protection Clause applies only to the privileges of "negroes as a class," not to classes of citizens in general.[73] But this resolution was inherently unstable. The decision was by the slimmest of majorities. Three justices (of nine) joined Justice Stephen Field in dissent, urging the broadest possible interpretation of the ban on unequal burdening. "What [Article IV, Section 2 of the Constitution] did for the protection of the citizens of one state against hostile and discriminating legislation of other states," wrote Justice Field, "the 14th Amendment does for the protection of every citizen of the United States against hostile and discriminating legislation, against him in favor of others whether they reside in the same or in different states."[74] Further, the Thirteenth Amendment does not restrict the prohibition against slavery to one class of citizens, to "negroes as a class." Any class can claim its benefit. Coupling the Fourteenth Amendment's dynamic approach to defining the protections accorded by the Thirteenth Amendment with the Thirteenth's capacious identification of the beneficiaries of those protections was all but inevitable. Finally, the Fourteenth Amendment also forbids states from depriving any person of life, liberty, or property without due process of law. And the Due Process Clause clearly applies to all persons, as individuals, not simply to unduly burdened classes or only to "negroes as a class." The dynamic approach that the Fourteenth Amendment applies to tracking the incidents of slavery could be applied to due process and equal protection as well.

The instability inherent in the resolution in the *Slaughter-House Cases* at first affected both due process and equal protection. Thirteen years after that decision, in 1886,[75] the Supreme Court extended equal protection to alien "subjects of the Emperor of China" who were arbitrarily denied permits to operate laundries in San Francisco: "The Fourteenth Amendment to the Constitution is not confined to the protection of citizens. . . . These provisions are universal in their application, to all persons within the territorial jurisdiction, without regard to any differences of race, of color, or of nationality. . . ."[76] But beyond implicit rejection of the narrow position in the *Slaughter-House Cases,* the Supreme Court offered no guidance as to which classes and what reasons would invalidate state provisions, and *Plessy v. Ferguson*[77] in 1896 put an end to further attempts to broaden equal protection for at least a generation.[78] The real energy in the wake of the *Slaughter-House Cases* focused on due process, not on equal protection.

It was a train of developments in due process and the political consequences of these developments that eventually led, in the 1930s, to a third crisis in constitutional governance, resolution of which would end in a reworking of the entire jurisprudential framework of constitutional governance. In 1877, four years after the decision in the *Slaughter-House Cases,* the Supreme Court in *Munn v. Illinois* upheld the power of Illinois to fix by law the maximum charges for the storage of grain in certain warehouses against a challenge that statutes regulating the use of private property necessarily deprive an owner of his property without due process.[79] Over dissents by Justices Field and William Strong, the Court held that states have the power to regulate property "affected with a public interest," thus cabining the police power of states within strict, yet reasonably capacious limits. But due process, dynamically construed, was to have other incidents that would further restrict the states' police power. In 1890 the Court condemned a Minnesota statute making rates established by a railroad commission final and conclusive as a taking of the railroads' property without due process.[80] The reasonableness of the rates, said the Court, was a question for judicial determination, requiring due process of law. In 1894 the Court struck down a statute that prohibited any person from effecting insurance on property in the state with companies not admitted to do business there, on the ground that the right of citizens to earn a livelihood by any lawful calling is a "liberty" protected by due process.[81] Yet, by far the most important assertion of due process limits on the states' exercise of their police power was *Lochner v. New York*[82] in 1905. It was *Lochner,* like *Dred Scott* before it, that through a chain of events would transform the ambiguities of the Fourteenth Amendment into a crisis of constitutional governance. Unlike *Dred Scott,* however, the political conditions precipitating the crisis took a quarter-century to develop.

Over dissents by Justices Oliver Wendell Holmes and John Marshall Harlan (who were joined by Justices Edward White and William Day), *Lochner* held unconstitutional a New York statute of the Progressive Era (1897) making it unlawful for bakers or confectioners to require or permit employees to work more than sixty hours per week or ten hours per day, on the ground that the statute deprives both employers and employees of a "liberty" to contract protected by due process. The Court rejected as unreasonable a legislative finding that the statute was necessary to protect the health of individuals who are following the trade of a baker, hence within the state's police power. *Lochner* thus heralded an era in which the Court was prepared to review legislative judgments about the propriety of a state's exercise of the police power, thus drawing lines about the police power far tighter than any before.[83]

The usual story in American constitutional history is that *Lochner* effectively disabled the states and the federal government from responding to the regulatory demands of a growing industrial economy. However, the aftermath of *Lochner* reveals considerable flexibility on the part of the Court towards the states' regulatory efforts. Thus, in *Muller v. Oregon,*[84] three years after *Lochner,* the Court rejected a due process challenge to an Oregon statute forbidding the employment of women "in any mechanical establishment, or factory, or laundry" for more than ten hours per day. Louis Brandeis's famous "factual" brief persuaded the Court that there was a compelling legislative basis for the restriction, unlike the restriction in *Lochner.* In 1917, in *Bunting v. Oregon,*[85] the Court even seemed to overrule *Lochner sub silentio,* holding that the Court would accept the judgment of a state legislature and supreme court that a statute forbidding the employment of any person in any mill, factory, or manufacturing establishment more than ten hours per day and providing payment for overtime at a higher rate was necessary for the preservation of the health of employees in these industries. The Court also decided cases against the regulatory power of the states. Two years before *Bunting,* for example, the Court struck down a Kansas statute making it a misdemeanor for employers to require employees to execute a "yellow-dog contract"—a promise not to join a union—on *Lochner* grounds.[86] In the two decades after *Lochner,* the Court showed a willingness to regulate the states' exercise of the police power on a case-by-case basis. It was not prepared to narrow the police power to activities, such as common carriage and government contracting, that are clearly in the public realm.

Nevertheless, in 1923, the Court began interpreting the police power more restrictively. In *Adkins v. Children's Hospital,*[87] the Court held that a law empowering a commission to fix minimum wages for women and children in the District of Columbia violates Fifth Amendment due process. The Court distinguished *Muller v. Oregon* as approving a statute regulating the hours of women, not their wage. *Adkins* accompanied a parallel retreat from the formula of *Munn v. Illinois.* Prior to *Adkins* the Court had sustained price regulation in fire insurance[88] and rental housing[89] on the ground that those activities are "affected with a public interest." In *Wolff v. Industrial Court*[90] in 1923, and in a series of decisions running through the early 1930s,[91] the Court uniformly held, when the issue arose, that activities regulated by the states were not "affected with a public interest."

The image of a Court implacably opposed to an expansive police power is thus accurate only for the period after 1923, not 1905, when *Lochner* was decided. Yet when the Great Depression struck, the extreme version of *Lochner* was ascendant, sharply constraining the regulatory powers of both the states and the federal government. The powers of the federal government were constrained as well by a contemporary understanding, rooted more deeply than the extreme version of *Lochner* in constitutional history and doctrine, of the allocation of powers in a federal system and the separation of powers within the federal government. These constraints focused on the power of Congress to regulate interstate, but not local, commerce, and the doctrine forbidding Congress to delegate legislative authority to another branch of government or to private groups. These other constraints led the Court to invalidate a series of enactments designed to meet the emergency caused by the Great Depression—gross domestic product halved and a quarter of the workforce unemployed.[92]

The ascendancy of the extreme version of *Lochner* was to be brief, ending three years after the Great Depression began and two years after the Roosevelt administration took office.[93] In an exceptional moment in American legal history, the groundwork for change was prepared by legal theorists who wanted states and the federal government to regulate economic activity more aggressively. These theorists—the American legal realists— began to undermine the jurisprudential framework on which *Lochner* and *Munn* depended immediately after *Lochner,* and certainly well before the Great Depression made political pressure against *Lochner* irresistible. *Lochner*'s jurisprudential framework had two principle elements; each had to be dealt with.

First, *Lochner* required that legal rules sustaining private economic activity have a source other than political fiat. Otherwise all matters would be "affected with a public interest" and subject to regulation, free of due process. If private law cannot trace its source to something other than ordinary politics, then the state that gave rules in the first place can alter them or take them away. Then immutable private law rules cease to function as a bulwark against regulatory incursion. So, the early realists set about attacking formalist or naturalist derivations of private law, all to prove that politics and only politics had a hand in creating it. The rather neutral-sounding rule requiring consideration in contracts was no different in this estimation than the quite specific Louisiana law at issue in the *Slaughter-House Cases,* granting a twenty-five-year monopoly to the Crescent City Live-Stock Landing and Slaughter-House Company "to maintain slaughterhouses, landings for cattle and stockyards." Both are naked political regulation of private economic activity. The rule of consideration is no more immune from political process than the Crescent City Live-Stock Landing and Slaughter-House Company.

Second, *Lochner* required the enforcement of legal rules to be transparent. If not, then judges could smuggle their own politics into decisions, and the vulnerability of private law to politics would shift from the legislative to the judicial arena, and, once again, states could exercise their police power unfettered by due process. Again, realists set to work challenging the capacity of judges (or anyone else) to follow rules unembarrassed by politics or temperament or to tell whether a fellow judge is following rules "correctly." Not only is the content of rules political, but the process by which the content impresses itself on single cases subjects rules to microscopic revision according to further politics and personal inclination. There is no escaping political regulation or regulatory administration in every branch of law, even those formally labeled "private." Realists carried out this two-pronged attack on *Lochner* relentlessly in the decades following 1905. Justice Holmes, who was many things but surely also a protorealist, dissented in *Lochner*. Holmes's theoretical work predates *Lochner,* and some of the work of the anti-*Lochner* realists was done, not in response to *Lochner,* but as an aid to the passage of the sort of legislation that was invalidated by *Lochner*. But *Lochner* turned Holmes and his allies from theorists into prophets, and there is no question that the movement Holmes helped form and represented picked up terrific steam once *Lochner* was decided.

The fruit of their labors, once depression hit, was a theoretical apparatus that could accommodate the regulatory demands—moral, political, and economic—triggered by the Great Depression against the objection of due process. The third crisis in American constitutional governance was resolved by a transformation of the jurisprudence in which constitutional interpretation—indeed all legal interpretation—would be conducted. Unlike the first two, the third crisis resulted in no new amendments to the Constitution. It developed no new structure or concept of constitutional governance. It did, however, more profoundly than they, affect the shape of the union and the texture of law in general.

The Court hinted at change in *Home Building and Loan Association v. Blaisdell,*[94] decided in January 1934. *Blaisdell* upheld a Minnesota law declaring a limited moratorium on mortgage payments against a challenge that the law violated Article 1, section 10 of the Constitution, impairing the obligation of contract. The Court justified the law as an appropriate "exercise of the reserved power of the state to protect the vital interests of the community,"[95] triggered by economic emergency. Chief Justice Charles Evans Hughes wrote:[96]

> [T]here has been a growing appreciation of public needs and of the necessity of finding ground for a rational compromise between individual rights and public welfare. . . . Where, in earlier days, it was thought that only the concerns of individuals or of classes were involved, and that those of the state itself were touched only remotely, it has later been found that the fundamental interests of the state are directly affected; and that the question is no longer merely that of one party to a contract as against another, but of the use of reasonable means to safeguard the economic structure upon which the good of all depends.

The Chief Justice added a brief but portentous statement: "What has been said on that point [the contract clause] is also applicable to the contention presented under the due process clause."[97] That was the hint. What the Court meant by the hint became clear two months later, in *Nebbia v. New York*.[98]

In *Nebbia*, the Court upheld against due process challenge a law empowering New York's Milk Control Board "to fix minimum and maximum . . . retail prices to be charged by . . . stores to consumers for consumption off the premises where sold." The Court accepted the New York legislature's justification of the law as a health measure (producers failing to receive a reasonable return relax their vigilance against contamination) and as a scheme to ensure the prosperity of a "paramount industry of the state."[99] But the Court was not returning to a more relaxed version of *Lochner,* or to *Munn v. Illinois.* Justice Owen Roberts announced a radical departure in the Court's due process jurisprudence:[100]

> The Fifth Amendment, in the field of federal activity, and the Fourteenth, as respects State action, do not prohibit governmental regulation for the public welfare. They merely condition the exertion of the admitted power, by securing that the end shall be accomplished by methods consistent with due process. And the guaranty of due process, as has often been held, demands only that the law shall not be unreasonable, arbitrary, or capricious, and that the means selected shall have a real and substantial relation to the object sought to be attained.

No longer must the state or federal government show that the matter regulated is "affected with a public interest." No longer need they persuade the Court that the regulation is a bona fide exercise of the police power. All due process requires is that the regulation be for the "public welfare" however the states or federal government choose to define it, that the regulation not be "unreasonable, arbitrary, or capricious," and that the means selected "have a real and substantial relation to the object sought to be attained." Not only was the extreme version of *Lochner* dead but also the flexible version, and even the capacious formula of *Munn v. Illinois.*

After *Nebbia,* the due process rights of the unified citizen of the Fourteenth Amendment would never again be an obstacle to the states or the federal government enacting laws in the interests of the people.[101] The Roosevelt administration and Congress were free to craft whatever schemes they saw fit, consistent with other provisions of the Constitution, so long as they were for the public welfare and consistent with the "real and substantial relation" test of *Nebbia.*

Historians have debated whether *Nebbia* was the turning point in the Court's stance towards the New Deal or whether the real change occurred three years later, in *West Coast Hotel Co. v. Parrish.*[102] After all, *Parrish* overruled *Adkins,* and the Court was far friendlier to New Deal programs after *Parrish* than it had been between *Nebbia* and *Parrish. Parrish* was handed down on 29 March 1937, just seven weeks after the Roosevelt administration unveiled its Court-packing plan on 5 February. The thought, which has achieved the status of myth in American scholarship, is that the Court changed course starting with *Parrish*, not *Nebbia*, in order to forestall the Court-packing plan. Recent scholarship, however, has debunked the myth.[103]

What is at stake is the character of the Court as a legal or as a political institution. If the Court responds to short-term political pressures, then it is a political institution like any other, having no greater claim to make legal decisions than Congress or the Executive, and certainly less when the judgments of the Court conflict with the desires of the democratic branches of government. The Court can legitimately make undemocratic decisions only if constitutional law is an autonomous discipline with its own practices and logic. If *Blaisdell* and *Nebbia* are the key decisions, then the source of the Court's constitutional revolution was not political pressure but the autonomous discipline of law. If *Parrish* is key, then the case can be made that the Court is a political institution responding to ordinary political pressures and illegitimately resisted the democratic will of the state legislatures and Congress during the First New Deal.

To hold that *Blaisdell* and *Nebbia* are key and that the Court transformed the meaning of unified citizenship under the Fifth and Fourteenth Amendments as a consequence of autonomous legal development is not to say that the Court was immune to politics of any sort whatsoever; it is to say only that the Court was not responding to ordinary political pressure. The Court was responding to politics of a very different sort—the politics of lawyers using the practices and logic of law to shape legal development.

Although *Nebbia* deprived due process of its role constraining exercise of the police power, due process was to play a significant role in the era following the Second World War. The spirit of *Lochner* has haunted American constitutional jurisprudence, in other guises, to this day.[104] The most significant role of due process in the post-*Lochner* era has been to constrain the government, not in pursuit of the public welfare, but in the methods by which that pursuit is carried on. Due process changed from a limitation on programs to a limitation on the implementation of programs. Unified citizenship was no longer a bar to government action, but a source of rights, both procedural and substantive, to ensure the fairness and integrity of government action. The story of the subjection of the operations of an expanded government to due process takes us into contemporary times.

VI

The American state thus faced the same challenge as Weimar in roughly the same era: Would constitutional government have the capacity to marshal its powers in the "interests of its people"? But Weimar faced this challenge without a constitutional history in which development followed repeatedly upon crisis. It never answered the *constitutional* questions of union. These had been answered for it in a monarchic political structure. It never developed a conception of citizenship against the sovereign. By the crisis of the 1930s, Americans had already tested the preconditions of constitutional government in action. The Weimar crisis set theory this task instead. In the United States, by contrast, the task for theory was a reconstruction of private law, with the aim of undermining the distinction between private law and government.

The question then in the United States was not, as it was in Weimar, whether a democratic government whose legitimacy sprang not from a preconceived monarchic notion of the state's rights and duties but solely from the free expression of differing and conflicting interests would be able to make hard decisions. After all, social and economic regulation in the United States before the New Deal was sufficiently sparse compared with the scheme laid down in Bismarck's Germany that American executives and legislatures had never been put to the hard tests of political accommodation that hobbled Weimar—along with defeat, occupation, and reparations. Also, prosperity and a patriotic war had shoved issues of social regulation from the spotlight during much of the period between *Lochner* and the Great Depression.[105] Rather, the question put to the American states by *Lochner* was whether, in the name of individual liberty, the judicial branch of government could stop executives and legislatures from implementing regulatory decisions they were otherwise perfectly capable of making.

As comparison with the American case makes clear, the reaction of legal theory in Weimar to the incapacity of the state to meet the regulatory demands made on it by economic crisis and social conflict was by no means the only possible reaction. Where the constitution precedes the state, as it did in the United States, the challenge to the state's capacity to meet these demands takes a different form than where the state precedes the constitution. The challenge to the regulatory capacity of the United States flowed from the Constitution itself, requiring reconciliation of the state's regulatory capacity with rights granted by the Constitution to individuals. The challenge to the Weimar state focused instead on the capacity of constitutional government to make politically necessary decisions. When crisis takes this specific form, then the answers provided by the Weimar theorists exhaust the ways in legal theory of meeting crises of the state and its constitution.

One can attempt to force the battle accompanying the crisis into the frame and, under the rules, of the given constitutional and legal order. One can try to hold together the fragile or even crumbling unity culturally and spiritually or organizationally and institutionally, and to strengthen the state against the battle as a Smendesque unity of integration or as a Helleresque unity of action and decision. Here it is of secondary importance whether this is done by preserving, changing, or even violating the existing constitutional and legal order. Finally, one can take up the battle, make a clear decision about friend and enemy, and choose sides—again, depending on the situation—and make it a matter of politics whether to preserve or abandon the frame and rules of the given constitutional and legal order.

There are no other answers, and they can hardly all be right at the same time. So the Weimar struggle over methods and aims persists in the ongoing quest for the right answer.

The Shattering of Methods in Late Wilhelmine Germany

INTRODUCTION

Stefan Korioth

The Weimar debate on the tasks, aims, and methods of the theory of the law of the state spans a discrete period in the development of public law in Germany. However, it would be simplistic to seek in Weimar alone the factors that triggered this debate; the Weimar discussion took up issues and provided answers to questions that were of longer standing. Just as the problems of the Weimar state were rooted in certain developments in the Empire, the Weimar debate had its background in the latter years of the Empire—between 1900 and 1918. Much of what developed into the principal approaches of the 1920s had already been tentatively reflected, and sometimes even tested, in individual problems of state law during those two decades. However, this prehistory of Weimar state law theory lacked clear programmatic contours and positions. Apart from attempts to further elaborate the legal positivism that had first emerged in state law theory at the beginning of the Empire, the specific character of this prehistory was to show the early beginnings of tendencies toward radical change. The latter trend tended to undermine the foundations of the constitutional positivism that had dominated state law theory almost unchallenged up to 1900. This happened gradually, often unnoticed, sometimes even by the authors themselves. No express questioning or radical critique of positivism took place; the fundamental debate on redirecting state law theory was reserved for Weimar.

The history of Weimar can be understood only against the background of what was gradually being called into question. Therefore, the subject of the following overview is, first, the basics of state law positivism. Only after this can we ask how, after 1900, the familiar paths of state law reasoning were abandoned and why state law positivism eroded.

I

State law positivism began to develop in 1850 and achieved its dominant position around 1880.

With the failure of the revolution of 1848, bourgeois hopes for a united, democratic German nation-state were shattered. Germany sank back into small monarchical states, linked loosely by the German Union [*Deutscher Bund*]. The bourgeois political liberalism of the first half of the century became economic liberalism; bourgeois interests no longer sought political participation in the state, but freedom *from* the state—particularly freedom of economic action.

Two works by the civil law scholar Carl Friedrich von Gerber (1823–91) contain terms that state law positivists elaborated into an entire school of thought. Disappointment in the political situation, as well as the inclination to make peace with it, is mirrored in Gerber's postulate that politics is "not the purpose, but simply the material"[1] of the law of the state. This postulate defines the tasks, as well as the limitations, of state law theory: to exclude the "purely political aspects" of the state while including its "legal aspects."[2] The theory of the law of the state was not intended to mirror political hopes—that is, to serve as a scholarly instrument of legal policy, as was often the case in the law of the state before 1850—but rather to begin to address the positive law of the state. This can be seen as the legal correlate to the bourgeoisie's acceptance of the political status quo in the years after 1850. Gerber's terminology refers to the manner in which the theory of the law of the state can do justice to its new task: the "creation of a theoretical system"[3] through formal "legal construction"[4] that would learn from and match the conceptual clarity achieved in private law. Only this could be the foundation of the "theoretical autonomy"[5] of state law.

The finest hour of this program, soon to be called "legal method" by its supporters, began with the formation of the Empire between 1867 and 1871. The bourgeoisie again proved incapable of creating a state responsive to its own interests; the leading role in creating the Empire was taken by the individual monarchic Länder. But German national unity was nonetheless achieved; the bourgeoisie quickly adapted to the new state, and the Empire's early decades were relatively quiet politically. Gerber's call for a systematic ordering of positive law and for the abolition of wishful political thinking from state law theory now met with strong approval, especially in the face of the need to interpret the Empire's constitution, the first codification of state law to apply to all of Germany. The task of systematically exploring the new legal order was essentially completed by Paul Laband (1838–1918), whose background, like Gerber's, was in civil law. Laband's *State Law of the German Reich* [*Staatsrecht des Deutschen Reiches*], which went to five editions between 1876 and 1914, was the most authoritative and influential elaboration of state law in the Empire and brought constitutional positivism to full bloom.[6] Laband formulated the credo of positivism in the introduction to his book in a few succinct sentences: Legal treatment of state law consists, on the one hand, "of the construction of legal institutions, of retracing individual norms to general concepts" and, on the other, of "deriving the consequences that result from these concepts." Both consist of "purely logical intellectual endeavor," for which "nothing can substitute." "All historical, political, and philosophical considerations" are "without significance" for state law doctrine. State law doctrine is nothing but a "conscientious and complete identification of the positive legal material and its logical mastery through concepts."[7] Laband's remarks on how concepts are constructed and their productive power indicate that his positivism was not a statutory positivism [*Gesetzespositivismus*], narrowly confined to the construction of statutes. With unmistakable pride in the productivity of legal concept-construction, Laband proclaimed: "A gap in the Constitution . . . must not be taken for a gap in the constitution of the state. The latter is an inconceivable concept; statutes may have gaps, but the legal order can no more have gaps than can the order of nature."[8]

What explains the sweeping success of this positivism, based on a conceptual, systematic understanding of law, in the years immediately following its formulation? Initially, positivism sought to establish the autonomy of the theory of state law, matching the theory of private law in methodological stringency. It did away with the desolate state of scholarship in the field of public law, which had most often been limited to listing positive norms, with, depending on the author's whim, historical, political, or philosophical trimmings. For the first time, attempts were made to offer a state law theory that could provide rational, logically grounded, and reliable answers in the field of constitutional law; in short, positivism established a doctrine of constitutional law. In addition, positivist procedure linked the field of law with the methods of the expanding natural sciences and the tendency, characteristic of nineteenth-century thought, to turn all of life into science. The positivist trust in "what is" corresponded to the general trend in the humanities that followed the collapse of philosophical idealism in the first half of the century.

State law positivism also had a salubrious political effect. Its pointed demand that the law of the state be isolated from all its determining factors neutralized the latent political conflicts of the Empire, especially the precarious balance of power between the monarchic and bourgeois elements in the political system.[9] The Constitution of 1871 avoided deciding between monarchic and democratic legitimacy. Laband's law of the state reflected this strategy: indeed, for Laband, the legitimacy of the legal order was not an issue, and he ignored the political aspects of law and the social reality that law might encounter or create. Over the first twenty-five years of the Empire, numerous objections were raised against Laband's doctrinal style—some of them of great substantive and methodological depth.[10] However, these objections died away before 1900, and they remained largely without effect in the decades following.

II

What changed during the last two decades of the Empire? The Gerber-Laband school of "legal method" remained dominant, but two new developments may be discerned as tendencies.

The first continued on the path of state law positivism. However, it sought to explain more precisely the autonomy of legal reasoning and argumentation and, in particular, to provide an epistemological basis for differentiating between state law doctrine, on the one hand, and sociological and political analysis of the state, on the other. Its critique of the positivism of Gerber and Laband was not aimed at the program of "legal method" but at the inconsistencies in how Laband and others put it into practice. The texts by Max Weber (1864–1920), Georg Jellinek (1851–1911), and Hans Kelsen (1881–1973) that follow reflect this school of thought, though Kelsen came to conclusions very different from those of Weber and Jellinek.

1. Weber's ideal of "value-free" science shared the efforts of the representatives of state law positivism to keep its doctrine free of political and sociological admixture. His belief that legal concepts and norms could be viewed from various perspectives was a precept of legal positivism. Although Laband had expressly acknowledged the value of historical and sociological research for law, he felt that the disciplines had no place in doctrines of positive law. Weber, on the other hand (notably in the text below), examined what the sociology of law could say about legal concepts and norms and what relationship it had to legal doctrine. Weber developed a dual sense of the "validity" of a legal norm: sociological validity is "factual probability," the "chance" that the state will take measures to implement law. This chance "is a . . . calculable possibility . . . like any possible event in inanimate or animate nature."[11] Validity in the legal sense, by contrast, is a "logical ought." Weber makes this distinction explicit in his principal sociological work, published posthumously: "The legal, or more precisely, the doctrinal view assigns itself the task of investigating the true meaning of sentences whose contents represent a system that is supposed to be decisive for the behavior of a particular group of people—that is, of investigating which factual constellations fall under these sentences and how." In contrast, the sociology of law is concerned with empirical validity: "The meaning of the word 'legal order'

then changes entirely. It means not a cosmos of norms whose correctness can be determined through logic but a complex of factual determinants of human behavior."[12] Are there points of contact between the two concepts of validity? In the text below, Weber refers specifically to the application of law by courts. Judicial decision making is determined not only by doctrinal, logical considerations but also—from a sociological point of view—by "personal attitudes" and "class conflicts." By addressing the relationship between norms and their application, Weber was addressing a problem that, prior to 1914, had also triggered other theorists' doubts about the foundations of state law positivism; we shall see this again in the writings of Carl Schmitt.

The methodological foundations of Georg Jellinek's work (starting in 1900 with his *General Theory of the State* [*Allgemeine Staatslehre*]) manifest a particular affinity with Weber's approach. (Presumably, the two authors influenced each other; it is certain that Jellinek and Weber communicated during the years they both taught in Heidelberg.) While Jellinek essentially acknowledged Laband's method in the field of state law doctrine,[13] it is his efforts to supplement state law positivism with social-scientific analysis that have lasting significance. Like Weber, Jellinek had a dual perspective, the most famous example of which is his "theory of the state's two-sidedness" [*Zwei-Seiten Lehre*], the centerpiece of his *General Theory of the State*. For Jellinek, the theory of the state broke down into a "social theory" and a "legal theory"; the sociological and legal aspects of the state could be distinguished depending on the epistemic goal of the observer. However, Jellinek was never able to specifically identify the relationship between the two, whether it involved a haphazard juxtaposition of state and legal theory or mutually dependent perspectives.

The duality of the legal and the socio-political perspectives is also characteristic of Jellinek's *Constitutional Amendment and Constitutional Transformation* [*Verfassungsänderung und Verfassungswandlung* (1906)]. Its focus is the problem of constitutional transformation, by which Jellinek means a change in the constitution that "leaves [the text of the constitution] formally unchanged and is brought about by facts that need not be accompanied by an intent to change, or awareness of changing, the constitution." Amendment, by contrast, indicates changes in the constitution's text, although unlike amendment of the American Constitution, amendments in German constitutional law (as in most constitutional systems) erase the old text in its entirety and replace it with a new one. Jellinek failed to achieve a deeper theoretical understanding of the problem; instead, he distinguished various types of constitutional transformation. That transformation might, for example, be the result of (incorrect) interpretation of constitutional norms by parliaments, governments, or courts. It might be limited to filling in constitutional gaps or extend to complete overthrow of the state's existing order. The most important motive for constitutional transformation is political necessity. It is instructive that Jellinek provides no clear doctrinal classification of the problem. In particular, he does resolve whether there are any limits to constitutional transformation—that is, any criteria for its constitutionality. Instead, he states somewhat helplessly that in constitutional transformation, "law and fact, otherwise kept strictly separate, merge into one another." Jellinek's failure to deal normatively with the phenomenon is attributable to his tacit adherence to the axiom of state law positivism that the theory of the law of the state must deal exclusively with the positive legal order. Taking this into account, one can understand why Jellinek believed that the "irrationality of reality" turned against the positivity of law in the process of constitutional transformation and why he acknowledged, almost resignedly, that "[a]ctual political forces operate according to their own laws, which are independent of any legal forms." The theory of the law of the state can merely track the success or failure of transformative strivings of political forces. "The *fait accompli*, the accomplished fact," Jellinek argues, "is a historical phenomenon of constitution-forming power, and attempting to fight it with theories of legitimacy is an impotent enterprise." Thus the methodological yield of Jellinek's treatise is ultimately quite meager. Constitutional transformation is understood and described as an empirical phenomenon; the influence of reality on law is acknowledged; but the issues raised by that influence are not normatively resolved. Jellinek does not offer a substitute for state law positivism but merely supplements it with a description of socio-political processes.

Weber's and Jellinek's twofold approach, in which norms claim validity as precepts while at the same time becoming social reality through behavior that obeys or transforms the norm, was soon sharply criticized by Hans Kelsen. Kelsen's 1911 speech, "On the Borders Between Legal and Sociological Method" [*Über Grenzen zwischen juristischer und soziologischer Methode*], summarizes the methodological postulates of his first major work, *Main Problems in State Law Theory Developed from the the Theory of the Normative Proposition* [*Hauptprobleme der Staatsrechtslehre entwickelt aus der Lehre vom Rechtssätze* (1911)], published in the same year. In his work, Kelsen subjects the state law theory of the last phase of German monarchic constitutionalism [*Spätkonstitutionalismus*] to radical examination and critique, finding repeatedly that the concepts of the Gerber-Laband school, contrary to the assertions of the two authors, are rife with methodological "syncretism," overstepping the bounds of the purely legal. Kelsen contrasts this "syncretism" with his own fundamental methodological postulate, influenced by neo-Kantianism,[14] according to which "is" and "ought" denote different, logically irreconcilable structures of thought. These different forms of thought constitute different fields of knowledge: "The contrast between 'is' and 'ought' is the basis of the division into explanatory and normative theoretical disciplines, knowledge of causes and knowledge of norms [*Kausal- und Normwissenschaften*]." Legal scholarship can be conceived only as knowledge of norms—its concepts may only come from the "world of 'ought'." Kelsen therefore rejects as a logical impossibility Jellinek's and Weber's argument that there can be different sides of one and the same object of knowledge: A concept, Kelsen maintains, cannot have two conceptual contents. Thus, for Kelsen the validity of a legal norm is an exclusively normative concept, and Weber's legal-sociological validity merely a question of the "efficacy" of a norm. Kelsen acknowledged only the normative side of Jellinek's "two-sides theory."

The significance of Kelsen's 1911 work lay in his attempt to determine precisely the methodological position of legal scholarship. He gave theoretical grounding and certainty, previously lacking, to the call, raised since 1850, for the methodological autonomy of state law theory. Kelsen's methodological rigor subjected legal scholarship to strict, exact, and objective scientific standards. The task of maturing a once epistemologically naive positivism (which Kelsen had undertaken even prior to 1914) ultimately led him to his "pure theory of law."

2. While Weber, Jellinek, and even Kelsen remained faithful to the tradition of the second half of the nineteenth century,[15] other authors distanced themselves from the positivist program even prior to 1914. Whether their goal in so doing was to overcome positivism or merely to supplement it remains uncertain, for the departures from positivism, undertaken with varying energy, did not occur at the level of methodology; instead, when treating specific issues, traditional methodological guidelines tended to be tacitly ignored. The trend in substance was far ahead of its methodological reflection; the methodological presuppositions of these works can be deduced only from their treatment of substance. This trend is manifested in the early works of Erich Kaufmann (1880–1972), Rudolf Smend (1882–1975), and Carl Schmitt (1888–1985),[16] the authors who during the 1920s were among the most prominent advocates of a departure from the Empire's formalist tradition of state law theory, of a turn from form to substance. The emerging anti-positivism in essence favored mobilization of the forces of "life"— the power of political facts and historical ideas over the sober, rational, often seemingly shallow technicality of positivism. The theories of state and law were directed toward life. While Kelsen's methodology was influenced by neo-Kantianism, the anti-positivist view corresponded (albeit still vaguely before 1914) to the contemporary philosophical school of "life philosophy" [*Lebensphilosophie*].[17] This school expressed an early discomfort with an increasingly complex world, manifested in the mechanization and industrialization of all areas of life. Traces of skepticism toward "the modern"—the massing of populations, democratization, the social pluralism of economic organizations and associations, and the isolation of the individual in a liberal society lacking in meaning and orientation—are evident in the pre-1914 legal writings of Schmitt, Smend, and Kaufmann. Smend, for ex-

ample, emphasized the state's own roots against the dynamic of society and the liberal and "rational" concept of suffrage.[18] Even prior to 1914, such arguments reflected concern over the stability of the state as a national union and an association through domination [*Herrschaftsverband*]. It comes as no surprise that these politically conservative writers after 1918 focused particularly on the problem of the "unity" of the state in the face of an increasingly differentiated organization of state and society.

Carl Schmitt's 1912 *Statute and Judgment* [*Gesetz und Urteil*], his first major work following his 1910 dissertation, made a clear break with Laband's positivism. Schmitt's subject was the application of law by judges. From the "gaplessness" of the legal order that he posited, Laband had concluded that the judge is nothing but the "*viva vox legis*" and the application of law, like the work of doctrinal systematization, nothing but logical operations and subsumption.[19] This view of judicial decision making allowed for no element of individual discretion, will, or even subjective bias. Schmitt did away with the concept of the judge as a "subsuming automaton." His response to the question with which he began—"When is a judicial decision correct?"—was that correctness depends not on whether the decision matches the statute, but on whether "a different judge would have arrived at the same decision." This was not intended as *carte blanche* to ignore statutes; rather, Schmitt's interest, given his assumption that the legal order has gaps, focused from the start on the exceptional case in which the judge finds no prescription for his decision in the statutes. Schmitt begins by emphasizing that the value of a judgment lies in large part in the fact that a decision was made at all. The power of legal practice and the beliefs of the judges give decisions their legitimacy. These factors are legally significant, without regard to the legality of the decision; they are the criteria of legal correctness. Such arguments foreshadow Schmitt's major themes of the 1920s: orientation toward the exception, the emphasis on the value of the act of deciding, and the distinction between legality and legitimacy, which he plays off against one another.

What were the reasons for this deep, albeit rather offhandedly executed, break with tradition? With the problem of law application, Schmitt had taken up a complex of issues which, to many lawyers of the late Empire, prevailing theory had failed satisfactorily to resolve; numerous works on the activities of judges had appeared during this period that acknowledged, in various ways, breaks with legal practice and doctrine. The "School of Free Law" [*Freirechtsschule*],[20] which grew stronger after 1900, went so far as to center its reflections around the problem of the judge who finds no certain statutory guidelines for making decisions. The Wilhelmine judge apparently no longer saw himself as a subsuming automaton and did not recognize himself in Laband's depiction. It makes complete sense that a new characterization of judicial activity—between faithfulness to statute and freedom from it—was sought at the end of the Empire: with the onset of rapid industrialization in the second half of the nineteenth century, the need for norms and the density of norms regulating individual spheres of life had grown steeply. At the same time, the state developed into an interventionist entity that sought to, and had to, regulate social processes more intensely. The increased density of norms—their proliferation and extension throughout society—led, on the one hand, to increasing judicialization; judges became more important. On the other hand, increased production of norms in legislation did not mean that judges could find ready-made solutions to legal conflicts in statutes. On the contrary, "constant intervention means constant statutory revision on the part of the lawmaker . . . but at the same time, a constant impulse towards greater flexibility of judicial decision making, because there is no other way of mediating between the cumbersome apparatus of norms and rapidly changing reality."[21] The concept of the judge who only applies statutes thus necessarily underwent a crisis. It could no longer explain the new role of the judge, let alone justify it. Schmitt's theory, which declared the judge to be empowered to create law outside given norms and emphasized the autonomy of legal practice (as against the codifying legislature and systematizing scholarship), filled precisely this vacuum. At the same time, it displayed skepticism of the nineteenth century's confidence that a farsighted, planned, and rational society could be created by means of statutes.

The fact that new developments in the social and socio-political realm were translated legally into a departure from state law positivism explains the crumbling of Laband's constructive formalism after 1900. The "legal method" reflected the political compromise achieved in 1871 and the subsequent, comparatively calm decades. Its strength lay in the neutralization of political antagonisms by formalizing law and ridding it of any political or social goals; however, for precisely this reason it was unable to stand up to the challenge of new political developments and needs.

Yet the Empire was far from being a static period in state and society. Rapid industrialization made the "social question"—the place of the working class in society and its relationship to the state—a pressing problem; with the rise of the Social Democratic Party, the compromise of 1871 between the monarchy and the bourgeoisie was increasingly called into question. Among lawyers, the first to deal with the resulting conflicts were the judges—another reason that reflection on the methodology of judicial decision making led to the first cracks in the traditional view. At the same time, intellectual life in Germany was marked increasingly clearly by a departure from rationalism and Enlightenment ideas of progress. Starting around 1900, a restlessness pervaded many spheres of life and quickly gave rise to radical cultural critique.[22] The art and literature of this period reflected ambivalence between the traditional and the modern. It comes as no surprise that it was during this period that state law theorists departed from the positivist tradition. They aimed to reestablish harmony between constitutional law and

its political framework, which they thought might be lost. They also emphasized the "life-world" and the "is," as opposed to the positivist retreat from the
state's reality, which seemed to have reached a dead end. Schmitt's focus on
the decision against the norm was reflected in remarks by Erich Kaufmann
on the role of scholarship: The theory of the law of the state had an obligation to "the real life of the state" and its functioning; "any scholarly work using the usual methods of formal jurisprudence must fail."[23] The struggle over
the foundations of state law theory that began after 1920 was intimated by
such statements, which contained, for the first time, explicit critique of the
uninvolved, distanced attitude of Laband's law of the state. From the point
of view of intellectual history, despite the semi-official position of Laband's
law of the state, the epoch from 1871 to 1914 can by no means be described
as a monolithic era of positivism.

ON LEGAL THEORY AND SOCIOLOGY

Max Weber

Max Weber, "Diskussionsrede zu dem Vortrag von H. Kantorowicz
'Rechtswissenschaft und Soziologie'," *Gesammelte Aufsätze zur Soziologie
und Sozialpolitik* (Tübingen: Mohr, 1924), 477–81. Originally appeared
in *Verhandlungsberichte über den 1. Deutschen Soziologentag* (Glashütten
im Taunus: Auvermann, 1911), 323–30.

We can view a specific legal precept [*Rechtssatz*]—for example, a clause of the
Civil Code—in two very different ways, or rather, a specific legal precept is
something very different according to the question we bring to it. We can,
on the one hand, ask about the "meaning" of the precept; that is, assuming
its existence as a general, hypothetical norm, we can ask: Can it, given its
meaning, be applied to cases X, Y, and Z in such a way that a judge, if
he wants to decide "*correctly,*" must decide thus and so? This is a question of
doctrine, not of fact, not a sociological question in any sense of the word, but
a purely legal question. On the other hand, we can view the same legal precept sociologically; immediately, it not only takes on a new meaning, but is
something completely different. What "*is*" the legal precept, sociologically?
The meaning of the precept is that there exists a specific factual *probability,* a
"chance" that once those fact situations X, Y, and Z are present, *factual* consequences of a specific sort will result, factual pressure in a specific direction
will be exercised in favor of those who turn in a specific way to specific institutions set up by the state—to the "courts," who are capable of spending the

money it costs and willing to let themselves in for the difficulties connected with it. This chance—that the economic or other interests involved, given the average, *common* "interpretation" of a printed sentence in a law code, *will actually* be backed by the protection of the state—this chance is, in principle, a possibility whose "probability" can be calculated—in principle, not in fact—as much as any possible event in dead or living nature. The claim of legal *doctrine* that a legal precept with a certain content "is valid" means only, in the language of sociology, that a specific *probability* exists that specific *factual* circumstances lead to a specific coercive interference by the state. . . .

Now, whether in individual cases these legal precepts are actualized through a judgment that is "*correct*"—if we look at the *meaning* of the legal precept, that is, if we ask a very different question from the sociological one—well, *that* depends on an enormous number of sociological circumstances and quite concrete things. Certainly, in certain circumstances, even on whether the judge had a lot to drink that morning. It depends upon the lawyer's education, it depends on thousands of concrete circumstances that, whether social in nature or not, are in any case pure facticity. The "validity" of a legal precept in its *sociological* meaning is a factual statement about empirical probability; the validity in its legal meaning is a logical "ought," and these are two very different things. What I have demonstrated here with a clause of the Civil Code, perhaps somewhat unclearly, may become clearer if I choose a different example. . . . When we look at the following sequence of sentences: "The United States has the right, as against its individual states, to sign trade treaties"—first sentence; second sentence: "accordingly, the United States has signed a trade treaty with Mexico"; third sentence: "this trade treaty is not consonant with the interests of the United States"; fourth sentence: "as the balance of payments of the United States is influenced unfavorably by it"; "the interests of the United States would have lain more in such and such a direction"; "it is the fault of the Constitution of the United States that something like that could occur"; "thus the mood in the United States is such and such," etc. If you take these individual sentences together and ask yourself what is *meant* in each case by "the United States," you would, I say, come to the conclusion: each time something different but never the *legal* concept, United States. The legal concept "United States" is, namely, a complex of legal norms whose meaning must be interpreted by legal scholars, while "United States" in the sense with which we deal with it in economics, sociology, politics, everywhere except legal scholarship, is a practically endless complex of parliamentarians of every possible stripe, of presidents and bureaucracy, the military, of coal mines and gold mines and blast furnaces and iron, what is or could be produced there, of workers and I don't know what else—perhaps something different in each of the cases mentioned, conceptualized differently from different points of view. But the

legal concept "United States" has the enormous advantage over the sociological concept "United States" that its content is in principle *logically* clear,
and for that reason the sociological concept and the collective concepts
of other disciplines regularly take the legal concept as an orienting principle, although the *legally conceptualized* system "United States" is a purely
ideal thought-construct, something that has no empirical reality in life as
such, but instead is something that is, as we used to say, "valid." It is something
that "exists," exists *empirically,* only to the extent that it *tends* to be thought
by lawyers in accordance with its *valid* meaning—thus in accordance, more
or less precisely, with the ideal *norm* of legal thought—not because it is *valid*
as this ideal norm, but because a certain chance exists that people, especially
judges, *act* in a specific manner that accords with it.

Thus: the doctrinal view—that is, the view of the meaning of constitutional law and state law—and the view of a legally ordered commonwealth,
for which, viewed doctrinally, they are supposed to be "valid"—are two entirely different things.

Now the question arises: *how is it logically possible* that sociological findings can nevertheless gain significance for legal considerations [Hermann]
Kantorowicz mentioned first, the unavoidable gaps in the legal system in
the logical sense. It is, he said, not a logically closed system. Granted! However, can we infer from this alone that the sociological view, which is so heterogeneous, is suited to help out? That is certainly not what Kantorowicz
meant to say; he must have meant only that from knowledge of the factual
structure of the society—or, as I quoted, of the commonwealth, which is
a quite heterogeneous legal term that we use for the sake of brevity—that
from this knowledge, under certain circumstances, the only possible—because the only reasonable—*purpose* of legal norms may be reckoned. He
himself has offered, as a classic example of what he believes to be logically
correct, the words of the Swiss Code, under which the judge is to decide the
individual case as he would craft the legal norm were he the legislator. This
is clearly not a sociological but a strictly Kantian principle, taken almost word
for word from the *Critique of Practical Reason.* . . .

Now, gentlemen, what results the recognition of this principle could have
for our jurisprudence is, in turn, a question that is very difficult to answer
sociologically. The position of a judge in England is different from that of a
judge here, and this is not at all a matter of practical indifference for the
consequences that would result if we would put this, at least *apparently* and
from the judge's perspective, very great power in the hands of the German
judge, whose social position is very different. However, this question would
lead us into legal politics, and we are staying away from that. But as far as facts
are concerned, we should remember that gaps in the law are already today
not the only instances, brought about by legislation itself, of adjudication

apart from law or contrary to it. For if it is correct that there can be two ways of finding law, "formal justice" and "Kadi justice," and if [Rudolf von] Ihering could say of formal justice that form is the enemy of arbitrariness, the twin sister of freedom—we won't ask whether he was right or not—then we should recall that as a matter of fact the institution of the jury trial opens the door here through which Kadi justice apart from and contrary to law enters. Often, jurors render a finding of manslaughter because they lack the courage to accept the consequence that someone found guilty of murder on circumstantial evidence will be condemned to death. Often jurors find a man innocent of the rape of a girl because the girl previously had sexual intercourse—in both situations, contrary to law. But jurors are not obliged to give reasons; there is no institution for rectification; despite all law, and despite the fact that the law's intent, of course, is to bind the jurors to its meaning, they evade it de facto. . . .

And now I come to legal history. . . . Essentially, all that my colleagues have talked about is that sociology is to serve legal history and that legal history is to be pursued sociologically—that is, that legal history should have as its subject the facts of legal life, the way in which law actually comes to life, and not what can be construed from some past legal norms. I would like to say one thing on that: The crucial question of what is relevant to legal history—and should therefore become its object—can be decided only from a systematic perspective. Research in legal history can only be conducted in such a way—it actually is only conducted in such a way—that, if I have before me a "legal source," by which I mean a source of knowledge of the law—be it a legal code, ancient legal sayings, a judgment, a private document, or whatever—I must necessarily first get a picture of it in legal *doctrine,* the *validity* of which legal precept it *logically* presupposes. I find this out by transporting myself back as far as possible into the soul of a judge of the time; and by asking how a judge of the time would have to decide in a concrete case presented to him, if this legal precept which I am construing doctrinally were taken by him as the basis of his decision. As soon as one looks at the actual process of research in legal history, this cannot be denied, even though you won't perhaps believe it at first glance. Only on the basis of these doctrinal considerations do I become capable at all of noticing that—as often enough happened—in such and such case the actual legal consciousness did not function this way, not in accordance with the ideally construable meaning that I had found. And only then does my eye really open to *how* the living law of the period de facto looked, that is, *how* it was actually expressed in real coercion; perhaps—indeed, probably—extremely contradictory, and differing from court to court. In other words, as a heuristic principle a legal-doctrinal construction is indispensable even for the law of the past, even for legal history. Thus I would consider it unjustifiable to make a distinction—

to view law that no longer applies only as a fact and not as a "norm," and the law that still applies not as a fact, but as a norm. The meaning of both can be viewed in two different ways.

CONSTITUTIONAL AMENDMENT AND CONSTITUTIONAL TRANSFORMATION

Georg Jellinek

Originally appeared in Georg Jellinek, *Verfassungsänderung und Verfassungswandlung: Eine staatsrechtlich-politische Abhandlung* (Berlin: Häring, 1906), v, 3, 8–10, 16, 19–21, 43, 44–45, 72.

The course of this treatise moves along the borderline between the law of the state and politics. I have always supported the methodological separation and the intrinsic connection of these two disciplines. Today, however, while state law in Germany has already experienced such rich legal elaboration, the need for supplementing and propelling political research, as detailed in the text, becomes greater and greater. . . .

By constitutional amendment, I mean change in the text of the constitution through a purposeful act of will; by constitutional transformation, I mean change that allows the text to remain formally unchanged and is caused by facts that need not be accompanied by an intention or awareness of the change.[24] I need hardly mention that the theory of transformation is much more interesting than that of change. . . .

Constitutional laws tend to be surrounded by special guarantees of inviolability. Many forms of impediment have been devised to protect them from precipitate change. Only where such forms are present can we speak of constitutional laws in a special legal sense. Where they are lacking, there is no legal difference between laws thus designated as constitutional law and others.[25] But the practical experience we have had with such impediments to constitutional amendment has not lived up to expectations. Certainly changes that catch the eye at first glance may be made only if the prescribed forms are observed. If a constitutionally limited voting right is replaced by a general one, and if a constitutionally general voting right is replaced by a limited one, this can only happen, of course, by way of a law that comes into being through the forms of constitutional amendment. Yet the limits of the constitution, like all limits drawn by law, are always unclear; there is no guarantee that statutes that are intended to be based on the existing constitution will, nevertheless, not violate it, thus resulting in an undesired, or at least not expressly desired, amendment of the constitution. Constitutional precepts are often unclear and elastic, and only the legislator gives them firm meaning through implementing laws, just as only the judge creates clear awareness of the content of the statutes he is to apply. Just as, given the same legal texts, jurisprudence is everywhere based on people's changing views and needs,[26] the same is true of the legislature when it interprets the constitution through specific laws. What seems to be unconstitutional in one period appears constitutional in the following; thus, through transformation of its interpretation, the constitution itself experiences transformation. And it is not just the legislature that can produce such transformation; the practice of parliaments, as well as government and judicial authorities, can also do this and in fact does. They must interpret statutes and thus also constitutional law, and in their hands constitutional law may gradually attain a very different meaning in the system of laws than was originally inherent in it. As far as parliaments are concerned, they must decide in the first place on the constitutionality of their resolutions. If a parliamentary resolution requires an act of government to become valid, the government may prevent a deviation from the constitution that is inherent in the resolution. However, if its view coincides with that of parliament, there is no practical means of preventing the deviation. When a chamber makes an unconstitutional resolution in unreviewable fashion, there is no chance at all to render the provisions of the constitution valid. From such unconstitutional behavior, if it is consistently practiced, a transformation of the constitution may ensue. . . . . . .

This gives us an opportunity to discuss a protective tool in the constitution which, at first glance, is lauded as the strongest bulwark against unconstitutional excesses by the legislature itself. This is the familiar American institution by which the courts are to judge the material constitutionality of laws. . . . . . .

Thus, however, the judge in America does indeed take the place of the constitutional legislature. Not without reason have people in America described the courts as the third house of the legislature. In deciding on the constitutionality of laws, the judge is subject to the enormous pressure of public opinion, often split along party lines, which in a democracy forces itself with irresistible power upon anyone in public life; thus in many cases the judge's view of the law in question, as objective as he may think himself, is politically colored. That is seen in the fact that judges refuse only in exceptional cases to recognize laws, because they tend to take account of the political necessity that led the legislature to act. In the first century of its activity (1789–1889), the union's Supreme Court declared an act of Congress unconstitutional in only twenty-one cases, while the same court, in the same period, found 177 laws of all the individual states violative of the constitution—that is, given the large number of individual states and their laws, even fewer state than union laws.[27]

This ratio explains why no country in the world has as few constitution-changing laws as the American union. Only three amendments to the constitution, made necessary by the end of the Civil War, have been adopted in a century. Such apparent persistence, however, is possible only because American jurists have advanced the doctrine of "implied powers." In the letter of the constitution have been slumbering as-yet unrecognized powers, which are discovered by the legislature and then definitively brought to life by the judge. The Americans like to say that there are only three documents in world history whose words have been as thoroughly interpreted as their constitution: the Bible, the Koran, and the Digests. Yet the highest art of the interpreters consists not in interpreting from, but interpreting into. "Be bright and lively in expounding, if you can't expound, then pound it in" [*Im Auslegen seid frisch und munter, legt ihr's nicht aus, so leget was unter*]—these words of the poet [Goethe] are the highest maxim for constitutional transformation through judicial interpretation. . . .

. . .

Closely connected with the question of constitutional transformation is that of gaps in the constitution. The previous discussion has given many examples of the existence of such gaps, which cannot be denied if one has recognized the fundamental relationship between state and law, and knows that the state is first and foremost a historical phenomenon that may systematize law but not create it.[28] However, the historic episodes through which states realize themselves are accessible to human foresight only to a highly imperfect extent; it is thus impossible for law that hopes consciously to affect the future to hold its norms ready for unpredicted and unpredictable events in the future. Thus historical experience also leads to the realization that every constitution is fraught with gaps, which often become evident only after a long time and cannot be closed by the conventional methods of interpretation and analogy. . . .

. . .

Such unexpected discoveries of the existence of constitutional gaps may lead to constitutional transformation, where the new factual situation achieves common law recognition and is granted normal meaning. But realization of constitutional gaps is generally the task of the legislature, as constitutional amendment is the most certain way of thoroughly closing such a gap.

So far we have looked at transformation and amendment of our constitution that leaves the basic elements of today's model intact. Now, however, I will dare to ascend to a higher standpoint and, with bold daring, point out the highest and deepest problem of constitutional transformation. And I will attempt this with the cool objectivity of the man of science who wishes not to express feelings and desires, but only the findings of passionless knowledge, freed as far as possible of everything subjective.

Incomparably more instructive than all the constitutional transformations discussed, which take on one or another part of the constitution, are those that, without any sudden disruption of the state itself, completely destroy the existing state system and have as their ultimate result the complete rebuilding of the state. Long periods of time and the effect of great historical forces are necessary to give rise to something like this. If we look backwards through history we must grant, in astonishment, how even the most solid foundations of a state entity upon which it rested, apparently unshakably, for many centuries can crumble, shake, collapse, without the hand of a purposeful legislature having shaken them. The doctrine of such slow death of a constitution has been little cultivated. It could die because the value of its institutions sinks so low that no one desires them anymore—that ultimately none can be found to place their wills in the service of such institutions. . . .
. . .

The development of the constitution provides us with the great doctrine—the great significance of which has not yet been sufficiently appreciated—that legal precepts are incapable of actually controlling the distribution of power in a state. Real political forces move according to their own laws, which act independently of any legal forms. . . .

ON THE BORDERS BETWEEN LEGAL AND SOCIOLOGICAL METHOD

Hans Kelsen

Originally appeared in Hans Kelsen, *Über Grenzen zwischen juristischer und soziologischer Methode* (Tübingen: Mohr, 1911; reprint, Aalen: Scientia, 1970), 5, 6–7, 10–15, 18–19, 20–22, 23–30.

The methodological contrast between sociology and jurisprudence taken as a starting point for the following discussion is one between "is" and "ought." Just as I may say of something that it is, so can I say of the same thing that it ought to be, and in each case I have said something completely different. . . .
. . .

The contrast between "is" and "ought" is one of formal logic, and as long as we remain within the limits of formal logical examination, nothing leads from one to the other; the two worlds remain separated by an unbridgeable chasm. Logically, inquiring why some concrete "ought" should lead back only to something that ought to be, just as asking why something "is" can only be answered with something that is. . . .
. . .

The contrast between "is" and "ought" is decisive for the fundamental distinction between all scholarly disciplines. The separation into *explanatory* and *normative* disciplines, into causality and normativity, is based on the contrast between "is" and "ought." While one discipline is aimed at what actually exists—the world of what is: *reality*—the other turns to the world of what ought to be—of *ideality*. While the first, explanatory causal science, attempts to describe the causal necessity of the actual behavior of nature—that is, aims to *explain* what actually occurs—the latter, the normative disciplines, aim to know not what actually occurs, but what *ought* to occur; they create rules that prescribe behavior, demand that something be or not be—that is, establish an "ought." While the causal or explanatory disciplines strive to find *natural laws* according to which the processes of real life actually do—and *must*, without exception—occur, the purpose and subject of the normative disciplines, which by no means desire to *explain* any real occurrences, are merely *norms* on the basis of which something *ought* to occur, but by no means must, in fact, may not.[29]

The natural sciences, in particular, belong to the explanatory or causal disciplines, as do the historical disciplines; among the normative disciplines are found ethics, logic, and grammar.

If I now call sociology—a natural science of human society that strives to find the natural laws of social life, to *explain* what happens in society just as it actually happens in reality—if I call this sociology an explanatory, causal science, I believe I will encounter little opposition. Not so if I include legal scholarship within the normative disciplines,[30] for this could easily lead to the following misunderstanding: One might think I had assigned to legal scholarship a normative, norm-creating function, independent of positive law. Then one would, quite correctly, have to reject the idea that legal scholarship has a normative character in this sense. But one does not have to.

It is true that what must be considered "normative" in the original sense are the acts by which authorities create norms for the behavior of subjects; "normative," in this original sense, is merely the creation of commands and prohibitions on the basis of the actual power of domination. As this is a function of *will,* not of thought, no science can ever be described as normative in the original sense of the word. It is not the theoretical discipline called "ethics" that is the moral lawgiver, but the human conscience, or the will of God, or some other authority considered able to exercise will. It is not the science of grammar that commands the rules of language, but society that creates *usage.* Neither, then, is legal scholarship normative in the sense of a law-creating authority. Instead, here, as in all cases in which we speak of *normative* disciplines, the term in question is to be used in a derivative sense. It cannot describe a particular type of will; it must describe a certain form of *thought,* an unusual point of view that differs from other disciplines in its specific direction, and which can be called normative, because it turns toward the world of what ought to be and because its goal is to comprehend norms. If legal scholarship, in particular, is counted as a normative discipline, it must also be pointed out that legal scholarship, whose task is by no means to explain actual occurrences causally, cannot take the content of norms or of the "ought" at which its reflections are aimed from the nature of things or innate reason, as natural law theorists have done, but exclusively from positive law.

Of course, when I speak of legal scholarship as a normative discipline, I am not thinking of all the methodologically quite varied sciences collectively labeled legal scholarship. Naturally, legal history, as a historical discipline, is an exception and must be assigned to the explanatory disciplines. As legal scholarship in the actual, more narrow sense, only dogmatic doctrinal legal scholarship comes under consideration, and even this I take into account only to the extent that it is concerned with stabilizing fundamental legal concepts—to the extent that it is a general doctrine of law.

The important border between legal and sociological method—which follows from the difference between a point of view targeted at a specific "is," namely, social events, and the other targeted at a specific, namely legal, "ought"—this border lawyers are tempted to cross by seeking, over and above a knowledge of legal norms, an *explanation* for the real events that the norms are supposed to regulate. Such a push toward reality is psychologically understandable. It manifests the general disposition of the human spirit, which devotes itself more easily and preferably to the real than to the ideal, to the material than to the formal, and an *explanation* of real occurrences between people is thoroughly justifiable and necessary. Nevertheless, it is inadmissible to attempt such an *explanation* with means that cannot, by nature, provide it, because they are constructed as tools of a specifically normative point of view, not to explain what is really happening, but to record what ought to be. . . .

. . .

One of the most frequently discussed problems of the general doctrine of law is the basis for the validity of positive law or for the binding power of the legal order. Let us leave open whether such a problem even falls within the scope of law or is not rather metalegal—perhaps a problem of ethics. The fact is that *lawyers* feel an obligation to solve it. However, it is certain that the problem can only be normative—that is, that the relevant question is why legal norms ought to be obeyed, and not why they are actually obeyed or disobeyed. The *validity* whose basis is sought is an "ought-validity," not an "is-validity." For an "is-validity"—the question why people obey a norm of social life, the question of the psychic motivation of social behavior—is exclusively a subject for sociology and social psychology and can be answered only with the specific tools of the explanatory disciplines.

So what answer do lawyers give to the question they pose of the basis for the validity of positive law? With a unanimity seldom observed among lawyers, the problem is solved by a generally accepted formula called recognition theory. It says that legal norms are valid only because, and only to the extent that, they are *recognized* as such by those at whom they are aimed. I do not think it is going too far in saying that this recognition theory[31] of our modern positivist legal doctrine is almost identical with the derided contract theory of natural law, that it contains the same methodological errors, and must therefore lead to the same reprehensible fiction. . . . For what can recognition of a legal order by a legal subject mean? Apparently, a real act of psychic will or judgment, through which agreement to the norm by those subject to it is expressed: an affirmation of the legal order. But what is gained by this real psychic act of recognition? Apparently only an explanation of the "is-validity" of the norm—that is, an explanation of why people actually obey the norm. When, and under what circumstances, does this act of recognition really occur? Is it found in all legal subjects, or only in the majority; is it found with or without differences of age, sex, use of reason, etc.?

To this supporters of recognition theory have the most curious answers. For such an act of recognition is, of course, just as difficult to prove in people as the contract that founds the state. People are born into a legal system just as they are into a state, and the objective, thoroughly heteronomous legal norms are "valid" for them regardless of their agreement. That claiming some process of recognition on the part of the legal subject is an obvious fiction is shown by the way in which the supporters of recognition theory further develop it. They explain recognition not as an individual act, but as habitual behavior in regard to the norm; they speak of unconscious and unintentional, indirect and coerced recognition, even for those who clearly manifest their opposition to the legal system through norm-violating behavior. They claim recognition sometimes by an overwhelming majority of fellow legal subjects, sometimes only by the *pater familias,* whom a modern, not at all insignificant author resurrected from Roman law purely for the purpose of recognition theory.[32] In the process, they simply forget that such a real psychic act or state—of which, indeed, not much remains if it is unconscious and unintentional—could be established only through empirical social-psychological research. Certainly no trace of that can be found among the construing lawyers. Thus they have no right at all to claim a recognition which, incidentally, is as unlikely as the social contract. Here, too, the claim of an actual process consciously contradicts reality—and is, in fact, a fiction. Because the question of the basis of an "ought," or a norm, can lead, again and again, only to an "ought" or a norm that is superior to the first, recognition—which implies something that actually is—cannot be an answer to the question of the basis of the validity of legal norms. . . . To the extent that recognition implies an affirmative act of will by the legal subject that must

coincide with the will of the state as expressed in the legal norm, one feels . . .
obliged to bring the concept of will into play. Anyone with even the slightest understanding of the theory of public and private law knows what a varied role this concept plays in all aspects of legal doctrine. Thus it has always
been the subject of thorough investigations, within the scope of private law,
criminal law, and the law of the state. However, this is not obvious at all, since
the problem is one that, at first sight, does not even belong in the field of
legal scholarship. The will is a fact of psychic life and investigating it the task
of psychologists. To the extent he must operate with the concept of the will,
the lawyer must be satisfied with the findings provided to him by psychology. However, hardly any lawyer who has dealt more closely with the problem of will in law could refrain from creating his own phenomenology of the
will and thereby come up with results that deviate remarkably from those of
psychology. These lawyers have obviously exceeded their competence, which
requires a special explanation. It lies simply in the fact that legal scholarship
can make nothing of the findings of psychology, because the concept of the
will in psychology is useless for the specific purposes of legal scholarship.
This fact alone could have caused doubt as to whether lawyers and psychologists really have the same *object* in mind when they speak of "will." And I
would like here to turn this doubt into certainty by attempting briefly to show
the sense in which legal scholarship uses the term "will." . . .
. . .

   The cornerstone of all construction in the law of the state is, to use the
words of the great scholar of state law Jellinek, the conception of the state
as a person—that is, as a subject of rights and duties. The foundation of this
state personality, the unifying substratum, is found by the modern law of the
state in the uniform *will* of the state. The existence of such a uniform will of
the state is assumed to be a necessary prerequisite by both currents into
which recent state theory has split. Now, what is this uniform will of the state?
The *organic* theory of the state—and this is the only one to be taken into consideration here, because it has developed most purely and to its greatest
extreme the method of construction to be criticized here[33]—answers this
question by explaining the will of the state, in accordance with the findings of social psychology, as a general will in the social psychological sense,
a *real* psychic fact arising from the social life of the people within the state
organization.
   Now, modern social psychology does indeed operate with the concept
of a common will, just as with that of a common consciousness. [Wilhelm]
Wundt[34] has already strikingly emphasized that such a common will cannot
be seen as a metaphysical substance differing and autonomous from individual will, but as nothing more than the expression of an actual congruence
in individual wills born of living together. It is obvious that this common will

is a "real" one insofar as it describes a relationship among real, actual psychic processes.

However, we must further ask whether the common will recognized by sociologists in a social community can be the same as that which legal scholarship understands as the "will of the state."

We will leave open the question whether, and in what way, the state can even be seen as a sociological unity; whether a sociological view of the social processes taking place within the borders of a state are not a multiplicity rather than a unity; in other words, whether the state is not perhaps exclusively a legal unity, merely a legal concept. Here it is enough to establish that in any case the element of will, the common will, does not provide a sufficient criterion to achieve that unity "state," as which the people living on a specific territory and under a uniform legal order—this territorial entity—appears in legal scholarship. For even a superficial observation of reality forces one to realize that it is impossible for a people that is to be seen as a legal unity to be the intense spiritual community that leads to a congruence of wills in all individuals—that is, to the social and psychic fact of the common will. A common will in the socio-psychological sense exists only to the extent that a true spiritual link exists through actual, mutual spiritual relationships, rather than a mere legal unity that has psychic connection and harmony among individuals neither as prerequisite nor as effect. The spiritual community that represents a common will in the sociological sense can just barely extend to those individuals in whom mutual spiritual relationships have actually engendered the same direction of will. Not even a *single individual* who does not evidence the same psychic quality of will can be considered part of this community, let alone a multiplicity, as a minority to be neglected by the majority. For the majority principle is a legal and—though it cannot be expanded on here—specifically normative tool of construction, which has no place in the explanatory methods of natural science or sociology.

If one actually adheres to the real psychic facts, and especially to the congruence of wills, the people living within the borders of a state must disintegrate into a multiplicity of groups; and because the creation of spiritual communities does not stop at the borders of a state, the residents of the border regions of two completely different states, living in the closest economic and other intercourse, must be able to form conglomerates of will just like those within the *borders of the state;* for a sociological view—that is, one directed toward the reality of what is, not the ideality of some norm— these borders, if they are not part of the concrete psychic processes of humans, do not exist at all. One need not be a Marxist to consider a common will that psychically unites an entire people to be a phantom, given the deep class divisions that rend the people of a state who form a legal unity. Finally, there is one more thing to consider: From a legal perspective, what is the content of the will of the state, on the unity of which the personality of the state is based? The content of the will of the state is the legal order—that is, law is the will of the state. Yes, only to the extent that the legal order—which is also the organization of the state—is undivided, is imaginable as an undivided state person, and what one calls the undivided will of the state is perhaps merely a formula for the undividedness of the legal order—of the organization. But I am getting ahead of myself. For now, it is enough to make clear the hair-raising results that must occur if one passes off the so-called will, whose content is the entire legal order, consisting of thousands of legal norms, as a real, social, and psychic fact, as the common will of the people of a state! On the basis of this view, every citizen would have to have the entire legal order as the content of his psychic will—and even more, this would have to be permanent, for the permanence of the legal order forming the will of the state is an idea indispensable for legal construction.

After what has been said, there can be no doubt as to how this whole theory, which sees the will of the state as a real psychic fact, as a common will, can be designated methodologically: It is a classic example of a fiction—the claim of a reality, in conscious contradiction to reality! And like a warning sign, the fiction always reveals the point where legal construction has gone astray!

STATUTE AND JUDGMENT

Carl Schmitt

Originally appeared in Carl Schmitt, *Gesetz und Urteil: Eine Untersuchung zum Problem der Rechtspraxis* (Berlin, 1912; reprint, Munich: Beck, 1969), 1, 71–72, 77–78, 79, 111–14.

The crucial question is this: When is a judicial decision correct?

In order to clearly delimit from the start this ambiguous question, the meaning of which will emerge step by step with hopefully unmistakable clarity in the following presentation, I will make it more precise: Upon what normative principle is modern legal practice based?

The inquiry is a legal one. It asks when a decision that has been made within judicial practice can be viewed today as legally correct. But not how decisions are actually made today, or whether the average decision is correct . . .

. . .

Since conformity to statute is worthless as a criterion, since criteria making reference to "prelegal" complexes of norms must ignore important facts of legal life, since a criterion must finally be found that is autochthonous within legal practice—the following formula will no longer seem paradoxical or provocative:

> A judicial decision is correct today if it may be assumed that another judge would have decided in the same way. Here "another judge" refers to the empirical type of the modern, legally learned lawyer. . . .

The formula contains a resolution, without contradictions, of the complications arising from the fact that, on the one hand, the statute's authority must be maintained, but that at the same time decisions must be made apart from and at times against the law; yet are defined as correct, although they can hardly be said to be "in accordance with the sources"—whether or not covered by precedents of the highest courts and their constant practice. The fact that a decision's "conformity to statute" is no longer identified with its correctness does not mean abandoning any objective standard and leaving everything up to the subjectivity of the judge.[35] . . .

. . .

. . . Naturally we are not talking about every single judge. The purpose of the hypothetical formula (chosen with full awareness) is not to point out something that would actually have happened if something else had not occurred. Nor is it aimed at determining the behavior of other judges in order to derive a law[36] under which the decision to be assessed should now be subsumed; it would be a psychological misunderstanding to see in it a call for observation of the mass-psychology of judges. Of course, such observation is possible, and an inquiry in that direction would be valuable—just as can be done with the precept "so act that the maxim of your will could always hold at the same time as a principle establishing universal law" without annulling or even touching its normative significance. Neither does the suggested formula have anything to do with a statutory command to the judge. It offers only a methodological principle for today's judicial practice. Reference to the "other judge" as an empirical type is only a manifestation of the constitutive significance of the cardinal requirement of legal specificity for the question of the correctness of a decision. Thus a judge wanting to decide correctly need not first codify, as it were, the views of other judges and then subsume his case under them. That would be the old error that views "conformity to statute" as the criterion of the correctness of a decision. Instead, he must strive to ensure that his decision corresponds to what is actually practiced. . . . However, at no point in the decision may the judge follow an absolutely *free* discretion, his particular subjectivity, his personal belief as such; the "other judge" is the normal, legally cultivated judge, where the word "normal" is used in a quantitative-average sense, not describing an ideal type, not qualitative and teleological. . . .

A judicial decision is correct if it is foreseeable and predictable. This

emerged from the cardinal requirement of legal specificity and the observation of legal practice. From the formula proposed, the response to the
question whether a judge may decide against the meaning of the language
of a statute follows with all desirable clarity. The psychological fact that every
judge would shun adjudicating contrary to law, and that he would refer to
the language of the statute rather than to the most obvious, urgent considerations of equity, gains its methodological significance from the fact that it
can be connected with the tenet of legal specificity. It is a historical fact, established countless times, that, without being able to refer to prescriptive
law, practice disregards the language and meaning of a statute. . . . A decision
that offends the meaning of the language of a statute—and this means a decision contrary to law . . . is correct under the same premises as every other:
namely, if it would have been made in the same way by the other judge (by
the whole judicial practice). It follows that the function of positive law in determining the law provides an argument against the unconditional rejection
of adjudication contrary to law insofar as the limits of the conclusiveness of
positive law necessarily follows from its foundations.[37] Where positive law
is capable of guaranteeing legal specificity and produces an unambiguous
practice, the decision's "conformity to statute" is proof of its correctness. But
as soon as elements from outside the positive statutory content unsettle this
practice and are able to change the law's actual validity, even by means of an
"interpretation," this congruence of the decision's "conformity to statute"
with its correctness disappears, and a judgment contrary to the meaning of
the statute can still be correct. The major reservation that will be advanced
against this recognition of adjudication contrary to law is based only on the
fact that so far the problem has been posed falsely; it always ends up with considerations of "legal certainty," which, however, is exactly what is taken as
the foundation here.[38] Here it is expressly denied that the individual judge,
regardless of his convictions, can make a correct decision contrary to law.
Nor can the strongest sense of justice, as such, displace the statute as the
standard of correctness. What is decisive is always the entire judicial practice that grounds the foreseeability and predictability of decisions, and thus
legal specificity. It must be repeated that the question of the creation of positive law through judicial practice does not belong here, where the issue
is exclusively that of finding a criterion for the correctness of decisions
that is practice specific. The actual predominance of clear positive norms
does seem so large, however, from the point of view of legal specificity, that
the ambiguous, extra-positive ones may appear in comparison to be mere
stopgaps. . . .

ONE

Hans Kelsen

INTRODUCTION

Clemens Jabloner

Hans Kelsen was born on 11 October 1881 into a modest bourgeois family in Prague. The family soon moved to Vienna, where Kelsen passed his *Gymnasium* exams in 1900. The economist Ludwig von Mises was among his classmates and friends. Kelsen studied law and earned a doctorate in 1906 with a quite unusual work, "Dante Alighieri's Theory of the State" [*Die Staatslehre des Dante Alighieri*]. In 1908, Kelsen had the opportunity to study for a time in Heidelberg with Georg Jellinek, at the time the leading authority on the general theory of the state. In 1911, Kelsen published his *Habilitationsschrift*, titled *Main Problems in State Law Theory Developed from the Theory of the Normative Proposition* [*Hauptprobleme der Staatsrechtslehre entwickelt aus der Lehre vom Rechtssatze*]. Kelsen became a university teacher in 1911 and held a chair in Constitutional and Administrative Law at the University of Vienna from 1919 to 1930. He took an active part in developing the Austrian federal constitution of 1 October 1920, and is rightly considered its creator. In addition to his work as a university professor, which led to the establishment of a "Vienna school of legal theory" whose influence extended far beyond Austria's borders, Kelsen served until 1929 as a member of the Austrian Constitutional Court; establishing the court's theoretical and constitutional basis remained at the center of Kelsen's commitment.

Austria's worsening domestic political situation led to Kelsen losing his

The introduction and selections from Kelsen were translated by Belinda Cooper and Stephan Hemetsberger.

position as constitutional court judge. In 1929 Kelsen accepted a chair at the University of Cologne, which he lost in 1933 because of his Jewish origins. Kelsen moved to Geneva and until 1940 worked at the University Institute of Advanced International Studies [*Institut Universitaire des Hautes Études Internationales*] and also occasionally at the University of Prague. In 1940, he left Europe for good and emigrated to the United States. He taught—with great difficulty[1]—first at Harvard Law School, and later in the political science department of the University of California at Berkeley. In 1945 Kelsen accepted a professorship at Berkeley. Apart from visits to Vienna and some official honors, Kelsen never returned to his home country. He died on 19 April 1973 in Berkeley.

I

At the core of Kelsen's extensive work lies his foundation and development of the Pure Theory of Law. His thesis of 1911 (*Main Problems*) was an initial, powerful attempt to solve the problems of the theory of the state through an exclusively legal methodology. Remaining true to his basic scholarly interests, Kelsen repeatedly turned to outlining a complete account of his theory. This includes the *Main Problems,* the *General Theory of the State* [*Allgemeine Staatslehre,* 1925], the first edition of the *Pure Theory of Law* [*Reine Rechtslehre,* 1934], the *General Theory of Law and State* (written in English, 1945), the second edition of the *Pure Theory of Law* (1960), and the posthumous *General Theory of Norms* [*Allgemeine Theorie der Normen,* 1979].

What are the essential elements of the Pure Theory of Law?[2]

1. The Pure Theory of Law is a theory about norms. Its object—positive law—is an order of "ought" and not of "is," of legal norms, not social facts. Only this normative approach does justice to the immanent meaning of law, which is its claim to validity. Thus, the Pure Theory of Law stands in opposition to a sociological jurisprudence that denies the possibility of a normative, doctrinal jurisprudence.[3]

2. The Pure Theory of Law is a positivist theory. Legal norms are the meaning of human acts of will. This discards all variants of natural law, whether they construe law as a product of a supernatural will or as a construction of reason. The task of doctrinal jurisprudence is in essence to ascertain as precisely as possible the will of the lawmaker.

3. The Pure Theory of Law is based on the separation of "is" and "ought": Its foundation is the epistemological dualism of facts and values, propositions and norms, cognition and volition. In this way, it rejects all legal theories that derive the validity of law from its efficacy. Ultimately, in order to justify the validity of law, one must assume what Kelsen termed the "basic norm" [*Grundnorm*]. This assumption is not applied

to just any "ought" order, but—in accordance with legal positivism—
only to those that are efficacious on the whole. However, social efficacy
is not the reason for law's validity but only an appropriate guide for jurisprudence regarding its interest in describing efficacious coercive
orders. The Pure Theory of Law relativizes the moral value of positive
law. It focuses on the interest in cognition and description of positive
law, which exists regardless of whether individuals obey, disregard, or
even fight the legal system; it is important to understand even an in-
humane legal system—if only to escape it.

4. The Pure Theory of Law leads to a strict separation of jurisprudence
   from policy. It also separates positive law from other systems of norms,
   especially moral norms. Since the Pure Theory of Law is relativist for
   epistemological reasons, it does not recognize absolute values. The
   cognition and description of positive law must thus be kept separate
   from its valuation. Thus, jurisprudence (whose focus is cognition and
   description) and policy (whose focus is the creation and formation of
   law) must be carefully distinguished. This position of the Pure Theory
   of Law is decisive for the role of jurisprudence in politics, since a jurisprudence that restricts itself in this way cannot be misused in the
   service of political goals.

5. The Pure Theory of Law separates positive law from jurisprudence,
   prescriptive legal norms from descriptive normative propositions. Legal scholars use normative propositions to describe a situation in legal
   terms. Jurisprudence cannot create legal norms.

All in all, the Pure Theory of Law thus has a dual function: on the one
hand, it is an epistemology, a methodology for lawyers, who base doctrine
on it; on the other, it is also a critical challenge to ordinary jurisprudence,
which Kelsen accused of distorting positive law for ideological reasons be-
neath the mantle of juridical constructions.

Kelsen continued to pursue this critique of ideology. His theoretical work
thus goes beyond conventional legal theory. Kelsen's contributions to the
critique of ideology and to the theory of *Weltanschauung* are by no means
unrelated to his legal writings; instead, they serve to provide the Pure Theory
of Law with a foundation in the sociology and history of knowledge. Kelsen
connects a fundamental critique of natural law with thorough reflections
on the "social history of knowledge." Kelsen's research in social philosophy
culminated in his treatise *Society and Nature* [*Vergeltung und Kausalität: Eine
soziologische Untersuchung* (1941, English trans. 1943)]. In this rich work,
Kelsen sought to prove that primitive society and mentality indicate that the
interpretation of nature initially involved the principle of responsibility, not
that of causality. For early humans, he found, there was no "nature" in our
sense of the word, but only "society," and society's basic rule was the principle

of retribution. Thus, early humans did not look for causes—even of a mystical sort—but for the agency responsible for evil or good fortune. Kelsen called this interpretation of nature "socio-normative." Even in the modern, scientific concept of causality, Kelsen saw residues of the older principle of retribution.

In the last phase of his work, this research led Kelsen to a close examination of Greek philosophy, as in his posthumous *The Illusion of Justice* [*Die Illusion der Gerechtigkeit* (1985)], which focuses on Plato's social philosophy. This was also a late contribution on an issue that played an important role in Kelsen's oeuvre since the 1920s: the theory of democracy. His work on the theory of democracy culminated in the second edition of *On the Essence and Value of Democracy* [*Vom Wesen und Wert der Demokratie* (1929)], which is published in part in this volume and will be discussed below.

II

In his 1929 essay "Legal Formalism and the Pure Theory of Law" [*Juristischer Formalismus und Reine Rechtslehre*] Kelsen's concern was to defend his method against attacks from all sides. The essay leads straight to the heart of the "struggle over methods and aims" [*Methoden- und Richtungsstreit*] in the Weimar Republic. In the politically overheated atmosphere of this period, Kelsen was an important participant in the bitter disputes among state law scholars. Behind the "struggle over methods and aims" lay deep and thinly veiled political differences—and often personal resentment as well.

The normative theory of the state in the Pure Theory of Law was attacked by both right and left; its "formalism" was denounced by conservatives as "liberalism" and by Marxists as "fascism." The following highlights some of the more prominent of the many battles Kelsen fought on behalf of his theory.

With his theory of integration, Rudolf Smend was at the forefront of the current in the German theory of the state that opposed legal positivism. In *The State as Integration* [*Der Staat als Integration* (1930)], Kelsen undertook "a debate on principles" (as the subtitle describes it), pointing to the lack of methodological clarity in Smend's concept of integration and revealing in particular its veiled political nature. According to Kelsen, Smend's conceptualization of the state exclusively in terms of the "not precisely constitutional" paths of the stream of the state's life in its extraconstitutional sphere (as Smend put it) could only result in a pseudoscientific legitimization of constitutional violations, when viewed against the backdrop of Smend's criticism of the Weimar Constitution, and especially of parliamentarism.

Kelsen's dispute with Carl Schmitt focused on the question—at first glance merely technical—of constitutional guarantees. Kelsen, as a theorist as well as a *homo politicus,* believed in a constitutional court—that is, the model of judicial review of legislation practiced by the Austrian Constitutional Court—as essential to the perfection of the constitutional state. The Weimar Constitution included no such institution, but rather the emergency powers of the president under Article 48. As early as 1924 Schmitt had spoken at a conference of professors of state law in Jena on the dictatorship of the president, interpreting the executive's emergency powers broadly. In 1931, he published *The Guardian of the Constitution* [*Der Hüter der Verfassung*], to which Kelsen responded with *Who Should Be the Guardian of the Constitution?* [*Wer soll der Hüter der Verfassung sein?*]. For Schmitt, the answer was the president, as guardian and protector of the German people's constitutional unity and wholeness, above party and directly connected with the "common political will of the German people." The president's corresponding powers were the supervisory power of dissolving legislative organs for constitutional violations, as well as the power to call a plebiscite, thus actualizing the people's political will. Schmitt opposed the establishment of constitutional courts because, in his opinion, the very idea of the judiciary does not include the task of passing political judgment on the constitutionality of legislative acts.

Kelsen, meanwhile, entirely in keeping with the Pure Theory of Law, demonstrated that there is no qualitative difference between statutes and judgments; that both are products of law; that the decision of a constitutional court, even if it is an act of legislation—that is, of creating law—does not cease to be an act of the judiciary—that is, of applying law; and last but not least that, because the element of decision is by no means limited to legislating but is also and necessarily contained in judging, both must have a political character.

Kelsen and Schmitt also differ in their ideas on the possibility of "civilizing" the political process and thus ultimately in their picture of humanity. While in Kelsen's system, legal acts are examined for error and, if necessary, annulled in judicial procedures, the emergency powers of the president are directed at the officials and politicians who perform these acts. On the one hand, the calm, formal, more or less everyday dispute in front of the constitutional court; on the other, emergency measures—abrupt and harsh conflicts in the political sphere that can lead to a state of emergency and the breakdown of the existing system. This dichotomy, however, was precisely Schmitt's focus.

Kelsen, who never belonged to a political party, nonetheless felt a certain sympathy toward the Austrian Social Democrats. This led him early on into intensive debates with the Austro-Marxists, the most prominent of whom were Max Adler and Otto Bauer. In opposition to the left wing of the Austrian Social Democratic Party, Kelsen supported a "neutrality" principle, according to which the state was to be an accidental and temporary equilibrium of classes. Kelsen's dispute with the Marxist and Austro-Marxist theories of the state culminated in *Socialism and the State* [*Sozialismus und Staat* (2nd edition, 1923)].

Within the ranks of professors of the law of the state, the critique from the left came from Kelsen's colleague Hermann Heller, who spoke in 1927 at a conference in Munich on "The Concept of the Statute in the Reich Constitution [*Der Begriff des Gesetzes in der Reichsverfassung*]."[4] Heller criticized Kelsen's method as a "rule-of-law based rationalism" [*rechtstaatlicher Rationalismus*] that portrays the creation of law as a series of norms, each derived mechanically from the next-higher norm. Kelsen responded that this assessment was based on a complete misunderstanding of the Pure Theory of Law. The hierarchical ordering of norms [*Stufenbau der Rechtsordnung*]— with its emphasis on the forms of delegation—by no means prevents administrative acts and judgments from being seen as the creation of law. (The insight into the hierarchical ordering of the system of laws and the discovery of the Janus-like "two faces" of the administration of law—the application of law and the creation of law—were contributed to the Pure Theory of Law by Kelsen's most important pupil, Adolf Julius Merkl.) While this was still a rather academic debate, the chasm between the two was finally revealed in Heller's last words in the Munich discussion, when he said Kelsen had felt called upon, in response to Smend's and his own remarks, to warn against "political invasion of jurisprudence from the right and the left." For Heller, "this very invasion" signified "the hope that the theory of the law of the state will become aware of its presuppositions in fact and consciousness, and that it will therefore be better protected against one-sided party politics and leave behind its unfruitful and arbitrary logism." With Kelsen's pseudo-pure forms, one might cobble together into a system any concepts, emptied of content and arbitrarily construed; however, they serve to comprehend the concepts of neither the state nor law, and least of all the state governed by the rule of law and the role of the statute in the constitutional state. After all, to Kelsen every state is ruled by law.

This brings us back to the "formalist" method that Kelsen defended in 1929; whether this method is in fact a typical product of liberalism remains to be examined.[5] In answering this question, we must distinguish carefully between a historical and sociological perspective and the point of view of legal theory. Like all theories, the Pure Theory of Law has specific conditions for its emergence and influence. The idea of the constitutional state under the rule of law, which stems from the liberal currents of the nineteenth century, encouraged and required the specialization of legal tools and the differentiation of legal discourse. The Pure Theory of Law was the culmination of this process. However, these historical and sociological facts say nothing about the value of the Pure Theory of Law as legal theory. After all, critical legal positivism proves its timeless explanatory power by the fact that it can describe every coercive order. If it is a primitive coercive order, however, the Pure Theory of Law cannot unfold its full explanatory potential.[6]

III

In contrast to his legal theory, which was only briefly and somewhat defensively expressed in his 1929 essay "Legal Formalism and the Pure Theory of Law," Kelsen's theory of democracy hardly needs any introduction. *On the Essence and Value of Democracy,* published almost in its entirety in this volume, speaks for itself and is rightly considered a classic text of modern political science.

According to a myth that stubbornly persists, value-relative, formalist legal positivism—Kelsen's in particular—bore significant responsibility for the fall of the Weimar Republic. In this context, Kelsen is often even placed in the same class as his most implacable adversary, Carl Schmitt. Such notions arise out of the reaction of the natural law school at the beginning of the second German republic. They are understandable to a certain degree, but in fact wrong.

An analysis of the theory of the state in Weimar shows that German democracy was, at the level of legal discussion, significantly weakened by widespread anti-republican, anti-democratic, anti-parliamentary, and thus by no means value-relative, positions. This is not the place to describe them. But it is also not true that nothing was done to oppose these positions. Kelsen himself is an example to the contrary.

Kelsen was not only a legal theorist; he applied his extraordinary analytic skills to an examination of the form of the state he believed to be best—parliamentary democracy. He was especially interested in democracy as a political idea. To emphasize only the main idea: As a way to create law, democracy realizes the idea of freedom; in order to function it must, as parliamentarism, accept a compromise with the division of labor that is a condition of all social and technical progress. Kelsen showed the degree to which this compromise requires fictions—a concept Kelsen used neutrally—in order to achieve the desirable identity of rulers and ruled.

Kelsen's text continues to have unbroken relevance. One has only to read his critique of the conventional concept of *Volk* and the demand flowing from this critique that foreigners living in the country for the purpose of work be granted equal political rights.

The element that connects the Pure Theory of Law with Kelsen's theory of democracy is value relativism. The main concern of his legal theory is that the validity of law cannot be based on prepositive values or norms, while the main concern of his theory of democracy is not to impose limits on decisions by the people—that is, by the majority. Such limits (on the content of the law to be created) are frequently called for with the argument that it is by no means certain that the majority will recognize what is right. However, according to Kelsen, such limits assume insight into absolute values and are ultimately possible only within the framework of a "metaphysical, and especially religious and mystical, *Weltanschauung*."

Kelsen by no means neglected the problem of democracy—the danger of its self-destruction. In *Defense of Democracy* [*Verteidigung der Demokratie* (1932)], Kelsen thus asked whether democracy should not defend itself against a majority that wishes to destroy it. But, according to Kelsen, posing this question already means answering it in the negative. A democracy that tries to assert itself against the will of the majority, even by force, has ceased to be a democracy. Rule of the people cannot continue to exist against the people.[7]

And the democrat, how should he behave? Kelsen answers in moving words: "One must remain true to his colors, even when the ship is sinking, and can take with him into the depths only the hope that the ideal of freedom is indestructible and that the deeper it has sunk, the more passionately will it revive."

MAIN WORKS

Preliminary Remarks: A complete bibliography of Kelsen's works would contain 392 titles. The following lists the most important works, with special emphasis given to writings originally in English and translations into English. Where new editions or reprints exist, the first and last editions are cited. It should be pointed out that a number of writings not available in English are available in other languages, especially Spanish.

The *Hans-Kelsen Institut* (A-1190 Vienna, Gymnasiumstr. 79; http://www.univie.ac.at/staatsrecht-kelsen) was created to preserve Kelsen's works. Among other things, it holds a collection of Kelsen's writings and a rich stock of secondary literature. A complete bibliography as of 1985 can be found in volume 10 (*Hans Kelsen: Ein Leben im Dienste der Wissenschaft*) of the Institute's publication series.

Hauptprobleme der Staatsrechtslehre entwickelt aus der Lehre vom Rechtssätze. Tübingen: Mohr, 1911. 2nd ed. Tübingen: Mohr, 1923. Reprint, Aalen: Scientia Verlag, 1984.
Über Grenzen zwischen juristischer und soziologischer Methode. Tübingen: Mohr, 1911. Reprint, Aalen: Scientia Verlag, 1970.
Das Problem der Souveränität und die Theorie des Völkerrechts: Beitrag zu einer reinen Rechtslehre. Tübingen: Mohr, 1920. Reprint, Aalen: Scientia Verlag, 1981.
Sozialismus und Staat: Eine Untersuchung der politischen Theorie des Marxismus. Leipzig: C. C. Hirschfeld, 1920. 2nd ed. Leipzig: C. L. Hirschfeld, 1923. Reprint, edited by Norbert Leser, Vienna: Wiener Volksbuchhandlung, 1965.
Vom Wesen und Wert der Demokratie. Tübingen: Mohr, 1920. 2nd ed. Tübingen: Mohr, 1929. Reprint, Aalen: Scientia Verlag, 1981.

Der soziologische und der juristische Staatsbegriff: Kritische Untersuchung des Verhältnisses von Staat und Recht. Tübingen: Mohr, 1922. Reprint, Aalen: Scientia Verlag, 1981.

Allgemeine Staatslehre. Berlin: Springer, 1925. Reprint, Vienna: Österreichischer Staatsdruck, 1993.

Das Problem des Parliamentarismus. Vienna and Leipzig: W. Braumüller, 1925. Reprinted in *Hans Kelsen oder die Reinheit der Rechtslehre,* edited by Friedrich Koja. Vienna, Cologne, and Graz: Böhlau, 1988.

Verhandlungen der Tagung der deutschen Staatsrechtslehrer zu München am 24. und 25. März 1927 (Diskussionsreden), 168–89. Berlin and Leipzig: de Gruyter, 1928.

Verhandlungen der Tagung der deutschen Staatsrechtslehrer zu Wien am 23. und 24. April 1928. Wesen und Entwicklung der Staatsgerichtsbarkeit, 222–25. Berlin and Leipzig: de Gruyter, 1929.

"Juristischer Formalismus und reine Rechtslehre," *Juristische Wochenschrift* 58 (1929): 1723–26.

Der Staat als Integration: Eine prinzipielle Auseinandersetzung. Vienna: Springer, 1930. Reprint, Aalen: Scientia Verlag, 1974.

"Wer soll der Hüter der Verfassung sein?" *Die Justiz* 6 (1931): 576–628. Reprinted in *Die Wiener Rechtstheoretische Schule,* edited by Hans Klecatsky, René Marcic, and Herbert Schambeck, pp. 1873–1922. Vienna and Frankfurt am Main: Europa Verlag, 1968.

"Verteidigung der Demokratie," *Blätter der Staatspartei.* 2. Jahrgang, no. 3/4. Berlin: 1932, 90–98. Reprinted in *Demokratie und Sozialismus: Ausgewählte Aufsätze,* edited by Norbert Leser, 60–68. Vienna: Wiener Volksbuchhandlung, 1967.

Reine Rechtslehre: Einleitung in die rechtswissenschaftliche Problematik, 1st ed. Vienna: Deuticke, 1934. Reprint, Aalen: Scientia Verlag, 1994. English translation: *Introduction to the Problems of Legal Theory.* Oxford: Clarendon Press, 1992.

Vergeltung und Kausalität: Eine soziologische Untersuchung. The Hague: van Stockum und Zoan, 1941. Reprint, Graz: Böhlau, 1982. English translation: *Society and Nature. A Sociological Inquiry.* Chicago: University of Chicago Press, 1943.

General Theory of Law and State. Cambridge, Mass.: Harvard University Press, 1945. Reprint, Birmingham, Ala.: Gryphon Editions, 1990.

The Law of the United Nations: A Critical Analysis of Its Fundamental Problems. London: Stevens, 1950. 5th ed. New York: Praeger, 1966.

"Was ist ein Rechtsakt?" *Österreichischer Zeitschrift für öffentliches Recht,* n.s. 4 (1951/52): 263–74. English translation: "What Is a Legal Act?" *American Journal of Jurisprudence* 29 (Notre Dame, Ind.: Notre Dame Law School, 1984): 199–212.

Principles of International Law. New York: Rinehart, 1952. 2nd ed. New York: Holt, Rinehart and Winston, 1966.

The Communist Theory of Law. London: Stevens, 1955. Reprint, Aalen: Scientia Verlag, 1976.

"Foundations of Democracy," *Ethics* 66, no. 1, pt. 2 (1955): 1–101.

What Is Justice? Justice, Law, and Politics in the Mirror of Science: Collected Essays. Berkeley and Los Angeles: University of California Press, 1957.

"On the Basic Norm," *California Law Review* 47 (1959): 107–10.

Reine Rechtslehre. Mit einem Anhang: Das Problem der Gerechtigkeit. Second, entirely new, expanded edition, Vienna: Deuticke, 1960. Reprint, Vienna: Österreichischer

Staatsdruck, 1992. English translation, without the appendix: *Pure Theory of Law.*
Berkeley and Los Angeles: University of California Press, 1967.
"Vom Geltungsgrund des Rechts," in *Festschrift für Alfred Verdross,* 157–65. Vienna:
Springer, 1960. English translation: "On the Basis of Legal Validity," *American Jour-
nal of Jurisprudence* 26 (1981): 178–89.
"What is the Pure Theory of Law?" *Tulane Law Review* 34 (1960): 269–76.
Staat und Naturrecht. Aufsätze zur Ideologiekritik. Neuwied and Berlin: Luchterhand,
1964. 2nd ed. Munich: Fink, 1989.
Essays in Legal and Moral Philosophy. Dordrecht: Reidel, 1973.
Allgemeine Theorie der Normen. Vienna: Mans, 1979 [posthumous]. English transla-
tion: *General Theory of Norms.* Oxford: Clarendon Press, 1991.
Die Illusion der Gerechtigkeit. Eine kritische Untersuchung der Sozialphilosophie Platons, Vi-
enna: Mans, 1985 [posthumous].

LITERATURE

Schriftenreihe des Hans Kelsen-Instituts (nineteen volumes since 1974).
Dreier, Horst. *Rechtslehre, Staatssoziologie und Demokratietheorie bei Hans Kelsen.* 2nd ed.
Baden-Baden: Nomos Verlagsgesellschaft, 1990.
———. "Hans Kelsen (1881–1973): Jurist des Jahrhunderts." In *Deutsche Juristen
jüdischer Herkunft.* Edited by Helmut Heinrichs et al., 705–32. Munich: Beck, 1993.
Ebenstein, William. "The Pure Theory of Law: Demythologizing Legal Thought."
California Law Review 59 (1971): 617–52.
Métall, Rudolf Aladár. *Hans Kelsen-Leben und Werk.* Vienna: Deuticke, 1969.
———, ed. *33 Beiträge zur Reinen Rechtslehre.* Vienna: Europa Verlag, 1974.
Walter, Robert. "Der gegenwärtige Stand der Reinen Rechtslehre." *Rechtstheorie* 1
(1970): 69–95.
Walter, Robert, and Clemens Jabloner. "Hans Kelsen (1881–1973): Leben—Werk—
Wirkung." *Der Einfluß deutscher Emigranten auf die Rechtsentwicklung in den USA und
in Deutschland.* Edited by Marcus Lutter, Ernst C. Stiefel, and Michael H. Hoeflich,
521–47. Tübingen: Mohr, 1994.

LEGAL FORMALISM AND
THE PURE THEORY OF LAW

Hans Kelsen

Originally appeared as "Juristischer Formalismus und reine Rechtslehre,"
in *Juristische Wochenschrift,* 58th Year, no. 23 (1929): 1723–26.

I. The Pure Theory of Law is nothing other than a *theory of positive law* and
pretends to be nothing else. It refuses to respond to the question of the cor-

rect law, without judging the dignity of this question. It wants to discover only what *is* in the law; not what *ought* to be. Let this be addressed with particular emphasis to those who counter the Pure Theory of Law by saying that law is not an "ought," but an "is"—a "reality." For it is the Pure Theory of Law itself that emphasizes—in relation to justice—the reality, that is, the *positivity* of law, regardless of the fact that this positive law—in relation to nature, that is, to the causally-determined actual behavior of people—is an "ought." The opposition between "ought" and "is" is relative, given that for scientific knowledge there is no absolute "reality." And the statement that law represents a reality says hardly anything; everything depends on determining what *kind* of reality, since it obviously cannot be the reality of nature. Only the Pure Theory of Law clearly recognizes the problem of the specific reality of law as the problem of the positivity of law and tries to solve it.

As a theory of positive law, it is primarily a general theory of law, providing the conceptual tools with which to seize a particular law intellectually. By separating form and content in the phenomenon of positive law, the concepts of legal form that prove their worth in every legal order are distinguished from concepts of legal content, which can be found only through comparative study of legal systems given by history and which represent a typology of legal content.[8] That this system of concepts must have a relatively formal character is self-evident to anyone not entirely a stranger to the principles of logic and method. For it is the task of the concepts of a general theory of law to master cognitively the immense wealth of positive legal material. Like all cognition, cognition of law must formalize its object. No one can reproach it for *this* "formalism." For precisely in this formalism lies that which is held up as a virtue, in contrast to the "formalism" frowned upon as a vice: its *objectivity*. "Only the formal is objective; the more formal a methodology, the more objective it can become. And the more objectively a problem is formulated in all the depths of the issue, the more formally it must be grounded" (Hermann Cohen, *Logic of Pure Cognition* [*Logik der reinen Erkenntnis*], 587). Those who do not understand this do not know what is essential to scientific knowledge. The endeavor of the Pure Theory of Law to capture the material assigned to it as exhaustively and precisely as possible in a system of concepts is the endeavor of every type of cognition in regard to its object. To disparage the Pure Theory of Law as "conceptual jurisprudence" for that reason—which occurs often—is a truly deplorable misunderstanding. Who would ever think of fighting a theory of physics for being "conceptual physics"? *Cognition* of law can be nothing but "conceptual" jurisprudence. How can one conceive without concepts? Certainly the *production* of law is something different. Concepts are not its purpose; it must create legal norms; it is a function of will, not knowledge; it must first produce the material that legal scholarship attempts to conceive. The failure of traditional jurisprudence to separate cognition and production of law—

legal theory and legal practice—makes a different improper and rightly rejected understanding of "conceptual jurisprudence" possible: namely, that highly pernicious practice of deducing legal norms from concepts prefabricated for this purpose and not extracted exclusively from the empirical legal material; of "scientifically" obtaining legal content from a concept of the law or the state, from a concept of property, of servitude, etc., even though the content could be created only in the legal processes of legislation or application of law. No theory but the Pure Theory of Law has taken such an energetic position against this conceptual jurisprudence, by emphasizing repeatedly that legal *scholarship* cannot be a *source* of law, that the derivation of legal *norms* from legal *concepts* is naked natural law, that not the slightest bit of new law can be gained from a cognition of positive law that remains within its boundaries. Only the Pure Theory of Law has exposed the highly unscholarly motives that lead, in traditional jurisprudence, to such a desperate struggle against the strict separation of legal theory and legal practice, which is what makes such unpleasant conceptual jurisprudence possible in the first place. The reproach of conceptual jurisprudence is aimed above all at legal formalism. It does not affect the Pure Theory of Law at all, because it has kept its *theoretical* character pure as no other legal theory has.

Therein lies the essence of its "purity": that it wants only to cognize, not to want; only to be scholarship, not politics. As paradoxical as it may be, it is accused of "formalism" for precisely this reason, although it is precisely this that protects it from the formalism that is rightly castigated as conceptual jurisprudence. For nearly two decades, the Pure Theory of Law has attempted in an immanent critique of traditional doctrine in all areas of jurisprudence to point out the great danger of *methodological syncretism* that mingles the *cognition* of a given state and its positive law with the aspiration to *shape* these objects in a certain way. For such shaping can correspond only to a subjective *interest,* be it that of a smaller or larger group. There is simply no interest that is not, as the interest of some, opposed by a contradictory interest of others. The so-called general interest of all is a clearly demonstrable fiction when it is understood as anything other than a *compromise* among opposing interests. But if scholarship of law and the state does not limit itself scrupulously to cognizing the reality of these objects—that is, to capturing them conceptually, analyzing their structures, elucidating existing relations; if it arrogates to itself, as scholarship, a creative and normative influence on the object given to its cognition, then what is merely the expression of a subjective interest presents itself as cloaked in the authority of scholarship, that is, equipped with the value of objective knowledge. *Scholarship becomes a mere ideology of politics.* It is one of the characteristic signs of our times that there are scholars who find the questionable courage to make a virtue of this necessity, denying the professional ethos of all scholarly work, abandoning the ideal of objective knowledge free of subjective interests—that is, free of political tendencies—and defending the right of methodological syncretism by proclaiming the inseparable link between legal scholarship and politics. In a society shaken by world war and world revolution, struggling groups and classes are interested more than ever in the production of useful ideologies, which make possible the most effective defense of the interests of those holding power as well as those striving to get it. That which reflects their subjective interests they would present as objective truth. Here, "scholarship" about state and law is made to serve. It provides the "objectivity" that politics itself is unable to produce. And—as though, even in this violation, it were unable to deny its nature—it truly provides it with disastrous "objectivity," to the right as well as to the left. And thus from the concept of the state, the conservative professor derives—in a strictly "scholarly" manner, of course—the impossibility of democracy and the necessity of some sort of fascism or corporative state [*Ständestaat*]; and on the basis of an equally "scientific" socialism, the revolutionary Marxist teaches the predictability of the dictatorship of the proletariat according to the laws of causality. And both explain a reality of state and law incompatible with their political ideals as a manifestation of "sickness" or "decay," concealing their political desires behind claims of an "organic" development that, remarkably enough, matches the results of their objective scholarly discoveries. It is only surprising that more of us do not see through the complete worthlessness of this "scholarship," which merely masks politics, with a method that permits the opponent to prove just the opposite. What is *not* surprising, however, is the fact that proponents of such legal "scholarship," on the right as well as on the left, are uncomfortable with a theory that prefers not to join this masquerade, a theory that refuses under any circumstances to pass off something that is merely a single possible, contingent structure of state and law emerging from particular interests as the outcome of scholarly knowledge, and thus as the necessary and general character of these social structures, simply because the theory would prefer to be scholarship and not politics. But how can one express one's dissatisfaction with the fact that one cannot learn through the study of the Pure Theory of Law what is the "true" state and the "correct" law; that one cannot find in the Pure Theory of Law a justification for one's own political ideals—that is, for a structure of social order matching one's particular interests? How can one express one's disappointment in the fact that the Pure Theory of Law not only fails to provide a useful ideology—for the right or for the left—but even combats scholarship that willingly offers such an ideology? Very simply: by arguing that the Pure Theory of Law is formalistic.

For this reason, it is an error to characterize the Pure Theory of Law as an offshoot of the liberal-individualist theory of states governed by the rule of law, as political democratism and pacifism. No one has unmasked as I have the democratic natural law hidden in some of the thinking of the traditional theory of the law of the state; no one has countered the subjectivist attitude of supposedly scientific liberalism as emphatically as I with the necessity of objectivist legal and state theory. No one has brought to light political liberalism's concept of the state governed by the rule of law as I have, as the absolutization of a one-sided standpoint. I have insistently explained that the pacifist-influenced view of the relationship between international and national law—what I call the primacy of the international legal order—is, from the standpoint of legal knowledge, of a value equal to the imperialist-oriented primacy of the national legal order. When I advocated democracy or pacifism, I never passed this judgment off as the result of objective scholarly knowledge, but declared it openly and honestly to be the consequence of a fundamental subjective value judgment far beyond any scholarly pretension. Doing scholarship does not force us to abandon all political judgment; it merely obligates us to separate the one from the other, cognition from volition.

And yet I must confess that I bear a share of the blame for the mistaken belief that the Pure Theory of Law is liberalism. A rash remark in the preface to my *Main Problems in State Law Theory* [*Hauptprobleme der Staatsrechtslehre*], published in 1911, can undoubtedly be cited against me. There is also a passage on legal formalism that I must describe as quite unfortunate. I would not find the courage for such a confession if not for the fact that not only my *Main Problems in State Law Theory* but also my numerous later writings bear witness that my actual scholarly work follows the principles I have developed here. I believe I have the right to be judged by this actual work and not merely by two sentences written in the preface of a book published seventeen years ago. One should not read only the preface of his first work when judging an author's life's work. But for those wishing to condemn the Pure Theory of Law as formalist liberalism without having read my work, I would like to call attention to the fact that my scholarly friends hail from all points on the political spectrum. That would hardly be the case if my theory possessed as one-sided a political character as it is accused of. What links the various supporters of the Pure Theory of Law is not a common political belief, least of all liberalism, democracy, pacifism. It is faith in a scholarly method that, as far as humanly possible, refrains from any political judgment.

II. Even though law, as already suggested, seen from a particular standpoint (a standpoint in which law is viewed side by side with and compared to other social phenomena), can be understood in its entirety as form—as

form of economics or power, etc.—it is still possible to judge the formation
of law in the legislation and administration of statutes as "formalistic" or not
formalistic. . . .

. . . By far the largest part of what is brought forward against legal formalism in the literature, with varying degrees of passion, is a dispute over the
methods of statutory interpretation. But when is an interpretation "formalistic"? It is telling that most lawyers who rush to make the charge of formalism are at a loss when asked for a more precise definition of this characteristic. And an analysis of the exceedingly frequent use of this word in the critical
literature would hardly reveal anything even approaching agreement on its
meaning. However, here it is enough to state that of the various methods of
interpretation, so-called plain meaning is for the most part described as "formalistic." And even this is not without exception. If one can give reasons for
a decision considered to be expedient or desirable only by showing that it can
be subsumed under the language of a legislative text, without coinciding
with the provable intent of the legislator, one will be highly unlikely to reject the decision as "formalistic." But if such a decision conflicts with interests one considers worthy of protection, then and only then will one call it
a formalistic interpretation. Though it must be noted that in a society in
which statutorily determined decisions or administrative actions or judicial
opinions have normative effects in individual cases, the reality of life ac-
knowledges no interests but knows only conflicts of interest; and the idea
that interests can be weighed like butter, that there is an objective measure
under which it is possible to determine the absolute higher value of one interest as opposed to another, is part of the most naive of illusions with which
practical lawyers, quite naive in this respect, have allowed themselves to be
lulled. It is also quite short-sighted when not merely a single decision but
the entire practice of a supreme court, or even the complete judicial authority of an entire country over a longer period are accused of "formalism,"
with the argument that only an incorrect scholarly doctrine of interpretation is to blame. Some people may not know any better. But on the whole,
we must assume that quite concrete interests are behind a particular
method of interpretation. And then it is simply the opposing interests that
would like to gain recognition through criticism of prevailing interpretive
methods by using the argument of formalism. Nothing is more easily understandable than the fact that the strict application of a statute that takes
little consideration of the interests of a particular group will be combated as
"formalistic" by that group's legal ideologues. In today's jurisprudence it is
self-evident that the interests that use this critique will present themselves
as the better interpretive method with higher "scholarly" standards.

Be this as it may, whatever may emerge in the battle against formalism in the field of interpretation cannot be held against the Pure Theory of Law. For until recently this theory had not even taken any position on the problem of interpretation.[9] And it has never opposed any possible method of interpretation. It is in no way possible to gain arguments for formalistic interpretation from specific positions in the Pure Theory of Law, nor against the opinion that courts and administrative authorities are to be bound by statute only to a very small extent, if this is a demand of legal policy or if positive law has accepted this principle. Only if the thesis negating the binding force of statutes is maintained in contradiction to positive law must it be rejected. However, it must be considered that the Pure Theory of Law in particular has emphasized the function that the *res judicata* effect of an individual norm has in its relationship with the general norm. The effect is that even an individual norm that contravenes the statute is statutorily sanctioned; this leads to the theory, developed by the Pure Theory of Law, of the *double legal order,* law's "double face" or "double basis," as we call it. . . .

The Pure Theory of Law, with its insight into the *hierarchical structure of the legal order,* has first grounded theoretically one of the main positions of the School of Free Law—that is, the assertion that the so-called application of law by courts and administrative authorities is true law *creation.* By seeing statutes merely as a frame that must be filled in by the law-producing action of the judiciary and administration, by seeing decisions and administrative action as merely the continuation of a process of law-production in which legislation represents only a preliminary stage, the Pure Theory of Law, based on the conclusions of the School of Free Law, emphasizes that generally it is a majority of individual norms, of decisions or administrative actions, that is possible on the basis or within the frame of a statute; that the opinion that, in a particular case, only one decision or administrative action is possible, only one is the "correct" one, is an illusion created by theory in order to provoke a sense of legal certainty in a law-seeking public, and in the law-seeking authorities a consciousness of being most strictly bound. It is already this attitude that prevents the Pure Theory of Law from preferring a particular interpretive method—let us say a "formalistic" one. *Cognitively,* all possible individual norms that refer to an individual case within the frame of the general norm must be considered of equal value, even though only one of them enters into the system of positive law by being adopted and becoming *res judicata.* The selection cannot occur by way of *cognition,* least of all through cognition of the statute, but through an *act of will* not justified only by reference to statute. To the extent a statute allows discretion—and it always permits this to a far greater extent than traditional theory had assumed before the emergence of the School of Free Law—concrete decisions or administrative actions can be justified only by recourse to norms other than those of positive law; no different than is the case with legislation, which, to the extent it is not determined by the constitution, is legitimized only by reference to morality or justice. Because the Pure Theory of Law is only cognition of existing positive law, not a prescription for its correct production, it neither provides directions on how to make good laws nor gives advice on how to make good decisions and take good administrative action on the basis or within the frame of statutes. Therefore it takes only minor account of the problem of interpretation. That it can be resolved with "scholarly" objectivity, that is, that one can cognitively determine which of several possible decisions or administrative actions falling within the frame of the law is the "best"; that norm *production* or—as one says in a veiled way—norm "extraction" on the basis of statute could be the task of legal scholarship: this is no less a self-deception than the idea that by using pure cognition one can find a "correct" content for statutes to be passed. If scholarship, conscious of its insurmountable limits, refuses to attempt to solve problems that will eternally fail to be solved with the specific means of that scholarship—if such scholarship is "formalistic," then being formalistic amounts to being honest, to not wanting to fool oneself and others. And in that case, the Pure Theory of Law, as scholarship, will gladly accept the accusation of being formalistic.

Certainly traditional jurisprudence has always claimed the title of scholarship for its decision on the question of the "correct" law—originally also for legislation, later only for the administration of justice. Lawyers' class interests are among the factors pressing for such an attitude. One tends to maintain this claim through the superficial cliché, sure of cheap success, that legal scholarship must serve "life" or even "pulsating life"! This is certainly an incontrovertible phrase. But one can serve life through scholarship by attempting with incorruptible objectivity to *understand* the nature of things, and thus the essence of state and law, and one can serve life through *politics* by *willingly* and *actively* implementing values, especially enacting and applying laws. Those for whom scholarship is not doing enough by serving objective knowledge actually expect it—through the demand that it "serve life"—to serve interests that, as cognition shows, can be none other than individual and group interests, even if they pretend to be objective values. It is not scholarship but politics that rails against the Pure Theory of Law with the accusation of formalism. And with this argument, the Pure Theory of Law cannot be refuted by scholarship, by a differing scholarly position; it can only be shouted down by politics with this slogan. But this the Pure Theory of Law does not fear. For the history of the human spirit shows that scholarship, and thus also the scholarship of state and law, has always freed itself from the bondage in which politics has always attempted to keep it, because the innermost nature of science forces it to be, if not something *more,* then at least something *other* than an instrument in the struggle for power. If there is any point at all upon which one can stand outside the arena of power, then it is science and scholarship. Even the science of power; which is then a pure theory of state and law.

ON THE ESSENCE AND VALUE OF DEMOCRACY

Hans Kelsen

Originally appeared as *Vom Wesen und Wert der Demokratie* (Tübingen: Mohr, 1929; reprint, Aalen: Scientia, 1963), 3–37, 53–58, 65–68, 93–104.

FREEDOM

In the *idea* of democracy—and I will first discuss this idea, rather than the political *reality* that approaches it to a greater or lesser degree—two postulates of our practical reason unite, two of the basic instincts of social beings press for satisfaction. The first is a reaction against the pressure flowing from the social condition—a protest against an alien will that subjugates one's own, against the torment of heteronomy. In the demand for *freedom,* nature itself rebels against society. The burden of an alien will that imposes a social order seems repressive, and even more so the more immediately the human being's primary feeling of his own value is expressed in a rejection of the greater value of others and the more fundamentally the person forced into obedience perceives that the one giving orders is a person like himself: The master and I are equal! What gives him the right to rule over me? Thus the very negative, deeply anti-heroic [10] idea of *equality* comes to serve the equally negative demand for *freedom.*

From the assumption that we are—ideally—equal, we can derive the claim that one ought not rule over the other. But experience teaches that if we wish to remain equal in reality, we must let ourselves be ruled. Yet this has not kept political ideology from linking freedom and equality. It is precisely the synthesis of these two principles that is characteristic of democracy. This was expressed by a master of political ideology, Cicero, in his famous words "itaque nulla alia in civitate, nisi in qua populi potestas summa est, ullum domicilium libertas habet: qua quidem certe nihil potest esse dulcius et quae, si aequa non est, ne libertas quidem est."*

It is possible for the idea of freedom to enter into the calculus of the social and even political ideas only through a transformation of meaning, which turns an absolute negation of social links in general, and therefore of the state in particular, into a special form of the same that, in conjunction

*De Re Publica, I.xxxi [47]: "Hence liberty has no dwelling-place in any state except that in which the people's power is the greatest, and surely nothing can be sweeter than liberty, but if it is not the same for all, it does not deserve the name of liberty." Trans. Clinton Walker Keyes, Loeb Classical Library (Cambridge, Mass.: Harvard University Press, 1943), 170–73.—EDS.

with its dialectic opposite, represents all possible forms of the state and even society in general: *democracy* and *autocracy*.

For society or even the state to exist, a binding order governing mutual behavior among people must be in force. There must be rule. But if we must be ruled, we want to be ruled only by ourselves. Social or *political* freedom is detached from *natural* freedom. A politically free person is one who is subject only to his own, not to an alien, will. The principal opposition between the different forms of the state and of society is thus introduced.

Seen from an epistemological perspective, for *society* to be possible at all as a system differing from nature, there have to be specific laws governing the social order in addition to the laws determining the natural order. Besides the *law of causality* there is the *norm*. Originally, from the standpoint of nature, freedom means the negation of social order, and from the standpoint of society, the negation of the (causal) laws determining nature (free will). "Back to *nature*" (or to "natural" freedom) merely means release from *social* obligations; onwards to society (or social freedom) means freedom from the laws determining the natural order. The contradiction is resolved only when "freedom" becomes the expression of specific laws, namely, the laws governing the social (i.e., ethical-political and formally legal) order; when the opposition between nature and society becomes an opposition between two different sets of laws, and thus two different perspectives.

One tends to contrast the citizen's political self-determination and his participation in forming the governing will of the state, as the *classical idea of freedom,* with the Germanic idea, which is limited to freedom from rule—in fact, to freedom from the state itself. However, this is not, in fact, a historical, ethnographic difference. The step from the Germanic to the so-called classical articulation of the problem of freedom is only the first step in the inevitable process of change, the denaturalization, to which original instinctual freedom is subject, as human consciousness progresses from its natural condition to a coercive legal order. This transformation of meaning in the concept of freedom is highly characteristic of the mechanics of our social thought. The enormous significance of the idea of freedom in political ideology cannot be overstated; it can only be explained as arising from a source deep in the human soul, from that basic instinct of enmity toward the state that sets the individual *against* society. And yet, in almost mysterious self-deception, this idea of freedom becomes merely the expression of a particular position of the individual *in* society. The freedom of *anarchy* becomes the freedom of *democracy*.

The transformation is greater than it appears at first glance. Rousseau, perhaps the most important theorist of democracy, poses the question of the best state—which for him is the problem of democracy[11]—with the words "To find a form of association that defends and protects the person and goods of each member with all the force in common, and in which each one, though united with all, nevertheless obeys himself alone and remains as free as before."[12] The extent to which freedom itself was the cornerstone of his political system is shown by his attack on the English parliamentary principle: "The English people thinks it is free. It is gravely mistaken; it is free only during parliamentary elections; as soon as they are over, it is enslaved, as if it were nothing."[13] As we know, the consequence Rousseau draws is that democracy must be direct. But even if the governing will of the state arises directly from referendum, the individual is free only at one moment, only while voting, and only if he votes with the majority and not with the outvoted minority. Therefore, the democratic principle of freedom appears to demand that the possibility of being outvoted be kept to a minimum; qualified majorities—if possible, *unanimity*—are seen as guarantees of individual freedom. Yet experience of the existing opposition of interests tells us that such majorities are so out of the question in the practical life of the state that even an apostle of freedom such as Rousseau demands unanimity only on the *basic contract creating the state*. And this limitation of the principle of unanimity to the hypothetical act of state-creation is by no means grounded in simple expediency, as is often assumed. The principle of unanimity in *concluding* the basic contract, arising from the demand for freedom, would mean, strictly speaking, that also the *continuation* of the order stipulated in the contract depends on everyone's ongoing assent, that, therefore, each person would be free at any time to leave the community and to escape the validity of the social order by refusing to recognize it. Here we see clearly the insoluble conflict between the idea of individual freedom and the idea of a social order that, in its truest essence, is possible only through objective validity—that is, through a validity independent of the will of those subject to its norms. Theoretically, this *objective* validity of a social order remains untouched, even if the content of the order is somehow determined by the will of those subject to its norms. Yet formal objectivity demands a material counterpart. In the extreme case that the "you ought" of the social imperative is conditioned on a "when and what you will" of the addressee, the order loses any social meaning. Therefore, if society and particularly the state are to exist at all, there must be the possibility of incongruity between the content of the order and the content of the wills subject to it. If the tension between these two poles, between "ought" and "is," were nil, and thus the value of freedom infinite, subjugation would be completely out of question. By allowing an order *created* according to the idea of freedom, thus hypothetically by contract, that is, unanimously, to be *developed* further through majority decision, democracy contents itself with merely approaching the original idea. The fact that we still speak of self-determination, saying that each is subject only to his own will when the will of the *majority* prevails, is a further step in the metamorphosis of the idea of freedom.[14]

But even one who votes with the majority is no longer subject to his own will alone. He discovers this as soon as he changes the will expressed in the vote. The legal irrelevance of such a change of will reveals only too clearly the *alien will*, or—speaking nonmetaphorically the *objective validity of the social order* to which he is subject. He must find a majority for his change of will if he, the individual, is once again to be free. And this accord between the will of the individual and the governing will of the state becomes more difficult, this guarantee of individual freedom lessens, the higher the majority necessary to create a change in the will of the state. It would be as good as eliminated, were unanimity required. Here we see a highly peculiar ambiguity of the political mechanism. That which earlier, at the founding of the state order, served to protect individual freedom, in accordance with the idea of freedom, becomes its shackle if it is no longer possible to escape the order. The founding of a state, the initial creation of a legal order or will of the state, almost never happens in experience. Generally, one is born into a finished state order, in whose creation one did not take part, and which one therefore approaches from the start as an alien will. Only the *furtherance* and *modification* of this order is at issue. From this point of view, however, the principle of absolute (and not super) *majority* represents the *relatively closest approach to the idea of freedom*.

From this idea the *majority principle* is to be derived. Not, however—as tends to happen—from the idea of equality. That human wills are equal is indeed a precondition of the majority principle. But this being equal is only figurative; it cannot mean that human wills or personalities can actually be measured or added together. It would be impossible to justify the majority principle by saying that more votes have a greater total weight than fewer votes. We cannot conclude positively, from the purely negative presumption that one person is worth no more than another, that the will of the majority should prevail. If one attempts to derive the majority principle only from the idea of equality, it does indeed have that purely mechanical, even senseless, character with which the autocratic side reproaches it. It would only be the roughly formalized expression of the experience that the many are stronger than the few; the maxim "might makes right" would be overcome only insofar as it would be raised to a legal principle. Only the thought that, if not all, then at least *as many people as possible shall be free,* that is, *as few people as possible should find their wills in opposition to the general will of the social order,* places us on the right track to understanding the majority principle. That equality is naturally assumed to be a basic hypothesis of democracy is shown by the fact that not only this or that person is to be free, because this person is not worth more than that one; instead, as many as possible are to be free. Accord between the individual will and the will of the state becomes easier, the fewer the individual wills necessary for changing the will of the state. The absolute majority is indeed the upper limit. Any fewer, and it would be possible that the will of the state at the moment of its creation would conflict with more individual wills than those with which it would harmonize. Any more, and a minority would be able to determine the will of the state against the majority by preventing a change in the will of the state.

The transformation in the concept of freedom, from the notion of the individual's freedom from state rule to the notion of the individual's participation in state rule, also signifies *democracy*'s detachment from *liberalism*. Because the demand for democracy is considered met to the extent that those subject to the state order participate in its creation, the ideal of democracy is independent of the extent to which the state order affects the individuals who create it—that is, independent of the degree to which it interferes with their "freedom." As long as state authority emanates from the individuals subject to it, democracy is possible even in the case of unlimited expansion of the state order over the individual—that is, complete annihilation of individual "freedom" and negation of the liberal ideal. And history shows that democratic state authority does not tend less towards expansion than autocratic state authority.[15]

Given the unavoidable distance between the will of the individual and the state order—the individual will, which forms the starting point of the demand for freedom, while the state order confronts the individual as an alien will, even in a democracy, where this distance is reduced to a minimum—a further transformation occurs in the notion of political freedom. The fundamentally *impossible freedom of the individual* gradually fades into the background, and the *freedom of the social collective* comes to the fore. The protest against being ruled by equals is as unavoidable in a democracy as its consequence: the shift in political consciousness to construction of the anonymous *person of the state* as ruling subject. From it, and not from externally visible persons, authority may emanate. A mysterious general will and an almost mystical general person are detached from the wills and personalities of the individuals. This fictional isolation occurs not so much with regard to the will of the subjects as with regard to the will of those who rule in fact, and who now appear to be nothing more than organs of a hypostasized ruling subject. In an autocracy, a *man* made of flesh and blood is considered the ruler, even if he is raised to the status of a god. In a democracy, the *state* as such becomes the ruling subject. Here the personification of the state hides the fact that man rules over man, unbearable to democratic sensibilities. The *personification of the state*, now fundamental to the theory of the law of the state, doubtlessly also has its roots in this ideology of democracy.

Once, however, the notion is laid to rest that one is ruled by his equals, one no longer resists the knowledge that the individual is unfree, to the extent that he must obey the state order. The subject of freedom shifts with the ruling subject. Nevertheless, it is emphasized emphatically that the individual, where he creates the state order in organic connection with other individuals, is "free" in this connection and in this connection only. The Rousseauian idea that the subject renounces all his freedom, only to gain it back as a citizen, distinguishes between *subject* and *citizen* and so suggests a complete shift of problems and views in social studies. In an individualist understanding of society the subject is the isolated individual; in a universalist understanding of society the citizen is only part of a greater organic whole, of a collective that, from an entirely individualist, freedom-based starting point, has a transcendent, metaphysical character.[16] The change of scene is so absolute that it is actually no longer correct, or at least no longer important, to claim that the single citizen is free. The correct conclusion, drawn by some authors, is that, because citizens are free only in the state, in essence it is not the single citizen but the person of the *state* that is free. This is expressed also in the maxim that only the citizen of a free state is free. As a fundamental demand, the freedom of the individual is replaced by the *sovereignty of the people*, or what amounts to the same thing, the *free state*.

That is the last stage in the transformation in meaning of the idea of freedom. Those who cannot or will not follow this concept's movement caused by its immanent logic may criticize the contradiction between the original and the final meaning; they must renounce the conclusions drawn by the most ingenious portrayer of democracy, who was not afraid to claim that the citizen is free only through the general will, and that those who refuse to obey this will, when forced to obey the will of the state, are *forced*—to be *free*. It was more than a paradox, it was a symbol of democracy that, above the prison doors and on the chains of the galley slaves in the Genoan Republic, one found the word *"libertas."*[17]

THE PEOPLE

The metamorphosis in the idea of freedom leads from the *idea* to the *reality* of democracy. Its essence can be comprehended only in the specific opposition, particularly characteristic of the problem of democracy, between *ideology* and *reality*. Many misunderstandings in the controversies over democracy arise as a result of the fact that one side speaks only of the idea, and the other only of the reality, of the phenomenon, each contradicting the other, because neither comprehends the whole: the reality in light of the ideology elevated above it, the ideology in view of the reality that carries it.[18] And this antagonism between idea and reality is significant not only to the basic principle of democracy, the idea of *freedom;* it can be seen in all its constituent elements, and therefore, in particular, in the concept of the *people*.

Democracy, according to its idea, is a form of state or society in which the will of the community, or, speaking nonmetaphorically, the social order, is created by those subject to it: by the *people*. Democracy is the identity of the leader and the led, of the subject and the object of rule; it means the rule of the people over the people. But what is this "people"? It seems to be a basic condition of democracy that a *multitude of human beings* becomes a *unity* in it. For democracy, the "people" as a unity is even more essential, as it is not only, or not so much the *object* as the ruling *subject*—or should be, according to the idea. And yet, the unity that appears under the name "people" creates the greatest problems for a study of reality. Split by national, religious, and economic conflicts, that unity is—according to sociological findings—more a bundle of groups than a coherent mass of one and the same aggregate state.[19] Only in a *normative sense can one speak of a unity*. For the unity of the people as a concord of thought, feeling, and desire, as a solidarity of interests, is an ethical-political *postulate* declared to be real by the national or state ideology by means of a fiction that is generally used and therefore no longer thought about. Fundamentally, only a *legal* element can be conceived more or less precisely as the unity of the people: the *unity* of the *state's legal order*,[20] which rules the behavior of the human beings subject to its norms. In this unity and through the content of its norms, the unity of the variety of human action is constituted, which the "people" as an element of the state, as a specific social order, represents. As that unity, the "people" is by no means—as is naively believed—an embodiment, a conglomerate, as it were, of human beings, but merely a system of the acts of single human beings determined by the state's legal order. For the human being never belongs *entirely*, that is, with all his functions, all aspects of his mental and bodily life, to the social community—not even to the one that affects him the most, the state,[21] and least of all to a state formed according to the ideal of freedom. Only very specific manifestations of the individual's life are encompassed by the state order. A more or less large portion of human life must always remain outside this order, and must be preserved *free of the state*. When the legal order of the state presents as a unity the variety of individual human acts, it creates a fiction. That fiction makes the unity "an embodiment of human beings," as though all human beings, belonging to the people merely by virtue of specific actions requested or forbidden by the state, actually formed this element of the state with their whole beings. This is the illusion Nietzsche destroys in his *Zarathustra* when he says of the "new idol," "State is the name of the coldest of all monsters. Coldly, it also lies; and this is the lie that crawls from its mouth: I, the state, am the people."[22]

　　If the unity of the people is only a unity of human actions regulated by the state's legal order, then in this normative sphere, in which "domination" means normative obligation, subordination to norms, the people as a unity is again only the object of rule. As ruling *subject,* human beings are recognized only to the extent that they participate in *creating* the state order. And it is precisely this function, crucial for the idea of democracy, which includes the "people" in the norm-creating process and at the same time reveals the unavoidable distance between this "people" and the "people" understood as the embodiment of those subject to norms. Not all those belonging to the

people as subject to norms or rule can take part in the process of norm creation—the form in which rule is necessarily exercised—or can form the
people as ruling subject. Democratic ideologues themselves often do not
realize what gaps they are concealing when they identify the "people" in the
one sense with the "people" in the other. Participation in creating the will
of the community is the content of so-called *political rights*. Even in an extreme democracy, the people as embodiment of those with political rights
represents only a small segment of those obligated by the state order, of the
people as object of rule. Certain natural limits, such as *age* and intellectual
and moral *health,* prevent the extension of political rights and thus of the
"people" in an active sense, and create barriers that do not exist at all for the
concept of "people" in the passive sense. It is typical that the democratic
ideology tolerates particularly extensive restrictions on the "people" as the
embodiment of those participating in rule. The exclusion of *slaves,* and today of *women,* from political rights does not at all hinder calling a state order
a democracy. And privileges based in the institution of *citizenship* are considered entirely normal, because it is seen as an institution essential to the
state—an error arising from the aforementioned tendency to limit political
rights.[23] However, experience with the latest constitutional developments
shows that political rights need not be linked with citizenship. Thus the constitution of Soviet Russia, breaking down thousand-year-old barriers, grants
full political equality to foreigners working in Russia. In the legal development characterized by the extremely slow progress of human thought,
in which aliens originally were outlaws and later received civil equality gradually and step by step, but today continue to lack political rights almost
everywhere, the Soviet constitution has thus wrought a deed of historic significance. It is, however, also true that Soviet Russia has taken regressive steps
in other respects that are all the greater (for example, certain categories of
citizens are excluded from political rights on the grounds of class struggle).

   If we want to advance from the *ideal concept* of the people to the *realist concept,* it is not enough to replace the embodiment of all those subjugated by
rule with the much narrower circle of those with political rights. We must
go a step further and consider the difference between the number of those
having political rights and the number actually exercising them. This difference varies depending on the degree of political interest but is always a
significant quantity, and can only be diminished by systematic education in
democracy. Because the "people" that represents the basis of the democratic
idea is the governing and not the governed people, from a realistic point
of view the concept in question could be narrowed even further. Among
the mass of those who, in actually exercising their political rights, take part
in forming the will of the state, we must distinguish between the undiscern-
ing crowd of those who unreflectively accept the influence of others and
those few who actually get involved in the process of forming the will of the

community, giving direction through autonomous decisions, as required by the idea of democracy. Such an inquiry happens upon the effectiveness of one of the most important elements of real democracy: *political parties,* which *unite* the like-minded to ensure their influence in shaping public affairs. These social entities generally still possess an *amorphous* character; they appear in the loose form of independent associations, and often not even in this, but without any legal form. Nevertheless, an essential aspect of the formation of the will of the community takes place within them: the *preparation* of the process—generally decisive for the direction of the common will—that is fed by impulses from the political parties, as from many underground streams, and that first comes to the surface in popular assemblies or parliaments, where it is directed into a single channel. Modern democracy is based upon political parties, whose significance increases the more the democratic principle is implemented. Considering this fact, one can understand the tendency—though still weak—to anchor political parties *in the constitution* and give legal form to what they have de facto long since become: organs forming the will of the state.

This would mean only another step in the process that has been accurately described as "rationalization of power,"[24] and that goes hand-in-hand with the democratization of the modern state.

However, the resistance faced by such rationalization in general, and the formation of political parties into constitutional organs of the state in particular, is not small. It was not very long ago that legislative and executive powers officially ignored the existence of political parties, or directly rejected them. And even today there is insufficient awareness that the *anti-party views* of the old monarchy, and the essential conflict between *political parties* and the *state* postulated in particular by the ideology of constitutional monarchy, are nothing more than poorly concealed *hostility to democracy*. That the isolated individual has no real political existence whatsoever, because he can gain no actual influence on forming the will of the state; that democracy is possible in earnest only if individuals *integrate* into communities for the purpose of influencing the common will from the standpoint of various political goals; that, therefore, *collective* entities uniting the similar wills of individuals as political parties have to insert themselves between the individual and the state[25]—this is obvious. Thus, one cannot seriously doubt that by discrediting political parties the political and constitutional theorists of constitutional monarchy launched an ideologically masked attack on the implementation of democracy. Only self-deception or hypocrisy can lead one to believe that democracy is possible without political parties. A democracy is necessarily and unavoidably a *party state*.

That is a simple assertion of fact. And this fact alone, of which one can convince oneself by a glance at the development of all historical democracies, refutes the thesis, still widespread today, that the essence of political parties is incompatible with the essence of the state—that the state by its *nature* cannot be erected upon social entities like political parties.[26] Political reality proves the opposite. What is presented here as the "essence" or "nature" of the state is—as is so often the case—in truth a particular, namely anti-democratic ideal.[27] What is it that makes a political party seem essentially opposed to the state? A party is, they say, merely a community of group interests, and therefore based on self-interest, while the state represents the common interest. That is, it is *above* interest groups, beyond the political parties in which they are organized. First of all, in addition to parties representing group interests there are also parties promoting a *Weltanschauung* that play an important role, particularly within the *German states*. However, one must admit that in reality they share the same grounds with associations representing group interests. But then a realistic understanding, going beyond the ideological appearance with which every apparatus of power surrounds itself, reveals historic *states,* for the most part, to be organizations functioning primarily in the interests of a dominant group. To pass them off for instruments of the collective interest of a solidary community means, at best, taking an "ought" for an "is" and the ideal for the reality, but generally only idealizing the reality for political reasons—which means justifying it. After all, the ideal of a collective interest *above* and beyond group interests and thus "supra-partisan" of a solidarity of interests of all members of the community irrespective of religion, nation, class, etc., is a metaphysical, or, even better, a metapolitical illusion that tends to be expressed in the highly vague terminology of an "organic" polity or organically organized polity, opposed to the so-called party state, to mechanical democracy. In answering the question of what other social groups should take the place of political parties as factors in forming the will of the state, it becomes apparent how questionable is this whole argumentation against political parties. For almost nothing remains but to assign *corporatist* groups the role held by parties today. These groups—whose political significance will be examined later—represent interests no less, and possibly even more, than do the political parties, as they can be concerned only with *material* interests.[28] Given the empirical and unavoidable opposition of interests, the common will, if it is not to express unilaterally the interests of one group alone, can only be a resultant, a compromise among opposing interests. Organization of the people into political parties means, in reality, creating the organizational conditions for such compromises, the possibility of moving the common will toward a median. Opposition to party creation and thus, in the end, to democracy itself, provides conscious or unconscious support to political forces whose goal is the absolute rule of a single interest group which, unwilling to take account of opposing interests, attempts to disguise itself as an "organic," "true," "well-understood" collective interest. Precisely because democracy as *a party state* only permits a will of the community to emerge as the resultant of party wills, it can do without the fiction of a supra-partisan "organic" collective will.

Irresistible developments lead in all democracies to the organization of the "people" into political parties; or rather, since the "people" as a political force does not previously exist, democratic developments integrate the mass of isolated individuals into political parties, thus releasing for the first time social forces that can somehow be described as the "people." When the constitutions of democratic republics—influenced, in this as in other areas, by the ideology of constitutional monarchies—deny political parties legal recognition, they no longer inhibit the implementation of democracy, as constitutional monarchies did; they only close their eyes to the facts.

Anchoring political parties in the constitution also makes it possible to democratize the formation of the will of the community *within this sphere.* This is all the more necessary because it is most likely the amorphous structure of this class that promotes a pronounced aristocratic-autocratic character in the process of forming the will of the community as it takes place here.[29] This is even the case within parties with extremely democratic programs. The reality of party life, in which important leaders can assert themselves even more than within the limits of a democratic constitution; this party life in which so-called *party discipline* continues to function—while in the relationship *between* the parties (that is, in the sphere of parliamentary will-formation), no one seriously expects an analogous *state discipline*—as a rule offers the individual only a very small amount of democratic self-determination.

The transformation from the ideal to the realist concept of the "people" is thus no less significant than the metamorphosis from the natural to a political "freedom." Therefore, one must admit that the gap between ideology and reality, even between ideology and the maximum chance of its realization, is extraordinary. One may thus take Rousseau's famous statement that there has never been a democracy in the strict sense of the word, and never can be, as it violates the natural order that the greater number governs and the smaller number is governed,[30] for more than a rhetorical hyperbole.

The reduction that the idea of democracy suffers within social reality is by no means completed when natural freedom shrinks to political self-determination through majority decision and when the ideal concept of the people shrinks to the much narrower concept of those possessing and actually exercising political rights. For only in a *direct democracy,* no longer possible as a political form given the size of the modern state and the variety of its tasks, is the social order in fact created through a decision of the majority of those possessing political rights and exercising them in popular assembly. The democracy of the modern state is *indirect, parliamentary democracy,* in which the governing will of the community is shaped only by the majority of those *elected* by the majority of those possessing political rights.

Thus political rights—and that is *freedom*—essentially diminish to mere *voting rights*. Of all elements mentioned so far that limit the idea of freedom, and thus the idea of democracy, *parliamentarism* is perhaps the most significant. It is the one that must be understood in order to comprehend the true essence of those entities today considered democracies.

THE PARLIAMENT

The struggle waged against autocracy at the end of the eighteenth and beginning of the nineteenth century was essentially a struggle for parliamentarism.[31] At the time, all conceivable political progress, the creation of a just social order, and the dawn of a new and better age were expected from a constitution that would provide popular representation a decisive role in formation of the state's will, thus ending the dictatorship of absolute monarchs and the privileges of the legal order based on estates. And although parliamentarism as the form of the state of the nineteenth and twentieth centuries can point to quite respectable achievements—the complete emancipation of citizens vis-à-vis the privileges of birth, later the political equality of the proletariat and the beginning of the moral and economic emancipation of this class in relation to the possessing class—the assessment of parliamentarism by historians of the time and political ideologists of today is not a favorable one. Parties of the extreme right and the extreme left reject the parliamentary principle more and more vehemently; the call for a dictatorship or a corporatist order is growing louder. Even among the parties of the center, one cannot help noticing a certain cooling towards the former ideal. Let us harbor no illusions: people have become somewhat tired of parliaments, though we are still far from having reached the point where—as some authors do—we might speak of the "crisis," the "bankruptcy," or even the "agony" of parliamentarism.

Doubts about the quality of the parliamentary principle were already expressed in the middle and at the end of the last century. But under the reign of constitutional monarchy, such anti-parliamentary tendencies understandably failed to gain much significance. They had no effect on the slowly but steadily growing democratic movement that focused primarily on parliament. However, it is a very different story to question parliamentarism in a situation of complete and unlimited rule of the parliamentary principle, as is the case today. Within the democratic parliamentary republic, the problem of parliamentarism becomes a fateful question. The existence of modern democracy depends on whether parliament is a workable tool to solve the social problems of our time. It is true that democracy and parliamentarism are not identical. But because direct democracy is practically impossible for the modern state, we cannot seriously doubt that parliamentarism is the only realistic form in which the idea of democracy can be fulfilled within today's social reality. Thus a decision about parliamentarism is at the same time a decision about democracy.

A not-insignificant cause of the so-called crisis of parliamentarism was a critique that incorrectly interpreted the essence of this political form and therefore wrongly assessed its value. But what is *the essence of parliamentarism*—its objective essence, not to be confused with the subjective interpretation that those involved or interested in the institution attempt to give it, for conscious or unconscious reasons? Parliamentarism is *formation of the governing will of the state according to the majority principle through a collegial organ elected by the people on the basis of a universal and equal right to take part in the full electoral process—that is, democratically.*

If we attempt to understand the ideas determining the parliamentary system, it becomes clear that the dominant idea is that of democratic self-determination; that is, the idea of freedom. The struggle for parliamentarism was a struggle for political freedom. This is easily forgotten today, when an often unjust critique is aimed at parliamentarism. Possessing a freedom that has become a matter of course and is therefore no longer appreciated, though it is guaranteed only by parliamentarism, many believe that they can do without this political standard. But the idea of freedom remains the eternal and fundamental dominant factor in all political speculations, even though—or precisely because—the idea of freedom by its essence negates everything social and thus everything political, thereby forming the counterpoint to all social theory and state practice. As we have seen, precisely for this reason, freedom in its pure form cannot enter the sphere of the social or even the political and the state but must amalgamate with certain elements.

Thus also within the principle of parliamentarism, the idea of freedom appears in a double nexus that limits its original force. It appears, first with the majority principle, whose relationship to the idea of freedom has already been examined, and whose real function in parliamentary systems we will return to. The second element revealed by an analysis of parliamentarism is the *indirectness* of will-formation; the fact that the state's will is not formed directly by the people itself, but by a parliament created by the people. Here the idea of freedom, the idea of self-determination, is linked with an indispensable need for *division of labor,* for social differentiation; that is, with a tendency that contradicts the primitivizing basic character of the democratic idea of freedom. For according to this idea, the entire will of the state, in all its manifold manifestations, would have to be formed directly through one and the same assembly of all citizens entitled to vote. *Each differentiation in the state organism by division of labor, the transfer of any state function to an organ other than the people, necessarily signifies a limitation of freedom.*

Parliamentarism thus presents itself as a *compromise* between the democratic demand of *freedom* and the principle of *division of labor* that is a condition of all socio-technical progress. However, the attempt has been made to disguise the considerable impairment suffered by the democratic idea when, instead of the people, the parliament—an organ very different from the people, though elected by it—forms the will of the state. On the one hand, it was impossible to accept seriously the primitive form of direct democracy, given the complicated social conditions involved, because one could not do without the advantages of the division of labor. The larger the state community, the less the "people" itself proves capable of *directly* developing the truly creative activity of forming the state's will—and the more it is forced, for purely socio-technical reasons, to limit itself to creating and supervising the apparatus forming the will of the state. On the other hand, however, one wanted to create the appearance, as if parliamentarism gave undiminished expression to the idea of democratic freedom, and *only* to this idea. The *fiction of representation* serves this purpose—the idea that parliament is only the *representative* of the people, that the people can express its will only in parliament, only through parliament—although the parliamentary principle is connected in all constitutions, without exception, to the provision that the representatives are to take *no binding instructions* from their voters, and that *parliament* is thus in its function legally *independent of the people*.[32] Yes, it was with this declaration of independence by the parliament with regard to the people that the modern parliament first emerged, clearly distinguishing itself from the old assemblies of estates, whose members were bound by the imperative mandate of their groups of voters and were responsible to them. The fiction of representation serves to legitimize parliamentarism from the standpoint of *popular sovereignty*. But this obvious fiction, intended to disguise the actual, essential impairment of the principle of freedom through parliamentarism, played into the hands of its opponents by allowing them to argue that democracy is built upon a blatant untruth. Thus in the long run, the fiction of representation could not fulfill its actual task of justifying parliament from the standpoint of popular sovereignty. Yet it fulfilled a function other than the one intended: it held the political movement of the nineteenth and twentieth centuries, under enormous pressure from the democratic idea, on a rational middle course. By making people believe that the great mass of the people could exercise political self-determination in elected parliaments, it prevented excessive strain on the democratic idea within existing political realities, a strain not without danger to social progress, because it would necessarily have been linked to an unnatural primitivization of political techniques.

The fictitious character of the idea of representation understandably did not enter the forefront of political consciousness as long as democracy was involved in the struggle with autocracy, and parliamentarism itself had not yet asserted itself completely against the claims of monarchs and estates. Under the reign of constitutional monarchy, as long as the popularly elected parliament had to be seen as the most that could be wrung politically from the once absolute monarchs, it made no sense to discuss the form of the state from the point of view whether parliament could really represent the will of the people completely. But as soon as the parliamentary principle—especially in the republic—had achieved total victory, as soon as parliamentary rule had replaced constitutional monarchy, basing itself on the principle of popular sovereignty, critics could no longer ignore the crass fiction underlying the theory, already developed in the French National Assembly of 1789, that parliament was essentially nothing but a representative of the people, whose will alone was expressed in the acts of parliament. Thus, it should come as no surprise that among the arguments advanced against parliamentarism today, the most important is the news that the will of the state formed by parliament is not at all the will of the people and that parliament cannot in fact express the will of the people for the simple reason that, in the constitutions of parliamentary states, no will of the people can be formed at all other than by the act of electing the parliament.

This argument is correct; but it can be used *against* parliamentarism only so long as one attempts to legitimize it through the principle of popular sovereignty, as long as one thinks its essence can be described *entirely* by the idea of freedom. In that case it is true that parliamentarism promised something it failed to carry out and will never be able to carry out. The essence of parliamentarism, however, as shown at the outset, can be described without having recourse to the fiction of representation, and its value justified as a specific, socio-technical means of creating the state's order. . . .

It is certainly no accident, but reflects a law of the structural formation of social bodies, that something like a parliament exists in every more-or-less technically advanced commonwealth. It is particularly remarkable that even in evident autocracies, monarchs feel urged to call to their support assemblies of men, called state councils or the like, that stand by them and in particular prepare, deliberate, and evaluate *universal* orders, *general* norms issued in the name of the monarch. If in a large commonwealth the people as such, in its entirety, is not capable of directly forming the will of the community, the autocrat is just as incapable of doing so alone, in part for the same reasons: lack of knowledge and ability, fear of responsibility. The fact that the members of this collegial body are in the one case appointed by the autocrat and in the other elected by the people is indeed significant—but certainly more from the standpoint of ideology than from that of the actual functions that this organ exercises in social reality. It is also certainly significant whether it possesses an advisory or decision-making function. Here too, however, an examination of the actual relationships—the psychological effectiveness rather than the legal form—might find no great difference between the legislative parliament in a democracy and the state council of an absolute monarch. This is particularly the case if we take into account that a very significant although not externally visible amount of legislative work even in modern democracies takes place not in parliament but in government; that government initiates legislation, directly or indirectly, in parliamentary democracies as in constitutional monarchies; and that, finally, the authority of the personalities joined in a state council frequently ensures this body a much greater influence on the absolute monarch than can be inferred from the constitution.

That within a technically developed social body a special, *collegial* organ of legislation emerges besides the organ of government (and the subordinate administrative apparatus) seems to be a necessity of social development, arising not least from the nature of the *process by which the state's will is formed.* It is presupposed here that the phenomenon, metaphorically described as the "will" of the community in general and the state in particular, is *not a real psychological fact,* because from a psychological point of view there are only *individual human* wills.[33] The so-called will of the state is only the anthropomorphic expression for the conceptual order of the community, which, set in a multitude of individual human acts, appears as their *meaning.* As the meaning of these acts, the order of the community is a complex of *norms,* of *ought*-provisions that determine the behavior of people belonging to the community and thus constitute the community as such. That members of the community ought to behave in a certain way—the conceptual content of the order of the community—this entirely ideal relation is expressed most vividly and thus, for the great mass of those concerned, most comprehensibly, if we say that the community, the state, hypostasized to a person, "wills"—as though it were a human being or superman—the members of the state to behave in a certain way. The "ought" of the state's order is presented as the "will" of a state person. "Formation of the will of the state" thus means nothing other than the process of creating the state's order.

This process is characterized essentially by a transformation from an initially *abstract* form, through a greater or lesser number of intermediate steps to a *concrete* form; from *general* norms to *individual* acts of the state. It is a process of *concretization* and *individualization* very different from the formation of the psychological will in the human being. Within this process, as two completely different functions or levels, the formation of the general, abstract norm is clearly distinguished from the issue of the concrete, individual act, of the single order or decision. Demonstrating the variety of these functions is a problem for legal phenomenology.[34] These two different functions or levels of the formation of the will of the community can be observed even in quite primitive social groups—although one must admit that the impulse to form a special organ for the creation of general norms exists only when the formation of the will of the community has developed from an unconscious, customary exercise by those subject to norms, to a process of conscious determination and fixation. Only the most superficial consideration, limited to the most primitive groups, could make one believe that the will of the community constituting the social group can come to life directly and exclusively in the form of *individual* imperative and coercive acts. This superficial consideration ignores the fact that a *general* order, present in the consciousness of all or certain group members, is necessary to make possible the functioning of those organs that issue individual acts of the community. The organs of primitive groups are much less able to decide and judge with free discretion, not bound by general norms, than those of a modern state; they feel bound to a great degree by general norms, all the more effective because they possess a religious or magical character. The social community comes to life in people's consciousness through general norms of mutual individual behavior, rather than through individual acts of the community. The function of creating *general* norms will always tend to produce a *collegial* organ and not an organ of one.

The attempt to remove parliament entirely from the organism of the modern state can hardly succeed in the long run. The essential issue can be only the *way in which parliament is appointed and constituted,* and the *type and degree of powers* it should have.[35]

. . .

THE MAJORITY PRINCIPLE

The *parliamentary majority principle* is perfectly suited to preventing class rule. It is telling that experience has shown it to be compatible with *protection of minorities.* For the concept of a majority assumes by definition the existence of a *minority,* and thus *the right of the majority* presupposes the *right* of a minority to exist. From this arises perhaps not the necessity, but certainly the possibility, of *protecting* the minority from the majority. This *protection of minorities* is the essential function of the so-called *basic rights* and *rights of freedom,* or *human and civil rights* guaranteed by all modern constitutions of parliamentary democracies. Originally, they offered *individuals* protection against executive authority, which, under the legal principle of absolute monarchy, was authorized to carry out in the "public interest" any restriction of the individual sphere not expressly prohibited by law. But as soon as administration and jurisdiction become possible only on the basis of specific legal authorization, and this principle of legality based on statute [*Gesetzmäßigkeit*] becomes ever more conscious, as in constitutional monarchy and the democratic republic, the establishment of basic rights makes sense only if it unfolds in a specific *constitutional form.*[36] This means that only a law created in a qualified, rather than a normal, procedure can protect the sphere composed of single basic rights against the executive and its restrictions. The typical form in which the constitution is qualified in comparison with ordinary statutes is a *heightened quorum and a special majority, such as two-thirds or three-quarters.* Although distinguishing in this way between ordinary statutes and the constitution would, in theory, also be possible in a direct democracy, in practice only a parliamentary legislative procedure can make this distinction. Where the people assembles, the presence of physical power is still too noticeable to allow more than submission to the *absolute* majority, and the absolute majority cannot refrain from imposing its will on a minority solely because it is somehow qualified. Only in parliamentary procedure is such rational *self-restraint* possible as a constitutional institution. It means that the catalogue of basic rights and rights of freedom turns from *protection of the individual from the state to protection of a minority,* a *qualified* minority, from the *absolute* majority. It means that measures encroaching upon certain national, religious, economic, or spiritual and intellectual spheres of interest are possible, not against the will of a qualified minority, but with its approval; that is, only when the majority and the minority *agree.* It may have appeared at first to be the principle of *absolute* majority that was most in tune with democracy on its path from idea to reality; but it now becomes clear that under certain conditions the principle of *qualified majority* is even closer to the idea of freedom, signifying a tendency to *unanimity* in the formation of the will of the community.

This is, then, what parliamentary procedure teaches us: that we must also distinguish between *ideology and reality* in the case of the majority principle. *Ideologically,* i.e., in the system of the democratic ideology of *freedom,* the majority principle means formation of the will of the community with the greatest possible accord with the will of the subject individuals. If the will of the community accords with more individual wills than it contradicts (and that, as shown earlier, is the case with the majority decision), the *maximum possible freedom* is achieved—with freedom assumed to mean self-determination. If we disregard the fiction that the majority also represents the minority, that the majority will is a *collective* will, then the majority principle appears to be the principle of *majority rule over the minority.* But in *reality,* this is hardly ever the case. First of all, social reality resists that which has occasionally, and quite accurately, been termed the "contingency of arithmetic." In reality, the issue is not numerical majority. Even where the so-called majority principle is fully recognized, a numerical minority can rule over a numerical majority—be it in disguise, where the group that rules merely seems to be the majority through some electoral artifice, or completely in the open, in the case of so-called minority governments, which may conflict with the *ideology* of the majority principle and democracy but are thoroughly compatible with the *real type* of the latter. For a study of social reality, the significance of the majority principle is found not in the fact that the will of the numerical majority wins, but in the fact that, with the *acceptance of this conception,* with the *efficacy of this ideology,* the individuals who form the social community *separate into essentially two groups.* The tendency to gain and form a majority has the final effect that *essentially only two groups face each other* in the struggle for power; the numerous forces within society that drive it into divisions and ruptures are *overcome, leaving only one single fundamental conflict.* The two groups may be more or less distinct in numerical strength; but in their political significance, in their social potency, there is little difference. It is above all this *power of social integration* that characterizes the majority principle sociologically.

But the fact that the efficacy of the majority principle does not so much depend upon the numerical majority is closely connected with the fact that, in social reality, *there is no absolute rule of the majority over the minority;* the will of the community formed according to the so-called majority principle turns out to be not a majority diktat to the minority but a result of the mutual influence exercised by both groups upon one another, a resultant of the clash of their political wills. A dictatorship of the majority over the minority is not possible in the long run, because a minority condemned to complete lack of influence would renounce, in the end, the continuation of a merely formal—not only worthless but even harmful—participation in the formation of the will of the community. By that, it deprives the majority—which by definition is not possible without a minority—of its very character. This provides the minority a means of gaining influence over the decisions of the majority. This is especially true in parliamentary democracy; for the entire parliamentary process, with its techniques of dialectic and contradiction, plea and counterplea, argument and counterargument, aims at achieving *compromise.* Therein lies the true significance of the majority principle in actual democracies. Thus it is better termed the majority-minority principle; by dividing the totality of those subject to norms into essentially only two groups, majority and minority, it creates the *possibility* of compromise in forming the collective will, after having prepared this final integration through the *pressure* to compromise, because compromise alone allows formation of a majority as well as of a minority. Compromise means deferring that which divides those who are to be united, in favor of that which unites them. Every exchange, every *contract* is a compromise, for compromise means *to be tractable.* Even a brief glance at parliamentary practice shows that the majority principle has proven its worth especially within the *parliamentary system* as a principle of compromise, a means of balancing political opposites. The entire *parliamentary procedure* aims at achieving such a median between opposing interests, a resultant of antagonistic social forces. It creates guarantees that the various interests of the groups represented in parliament can articulate and manifest themselves in a public process. And if parliament's specific procedure of dialectic and contradiction has any deeper meaning, it can only be the creation of a synthesis somehow from the confrontation of thesis and antithesis of political interests. But that cannot mean a "higher," absolute truth, an *absolute* value above group interests, with which parliamentarism is often wrongly saddled by those who confuse its reality with its ideology, but a *compromise.* . . .

Application of the majority principle is limited by certain more or less natural barriers. The majority and the minority must be able to *come to an understanding* with each other, if they are to *be tractable.* The factual conditions for mutual understanding of those involved in forming the social will must therefore exist: a society with a relatively homogeneous culture, in particular with the same language. If *nation* is above all a community of *culture* and *language,* then the majority principle makes complete sense only *within* a uniform national body. The least that follows is that, in supranational, international communities, especially in nationally mixed, so-called multinational states, decisions on national cultural issues must be taken from the central parliament and left to autonomy—that is, to representative bodies of national communities (subgroups) organized according to the personality principle. The familiar argument that the majority principle would lead to absurd results if applied to today's humanity as such touches not so much the principle itself as its exaggeration in cases of excessive *centralization.*

And from this standpoint must also be judged the Marxist view that the majority principle can be applied only to a society founded in its members' complete commonality of interests, but not in one divided by *class conflict,* because it is suited only to overcoming subordinate, merely technical differences of opinion but not to resolving vital conflicts of interest.[37] First of all, basic harmony of interests in all areas does not exist right from the start in any human society; such harmony must be created through constant, continually renewed compromise, as even the most subordinate differences of opinion can become vital conflicts of interest. Aside from this fact, such a *rejection of the majority principle* as a basic form of democracy, and especially of parliamentarism, for a society divided by class, is grounded not so much in a *cognitive* insight into the inadequacy of the principle in the particular case, as in a—rationally unjustifiable—*will* to overcome class conflict not through peaceful resolution, but through revolutionary violence; not democratically, but autocratically and dictatorially. The majority principle is rejected because—rightly or wrongly—the compromise for which the majority principle provides the requirements is rejected. Because in reality it is compromise that comes close to unanimity in creating the social order by those subject to this order the majority principle also proves its value in light of the idea of political freedom that ideally requires unanimity. The materialist view of history teaches that social developments necessarily lead to a state in which essentially two groups face each other as *classes* with adverse interests, and a Marxist theorist recently demonstrated[38] that the relationship of these classes can and must result in a certain balance, and that from the economic side a disturbance or elimination of the balance now reached can hardly be expected in the foreseeable future. If this is true, then the question for socialist theory is no longer that which has so often been posed: formal *democracy* or *dictatorship?* Then democracy is the only natural, adequate expression of the actual state of power, the political form that a social situation qualified by class conflict will seek repeatedly against attempts at dictatorship, even if these enjoy temporary success. Then democracy is the center of gravity to which the political pendulum must always return after swinging right and left. And if the issue is the actual state of power in society, as the Marxist critique of so-called bourgeois democracy emphasizes, then the parliamentary democratic state with its fundamental duality constituted by the majority-minority principle is the "true" expression of today's society, split as it is into essentially two classes. And if there is any form at all that possibly keeps this tremendous, regrettable but undeniable contrast from being driven on a bloody, revolutionary way to catastrophe and instead resolves it peacefully and gradually, then this form is parliamentary democracy. Its ideology may be a *freedom* that remains unattainable in social reality, but its reality is *peace.* . . .

FORMAL AND SOCIAL DEMOCRACY

Marxists contrast a democracy based on the majority principle, a *formal, bourgeois* democracy, with a *social, proletarian* democracy—by which they understand a social order that guarantees those subject to its norms not only a formally equal share in forming the will of the community, but also an *equal amount of goods*—equal in some sense or other. This contrast must be rejected most decisively. It is the *value of freedom* and not the value of equality that primarily characterizes the idea of democracy. Certainly the idea of equality plays a role in democratic ideology; but it does so only in an entirely negative, formal and secondary sense. Because all are to be as *free* as possible, and thus equally so, all are to participate in forming the will of the state, and thus in equal measure. The struggle for democracy is, *historically,* a struggle for political *freedom;* that is, for popular participation in the legislature and executive. The idea of equality, to the extent it is something other than the idea of *formal equality in freedom*—that is, equality of political rights—has nothing to do with the concept of democracy. This is shown most clearly by the fact that equality, not in the sense of formal political, but of material and economic being equal of all, can be implemented not only in democratic, but also in autocratic and dictatorial forms of state—in the latter, perhaps even more successfully than in the former. Quite aside from the fact that the equal amount of goods to be assured all citizens by a "social" democracy is also meant to be an *abundant* amount, the concept of equality can take on such varied meanings that it becomes downright impossible to combine it with the concept of democracy. This "equality" means more or less the same as *justice,* and is just as ambiguous. Marxist theory, or at least a certain more recent variant of it, especially the Bolshevist doctrine, tries in the name of "democracy" to replace the ideology of freedom with the *ideology of justice.* But it is an obvious misuse of terminology to use the word "democracy," which represents—whether from an ideological or realist point of view—a specific *method of creating a social order* to refer to the *content* of this social order, which has no essential relationship to its method of creation. Such terminological manipulation has the dubious effect, if not the intention, of supplying a political state of evident *dictatorship* with the great justifying power and emotional force of the word "democracy," a power and force it enjoys thanks to its ideology of *freedom.* One simply denies the difference between democracy and dictatorship, using the social concept of democracy as opposed to the *formal* concept, and declaring *dictatorship,* which supposedly assures social justice, to be "true" democracy. The side-effect of this is to unjustly disparage the democracy of today, and with it the merit of the group that was instrumental in bringing it about, sometimes against its own material interests.

It strikes one as particularly curious that it is the socialist ideal whose implementation requires democratic methods to be tossed overboard, as since the time of Marx and Engels, one of the basic assumptions of both the political and the economic theories of socialism has been that the exploited, impoverished proletariat forms the overwhelming majority of the population, and that this proletariat must only become conscious of its class condition in order to organize in the socialist party for the class struggle against a vanishing minority. Precisely for this reason socialists were the ones to demand democracy, because they felt sure of a power whose possession was decided by the majority. However, the emergence of *bourgeois democracy* in the first half of the nineteenth century, and, even more, its stable continuity and progressive democratic development in subsequent years, were no longer completely consistent with the assumptions of socialism. Why does simple political democracy not become economic democracy? Why do bourgeois capitalist rather than proletarian communist forces rule if the socialist-educated proletariat forms the majority, and a universal, equal right to take part in the full electoral process ensures this majority the power in parliament? Of course, this question is valid only where true democracy prevails, where universal and equal political rights undeniably exist. But this is the case in the great democracies of Western Europe and America; it is even the case in Germany and Austria. Reference to the practice of electoral regulation, such as gerrymandering, impeding the exercise of the right to full participation in the electoral process for certain categories of voters, and so forth, and particularly to the powerful influence of the capitalist press, are absolutely insufficient to explain the situation. The reason that bourgeois democracy remains stuck at the level of political equality, that political equality does not lead to economic "equality," is that, contrary to decades of socialist teaching—as is shown all too clearly in the concrete lesson of the most recent revolution, particularly in Russia—the proletariat, interested in economic equality and the nationalization or socialization of production, does not, or not yet, make up an overwhelming majority of the people; in fact, in those places where socialism actually has achieved sole power through the proletariat, it is only a weak minority. That is the reason for the fundamental change in political methods by some factions of the socialist party; that is the reason why democracy, which Marx and Engels considered compatible or even identical with the *dictatorship* of the proletariat, had to be replaced with a dictatorship that represents itself with the absolutism of a political dogma and a party rule implementing this dogma. Thus the democratic ideal is being abandoned by the left wing of the proletarian party, in the belief that the proletariat cannot now, or in the foreseeable future, take power in this political form; and by the right wing of the bourgeois parties, because it believes the bourgeoisie cannot, or cannot much longer, defend its power in this political form. This is a clear symptom that the forces of both groups are approaching a state in which they actually hold a balance.[39]

DEMOCRACY AND *WELTANSCHAUUNG*

If, as has been shown above, democracy is only a *form*, only a *method* of creating a social order, then its *value*—which remains to be explored—appears highly problematic. For a specific rule of creation, a particular form of state and society, does not at all answer the obviously far more important question of the *content* of the state's order. To solve social problems, the material structure of a state's or society's order seems crucial—whether it is socialist or capitalist, whether it greatly restricts the individual sphere or limits such restrictions to a minimum, in short: not so much *how* norms are created, as what is established by them. Does one not unduly overvalue form at the expense of content when political discussion turns primarily on the choice between democracy and autocracy? And the ideology of democracy in particular has a pronounced tendency to pose the crucial question in this way, while the ideology of autocracy forces questions of state *form* into the background. Assuming that the question of the form of the state has been decided, that the state's order may be determined only by those for whom it claims validity, only then does the actual task become apparent: what content should the people give the laws it creates? Not even a radical democrat would be able to claim that the issue of state *content*, that is, the correct, best content of the state order, is determined once the issue of the *form* of the state is decided. Only one who believes that the people, and *only* the people, possesses the truth, insight into the good, could think this way. Such a view cannot be justified except through a religious-metaphysical hypothesis under which the people, and *only* the people, achieves its wisdom in some supernatural way. This would mean believing in the divine right of the people—a belief that is no more acceptable than the divine right of princes.

It is true that various apologists for popular sovereignty have made similar claims; even Rousseau was not far from it when he justified the binding force of majority decisions, the authority of the majority, by saying the minority was *mistaken* about the *true* content of the *volonté générale.* But anyone can see that here the defenders of democracy employ an argument alien to its essence. The personal relationship to the absolute, to a divinity as whose messenger, instrument, or son the single, individual autocratic leader appears, may bolster his charisma and his claim to the people's faith. But it cannot be transferred. If democracy really took relationship to the absolute as a justification, it would be an ass in lion's clothing. On the other hand, one need not be a pessimist and believe Ibsen's bitter words that the majority is always wrong and therefore the people are entirely incapable of insight into what is right; to be skeptical of democracy, one need merely question whether *only* the people, *only* the majority, is capable of cognition of the true and the good. The situation would, in fact, seem hopeless for democracy if we assumed that cognition of *absolute truth,* insight into *absolute values,* were possible. For in the face of the overarching authority of the absolute good, what can exist besides the *obedience* of those to whom it brings salvation; unconditional and thankful obedience to him who, possessing the absolute good, knows and demands it; an obedience that can be based only in a *belief* that the authoritative person of the legislator possesses the absolute good, to the extent that *cognition* of the same is denied to the great mass of those subject to the norms.

At this point, where democracy seems to have lost any chance of justification—precisely at this point—its defense must begin.

For that is the great question: *whether* there is cognition of absolute truth, insight into absolute values. That is the basic conflict between *Weltanschauung*s and views of life under which the conflict between autocracy and democracy can be subsumed. Belief in absolute truth and absolute values provides the conditions for a metaphysical, and especially religious-mystical *Weltanschauung.* But the negation of these conditions, the opinion that only relative truths, only relative values can be attained by human cognition, and that every truth and every value—like the people who discover them—must thus be ready at all times to retreat and make way for others, leads to a *Weltanschauung* of criticism and positivism, defined as a philosophical and scientific school of thought based in the positive—that is, the given, the perceivable, a changeable and constantly changing *experience*—that rejects the assumption of an absolute transcending this experience. This conflict of *Weltanschauung*s corresponds to a conflict of values, especially in fundamental political attitudes. The metaphysical-absolutist world view corresponds with an autocratic, the critical-relativist with a democratic attitude.[40]

Those who hold absolute truth and absolute values to be inaccessible to human cognition must consider not only their own, but also foreign, opposing opinions to be at least possible. Thus *relativism* is the *Weltanschauung* that the *democratic idea* presumes. Democracy values each person's political will *equally*, just as it respects equally any political belief, any political opinion, which is after all expressed by the political will. It therefore gives every political conviction the same chance to be articulated and to *compete* freely for people's minds and hearts. Thus the dialectic procedure in popular and parliamentary assemblies, unfolding in plea and counterplea, preparing for the creation of norms, has been correctly recognized as democratic. The rule of the majority, so characteristic of democracy, is distinguished from every other sort of rule in that it not only—according to its innermost essence—conceptually requires an opposition, the minority, but also recognizes and protects it politically through basic rights and the principle of proportionality. But the stronger the minority, the more the politics of democracy become the politics of compromise; just as nothing is more typical of the relativist *Weltanschauung* than the tendency toward mediation between two opposing standpoints, of which neither can be adopted completely, unconditionally, and in full negation of the other. The relativity of values upheld by specific political beliefs, the impossibility of claiming—despite all subjective devotion or personal conviction—*absolute validity* for a political program, a political ideal, imperatively forces a rejection also of *political* absolutism—be it the absolutism of a monarch, a priestly, noble or warrior caste, a class or an otherwise privileged group. One who claims *divine* inspiration, supernatural illumination for his political desires and actions may have the right to close his ears to human voices and impose his will, as the will of the absolute good, upon a world of unbelievers blind enough to have a differing will. That is why the motto of the divine right of Christian monarchy could be "authority, not majority," a motto that has become the target of anyone who advocates intellectual freedom, science freed from miracles and dogmas, based in human reason and critical doubt, and, politically, democracy. One who appeals only to earthly truth, whose social goals are steered only by human knowledge, *can hardly justify the coercion inevitable for implementing the social goals except through the agreement of at least the majority of those for whom this coercive order is supposed to be beneficial.* And this coercive order may be constituted only in such a way that the minority, which is not absolutely wrong, absolutely without rights, may at any time itself become a majority.

This is the actual sense of the political system we call democracy, which may be offered as an alternative to political absolutism only because it is the expression of a political relativism.

Chapter 18 of the Gospel according to St. John describes an occurrence in the life of Jesus. The simple, in its naïveté lapidary, presentation is one of the most wonderful in world literature; and without intending to, it becomes a tragic symbol of relativism—and democracy. It is the time of the Easter celebration, when Jesus, accused of claiming to be the son of God and King of the Jews, is brought before Pilate, the Roman governor. Pilate ironically asks him, who in the Roman's eyes can only be a poor fool: "So you are the King of the Jews?" And Jesus, deeply serious and filled with the glow of his divine mission, answers: "As you say. I am a king, and was born and came into the world to bear witness to the truth. Let all who are from the truth hear my voice." Then Pilate, this member of an old, tired, and thus skeptical culture, says: "What is truth?" And because he does not know what truth is, and because he—as a Roman—is accustomed to thinking democratically, he appeals to the people and calls for a vote. According to the gospel, he went to the Jews, and said to them: "I can find no guilt in him. But it is a tradition among you that I set someone free for you at the Easter celebration. Do you want me to give you the King of the Jews?" The plebiscite went against Jesus. Everyone cried out, saying: "Not this one, but Barabbas." But the chronicler adds: "Barabbas was a thief."

Perhaps one, perhaps the faithful, the political faithful, will argue that this particular example speaks against democracy rather than for it. And this argument must be accepted, but only on one condition: of their political truth, which must, if necessary, be imposed by political force, the faithful be as sure as was the son of God.

TWO

Hugo Preuss

INTRODUCTION

Christoph Schoenberger

The Weimar Constitution had no more passionate defender than the person who drafted it. No German law professor bound his name so unreservedly to the Weimar Republic as Hugo Preuss.

On 15 November 1918, six days after the fall of the monarchy, Friedrich Ebert, the Social Democratic chairman of the Council of People's Deputies and later president, appointed Preuss to a high post in the government: *Staatssekretär des Inneren*. His main responsibility was to draft a democratic constitution. Preuss, a bourgeois left-liberal, was at the time the most left-leaning scholar of the law of the state in Germany—Social Democratic professors of the law of the state had been unthinkable under the Kaiser. By appointing him, Ebert sought to bridge the divide between his Social Democrats and the middle class. He hoped to mollify bourgeois fears of a social-revolutionary dictatorship, the "authoritarian state in reverse" against which Preuss had warned in a famous newspaper article in the days after the November Revolution.[1] At the end of 1918, Preuss completed a draft that decisively influenced the Weimar Constitution, although it underwent significant changes in the National Assembly. This "paternity" strengthened his deep inner bond with the Weimar Republic; his death in 1925 at the age of sixty-four spared him the experience of its failure.

During the Empire, Preuss had been an outsider among fellow scholars of the law of the state—unlike, for example, Gerhard Anschütz, one of his generation's few other pro-republican scholars of state law. Preuss was never offered a professorship at a German university; political and scholarly reservations as well as anti-Semitic prejudice kept him from the centers of scholarly life in the Empire. It was not an accident that he taught at the far less respected Berlin College of Commerce [*Handelshochschule*], a private school founded by the Berlin business community. The College of Commerce was an institution of the urban liberal bourgeoisie, the social class to which Preuss, a financially independent member of the Jewish upper class and an active left-liberal municipal politician, felt the closest ties. Here Preuss's career coincided with his scholarly and political interest: the self-organization of a free citizenry.

Preuss believed that citizens should organize themselves in locally self-governed communities, which would ultimately be supplemented by parliamentarization and democratization at the level of the Länder and the Reich. His personal involvement in local Berlin politics, as city councilor and honorary member of the municipal council [*Magistrat*], served this end at the local level. Historians of the Empire have sometimes viewed such liberal influence in local politics as indicative of the potential for liberalizing imperial Germany as a whole.[2] This is certainly what left-liberals like Preuss had in mind. But it should be noted that the strong position of liberals in the cities was largely due to the restricted franchise that applied to local elections. By contrast, the introduction of universal suffrage for Reichstag elections in 1871 seriously reduced liberal influence at the federal level and strengthened the Social Democrats and the Catholic Center Party. Preuss's political fate at the national level during the Empire mirrored the different conditions there. His efforts to win a Reichstag seat were unsuccessful both in the Empire's last Reichstag elections of 1912 and in the elections to the National Assembly and the first Reichstag of the Weimar Republic in 1919–20. Preuss, who joined the newly founded left-liberal German Democratic Party [*Deutsche Demokratische Partei*, DDP] after the end of the monarchy, ultimately proved to be too much the scholar and too little the politician.

His scholarly work centered on citizen self-organization as well. In 1889, he successfully defended his *Habilitationsschrift* under Otto von Gierke at the University of Berlin. That work, *Municipality, State, and Reich as Territorial Corporations* [*Gemeinde, Staat und Reich als Gebietskörperschaften*] and his later historical work on the development of German towns since the late Middle Ages were strongly influenced by Gierke's *Theory of Associations* [*Genossenschaftslehre*]. Gierke thought that the possibility of creating associations and cooperatives was the basis of human history in general. According to him, associations of all kinds, from the family to the state, were able to combine diversity and uniformity.[3] Gierke's theory owed much to the tradition of the failed German revolution of 1848 and the Paul's Church Constitution drafted by the National Assembly in Frankfurt.

Gierke and Preuss, influenced as they were by the liberal ideals of 1848, opposed the legal positivism of Paul Laband that dominated state law scholarship during the early decades of imperial Germany. Laband viewed the law of the state as a creation of state power and attributed this power to the monarchy and its bureaucracy alone. His canonical *State Law of the German Reich* [*Das Staatsrecht des deutschen Reiches* (1876–82)] therefore dealt only grudgingly with the Reichstag's position in the Wilhelmine system. Laband considered parliamentary institutions to be mere formal limitations to an elementary state power that remained firmly in the hands of unelected bureaucrats.[4] Gierke, on the other hand, insisted on the crucial importance of the Reichstag, on the significance of basic rights and on the right of citizens to participate in public affairs in general. But Gierke was in favor of neither parliamentary government nor modern democracy. Preuss later radicalized Gierke's position, advocating gradual parliamentarization and democratization of the Wilhelmine system, which he termed an "authoritarian state" [*Obrigkeitsstaat*]. Long before Hans Kelsen, Preuss rejected the very concept of sovereignty, which was for him a relic of the monarchic-bureaucratic-absolutist tradition. A state built according to the principles of Gierke's *Theory of Associations* could no longer be fixated on sovereignty; instead, the state would be characterized by popular self-organization at all levels—from the municipalities to the Länder and the Reich.

During the First World War, Preuss became one of the most outspoken critics of Wilhelmine Germany's political system. His impassioned *German People and Politics* [*Das deutsche Volk und die Politik* (1915)] dealt harshly with the Empire from a practical political perspective. In this wartime book, Preuss bemoaned the weakness of the German liberal tradition, which he claimed gave Germany a fundamentally different nature than the western democracies. The German idea of freedom, he argued, was traditionally apolitical and aimed only at protecting a private sphere of freedom against the alien, authoritarian power of the state. Freedom was only freedom from the state, not freedom *in* the state. For Preuss, the German party system reflected this tradition. Since the Reichstag had no direct influence on the formation of a cabinet, the German parties had developed stubborn ideological convictions and a strong oppositional spirit. They lacked the ability to compromise, let alone to take practical responsibility:

> Despite the constitutional structure and local autonomy, the state appears again and again—above all in cases of conflict—to be embodied by the sole executive with its army and bureaucracy. Faced with this state, parliament and local government are an alien, heterogeneous element and can at best serve as external limitations. Not only does the attitude of the executive involuntarily follow this pattern; so does, involuntarily, the effort of the political currents called upon to practice eternal opposition in the German Länder. This effort always tended far more toward the negative side, the protection of individual and private freedom from encroachments by the state—the authoritarian

bureaucracy—than toward the positive side, the conquest of state power and responsibility for one's own party.[5]

Preuss, in contrast, wanted freedom to be thought of as the freedom to co-operate in the community of citizens. With the end of the monarchy, he had the opportunity to translate his ideas into action.

Preuss drafted the Weimar Constitution, defended the draft before the National Assembly, and was closely involved in working out the final version of the document, which was promulgated on 14 August 1919. However, the Weimar Constitution did not reflect Preuss's wishes in every respect, particularly with regard to Germany's new federal structure. Preuss was convinced that the young republic could succeed only if its territorial boundaries, until then coupled with the dynasties of the individual Länder, were to change fundamentally. He proposed, on the one hand, unifying the underpopulated dwarf states of the Empire into larger territories, and, on the other, dividing Prussia into several separate Länder. In Preuss's view, the dissolution of Prussia, which had exercised a de facto hegemony during the Empire, was indispensable to the formation of a parliamentary democracy at the national level. He was convinced that the end of the dynasties signaled the coming of a unitary German nation-state—a state that could not bear the weight of an overgrown Prussia.[6] Preuss underestimated the tenacity of German federalism, however, and was unable to put his views into practice. A thorough restructuring of territorial divisions did not occur, nor did the breakup of Prussia. The continued existence of Prussia, which comprised three-fifths of the territory of Germany and its population, would be an obstacle to the development of the constitution, as Preuss had predicted. Ironically, democracy in Prussia, under the leadership of the Social Democratic minister-president Otto Braun, proved far less crisis-prone than its national counterpart.[7]

By contrast, the central institutions recommended by Preuss for the Weimar Constitution did succeed in gaining the support of the National Assembly, in particular his conception of the relationship between Reichstag, cabinet [*Reichsregierung*], and president [*Reichspräsident*]. In Preuss's model, the president would appoint a chancellor to head the cabinet, who would at the same time require the confidence of the Reichstag. The president, directly elected by the people, would have a status equal to that of the Reichstag. In case of conflict between president and Reichstag, the president would have the right to call new elections "to lodge an appeal against the people's representative with the people themselves."[8] This system was intended, on the one hand, to lead to an equilibrium based on separation of powers; on the other hand, it was to guarantee the democratic rights of the people against parliament.[9]

The new constitutional system weakened parliamentary institutions from the start. The Reichstag still had to grow out of the oppositional role to which it had become accustomed during the Empire. The new system, however, favored the persistence of behavior held over from the monarchy, as it ensured the presence of an executive ready for action and supported by the civil service and the military. The existence of a popularly elected president relieved the parties in the Reichstag, which were deeply split by social and religious differences and unused to the necessity of compromise, of the responsibility to form a cabinet. With the president as an *Ersatzkaiser,* a reserve authority stood at the ready that could easily head the state administration should the Reichstag fail to act. This "reserve constitution" became reality at the end of the Weimar Republic, when a presidential cabinet replaced the Reichstag as the primary legislative body. Preuss, who had denounced the weaknesses of the imperial constitutional system so unsparingly during the First World War, proved in his Weimar draft constitution to be far more influenced by the legacy of the constitutional monarchy than he himself realized. His system was one-sidedly aimed at weakening the Reichstag but took no practical precautions against the danger of a dictatorship of the president.

Preuss's idealistic conception of cooperative democracy prevented him, like so many other Weimar democrats, from paying enough attention to the great significance of parties in a democratic state. Apart from exceptions such as Gustav Radbruch and Hans Kelsen, even democratically oriented state law scholars left the discussion of parties to conservative authors such as Heinrich Triepel, who bemoaned their influence over representative bodies and flirted with the idea of a parliament of estates. Even pro-republican scholars such as Preuss conceived of democracy more as an organic unity of the people than as a system for the orderly resolution of conflict. In their minds as well, the president easily developed into a guardian of the unified popular will facing a parliament splintered into opposing parties.[10]

Preuss continued his political, journalistic, and academic engagement on behalf of the young German democracy until his death in 1925. He was especially hurt by the accusation of right-wing nationalists circles, often accompanied by anti-Semitic attacks directed at him personally, that the Constitution was "un-German."[11] Improvised in a climate of wartime defeat, saddled with enormous problems of foreign policy and economics, the Weimar Republic was unable to fulfill the task formulated by Preuss during the First World War as the goal of German constitutional development: "to synthesize antitheses and interests in common work and common responsibility for the commonwealth, the *res publica.*"[12]

MAIN WORKS

Gemeinde, Staat und Reich als Gebietskörperschaften: Versuch einer deutschen Staatskonstruktion auf Grundlage der Genossenschaftslehre. Berlin: Springer, 1889.

Die Entwicklung des deutschen Städtewesens. Vol. 1: *Entwicklungsgeschichte der deutschen Städteverfassung.* Leipzig: Teubner, 1906.
"Selbstverwaltung, Gemeinde, Staat, Souveränität." In *Staatsrechtliche Abhandlungen: Festgabe für Paul Laband zum fünfzigsten Jahrestage der Doktor-Promotion,* vol. 2, 197 ff. Tübingen: Mohr, 1908.
Das deutsche Volk und die Politik. Jena: Diederichs, 1915.
Deutschlands republikanische Reichsverfassung. 2nd ed. Berlin: Neuer Staat, 1923.
Um die Reichsverfassung von Weimar. Berlin: Mosse, 1924.
Staat, Recht und Freiheit: Aus 40 Jahren deutscher Politik und Geschichte. Tübingen: Mohr, 1926.
Reich und Länder: Bruchstücke eines Kommentars zur Verfassung des deutschen Reiches. Aus dem Nachlaß herausgegeben von Gerhard Anschütz. Berlin: Heymann, 1928.

LITERATURE

Bilfinger, Carl. "Reich und Länder." *Zeitschrift für Politik* 19 (1929): 63 ff.
Feder, Ernst. *Hugo Preuss: Ein Lebensbild.* Berlin: Hapke & Schmidt, 1926.
Gillessen, Günther. "Hugo Preuss: Studien zur Ideen- und Verfassungsgeschichte der Weimarer Republik." Dissertation. University of Freiburg, 1955.
Grassmann, Siegfried. *Hugo Preuss und die deutsche Selbstverwaltung.* Lübeck and Hamburg: Matthieson, 1965.
Hamburger, Ernest. "Hugo Preuss: Scholar and Statesman." Leo Baeck Institute, *Yearbook* 20 (1975): 179 ff.
Heuss, Theodor. "Hugo Preuss." In Hugo Preuss. *Staat, Recht und Freiheit,* 1 ff. Tübingen: Mohr, 1926.
Hintze, Hedwig. "Hugo Preuss: Eine historisch-politische Charakteristik." In *Die Justiz,* vol. 2, 223 ff. Berlin: Rothschild, 1926–27.
Lehnert, Detlev. "Hugo Preuss als moderner Klassiker einer kritischen Theorie der 'verfaßten' Politik: Vom Souveränitätsproblem zum demokratischen Pluralismus." *Politische Vierteljahresschrift* 33 (1992): 33 ff.
———. *Verfassungsdemokratie als Bürgergenossenschaft. Politisches Denken, Öffentliches Recht und Geschichtsdeutungen bei Hugo Preuss—Beiträge zur demokratischen Insitutionenlehre in Deutschland.* Baden-Baden: Nomos, 1998.
Mauersberg, Jasper. *Ideen und Konzeption Hugo Preuss' für die Verfassung der deutschen Republik 1919 und ihre Durchsetzung im Verfassungswerk von Weimar.* Frankfurt am Main: Peter Lang, 1991.
Schefold, Dian. "Hugo Preuss (1860–1925): Von der Stadtverfassung zur Staatsverfassung der Weimarer Republik." *Deutsche Juristen jüdischer Herkunft.* Edited by Helmut Heinrichs et al., 429 ff. Munich: Beck, 1993.
Schmidt, Gustav. "Hugo Preuss." In *Deutsche Historiker,* vol. 7. Edited by Hans-Ulrich Wehler, 55 ff. Göttingen: Vandenhoeck & Ruprecht, 1980.
Schmitt, Carl. *Hugo Preuss: Sein Staatsbegriff und seine Stellung in der deutschen Staatslehre.* Tübingen: Mohr, 1930.

THE SIGNIFICANCE OF THE DEMOCRATIC
REPUBLIC FOR THE IDEA OF SOCIAL JUSTICE

Hugo Preuss

Originally appeared as *Die Bedeutung der demokratischen Republik für den sozialen Gedanken* (1925), in Hugo Preuss, *Staat, Recht und Freiheit: Aus 40 Jahren deutscher Politik und Geschichte* (Tübingen: Mohr, 1926), 481–96. It is the text of a speech that Preuss gave to the General Association of Free Employees [*Allgemeiner freier Angestellten Bund*], which was a trade union of white-collar workers.

Of the value and dignity of the republic and of democracy in general I do not believe that I need to speak. I know that the AfA-Bund [*Allgemeiner freier Angestellten Bund,* General Association of Free Employees] is supposed to be "apolitical" in a certain sense; yet it is not so apolitical as not to be pervaded by the value and dignity of democracy, without my having to preach it. One would have to be politically blind not to discern clearly in the great course of recent history the direction in which historical development is moving with an internal necessity. If we look back one and a half centuries—a short span of time in the historical context—this period, especially its final decades, is filled with the incomparable triumph of democratic principles around the world. It starts with the Declaration of Independence by the United States and ends with the world war. One and a half centuries ago, when the United States entered the community of nations, it was the first and only large, modern, democratic republic. And after one and a half centuries had past, the last three anti-democratic powers collapsed in the world war—we, unfortunately, along with them. It is of world historical significance that not only Germany and Austria fell before the superior power of the coalition, but first of all Russia, which had been on the side of the victors, on the side of the superior power. This certainly does not prove that the allied and associated democracies of the West had led a crusade for democracy, as they claimed in their wartime propaganda. Yet it proves much more. It proves that in the great conflicts and decisions of the modern world with its tremendous mass movements—in these battles in which not only the military, but whole peoples, determine victory or defeat in their social entirety by summoning all their social strength of soul and technical potential—that in these times the anti-democratic form of government is simply no longer capable of competing with the great democracies. In short, it is so clear and apparent that the development is strengthening and securing the spread of the democratic principle and asserting it everywhere, that one could hardly deny it even if one wished to.

Yet, some say, all that may be true, but the democratic state simply does not suit Germany. It contradicts the German character! Democratic institutions are "Western." Yes, gentlemen, as I said at the beginning, I do not believe I need to refute that in front of this audience. They would be a strange people, these Germans, if they alone were incapable of keeping step with the political development of all civilized humanity. This claim is suspiciously reminiscent of those who glorified Russian czarism and desired to protect "Holy Mother Russia" from infection by the "rotten West." It is generally those in power, favored by the historical destiny of a country and its people and by particular circumstances, who fear nothing so much as that their subjects could enter the great stream of general political and social development. The beneficiaries and followers of the power of princely dynasties, as well as the princely bureaucracies, also insisted that the German character and the true German national feeling stood in opposition to a unified national state. German nationalism, they said, could only feel at home in Prussia, or even more in Bavaria, and then, *secundum ordinem,* down to the Lippe and the Reuss. One is bitterly reminded of [Gotthold Ephraim] Lessing's despairing words, uttered at the height of princely sovereignty: "The true German national character is to have no national character." But praise God, these times are behind us. Democratic freedom and national unity belong together, and why they belong together will be discussed later. But is it not already proven by the fact that we survived the terrible collapse of the old powers and the six equally terrible years of peace on this foundation of democratic and national unity? We could not have done it on any other foundation. But I do not need to discuss this further here.

In this circle, however, dedicated to social policy, the question formulated in my topic does arise: the social significance of the democratic republic. This certainly does not mean that I expect you to be small-minded enough to gauge great principles of the state's communal life and its historical development according to the personal advantages they bring or some other facet of social or trade union policy. I know that your opponents accuse you of this, but it does not touch you. But on the other hand, the republic and the democratic idea would be nothing but sounding brass or a tinkling cymbal* if the democratic idea were not closely linked with the social idea; if the free people's state that we hope to realize in the democratic republic meant nothing for the freedom and for the moral and material improvement of the people—that is, in general, the working people—in their own state. However, two opposing parties claim that democracy and republic mean nothing for the social idea and social progress.

You all know the term "formal democracy" used as an attack. Formal democracy—and there are many who mean the Weimar Constitution in

*Preuss quotes from 1 Corinthians 13:1.—EDS.

particular when they say this—is said to be socially meaningless as long as the capitalist economic order has not been destroyed. In this view democratization of the state without socialization of the means of production is form without content, the equal rights of democratic freedom are as much of a lie as the private-law freedom of the so-called free-labor contract between the owners of the means of production and the proletarian who possesses only his labor power; just as the worker continues to be exploited through free-labor contracts, so also does he remain unfree under the freedom of democracy and the republican constitution. And this is where the opposing side chimes in: No, not only does he remain unfree, but he is even less free and more helpless in the democratic republic; for in the democratic republic, the property-owning classes rule without scruple or restraint. In the capitalist economic order, there is only one road to effective social reform, effective social progress, and that is a strong monarchy, they say, a strong monarchy that stands above the interests and aspirations of the ruling economic classes and is immune to class egoism, but which must also have the power to rein in the ruling economic classes and circles, to set restraints and to force them to take measures of social reform. And then, naturally, they go on to praise specifically the social kingship of the Hohenzollerns, and they quote the old Fritz, who is supposed already to have said that he would like to be a king for the beggars.* These are the two opposing parties, in whose cross-fire the democratic republican constitution stands with regard to its connection with the social idea.

"Formal democracy!" Yes indeed, in a sense every constitution, like every legal order, is formal. It creates formal barriers between individuals and groups. Is, for example, the Soviet constitution (if one can speak of a constitution) not formal? It determines above all purely organizational forms and the rights to participate in the full electoral process and to vote. It is even more formal in creating, purely formally, an endless chasm between the minority of those with rights and the great mass of those excluded from them. These are formal barriers. Because every constitution, like every legal order, is in itself a formal element, no constitution as such can create a new society. It would be exciting false hopes to claim that any constitution, however it may be formulated, could immediately and directly create a new social landscape. Nevertheless, the value of a constitution for the idea of social

---

*The supporters of the monarchy in Imperial Germany had argued that only the monarchy could guarantee social justice, because it stood above the various interest groups. They referred to a celebrated remark of Frederick the Great, who, as Prussian prince, is supposed to have said that as king he would be "a king for the beggars" ["Quand je serai roi, je serai un vrai roi des gueux."]. See Eckart Reidegeld, "Schöpfermythen des Wilhelminismus: Kaiser und Kansler an der 'Weige des deutschen Sozialstaates'," in Lothar Machten, ed., *Bismarcks Sozialstaat: Beiträge zur Geschichte der Sozialpolitik und zur sozialpolitischen Geschichtsschreibung* (Frankfurt and New York: Campus, 1994), 269.—EDS.

justice can vary enormously. I believe that the value of a constitution for the idea of social justice can be determined by looking at its structure, the "formal" structure in which the constitution shapes the organization of government. The constitution may benefit and promote positive social development and leave it the most leeway legally, or it may limit social justice through privileges on the one hand and deprivation of rights on the other, and set artificial barriers and obstacles to the natural development of positive social movement. A constitution, even in the democratic republic, cannot create the "social state of the future" (to use an older expression). That is beyond the powers of a mere legal order. However, its value from a social point of view will be judged according to how its legal norms—the legal limits and restraints it sets—perform in regard to the law of progressive socialization. Although, or perhaps because, I am not a socialist, I can refer to progressive socialization with a clear conscience. It is an undeniable truth. Of course, one must not expect of it the sudden fulfillment of any socialist schema. But with shrinking space on earth, due as well to the growth of mankind and the conquest of distance, the law of progressive socialization has a certain natural inevitability. One need only consider the development of common means of transportation, light sources, energy sources, water sources, etc., with all their consequences. The present situation, with the consequences of the world war, offers indirect evidence. At first, a socialist deluge was expected, hoped for, or feared as a consequence. In fact, we see the opposite: an ebbing of socialization despite a socialist electorate and the swelling of an anti-social super-capitalism; for the world war temporarily pulled mankind apart, not only intellectually but also economically. By making international exchange and traffic more difficult, it also increased physical distances to a certain extent. As long as this situation continues, it limits or interrupts the efficacy of the law of progressive socialization.

However, it makes a significant difference whether a legal order hinders the development of the law of progressive socialization, whether it, as we can also say, hinders the intensification of social life—through artificial restraints, legal inequality, privileges and deprivation of rights—or whether it smoothes the path through democratic equality. Smoothing does not immediately lead to an ideal goal; neither do restraints hold off the goal forever. The development simply takes a longer or shorter time; and above all, it progresses either through healthy, peaceful internal development or through internal struggles and convulsions. That is the whole difference. But it is important enough for those who have to live with it.

I would like to illustrate this with an example. The free-labor contract certainly brings only formal equality of rights. When the employer and the employee, formally equal, make a legally free contract, they are not economically and socially equal; the economic and social differences at first remain unchanged. Here we see a spectacle that is often repeated in similar circumstances. There was a time and there were people who celebrated the free-labor contract as the ultimate in economic and social wisdom and who said: Children, what else do you want? The thousand-year Reich has been achieved! That was foolish; it was lack of political awareness. And it is partly for this reason that the opposing side now can claim, in contrast to this sense-less overestimation, a swindle, a complete nothing, a lie; the free-labor con-tract is worthless! Gentlemen! For social policy it is neither the ultimate wisdom, nor is it socially worthless. It is even eminently valuable. Ask your-self: Is not the free-labor contract the starting point for the entire recent upward movement in social policy? Would this even be imaginable without the "formal" legal prerequisite of the free-labor contract? Would this entire development be imaginable under conditions of slavery, bondage, serfdom, indentured servitude, and guilds? No, these legal conditions had to outlive themselves, they had to make room for the new, "formal" right of the free-labor contract in order to create the opportunity and precondition for all the things that seem obvious to you today, since they have become so normal: the right to form unions, their movement and activity, collective bargaining agreements, etc. Just ask yourselves, in a quiet moment, what the necessary precondition to all these things is. The free-labor contract! Certainly, the free-labor contract did not in itself create the upward social movement, other movements and struggles did this. But the disgraceful "formal" right of the free-labor contract was the precondition to and root of all these modern weapons in the onward pressure of social policy. And now, to leave this example, constitutionally granted "formal" democracy offers in a similar, but much broader and larger sense, the basis, the starting point, the pre-condition for a rich and vigorous, though gradual, step-by-step unfolding of the social idea.

The democratic constitution contributes nothing to social progress? The supporters of the old say: Did not the social kingship do more? The demo-cratic constitution does not speak of the "poor man" who must be "raised." The so-called social kingship spoke quite a lot of him. Yes, gentlemen! The older among you still recall the large employers, who were in a certain sense extremely active in regard to "social policy"; they created a wealth of well-meaning rules and beneficial social institutions—and they strongly empha-sized what they did. But is it not remarkable that those who were to be fa-vored by these measures saw them as a means of oppression! No fair person would deny that in a material sense the results were excellent. But why did those on the receiving end, if they were of firm character and clear head, experience at least, let us say, an uneasy feeling? Because they felt, and rightly so, that these social measures were not an end in itself; they were rather the means to an end, to a goal of power, stricter control and tighter shackles. Nonsocialists must never forget that, despite certain errors and mistakes, socialism always heavily and rightly emphasized, despite the importance of material questions, that the human being, and therefore the worker, does not live by bread alone; that to him ideal claims, claims to freedom, are just as much a necessity. For those "social" welfare measures, one is justifiably convinced that many a grant of bread and other material things occurs at the cost of personal freedom, dignity, and autonomy. What for the individual large employer is a matter of business policy and personal advantage, is on a larger scale and in modernized form what the social policy of the eudaimonic police state and of the Kaiser used to be. I do not deny that liberals and Social Democrats made political errors in dealing with these things. But what is now extolled in so many beautiful speeches—that real social improvement was achieved from above, that a real social, I won't say reconciliation, but rapprochement between the various segments of this one people through the instrument of social policy was reached; that is beyond question. For just like the policy of the enlightened absolutist employers (if we may so characterize them), authoritarian social policy was also a means to an end. The obvious proof of this is the fact that legislation concerning social policy was framed within anti-Socialist legislation—emergency legislation. The aim of this legislation was not social improvement in itself; it did not indicate that the social idea had penetrated the state; it was a means to the goal of power. We need not express it as impolitely as did Marx and Engels, speaking of the deception of royal Prussian government socialism; but those who follow these things more closely know what Bismarck learned from Louis Bonaparte in regard to this social policy as an instrument of power. It is simply an embarrassment to ascribe merely to Social Democratic agitation the astonishing fact that Germany, the country with the most progressive legislation concerning social policy, is at the same time the country whose working class is most alienated from the state, the life of the state, and the nation. During the war, as a member of the Reich Committee for the Welfare of War Invalids, I once went to Brussels at the invitation of the former governor-general of Belgium, von Bissing. Some of you will remember that Herr von Bissing made great efforts to explain to the Belgians how far ahead of their fatherland Germany was in social policy. He thought that with this he would propagandize Germany to the Belgian workers in a particularly clever and cautious way. And one must admit that Belgium was as backward in social policy as Germany was progressive. Despite Germany's exemplary social policy, the Belgian workers wanted nothing to do with its control. For *politically* they were more closely linked with their state than the German workers unfortunately were or could have been with the German state until the war, despite social policy from above—a result of the authoritarian system that excluded broad sectors from the life of the state.

Is not there a strong nexus between the idea of the republic—the *res publica,* the *res populi,* the affair of the people, what is shared by the entire people—and the social idea, in and of itself? Seen in broad terms, two structures of the state face one another here. The socialists call each other *comrade*. And the republic, and the democratic principle, rest on the *cooperative* principle of organization from below. Authority is not derived from above but from the community of comrades, of citizens; it rises from narrower to ever wider associations, from bottom to top. It is the cooperative structuring of the state. It faces the authoritarian structuring of the state from top to bottom that claims an authority given *a priori*. Max Weber has defined state power as the "monopoly of the legitimate use of force." If this monopoly of the legitimate use of force is not in the hands of the entire population but of a dynasty, a class, a caste, a ruling body, they are forced like every creature, in line with the drive for self-preservation, to use their power and force, first of all to obtain the monopoly. They must follow policies that cannot arise from the cooperative spirit of the entire population. They assure their own preservation, the assertion of their own control, anchored in all sorts of formal legal regulations and a corresponding administrative practice.

To be sure, democratic equality cannot be equated with the fiction of complete personal equality. First of all, people are not equal but very unequal. It has been said that, just as on a tree not one leaf is like the other, so not one person is really like the other. And further, political organization, like every organization, is differentiation and division of labor, hence, inequality. But why, then, is the right to take part in the full electoral process, political equality in general, the basis of every democratic form of state? Because at least at today's level of social, cultural, and economic conditions, any formal difference in the allocation of political rights to individuals leads to despotism, privilege, and deprivation of rights; a just allocation of different rights according to differences in personality is impossible. Those who would like to introduce an "organic" right to take part in the full electoral process, as they like to call it—that is, an unequal right—insist that the highest legal principle is not equal treatment for all, but equal for equals, unequal for unequals. But against what standard can one justly measure the allocation of political rights? Once, it could be done, when the rights of the estates still existed—before they were in ruins and could only be upheld in the flow of times through trickery and violence. At a time when they were still vital, the legal order had strict measures and could do justice to mass phenomena according to them. Individuals could still fall under the wheels of life, but these were individual cases. In general, the knight was a knight, the peasant a peasant, the trader a trader, the wage laborer a wage laborer in his entire nature and manner. It always happened that some were declassed upward or downward, but these were exceptions. But in this regard, modern social development (to summarize) involves differentiation of individuals and integration of classes. I know that it contradicts some of this audience's feelings, but I must openly express my scholarly conviction: Our development is not characterized by a deepening of class oppositions; rather, it integrates the classes.

The mental and intellectual differences, the typical features of classes are leveling out; they level out to the same extent that individuals differentiate and become intellectually more varied. Today, gentlemen, the worker is not simply part of the mass phenomenon of workers; everything depends on individuality. I know "workers" who are statesmen in their entire individuality and mentality. And there are members of classes formerly called upon by law to govern, who in their mentality are not the least statesmen. The fact that they are not workers is certainly not a result of their being too good for it intellectually and being destined for something else because of their mentality. I do not want to go into this more deeply. If you follow me and quietly extend it according to your own personal experience, you will find confirmation in many examples. And if you know family histories, you will see how great the changes have been within a few generations! Differentiation of individuals out of their classes, and integration and equalization of various classes and vocations. Economic conditions also help to blur these boundaries. And because this is the essence of modern development, the legal order can no longer link varied rights to a variety of fixed, large groups. Thus democracy in the sense of equality, unconditional equality, is not a doctrinaire quirk, not a dogma made up in someone's study, but the natural, just consequence of all recent economic, social, cultural, and intellectual development.

Law in a democracy has realized that to turn political valuations into legal distinctions would be purely arbitrary; for the fixed, large, cultural, intellectual, etc. mass phenomena to which they could be linked no longer exist. However, individual differences cannot be measured using "formal" law. Does democracy therefore mean atomization, dissolution into mere unconnected individuals? Oh no, not into unconnected individuals; they simply are no longer divided into artificial, falsely formed groups forced together through a law that has become unjust.

On the basis of modern development, there is a remedy for atomization in keeping with and based upon democratic equality, which is also necessary and indispensable for the new state: the people's free *self-organization* in *parties*. This avoids atomization and gives the people the means of acting politically in a democratic sense. Perhaps you will interject: Wait! Do the political parties in Germany really provide the people with the means of acting politically, or should one maintain the opposite? Democratic self-government is still in its infancy here. We have inherited our party system from the old days of the old authoritarian state, where playing political games was a more-or-less sensible way of passing the time without any true, serious responsibility for the fate of the people. They will have to change and reform themselves under the harsh necessity of the responsible task that popular self-government poses. Thus, our old party system is experiencing ferment and decomposition; something new is happening. Certain parties would like to use social conflicts of interest to drive apart the political trends that belong together from internal necessity for the future of our people.

All liberal political trends must be rooted in the social idea, if they are not to betray themselves. One often hears of the contradiction in principles between liberalism and democracy, namely, social democracy. Gentlemen, this contradiction is not genuine, not true. Read the father of classical liberal economics, Adam Smith. If you really read him, you will have to say that the man is not the father of the Manchester guild; he is much more what today we would call social-liberal. He certainly is, and this also is what liberalism was originally. That is why liberalism had to grow into a socially oriented democracy. Only later does one find a different trend, a distortion of liberalism— when, as Alfred Weber described it, competitive capitalism changed into monopoly capitalism. That was an important change. The idea of free movement for all, the search for freedom of economic development in opposition to the state, were no longer the true leitmotifs; they declined to mere propaganda and advertisement. Instead, in reality, the real issue for this trend was and is until today control by private economic interests over the entire state, over the public interest. Monopoly capitalism is necessarily antidemocratic and anti-social—what competitive capitalism is not, so long as it is healthy and fresh. In contrast, the democratic and the social ideas are rooted together in the cooperative principle of the commonwealth, the democratic, the republican state. Gentlemen, it was under the aegis of imperial social policy that monopoly capitalism, with its anti-social and antidemocratic instincts, became far stronger. It became one of the driving forces behind that means of power, behind the whip of the emergency laws, when the carrot of social policy with its legislation was proven politically ineffective. It was one reason for the alienation of broad sectors of the population from the state and finally for the collapse that we experienced with horror.

Lulled by the dream of security in the good old days, no sector of the German people was prepared for that collapse. If one considers this, one must realize—as will future historical investigation—that those trends and movements of the people who were not attached to the old system come hell or high water, as well as those who in fact opposed it, did an incredible rescue job after the collapse. I have always emphasized that the attitude taken by the Majority Social Democrats in those terrible, critical days was a stroke of luck for Germany. It was statesmanlike, it was national in the true sense of the word, and it gave credit to its name, social and democratic. It is really not so much a question of how the two parts of the word are connected, whether democratic and social or social and democratic. It is just a difference in emphasis. What counts is not to allow the democratic and the social principles to be turned against one another, playing into the hands of those who, as anti-nationalists and anti-democrats, serve the cause of reaction and monopoly capitalism. In that terrible emergency, after all the gods or idols had collapsed in the great twilight of the gods; after the world war, this horrible judgment of the world, had revealed the old system's loss of vitality, the only possibility of salvation proved to be the fact that the new state could be erected on the elemental community of democratic, social, and national ideas, all inseparable from one another.

A nation that no longer believes itself held together by subservience to hereditary dynasties—what is it but a cooperative community, the cooperative community of a people sharing common historical experiences, a common language, a common culture, a people that wishes to be itself, developing through its own individuality, its own character, its own intellectual gifts as a full-fledged member of the international community? For this national community to hold together strongly and firmly, it must—on a cultural and intellectual level that a people such as ours achieved long ago—live in a state based on the rule of law that facilitates and makes possible the betterment of all members of the people and gives it free rein by refraining from limiting and harming the natural development of this upward movement through outdated privileges, legal inequalities of a "formal" yet legally binding type. The necessity of democratic equality of which I spoke previously must become the reality of this state based on the rule of law.

Common work on the common democratic state, on the *res populi,* the affair of the people, at the same time creates common ground for the various economic and social interest groups and classes. This is not the sweet song of eternal social peace and harmony. We should not believe that economic and social struggles, or party struggles, will disappear even in the most attractive democratic order. That would be marasmus; everything would suffocate in such stagnation. But the struggles would lose much of their poison if they were framed by the common object of democratically equal comrades, by the political commonwealth. Common political activities—getting acquainted, standing shoulder-to-shoulder, collegial political relationships—create mutual respect and temper harshness, and the attack of monopoly capitalism will be countered by the great mass of voting citizens with their superior weight.

When we consider under what conditions of external and internal distress the democratic German republic was born and lived its early years, we must say, despite everything that, God knows, we do not approve of in this German republic, it did good work. It would not have been possible to hold the German Reich together without the democratic and social communal spirit. Without this communal spirit, without the commonalities of the national, democratic, and social principle, everything would have come apart at the seams. Pure power politics, pure authoritarian power could not have kept

the Germans on the Rhine and the Ruhr within the Fatherland. Not because they were ordered from above, but because they wanted from below,
they remained loyal to the nation. It would be triply pernicious from this
point of view if one did not attempt to lead the social struggle into calmer
paths where possible—if one were to fan the flames of social bitterness and
embitterment in Germany's democratic, national, and social republic.

Certainly weaknesses, grave weaknesses, did the state reveal during this
period and continues to reveal today. When the so-called bourgeoisie feared
that the red wave of socialism would close over their heads, in reality monopoly capitalism was celebrating its orgies. In those early days, when there
was weeping and gnashing of teeth in many circles I knew, when people sat
behind lowered blinds and only timidly passed a lantern, then I said, my
God, I am not afraid of socialism but of social reaction. It will not be caused
by what really happened, but by your fear. And unfortunately, that was often the case. The fact that great parts of our bourgeoisie were impoverished
under the Weimar Constitution was not caused by the Weimar Constitution
or by its social content, nor by socialism, which may have done many wrong
things and unfortunately may not have done some right ones. But the responsibility lies with the orgy of monopoly capitalism. Lately, monopoly capitalism does not seem to be doing so well; and while until now it was closely
linked with all the reactionary opponents of democracy and the republic,
in accordance with its anti-democratic and anti-social nature, today one
can observe something resembling an affectation of reconciliation. It almost
seems as though the monopoly capitalists would begin to recognize the republic "formally." Maybe they recall how it was often scornfully said that it
was only a formal democracy; and they have neither great respect for nor
great fear of the simply formal. There is some indication that a great transaction could take place: recognition of the republic as a formal constitutional schema and, in return, a united "bourgeois" front against socialism.
This is not without dangers. But I must say, such a price is too high for the
recognition of the "formal" democracy and republic by its opponents. If the
content withers, the shell will also shrivel away. Whoever does not want this
to happen must, I believe, whatever narrow party basis he may stand upon,
stand together with all who wish to truly preserve the Weimar Constitution,
the republic, its close link to the forward movement of the social idea so that
the republican form will not be robbed of its democratic and social content.
All supporters of the democratic, national, and social republic, supporters
of its true spirit belong together in opposition to attempts at domination
made in manifold guises by anti-democratic, anti-social monopoly capitalism. The nuances may vary in what the supporters seek in terms of political
freedom, national unity, and social advancement; but their goals are linked
at the core. In any case, in our modern age and under its conditions, the one

cannot be achieved without the other. One must serve all three, must fight for them together—national unity within the international community, political freedom and democratic equality, and social advancement according to natural development. This, gentlemen, I consider—and I would be happy if you would consider it with me—to be the significance of the democratic republic for the social idea.

THREE

Gerhard Anschütz

INTRODUCTION

Walter Pauly

Gerhard Anschütz did not owe his standing in the state law theory of the Weimar period to conceptions of state and constitutional theory, as did Hermann Heller, Rudolf Smend, and Carl Schmitt, nor to a position on state law grounded in legal theory, as did Hans Kelsen; his prominence was due instead to doctrinal works on existing public law. He succeeded in writing the classic commentary on the Weimar Constitution, one of the few works that went to fourteen editions in the Weimar Republic, and with his temporary colleague on the Heidelberg faculty, Richard Thoma, edited the two-volume *Handbook of the German Law of the State* [*Handbuch des deutschen Staatsrechts*], a unique encyclopedia that collected pieces by numerous scholars. Citations from both works continue to this day to carry great weight.

Anschütz had already become a scholarly authority during the Empire; his appointments in Tübingen (1899), Heidelberg (1900), Berlin (1908), and, at his own wish, his return to Heidelberg (1916) document this, as do his assumption of Georg Meyer's successful textbook on German constitutional law and the inclusion of his article on German constitutional law in the *Encyclopedia of Jurisprudence*. He began publishing in 1891, at the age of 24, with a dissertation written under Edgar Loening in Halle: *Critical Studies on the Theory of Legal Propositions and Formal Law* [*Kritische Studien zur Lehre vom Rechtssatz und formellen Gesetz*]. It was—like his later lecture, "Theories of the Concept of Legislative Power," given following his

Habilitationsschrift—a contribution to the concept of the "statute," and thus to the scope of parliamentary cooperation in the process of creating law. According to Anschütz, for acts interfering with the freedom and property of individuals, the monarchic executive needed statutory authorization and to that extent the agreement of parliament—the "provision of legality" [*Vorbehalt des Gesetzes*].

While the dissertation was still clearly influenced by the conceptual legal method of Carl Friedrich von Gerber and Paul Laband—its construction was largely conceptual—the second study focused on the text and genesis of the relevant constitutional norms. Here Anschütz changed his position from a constructivist legal positivism [*Rechtspositivismus*] to a statutory positivism [*Gesetzespositivismus*] based on an historical and genetic understanding of norms. His commentary on the Prussian constitutional charter that appeared in 1912 also followed this method and thus became in many ways more traditionalist than had it followed a doctrinal approach guided by von Gerber's and Laband's conceptual legal method. Thus Richard Thoma[1] praised the fact that at least in part it took the rights of Prussian citizens seriously as individual rights but at the same time criticized Anschütz's argument that these rights did little more than mirror the provision of statutory legality.

Anschütz's strict statutory positivism placed him in conflict with other leading contemporary scholars of the law of the state. Unlike Paul Laband, he denied the existence of a legal resolution of a conflict where monarch and parliament could not agree on the budget, stating: "Here the law of the state ceases; the question of how to proceed when no budget exists is not a legal question."[2] He accused Rudolf Smend of confusing law and politics, of interpreting the constitution with his integrationist approach—if not counter to, then at least far beyond the text.[3] He criticized Erich Kaufmann as a natural-law thinker for seeking to bind the legislature to the principle of equality, although this was not stated explicitly in the constitution.[4] He also questioned the doctrinal conclusions Hans Kelsen had drawn from his legal theory as lacking historical understanding.[5] He criticized as unfounded in the text the substantive limits on constitutional amendment asserted by Carl Schmitt as a consequence of his concept of the constitution.[6] Anschütz's statutory positivism placed constitutional law within narrow bounds. The field of constitutional *policy*, to which he also devoted himself throughout his lifetime, began for him beyond these bounds.

Impressed by southern Germany's social structure and mentality that he had come to know and appreciate in Tübingen and Heidelberg, the Prussian Anschütz developed increasingly in the course of the Empire into an advocate of the democratic idea. In his writings on constitutional policy during the First World War, he demanded the elimination of the three-class electoral system in Prussia and the introduction of the parliamentary system in the Reich, especially the responsibility of the chancellor [*Reichskanzler*] to the parliament [*Reichstag*]. This began to be realized only in 1918, when collapse and revolution were imminent. Thus it is not surprising that in 1919 Anschütz participated, as a drafter and adviser, in the creation of the democratic constitution. He identified passionately with the Weimar Constitution and the state it created; he was more than a mere "republican of convenience" [*Vernunftrepublikaner*].[7]

Thus it was no accident that Anschütz chose "The Three Guiding Principles of the Weimar Constitution" as the subject of his speech in the auditorium of Heidelberg University on the *dies academicus* in 1922. Anschütz expected agreement when he linked the democratic and national ideas, and was surprised to be interrupted precisely at this point by loud scraping of feet—the traditional expression of student dissatisfaction, unprecedented at an academic ceremony. Anschütz agreed with Thomas Mann, who, in a speech on German youth also held in 1922, had remarked: "Let them scrape. It doesn't matter, I will finish speaking and put my heart and mind into winning them over."[8] However, this was a difficult enterprise, doomed to failure. Major segments of the young rejected democracy, the victors' form of government, as alien and considered the national idea besmirched by Anschütz's linkage. Among his colleagues, Anschütz found agreement here and there, but mainly was subjected to pointed criticism: The speech was labeled political, hence unscholarly. The reactions to his speech indicate the extent to which the Weimar Republic was a democracy without democrats from the beginning. Until the Nazi seizure of power Anschütz sought to defend the Weimar state by publicly professing his allegiance to democracy.

On 31 March 1933, when democracy succumbed to National Socialism, Anschütz requested emeritus status, with the justification that he could not teach National Socialist state law because of his lack of "inward connection" to it. With this personal, ethical decision, Anschütz's colleagues felt under pressure to do likewise. In a letter to him of 22 October 1933, Richard Thoma, agreeing with Heinrich Triepel, justified his coming to terms with the new rulers as not signifying sympathy, and accused Anschütz of a "rash lack of consideration for younger colleagues (in some cases not even entitled to a pension)." Anschütz lived in seclusion in Heidelberg during the Nazi period and wrote his memoirs. He died in 1948 after a traffic accident.

MAIN WORKS

Kritische Studien zur Lehre vom Rechtssatz und formellen Gesetz. Berlin: Breitkopf & Härtel, 1891.

Der Ersatzanspruch aus Vermögensbeschädigungen durch rechtmäßige Handhabung der Staatsgewalt. Verwaltungsarchiv. Vol. 5, 1–136. Berlin: Heymanns, 1897.
Bismarck und die Reichsverfassung. Berlin: Heymanns, 1899.
Die gegenwärtigen Theorien über den Begriff der gesetzgebenden Gewalt und den Umfang des königlichen Verordnungsrechts nach preußischem Staatsrecht. 2nd ed. Tübingen and Leipzig: Mohr, 1901.
Die Verfassungs-Urkunde für den Preußischen Staat vom 31. Januar 1850: Ein Kommentar für Wissenschaft und Praxis. Vol. 1. Berlin: Häring, 1912.
"Deutsches Staatsrecht." In *Encyklopädie der Rechtswissenschaft in systematischer Bearbeitung,* vol. 4, edited by Franz von Holtzendorff and Josef Kohler, 1–192. Munich, Leipzig, and Berlin: Duncker & Humblot, and J. Guttentag, 1914.
Die preußische Wahlreform. Berlin: Springer, 1917.
Zukunftsprobleme deutscher Staatskunst. Berlin: Heymanns, 1917.
Parlament und Regierung im deutschen Reich. Berlin: Liebmann, 1918.
Georg Meyers Lehrbuch des deutschen Staatsrechts. 7th ed. Munich and Leipzig: Duncker & Humblot, 1919.
Das preußisch-deutsche Problem. Tübingen: Mohr, 1922.
Drei Leitgedanken der Weimarer Reichsverfassung. Tübingen: Mohr, 1923.
"Der deutsche Föderalismus in Vergangenheit, Gegenwart und Zukunft." In *Veröffentlichungen der Vereinigung der deutschen Staatsrechtslehrer.* Vol. 1, 11–34. Berlin and Leipzig: de Gruyter, 1924.
Handbuch des deutschen Staatsrechts. Edited with Richard Thoma. 2 vols. Tübingen: Mohr, 1930–32.
Die Verfassung des deutschen Reichs vom 11. August 1919. 14th ed. Berlin: Stilke, 1933.
Aus meinem Leben: Erinnerungen von Gerhard Anschütz. Edited by Walter Pauly. Frankfurt: Klostermann, 1992.

LITERATURE

Böckenförde, Ernst-Wolfgang. "Gerhard Anschütz." In Ernst Böckenförde, *Recht, Staat, Freiheit,* 367–78. Frankfurt am Main: Suhrkamp, 1991.
Forsthoff, Ernst. "Gerhard Anschütz." *Der Staat* 6 (1967): 139–50.
Giese, Friedrich. "Gerhard Anschütz zum Gedächtnis." *Süddeutsche Juristen-Zeitung.* Heidelberg: Lambert Schneider, 1948. Cols. 333–36.
Jellinek, Walter. "Gerhard Anschütz zum 80. Geburtstag." *Süddeutsche Juristen-Zeitung.* Heidelberg: Lambert Schneider, 1947. Cols. 1–4.
Pauly, Walter. "Zu Leben und Werk von Gerhard Anschütz." In *Aus meinem Leben: Erinnerungen von Gerhard Anschütz,* edited by Walter Pauly, xi–xliv. Frankfurt: Klostermann, 1992.
Thoma, Richard. "Gerhard Anschütz zum 80. Geburtstag." *Deutsche Rechts-Zeitschrift* 2 (1947): 25–27.

THREE GUIDING PRINCIPLES OF
THE WEIMAR CONSTITUTION

Gerhard Anschütz

Originally appeared as *Drei Leitgedanken der Weimarer Reichsverfassung: Rede gehalten bei der Jahresfeier der Universität Heidelberg am 22. November 1922* [Speech to the Annual Gathering of the University of Heidelberg on 22 November 1922] (Tübingen: Mohr, 1923).

Fellow Citizens!

The tradition of our alma mater requires that the rector speak at today's celebration on a subject of his teachings and work. The teacher of the German law of the state thus finds himself—beginning with the search for a suitable theme—faced with a task that is neither easy nor pleasant.

Under pressure of the terrible fate that has befallen it in recent years, the German legal system, along with the state, has fallen into disorder and confusion. The revolution neither completely designed the public law that had prevailed in Germany, nor has it designed a new public law that is uniform. Alongside remnants and ruins of the old, we see a growing wealth of new creations, some of them incomplete shells that themselves resemble ruins. Feverish legislation, encouraged constantly by pressing emergencies and exigencies of the moment, creates an army of wavering formal statutes that, having barely a chance to take force, must be soon be revised. It is an unpleasant situation, not least for scholarship, since it is almost impossible in many areas of the law of the state and administrative law to follow the continual changes in the material, to retain a clear overview, to ensure the clarity and order of concepts. A chaos, about which, unfortunately, one cannot yet say when and how it will form into a cosmos.

And all this is still not the most unpleasant aspect of our public law. The entire situation is, naturally, only a symptom of the illness imposed upon our state by the loss of the war and its consequences. We view this deathly ill state with deep, often despairing concern. Is it even necessary to describe our situation? A dictated peace cloaked in the garb of a treaty that mocks the defeated, more vile than any that has ever been forced upon a great nation, has robbed us of land and people that are ours and loaded us with unbearable burdens. The union of our enemies, with the deadly arch-enemy in the West always at their head, has suborned our finances, our economy, our entire national life to control and tutelage to such an extent that one would have to be an expert in the legal art of differentiating between law and fact to be able to claim that the German Reich remains a sovereign state. Internally as well, the externally powerless state—how could it be otherwise?—

is no longer in command. Here I am thinking not of the special situation in the occupied territories but of a general phenomenon: The internal opponents of state power, who without directly combating it threaten to outgrow it—the social and economic powers, labor and business associations, created through a concentration of people and capital, that the state often can no longer control and that will be joined at the first opportunity by the forces of the streets—a rival to state power! All of this taken together provides a bleak picture of *a state in crisis,* the further development and consequences of which remain completely in the dark.

And yet we do not want here to succumb to unrelieved pessimism. Let us recall that in all our national misfortune a last possession is left to us, at the same time the greatest good that a people like the German—sure of itself, yet suffering from internal divisions and conflicts—can call its own. This greatest good is the state organization of our national unity, *our Reich.* Certainly even this last possession is not unthreatened. French politics is at work, sometimes secretly, sometimes hypocritically hiding its aim, sometimes with cynical openness—according to circumstances and by turns—to tear to pieces the Reich whose destruction it did not achieve at Versailles. And in Germany, too—a shame that cannot be denied—there exist corrupt sentiments that degrade the idea of the Reich, because they do not like its present *constitution,* that even attempt to uproot the idea of the Reich, because they are more concerned with particularistic special interests than in the weal and woe of the nation. We know this; but we also know that these Reich-corrupters are just a small crowd and that, as long as we others are unified against them, as long as the overwhelming majority of the German people wants the Reich and the national unity it embodies, the French will not achieve their goal, this old and constantly renewed goal—not even with the help of the eastern vassal states that have been built up behind us so that they can attack at the right moment in support of their great friend.

The Reich must remain ours, and it will remain ours so long as we are united.

I would like to speak today about the political type, the legal essence of our Reich, as represented by its current basic law, the Weimar Constitution of 11 August 1919; and I would like—with some doubts as to the correctness and completeness of the title—to describe my task with the words:

Three Guiding Principles of the Weimar Constitution.

Twice in a period of seventy years the German people, in contrast to its deeply rooted propensity for being led from above by historically legitimized power, has roused itself to take its fate into its own hands, to help itself out of the difficulties of the time, to reform its state from the bottom up, and to do all this *itself* through a freely elected constitutional assembly, a national assembly. The first time, what the national will had intended was unsuccessful;

it is well known that the meeting of the National Assembly in Paul's Church in Frankfurt created a Reich *constitution,* but not a Reich that could be served by this constitution. The Frankfurt Constitution of 1849 remained a document, an honorable legal monument; it did not become law. The second time, in 1919 in Weimar, the will became reality. This time, however, despite all the obstacles in its way, the task was not as difficult as it had been seventy years ago; it was not necessary first to create the national state, for it had already been formed in the great period of the fulfillment of our dream of unity, 1866–71, and the task of the Weimar Assembly was only to give the existing Reich a new constitution in place of the old one that had been destroyed by the revolution.

The crucial guiding principles of both times, of Frankfurt in 1849 and Weimar in 1919, correspond to a great extent despite all the differences between the two epochs. The work of Paul's Church in Frankfurt and the Weimar Constitution are much more closely related than either is to the third German constitution that separated them and that ruled us until the collapse of 1918: the Bismarck Constitution of 1871. Between the men in Paul's Church in Frankfurt and those in the Weimar Theater stands the founder of the Reich: Bismarck. Overall he is closer to those in Frankfurt than to those in Weimar but is so far removed from both camps that his work stands out sharply from what Frankfurt wanted, as well as what Weimar then achieved— a distance that must be grasped by anyone wishing to achieve clarity on the basic questions of the German law of the state.

The distance between the Weimar Constitution and its predecessor, the Bismarck Constitution, is apparent in the following, to mention only the most important points:

1. Far more clearly and strongly than its predecessors the Weimar Constitution emphasizes the *statehood of the Reich,* its character as an independent national state that is more than, and different from, the sum or union of its member states.

2. The relationship of the Reich to its member states, the Länder, previously structured in favor of the latter, looks different today. The standard is no longer federal but in conformity with the opposite principle, *unitary.*

3. A particularly deep chasm opens up when we look at the differences in the *form of the state* then and now. In place of the old monarchic Germany a new one has appeared, *democratically* structured in Reich and Länder, and *republican.*

Statehood of the Reich, unitary Reich, democratic Reich; before us are the three great principles of the Weimar Constitution. Thus we enter the area that we would like to examine more closely.

I

Statehood of the Reich. I have already tried to explain what this means. "The German Reich is a state" means it is more and other than merely an association of the particular powers that have taken over German soil in the course of the centuries as opponents of national unity. The Reich is not both the unity of these particular powers, *the Länder,* and the *unity of the German people;* it is the German people united across Länder borders under a supreme power. Thus, even if one wants to see the Länder, too, as entities possessing statehood, as states of lower degree and rank, and therefore to consider the Reich's entirety to be a common state [*Gesamtstaat*] made up of single states [*Einzelstaaten*]—even then, the Reich is also a state and essentially equal to other large nation-states such as England and North America, France, Italy, etc. The Reich does not offer the Germans a substitute for a state; *it is the German state.* This is not merely a political wish but legal reality, the unequivocal, stated will of our constitution. To estimate the progress this implies for our national unification correctly, we must look backwards and compare in hindsight the present with the earlier stages of the movement towards unity, especially the position taken by the Bismarck Constitution on the question of the statehood of the Reich. What was the meaning of the great popular movement that gripped Germany, like other divided nations, in the nineteenth century—what was the aim of our search for unity? The meaning and aim lay ever in the wish to escape from all these small and medium-sized states, from all these many states, and to replace or place *above* them one state, a national state: *the Reich.* That is how the generation that fought the wars of liberation already thought more than a hundred years ago. They did not forget that divided Germany had once been a single state, a mighty imperial Reich; they knew that this state had collapsed and wished to regain it. They could not fulfill this wish for unity but instead were diverted in a petty and deplorable fashion when the German princes, unable to sacrifice even the least rights of sovereignty to the national idea, united in 1815 in the Deutsche Bund, a protective union that was mainly intended mutually to secure allied dynastic interests, but which had *nothing* to do with the idea of national unity, the *idea of the Reich.* Our long-suffering people accepted this situation, first until 1848. Then it rebelled. Out of the revolutionary movement of the time came the Frankfurt National Assembly of which we have already spoken, in Paul's Church. The German Reich that it hoped to create and to which it hoped to dedicate the constitution it wrote had, in accordance with the will to national unity, all the characteristics of true statehood: It was to be not a contractual relationship between individual states, not a union of princes, but the state organization of the German people in the form of a democratic, constitutional, imperial Reich—a state about which one may argue whether it was or would have become a federal state [*Bundesstaat*] or a centralized state [*Einheitsstaat*], *but in any case a state.* But, as mentioned, the founding of the Reich did not succeed, the Deutsche Bund came back into force. What then finally smashed it half a generation later was not a popular movement but the German policies of Prussia and its brilliant leader. What did Bismarck put in place of the Deutsche Bund? What was the Norddeutsche Bund of 1867 and its extension, the Deutsches Reich with its Constitution of 1871? Was it a state, or something else, a mere union of states [*Staatenbund*] that in certain respects achieved the same as a state?

The Constitution of 1871 provided no clear answers to these questions. Sometimes its text seemed to speak more for a union of states and was gladly interpreted as such by those who had an interest in this; for example, the introductory words, in which the Reich is described as an *"eternal union"* of German princes and free cities, or the provisions reserving powers from the central state, or the treaty with Bavaria appended to the constitution. Bismarck himself spoke only once about the basic plan of his work—whether a state or a mere union—and then with apparently intentional ambiguity. The guidelines he provided in the autumn of 1866 for drafting the Norddeutsche Bund's constitution stated at one point: "It will be necessary *in form* to adhere more to a *union of states,* but *in practice* to pursue a *federal state,* with elastic, unassuming but far-reaching wording." Now, this did not mean that the structure of German unity should be a union of states but instead that it should as far as possible simply *resemble* a union of states, because (we may add this in revealing the motive) the dynastic and other particularisms with which we must deal would otherwise become uneasy. Here, as always, Bismarck used his characteristic combination of courtesy and cleverness to make the work of unity palatable to the German princes. For them he veiled the statehood of the Reich in a union of states; in any case, he veiled it. And thus it is not surprising that a tendency became apparent in scholarship that preferred the veil to the picture behind it, a view that advocated the Reich as more or less a union of states. This tendency was led by the Munich professor Max von Seydel, the most radical advocate of the Reich as a union of states among German state law scholars in Bismarck's period; he was joined by certain others, some of them without specific political views, such as Eugen von Jagemann and Otto Mayer, and more recently by the Austrian Leo Wittmayer. However, the large majority of German theorists of the law of the state rejected this view. At the beginning of the 1870s, Albert Hänel had already spoken up with great energy for the statehood of the Reich, and another master of our discipline, Paul Laband, at the same time presented the theory of the Reich as a federal state that would soon prevail, in which the statehood remaining to the Länder did not cripple the statehood of the Reich; the Reich was a sovereign common state consisting of nonsovereign single states—a *federal state*. Thus we scholars learned and taught—and I, for my part, never doubted—that Laband and Hänel were right, as opposed to Seydel and even Bismarck. But I must admit that as a result of the ambiguity of the constitution it was often difficult to refute opposing arguments. For those who were not willing to accept the Reich as a mere union of states, the old constitution presented many rough spots and contradictions that were more than so-called blemishes. In short: that the Reich of 1871, though also a union, was mainly a *state,* not merely a union, was not an entirely undisputed, agreed-upon fact.

Then came the Weimar Constitution, which brought with it the clarity that had been lacking until then, based upon the new political foundations created by the revolution. The old constitution disappeared, and with it also that which had been called, rightly or wrongly, its "contractual" elements, including the treaties and alliances made in November 1870 with the southern German states. And the new structure was executed not through agreements between the states, not on a treaty basis, but through an act of the national will to unification, through the decisions of the constitution-making National Assembly, possessing complete sovereignty in regard to the Länder. We encounter the distance between then and now in its full solemnity when we compare the introductory words, the preambles that precede the texts of both the old and the new constitutions. The old preamble declares that the king of Prussia, in the name of the Norddeutsche Bund, creates an "eternal union" with the monarchs of the southern German states, "for the protection of the federal territory and the laws in force within it, as well as for the promotion of the welfare of the German people." "This union will carry the name of the *Deutsche Reich* and will have the following constitution." The new preamble is very different: "The *German people,* united in its tribes and inspired with the will to renew and consolidate its Reich in freedom and justice . . . has given itself this constitution." There is no more talk of the single states, the German Länder that had in the meantime become republics. They no longer appear as Reich-founding or constitution-making factors, nor even as the building blocks from which the Reich is formed. The Reich is no longer a union of member states but a commonwealth of the entire German people, which rightly describes the Reich as "*its* Reich." The Reich is the German people, united by the authority that arises from itself. A people united under a higher authority: that is what is considered a state, *that is the image of the state. Today* no further argument is possible about the statehood of our Reich. Only now—may we confess this without negating Bismarck and his work—only now, after the overturn of the state and on the basis of the new constitution, have we *indisputably* reached the degree of unity to which we, as a great nation, have an undying claim: *state unity.* Only now is the notion of the statehood of the Reich free of all dross. Seydel once held that a German Land that single-handedly separated from the Reich did not commit treason but at the most breach of contract; on the same conceptual basis, [Eugen] von Jagemann even declared the governments of the German Länder justified in dissolving the Reich and replacing it with another Reich and another constitution, since it was nothing but a contract signed by them. But today, such views are simply impossible, completely out of the question. We can thank the Weimar Constitution for this; it is one of the greatest national and political advances that constitution has given us.

It would have been surprising had this advance escaped the deadly enemies of our unity. Thus, it did not escape the French, and the conclusion they drew is too typical, too French, for me to keep it from you. Not long ago, a respected representative of French jurisprudence, Professor [Henri] Berthelémy in Paris—with the quick eye of hate, and commendably revealing the actual goals of the war—explained to his countrymen that France had *lost the war, politically speaking;* for what Bismarck had failed to achieve was achieved as a result of the revolution following the German defeat: the German people were fused into a *state.* And as I have been told, Herr B. is by no means alone in this opinion.

II

With the theoretical energy that characterizes us, we Germans love to argue with each other about the fundamental theoretical principles of our state. Just as the statehood of the *Reich* was once disputed, so we argue today about the statehood of its members, the *Länder.* The controversy surrounding the question whether the Länder are really still states or only provinces of the Reich, self-administering bodies of a special kind, is naturally not without significance; after all, the decision whether the Reich is a *compound state* or a unified state depends upon it. If one accepts the statehood of the Länder, it is a compound; if one rejects it, it is a unified state. Thus the question is not unimportant; yet at the same time I would prefer not to address it here and now, as such a discussion would, as Bismarck would say, lead us too far afield into the sand of professorial disputes. In my opinion, the position of power remaining to the Länder under the new constitution is sufficient to allow scholars to label them states even today; and since, in addition, during the annoying conflict between Bavaria and the Reich that we recently experienced, their undamaged quality as states was officially confirmed to the Länder by the Reich at the express wish of the Bavarian government, I see no reason to consider this an open question. Thus the German Reich appears, now as before, to be a common state divided into single states, a *compound state,* for which it would then be necessary to examine—a question that we will not touch upon here either—whether it corresponds to the special concept of a *federal state*. However, it is certain—and here we come *to the second great guiding principle* of the Weimar Constitution—that the relationship of the Reich to the Länder is distinctly unitary, much more unitary than in the Reich of the Bismarck period.

The unitary state and its counter-concept, the federal state, are organizational forms of compound states, especially of the federal state. Should the relationship between the central power and the regional powers tend toward a centralized state, as a result of the predominance of the former and corresponding weakness of the latter, the whole in its statehood is considered centralized: "*unitary*"; if the situation is reversed, and it gravitates toward a union of states, it is described as unionlike: "*federalist.*" It is remarkable that unitary and federal statehood are not characteristics that exclude each other, that exist in a federal state completely or not at all, but can exist to a greater or lesser degree, so that it is quite possible that the constitution of a federal state can at the same time possess unitary and federal characteristics. Our constitution itself can serve as an example of this.

Unitary was the basic mood of the revolution; unitary in spirit were the overwhelming majority of members of the constitution-making National Assembly. It was only natural that the unitary principle would prevail in the work of Weimar. And that is what happened. The unitary characteristics of the Weimar Constitution leap to the eye. The number of matters for whose regulation the legislature of the Reich is responsible has increased conspicuously in comparison with the past. Important branches and objects of administration have been taken from the Länder and transferred to the Reich; for example, foreign policy, the military, railroads and waterways, mail and telegraph. The financial sovereignty of the Länder has been greatly reduced by the fact that all significant tax sources have been taken over by the Reich and are exploited in its own interest, under its statutes and by its own officials. The *organization* of the Reich as well is mainly unitary, for of the three main organs, two—the parliament [*Reichstag*] and the president [*Reichspräsident*]—are elected directly by the people of the Reich, without a right of cooperation by the single states; only the filling of the less-powerful third main organ [*Reichsrat*] is reserved to the Länder, that is, their governments. Also unitarily conceived is the fact that under Article 18 of the Constitution the territories and borders of the Länder are at the disposal of the Reich's sovereignty. The division of the Reich into Länder, the entire intra-German border network, is thus completely at the disposal of the Reich; this border network can be changed whenever the overwhelming interests of the Reich require it by a Reich amendment to the Constitution and, if the Länder involved agree, or if they do not agree but the population involved does, even through a simple Reich statute. No irrevocable right of the Länder to territorial and border integrity, not even a right to the *existence* of the single Länder, is recognized as against the territorial sovereignty of the Reich. In no other point is the subordination of the regional to the national interests followed through so unrestrainedly as here.

The unitary principle is thus the prevailing one of our constitution, there can be no doubt of that. However, there is no lack of institutions which, whether one considers their *form* federalist or not, nevertheless, are federalist in substance, to the extent that they satisfy the interests of the Länder—on the one hand, in an autonomy that is not too narrowly drawn, and on the other in equally broad participation in creation of the Reich will that governs them. The foremost of these institutions is the Reichsrat, the successor to the old Bundesrat, with its numerous responsibilities in the areas of Reich legislation and administration—it would be going too far afield for me to list them—that, though much weaker than similar rights of the Bundesrat, are strong enough to allow the Länder forcefully to represent their special interests. Second, there is the provision in the Reich constitution according to which, now as before, execution of Reich statutes is the responsibility of the Länder; that is, it is ensured by Länder authorities and can be transferred to Reich authorities only in exceptional cases, under special Reich statutes (as has occurred, for example, in the area of taxation). Thus, the Länder governments have the opportunity to interpret and apply Reich statutes in ways that conform to the character of their Länder. A third concession to the federalist idea lies in the Reich constitution's provision that Reich bureaus in the single Länder generally be staffed with citizens of the Land, and that Länder characteristics be taken into account in the organization of the Reich armed forces.

These pro-Länder institutions in the Constitution do not go far enough for some people, who say they contain too little of the spirit of true federalism. In the region in which this view is most widespread, in Bavaria, one hears again and again in increasing measure the call for a general revision of the Constitution in a more federal direction. A discussion with those who demand this is made somewhat difficult by the fact that they lack a clearly defined program. However, it is possible to gauge more or less the direction in which they are moving. The issue is to reduce the Reich to something that, under the Weimar Constitution, it neither is nor is to be: *a union of single German states*—perhaps not a union of states as a matter of mere international law, perhaps only a loose constitutional federative relationship of the type imputed to Bismarck's Reich by Seydel and the like; a federative relationship entered into not for its own sake, not even so much for the sake of the German nation, but first for the sake of the federated, *the single states* to their advantage above all. It is hardly necessary to point out that if such views were to dominate the law of the state, it would mean a fundamental alteration in the work of Weimar. For the Reich of today, as we have already seen, did not emerge *from* a union, nor was it created *as* a union of single states; it is the commonwealth of the German people, created by the people itself, a state in which the unity of this people, not the multitude of single states, emerges as the bearer of supreme authority.

Precisely because the constitutional revision desired by the opponents is not an incidental question, but one involving issues of the highest principles, altering the existing foundations, I expect agreement with my view that *today is not the time* for such changes. The times demand of us that we seek rescue from our afflictions, which cry out to Heaven, but not that we alter articles of the Constitution or even its *foundations*. The need of the moment is not to *revise* the Constitution, but to settle our differences under it, to recognize it as the supreme ordering of German affairs, determined by and for all; while its opponents, if they wish, may continue to call it by the completely unsuitable epithet "emergency constitution." This of course does not mean that private discussions on basic constitutional principles are impossible, and this is such a private discussion.

What I have to set against the spirit of the federal state is first of all a confession.

I confess that I am one of those to whom, in case of conflict, the Reich is everything, the single state nothing. For me, the German state was always embodied first and foremost *in the Reich,* not in the Länder. The Reich is not a union of German Länder, on no account an emanation of particularism; it is the state representing national unity. The Reich is necessary to our survival, its existence is not open to discussion; whether it is to be divided into Länder, and if yes, into which ones, is a question of expediency and open to discussion.

That had to be stated at the outset. Besides, there is no reason—and thus I return to our original subject—to alter that of which we are speaking, the existing relationship between Reich and Länder. For this relationship is one under which both can live: not only the Reich but also the Länder. As evidence of this, I remind you of the pro-Länder institutions in the Weimar Constitution: the Reichsrat and the execution of Reich statutes by the Länder governments. In my opinion, the Länder have no reason to complain—of course, assuming they remain aware of their position. This position is not that of sovereign members of a union of states, but of *members serving a federal state!*

There is yet another reason for rejecting the revision of our constitution in a more federal direction. The Weimar Constitution is elastic and wide-meshed enough to leave room for further development of the relationship between Reich and Länder conditioned by time and circumstance, without its being formally altered. In particular, there is nothing standing in the way of a further development that I—here again, I do not hesitate to confess my convictions—would desire in the national interest: *further development of Germany into a centralized state.*

Do not misunderstand me. I am not thinking of a centralized state as a result of formal constitutional change to be taken in hand today or tomorrow. Anyone who would call now for such constitutional change would, through untimely arousal of political conflicts and passions, be open to the same charge that I previously raised against plans for a revision of the Constitution in a more federal direction. For we must admit that a large sector of the German people does not support a centralized state, at least not an openly declared centralized state. In this regard, there is an undeniable difference between Prussia, northern Germany in general, and the southern part of our Fatherland, especially Bavaria. Unitary views have always been more at home in the north; in southern Germany, federal views are more common. The contrast in public opinion became visible in December 1919, when the Prussian constitutional assembly made the tactically perhaps mistaken, though otherwise notable decision to openly declare support for the notion of the centralized state, and called upon the government to act towards its realization. I believe that the centralized state would by now be accepted not only in Prussia, but in the other northern and central German states. It is different here in the south, with Bavaria always at the forefront. Here, the centralized state—*the word even more than the thing itself*—is thoroughly unpopular. At the moment, it is difficult to do anything about this, especially without using means that resemble force or would be perceived as such, among which I would include thoughtless outvoting in the Reichstag and Reichsrat.

Those who cherish the great idea of the national centralized state must have patience. And they must be content if they do not live to see the realization of their idea. *We must be able to wait, and we are able.* For, and I trust in this, time is on our side. Things will develop, not only *around us,* but also *within us. Within us:* on this it will mainly depend. What will bring us the centralized state is not an order of the legislature but a change in convictions. It is to be hoped that the apparently indestructible spirit of particularism that inhabits our people will progressively learn that the reacquisition and reassertion of all that we have lost is only possible through strict inclusion and combination of all national forces, a combination that only the centralized state can bring about. And to the extent that this belief in unity progresses, the Länder will change not according to the letter of the Constitution, but (if I am permitted the expression) according to their own self-assessment. The independence of the Länder will gradually fade, even in the eyes of those to whom it is so important today.

I thus imagine this progress towards a centralized state, in summary, as what Georg Jellinek would call a *constitutional transformation:* a gradually advancing shift in people's convictions and, linked with this, in the political dynamic—in contrast to a constitutional *amendment,* that is, the formal revision of the formal law of the state by legislative decision. This transformation will not lead to the disappearance of the Länder. That which has so often been said to the opponents of the centralized state, especially those who reject it for fear that it would destroy the colorful variety of German life and replace it with bleak monotony and uniformity, must be repeated again and again: *A centralized state does not exclude administrative decentralization.* One could decentralize the centralized state so much that all the unique characteristics of our peoples and regions would retain the scope they deserve. The bearers of this decentralization would be the Länder, within their present borders or within new ones given them under Article 18 of the Reich Constitution. They could continue to exist under the centralized state, with rights and freedoms that need be no fewer than those they possess today; with autonomy over wide areas left to them by the Reich, with the right to influence legislation and administration by means of the Reichsrat, and with the right to execute Reich statutes under Reich supervision. They would continue to exist with the status of large, strong, free *self-governing administrative bodies* that, by sacrificing their independence (today only formal anyway) are, and want nothing else than to be, members that willingly serve their whole, the whole Reich.

This goal is not new. Its result is nothing other than what one of the greatest sons of this university, Heinrich von Treitschke, once pronounced: *"the centralized national state with a strong self-government of autonomous provinces."* Like him, I speak of ideas as if of things to come; like him, with the assurance of those who have faith.

III

We became a state late, and still later a people's state. The triumphal march of the democratic idea, which elsewhere in the world overturned thrones and expelled dynasties, turned monarchies into republics or monarchs into largely decorative heads of state receiving their power and dignity more from below than from above; this triumphal march was long forced to halt before the gates of the German state. The year 1848 shook the foundations of the monarchy, just as Paul's Church in Frankfurt hoped to create its German Reich as an *imperial Reich* in form, though in reality a people's Reich, a democracy. But the monarchy held firm against this onslaught; and it was then so strongly stabilized by Bismarck, and so firmly secured in the Reich and Länder by the union of princes on which the Reich Constitution was based, that for the foreseeable future it seemed immune to the democratic spirit, even if only in the modest form of monarchic parliamentarism. Today we know that the era so characterized, imperial Germany, was not an epoch, but merely an episode. With the collapse of our old state's political and military forces in the world war its central institution, the monarchy, also collapsed. We do not want to discuss how this happened or who is to be blamed. The correct view is most likely that the monarchy was brought down neither by foreign nor by domestic forces, neither at the dictate of the enemy alliance nor by a conscious, popular revolutionary decision; that it was not overthrown on purpose at all, but *collapsed* from and in its own weakness, failing at the decisive moment, overwhelmed by the huge tasks of the world war. The fact is that the German people, abandoned by Kaiser and princes in those dark November days that recently had their fourth anniversary, was thrown back upon itself. We had to help ourselves without our hereditary princes, and help ourselves we did. That is the significance of the events we call the revolution; that, above all, is the meaning of the work of Weimar.

The Weimar Constitution is a *democratic* constitution, both in origin and content.

Unlike its predecessor of 1871, its *origin* was not an agreement among the German states, but—like the Frankfurt Constitution of 1849—an act of the German *people*. Thus its introduction states: "The German people has given itself this constitution"; this of course should not be understood literally, as if the entire people itself accepted the Constitution through plebiscite, but rather to mean that the people acted through a parliament that it elected and empowered: the National Assembly of Weimar. We should recall that the elections to this constitutional assembly took place on the basis of an extremely free right to take part in the full electoral process and with the participation of all political parties—*all*, including those that rejected the new state that was being created. Even these opponents consented to democracy in one main point; in their opinion, too, the new Germany could not be created otherwise than through the self-organization of the people, through the will of constitutive popular representation. If in addition one considers the fact that the Constitution was accepted in the National Assembly by a majority of more than three quarters of those voting, it is clear how foolish the contention is; I would not even mention it had it not recently been made by a politician who otherwise wishes to be taken seriously (Dr. Heim)—that the Weimar Constitution was adopted against the will of the majority of the people, that is, undemocratically.

Like its origin, the *content* of the Constitution reflects the democratic idea in all its purity. The very first article states the guiding principle: "State power emanates from the people." The state power spoken of here, *Reich* power, is located and has its source not outside of and above the people, but in it; it is synonymous with the common will of the entire people. Two of the major organs that are to create, explain, and execute this common will, the Reichstag and the president, are filled by popular election, so that not only the *legislature,* but also the highest bearer of the *executive* are direct agents of the national will. Only the third main organ, the Reichsrat—not powerless, just less important than the first two—consists not of representatives elected by the people but as we have seen, of members appointed by the governments of the Länder; this, however should not be seen as an anti-democratic concession but as a federal counterweight to the strictly unitary formative principle of the first two organs. However, above all these organs, as the highest extraordinary organ of the Reich, stands the entirety of those entitled to vote for the Reichstag: the electorate, the people in that sense, which can be called upon by the president, by a certain portion of the electorate, or by the Reichsrat to make the most important and final decision, the "plebiscite" in certain cases; for example, when a statute passed by the Reichstag is to be changed against its will, or a statute not wanted by the Reichstag is to be passed, or the president is to be removed before his term has expired. If one adds to all this the fact that the Constitution also prescribes to the Länder a democratic, republican form and thus forbids them not only a return to monarchy but also the introduction of undemocratic forms of government, such as, in particular, the dictatorship of the working class or proletariat—it becomes apparent with what energy and consequence a democratic view of the state is expressed and implemented in the Weimar Constitution.

We put the people's state into practice; everybody must admit that much. Less unanimous is the judgment whether democracy is right for Germany. Here the political standpoint matters, and opinions part.

Do not expect me to go fully into the problems related to the essence and value of democracy. But I will say several things about it here.

The question whether democracy should be retained or eliminated is usually identified with another either/or; namely, the alternatives *republic or monarchy*. But this equation is not accurate; for there are very undemocratic republics, and monarchies that are quite democratic. The law of the Bolshevik state, as the tyranny of one class over another, as an oligarchic dictatorship, has nothing in common with democracy; on the other hand, only one who allows himself to be fooled about the basic plan of the edifice of the state by looking at its facade could claim that modern parliamentary monarchies like England and Italy are more than merely formal monarchies, while in reality they are nothing less than democracies. However, we do not want to be sidetracked by these inconsistencies. Fortunately, Bolshevism is out of the question for Germany; and restoration of a monarchical form of state—assuming that it were desirable—faces insurmountable obstacles at the moment, *even if* it were to be a parliamentary-democratic monarchy, and thus something very different from what we had until the overthrow. Those who believe that our former enemies and their accomplices all around us would permit us to restore the imperial system, even as a democratic imperial system, belong in the class of political dreamers. But even from a purely internal point of view, the remonarchization of Germany—if one imagines it occurring legally, and not through a victorious civil war by monarchist against republican Germany—is completely impossible for the foreseeable future. And precisely because it would involve the incitement of internal struggles that would destroy everything—truly everything—we possess in terms of national unity and harmony, any *attempt* to introduce a monarchist revision of our constitution must be met with the same or even stronger objections than those made previously against suggestions for a constitutional revision in a more *federal* direction. Again, it makes no difference what variety of monarchy is being sought. In Germany, at the moment, there is not even room for an imperial system that is intrinsically democratic; the supporters of such an imperial system should tell themselves that this is not the time for constitutional debates beyond simple disputes over technical details. The work of Weimar came about through compromise—reached arduously but in the end with an impressive, even awe-inspiring majority—between great formative forces, between the bourgeoisie and the workers; it is important to honor this compromise in the overriding interest of national unity, which must be preserved internally and proven externally. A right-wing politician recently spoke once again of the form of the state "that we need." The form of the state that we need, and the only one we can use today, is that which is supported by the greatest possible majority of the people. And that, today, is democracy in the form of the republic. In the present need and distress of our country, we cannot afford a battle, or even a mere campaign, on the question "republic or monarchy," for the question to be decided—as those who are involved must realize—is in reality not "republic or *monarchy*," but "republic or *anarchy*." It is not too much to ask of the opponents of the existing form of the state that they understand this and cease for the time being to treat what exists, and rightly exists, as an open question.

We are, in general, not asking much of them. Politically, it would be a great step forward if the opposition about and to which I am speaking could bring itself to admit not only that we *must* accept the principle of democracy, but that we *can*.

The *principle*, I say. That is all that matters. Not the specific shape of the principle in the Weimar Constitution. The details are open to discussion, if not now then in a quieter period. But accord could and should already prevail today *on the spirit that pervades the whole, the democratic idea of the state.*

Certainly we are a long way from such accord. Large groups, particularly in the class to which we academics belong, the educated bourgeoisie, reject democracy even today. But are not they led more by surges of emotion, more by agitation, than by insight? Are they fighting against democracy or rather against a bogy that has been made of it? Ordinary anti-democratic politics are not always free of the resentments of a social class that feels pushed back by other classes—a resentment, however, that should not be aimed against democracy, but should instead focus upon regaining ground on the basis of democracy. With reference to the bogy that has been set up, the popular distortions of the democratic principle about which I am thinking provide an unflattering view of the political insights of those who take them as true.

One hears, for example, that democracy is the equivalent of weak, and monarchy of strong, state power. As if—good heavens!—in the world war, which was very much a contest between the democratic and authoritarian-monarchic forms of state, the democratic Western powers were not stronger in every respect! And as if the present weakness of state power in Germany could be traced to its democratic organization and not rather to the lost war, lost not by the new state, but by the old. Then it is said that democracy, "where everyone has his say," prevents uniform, firm leadership and the rise of out-standing statesmen. That the opposite is the case is shown by a glance at the impressive power and steadiness which directed the foreign policy of the great democracies of the West not only during the world war, but long before; while the achievements of our monarchy during the same period in terms of the uniformity, steadiness, and firmness of the high command as well as of the selection of the leadership are a chapter too painful for me to pre-sent here.

Finally, there is the attempt to place the democratic principle in the wrong; better put, to discredit it by calling it un-national or anti-national. That attempt is doomed to fail from the start through the inferiority of its means. These opponents are very often under the influence of a political vice that is unfortunately widespread in Germany and that makes certain parties claim patriotism and national spirit for themselves alone and deny them to others—a bad habit that I simply record, without condescending to discuss it. Aside from this, the attempt to discredit of which we are speaking unveils a strange ignorance of the intrinsic connections between national-ism and democracy, connections that become apparent when one recalls the gradual advance of democratic ideas since the days of the American Decla-ration of Independence and the first French Revolution. The consolidation and deepening of the view of the state based on the nationality principle, *nationalism,* goes hand in hand with this slowly yet inexorably advancing de-mocratization of the world to such an extent that it is sometimes difficult to say which is the cause and which the effect—whether democratization had nationalist effects, or the growing national consciousness of peoples made their states democratic. The latter appears more correct to me, and I would like to indicate briefly why. Not every people is a nation, but only those con-scious of their unity and individuality. This self-consciousness normally does not remain mere *knowledge,* but increases sooner or later, depending on the people's political talents, to a desire: to the will to create an independent state for itself and shape this state as the people wishes and wills.

This is the spirit of democracy. Monarchic institutions are not incom-patible with this—since in general (and I emphasize this again) the demo-cratic state need not necessarily be a republic—but only so long as the bearer of the crown bows to the genius of the nation, so long as he aspires to be nothing more than the servant of this genius, the executor of the national will. Thus we recognize that the national and the democratic notions are *not contradictions, but sisters, children of one spirit;* this spirit is *the right of self-determination of peoples, demanded by their self-consciousness.* Once awakened, this self-consciousness will grow and act; in the short or long run, it will lead forcefully to a state in which bearers of power who claim to be outside of and above the people will have no place, and only those authorities will govern *that emanate from the people themselves.*

Thus, after casting off certain errors, we arrive at the heart of the democratic principle, the democratic state view; this is the notion of the *unity of state and people.* The state is not an institution outside of us; we ourselves, the association of the entire people, are the state; *we are the state.* The monarchy need not stand in the way of this unity of state and people, but experience shows that it often did, especially, unfortunately, here as well. Our monarchy was afflicted to the end with the remnants of an absolutism and patrimonialism that had otherwise been overcome, of a doctrine of divine right that no longer contained any truth; this gave our state the character of an institution that transcended the people and that, embodied in princes ruling in their own right, enforced its mission, which was said to come from outside and above, upon the people. This was a constitution and a view of the state that necessarily led to the disastrous situation in which the mass of the people no longer considered the state their own, but something *alien*—an alien force that lost respect and moral justification to the same degree that the people matured and desired a state for themselves.

This turning point has now arrived, the situation has changed. *We are the state.* We the people are no longer the object of a state force that derives its force from some "above"; we have ourselves become the subject of state power. The power of the state is the will of the people; the "authorities," that is, the entirety of those fellow citizens called upon to implement state power, are only servants, organs of popular will, organs whose power is and can only be rooted in popular will. The state is a power not transcending us, but *immanent in us,* to which we are all subordinate, but in which we are also participants, which involves all of us and for which we should all feel responsible as dutiful citizens.

Collection of all popular energies in the state, dutiful cooperation by all towards the state, responsibility of all for the state—that is the essence and value, the ethos of democracy. Democracy had to come at last, and it is good that it came. For if we want to preserve the idea of the state at all, if we still consider the state as a sovereign power overriding all single interests in the interest of the general public, such power can be borne by none other than the entirety of the people itself, by its affirmation of the state, by the national solidarity of all forces living in it. *Our state will be democratic, a people's state, or it will not be.*

We see again and again—the thought is important enough to me that I will end with it—the close kinship between the democratic and the national idea. Both ideas are basically *one;* both herald the great, proud notion of a people that rules itself. Nationalism aims to produce and consolidate this unity in the consciousness of the people; democracy seeks to put it in practice through the will of the people. We are reminded of the spirit of [the Swiss founding fathers taking] the Rütli oath: *"We want to be one single people of brothers"*—of brothers who, we may add in a democratic sense, regulate and administer their common affairs through common decisions, not subordinate to a paternal power.

My esteemed listeners, especially you students, my dear young friends, I have tried to impress upon you the great ideals of our Reich Constitution, ideals that I, so help me God, did not read into the Constitution, but only read out of it.

It is far from my intention to imply that the work of Weimar contains ultimate wisdom. Many of its details may be open to attack, others wrong. But the guiding principles are good—good in the relative sense that is characteristic of political value judgments. They are good because they accord with our internal relations of power, and because they genuinely reflect the political views of the majority of our people. And that for now, for the time being, is the most important thing. Admitting all this, we should not see in the Weimar Constitution a talisman that will bring us good and protect us from evil. We must be careful not to overestimate the significance of this, or of *any* other constitution. A good constitution is only one of the prerequisites if a state is to live and blossom. What we need are not only good constitutional institutions, but also the right people to embody and give life to them. Here, too, the important thing is: not rules, but men. A good constitution can guarantee that the choice of such men, the *selection of leaders,* is carried out correctly, that is, that the contest of political forces brings those relatively most competent to the positions most suitable for them. And it is a lot if it guarantees this. But every choice requires material, people among whom to choose, broad classes from which *more* statesmen than actually needed are constantly emerging—in the end, it requires an entire people that thinks and feels politically. These are conditions that no constitution can create, that on the other hand are *prerequisites* for every constitution, especially that of a democratic state.

It is *up to us* to make these prerequisites a reality—up to us, and especially *to you young Germans* who are the future of our people, who have the difficult duty to be more, to achieve better than the generation that preceded you and that—it must be said—failed politically in so many things.

You shall not only train the man within yourself, but even more the *citizen,* the *citizen of the state*. Three virtues you should have: joy in sacrifice, a citizen's sense of responsibility, love of fatherland; love of fatherland, however, is the greatest among them. Love your German fatherland more than all of these and more than yourselves, and more than your narrow homelands, for it is not the narrow homeland that is first and most important, but the nation; and there is no Bavarian or Prussian, but only one German nation. As [the Prussian reformer of the Napoleonic era] Freiherr vom Stein once said: "I know only one fatherland, and it is called Germany; therefore I can devote my whole soul only to all of Germany, and not to a part of it."

Love of fatherland is something that can tolerate no conditions. Therefore do not be like those whose love of fatherland depends on the degree to which they like the constitution and the men who govern; such people are bad patriots, for they love their party dogmas more than their fatherland. You should be proud of your German fatherland, for Germany does not become worse because others speak badly of it, nor because it is sick and unhappy. You should have a sensitive and passionate national pride that is to the citizen what honor is to the man; here too one can say, better too thin-skinned than too thick-skinned. And just as no love can exist without hatred of the deadly enemies of that which one loves, so too the love of fatherland. Just as it is holy, so too is the hate it demands. But do not turn your hatred against your fellow citizens, turn it where it belongs. The enemy is not to the left and right, *but on the Rhine;* there he is, the only one with whom there can be neither peace nor reconciliation, I do not need to name him.

Our Heidelberg has often been accused of tending to internationalism in the negative sense of the word. I find the accusation unjust; it is based on externals. In any case, it was not always justified. I previously mentioned Freiherr vom Stein; let me conjure up the great shade once again. With regard to the works of our romantic poets that were created here, especially with regard to those of Achim von Arnim and Clemens Brentano, works that contributed more than a little to the awakening of German spirit and German national feeling in the period before the wars of liberation, Stein once said that in Heidelberg a good deal of the fire had been kindled that would later consume the French. The day will come when this fire will flare up again. May it then again be rightly said of our city, and especially of our university, that it protected and fed the holy flame with a loyal hand.

FOUR

Richard Thoma

INTRODUCTION

Peter C. Caldwell

Of the leading representatives of the statutory positivist approach to public law in the Weimar Republic, Richard Thoma produced the most coherent political theory of the Weimar constitutional system. He developed this theory in numerous essays and expositions of legal problems, in journals, in Festschriften, and in his many contributions to the *Handbook of the German Law of the State* [*Handbuch des deutschen Staatsrechts*], edited by him and Gerhard Anschütz in 1930 and 1932. Thoma provided a political and legal account of parliamentary democracy expounded from a left-liberal political and a neo-Kantian philosophical position. Both positions owed much to the Heidelberg milieu and the circle of scholars around Max and Marianne Weber in which Thoma was trained. The product was a theory of the way the Weimar Republic was supposed to function, had the left-liberal, social-democratic, and Christian-democratic political assumptions at its basis been realized in German political culture.

Thoma was born in 1874, the son of a factory owner in Todtnau, a town in the Black Forest region of the southwestern German state of Baden.[1] In the years after 1848, southwestern Germany and Baden in particular had become the training-ground for the theory and practice of left-liberal democracy in Germany. It was in Baden, for example, that the Social Democratic faction first entered into voting agreements with liberals during the Empire. A major theme of Thoma's mature works was the development of social reforms in tandem with Social Democracy.

Thoma wrote his dissertation in 1900 on issues of property law in the new civil code, which went into effect in the same year. Six years later, at the University of Freiburg, he wrote his *Habilitationsschift,* titled *The Police Command in the Law of Baden* [*Der Polizeibefehl im Badischen Recht*]. From this time on, Thoma quickly gained a reputation among legal scholars across Germany.[2] In 1908, he received a professorship at the Kolonialinstitut in Hamburg; in 1909, he returned to the southwest to accept a professorship in Tübingen; and in 1911 he was called to Heidelberg. He remained there until 1928, when he accepted a position at Bonn, where he stayed until his death in 1957.

Thoma's work spanned half a century and four state forms in Germany. His works prior to 1918 already show some of the basic issues that would preoccupy him until his final days. These issues are apparent in his 1910 essay "The Idea of the State Based on the Rule of Law and Administrative Law Scholarship" [*Rechtsstaatsidee und Verwaltungsrechtswissenschaft*].[3] The dry title of the essay conceals a burning political topic: how to combine the rule of law with administrative activity in the early years of a modern welfare state. Thoma argued that conceptions of the state based on the rule of law from the mid-nineteenth century had posited a substantive idea of what *Recht* was, based on individualistic notions of personal and property rights. But these substantive notions had to be replaced with a more formal notion of *Recht* at the end of the nineteenth century, when "the creative forces of national and the socialist ideas" overcame "individualist" conceptions.[4] Like other left-liberals and like later reformist socialists, Thoma linked the words "national" and "socialist" to develop the idea of an interventionist ("social") republic based on legal principles—a republic that would provide for the "emancipation of the fourth estate" and initiate social reform legislation.[5] This combination of ideas prefigured the underlying logic of the Weimar Republic, which combined republicanism and an openness to substantive reforms in its constitutional structure.

At the same time, Thoma insisted that openness to social law would not undermine the formal structure of law. Indeed, he called for a more rigidly formalist approach to administrative law to preserve the rule of law. First, all administrative acts were necessarily subordinate to a statute approved by the legislature (in the case of the Empire, the monarch and the Reichstag). The statute was "omnipotent," the highest expression of the state's authority; it set the framework within which the administration could operate.[6] Second, basic rights would create an additional set of limits to the actions of the administration.[7] Finally, Thoma stressed the necessary presence of a strong parliamentary system equipped with the institution of ministerial responsibility. The responsibility of ministers to the assembly was not, however, fully developed in the Empire. In spite of being a member of the right-liberal National Liberals, Thoma cast doubt on the *Rechtsstaatlichkeit* of the Bismarck Constitution of 1871 while still basically affirming the existing Reich.[8]

At first somewhat hesitant in his support of the new Weimar Republic in 1919, Thoma soon became one of the republic's leading supporters. He gave speeches to the left-liberal German Democratic Party, worked with an organization of university educators who were "faithful to the constitution," and published numerous works in defense of the Weimar democracy.[9] As one of his colleagues wrote in an obituary: "He did not, like so many others of his generation, merely accept the first democratic constitution of the Reich; he loved it."[10]

By "democracy" Thoma meant the kind of liberal-democratic system adopted by the Weimar Constitution. Like his fellow left-liberals Anschütz and Hugo Preuss, Thoma repeatedly rejected rule by "the plebeian." As he wrote in the essay below, the election of the National Assembly on 19 January 1919 was a decision for "responsible government" based on competing parties whose representatives were elected by rules of general suffrage— not rule by an autocratic minority. In other words, parliamentary democracy was still based on an aristocratic principle of indirect representation and not direct (plebiscitary) democracy, while at the same time the "aristocratic" electors were responsible to periodic popular votes.

The democracy Thoma had in mind, then, was anything but the "series of identifications" of people and state invoked by Carl Schmitt.[11] To Schmitt, Thoma would respond: To proclaim a magically unified, republican whole was to ignore the reality of fragmented interests of the German people. Democracy had to involve representation of concrete interests. Therefore, Thoma argued, it required different, contending political parties. From here it was only a short step to assuming (with Hans Kelsen) that only proportional voting rights could adequately represent the many interests of the German people, without allowing a majority to trample the interests of a minority.[12] At the same time, Thoma had great faith that the combination of proportional representation with the parliamentary system would create a truly democratic decision-making process. For this reason, he argued that the right of the Reichstag to amend the Constitution through a two-thirds vote was in theory unlimited. This idea of free, democratic self-determination, he argued, was "daring, perhaps, but sublime in its logical consistency."[13] The key to his argument, however, lies in the distinction between theory and practice: theoretically, i.e., from the point of view of existing legal forms and procedures, Article 76 was unlimited. But in actual practice, Thoma pointed out, a whole range of limits to "parliamentary absolutism" existed— from minority parties' right of inquiry to public opinion to the plebiscitarian right of popular initiative.

Thoma made a similar distinction between theory and practice in his essay on the limits of judicial interpretation of constitutional law in a democracy. He laid out this argument in a brilliant speech to the first meeting of the Association of German Teachers of the Law of the State [*Vereinigung der deutschen Staatsrechtslehrer*] in 1922. The essay, on the judiciary's right to review legislation, is a perfect example of the way a sharp-minded legal scholar in the neo-Kantian tradition of Max Weber would proceed with analysis. First, he confronted efforts either to affirm or to deny the right of judicial review on the basis of a reading of existing law. The relevant statutes, he argued, did not provide an explicit answer to this question. There was, then, no legal answer to the problem; this was "an authentic problem," to be solved "with the will, not with logic."[14] A problem of the "will" meant, in this case, a problem to be solved through an analysis of values and desires, not of an existing legal system. Thoma phrased the problem in a way that stressed the values of the Weimar Constitution: "Can German jurisprudence continue to adhere to the basic principle of the nonreviewability of statutes, which has been quite satisfactory in legal politics, or is it compelled to give it up to rush to the aid of the threatened new constitutions?"[15]

Thoma rejected the judiciary's right to review statutes on political grounds: There were sufficient other defenses of the Constitution such that granting judges this right—and deviating from existing doctrine—seemed unnecessary. During these same years the higher levels of the judiciary did begin to develop systems of judicial review, often making questionable judgments in the process. Thoma viewed these new practices as autonomous claims, almost usurpation, of power by the courts: a "gerontocracy of the judiciary."[16]

The strength of the positivist tradition lay in its ability to outline the way a given system of law should function. Thoma and Anschütz's *Handbuch des deutschen Staatsrechts* was, in this respect, one of the best practical works of German political science before 1945. The dark side of the positivist tradition lay, however, in its utter dependence on the workability of the political system. By 1932, when the second volume of the *Handbuch* was published, the Weimar constitutional system had become paralyzed. During the final months of its existence, the positivist tradition was unable to offer any politically acceptable way out of the crisis.[17]

Thoma continued teaching under National Socialism, but restricted himself to the less immediately political area of administrative law. He published only one major work during the Nazi period, an essay from 1937 that dealt with the financial policies of the new *Volksgemeinwirtschaft*, or the "common economy of the Volk."[18] The book contains praise for the "insight" and "saving deeds" of "our Führer, Adolf Hitler." In this respect, Thoma offered no critical perspectives.[19] The argument can be made, however, that his work indicated the limits to expansive financial policies. In this way it seems to have supported Hjalmar Schacht's calls for limiting deficit spending on rearmament. It is unclear whether Thoma intended this work as a strategy to counter Hitler's rearmament policies or as a reflection on the existing system.

After the Nazis were defeated in 1945, Thoma regained a prominent position in public life. He published an important defense of parliamentary democracy in 1948—no longer filled with the enthusiasm of the 1920s, but still supporting the institutions of liberal democracy.[20] He served as an adviser to the Parliamentary Council during its discussions on basic rights in the Basic Law of 1949. In his last essays, he developed an important, critical commentary on the rights and the place of the Federal Constitutional Court [*Bundesverfassungsgericht*], completed as blindness was slowly setting in.[21] In this and other works, he repeated virtually verbatim the arguments he had made against an extensive application of the equality clause in the Weimar Republic, which had been part of his general critique of judicial review.[22] In 1949, Thoma served as honorary chair of the newly reorganized Association of German Teachers of the Law of the State in its first meeting since 1932. He died on 26 June 1957, in Bonn.

MAIN WORKS

Der Polizeibefehl im Badischen Recht, dargestellt auf rechtsvergleichender Grundlage. Tübingen: Mohr, 1906.

"Rechtsstaatsidee und Verwaltungsrechtswissenschaft." *Jahrbuch des öffentlichen Rechts der Gegenwart* 4 (1910): 196–218.

"Der Vorbehalt des Gesetzes im preußischen Verfassungsrecht." In *Festschrift für Otto Mayer*, 167–221. Tübingen: Mohr, 1916.

"Das richterliche Prüfungsrecht." *Archiv des öffentlichen Rechts* 43 (1922): 267–86.

"Der Begriff der modernen Demokratie in seinem Verhältnis zum Staatsbegriff." In *Hauptprobleme der Soziologie: Erinnerungsgabe für Max Weber*, edited by Melchior Palyi, 37–64. Munich: Duncker & Humblot, 1923.

"Zur Ideologie des Parlamentarismus und der Diktatur," *Archiv für Sozial-Wissenschaft und Sozial-Politik*, vol. 53 (Tübingen: Mohr, 1924): 212 ff. English translation: "The Ideology of Parliamentarianism and Democracy." In Carl Schmitt, *Crisis of Parliamentary Democracy*, translated by Ellen Kennedy, 77–83. Cambridge, Mass., and London: MIT Press, 1985.

"Grundrechte und Polizeigewalt." In *Festgabe zur Feier des fünfzigjährigen Bestehens des Preußischen Oberverwaltungsgerichts 1875–20. November 1925*, edited by Heinrich Triepel, 183–223. Berlin: Heymann, 1925.

"Die juristische Bedeutung der grundrechtlichen Sätze der deutschen Reichsverfassung im allgemeinen." In *Die Grundrechte und Grundpflichten der Reichsverfassung. Kommentar zum zweiten Teil der Reichsverfassung*, edited by Hans-Carl Nipperdey, vol. 1, 1–53. Berlin: Reimar Hobbing, 1929.

"Sinn und Gestaltung des deutschen Parlamentarismus." In *Recht und Staat im neuen Deutschland*, edited by Bernhard Harms, vol. 1, 98–126. Berlin: Reimar Hobbing, 1929.

Handbuch des deutschen Staatsrechts. Edited by Richard Thoma and Gerhard Anschütz. Tübingen: Mohr, 1930–32.

"Gegenstand-Methode-Literatur." In *Handbuch des deutschen Staatsrechts,* vol. 1, 1–13.

"Das Staatsrecht des Kaiserreiches." In *Handbuch des deutschen Staatsrechts,* vol. 1, 69–80.

"Das Reich als Bundesstaat." In *Handbuch des deutschen Staatsrechts,* vol. 1, 169–86.

"Das Reich als Demokratie." *Handbuch des deutschen Staatsrechts,* vol. 1, 186–200.

"Die rechtliche Ordnung des parlamentarischen Regierungssystems." In *Handbuch des deutschen Staatsrechts,* vol. 1, 503–11.

"Die Funktionen der Staatsgewalt, Grundbegriffe und Grundsätze." In *Handbuch des deutschen Staatsrechts,* vol. 2, 108–59.

"Der Vorbehalt der Legislative und das Prinzip der Gesetzmäßigkeit von Verwaltung und Rechtsprechung." In *Handbuch des deutschen Staatsrechts,* vol. 2, 221–36.

"Das System der subjektiven öffentlichen Rechte und Pflichten." In *Handbuch des deutschen Staatsrechts,* vol. 2, 606–23.

"Die Notstandsverordnung des Reichspräsidenten vom 26. Juli 1930." *Zeitschrift für öffentliches Recht* 11 (1931): 12–33.

Die Staatsfinanzen in der Volksgemeinschaft: Ein Beitrag zur Gestaltung des deutschen Sozialismus. Tübingen: Mohr, 1937.

Über Wesen und Erscheinungsformen der modernen Demokratie. Bonn: Dümmler, 1948.

Grundriß der allgemeinen Staatslehre. Bonn: Dümmler, 1948.

"Über die Grundrechte im Grundgesetz für die Bundesrepublik Deutschland." In *Recht, Staat, Wirtschaft,* vol. 3, edited by Hermann Wandersleb, 9–19. Düsseldorf: Schwann, 1951.

"Ungleichheit und Gleichheit im Bonner Grundgesetz." *Deutsches Verwaltungsblatt* 66 (1951): 457–59.

LITERATURE

Festschrift für Richard Thoma zum 75. Geburtstag am 19. Dezember 1949. Tübingen: Mohr, 1950.

Giese, Friedrich. "Richard Thoma." *Juristenzeitung* 12:18 (1957): 589–90.

Maus, Ingeborg. "Entwicklung und Funktionswandel der Theorie des bürgerlichen Rechtsstaats." In *Rechtstheorie und politische Theorie im Industriekapitalismus,* edited by Ingeborg Maus, 11–82. Munich: Wilhelm Fink, 1986.

Mosler, Hermann. "Richard Thoma zum Gedächtnis." *Die öffentliche Verwaltung* 10 (1957): 826–28.

Rath, Hans-Dieter. *Positivismus und Demokratie: Richard Thoma, 1874–1957.* Berlin: Duncker & Humblot, 1981.

Scheuner, Ulrich. "Zum Gedächtnis von Geh. Hofrat Prof. Dr. Richard Thoma (1874–1957)." *Neue Juristische Wochenschrift* 10:36 (1957): 1309.

Schüle, Adolf. "Richard Thoma zum Gedächtnis." *Archiv des öffentlichen Rechts* 82:2/3 (1957): 153–56.

THE REICH AS A DEMOCRACY

Richard Thoma

Originally appeared as *Das Reich als Demokratie,* in *Handbuch des deutschen Staatsrechts,* edited by Richard Thoma and Gerhard Anschütz, 2 vols. (Tübingen: Mohr, 1930–32), 1:186–200. Translated by Peter C. Caldwell.

I

[T]he Weimar Constitution begins with the words:

> The German Reich is a Republic. State power emanates from the people.

These words fulfill two concepts that express a symbolically solemn content and at the same time provide a legally binding provision with a quite precise meaning. *Republic* means the negation of all power of domination by a single person, be it a hereditary monarch or a monarch irremovable for life, conveyed by vote or by co-optation. But republic also means affirmation and construction! The positive and original sense of the word conceives of the state as a *res publica,* as a *commonwealth,* in which all citizens participate, in which all domination is bound to serve the parts, and each part is bound to serve the whole. Republic in this sense makes the subject a citizen; it obliges and entitles him to the sentiments and the engaged readiness that Friedrich Naumann couched in the words: "We are the state." These words express a pride in freedom and the humility of responsibility with the same force.

The *people,* from which all state power is supposed to emanate, means similarly not just any concept of people, not any arbitrarily bounded active citizenry, ranked, perhaps, according to differing political rights. What it means is the totality of all adult Germans, conceived as a united association enjoying equal rights, including both those without property, of the lowest social strata, and those with wealth and education, of the highest social strata. Thus it signifies *an active citizenry enjoying a universal and equal right to vote and to take part in the full electoral process.*[23] "The people" in Article 1, paragraph 2 refers to the nation, i.e., to the Germans as such, not differentiated in one way or another.

Thus the first article of the Constitution proclaims what the following articles in fact organize: *democracy,* and with it, if one wants to express it thus, *popular sovereignty.*[24]

A *vast* democracy! The number of its active male and female citizens at present exceeds forty million.

A *poor* democracy! Of the heads of families and individuals assessed for the federal income tax in 1928, only around 370,000 showed a taxable income in the calendar year 1927 of more than 8,000 marks. Of these, only those assessed with more than 50,000 marks of taxable income a year could be considered well-to-do or even rich. That was, however, fewer than 17,000! Before the war, 15,547 people with more than one million marks were assessed property taxes. Their number has declined to 2,335.[25] In addition the buying power of the currency has sunk around 30 percent, and the tax burden has multiplied. It is no wonder that the economically independent "gentleman-politician"—characterized by his social condition, not his political tendency; he was and presumably still is to be found among the Social Democrats and to a considerable extent in the English Labour Party—has become rare in German democracy.

An *oppressed* democracy: The men and women productively active in the economy have to maintain the hundreds of thousands left injured from the war and on-the-job accidents, the surviving dependents that need support, as well as around a million unemployed and in addition countless other [victims of] poverty. And what is left over from the year's social product is drawn out of the country by the suction-pump of reparations payments. The misery of daily economic struggle, compensated by the sensations of movies and sporting events in recreational hours, permits only the fewest to train themselves seriously in politics through press and assembly.

A *threatened* democracy: In order to maintain itself, it had to crush the social-revolutionary rebellion of the years 1920 and 1921 in bloody civil wars. Today it sees itself confronted by a fascist rebellion that is growing in public and arming itself in secret.

II

The word "democracy" can be found neither in the constitution of the Reich nor in those of the Länder. There is no definition of the democratic established in positive law. And for ages, the concept has been iridescent with different meanings and colorations in the theory of the state and in practical usage. It can signify more form or content, more a "least" or more a "best" or "worst." No politician or theorist can be prevented from making use of a concept of democracy that would permit him to assert that the German Reich, in its constitutional construction or in its political reality, is not at all what one has to understand by democracy, or at least not what is to be true or authentic democracy—meant as criticism, or as praise.[26]

Thus it is superfluous—at least for investigation and description, the aims of scholarship about positive German state law—to argue over whether the German Republic under its present-day constitutional law "really" presents itself as a democracy. It is enough to indicate that a *concept of democracy* has been in vogue for decades in the entire world of western culture, which refers solely to whether all holders of the power of domination in a state arise, directly or indirectly, from popular elections and whether these elections take place according to a truly universal and equal suffrage.[27] What matters for this usage is thus, on the one hand, the full political emancipation and equality of rights of the lower stratum of society, and, on the other hand, the abolition of all stable, irremovable governmental authority, and instead *governmental authority, with a time limit or subject to recall, on the basis of democratic rights to take part in the full electoral process.*

Democratization is the name for the venture of western civilization, epoch-making in world history, to draw the working classes into the state on the basis of equal rights, in spite of—or because of—their increasing numbers, outgrowing all other classes and groups. It is the attempt to take the regulating power of domination from a lord and master over a society split by interests and give it to a creature and servant of a nation, conceptualized as somehow fundamentally solidary in its interests.[28] It is a resultant of the most varied components and developments, among which the unfolding of the idea of freedom, equality, and fraternal solidarity weighs, if not the heaviest, then also not the lightest. Born of the ethics and metaphysics of Christianity, transformed into an inner-worldly enthusiasm for the dignity and happiness of the human, democracy dares to seek the solution to national, social, and cultural problems by way of the free self-determination of individuals, classes, and nations.

One can define a state as a *democracy* in this sense *to the extent that its state law summons all strata of the people to equal rights to take part in the full electoral process and, should the occasion arise, to an equal right to vote directly in a plebiscite, and builds all power of domination either directly or indirectly on this foundation, which necessarily includes freedom of the press, of assembly, and of associations.*

The majority of the Council of People's Delegates decided for the democratic way in *this* sense of the word in the months of revolution, in opposition to the dictatorial minority of the Workers' and Soldiers' Councils. In *this* sense, the Weimar National Assembly decided for the construction of a democracy[29] in opposition to reactivating a governmental authority based on hereditary monarchy, to limiting or relativizing rights to take part in the full electoral process, to paralyzing the democratic representative assemblies through first chambers based on occupation or even birth, and so on.

Democracy or the people's state signifies an exclusive opposition to what Hugo Preuss called the "authoritarian state," by which is meant a state with stable and irremovable authority: "autocratic government" [English in the original] as opposed to "responsible government" [English in the original].

Now a constitution, according to which all holders of the highest legislative and governmental power emerge from the votes of the people or from the votes or other powers of designation of popularly elected state organs, cannot be called to life or kept alive unless some groups form freely within society and present their leaders as candidates for the different elective offices (member of parliament, president, minister, etc.). Therefore every state based on "responsible government" [English in the original] is necessarily and according to plan a *party-state* (in a general sense, free of any value judgment). And it is necessary and self-evident that the decision of the *majority* always has to be binding for the minority, whether in the election of representatives or heads of state, in a vote in the representative assembly, or in a referendum of the citizens themselves. The distinction between the stable authoritarian state and the party-state with legitimately removable governments is not based on "authority or majority," as Friedrich Julius Stahl maintained in former days. It is based on whether authority should lie in the hands of an irremovable minority group or in the hands of a government borne by the *trust of a majority*. Only an "elite" can govern. The question is, who or what does the electing.

A party-state can be constructed in a highly undemocratic way. It is a democratic party-state only when it broadens its base to the ultimate possible point, i.e., to a truly universal and thoroughly equal suffrage. In other words, it must renounce elevating an individual or a small group to rights of domination that cannot be withdrawn, a privilege characteristic of the authoritarian state; and in addition it must renounce all other constitutionally based privileges, such as prerogatives based on birth, census-based rights to take part in the full electoral process, gradation of those rights according to income classes, and so on. Then the state is no longer a state constitutionally based on privileges but a democracy, no longer a "class state" but truly a *common*wealth, and has at least the chance to get rid of all plutocratic or ochlocratic degenerations for ever.

If the German Republic thus exhibits the constitutional *form* of a democracy, then the next question is whether it is not also determined in *substance,* directed toward goals, oriented toward ethical-political ideas. In fact, in the National Assembly and its Constitutional Committee not only were highly different and contradictory ideas asserted about how a just German people's state should be organized and operate. Rather, *one* group of such ideas and considerations predominantly succeeded and made only a few concessions to the opposing group. Until more precise analyses have been carried out and more appropriate expressions found, one can characterize the two complexes of ideas as democracy of a more radical and egalitarian stamp and democracy of a liberal stamp. I have characterized the two tendencies as follows: [30]

> The basic tendency of *radical* democracy is *egalitarian.* Carried to an extreme, its realization in the constitution would lead to a dwarf democracy with completely unrestrained popular resolutions and offices filled in succession or by lottery; in the economy, to communism. In the practice of modern constitutional politics, radical democracy prefers the plebiscite over legislation

through representative assemblies; in representative assemblies it prefers the imperative over the free mandate; in filling offices and courts it prefers the popular vote and *recall* [English in original] over legally determined appointments, and so on. All this characterizes *one* kind of democracy.

The basic tendency of *liberal* democracy is *anti-egalitarian.* It demands the equality of rights as the basis of political and social life, in which the natural inequality of humans with respect to character and ability will finally be able to work itself out completely, undisturbed by privileges of birth or of wealth. One may characterize Kant, and [Immanuel Hermann] Fichte even more, as its philosophers. The word "liberal" should not hereby signify an opposition to "socialist."

On the contrary, perhaps no one has defined the principle of democracy of the liberal stamp more sharply than the Swedish socialist [Gustav Fredrik] Steffen, at home in the intellectual world of John Stuart Mill and the Fabian Society, when he says: "A deeply rooted aristocracy is the salt of a vital democracy." [31]

What it excludes is, of course, only an aristocracy based on heredity, estate, or property; it includes, however, and emphasizes personally gained higher qualification for offices based on education (the *Bildungszensus* of Max Weber). The selection should be democratic, but not necessarily direct: It includes the possibility of selection by electors. The hope, moreover, often raised to the level of utopia, is that direct and indirect democratic selection will raise the most able and most worthy, and that through the principle of representation and other selections the principle of democracy will not be dissolved, but "ennobled" (J. C. Bluntschli). The fervor of liberal democracy, however, lies at least as much in the demand for guarantees of individual freedom.

In the sense of these concepts, *German democracy* proves to be one of an *overwhelmingly liberal stamp,* with some concessions to popular referenda in tune with radical democracy. Moreover, the plebiscitary elements of the constitutional structure do not so much arise from an ideology or the superstition that the masses—themselves in part indifferent, in part seducible by demagogues—possess a higher wisdom as from the need for a corrective against deformations of parliamentarism and rigidification of the parties. And in part they arise from the hope that occasional plebiscites on major and generally comprehensible questions will have the effect of drawing the people to take a responsible interest in politics. Common to all German democracy—socialist as well as "bourgeois"—is the conviction that politics and legislation forced on the majority by a minority are not worthy of a free and cultured nation, that such domination by force is unable to solve the great problems of social reform, economic reconstruction, the unity of the Reich, and the unfolding of culture in the sense of a national community, and that it cannot truly become master over the enmity of classes, branches of economic production, confessions, and particularisms.

As Friedrich Meinecke shows, . . . it is not so much doctrines that have determined the spirit and details of the German constitution and make it conceivable, as practical reflection on how the task of mastering a particular and almost desperate historical and political situation can be solved.[32]

These analyses and intimations only lead through the outer courts to a deepened scholarly insight into the German democracy's spirit and mode of operation, its social and political preconditions, the dangers of its degeneration, and the chances of its accomplishment. And it is the task not only of scientific politics, of sociology, and of the philosophy of the state, but also to a significant extent of legal scholarship to penetrate these problems. But that is not the task of this *Handbook*, which is dedicated to the depiction of positive German state law. The most important and indispensable preliminary question for grasping the law of a democratic party state, namely that of the type and significance of the political parties that realize it, is investigated and depicted separately [in another chapter of the *Handbook*]. Here is the place to discuss the foundation and blueprint of the *legal* structure of the German Republic.

III

A democratic constitution claims to be based on the "people's will." A constitution and those who hold power on its basis count as democratically legitimate only if they rest on a resolution of the will made in full freedom by the entire citizenry. Naturally, this resolution can in practice only be the agreement of a decisive majority of all adult citizens of the state. *The Weimar Constitution rests on the foundation of such a plebiscite.* It took place on 19 January 1919, when the Germans answered the summons of their revolutionary governments in the Reich and the single states, elected a National Assembly, and empowered it with a full and unlimited mandate for the proclamation of a new political organization of the nation. This was the beginning of the new, democratic legitimacy of German political life.

Only from a *legal* point of view can one consider what the majority of this National Assembly decided to be the decision of the German people. For the so-called representation of an absent multitude through some council or individual "representing" it always remains merely an idea or a fiction. In reality it was the 262 delegates who agreed to the constitution, drafted by the Constitutional Committee of the National Assembly in cooperation with the government of the Reich and in contact with the governments of the Länder, with some considerable regard for their wishes; they wanted the constitution and established it. But three considerations show that in this case the fiction was uncommonly close to reality, and that the assertion of the Preamble and of Article 181—that the German people had decided on this constitution "through its National Assembly" and "given" it to "itself"—accords with the truth. First, each voter who gave his vote to one of the three great parties of the so-called Weimar Coalition knew full well that these parties were resolved to establish a thoroughly democratic constitution. Next, the proportional voting law made sure that the strengths of the parties in the National Assembly represented, certainly not a mirror image, but an essentially true picture of their strengths among the active citizenry. Finally, with the rule that amendment of the Constitution would require a two-thirds majority, the National Assembly put a sensitive fetter on all future Reichstags for the purpose of consolidating the new order. Alongside this normal method of constitutional amendment, however, it also opened the gates to a second, extraordinary *pouvoir constituant,* that begins with the popular initiative and, if the Reichstag resists, is decided by plebiscite (according to Articles 76 and 73). Certainly this type of constitutional amendment requires the consent of more than half of all those entitled to vote. Practically, then, it is even more difficult to obtain than the ordinary method; for a statute that has so many opponents that it cannot obtain a two-thirds majority in the Reichstag, it will be difficult to get more than twenty million "yes" votes from the mass of those entitled to vote, who are in part quite indolent. In principle, however, the National Assembly subjected its constitution to plebiscites, that is, to plebiscites of a *simple,* though to be sure positive and active, majority.

Thus the Weimar Constitution is not only historically based on authorization by the majority of the nation, but also at present always based on its freely revocable sufferance. The opinion that the doubled *pouvoir constituant* regulated by Article 76 cannot be without limits, that one cannot have "really decided in Weimar for a system of apparently legalized coup d'état," fails to appreciate the idea—daring, perhaps, but sublime in its consistency—of free, democratic self-determination.[33] Certainly this freedom can be demagogically misused. But how would it be freedom otherwise? However, from the standpoint of democracy and liberalism, from which interpretation must begin, it would be impossible to evaluate what the resolute and undoubted majority of the people wills and decides in a legal way as a coup d'état or rebellion, even if it subverts the basic pillars of the present Constitution!

The doubling of the *pouvoir constituant* and in general of the legislative process, which ordinarily culminates in a resolution of the Reichstag but in extraordinary cases can culminate in a popular referendum, presents legal theory with difficulties that up to now have been relatively little discussed, even though they are as characteristic of the constitutional law of the Länder as of that of the Reich and in both cases of the same practical relevance. It is left to the theory of the functions of the state . . . to determine whether, to what degree, and with what duration a statute sanctioned by referendum is of higher rank than one voted by parliament. The latter, looked at closely, is not sanctioned at all, but becomes ripe for promulgation by the mere passage of time (during which popular referenda can be demanded or ordered, and objections of the Reichsrat or of the Prussian State Council* lodged).[34]

For the present, the pillars of the Weimar constitutional edifice—its *"plan of government"* [English in the original], to say it less loftily with an expression that is difficult to translate—stand unshaken. And whoever has comprehended the beneficial force of steady development and grasped the questionable nature of *all* conceivable constitutional systems, whether they have grown over time or been created, will wish it durability and show it respect, even if he is unable to share my personal conviction as to its relative excellence.

IV

This "plan of government," that is, the organization of the power of domination and the order of cooperation amongst state organs, is constructed in such a way that it places the representative assembly, the Reichstag, in the commanding center. Therefore, the German Republic is a democracy ruled predominantly indirectly, i.e., through representation—by parliament. At the same time, however, it is a democracy that separates powers in a genuine way and balances the national parliament with a whole system of counterweights. Some arise from the decentralization of the federal state. Others from the powers of the directly elected president. Still others from permitting popular initiatives and referenda. Added to that are important rights of the minority within parliament and the indirect counterweights of the bureaucratic organization and the institutions implementing the "rule of law." The German Republic is a democracy that one surely calls "mixed," because of the interplay, established in Reich and Länder, of representative-parliamentary (indirectly democratic) with plebiscitary (directly democratic) elements. Only the term "mixed parliamentary-plebiscitary-federal-bureaucratic-rule-of-law" would indicate its full complexity.

This is the place to provide a concise *general picture of the structure of the German people's state,* prior to the detailed exposition in the chapters that follow.[35]

1. The representative assemblies of the German people in the Reich, the Länder, and the municipalities are based on *proportional representation.* This above all gives German democracy its peculiar character, distinguishing it from the other democracies in large states. In England, France, and (in somewhat different conditions) in the United States of

---

*Article 40, paragraph 4 of the 1920 Prussian Constitution reserved to the state council in Prussia the right to examine all statutes, including those of the Reich, before their promulgation, although it had no legal right to alter any statute.—TRANS.

America, with their majority voting, the possibility—and often enough
the reality—exists that minority parties (because of their relative majority) come to power and force upon the nation possibly years of political action and legislation, of which the overwhelming majority of the
active citizenry disapproves. If democracy is supposed to signify guidance of the state through "leader personalities" and representative majorities that by and large have the trust and assent of the majority of the
nation behind them, then once the political will of the people has crys-
tallized into a multitude of parties and interest groups (and not merely
a duality, as at present in America, which is now only gradually getting
serious about the economic, cultural, and foreign-policy problems of
the present-day state), democracy cannot be realized except through
proportional representation. Proportional representation has its dark
side, and at present in Germany has been implemented in an exaggerated manner in need of reform. . . . *But its abolition would destroy democracy!* Artificially implementing a two-party system would deepen class
divisions and lead a socialist Reichstag majority that might arise into
the temptation of a proletarian, and a "bourgeois" Reichstag majority
into the temptation of a fascist dictatorship. Furthermore, it would almost inevitably have to go hand in hand with the abolition of direct
popular legislation. For against a real (not merely so-called) minority
government and legislature, popular initiatives would pile up intoler-
ably. Already at present, the relatively greatest role in practice in the
mid-sized and small German Länder is played by initiatives and referenda for dissolution, which aim at new elections for a Landtag that os-
tensibly no longer accords with real majority conditions.

2. The *Reichstag* is the normal legislator (Article 68) and even the legislator of the constitution, if it has a qualifying majority (Article 76). The
combination of party groupings making up the majority at a given time
is, moreover, what essentially determines the general direction of politics and to a great extent as well the leading figures of the Reich government. Article 54 of the Constitution has expressly established the
so-called *parliamentary system of government.* According to this system, a
parliamentary majority can in the Reich recall the entire ministry and
each individual minister, and thus indirectly force the head of state of
the Reich to name a government acceptable to the *majority* and, in the
Länder, which lack a head of state, elect such a government directly.
The meaning of the system is multiple. First, it effects a monistic union
of powers, guaranteeing the unity of the legislature and the executive,
in opposition to a division of powers, which is in a specific sense "constitutional," as was characteristic of the monarchic constitutionalism of
Germany and is characteristic of the American presidential republic.

Also, it guarantees the democratic principle of majority rule. Finally, one hopes it will enlist, school, and sift political talent that can rise to responsible statesmanship through service to a party, the proof of parliamentary mandates or other functions.

Out of clear insight into the possibilities for degeneration in a parliamentary party state, however, the National Assembly hedged in majority rule with a whole system of safeguards, limits, and counterweights. These can be arranged into the six groups of institutions sketched next.

3. *Counterweights of a direct democratic variety*—popular initiatives and referenda—have been built into the constitutional law of Reich and Länder with the intent that they might become effective as a corrective against one-sided parliamentary and party rule. Until now they have been almost exclusively misused demagogically and have remained, as is fitting, without effect. But this should not seduce one into thinking that the institutions at issue here are imprudent and scarcely worth maintaining. Different circumstances are conceivable, under which they could prove to be a desirable solution to political difficulties and valuable guarantees of political freedom.

4. A *president*, elected by the entire people for seven years, faces the Reichstag. To him are reserved an abundance of the most important governmental powers, all of which he can exercise, however, only with the countersignature of a minister (Article 50), so that he is and ought to be bound to a majority government dependent on the Reichstag. In this way, he remains more or less "capped" by parliament, as historically first befell the English king. He is elected by the people, like the American president, who actually governs, and positively thrust aside from governing independently, like the French president, who is elected by parliament. This combination of a parliamentary system of government with a head of state appointed by popular election, devised by Hugo Preuss, was a genuine and thus daring gamble. Only the experience of decades can judge whether it has succeeded. The president is strong in the negative, insofar as he refuses, for example, the chancellor's suggestion of an official appointment, a dictatorial measure, dissolution of the Reichstag, a directive for a popular referendum, ratification of an international treaty, or pardoning a condemned person. He could raise himself up to an independent political act were he to combine the dismissal of a majority government with the simultaneous dissolution of the Reichstag (Article 25) and the naming of a chancellor of his choice to countersign the entire action. It would depend on the result of the new election whether or not the new chancellor stays in power.

It is significant, furthermore, that the president functions as the independent guarantor of the constitutionality of statutes (Article 70).* Most significant, finally, is his quiet influence, not graspable in legal terms, which he is able to exercise as a prominent personality and as the chosen one of millions.

5. With some strength, the democratic will of the governments of the Länder is able to balance the majority of the Reichstag, and thus become a *federal counterweight*. . . .

6. Through the richly developed catalogue of *"Fundamental Rights and Duties of Germans,"* the Constitution seeks in part to secure the most important rights and freedoms of citizens, municipalities, and churches, and in part to put the Reich and Länder at the service of certain conserving or progressive goals. This catalogue signifies above all a comprehensive *substantive determination and legitimation* of the newly ordered state.[36] However, inasmuch as not a few of these norms have the binding force of constitutional law, and thus can be neither modified nor infringed by a simple majority in the Reichstag, they form at the same time a most important element of the hedges surrounding the parliamentary powers. To that extent they form part of the institutions protecting minorities as well as the institutions of the German state based on the rule of law [*Rechtsstaat*]. The "genius" of the work of Weimar in the realm of "substantive integration" (Rudolf Smend) is most clearly expressed in the social-liberal intentions of Articles 151 and 162.** These two articles recognize the economic freedom of the individual, but only within the limits of an order that corresponds to "justice aiming at an existence worthy of a human being for all." They stress interwovenness in the world economy and in international law (Article 4), but also oblige German foreign policy to commit itself to an international labor law that "strives for a universal minimum of social rights for the entire working class of mankind."

7. Combining the democratic majority principle with a *protection of minorities* that is, of course, only relative is certainly not characteristic of democracy in general (as Kelsen assumes), but of democracy with a liberal stamp. The combination is realized above all in proportional representation, evaluated above. The protection of minorities receives its most important augmentation through the wall of a two-thirds majority erected by Article 76, which secures not only the Constitution's

*According to Article 70, the president promulgates all laws "that have been adopted in accordance with the constitution."—TRANS.
**Article 151 regulated "economic life"; Article 162 called for a uniform code of labor law.—TRANS.

provisions dealing with the state's organization, but also, as the preceding section mentioned, a wealth of substantive provisions. Another most important minority right is the right to committees of investigation (Article 34), which under certain circumstances could throw light on illegalities or unfair practices of the majority government. Finally, the minority right to suspend the proclamation of a statute (Articles 72 and 73) is a component of the legislative procedure.*

8. The *principle of the rule of law* requires that the powers of the public authority and the rights and freedoms of citizens and their corporate bodies be as clearly and precisely delineated as possible, and above all that the legality of the life of the state be guaranteed by the right to invoke independent courts in legal disputes of all kinds. This principle remains incomplete in the German state law and administrative law, to be sure, but it has been implemented in such breadth and in so many forms that here one cannot even begin to hint at the ways it has been realized. . . . Fundamental to the legal structure of German democracy and of significance for the systematic limitation of parliamentary majority rule, however, are the fortifications and guarantees of the rule of law, in particular with reference to the following two groups.

a. To decide the many conflicts in state law, an independent *court for disputes over the law of the state* [*Staatsgerichtshof*] has been organized (see, in particular, Articles 15, 19, and 108). Furthermore, *the courts* have claimed for themselves the authority to *review* statutes approved by simple majority in Reich and Länder for their substantive conformity with the Constitution, and, should the occasion arise, not to apply them.

b. Democracy has not just allowed to persist—and further extended—in Reich and Länder the numerous "self-administering" municipalities and other corporate bodies, as well as a richly developed bureaucratic organization, and not just by and large taken over from the authoritarian state the civil service and its law, but it has also placed the duly acquired financial rights and the most important of the other *rights of civil servants,* in enhanced measure those of judges, under the protection of carefully sharpened articles of the Constitution (especially Article 129). Here lies a significant, sometimes politically very palpable limitation to the free discretion of parliaments and parliamentary governments. . . . The German Republic has been democratized from root to branch in the constitution of the munic-

*Article 72 allowed for deferral of the promulgation of a law for two months if two-thirds of the Reichstag so demanded. Article 73 allowed for referendum in such a case, if 5 percent of the voting population so demanded.—TRANS.

ipalities and the Länder. In wise self-restraint, it is democratized only to a precisely limited extent in relation to its "administrative staff."[37]

All these types of minority rights, basic rights, and institutions for the protection of rights, which not infrequently benefit the opponents of democracy, involve checks to majority rule, which a democracy of a liberal stamp imposes upon itself freely, out of idealistic motives: to protect civil and political freedom and to serve the ideal of the rule of law. Making it harder to effect constitutional amendments—which is hard to justify in doctrine, but evident in practice—serves at the same time the continuity of the life of the state.

This, then, is the system of "checks and balances" [English in the original] with which the Constitution prohibits rule by parliamentary majority beyond certain extreme limits. If one surveys this richly developed system of counterweights and limitations in toto, it follows that nothing is more perverse than to complain about a supposed parliamentary absolutism of the German Reichstag. "The Reichstag"—that is, an assembly of close to 500 representatives of the most highly opposed political tendencies, split into six large and constant party groupings and a number of smaller and fluctuating groups— this Reichstag, whenever in its normal activity a political task is at all *important* and controversial, produces at best a simple majority, and then usually only at the cost of painful coalition and compromise. The simple majority, however—the Reichstag in its normal activity—is fenced in or diked from several sides here; it finds limits in the Constitution, so rich in content, and in adversaries well-armed by law: the Reichsrat, the popular referendum, the president, the courts, and its own minorities. Only if the majority coalition, brought together to form a government, is able to convince a large enough part of the opposition of the necessity of legislation or some other step may a two-thirds majority come together. Then, to be sure, the dikes will be inundated, the Constitution can be suspended or amended, the Reichsrat overcome, the president impeached or put to a referendum of recall. But in this form, too, the Reichstag is not absolute; set above it still are dissolution and popular referendum, to which the president, the Reichsrat and popular initiative can appeal, so that the "residue of sovereignty," as the authors of the seventeenth century said, remains in all cases in the direct popular referendum. As a rule, however, this referendum is not at all necessary. For, as a result of proportional representation and in light of the dependence of each party grouping on the opinions and voices of its adherents as they emerge from the press, assemblies, and resolutions of associations, it is virtually impossible that a resolution by two-thirds of the Reichstag would come about whose expediency or at least inevitability a majority of the active citizenry would not recognize.

Naturally, one cannot simply maintain the same of the resolutions of a simple Reichstag majority. It is, however, precisely the proper sense of parliamentarism in German liberal democracy that in the normal course of state affairs deciding on the general direction of politics, filling the ministries, issuing laws, and drawing up the budget should be entrusted to a relatively small number of chosen individuals, namely, the representatives, not to the broad masses of an untrained and demagogically susceptible active citizenry.

Naturally, whether a decision is made by the Reichstag or by popular referendum—and in both cases whether the decision is constitutionally normal or extraordinary, amending or suspending the Constitution by a qualifying majority—there always remains, despite all minority rights, an outvoted and thus in some sense "violated" minority. Thus, one of the most popular accusations either against parliamentarism or against democracy is that they are a despotism of the majority and violate the minorities.

Frequently this critique derives from mere thoughtlessness and can be dispatched, since it belongs to the essence of the state to consider and to decide, since every measure offends some interest and quashes some contrary opinions, and since in a democracy it is, after all, only the majority that rules the minority, which can one day become the majority. In privilege-based and authoritarian states, on the other hand, a minority rules definitively over the majority, and therefore this nondemocracy can scarcely escape the socialist accusation of being a class state.

The critique can also be understood in a deeper sense; then it originates in either the disappointment that democracy has caused the social revolutionaries, or in the deeply rooted fears harbored by the upper strata of property and higher education against the economic and cultural consequences of the state of the common man, which is how, in any event, democracy presents itself. The fear is that a minority, conceived as a cultural elite, will gradually be violated, that the Patrician will be overrun by the Plebeian.

To recognize these dangers clearly, and, in the spirit and deed of national solidarity and of bond of fate, to eradicate them, this is the great task of national-democratic social and cultural policy.

FIVE

Heinrich Triepel

INTRODUCTION

Ralf Poscher

Heinrich Triepel's significance for the law of the state of the Weimar Republic was the result not only of his scholarly undertakings but also of his practical efforts.

Born on 12 February 1868 in Leipzig, Triepel completed his studies in Freiburg and Leipzig and, with the support of his teacher, Karl Binding, progressed rapidly through the early stages of his academic career. In the winter semester of 1900–01, he succeeded Gerhard Anschütz in Tübingen as professor of the general and German law of the state, international law, and the theory of the state. After appointment at Kiel in 1908, he became a member of the law faculty in Berlin in 1913.

Immediately after the war, Triepel devoted great effort to strengthening the discipline of public law institutionally. In 1920, together with Otto Koellreuther, he became publisher of the Archive for Public Law [*Archiv für öffentliches Recht*], thus ensuring continuity for the forum founded by Paul Laband. In 1921, thanks to Triepel's initiative, state law theory formed a topic at the German Jurists' Congress [*Deutsche Juristentag*] for the first time. Triepel himself gave the inaugural speech, on the distinction between statute and regulation.[1]

Even more important than the inauguration of law of the state as a discrete field at the Jurists' Congress was the founding of the Association of German Teachers of the Law of the State [*Vereinigung der deutschen Staatsrechtslehrer*]. With this, Triepel was responding to the wishes of other colleagues as well.

The association was intended neither to be a trade association nor to have a political agenda, but to "provide the basis for a working group that was urgently desired under the exigencies of the present and was possible despite antagonisms of scholarly method and political viewpoint."[2] From its first meeting in 1922, the association did full justice to the role Triepel intended for it.[3] Its meetings were important stimulus for the Weimar law of the state. Thus presentations by Kaufmann, Smend, and Heller at the 1926 and 1927 meetings took the struggle over methods and aims to new heights. It is due not least to debates mandated by the association's charter on set topics—in which Triepel was consistently one of the most active participants[4]—that the minutes of these meetings are today among the most lively documents of Weimar state law theory.

I

Triepel first gained lasting international recognition in the field of international law through his 1899 work *International Law and National Law* [*Völkerrecht und Landesrecht*]. Developing the consequences of the concept of sovereignty, Triepel depicted the relationship between international law and national law as a relationship between independent legal systems. He thus founded the so-called dualist theory, which he defended in 1923 against monism, which Hans Kelsen especially advocated.[5]

Although Triepel went on to be active in the field of international law after 1908 as publisher of the respected *Recueil Martens,* his interests gradually returned to the law of the state, with which he had already dealt in his dissertation on the Interregnum. With his focus of interest, his methods also shifted. While his work on international law was still written entirely in the style of the conceptual legal tradition of Carl Friedrich Wilhelm von Gerber and Laband, Triepel developed increasingly into an opponent of positivism. This was already apparent in the subtitle of his 1907 monograph on unitary and federal elements in the Reich, *A Constitutional and Political Study* [*Eine staatsrechtliche und politische Studie*]. Besides an examination of the Constitution, Triepel offered a detailed portrayal of the historical development of constitutional reality, including an analysis of the positions of political parties. Triepel had not yet brought the law of the state and politics into an alliance. Still, this work showed Triepel's lively historical and political interests, by no means limited to Germany, as his numerous references to Swiss and American constitutional law attest.

Triepel found his lifetime subject in the federal state. He returned to these issues again and again. Even in his last year of life, he took up the subject and wrote on the federal reorganization of Germany.[6] His most extensive work on state law in the Reich, *Reich Supervision* [*Die Reichsaufsicht*] of 1917, was devoted to that subject. Here, too, Triepel preceded his legal examination with a historical, comparative law investigation. He turned explicitly against the conceptual approach with which the supervisory powers of the Reich had previously been constructed. "The conceptual construct serves only . . . to derive a desired construct through inference from an arbitrarily created concept."[7] He emphasized the necessity of asking, in contrast, about the intent of the Constitution and its historical development.[8]

His speech inaugurating his rectorship in 1926 can be seen as a methodological reflection on the departure from state law positivism already completed by the First World War. In the teleological method he had come to know as an instrument of the jurisprudence of interests [*Interessenjurisprudenz*] during his period in Tübingen,[9] Triepel found a tool that mediated the legal and political aspects of the law of the state and also provided legal legitimacy to his historical and political interests. In this way, Triepel showed himself more an improver of the old than the originator of a new methodology.[10] Like conceptual jurisprudence, the teleological method in the law of the state was inspired by private law. His approach broke with positivist methods without having to break with the content of positivism. Teleological argumentation was also found among Weimar positivists such as Richard Thoma.[11] Therefore, the speech was seen not only as a settling of accounts with positivism but also as a rejection of the idealist method [*geisteswissenschaftliche Methode*][12] that Günther Holstein had promulgated with a strong critical, anti-positivist impetus only a year earlier.[13] It was not even mentioned by Triepel, either in this speech or later.

II

"I am . . . neither an absolutist nor a democrat, but if someday I would have to decide unconditionally and without further ado for absolutism or democracy, I would, without thinking twice, prefer monarchic absolutism as the lesser evil . . . in the certainty that it is ultimately better to live under the enlightened or unenlightened despotism of a single person than under the despotism of the never enlightened rabble."[14] This and other political confessions[15] in the Empire already suggest that Triepel, who considered himself a strong supporter of the rule of law,[16] was less than enthusiastic about the prospects for the Weimar Republic. As a democratic form of state, only a presidential democracy on the American model seemed to him to have any chance of success. His attitude towards the semi-parliamentary system of the Weimar Constitution was skeptical, though always constructive.[17] In Weimar, he was conservative in the sense that he wished to retain "eternal justice"[18] in the new age. Thus Triepel was the first to develop the equality principle of the Weimar Constitution into a principle of justice binding on the legislature. To him, freeing the legislator from all legal restrictions seemed unacceptable even under monarchic constitutionalism, but "in a democratic republic . . .

downright impossible."[19] His plea for a constitutional court with abundant powers accords with this view.[20]

Triepel considered the party-state a defect of Weimar, and the history of the Republic did little to make him doubt his assessment. Nevertheless, to his credit, he was one of the first to make the role of parties in the constitutional state the subject of a legal treatise. In his 1927 address inaugurating his rectorship, *The State Constitution and Political Parties* [*Die Staatsverfassung und die politischen Parteien*], he diagnosed party rule as a sickness of the commonwealth and contrasted modern mass democracy with an idea, not lacking in nostalgia, of liberal constitutionalism with a parliament of notables.[21]

His addresses reflect the ambivalence with which Triepel initially approached National Socialism. To him, bolshevism and fascism, in which a single party rules the state,[22] epitomized a society perverted into a party-state. Thus after the "enabling law" [*Ermächtigungsgesetz*], which gave Hitler's government almost unlimited legislative power, Triepel did not mourn the passing of the Weimar multiparty state. He still cherished the hope that "time will succeed in stripping from the now victorious party the dress of a party, and in transforming it into a community encompassing the entire nation, in which everyone feels able to incorporate himself in *freedom*."[23] Triepel yearned for a self-administering, cooperatively organized commonwealth.[24] But there is an air of desperation in Triepel's willingness to take Hitler at his word with his talk of legality and law and demands for a "national revolution" to end un-German radicalization and respect for the freedoms in the Weimar Constitution.[25]

During the national socialist regime, Triepel withdrew into works focusing largely on history[26] and the history of constitutional doctrine.[27] He did not take part in the legal idealization of the regime. His distance from the German situation in 1938 is evident in the chapter titled "The Essence of the Leader and of Leadership" [*Wesen des Führers und der Führung*] in his major study on hegemony.[28] The Jewish background of his wife, Marie Ebers, also stood in the way of any closer relationship with the Nazi movement.

It was commensurate not only with his advanced age but also with the distance between Triepel and his time that at the end of his life he wrote, from an aesthetic perspective, *On the Style of Law* [*Vom Stil des Rechts*]. Only with the eye of a scholar sweeping the centuries could he make himself believe as early as 1946 that, next to the beauty of German law, "the ugly blots that emerged in the recent past will somewhat fade."[29]

Heinrich Triepel died on 23 June 1946 in Grainau, Upper Bavaria.

MAIN WORKS

Das Interregnum: Eine staatsrechtliche Untersuchung. Leipzig: Hirschfeld, 1892.
Die Entstehung der konstitutionellen Monarchie. Leipzig: Seele, 1899.

Völkerrecht und Landesrecht. Leipzig: Hirschfeld, 1899.

Unitarismus und Föderalismus im deutschen Reiche: Eine staatsrechtliche und politische Studie. Tübingen: Mohr, 1907.

"Die Kompetenzen des Bundesstaats und die geschriebene Verfassung." In *Staatsrechtliche Abhandlungen: Festgabe für Paul Laband zum 50. Jahrestage der Doktor-Promotion,* vol. 2, edited by Wilhelm von Calker and Fritz Fleiner, 249–335. Tübingen: Mohr, 1908.

"Staatsdienst und staatlich gebundener Beruf." In *Festschrift für Karl Binding zum 4. Juni 1911,* vol. 2, 1–85. Leipzig: Meiner, 1911.

"Zur Vorgeschichte der norddeutschen Bundesverfassung." In *Festschrift für Otto Gierke zum 70. Geburtstage,* 589–644. Weimar: Böhlau, 1911.

Die Zukunft des Völkerrechts: Vortrag gehalten in der Gehe-Stiftung zu Dresden am 11. März 1916. Leipzig and Dresden: Teubner, 1916.

Die Reichsaufsicht: Untersuchungen zum Staatsrecht des deutschen Reiches. Berlin: Springer, 1917.

Konterbande, Blockade und Seesperre. Berlin: Mittler, 1918.

"Die Entwürfe zur neuen Reichsverfassung." In *Schmollers Jahrbuch für Gesetzgebung, Verwaltung und Volkswirtschaft,* vol. 43, 55–106. Munich and Leipzig: Duncker & Humblot, 1919.

Virtuelle Staatsangehörigkeit: Ein Beitrag zur Kritik der Rechtsprechung des Französisch-Deutschen Gemischten Schiedsgerichtshofs. Berlin: Vahlen, 1921.

"Streitigkeiten zwischen Reich und Ländern: Beiträge zur Auslegung des Artikels 19 der Weimarer Reichsverfassung." In *Festgabe der Berliner Juristischen Fakultät für Wilhelm Kahl zum Doktorjubiläum am 19. April 1923,* edited by Theodor Kipp and Heinrich Triepel, article 2. Tübingen: Mohr, 1923.

Goldbilanzen-Verordnung und Vorzugsaktien: Zur Frage der Rechtsgültigkeit der über sogenannte schuldverschreibungsähnliche Aktien in der Durchführungsbestimmung zur Goldbilanzen-Verordnung enthaltenen Vorschriften. Ein Rechtsgutachten. Berlin: de Gruyter, 1924.

[as editor] *Staatsrecht und Politik: Rede beim Antritte des Rektorats der Friedrich-Wilhelms-Universität zu Berlin am 15. Oktober 1926. Beiträge zum ausländischen öffentlichen Recht und Völkerrecht,* Heft I. Berlin and Leipzig: de Gruyter, 1927.

Die Staatsverfassung und die politischen Parteien. Berlin: Liebmann, 1927.

Die Hegemonie: Ein Buch von führenden Staaten. Stuttgart: Kohlhammer, 1938.

Delegation und Mandat im öffentlichen Recht. Eine kritische Studie. Stuttgart and Berlin: Kohlhammer, 1942.

Vom Stil des Rechts: Beiträge zu einer Ästhetik des Rechts. Heidelberg: Schneider, 1947.

LITERATURE

"Bibliography." *Archiv des öffentlichen Rechts* 91 (1966): 549–57.

Gassner, Ulrich M. *Heinrich Triepel: Leben und Werk.* Berlin: Duncker & Humblot, 1999.

Hollerbach, Alexander. "Zu Leben und Werk Heinrich Triepels." *Archiv des öffentlichen Rechts* 91 (1966): 417–41.

Kaufmann, Erich. "Heinrich Triepel." *Deutsche Rechtszeitschrift* (1947): 60–61.

Kohl, Wolfgang. "Triepel, Heinrich." In *Biographisches Lexikon zur Weimarer Republik,* 345–46. Munich: C. H. Beck, 1988.

Leibholz, Gerhard. "In Memoriam Heinrich Triepel." In *Deutsche Verwaltung,* 141–42. Hamburg: Rechts- und Staatswissenschaftlicher Verlag, 1949.

Scheuner, Ulrich. "Triepel." In *Staatslexikon,* 7: cols. 1044–45. Freiburg: Herder, 1962.

Smend, Rudolf. "Heinrich Triepel." In *Die moderne Demokratie und ihr Recht: Festschrift für Leibholz zum 65. Geburtstag,* edited by Karl Dietrich Bracher, 2:107–21. Tübingen: Mohr, 1966.

LAW OF THE STATE AND POLITICS

Heinrich Triepel

Originally appeared as *Staatsrecht und Politik: Rede beim Antritte des Rektorats der Friedrich Wilhelms-Universität zu Berlin am 15. Oktober 1926* [Speech Inaugurating the Rectorship of the Friedrich Wilhelm University in Berlin on 15 October 1926], in *Beiträge zum ausländischen öffentlichen Recht und Völkerrecht, Heft* I, edited by the Max-Planck-Institut für Ausländisches Öffentliches Recht und Völkerrecht (Berlin and Leipzig: de Gruyter, 1927), 5–40.

Honored gathering! Respected colleagues! Dear fellow-students!

. . . Carl Friedrich von Gerber's book on public law contains the clearly outlined program of a new school that makes it its business to cleanse the theory of the law of the state of everything political. Literally, he says that *conceptual legal constructions* should take the place of political and philosophical *raisonnements.* The meaning is: What is law can be understood only through what is law. Considered from the standpoint of legal scholarship, the political can only be the material, never the goal. In the law of the state, one must employ the entire sum of *legal concepts,* analyzed in their simplicity and unspoiled purity in private law, either directly, or where this is not possible because of the variety of material content, then in such a way that they are altered according to the principles of exact interpretation and consistency developed in private law. Gerber then immediately illustrates the usefulness of this method by way of a particular problem in which the "legal nature" of the rights of the monarch, the civil servant, and the subject in public law are revealed. In it, we encounter a series of constructions that would later play a major role—for example, the view that a monarch's rights are his "own" and "genuine" rights, and the claim that the subject's so-called rights of freedom are not rights but instead simply express certain effects of legal precepts on the exercise of state power. Practical consequences are immediately drawn from the conceptual construction—for example, the consequence that in public law almost none of a citizen's rights can be enforced in court.

The new method, which incidentally can be traced back to earlier suggestions by [Wilhelm Eduard] Albrecht, was later employed by Gerber in his appealing *Principles of the German Law of the State* [*Grundzüge des deutschen Staatsrechts*]. Then [Paul] Laband—Gerber's intellectual executor, as [Ernst] Landsberg aptly called him—took over the method and treated it with consummate artistry. And Laband's *State Law of the German Reich* [*Das Staatsrecht des deutschen Reiches*], the first volume of which appeared exactly fifty years ago, completely dominated more than one generation of German public law scholars and exercised an influence even beyond Germany's borders, particularly in the Romance countries. Few from my generation failed to be entranced by the Gerber-Laband school when we began our careers. Its effect was checked neither by the strong opposition of [Otto] Gierke and Edgar Loening nor by [Felix] Störk's courageous, if somewhat misdirected, attack.

In treating problems of the law of the state, this school was interested in nothing but analyzing public law relations by establishing their "legal nature," discovering the general legal concepts to which they were subject, and developing conclusions from the principles discovered. This analysis means, all in all, an unfolding of the logical elements of which the concept of a legal institution is composed. Any teleological examination is frowned upon, for the goal served by a legal institution lies beyond its concept. The conclusion thus follows of itself that the law of the state must shun all *political* considerations, since they include considerations of goals. The school bestows the honorable title "strictly legal" only upon writings that avoid any contact with the political as with the Evil One. Those who do not bow to this tyranny that on occasion almost resembles a court of the Inquisition are, at best, ignored. . . .

Now it is true that the word "politics" is ambiguous, and thus the relationship between the conceptual approach of public law scholarship and the "political" could be structured in various ways.

One can understand politics as state *action;* one might see politics, as does [Johan Caspar] Bluntschli, as leading the state and influencing it, as a "deliberate handling of all practical problems in and around the state" [*bewußte Staatspraxis*]. We need not concern ourselves with the question of where to draw the dividing line between the truly political and other state activity— perhaps by using the idea of integration that Rudolf Smend fortunately introduced into the world of state law. For in any case, states' political action, as well as mere technical administration, can support an assessment not only from the standpoint of expediency but also from that of law. Basically, the law of the state has no object other than the political. Thus, a scholar of the law of the state cannot avoid judging political processes and intentions by the standards of public law. . . .

Until a few decades ago, politics was seen as the theory of the state per se, more or less in the way in which it was treated in antiquity. Thus [Georg] Waitz, for example, refers to politics as the scholarly discussion of the conditions of the state, with consideration of the historical development of states as well as states of the present day. Under this view, constitutional law is part of a comprehensive political science, and the question arises whether the law of the state should be practiced with or without considering the other aspects of this theory of the state. The question remains the same, however, or shifts only superficially, if we assume that the formerly unified concept of politics has dissolved and that the state has now become the object of various disciplines, with one examining its legal aspects and others considering it from the historical or social or psychological or some other standpoint. Whether there can also be politics in a more narrow sense—and with it a scholarly theory of state interests—is controversial but immaterial to us for the time being. For the question is solely whether it is methodologically correct for scholarship to place the law of the state in relation to other disciplines concerned with the state. Everyone would probably agree to this without reservation, were it not being fought passionately in the interests of methodological purity by the newest trend, which likes to describe itself as the logical legacy of the Gerber-Laband school. The young Austrian school led by [Hans] Kelsen, taking as its starting point the epistemologically irrefutable contrast between the "is" and the "ought," would exclude any *causal* considerations from jurisprudence in general and the law of the state in particular, since it is a *normative* discipline. *Political* discussions are rejected with particular hostility as alien to law, because they are said to be discussions of goals. Although Laband was still willing to admit that the purposes of a legal institution could influence its legal structure and be important in understanding it, such a thought would be anathema to Kelsen, who would declare it "meta-legal," as it is unattractively called. In this way law, as mere form, is of course and deliberately emptied of any content. Kelsen has gone so far as to call the state a mere legal concept, a point of reference for certain actions; in the end he has equated it with the legal order itself—that is, with a system of norms.

Now, the critical distinction between knowledge gained from legal logic and from causal science is an undeniable advance. But it is a different question whether the brusque one-sidedness with which the latest trend limits legal scholarship to the formal is a benefit. If we assume, without accepting, that the lawyer is no longer doing jurisprudence, but sociology, history, or whatever when he supplements formal, logical, conceptual work with social, historical, ethical, and other considerations, this seems merely a matter of labeling, of no significance to the substance of the issue. But it is this supplementation against which they inveigh. The masters of the new school banish any legal thought that cannot be certified as logical from the field of jurisprudence, as the guild-master chased the bunglers from the town precincts. Certainly the law of the state may be pursued with such methodological exclusivity; but the cost, in the end, is the impoverishment of our scholarship, which must indeed pay a high price for the glory of methodological purity. Methodological syncretism, as Adolf Menzel correctly states, is not a crime against the crown! Where would we be today if we had pursued church law without church history, trade law without considering business economy! In the same way, however, the law of the state cannot be carried on without consideration of the political. Even [Samuel] Pufendorf was incensed at scholars of the law of the state who treated the German Constitution without knowing the *res civiles*—that is, politics. He scoffed that they were as suited to their work as donkeys to violin playing. What would that old fighter say to those most modern scholars of the state who do not even want to know anything about politics! The logical purism that protects jurisprudence from any contact with other disciplines, that makes it an esoteric doctrine comprehensible only to the initiated, and that gives all state institutions, constitution, parliament, kingship, self-government, and much more the appearance of bloodless schemes and leaves their ethical content uncomprehended; this must necessarily lead to the withering away of the theory of law and state. Let us hope that our next generation of public law scholars, more interested in life than the last, will turn their energies to placing the norms of the law of the state in the closest of contact with the political forces that create and form them, and which, in turn, are mastered by the state's laws—a task we have only just begun to take on and which has been far better accomplished by foreign, particularly Anglo-Saxon, theory of the law of the state than by the German.

However, it is not even correct that legal scholarship, even if taken in the most narrow sense, must limit itself to constructs of a formal logical conceptual quality for the sake of its object. The logical school of law has fallen back on a concept of law that, though not wrong, is arbitrarily narrow. It cannot reasonably be disputed that the law concerns an "ought," not an "is." However, our discipline deals not only with the transcendental content of law but also with empirically existing legal orders consisting of rules that govern the ordered communal life of people, rules that come and go and differ according to places and times. Therefore, despite everything, every legal system is in itself a "given," an "is," and this fact cannot be understood without considering the social relationships that the law orders with its norms. Further, the rules of "ought" in law are always an expression of universal valuations, and their meaning refers to objects seen as means for achieving certain ends. Thus one cannot arrive at an understanding of legal precepts at all unless one has an image of the goals to which the legal refers and of the *interests* whose recognition, disapproval, or balancing form the primary task, or, if you will, the prerequisite of the legal system. Now if we describe as "political"—this is yet another new meaning of this dubious word—anything referring to state goals or their distinction from individual goals, it is clear that a comprehensive understanding of the norms of the law of the state is not possible at all without inclusion of the political.

Looked at in the light, it is a mere self-deception for jurisprudence to believe it can construct the entire substance of the legal order formally, logically, and without value judgments. Let us look somewhat more closely at the operation commonly called "legal construction." First, some simple examples. One constructs when one understands the contract concerning a visit to the theater as a work contract, i.e., a contract for the production of work, namely the performance. One does this in order to apply the civil code provisions on work contracts to the relationship. Or, if I may present an example from the law of the state, there are lawyers who construct the abdication of a head of state as an act of government, in order to bring the act within the scope of the constitutional provisions that require government acts by the head of state to be countersigned by a minister. What does such a construction consist of? Strangely enough, many different explanations are offered. Max Rümelin, who I believe has most closely studied the issue, sees construction as assigning a single phenomenon a place within the system by analyzing and synthesizing its conceptual elements. I will accept this definition. However, somewhat differently from Rümelin, I would like to see construction not as the linkage of a factual predicate to its legal consequence, but as the classification of a factual predicate or a legal consequence within the system for the purpose of such linkage. Construction always refers to legal phenomena or events that cannot easily be subsumed under an established concept. If we bring a blow with a stick under the concept of bodily harm, this is mere subsumption, not construction. Construction is only the preparation in a subsumption that has yet to occur; its purpose is to make the legal phenomenon ready for subsumption. Again, unlike Rümelin, I consider it immaterial whether the concept under which a phenomenon is included is already known or newly created. Numerous concepts familiar to us today, some of which have already become statutory concepts, were originally created by scholars for the purpose of construction—think of the legal transaction, or of rights *in rem* and *in personam,* or of confederation and the federal state; it was a construction when Georg Jellinek invented the concept of "state fragment." The only requirement is that the new concept should work to further the system—perhaps to remove a phenomenon from subsumption under other already familiar concepts, thus giving it a place in the system.

We will thus have to distinguish between two types or two levels of construction. For the first, it is enough to present familiar legal materials as a unity by viewing individual legal precepts as flowing from higher principles, and seeing these, in continuous upward progression, as deriving from concepts placed at the top of the large pyramid. This seeks to view the single as part of the whole, and the whole with its inner connection and cohesion. It is construction for its own sake. We might describe it as *comprehending,* or, to paraphrase Max Weber's well-known formulation, as *understanding* construction. A second step, not always taken but quite obvious, consists of taking from the postulated unity of the legal order the authority to derive new legal precepts from the discovered principles—that is, to fill the gaps in the familiar legal material. From the standpoint of the constructing lawyer, what is filled only seems to be a gap, as for him consequence and analogy are mere logical operations that only confirm what is already contained in the existing legal material. Thus here, construction is used for finding law. Philipp Heck has called this the method of inversion. We will call it the *gap-filling* construction. It is not always possible to tell immediately whether a legal construction aims to reach only the first level or has its eye on filling a gap. The Gerber-Laband school is at any rate devoted to construction in the fullest sense. One may have doubts about its legacy in the Kelsen school, as here jurisprudence is no longer viewed as a practical discipline whose task it is to prepare the administration of law by interpreting the existing and finding new law.

It seems to me to be the failure to distinguish between understanding and gap-filling construction that leads to a disagreement about the historical, and especially the intellectual-historical, foundations upon which the jurisprudence of construction is based. It has been said that the displacement of the politicizing method of the law of the state by the approach of construction may be explained by the fact that the period in which our nation still struggled to find its constitutional form has been superseded by a period of quiet in constitutional politics. This is undoubtedly true to a certain degree. But this would have explanatory power only for the law of the state, while the predominance of construction in the second half of the previous century was found in all areas of legal scholarship. How can this be explained? Many trace it back to the effects of the *historical school of law,* others to the influence of Hegel—which would, incidentally, not necessarily be a conflict. I consider both of these to be incorrect, or only partially correct.

There is no doubt that even the leaders of the historical school of law use construction in their presentation of subsisting law. [Friedrich Karl von] Savigny's famous monograph on possession is, for many, a model of jurisprudential construction, and Albrecht's *Gewere* forms the Germanist counterpart to it. But is not Savigny's inclination toward construction a part of the natural law residues one rightly believed to have discovered in his thought? Besides, his methods were surely far more understanding than they were gap-filling constructions, except, perhaps, for the last part of his system: international private law. Since Savigny, the process of bringing to light the conceptual and of building it into a system has endowed jurisprudence with the dignity of a science. [Georg Friedrich] Puchta and [Friedrich Ludwig von] Keller were the first to consciously and energetically take the step down from constructed concepts to the solution of individual cases not settled so far by law. But for Puchta the special influence of dialectical philosophy probably played a role. Admittedly, even someone like [Karl Friedrich] Eichhorn had not scorned construction—for example, in proving the impossibility of establishing a federal court on the basis of the "nature" of the Deutsche Bund as an association under international law. However, the basic ideas of the historical school lead not to a method of construction but away from it. The doctrine of the logical completeness of law is a legacy of natural law and did not, as many believe, develop out of the historical school. Its most persistent advocates—recall, for example, Wilhelm Arnold—were determined opponents of construction. When others adopted the method of construction, they did so despite the school's basic principle. For according to this, law is after all the life of the people, seen from a particular angle. How could this lead to logically deriving legal precepts from invented concepts? [Alfred] Manigk has shown convincingly that the gap that has opened between the historical school and modern teleological jurisprudence is by no means unbridgeable. It is true that the historical school had to oppose any attempt to fill gaps in the law with subjective value judgments. However, it was certainly able to acknowledge the law creating power of objective values that exist in society and are thus universal; for these, too, are the result of history, part of the stream of history. As far as the relationship between the law of the state and the political, in particular, it may be true that the quietistic bent that clung to the historical school of law brought in its wake an aversion to political *raisonnement,* "which breathes the spirit of obsession for reform." And after all, the chief advocates of the antipolitical school in the law of the state, Gerber and Laband, came out of the historical school. Yet they were already more-or-less degenerate children of the great mother. About Gerber—who characteristically called Puchta, not Savigny, his master—Gierke made the harsh judgment that he had killed the German soul in German law with his romanist constructions. But the example of [Rudolf von] Gneist, certainly a son of the historical school of law, proves that even this school could achieve a relationship to the political.

The result is similar when we try to trace the jurisprudence of construction back to Hegel. Hegel unquestionably exercised a great influence on the lawyers of the first half of the previous century, and to some extent even beyond. Public law and, besides criminal law, the law of the state and international law in particular bear his mark—[Romeo] Maurenbrecher, the young [Johann Stephan] Pütter, [August Wilhelm] Heffter, [Carl Viktor] Fricker, finally Otto Mayer, besides some who were only superficially touched by Hegel. Undoubtedly, specific elements of Hegel's philosophy can be found in the jurisprudence of construction. When [Rudolf von] Ihering, in his younger period, oriented towards construction, was sustained—like Puchta and others—by the belief that a "higher" jurisprudence led to production of new legal material by virtue of the inner dialectic of legal relationships, this was obviously Hegelian thinking. Some concepts that were formed and played a role in the period of the jurisprudence of construction can be traced directly to Hegel. Yes, Hegel expressly, though admittedly with a pronounced tone of contempt, ascribed to legal scholarship the task of collecting, deriving, splitting given legal provisions through deduction from the positive legal material. But according to him, this was all merely a matter of the external order, a matter of understanding; it had nothing to do with true comprehension, with reason. Hegelian constructions cannot be compared with the constructions of jurisprudence at all. Those who assume the opposite confuse formal logic with Hegel's metaphysical logic, the conceptual in the ordinary sense with the Hegelian concept, which is the living spirit of the actual, developing in incessant progression. Thus Hegel's construction is only understanding construction, and even when it refers to law, it is construction through history. State and law take their places in the unfolding of the spirit in history. Hegel's construction thus leads beyond law; it does not serve the conceptual systematic of law itself. Therefore it comes as no surprise that, of the latest offshoots of Hegelianism in public law, neither Lorenz von Stein nor Gneist, the historically oriented Hegelians, but only Otto Mayer cultivated legal construction in the technical sense. And conversely, the latest guise of construction in state law theory, Kelsen's logic of norms, does not have the slightest connection to Hegel. How could it in a school that is consciously ahistorical, while Hegel was historically oriented, branding the creative self-movement of the spirit as axiomatic, that is, in a school that ultimately has the state disappear entirely into law, when for Hegel, law merges entirely into the state. In fact, the logical school itself seeks its point of departure not in Hegel but in Kant—whether rightly or wrongly is another question. The jurisprudence of construction shares its preference for the system and its belief in the completeness of that system not only with Hegel, but with all of idealist philosophy—perhaps with philosophy in general.

But the main point is that legal construction existed long before the historical school of law and long before Hegel; one might even say it has existed since people began to feel and satisfy a need for an immanent order in legal material, except that it was not always consciously treated as a method or as the only method. Often it was used only to model systems or for didactic purposes; often it served only as understanding, not as gap-filling construction.

Roman lawyers were already using construction—how exquisitely Ihering has described Paulus the constructor!—and glossators as well as post-glossators have used construction, as have Scholastics and Ramists, the Syntheticists and Systematicists of the sixteenth century, as well as natural law scholars and those of the Enlightenment. We find construction to an especially great extent in natural law. Except here it takes place first at another level; first, natural law as such is mastered through a priori concept formation and deduction, and the outcome is employed in positive law only if the lawyer wishes to employ natural law to fill gaps in positive law. Not all, but most natural law scholars have taken this second step. What is it but gap-filling construction when Hugo Grotius, for example, seeks to prove the inalienability of the demesnes—there was disagreement on whether or not state property could be sold by the monarch—by interpreting the rights of princes to the demesnes as usufruct, and when [Augustin von] Leyser tries to refute this by branding the ruler the true owner by virtue of the original social contract? Certainly, in natural law jurisprudence logical deductions from concepts often coexist peacefully side by side with considerations of purpose and value. To remain with the example of the demesnes, Pufendorf agrees with Grotius's theses and their justifications, but points to the necessity for the state to protect the economic needs of the respective government successor, and thus remove the demesnes from the control of the monarch. In any case, however, it is certain that the method of construction in finding law was quite familiar to natural law—except that natural law replaced the Roman legal concepts, from which German scholars of the law of the state originally constructed public legal relationships, with a different basis for construction. . . .

None of these various ways of describing and finding the law can be related to any particular legal philosophy. On the contrary, each attempted to accord with its period's *Weltanschauung*s and forms of cognition. They are as related to the conceptual realism of scholasticism as to the abstracting tendency of the Enlightenment and of Kantian and post-Kantian idealism, and finally to the positivist narrowing of thought in general in the most recent eras—a way of thinking that does not look beyond the subject matter and only considers valid what it can extract from it. All the types of the jurisprudence of construction have in common only *one* principle. It is, if I may say so, a professional lawyer's view. The method of construction aims to serve the needs of the theorist and the practitioner, to create certainty about the legal precepts that guide life in society. Legal *certainty* is necessary to reassure the citizen whose interests are affected by law, as well as to reassure the conscience of the legal researcher and of the lawmaking authority. The infallibility of the logical conclusion, the obviousness of its outcomes, alone seems to be capable of creating this reassurance. Thus it was believed that the best legal method was found in operating with crystal-clear concepts and granite-hard deductions, guaranteeing firm predictability of results.

Thence also the popular comparison of jurisprudence with mathematics, the description of law-finding as "calculating with concepts," the demand that legal doctrine determine for each his own with mathematical precision. It has been claimed repeatedly, from Leibniz to Wolff and Kant, that legal scholarship is related to mathematics. Hints of this may be found even in Savigny. Even more recently this idea has appeared among philosophers, for example in [Wilhelm Max] Wundt and [Hermann] Cohen; and Kelsen, a student of Cohen's, calls jurisprudence a geometry of the total legal phenomenon, though he also admits that this comparison does not work in every respect. At one time the matter was taken quite literally, and there were even attempts to solve questions of the law of the state through simple arithmetic. A famous debate turned on the question whether, in a dispute between the three *curia* of the old Reichstag, the Kaiser could join the majority and elevate their decisions to Reich law—whether he could, for example, join the college of electors and the council of princes to override an opposing vote by the free cities. Here, some based their views on the doctrine, defended by [Dietrich] Reinkingk, that the Kaiser and the Reichstag possessed sovereignty [*Majestät*] *pro partibus indivisis*—thus the Kaiser held half and each of the three estates one-sixth. From this, it was derived with mathematical certainty that the Kaiser and the two Reich estates together, with ten-twelfths, or the Kaiser even if he had only one estate on his side, with eight-twelfths, would be able to achieve more than the remaining two- or four-twelfths. Pütter still had to fight such nonsense.

But what is the truth about the apodictic certainty that is the aim of the intellectualist methods of formal logic? It is nothing more than deceptive facade. No lawyer has yet achieved a reasonable result using this alone, and if he thinks so, he deceives himself; for a seemingly pure logical analysis and synthesis of concepts, if it is to make sense, cannot be made at all if not supported by value judgments. . . . Even more so concept-creation and concept-classification growing out of a legal construction cannot be achieved without teleological ingredients. Thus it can easily happen that the constructor is seduced into filling a concept from the start with what he hopes to take from it later—thus arriving, by hook or by crook—at the desired result in a bona fide way. In the law of the state in particular, hundreds of constructions can be found with which results considered useful are brought about in this way. One example in place of many: A young scholar of the law of the state was once interested in the aforementioned question whether the abdication of the monarch required countersignature by a minister. It required this only if it were an act of government. Now, in order to have it appear to be one, the scholar broke it down into two acts: the monarch's petition to the state to release him from office—this petition was made by

the ruler as an individual—and the grant of release, which he accepts as
a state organ, and whatever he does in this capacity must be countersigned.
Few would be satisfied by such an artificial construction. It would never have
occurred to the scholar had he not wanted by all means to arrive at an outcome that was, in his eyes, a political necessity. In reality, abdication is a declaration made by the monarch not in the name of the state, but to the state;
that is, it is definitely not an act of government. Thus if one wishes, in opposition to the text of the constitution, to require a countersignature on it, this
might be achieved if, judging the relevant political interests, the legal principles of the constitution referring only to genuine acts of government are
extended by analogy to cases in which it seems reasonable for a personal decision by the head of state that strongly affects the national interest to be
treated like an act of government. However, I do not believe that the analogy
would be justified in this case, because I believe it absolutely imperative, in
the state's interest, that the head of state be able to decide with complete
freedom whether he considers his remaining in office or his removal to be
necessary.

The jurisprudence of construction in the law of the state is not loaded
with goal-oriented political considerations, consciously or unconsciously,
not when it deals with modest questions of detail. It is no exaggeration when
I say that the majority of theories of state that have become influential for
the law of the state—a majority of them legal constructions—were posited
with regard to political goals and used to justify political acts. The doctrines
of the state or social contract, of sovereignty, and of separation of powers
were not mere products of theoretical speculation, but have been from the
start the pillars of state and church policy. This can be followed into the modern period. The doctrine of the legal person of the state, like its opposite, the
private-law construction of the state, were, as Albrecht correctly saw, decisive
elements in the programs of political parties. The construction of the right
of the monarch as his own right to state power, the concept of the bearer of
state power, the formulation of the concept of the federal state were fashioned or used as crutches for political movements. Even Laband's doctrine
of the contrast between statutes in the material and in the formal sense, apparently politically quite neutral, grew out of the Prussian budget conflict
of the 1860s; it certainly had a political tendency, and the passion with which
it was fought by [Albert] Hänel had a political background. Gierke correctly
perceived an "unmistakably absolutist streak" in Laband's law of the state
[*Reichsstaatsrecht*], and something similar may be observed in Otto Mayer's
supposedly entirely apolitical administrative law constructions.

Yet in all these cases, it ultimately became clear that the most contradictory conclusions could be drawn from concepts; one could interpret the concepts more broadly or narrowly without being logically incorrect, and their
so-called rightness generally depended only on the breadth of the inductive

soil from which they sprang. Hobbes could have based his absolutism on the social contract as easily as the Monarchomachs or Milton and Sidney based on it the right to resist and depose, and Rousseau his democratic doctrine. The organic theory of the state could be used by [Nikolaus Thaddeus von] Gönner as the starting point for absolutist, by the Romantics for feudal, and by Hugo Preuss for democratic conclusions. The concept of sovereignty was formulated by [Jean] Bodin so as to support the French kingdom in its foreign and domestic policy. . . .

Thus it becomes clear that the logical school of the law of the state quite correctly accuses traditional scholarship of having used political goals and values to mold its own concepts, often in contradiction with its own basic methodological views. But we draw different conclusions from this than the intellectual purists. It is *not* our opinion that teleological considerations should be banned from legal theory. We believe that, instead of hiding behind the mask of logic, they must openly seek and claim their place in legal doctrine. Because law itself is nothing but a complex of value judgments on conflicts of interests, the teleological method is the suitable method for the object of legal theory. Thus in the law of the state too, we are not afraid of, but *demand,* a linkage of *political* considerations with logical, formal conceptual work. Today we make a stricter distinction between purely political and legal considerations than did the liberal public law scholars of the time of [Carl von] Rotteck and [Karl Theodor] Welcker or the conservatives, such as [Friedrich Julius] Stahl and others; we do not desire a return to the days when the law of the state was replaced by politics. And we especially loathe it when political trends try to distort the subsisting law. But we so little avoid the political that we even declare ourselves unable to interpret law without considering the political. Yet far be it from us to scorn legal construction as such. On the contrary, we recognize in it perhaps not the only, but certainly one valuable, and as yet unsurpassed, means of modeling systems, without which we would have had a difficult time mastering the material. We scholars of public law, especially, have much to be grateful for in this respect. Otto Mayer's method of construction was what actually allowed us to master the virtually limitless bulk of administrative law. Thus we make obeisance to *understanding* construction. We even appreciate construction, though with some reservations, when it serves as preparation for the second main task of the lawyer—supplementing the legal material by developing new legal precepts. For it provides us with comfortable labels we temporarily may give to legal phenomena that have yet to be examined, until we pass final judgment on them according to a principled weighing and judgment of interests. Thus construction may serve as a "hypothesis for subsumption and analogy." But should it try to play more than this heuristic part, should it dare to take on *gap-filling* functions, should it even behave as though it were the only method of salvation, then we will throw down the gauntlet.

It cannot be ignored that instrumental jurisprudence is exposed, and sometimes succumbs, to the danger of shallow relativism or raw utilitarianism; even Ihering did not always escape this danger. For the law of the state, above all, a method that bases all its interpretation and gap-filling on values seems questionable. "A state," said Gerber, "based on opinions can have only an insecure, unstable existence." But is the formal method of logic based any less on "opinions"? There is no doubt—and I ask you, my fellow students, always to remember this—that many public law concepts and axioms wearing the guise of the purely legal are nothing more than manifestations of political, even party-political tendencies. But teleological jurisprudence is forced to show its colors. It makes no secret of the fact that its results depend on value judgments. For a jurisprudence of interests that sets itself the task of "weighing" interests against each other must, if it is not to stop halfway, spell out the standards against which this weighing takes place. Instrumental jurisprudence makes it obvious, generally even to the untrained eye, when it reaches the border between subjective and objective assessment of interests. It is clear, however, that its task is to seek the standards it will follow in the objective sphere. We are all subject to error, and it can happen that we confuse subjective belief with objective validity. But such error is easier to discover than the mistake of logical construction. In any case, when we interpret and fill gaps we consider it our duty, in the law of the state as in private law—for there is only one legal method—we consider it our duty to stick, first of all, to the values we see expressed in laws. If this fails to help us, we are obliged to apply the standards we find in the legal consciousness of the legally bonded community. Even if we ultimately look into our hearts—if we decide, as required by the by-now classic provision of the Swiss civil code, on the basis of the rule we would create if we were legislator—we do not act according to individual caprice. The legislator also must create its norms not capriciously, but on the basis of factually justified considerations. Thus perhaps it could be better put as follows: In case of necessity, we decide as we *would have to* if we were the legislator. After all, our consciousness is merely part of an extra-individual spirit. When we look into our hearts, we are also reaching for eternal stars. For the jurisprudence of interests, the guiding star remains the *idea of law,* eternal *justice.* To serve only this is our duty; to serve it faithfully should be our vow.

SIX

Erich Kaufmann

INTRODUCTION

Stephen Cloyd

Erich Kaufmann (1880–1972) was a critical influence in reasserting the importance of history and sociological ideas in legal and state law scholarship. His 1921 *Critique of the Neo-Kantian Philosophy of Law* [*Kritik der neukantischen Rechtsphilosophie*] offered a penetrating and influential critique of the foundations and reasoning of the then-dominant school of legal positivism. For this, he is considered one of the founders of a new "idealist" [*geisteswissenschaftliche*] movement in Weimar legal scholarship, a movement that brought broader cultural and sociological perspectives to state law theory. While he never produced a comprehensive theoretical synthesis, his individual contributions taken together evolved a clearly articulated perspective on the most fundamental questions. He served both the Weimar Republic, and later, the Federal Republic, as a legal adviser and advocate on issues that mixed state law with international law, and published in both fields. His work reflected a unique combination of practical experience and philosophical and historical interest in the foundations of legal order.[1]

Kaufmann was a Protestant conservative. Born in Demmin, Pomerania, in 1880, he left Berlin's Königlichen Französischen Gymnasium and entered the University of Berlin in 1898. He intended to study philosophy and literary history but ended up studying philosophy and law. Although impressed by Wilhelm Dilthey and Georg Simmel, who were ornaments of the Berlin faculty, he was not really drawn to their perspectives. The Berlin law faculty's emphasis on the historical roots of law, however, may have had a latent influence. In any case, his philosophical hunger soon drew him elsewhere, to hear

Heinrich Rickert in Freiburg, from there to Heidelberg, Halle, Erlangen, and Kiel.

During this time, he considered himself a neo-Kantian. But his 1906 doctorate at Halle betrayed the influence of Otto Gierke's historical work. In 1908 Kaufmann completed his postdoctoral dissertation—the *Habilitationsschrift*—under Albert Hänel at Kiel. Hänel was a student of Robert von Mohl and a sensitive follower of Gierke, and his work pointed in the direction Kaufmann wanted to go. Hänel saw that law was a product of the state and institutions and urged scholars to study it from cultural and social perspectives, as well as with the more abstract methods of construction. Kaufmann's 1911 study, *The Essence of International Law and the Clausula rebus sic stantibus* [*Das Wesen des Völkerrechts und die Clausula rebus sic stantibus*], was dedicated to and well received by Gierke himself.[2]

The influence of Gierke and Hänel and his own reading of Hegel convinced Kaufmann not just that historical perspective was essential but that history offered the only insight into the problem of justice. Justice could not be discovered in the relational concepts of the science of jurisprudence, because it was a product of real, concrete institutions that could be understood only in the light of cultural history. Kaufmann also, more gradually, came to believe that despite their different historical expression, institutions were rooted in natural laws which provided an ethical foundation that could not be relativized by historical or other forms of scholarship. The insistence, on the one hand, on historical understanding, and on the other, an assertion of the limits to historical relativism set by natural law are at the heart of Kaufmann's work. From a perspective that he termed "objective idealism," he criticized both the positivist doctrines that Weimar's constitutional lawyers inherited from Imperial Germany and the work of scholars who had joined him in turning toward historical, sociological, and cultural perspectives.

Before the First World War, Kaufmann had adopted a Hegelian view of the state that emphasized unconditional sovereignty as a political necessity. He defined the state as "the organization that a people gives itself in order to knit itself into world history and to preserve its own character in world history." The self-preservation of the state was therefore "self-preservation for the purpose of participation in the cultural goods of humanity . . . in world history." Because there was no higher temporal good than this, the legal order of the national state was absolute by definition, as "the sovereign and universal . . . [order] that contains all others, limits them to their relative spheres and maintains and protects them within these." Kaufmann viewed the sovereign power of the state as the ultimate motor of all cultural development because it sought to mobilize all the physical and moral resources available: "From the consideration of power, the state becomes a welfare-state and a moral institution." In 1911 he wrote that "the social ideal is not the community of freely willing persons, but . . . victorious war," anticipating with these words what came to be called "the ideas of 1914."[3]

Germany's defeat and subsequent collapse after the First World War transformed Kaufmann's perspective, helping him to evolve a broader and more fruitful approach to the law of the state and politics. Returning wounded from the front in 1917, he remained conservative, a patriot, and even a nationalist. But his aggressive certainty about Germany's role in the world gave way to a greater concern about how the nation could best realize its own heritage within. He focused now on the limits of legal and constitutional order, and on the broader cultural and ethical foundations on which the Constitution and the laws rested.

In his 1921 *Critique of the Neo-Kantian Philosophy of Law* [*Kritik der neukantischen Rechtsphilosophie*], Kaufmann argued that German political and legal thought had played a role in the German defeat. German political philosophy and philosophy of law broke down because they lacked a sociological foundation. "Because we had no philosophy of law or philosophy of the state, because state and society were only supported by fading legacies, the legacies of Kant, Hegel, Stahl, and Marx, and not by their own living social philosophy, in the end both stood on insecure foundations and collapsed in the great historical test that the German spirit, like the German state, had to undergo in the world war." This, according to Kaufmann, was why the "spiritually duller and weaker nations" had proved "sociologically stronger" in the war.[4]

Kaufmann's *Critique* attacked the then-dominant school of liberal positivism on several levels, but the core of his argument concerned its failure to relate constitutional and legal issues to their social, material, and political foundations. "In neo-Kantianism the *intelligible* ordering of the legal world is degraded to *abstract generality* or even to a *technical-legal formalism* and the meta-legal/sociological is degraded to value-free material for classification." This reduction was politically dangerous. "Our conception of social phenomena has taken on a *sterile, static,* and *formal-juridical* perspective, and this leads to an *underestimation of sociological forces,* as well as to an *overestimation of legal forms* which are equally dangerous in domestic and foreign policy."[5]

Kaufmann's *Critique* was quickly cited by other scholars who were dissatisfied with formalism, including Hermann Heller, Rudolf Smend, and Carl Schmitt.[6] Kaufmann's plea for a broad sociological perspective and the sense of the openness and unavoidable fragility of a living constitutional order that he conveyed in the work helped push Weimar state law theory and law along new more sociologically and historically oriented paths.

At the same time, however, Kaufmann's *Critique* offered a warning. Blind to the "concrete spiritual values" that shaped social reality, neo-Kantianism encouraged contempt for such values on the one hand and hopeless relativism on the other. When concrete values were replaced by abstraction, the result was "a theory of knowledge that lacks a concept of truth, psychology without a soul, jurisprudence without a concept of law and a formal ethics of conviction without a concept of morality." Neo-Kantian rationalism promoted the opposite of what its proponents intended; it appeared as "the direct predecessor of the self-despairing Spenglerian atmosphere, the most recent disease . . ." of the German soul.[7] The reaction against oppressive formalism threatened to go too far and end in nihilism. Faced with the crisis of building new, living constitutional forms, Germany needed to reject both rationalism, whose forms were sterile, undying only because they had never lived, and "an unrestrained vitalism and complete dissolution of law in sociology." Kaufmann was confident that "the inexhaustible metaphysical and mystical depth of the German spirit" would not fail to meet this challenge.[8]

Kaufmann's response to the crisis reflected his understanding of the limits of reason. His 1922 essay on the conservative party and its history offered his strongest assertion of those limits. Conservative thought did not pursue "less clear and less rational thought than rationalism" by respecting the power of the nonrational. Conservatives knew full well that all thought was "a rational endeavor." At the same time, however, they perceived "the limits inherent to all rational thinking and to the comprehension of living reality by means of concepts." In accepting these limits, conservative thought took up a theme of Kant's own thought, "only it reacted against . . . the hubris of reason believing that it can grasp the essential, the heart of the matter, through a rationalizing, causal, or teleological analysis of life." Rational thinking itself was "only a particular and thus finally irrational activity of the human spirit."[9]

Kaufmann would, in his later work, always be at his best and most interesting when he was thinking about questions of limits: the limits to reason, to understanding, to law and the expression of will. He found positive law to be limited in the same way that reason was limited. This, however, did not mean that there were no "foundations." Kaufmann came to believe that the idea of natural law recognized an essential truth, that certain principles of justice were objectively given, and his 1926 conference paper "Equality before the Law" stated this, though without elaboration. Influenced by the antifoundational legacies of both the historical school and legal positivism, most of his colleagues in the Association of German Teachers of the Law of the State [*Vereinigung der deutschen Staatsrechtslehrer*] vehemently rejected his arguments.[10]

The contrast between Kaufmann's views and his colleagues' may have been due to Kaufmann having acquired, at this period, practical experience that encouraged him to reach for such foundations. After 1922, he served as an adviser to the German government and its legal representative on issues of German minority rights and property in Poland and in other occupied territories, and as Germany's legal representative to the international arbitration-tribunal set up under the Dawes Plan. Working between legal cultures, and beyond the shadow of positive law, Kaufmann had to pursue a more fundamental definition of justice, which in turn influenced his view of state law theory.

Natural law, Kaufmann argued, set forth principles of justice that stood above positive law, and to which legislators were bound as well. Every positive order had to be rooted in these. "Only if certain highest principles of justice remain valid can legislation truly be accounted as law." Kaufmann spoke of his conviction that "that which lies beyond historical change and beyond applicable positive law is not less real than the given positive order, yes, that this is the truly real, in which we are rooted by the best that is within us . . . if we wish to make law and judge legal matters."[11]

The publication of Rudolf Smend's *Constitution and Constitutional Law* [*Verfassung und Verfassungsrecht*] in 1928 finally led Kaufmann to give a more complete account of his own position. Smend appeared to regard the psychological and cultural conditioning of citizens through their participation in politics as the only foundation for political institutions and constitutional order. Kaufmann held that, in exploring the psychological processes and the cultural dynamics of constitutional life, Smend treated the resulting institutions as historically contingent and without essential content. Kaufmann himself, by contrast, believed that institutions did possess essential ethical contents, that there were real and fundamental categories, problems, and underlying laws of political organization and constitutional life. He found Smend's approach too value-neutral.

Both men belonged to the broader "idealist" tendency that was critical of neo-Kantian formalism and had supported one another in their arguments. But Kaufmann had moved to a distinctive position.[12] His appeal to natural law complemented his concern with cultural history and with sociological realism. He argued that society was objectively differentiated into institutions whose goals or teleology reflected natural law; although this differentiation and the form of the resulting institutions might be historically determined, the goals embodied in social institutions as such revealed ultimate norms. Thus, through these goals, Kaufmann insisted, social reality revealed itself as a more fundamental reality than any ordering created by law.[13]

The idea of law could not, he argued, even be recognized and understood in the abstract provisions of law, but only within the structure of real, objective institutions. Only in the context of such institutions could the notion of justice itself have meaning.[14]

Kaufmann first fleshed out these ideas in two fundamental papers, his 1931 paper "On the Problem of the People's Will" and his 1932 paper "Hegel's Philosophy of Law." In the 1931 paper, Kaufmann gave the idea of "people's will" [*Volkswille*] sociological definition. What is original in the essay and characteristic of Kaufmann is its emphasis on limits. The people's will could be formed and represented only through particular institutional arrangements with inherent limitations. At the historical moment, Kaufmann felt his countrymen had lost sight of those limitations, and he sought to illuminate some of the political and ethical dangers.

Kaufmann feared political relativism. He feared for the fate of the Constitution in a world contested by ideologies, but without standards to judge their truth and ethical justification. He offered a sophisticated explanation of how natural law could limit such relativism. "Legislated" [*gesetzte*] law, he argued, could "be understood only on the basis of unwritten law," thus "even the *pouvoir constituant* is not an absolute sovereign; even it is bound to preexisting unwritten fundamental principles and to particular real categories."[15] His work pioneered the arguments with which some German constitutional lawyers would assert natural law as an essential defense of rights and institutions after 1945, when the necessity of such limits had become apparent to all.

The Third Reich brought an end to Kaufmann's government service. It is worthy of note that his most important professional works between 1933 and 1945, all concerning matters of international law, were published abroad in French. In Germany, he was an intellectual supporter of Hitler's conservative opponents. The regime stripped him of his teaching privileges, and in 1939 he emigrated to the Netherlands, where he remained until 1945.[16]

After the Second World War, Kaufmann once again helped reestablish Germany's relationships with its neighbors and occupiers under international law. The founding of the Federal Republic then brought him new tasks as legal counsel to the chancellor's office and the German Foreign Office, especially in matters concerning the occupation and partition of Germany. For his services, he received many honors, including the civilian *pour le mérite* (1952) and the Great Service Cross of the Federal Republic in 1955, among others.

MAJOR WORKS

Gesammelte Schriften. Edited by Albert Hilger van Scherpenberg et al. Volume 1: *Autorität und Freiheit.* Volume 2: *Der Staat in der Rechtsgemeinschaft der Völker.* Volume 3: *Rechtsidee und Recht.* Göttingen: Otto Schwartz, 1960. Abbreviated below as "GS" with volume and page numbers.

Auswärtige Gewalt und Kolonialgewalt in den Vereinigten Staaten von Amerika. Berlin: Duncker & Humblot, 1908.

Über den Begriff des Organismus in der Staatslehre des 19. Jahrhunderts. Heidelberg: C. Winter, 1908. GS 3: 46–66.

Das Wesen des Völkerrechts und die Clausula rebus sic stantibus—Rechtsphilosophische Studie zum Rechts-, Staats-, und Vertragsbegriffe. Tübingen: Mohr, 1911.

Grundfragen der künftigen Reichsverfassung. Berlin: Noss, 1919. GS 1:253–96.

Kritik der neukantischen Rechtsphilosophie. Tübingen: Mohr, 1921. GS 3:177–246.

"Über die konservative Partei und ihre Geschichte." In *Schriften der Deutschen Gesellschaft für Politik an der Universität Halle-Wittenberg,* no. 2, edited by Heinrich Waentig. Bonn and Leipzig: Deutsche Gesellschaft für Politik an der Universität Halle-Wittenberg, 1922. GS 3:133–75.

Die Gleichheit vor dem Gesetz im Sinne des Art. 109 der Reichsverfassung. Berlin and Leipzig: de Gruyter, 1927. GS 3:246–65.

"Zur Problematik des Volkswillens." In *Beiträge zum öffentlichen Recht und Völkerrecht,* no. 17, edited by Viktor Bruns. Berlin and Leipzig: de Gruyter, 1931. GS 3: 272–84.

"Hegels Rechtsphilosophie." In *Hegelfeier der Friedrich-Wilhelm Universität zu Berlin am 14.11.1931,* edited by Eduard Spranger, 15–24. Berlin: Preussische Druckerei und Verlag, 1932. GS 3:285–96.

"Die Anthropologisch Grundlagen der Staatstheorien—Bemerkungen zu Rousseau, Luther und Kant." In *Rechtsprobleme in Staat und Kirche-Festschrift für Rudolf Smend-Göttinger Rechtswissenschaftliche Studien,* edited by the Rechts- und Staatswissenschaftliche Fakultät der Universität Göttingen, 177–88. Göttingen: Schwartz, 1952. GS 3:363–74.

"Die Grenzen der Verfassungsgerichtsbarkeit." In *Veröffentlichungen der Vereinigung der Deutschen Staatsrechtslehrer,* no. 9, pp. 1–16. Berlin: de Gruyter, 1952. GS 3: 500–514.

"Die Grenzen des verfassungsmäßigen Verhaltens nach dem Bonner Grundgesetz, insbesondere: Was ist unter einer freiheitlichen demokratischen Grundordnung zu verstehen?" In *Verhandlungen des 39. Deutschen Juristentages in Stuttgart, 1951,* no. 39, edited by the Deutscher Juristentag, 417–31. Tübingen: Mohr, 1952. GS 1:515–28.

"Carl Schmitt und seine Schule—Offener Brief an Ernst Forsthoff." In *Deutscher Rundschau,* 1013–15. Berlin: Deutscher Rundschau, 1958. GS 3:375–77.

LITERATURE

Bauer, Wolfram. *Wertrelativismus und Wertbestimmtheit im Kampf um die Weimarer Demokratie.* Berlin: Duncker & Humblot, 1968.

Castrucci, Emanuele. *Tra organicismo e 'Rechtsidee': Il pensiero giuridico di Erich Kaufmann. Per la storia del pensiero giuridico moderno.* Edited by Emanuele Castrucci. Milano: Giuffre, 1984.

Cloyd, D. Stephen. "Weimar Republicanism: Political Sociology and Constitutional Law in Weimar Germany." Ph.D. diss., University of Rochester, 1991.

Freiherr von der Heydte, Friedrich August. "Das Rechtsphilosophische Anliegen Erich Kaufmanns. Versuch einer Deutung." In *Um Recht und Gerechtigkeit. Festgabe für Erich Kaufmann zu seinem 70. Geburtstage -21. September 1950,* edited by Hermann Jahrreiss et al., 391–400. Stuttgart and Cologne: W. Kohlhammer, 1950.

Heller, Hermann. *Hegel und der nationale Machtstaatsgedanke in Deutschland: Ein Beitrag zur politischen Geistesgeschichte.* Leipzig: Teuber, 1921. In *Gesammelte Schriften.* 2nd ed. Edited by Christoph Müller. Tübingen: Mohr, 1992.

Rennert, Klaus. *Die "geisteswissenschaftliche Richtung" in der Staatsrechtslehre der Weimarer Republik: Untersuchungen zu Erich Kaufmann, Günther Holstein und Rudolf Smend.* Berlin: Duncker & Humblot, 1987.

Smend, Rudolf. "Die Vereinigung der Deutschen Staatsrechtslehrer und der Richtungsstreit." In *Festschrift für Ulrich Scheuner zum 70. Geburtstag,* edited by Horst Ehmke. Berlin: Duncker & Humblot, 1973.

————. "Zu Erich Kaufmanns wissenschaftlichem Werk." In *Festgabe,* edited by Hermann Jahrreiss, Bodo Börner, and Klaus Stern, 103–22. Cologne: C. Heymann, 1984.

Wendenburg, Helge. *Die Debatte um die Verfassungsgerichtsbarkeit und der Methodenstreit der Staatsrechtslehre in der Weimarer Republik.* Göttinger Rechtswissenschaftliche Studien, vol. 128. Göttingen: Otto Schwartz, 1984.

ON THE PROBLEM OF THE PEOPLE'S WILL

Erich Kaufmann

Originally appeared as *Zur Problematik des Volkswillens,* in Viktor Bruns, ed., *Beiträge zum öffentlichen Recht und Völkerrecht,* vol. 17 (Berlin and Leipzig: de Gruyter, 1931). Reprinted in Erich Kaufmann, *Gesammelte Schriften,* edited by Albert Hilger van Scherpenberg et al., vol. 3 (Göttingen: Otto Schwartz, 1960), 272–84. Translated by Stephen Cloyd.

The concept of the "people's will" [*Volkswille*] presupposes the concept of the "people's spirit" [*Volksgeist*]. Both concepts stem from the political and legal philosophy of the eighteenth century and found their classic expression more than one hundred years ago. The psychologism and positivism of the second half of the nineteenth century and the early twentieth century frequently denied them or believed they ought to epistemologically dissolve and undermine them. I do not overlook the fact that they need a new foundation. However, I believe that the contemporary philosophical trend, turning away from neo-Kantian epistemological theory toward ontology, with its characteristic renaissance of Aristotle, Thomas Aquinas, and a Hegel who is once again being correctly understood, may succeed in providing the foundation for a new ontological treatment of the problem. Insofar as I regard the problem as an ontological one, I oppose the philosophers and scholars of the humanities who believe that they are able to discover or create a specific kind of idealist thinking, or even a humanistic logic distinct from that of the natural sciences. This belief overlooks the ontological laws common to both spheres and ignores the fact that the reality forming the object of the humanities also has its own laws that make possible not only knowledge but also action. The two great spheres of knowledge differ not in their thinking, but in their objects. The objects of the humanities are also real, transsubjective external objects, which the knowledge-seeking subject wishes to comprehend or reveal.

People's spirit and people's will are real entities with a specific structure of being. They do not exhaust their mode of being in the psychic acts of the individuals who make up the people; they are not the product of integration or the result of acts taken to unify wills. But they are also not mere intellectual constructs; they cannot be regarded as such even if one recognizes and affirms the objectivity of the intellectual constructs as detached from specific acts of the individuals who produce or reproduce them, and their facticity transcending and binding the subjects. They are neither intellectual constructs like the propositions of mathematics or logic or like a melody, a building, a legal system, nor comparable to a Beethoven symphony interpreted by a particular artist, nor to a legal order as interpreted by a particular supreme court, nor, finally, to the way of being of a particular dead or living language. The wholeness of all these phenomena that may possibly be called intellectual constructs is of a different kind than that of the phenomena of people's spirit and people's will. The latter have a different kind of reality than the former.

Ontological research has not yet addressed all these phenomena of the humanities. The epoch in which it was self-evident that the single tree of a philosophical system would also bear the fruits of the philosophy of history, of law, and of the state seems to have ended, at least for the time being, with Hegel's death. It seems rather that it has become the task of specialized disciplines, should they focus on the foundations of their own areas of research, to find their own way. Here, however, I want to resist the temptation to open up the question of the mode of being or ontological structure of the phenomena of people's spirit and people's will. I do not even want to debate the question—even though it is in fact of central importance for our problem—of the embodiment of the character of collectivities as personalities with the opposing views of the most impressive ethical thinkers of recent times, Max Scheler and Nicolai Hartmann. Nor do I want to analyze the concept of will.

I want only to consider a few structural laws of these phenomena and, by presenting such structural laws, contribute to the great problem of what constitutes the mode of being of the people's will. Looking at concrete and contemporary constitutional problems, I shall attempt to develop a few precepts of constitutional theory. I will thereby avoid the misuse of the history of ideas in constitutional theory; the refusal to see, beyond pure ideology, any genuine idea; the mistakes of adopting too much typology while overlooking the essence typologically differentiating itself, and of allowing for too much idealist dynamism while ignoring the substance and its constant, stable, inherent laws.

The people's spirit is an objectively real entity that shows its effect in and through individuals and that is just as basic a reality as the spiritual life of the individual. As a reality that embraces generations it has its own laws, distinct from those that order the spiritual life of the individual. With his birth the individual is received into it and molded by it; and after he is thus received and molded, he carries it further along, and weaves his fiber into its cloth. The people's spirit has diverse effects on the individuals, and the individuals bear it in different ways. It is deposited in particular emotional and spiritual values, above all generally in particular presentations of value, especially ethical ones—in traditions, manners, legends, symbols, poetry, music, language, and so on. But it is only deposited in them and it is not consumed by them. Spirit must always actualize itself in forms. Thus, all of these phenomena are necessary forms of expression for the people's spirit but are not the people's spirit as such. It is rather the final source and substance irreducible to anything simpler that manifests itself in all these forms of expression. It is a temporal entity, possessing all that belongs to the nature of the temporal; exactly for this reason it is a spiritual substance that is not completely consumed by time but rather reveals itself, unfolds and realizes itself through the temporal.

Because the concept of the people is at heart a political concept, it is above all the political experiences that a people, as a people, has had, that form the substance of its people's spirit, and influence and determine its willing and its acting: The memory of political heroes, of power and fame, of social upheavals, of humiliation and insult, of poverty and suffering, of rebellion, rise, and freedom.

As a political entity, the people must possess a political will. This political will is first of all a will to live and a will to matter. It is, in other words, the will to be a people and the will to have an independent state as the politically unified will of the people. Further, it is will to form, not a will to romantic or classic self-fashioning but the will to forming and ordering the social forces within and to cooperate in forming an international order and to fit into it. It is, in short, the will to fulfill the eternal tasks of the state, according to the sometimes constant, sometimes changing spatial and temporal particularities of the people and to do this with the people's own particular ethical and spiritual powers and talents.

As real as the will of the people is, it is in essence unshaped as well as in need of shape. Within it there ring and swing the most varied, thwarting, and even opposing movements; it contains within itself endless possibilities, but of course only the possibilities of its concrete self. A different choirmaster can make it sing with a different tone. Great events that touch the people's innermost will to live and to matter can call forth powerful and unified responses, in the presence of which conflicting sentiments retreat or fall silent. The will of the people can manifest itself only through individual personalities and in individual personalities; only there can its multitude of inherent possibilities take concrete form and can it become an acting will. It requires personal shapers and bearers, by its very essence it requires *representation*. The greatest and most portentous error ever made in political theory is Rousseau's dictum "La volonté ne se représente pas." The concept of representation is one of the decisive basic categories of all spiritual and value-laden conduct; a topic now so often intellectually trivialized, it desperately needs more serious investigation and clarification.

The representatives of the people's will are those individual persons who, as members of the people as a whole, have the ability to shape the previously unshaped people's will within themselves and to shape it in such a manner that the people feels and accepts it an expression of its own will. In themselves they represent the totality of the people to the people itself as well as to the external world: they become organs. How this happens and when it is achieved cannot be put into a purely rational formula, especially since the opposition to certain strongly expressed currents of the people's will may be in highest harmony with it. The seemingly unpopular can be the truly popular.

The mission of the shapers and bearers of people's will is to recognize the situation and the task at hand, to will the goal and to carry out the recognized and willed goal in reality, a reality that always, on the one hand, has to be able as well as ready to assimilate to the goal, as, on the other hand, it will resist the assimilation. Only single personalities can do all of this, and they can do it only when they know that they are representative organs of the people, are known by the people as such and are such in substance.

It is a pure question of charisma, how, if, and to what extent this goal is ever achieved. No legal or constitutional arrangement can guarantee its realization. A constitution can do nothing more than create and establish frames in which the people's actual ethical and charismatic powers can find expression in a legal order. It is pointless to expect or demand something more or something different. The law in its formality neither creates charisma nor makes it superfluous. It sets up norms assigning competence, norms regulating procedures, and norms of behavior to ensure the orderly progress of the process of forming the will. It assumes that the people possesses a fund of ethical, intellectual, and political powers. Its true and only function is to provide a frame for all healthy and constructive social forces. Every hyperspiritualization of constitutional *law* ignores its essence and limits.

Of course, one cannot expect that in every moment the gifts of insight, of will, and of realization as of the capacity for substantial representation will be embodied in particular persons or that exactly those persons will occupy the right legal positions. This comes to pass only on rare and happy historical occasions. The cry for the leader of genius is a hysterical cry and a cry of impotence. A great deal has already been accomplished if the interplay of constitutional norms regularly brings men with but one of these gifts to the right positions who understand how to surround themselves with supplementary advisers and assistants. This must always be the goal in implementing the provisions of constitutional law.

In the broadest sense, every organ that serves to form, express, and realize the will of the state is within its own sphere an organ of people's will—including the monarch, the head of state of a republic, the civil servants, the
military. In a special sense we are speaking of organs of people's will in reference to bearers who are established not according to the organizational
principle of hierarchical unity but according to that of associational pluralism. What does that mean and how is it possible?

In constitutional theory the meaning of the bearers of the people's will
in the special sense takes into account that the plurality does not only accept and approve the government and its activities in silence and express its
approval in periodic acclamations—although without at least *this* acceptance or approval it would be impossible for the state to rule or the will to be
formed. The meaning of the bearers of the people's will lies in providing the
plurality as such with constitutional forms in which it proclaims, through
explicit, formalized, and normativized acts, that it accepts the actions of the
authorities and confirms and approves them as an expression of the will of
the people as a whole. This can take place in two different forms: either in
the form of the so-called direct plebiscite, or in a manner that confers the
vote on the substance upon a popular assembly and limits the so-called direct expression of the people's will to the election of representatives.

Fundamentally, it makes no difference here whether one is discussing
the different kinds of Roman *comitia,* a larger or smaller circle of active citizens, an assembly of notables, the representative bodies of the feudal estates, or modern parliaments. Those distinctions are decisive from the perspective of more-or-less developed democracy and from the perspective of
social strata claiming the right to political influence, but for the laws expli-
cated here do not matter, since these laws are the same for all different kinds
of pluralistic will-formation.

First, in this context, one should note that even in so-called plebiscites, the
people's will is far from being expressed directly, i.e., in a manner unmediated by representation. The people's will is neither more nor less present in
a real sense in the eligible active citizens, even when they are taken as a
whole, than it is in every other bearer and shaper of people's will. The totality of active citizens is a representation of the people's will for particular
purposes, and this totality is also a representation of the people's will only
insofar as the spirit of the people lives within it, and is interpreted by it correctly. Even the totality of active citizens is not the people in its unmediated,
generation-spanning, living unity. Quite apart from the children, the aged,
the sick, the absent, and those excluded from active citizenship, all of whom
are also vessels and bearers of the people's will, it is always only the generation of the moment that speaks in and for the moment, but that ideally is supposed to speak as the representative of the people as a reality transcending

the generations. Even for it the sentence "La volonté ne se représente pas" is a falsehood.

By their very nature, so-called direct plebiscites do not permit the plurality to take positive, substantive action. It can only answer the question that is put to it with a yes or a no. In such a plebiscite the plurality can only approve or disapprove the content from without and from above, whether it concerns legislative proposals, the dissolution of established organs of the state, a decision about the political division of territory, or any other issue. Everything depends on the content of the question—and the plurality cannot participate in or even exert influence over its formulation. Here there is no deliberation, no discussion, no possibility of amendment—only consent or denial of consent. This is the first law of formation of the people's will: The more directly the people as plurality wishes to speak, the less influence it will have on the substance of what actually happens.

Representative bodies serve to increase the influence of the plurality at the cost of a loss of immediacy. But even to the representative body as a pluralistic organ, true action, the exercise of dominion, remains forbidden by nature, whatever may be said in the text of the constitution or in some political ideology. When it comes to a final vote, the culmination of all their efforts, even representative assemblies can only say yes or no, only consent or deny consent to the matter put before them. But—and herein lies their specific character—they are able to do this following deliberation. This is not governmental or administrative deliberation concerning actions to be taken; rather, the specific character of parliamentary deliberation lies in the fact that it aims at either consent or denial of consent. Parliamentary deliberation is at one and the same time public deliberation, of course to crystallize the truth out of a dialectic of argument and counter argument, but rather to say publicly everything that seems necessary to justify parliamentary action and influence the electorate. Parliamentary speeches are essentially intended to be overheard by the public, in order to maintain contact and ties with the electorate and to give it an inner sense of participation in the parliamentary process. Parliamentary deliberation takes continual account of the electorate's consent or denial of consent.

Deliberation offers the possibility of amending the issue at hand, and can even advance to a form of collaboration, when consent is made conditional on changes or certain conditions. But there are essential limits to these possibilities. Whatever the written constitution may decree or a constitutional ideology say, even parliament remains, in the final analysis, an organ of consent and denial of consent: it can never become an active organ. Even parliamentary government does not mean government by parliament but remains government by government, which bears its own independent, unique responsibility for that which is its task and its task alone: to act and to govern.

If it rejects unjustified demands for collaboration or requests for amendments for which it does not wish to be held responsible, it forces parliament to express either confidence or no-confidence in the government, to give consent or to deny it. Or it can dissolve parliament to appeal to the electorate in order to determine whether the actions of those elected are to be approved or disapproved. The "action du parlement sur le gouvernement" is balanced by the "action du gouvernement sur le parlement."

Thus, a denial of consent by parliament is also responsible in the sense that every denial of consent, whether it concerns vital bills or the survival of a particular government, carries with it the duty to consent to something else. It is therefore an inherent law of parliamentary government that a parliament capable only of denial, but incapable of consent, eliminates itself. Such a parliament violates the unwritten fundamental laws—so essential that they need not be written—upon which its existence itself rests and thus also violates the constitution that depends upon its own functioning. It is parliament that would be guilty of the initial violation of the constitution, not the government that, called to action and independently obligated, would govern without the consent of a parliament incapable of giving consent. For the most extreme case there ultimately exists implied emergency power that belongs, together with the emergency law formalized and normativized in the constitution, to the fund of unwritten natural law inherent in every constitution.

On the other hand, the more tactfully and responsibly a parliament respects the inherent limits of its rights of amendment and its opportunities for collaboration, and remains conscious that the end of all of its deliberations is either consent or its denial, the more smoothly the parliamentary system will function. Then the head of state, who, however the text of the constitution may define him, is the chief and final governor of the formation of the will of the state, is less likely to need to act. Then his function will remain limited to dotting the i's, as Hegel put it. The law that the weakness and failure of one organ strengthens another, or that the strength and effective functioning of one organ may reduce the importance of another, applies to every form of government. It reflects the organic character of the people's community.

Parliament is, of course, only the frame into which the extra-parliamentary forces of the people, organized into political parties for the sake of political effectiveness and influence, are gathered in order to form majorities on the floor of parliament that can support a government. If this parliamentary frame and floor were swept away, that would not destroy the existing social and political powers outside parliament; rather, it would abandon those forces to unstructured and irresponsible conflicts. Naturally, the more divided the populace, the more difficult it is to bring and keep these forces together so that they form a parliamentary majority; but on the other hand the necessity to do so, and to give the political conflict organizational, legal, and ethical form by means of parliament, will be all the greater. The less successful this undertaking is, the stronger must be the powers of the government: They must be stronger than the strongest powers available to extra-parliamentary social and political forces. However, since the ultimate source of the powers of government is always the extra-parliamentary forces of the people, this dialectic can lead to a situation where a people in which the internal conflicts are more vigorous than the unifying power of a shared political fate and more powerful than the compulsion for ordered political action will be drawn into the maw of civil war.

The purely plebiscitary form of government, Bonapartism, requires a Bonaparte; if he is lacking, the bureaucracy, which decides by itself what questions the plebiscite will answer, will be all-powerful. The plebiscitary form of government always remains precarious, because no one can say from where the new Bonaparte will arise, if the present one loses the plebiscite. The so-called direct expression of the people's will, which can only say yes or no, reduces the influence of the plurality to a minimum. If parliament is conscious of its responsibility and its limits and uses its power to deny consent accordingly, it will at the same time always be a parliament capable of consent. This is the truth within the somewhat romantically expressed thesis that parliament also has the function to provide a forum for the selection of leaders. If its composition properly reflects its institutional essence, it will provide what is lacking in a purely plebiscitary system and be the natural reservoir from which individuals can come forth who have the ability to gather behind a new consent after consent has been denied.

This raises the great problem of the right to take part in the full electoral process, the problem of the so-called direct expression of the will of the people, concerned not with deciding particular substantive issues or discarding particular persons, but with the positive activity of choosing particular persons as the parliamentary trustees.

Here we encounter the by-now familiar law that the people in its so-called immediacy can only give or deny consent. It can only say yes or no to candidates presented to it from without and above. The plurality can put up no candidates. The principle that only individuals can act and that the plurality is restricted to either giving or denying consent is valid not only where there are established legal norms and forms for forming the will, but in all cases where a plurality is supposed to be effective: in every club, in every group, every business corporation, every association, every organization, including political parties. Robert Michels demonstrated clearly that this law of the elite applies to the whole social sphere.

The manner in which candidates are chosen is not regulated by norms; thus the creation in political parties of the more-or-less anonymous organizations that fulfill this function and that, of course, succumb to the same law. Those who want candidates other than those that the parties present, who want the parties to be divided according to a set of principles different from those according to which they have formed, are without a voice. The law concerning immediacy in the expression of the people's will also applies to electoral arrangements.

There is a second law in addition to this first: The truer the reflection of existing forces and their numerical strength among the people one seeks by means of proportional representation, the more empty of content and influence shall be the will of the people at elections.

The practice of proportional representation is intended to gather together all the votes within the borders of the state and to insure that no voter's voice is lost and that parliament reflects the relative strength of the parties with the greatest possible mathematical accuracy. As a result, proportional representation causes a mobilization of all the parties against one another. It does not permit an inward reconciliation by the voters themselves within a local voting district. Every member of parliament is elected only by the voters of his own party; they are the only people he needs to take account of, since he is dependent only on their consent. Thus, proportional representation has a tendency to radicalize political and parliamentary life. It manages to ferret out all the preexisting conflicts among the people and it will make them bigger and cruder. Every conflicting ideological, political, social, and economic interest may serve as the basis for building a party and putting forward an electoral list. Proportional representation can strengthen the large parties, but can also threaten them with splintering. It can unite widely scattered but valuable minorities but at the same time encourage the formation of splinter parties, particularly of parties based on economic interest. Its effects are unpredictable precisely because of its purely arithmetic character. As a result, it does not create a mirror image, as it seeks to do, but rather projected images with a variety of views and perspectives thrown on parliament lying side-by-side and overlapping according to the positions of the parties. The idea that what is being elected is an organ with essentially determined functions and limits is obscured by the numerical addition of party loyalties.

Once the voter has cast his declaration of loyalty into the big adding machine at the polls, his work is over. It is then once again the party organizations' responsibility to determine how the results will influence the formation of a majority in parliament. But the formation of a majority capable of giving consent is the truly decisive act of political will in parliamentary life. Proportional representation excludes the voters from precisely this decisive act.

To be sure, in the majority-based electoral system circumstances may dictate that many voters' ballots have no influence. But then ballots are not reduced to mere declarations of party loyalty. The vote, especially in run-off elections, elicits less party loyalty; it aims, rather, at the real goal of an election: at the formation of a particular parliamentary majority. It is less true to party but, as a result, has greater influence. The vote may count for less, but it possesses a richer political content and is a stronger declaration of the will to form politically. The voter himself is called upon to participate in the inner reconciliation of party conflicts to create a majority will, an all-important creation from which proportional representation excludes him. The voter gains what the party machine and the party bureaucrats lose. A majority of the members elected to parliament are not elected by supporters of their own party alone. Such a representative needs the support of the coalition formed by reconciliation within the local election district, which has not elected him as an anonymous number from a list. All this may be more successfully achieved when the second round is not a true runoff election but, like the election of the president [*Reichspräsident*], an unrestricted election. Elections are not about party statistics: Their goal is to consent or deny consent to individuals who are to form an organ, whose function is to consent or deny consent to a government formed by specific individuals and a particular governmental policy. In comparison to proportional representation, the majority ballot increases the influence of the voter at the expense of numerical-statistical veracity, just as the creation of a representative body increases the influence of the plurality at the expense of immediacy.

Those nations which, either out of conscious or instinctive insight into the purposes for which a parliament is called and is alone prepared, have, as in England, completely rejected the proportional ballot or, as in France, having tried it, abolished it. In the Weimar National Assembly, Friedrich Naumann warned against it as incompatible with the parliamentary system.

The more direct, pure, and numerically exact one seeks to make the expression of the people's will, the more one takes away its influence, content, and will. This is the insight, confirmed by experience, that must be gained by a constitutional theory aiming at a recognition of the inherent laws of the formation of the people's will and avoiding formalistic and ideological, i.e., also historicist, constitutional interpretation. Not everyone who mocks his positivist chains is free.

Action; consent and denial of consent; deliberation with regard to action; deliberation with regard to consent or denial of consent; these are the fundamental categories of each and every constitutional life—whether the constitution is democratic or takes some other form. Only knowledge of the essence, the limits, and the variance of these fundamental categories can make possible an understanding of constitutional history, constitutional law, constitutional politics, constitutional sociology and also of the history of political ideas with its truths and errors. A genuine constitutional theory must find its way to the insights that lie behind all these disciplines and perspectives and that serve as the foundation of them all. Everything that has ever happened in constitutional history is bound to these categories and the laws they obey; they are the only basis for understanding the origin, survival, and dissolution of individual constitutions, for judging their success and failure. Just as everything individual is a distinct and concrete variant and expression of a universal, so the individuality of a constitution rests on how individual peoples have in their individual spirit succeeded in giving these categories ethical and spiritual content in particular historical contexts.

It follows that the necessary point of departure for all constitutional theory is an insight into what the people's spirit and the people's will actually are. All questions of constitutional form retreat before the significance of this reality. Only this insight can convey understanding of what the institution of norms and establishment of forms in constitutional law means and can achieve. Only this insight can secure comprehension of what it is that good political sense and the formative power of the ethic have to accomplish in this legal framework, whatever social strata may be the leading influence. A morally uncorrupted people's will, instinctively or insightfully aware of the intrinsic laws of political life and of the imperatives of the historical moment, will shed illusions and ideologies alien to its essence and reality and create the forms and organizations that it needs, and it will know how to wield these forms and organizations with political and ethical insight.

SEVEN

Rudolf Smend

INTRODUCTION

Stefan Korioth

Rudolf Smend (15 January 1882–5 July 1975) was born into a family of lawyers and theologians. His scholarly work, though of comparatively limited volume, was crucial to the development in Germany in this century of the theories of the state, broadly conceived, and of the law of the state, conceived as a matter of doctrine. The main themes of Smend's work were legal and constitutional history, state and constitutional theory, and finally, especially after 1945, Protestant church law and the law of church and state. Smend focused on the fundamental concepts of state and constitutional theory; he was less concerned with doctrinal, systematic ventures into positive law. At the core of his work was the "theory of integration," created in the 1920s. This theory is Smend's own attempt to oppose a theory of state and constitution, in a very specific sense "idealistically" [*geisteswissenschaftlich*] and "sociologically" oriented, to the state law positivism associated with the names of Carl Friedrich von Gerber, Paul Laband, Georg Jellinek, and Hans Kelsen.

Smend's dissertation, which he presented in Göttingen at the age of 22, elaborated the principles of Prusso-German law of the monarchic state, using as an example the Prussian Constitution of 1850; he compared it with the Belgian Constitution, which contained some of the same wording but was based on the principle of popular sovereignty. This comparative approach was already leading Smend not to limit his constitutional interpretation to the interpretation of texts and the construction of concepts but to bring in the historical and political background of constitutional law to explain the differing meanings of identical constitutional provisions.

In 1908, Smend completed his *Habilitationsschift,* an examination of the *Reichskammergericht* (the highest court of the Holy Roman Empire) from the perspective of legal history, in Kiel under Albert Hänel, one of the strongest critics of Laband's positivism. Only a year later, Smend was named professor at Greifswald. This appointment was followed by chairs in Tübingen (1911), Bonn (1915), and Berlin (1922). Smend refused to collaborate with the Nazi regime, limiting his publications between 1933 and 1945 to legal history; in 1935, he was forced to surrender his chair in Berlin and accept one in Göttingen. He worked in Göttingen until his death, serving from 1945 to 1946 as the university's first postwar rector. From 1945 to 1955, Smend was a member of the Council of the Protestant Church in Germany [*Rat der Evangelischen Kirche·in Deutschland*], the church's leading body.

Smend's attempts to overcome state law positivism in the theories of the state and of state law began in the final years of the Empire. His most important work during this phase, a precursor of his theory of integration of the 1920s, was the 1916 study *Unwritten Constitutional Law in the Monarchic Federal State* [*Ungeschriebenes Verfassungsrecht im monarchischen Bundesstaat*]. Smend began by analyzing the political practice of the federal system under the Empire and discovered many elements that contradicted the norms of the Constitution of 1871. He then applied his new approach: Smend abandoned the dichotomy, typical of state law positivism, of "is" and "ought," of constitutional reality and constitutional norms which, where the two diverged, allowed only the verdict that state practice was unconstitutional. Instead, Smend demanded that state law theory mediate between norms and reality. He believed that the views of political actors should be included in the interpretation of constitutional norms. This approach, which Smend had not yet theoretically grounded during the Empire, took issue with a type of legal thinking that reduced the constitution to the "immanent logic" of its written words. The doctrinal result of this work of 1916 lay in the development of "unwritten" federal rights and duties. These culminated in the "federal comity" [*Bundestreue*] that the central government and individual states owed one another even if it was not an express constitutional norm. Smend thus established a legal device with long-term effect. Even in the entirely altered context of the democratic federal state under the Basic Law of 1949, the Federal Constitutional Court [*Bundesverfassungsgericht*] still uses the concept "federal comity," citing Smend's pre-Weimar work, in treating the relationship between the federal government and the Länder.

Smend's main work is *Constitution and Constitutional Law* [*Verfassung und Verfassungsrecht*] of 1928. This work was the first comprehensive presentation of the "theory of integration." The book and the theory are divided into three parts, which Smend considered interdependent. In the first, Smend outlined a philosophical theory of the state. Building on it, he explained in the second part the meaning and function of the constitution. Finally,

Smend attempted to infer concrete consequences for the interpretation of the Weimar Constitution from the integrationist view of state and constitution. This tri-partition makes it difficult to reduce the central concern and theoretical locus of the theory of integration to a pithy formula. Smend himself considered the focus to be a "legal theory of the correct, complete interpretation of the constitution"[1] based on certain premises in the theory of the state.

The book is difficult to read, for a variety of reasons. One is its very spare formulation; Smend treats his broad theme in less than two hundred pages, with much merely hinted at or sketchily developed. Kelsen, who reacted to Smend's work with a sharp polemic, found in this type of presentation, certainly too harshly, "a complete lack of systematic cohesion, an uncertainty of views which avoids clear, explicit decisions, prefers to indulge in intimations, and burdens every halfway comprehensible position with cautious qualifications."[2] A further reason for the book's difficulty lies in its methodological basis, which goes beyond the narrow realm of legal scholarship to involve philosophic edifices of thought. Kelsen, Smend's main scholarly antagonist, had consistently based his *Allgemeine Staatslehre* [*General Theory of the State* (1925)] on neo-Kantian epistemological premises, and on this basis subjected all traditional basic concepts of state and law to a radical examination and revision. This had set the standard of methodological stringency for the debates about theoretical foundations in the 1920s; no new concept could survive if it did not live up to it. Smend took up the challenge. In an effort to free the theory of state and constitution from its positivist context, Smend took as his basis, in methodological opposition to Kelsen, the phenomenological method of Theodor Litt and his Hegelian philosophy. Kelsen's epistemological credo was characterized by numerous dualisms, such as the gap between the knowing subject and the known object, between nature and spirit, between causally determined, explanatory natural sciences and normatively determined and idealist humanities [*Geisteswissenschaften*], which included legal scholarship. Smend countered with an attempt to overcome these divisions. He met Kelsen's radicalization of state law positivism with a phenomenological analysis, in which social reality was seen as a universe of meaning whose laws could be described by empathetic understanding: "The phenomenological structure of the ego in idealist scholarship is not that of an objectifiable element of spiritual life in a causal relationship with this life. The ego is not conceivable first in itself and then as causal for spiritual life, but only to the extent it spiritually exists, expresses itself, understands, takes part in the spiritual world; that is, the extent to which it is in some general sense a member of the community, intentionally connected to others."[3] Smend's theory thus attempts to "understand" state and constitution as a constantly developing link among spiritual and social, individual and collective factors. On this methodological basis, Smend distinguishes himself clearly from a positivist reductionism, where the state is only a legal person, equipped with rights and duties and, as such, bearer of the state's will. He rejects just as sharply Kelsen's identification of the state with the legal order, which makes state theory *per se* a science of norms. In contrast, Smend sees the state as part of an "integrated" spiritual reality, that is to say, a spiritual reality emerging from the interaction of individual life-processes. "Integration" means the continuous, unifying joinder of citizens in a state, not in the sense of a hypothetical or historical social contract, but in that of the citizens' spiritual experience of belonging and spiritual union. This spiritual reality of "state-ness" is not static, nor is it a "natural fact that must be accepted";[4] instead, it is constantly reemerging, as citizens' actions and experiences come together as events creating, embodying and symbolizing state unity. The state "exists and is present only in this process of constant renewal, continuously being-experienced-anew; it exists . . . because of a plebiscite repeated daily."[5] Smend developed a dynamic concept of the state that was at the same time oriented towards harmony. "State-ness" is a continuous process in which citizens are integrated into the state, in part through their own actions, in part passively through their experience of state action (including parades, flags and other state symbols). To Weimar, shaken by crisis and torn by ideological controversy, this concept of the state provided, at least on the level of theory, a contrasting positive image of unity. After 1945, Smend would say in retrospect that the objective basis of the theory of integration was "the sight of the political chaos of the sickly constitutional state of the 1920s, out of which emerged a desire to offer in contrast the original healthy sense of the life of the constitution."[6] But the theory of integration also reflected the traumatic experiences of the First World War, widely perceived as the collapse of the Enlightenment ideal of progress. Smend deliberately countered the "dead-end of the Enlightenment," its confidence in rationality, with the at least partial irrationality of the experience of integration.

Smend related the essence and function of the constitution to the dynamic of the state as a spiritual embodiment of human life and experience. To him, the constitution was the legal ordering of the process of integration; its purpose was to stimulate and channel this process, keep open opportunities for further development, and finally, normativize values upon which citizens agree—among which Smend included, especially, guarantees of basic rights. "The constitution is the legal order of the state, or more precisely, of the life through which the state has its reality—namely, of its integration process."[7] Smend thought it especially important that the dynamic of state's life could have an effect on the content of the constitution. He would permit the content of a constitution to develop fluidly even without formal constitutional amendment. Smend maintained that the "stream of political life" could deviate from "constitutional paths" as long as this conformed to the spirit of the constitution. "Thus it is the spirit of the constitution itself, its focus not on the details but on the totality of the state and the totality of its integration process, that not only permits but even requires such elastic, supplementary constitutional interpretation deviating greatly from every other kind of legal interpretation."[8] This is, at the same time, the central problem of his constitutional concept: dynamizing the constitution endangers its normativity. Smend underestimated the constitution's task of creating order through law. For him, the stability of constitutional law, which ensures predictability, took second place to the elasticity of a constantly changing constitutional system.

In the history of ideas, the theory of integration was an important aspect of the movement in the 1920s against state law positivism, which defined the constitution as a rigid organizational charter charged with creating state bodies, determining and delimiting their powers, and establishing the citizens' rights and duties vis-à-vis the state. Smend's theory shared the anti-positivist views of Carl Schmitt, Herman Heller, and Erich Kaufmann. However, in his reformulation of state and constitutional theory, Smend went very much his own way, one which had little in common with the concepts of the other innovators. The theory of integration received major attention in the final years of the Weimar Republic and was the subject of lively debate. Though its detractors were vehement (as evidenced by Kelsen's harsh rejection), Smend's integration theory also received widespread approval.

After 1933, scattered attempts were made to use a modified version of Smend's concept of integration to explain the Nazi state, presenting it as an example of a functioning system of integration. Smend himself did not take part in such efforts. These ended abruptly; influential legal scholars after 1933 were united in their rejection of the theory of integration.[9] Critics after 1945 wrongly accused the theory of integration of an implicit inclination toward the Nazi state, with its Führer and national community [*Volksgemeinschaft*]. It is true that Smend occasionally mentioned Italian Fascism in his *Verfassung und Verfassungsrecht,* and perhaps even considered it possible that more effective forms of integration could emerge in that context than in parliamentary democracy. But that was as far as he went. Nothing Smend published after 1933 could be construed as acceptance of the new system. But the fact that others attempted, though timidly, to instrumentalize the theory of integration in this way illuminates a fundamental problem: In Smend's writings, integration of citizens in the state is emphasized as the destiny of the state; the way in which state unity is to be produced becomes less important. All that is clear is that integration is neither struggle nor division into friends and enemies but instead an experience of spiritual community. This gentle, aestheticizing theory was an entirely understandable response to Weimar. However, Smend's model of harmonious normalcy overestimates the chances for deliberate inclusion of individuals in the state. His fixation on the state as a unified structure also lacks a clear perspective on the specific conflicts of the democratic, pluralist state; the theory of integration fails to reflect economic problems, nor does it take account of parties and associations—groups positioned between the state and the individual. The theory of integration is state-centered and remains bound to the relationship between the individual and the state. Thus Smend never dealt with the actual circumstances and problems of Weimar. Though he diagnosed its crises, he restored lost harmony and normalcy in a theoretical concept of state unity that failed to go far enough in describing the conditions for and difficulties of creating that unity.

After 1945, Smend admitted some of the one-sidedness and limitations of his theory of integration, but he never elaborated it further. Elements of Smend's theory of integration nonetheless continue to be cited as authority, and among German constitutional law scholars there is a current that follows Smend and is a decisive element in contemporary debates. But even they have failed to elaborate the theory of integration further. What the contemporary discussion owes Smend is, in particular, the question, first posed by him, of the meaning and function of the constitution. Smend's post-positivist understanding of the state and its constitution is one of the reasons for the interest shown today by German constitutional scholars in the role played by the constitution in the reality of the political process.

MAIN WORKS

Die Preußische Verfassungsurkunde im Vergleich mit der Belgischen. Göttingen: Dietricksche Universitäts Buchdruckerei (with Friedrich Kaestner), 1904.

Das Reichskammergericht. Erster Teil: Geschichte und Verfassung. Weimar: H. Böhlau, 1911.

Ungeschriebenes Verfassungsrecht im monarchischen Bundesstaat. Tübingen: Mohr (Paul Siebeck), 1916. Reprinted in Rudolf Smend, *Staatsrechtliche Abhandlungen und andere Aufsätze,* 2nd ed., 39–59. Berlin: Duncker & Humblot, 1968.

"Das Recht der freien Meinungsäußerung." In *Veröffentlichung der Vereinigung der deutschen Staatsrechtslehre* 4 (Berlin and Leipzig: de Gruyter, 1928), 44–74, 96–97. Reprinted in Smend, *Staatsrechtliche Abhandlungen,* 89–118.

Verfassung und Verfassungsrecht. Munich and Leipzig: Duncker & Humblot, 1928. Reprinted in Smend, *Staatsrechtliche Abhandlungen,* 119–276.

Bürger und Bourgeois im deutschen Staatsrecht. Berlin: Preußische Druckerei und Verlags-AG, 1933. Reprinted in Smend, *Staatsrechtliche Abhandlungen,* 309–25.

"Staat und Kirche nach dem Bonner Grundgesetz." In *Zeitschrift für evangelisches Kirchenrecht* 1 (Tübingen: Mohr, 1951). Reprinted in Smend, *Staatsrechtliche Abhandlungen,* 411–22.

Das Bundesverfassungsgericht. Karlsruhe: C. F. Müller, 1962. Reprinted in Smend, *Staatsrechtliche Abhandlungen,* 581–93.

"Integration." In *Evangelisches Staatslexikon,* 2nd ed., edited by Hermann Kunst,

Roman Herzog, and Wilhelm Schneemelcher, cols. 1023–27. Berlin: Kreuz-Verlag, 1975.

LITERATURE

Badura, Peter. "Staat, Recht und Verfassung in der Integrationslehre." *Der Staat* 16 (1977): 305–25.

Bartlsperger, Richard. "Die Integrationslehre Rudolf Smends als Grundlegung einer Staats- und Rechtsphilosophie." Dissertation. Universität Erlangen-Nürnberg, 1964.

Friedrich, Manfred. "Rudolf Smend." *Archiv des öffentlichen Rechts* 112 (1987): 1–25.

Kelsen, Hans. *Der Staat als Integration: Eine prinzipielle Auseinandersetzung.* Vienna: Springer, 1930. Reprint, Aalen: Scientia Verlag, 1974.

Korioth, Stefan. *Integration und Bundesstaat. Ein Beitrag zur Staats- und Verfassungslehre Rudolf Smends.* Berlin: Duncker & Humblot, 1990.

Mayer, Hanns. "Die Krisis der deutschen Staatslehre und die Staatsauffassung Rudolf Smends." Dissertation. Universität Köln, 1931.

Mols, Manfred. *Allgemeine Staatslehre oder politische Theorie? Interpretationen zu ihrem Verhältnis am Beispiel der Integrationslehre Rudolf Smends.* Berlin: Duncker & Humblot, 1969.

Rennert, Klaus. *Die "geisteswissenschaftliche Richtung" in der Staatsrechtslehre der Weimarer Republik. Untersuchungen zu Erich Kaufmann, Günther Holstein, und Rudolf Smend.* Berlin: Duncker & Humblot, 1987.

Scheuner, Ulrich. "Rudolf Smend." In *Rechtsprobleme in Staat und Kirche: Festschrift für R. Smend zum 70. Geburtstag.* Edited by Konrad Hesse, Siegfried Reicke, and Ulrich Scheuner, 433–43. Tübingen: Mohr, 1962.

CONSTITUTION AND CONSTITUTIONAL LAW

Rudolf Smend

Originally appeared in *Verfassung und Verfassungsrecht* (Munich: Duncker & Humblot, 1928), reprinted in Rudolf Smend, *Staatsrechtliche Abhandlungen und andere Aufsätze,* 2nd ed. (Berlin: Duncker & Humblot, 1968), 121–23, 124, 125–27, 136–38, 139, 140, 141–47, 148–49, 150–70, 171–80, 187, 188, 189–92, 192–93, 195–96, 197–98, 233, 235–36, 237–42.

Part One
Principles of the Theory of the State

THE CRISIS OF THE THEORY OF THE STATE

For some time, the theories of the state and of state law have been undergoing a crisis in Germany, or at least a transition. This situation is naturally less serious in the discipline of the law of the state than in the area of state theory. Neither spiritual nor political changes have destroyed the technical tools of the lawyer; thus, a broad common basis remains for supporters of the old and of the new, limiting the crisis to a conflict of aims—the extent of which, however, has yet to be widely acknowledged.[10] In the theory of the state, in contrast, as in politics, the scene is one of collapse and abdication. For it is abdication when Georg Jellinek's quarter-century-old, deservedly representative version of the general theory of the state robs the whole range of major problems of state theory of their gravity and significance through epistemological skepticism, by bringing either the correctness and serious-ness of the questions asked or the material for a response to nought.[11] It is indicative of the period that the valuable sections of this book that remain are memorials in the history of ideas that the book erected to those that it simultaneously declares (expressly or implicitly) methodologically dead. It is also indicative of the inescapable conclusions to be drawn from Jellinek's theory of the state that Kelsen's new solution to the same problem of the his-tory of human error lacks even the obeisance that in the previous generation went without saying.

It is characteristic of this unique situation that, according to the first prin-ciple of the greatest and most successful school of state theory and state law in the German-speaking world, the state may not be considered an aspect of reality. This situation signifies a crisis not only of state theory but also of state law. For without a well-founded body of knowledge about the state, there can in the long run be no fruitful theory of state law—without it, in the long run, no satisfactory life to state law itself.

The crisis of the theory of the state did not originate in war and upheaval. Historically it is a spiritual event and even more so a scholarly event. It has been rightly traced to neo-Kantianism, or, more generally, to a type of scholarly attitude of which neo-Kantianism is the philosophical representa-tion.[12] It is no accident that Kelsen's methodology is based on neo-Kantian attacks on positivism abandoned long ago by neo-Kantianism itself.[13]

But it would be incorrect to search for the preconditions and effects of this phenomenon solely in scholarship, especially in the field of state and state law theory.

Its extra-scholarly preconditions become clearer in the works of those German theorists who currently take a fresh look at the state outside the narrow bounds of the legal discipline, such as Max Weber or [Friedrich] Meinecke. There, at least, a real, positive theory of the state is developing—of the state as an "enterprise," whose immanent teleology forces the indi-vidual to live heteronomously under the demonic embodiment of its means and with inescapable moral culpability; of the state as a natural force and des-tiny and of the living idea of its "reason" [*Staatsräson*] leading to an insoluble antinomy of might [*Kratos*] and right [*Ethos*]—in both cases, self-contained, autonomous predestined forces, in relation to which the individual is more or less object and victim. Here, theoretical skepticism is predicated upon a truly German practical alienation from the state—these views are liberal in the sense of deepest inner nonparticipation in the state. We will see shortly how this shortcoming turns here, and elsewhere, into a fundamental error in epistemological foundations.

These theoretical views have consequences. A particularly striking example is provided by the field of political ethics. The fatal perplexity in this field, and so cuttingly expressed in the writings of [Ernst] Troeltsch, Max Weber and Meinecke, is a failure of theory; but it also explains and heightens the uncertainty of our practical behavior, rather than contributing to the clarity and certainty so desperately wanting in Germany. Again, on top of an unambiguously prevalent ethical skepticism, theoretical agnosticism and inner alienation from the state are manifestly at work here.

Based in this theoretical and practical alienation from the state, the German's two main political shortcomings grow steadily, often in the same soul: apolitical abstinence in regard to the state and, at the same time, apolitical worship of power. They are two sides of the same coin; inner uncertainty with regard to the state vacillates between under- and overestimation of the state. The crisis in the theory of the state takes the form of an inability to deal with this problem in nonprofessional, nonlegal literature on state theory. But the reasons are always the same.

Successful attempts have already been made from various directions to overcome the current situation. The following discussion follows in the footsteps of these attempts. It is limited to a single problem in state theory—one that is, however, the most important to the lawyer, and that illustrates with particular clarity the extent to which all work in the law of the state is predicated upon preliminary work in the theory of the state. Despite these concrete limits, a certain overemphasis of methodological and state-theoretical foundations was unavoidable, given the present footing of the inquiry.

METHODOLOGICAL PRINCIPLES

. . .

Legal formalism requires methodological elaboration of the material—not to say the sociological and teleological[14]—content that is the prerequisite and substance of its norms. In particular, therefore, the theory of the law of the state requires a material theory of the state. But this theory also stands on its own apart from this, as the idealist body of scholarship [*Geisteswissenschaft*] on the life of the state as autonomous spiritual and cultural sphere.

In this there is agreement, at least in a general sense, as long as one is not from Vienna. In contrast, agreement on the methodological foundations of such a theory of the state cannot yet be discerned even from afar.

The following exposition attempts to lay such a foundation, suggestively and provisionally.

. . .

The weakness of the material theory of the state to date is most clearly evident in certain antinomies in which it inevitably entangles itself. The problems of individual and community, individual and state, individualism and collectivism, personalism and transpersonalism surface everywhere as insoluble difficulties.[15] Often this is expressly recognized; in such cases it is generally seen as a question of a hierarchy of values and is settled in terms of a unilateral decision for individualism or collectivism, or, in more modern form and often in relativist discomfort, in terms of an insoluble "tension" between the two. In fact, however, it is not primarily a problem of values but one of structures.

As a problem of structures, it exists in all idealist bodies of scholarship and is everywhere equally insoluble, so long as the ego and the social world are made to confront one another in harsh substantiality. Such confrontations, however, and the objective isolation of both spheres are taken for granted in naive thinking by dint of its tendency to unconscious, mechanistic spatial categorizing. Legally trained social theorists also tend in this direction, as they are accustomed to strict distinction between the legal spheres of the physical person on the one hand and the legal person on the other.

But this way of thinking cannot be applied to any area of idealist scholarship.

The phenomenological structure of the ego in idealist scholarship is not that of an objectifiable element of spiritual life in a causal relationship with this life. The ego is not conceivable first in itself and then as causal for spiritual life, but only to the extent that it spiritually exists, expresses itself, understands, takes part in the spiritual world; that is, the extent to which it is in some general sense a member of the community, intentionally connected to others. It can only fulfill and shape its essence through spiritual life, which is social in structure.[16]

Even less is it the case that there is a collective ego based on itself. Collectivities are merely the unified structures of the experiences of meaning by individuals; not their product, however, but their necessary essence. Development of essence and creation of meaning are necessarily "socially linked"; they are essentially a meshing of individual and super-individual life.[17]

Psychology can isolate and objectify the individual; but in this way it gives up all claim to insight into spiritual life itself.[18] The sciences of an objective structure of meaning of a cultural domain can, in the same way, isolate their object as an objective system and focus exclusively on its immanent content.[19] One way or the other, life, the process of life, the reality of culture are not understood; they can be understood only from a perspective predicated on their phenomenological structure and proceeding in opposition to those objectifications of the individual soul and systems of meaning.

Thus, no science of spiritual life can interpret its most important objects—the individual, the community, the objective context of meaning—as isolated elements, factors, subjects or objects of the spiritual life, whose relationship to one another must be examined, but only as elements in a dialectic order whose parts are, at most (as in the examples mentioned), polarly paired with one another.[20] Every science of spiritual life here has its a priori—not a transcendental one, but one immanent in the structure of its object, which, found in the special manner of phenomenological abstraction, will here be presupposed.[21]

If a shift to idealist methods has correctly been demanded as a current necessity for the theory of the state and state law theory,[22] the direction here described is the one to be taken by this shift. Idealist scholarship is the scholarship of understanding, and here we are dealing with clarifying the conditions of such understanding, as they have always been taken for granted—empirically and generally unconsciously—in the practice of the individual idealist disciplines. Only the dialectic of the concept of the ego[23] gives it the "inner elasticity, mobility in its limbs and joints,"[24] without which it is impossible to integrate the ego into the structure of social reality and to avoid absolutizing or objectivizing and isolating it. Only the dialectic of the concept of the collective can effectively counter both the fateful objectivization and substantialization of the spiritual world into an anti-ego and any "organic" social theories.[25] Only as a dialectic structure does the entirety of the spiritual world become understandable—the world that prevailing sociology attempts in vain to break up into "relationships" or "mutual effects" between fixed points.[26]

. . .

INTEGRATION AS THE STATE'S FUNDAMENTAL PROCESS OF LIFE

The theories of the state and state law deal with the state as part of spiritual reality. Collective spiritual structures as parts of reality are not static substances but units of meaning of real spiritual life—spiritual acts. Their reality is that of functional actualization, reproduction, or more precisely, of continual spiritual achievement and formation (which can be progress or degeneracy, depending on their value)—only in this process and by dint of this process do they, or will they, renew their reality from moment to moment.

Thus the state, in particular, is not a static whole that issues individual manifestations of life, laws, judgments, diplomatic and administrative acts. Instead, it only exists at all in these various manifestations of life to the extent they are activations of an overall spiritual context, and in the even more important renewals and formations that act upon this context itself. It exists and is present only in this process of constant renewal, continuously being-experienced-anew; it exists, to borrow [Ernst] Renan's famous characterization of the nation, because of a plebiscite repeated daily.[27] It is this central process of state life, or if one prefers, its central substance, which I have elsewhere suggested be called integration.[28]

Here "state-ness" has its pivotal point in reality, from which state and state law theory must start. If they do not, they are left with the almost unavoidable alternatives of either attaching state-sociological machinery to certain rigid, unacceptably substantialized carriers of those sociological forces, to individuals or to an entire state, ambiguously viewed half legally, half spatially;[29] or of joining Kelsen in denying that the reality of this world is an object of state theory; or of retreating finally into an aestheticizing agnosticism.[30]

Though all spiritual life is self-creation of the individual and at the same time of the community, the significance of this creation for the community is more evident, as the justification of its spiritual reality, than it is for the individual person, who has a biological existence independent of that life.[31] The state exists only because, and to the extent, it constantly integrates and is formed in and of individuals—this constant process is its essence as a spiritual and social reality . . .

. . .

If what the state is supposed to be in essence and beyond its empirical manifestation is a sovereign union of wills and the state's ongoing integration into reality as such, it is the task of empirical observation to show the factors in actualizing this.

. . .

Until now, the literature on the theory of the state has not posed, and therefore not dealt with, this problem. . . .

More substance is found in the descriptive political literature, particularly when it takes account of the problem or aspects of the problem from the practical side, and especially when it involves the world of the Anglo-Saxon states. But the great treasure-trove today for studies in this area is the literature of fascism. It does not aim to provide a comprehensive theory of the state; its subject is rather new ways and means of state formation, state creation, life of the state—precisely what is described here as integration.[32] Its systematic exploration from the standpoint of integration theory would bring a rich yield, the value of which would be independent of the value and future of the fascist movement itself.

What has become conscious here, in a movement for systematic formation of a new national and state community based on endless reflection, has usually remained unconscious. Thus it is no surprise that the theories of the state and of state law have nothing to say on it. Rationalism sees only that which is conscious and accessible to naturalist thought; irrationalism is mired here in the agnosticism of organic theory. It is telling that constitutional legislators coming out of a theoretical background, like those of Weimar, overlooked this central problem of constitutions; while the Bismarck Constitution, as will be shown, is an unreflected but perfect example of an integrating constitution.

The spiritual life processes being discussed here, simultaneously those of the individual and of the whole, occur in the main without full awareness of their own meaning. Therefore, they still cannot be explained by recourse to the laws of causality but are understandable only by placing them in their context of meaning as an actualization of the laws of spiritual value.[33] The developing spirit does not know the meaning of its developmental stirrings; the mature spirit, by dint of the "cunning of reason," does not necessarily know the cultural context in which its activity exercises an influence.[34] Nevertheless, they become understandable not because of their consciousness but because of their objective spiritual connections. This is a late stage of spirit, which comes to know itself through insight into its own inherent logic (a logic of norms and values).

The following overview of the three types of integration is only an initial, preliminary effort. In particular, the tripartite division used here has been chosen for purely practical reasons.

The phenomena listed under the various types do not exhaust the relevant material; they are meant only as examples.

Of these examples, in the end, none is pure in the sense that it belongs only to the type under which it is listed. There is no leadership, no guidance of a group, that is not leadership in the name of an objective content or toward an objective end. There is no group-forming motion that does not contain active, leading, and passive participants and that is without an objective meaning or purpose. And there is no fulfillment of meaning or purpose without leadership and active group life. The following isolation of types of integration and of specific cases subsumed under them is offered only with the reservation that every real process of integration contains all these elements; it is, at most, primarily characterized by one of them.

PERSONAL INTEGRATION

Integration by persons is the type of integration most often dealt with in the literature, especially in the sociology and ideology of "leaderism" [*Führertums*].[35] However, it enjoys this preferred status thanks not only to its actual significance but also to practical and theoretical errors. Practical to the extent that, especially for the defeated in the world war, the cry for a "leader" was an expression of their own powerlessness, helplessness, and confusion,[36] from which they were gradually freed, not through the genius of a few individuals alone but only through the combination of statesman-like leadership and increasing consolidation of a people's will embodied by this leadership, under improving political conditions. It is liberal, or, as Hugo Preuss would say, authoritarian thinking to seek the problem of state leadership only in the leaders and not at least equally in those to be led. Theoretically, it results in a view of the led as an inert mass (as in physics), worked upon by an outside force[37]—mechanistic thinking that overlooks the necessary spontaneity and productivity of the led. They are stimulated to group life, but soon live this life as their own. In their experience, the leader is not the sole force, and they themselves are not objects to be passively pushed around; instead, they are alive, while their leaders are the living incarnation of the social and spiritual development alive and active within them.[38] Only this view corresponds theoretically to the basic structure of spiritual life in general, essentially breaking free of the paralyzing passivity of a leaderist ideology that expects everything of a political magician and therefore demands nothing of the members of the national community.

There is no spiritual life without leadership—least of all in the formation and normativization of a common cultural will. A function so apparently cooperative as the formation and maintenance of basic legal convictions proves upon closer inspection to be a constant process of leading and being led.[39] In state life, it simply appears with particular clarity and is especially multi-faceted—the latter to such an extent that not even an overview of the most important types can be attempted here. The following will develop only the essence shared by all state leadership, which so far as I can see has not yet been sufficiently highlighted by theorists.

The questionable mechanistic leaderist ideology sees in the leader merely a technician carrying out foreign and domestic policy goals that are set and are to be fulfilled objectively. But, in fact, he always has a second responsibility: In carrying out these objective functions, he has, apart from his technical success, to prove his worth as leader of those he leads. This is most apparent for party functionaries, journalists, government ministers; they fall as soon as they lose the backing of their voters, readers, etc., and their job is, above all, to hold together the political group that supports them. In government responsible to a parliament, this is raised to the status of a major constitutional institution; the cabinet, quite apart from its technical achievements in government and administration, is supposed to create and hold together a parliamentary majority, and thus—mediated by means of functional integration to be discussed later—integrate not merely a few citizens into a governing coalition but the entire citizenry into national unity.[40]

But the job of the "tenured" state functionary is essentially no different. The most obvious example is the monarchy. Again, it is an insufficient, mechanistic view of its essence to explain and justify or reject it by listing either its technical advantages in military leadership and foreign and domestic policy, and the kings who were statesmen and military leaders; or its technical weaknesses, and the monarchs who were unequal to these tasks. Historically, the most unsettling example of such misjudgment of the meaning of monarchic responsibility was Wilhelm II's method of governing, in which he invested his personal energy in the technical aspects of government—both misplaced for the monarch and more dubious than ever before—leading to unavoidable dilettantism. He thus completely ignored the imperative responsibility of representing in his own person the embodiment, the integration of the entire nation. The whole point of the position of all heads of state is more or less to "represent" or "embody" the unity of the citizenry; that is, to be a symbol for them, as are flags, coats of arms, and national anthems in a more substantive, functional manner.[41] This unity itself, however, is not something firm or static that is merely made visible, shown, or recalled. Rather, it exists as a spiritual reality only in the continuous flow of spiritual life; all "representations," "embodiments," symbols of the type described here are solidified stimuli for and forms of this ever-renewing experience. The unique quality of monarchic integration[42] lies in the fact that the legitimate monarch symbolizes above all the historic stock of common national values; that is, he simultaneously represents a case of integration through substantive values. He plays more or less the role that, in a republic, can be filled in the main only by historic or even mythic figures, such as [Wilhelm] Tell or [Arnold] Winkelried.[43] The ovation for the sovereign is not so much a way of honoring his person as an act of "the self-awareness of a unified citizenry,"[44] or more precisely, an actualization of this self-awareness, a renewal of its self-perception, as Thomas Mann characterized it.[45] Thus the task of the personality at the pinnacle of the state is not technical in nature; it does not lie primarily in specific state transactions, but in the nature and attitude of the personality. There are those who are unsuited by nature to integrating functions;[46] there are attitudes incompatible with this task.[47] Here the contradiction between technical and integrating personal functions becomes particularly apparent.

In the process, the integrating effectiveness of the monarchic personality can sometimes dissolve into the institutional embodiment of the political tradition and sometimes create and develop it further. But its effects on the members of the state are always determinative, integrating, stimulative of political life; in the case of creative personalities, this integrating effect on individuals is not only invigorating but also formative. Old Schlözer already saw this quite keenly: "Two eyes of Friedrich the Eagle close, and six million people are refashioned."[48]

Despite the opposition between integrating and technical activities on the part of the state, the administrative and judicial bureaucracies are also part of the circle of integrating persons. Since rationalism, and certainly since Max Weber's brilliant account, a prejudice has existed here that is difficult to overcome; it sees the bureaucracy as merely a rational machine and its officials as nothing but technical functionaries.[49] It is true that this sharply characterizes the difference between the essence of bureaucracy and its officials and the essence of statesmanlike activity and personality. But it ignores the fact that it is impossible to isolate the essence of a spiritual activity, least of all an activity taking place in the name of the social whole. Not only is the judge or the administrative official not an *être inanimé;* he is also social, as a spiritual being. His activity is a function within a spiritual whole; it is determined by the whole, orients itself according to it, and its acts determine the essence of the whole. If, for example, the ethic of public service demands that the official fulfill his task not only correctly but also in the spirit of the public—as its friend—this ethic does not demand something special and supererogatory but simply requires a certain coloring of an element in itself self-evident and unavoidable: that public activity under all circumstances be in a fluid relationship of influencing and being influenced by the official's circle, his "public." Such an official is in error if he sees his activity exclusively as a mere technique of appeal-proof decision making, as an elegant piece of administrative business or dull paperwork; he thereby inculcates a certain spirit that surrounds and affects him, and that he in turn directs and substantively fashions through his judgments, welfare, and administrative work of all kinds. Thus, the socialist critique of "bourgeois" judges, the way of thinking that takes literary form in *Justiz,** is not entirely incorrect in its theoretical foundations. Here is a task for the theorists of public functions and for the practical educators of future civil servants that has not yet been sufficiently undertaken.

However, the bureaucracy differs from other types of integrating persons in that the integrating effect is not its main task; it is subordinate to its task of specific, practical, technical acts of state business. In contrast, those chiefly called upon to carry out integrating functions comprise the category of political functionaries.

. . .

FUNCTIONAL INTEGRATION

In addition to integrating persons, the second formal—in contrast to substantial—element in the life of all human societies involves integrating functions or processes, collectivizing forms of life. To my knowledge, they have not yet been treated comprehensively in the literature. The most valuable groundwork has been laid here by social psychologists, whereas here as well legally minded theorists of state functions ignore the problem.

*A rather left-wing legal journal.—EDS.

The following is not an attempt to exhaust the subject or even to systematize it but simply to illustrate it in light of some especially important examples.

They all involve processes whose point is a social synthesis[50] seeking to make some spiritual content a common experience, or to strengthen this experience, with the dual effect of intensifying the lives of both the community and the individuals involved. The process itself can be found in the sensory arena, and can accompany, stimulate, and symbolize the spiritual content; the best-known example, since Karl Bücher's famed study of "work and rhythm," is the acoustic or motor rhythm of working together. It is also employed in state life, in marching troops or demonstrating parades, as a type of integrating confluence, primarily of those moving physically, but also, by dint of its emotionally inclusive demonstrative effect, of those not directly involved in the physical movement. Thus Friedrich von Wieser described the creation of powerful associations and of power (and thus the foundation and maintenance of the state) as a procedure for forcing the masses to fall in step and to synchronize their feelings and wills in an all but military fashion;[51] in the age of fascism and the *Reichsbanner Schwarz-Rot-Gold,** this is in part an objective description of reality (including its aura), and in part accurate symbolism.

. . .

The integration processes of a certain type of community are unique in that they are mainly processes of production, actualization, renewal, and development of the meaning that comprises the substantive content of the community. In national life, therefore, they are primarily processes of formation of the popular will. However, this is true not (or not only) in the legal sense—that is, in the sense of will formation that is legally significant, legally transacted in the broadest sense—but, in general, in the sense of ever-new production of the national community as a union of wills: that is, in the sense of ongoing creation of the conditions for the expressions and achievements and especially for the above-mentioned legally transacted consequences of the national community of will.

Natural law theory took as the basic sociological category[52] of its theory of the state not domination, but contract; not merely out of rationalist individualism,[53] but for good reason. As a social phenomenon, domination is never final, but always in need of legitimation, and at the same time, its essence is determined by this legitimation, as Max Weber, above all, has shown. There are always other values and orders behind it, from which it is derived; or, in the terminology used here, integrating factors that have already established, and continue to establish, a community in which domination can be exercised. A type of state based largely on domination thus

*The "Reich Flag Black-Red-Gold," a Social Democratic mass organization.—EDS.

requires a world of largely static substantive political values and orders in the name of which, and through which, this domination can legitimately be exercised.[54] In contrast, contracts, votes, and the majority principle are more simple, ordinary forms of integration.[55] Through them, the spiritual logic of social values has its most direct impact. They are based in the very battle that they bring to an end; the fact that they can bring it to an end has to do with the special quality of the battle, with its tendency towards integration.[56] The principles of formless unanimity and formalized majority[57] are the forms through which such battles are ended, and the majority principle is completely misunderstood if it is seen merely as a rational consequence of the will for community[58] or as a reflection of the belief, lost today, in the rightness of the will of the majority.[59] It originated historically as the formalization of battle and of the informal, in large part directly physical, subjugation of the minority[60] within a group held together by shared values and, especially for this battle—by rules of battle—and seeking in this battle to relieve tensions and increase unity. Under healthy political conditions, the experience of fighting internal political battles is one of beneficial release of tensions, a catharsis similar to that felt at the end of a game.[61] The deeper reason for this beneficial, cathartic effect is independent of satisfaction over a substantively correct outcome or gratification over the creation and preservation of formal unity; the battle itself is an essential integrating act in the life of the community and thus at the same time a heightening of the emotions in the life of the individual, whether part of the majority or of the minority.[62]

The problem we are dealing with here is the actual subject of one of the most interesting and instructive controversies in state theory in recent years: the dispute between Carl Schmitt and Richard Thoma on the essence of parliamentarism.[63] It is at the actual heart of the issue, but is not recognized by either of the adversaries, for different reasons.

According to Carl Schmitt, the parliament as developed in the nineteenth century has lost its previous basis and its meaning because the "idea," the "principle" of parliament—that is, the principles of openness and discussion and the accompanying guarantees of truth and justice—have died out today in both political belief and political reality.[64] Thoma has rightly (though with insufficient justification) declared this deduction to be all too ideological and literary. In fact, an institution stands and falls not with its ideology but with what Carl Schmitt himself calls its vitality, substance, and strength.[65] The one, however, is not identical with the other, and rationalism in particular tends to conceptualize such political "strength" in an abstract and ideological form;[66] that is, in our case, to rationalize a system of political integration as a mechanical, teleological mechanism for implementing ultimate abstract values. Here ideology can deteriorate while integration remains; in France, the ideology of the parliament has long since succumbed to the unique strength of the country's political satire and to practical experience, but the parliament lives on because it is still the appropriate form of political integration for a latinate bourgeoisie accustomed to a certain perceptual clarity and rhetorically theatrical dialectic in the political process.[67] In more strongly democratic Germany, this type of integration, tailored to a limited, newspaper-reading bourgeoisie, fails. Here the originary ideology is just one element of integration that could, if necessary, be dispensed with in structural transformation. Belief in the exclusive significance of ideology is rationalism, or (as in Carl Schmitt) conceptual realism.[68]

If Thoma is thus not unjustified in criticizing Carl Schmitt's far-too-exclusive focus on the history of ideas in dealing with the "death knell of the parliamentary state,"[69] Schmitt's anti-critique is, nevertheless, completely correct, to the extent that he accuses Thoma of an essentially technical view of constitutions.[70] It is true that an institution can remain vital by dint of a metamorphosis in purpose or transformation in structure. But it is inadmissible to claim that the creative—that is, integrating—discussion of early liberal parliamentarism is being replaced by "creative discussions in party caucuses, the cabinet, inter-party discussions, talks with experts and businessmen."[71] The latter are techniques to accomplish certain political deals; the former was an integrating institution as an end in itself, that is, one that determined and grounded the essence of the nation and the state. But techniques and institutions are among the highest categories of idealist thought and must not be confused.[72] It is not by chance that Thoma refers to Max Weber in this context—to the classic example of such confusion in the theory of the state and especially of the constitution. The principled contrast between the way of thinking presented here and that of Weber and Thoma was already hinted at earlier; its relevance to the outcomes in a theory of the state will be acknowledged later.

Elections, parliamentary negotiations, cabinet formation, popular referenda—all are integrating functions. That is, they can be justified not only—as is taught by the prevailing theory of state bodies and functions, due to its background in law—because representatives [73] of the state or the entire nation are granted authority to act, and then, by dint of this authority, make valid legal declarations and transactions for and against those represented. Nor is it, as constitutional technicians claim in the spirit of Max Weber, because good decisions are made and good leaders selected. This fails to illuminate the spiritual process upon which it is based, the understanding of which should be the main task of idealist scholarship. But this process is the main point of these procedures: they integrate—that is, they do their part to create the specific political individuality of the entire nation, and thus the condition for its legally comprehensible activity, whether good or bad in content. It makes no difference to the ultimate significance of a parliamentary state whether parliament actually makes decisions,[74] and whether, in particular, its decisions are good; what matters is whether the parliamentary dialectic within the parliament and among the citizenry leads to group for-mation, association, creation of a specific common political attitude[75]—just as election law serves first of all to form parties and then to create majori-ties, rather than simply to bring forth individual deputies.[76] In the parlia-mentary state, the nation has no a priori political existence, becoming ever more politically qualified from election to election and cabinet formation to cabinet formation; instead, it owes its existence as a political nation, as a sovereign union of wills, primarily to the political synthesis in which it gains, over and over again, its existence and reality as a state. This process, though, is never the only factor integrating a citizenry, the only political condition of its capacity to will and act politically; but within the meaning of a parlia-mentary constitution, it is the ultimate one, by which specific political indi-viduality is primarily established.

The effectiveness of this as of every other integrating function depends upon two elements: that its principle (here, that of the majority) has inte-grating power at all, and that it has this power for the entire citizenry.

That it has this effect at all is determined by values not questioned in the political battle, but underlying it and giving the battle itself rules and the meaning of an integrating function in group life. Parts of the group that are not sufficiently connected to the whole through such values will easily with-draw from the rules of the battle, and thus from its integrating effect—for example, through obstruction.[77] Or the rules will be followed, not in their fullest sense, but only as the rules of intercourse between hostile powers are followed; an example is the problematic state of nationalities whose parlia-ment, as one said of the Austrian Reichsrat, is often merely a "a congress of nationalities for particularistic transactions," and no longer a way of creat-ing solidarity in constitutional life. On the other hand, forms of state that provide for integrating battles in their constitutions have the advantage of more easily hindering the relegation to permanent minority status of certain sectors of their populations which, under static constitutions that provide for permanent representation of certain objective values they re-ject, can be placed in permanent minority status and thus be permanently alienated; whereas the constantly renewed battle for power in the parlia-mentary state reassures them by offering the possibility of future participa-tion in power, pulling them actively into state life through the battle for such participation.

The second requirement of the proper integrating effect of constitutional life is everyone's internal participation in it. If the state and the form of state, as well as the law, depend on the recognition of those subject to them,[78] this "recognition" of the state is consummated through the individual subject-ing himself to the impact of the most essential factors of state integration. Participation in the life of the representative state can be that of an active voter or an avid newspaper reader. One cannot doubt the effectiveness of this impact; [Alfred] Vierkandt has quite correctly pointed out that the "spectators" in a group are often even more active than the apparently acting ones.[79] This "spectator" role occurs in the most manifold shadings; because sharing encompassing connections of experience is generally possible only indirectly, only through the technique of "reporting" and other "social mediations," the individual can variously determine the extent of the mediation he enjoys—from extensive newspaper reading to having the attitude that politics is for those with time for it, and limiting oneself to those contacts with the political world that are completely unavoidable for a contemporary in possession of his senses. And this variety among observing participants only manifests the fundamental variety among types of emotional and "sociological" participation—from the activity of the leader and the politicized citizen to Friedrich von Wieser's completely "passive mass," which approves of the state because it approves of some other, perhaps purely personal, values and therefore—simultaneously and generally unconsciously—approves of the endless linkage of all the other values, not the least of which is the state, upon which these are conditioned. It thus becomes unavoidable that the observing participants march, only partially aware of what they are doing, in step with the state.[80] This variously shaded, manifold, and, in the most diverse sense, indirect political integration of the individual deserves most careful study as one of the most important, if not the most important, fact of politics. Only this mediation through personal leadership first makes the leader an integrating factor.[81] On the other hand, this mediation is what the advocates of modern political theory and practice essentially attack; they would like to replace democracy, liberalism, and parliament by direct action, or, as its fascist variant might better be described, by direct integration. According to [Georges] Sorel, only in direct action is the individual unmediatedly involved and politically alive; fascism depends on unmediated integration through corporativism, militarism, myth, and countless other techniques, in the paradoxical awareness that only a relatively small citizenry can live in a mediated relationship with the state, while the mass citizenries of modern democracies are not quite included in the delicate and somewhat literary forms of the representative bourgeois state, and require elemental plebiscitary, syndicalist, sensual, and in any case unmediated, political forms of life in modern times.

Besides integration through a constitutionally prescribed parliamentary or plebiscitary battle, a second integrating function is domination. It is even more unmediatedly determined by substantive values than is the integrating battle; while battle requires only a general community of values, in this case domination is grounded in specific values—irrational ones that give it legitimacy, rational ones that primarily justify it as administration.[82] Domination is the actualization of these values and thus a form of life of the community held together by these values. To be subject to one and the same source of domination with all its consequences, its government and administration, its lawmaking and legal decisions, means, in addition to the community of values so established, above all a community of experience of these formal communal functions; where the system of these functions, while it does not form a unity as closed and identical for everyone as the parliamentary or plebiscitary constitutional system, still grips each individual all the more emphatically, multifariously, and repeatedly. Domination is also the most general form of functional integration to the extent that all constitutional life in all forms of state in the end aim to create and express the dominating will. In any case, it too is a form of life encompassing the whole as well as the individual who carries it and makes it possible and who experiences it, thus acting in spiritual interaction with the whole and with others, standing in a relationship of integrating spiritual interchange even as the object of domination.

This understanding of domination is impossible if one understands it, according to the logic of norms, as the validity of legal norms;[83] or if one conceives it, in the popular spatial image, as the overpowering of the subordinate by a position of greater rank and power, or defines it—in an objectivization that is impermissible in idealism—as a chance for obedience,[84] that is, a situation understood in terms of cause and social technology. Here, as everywhere, the methods of causal science and the logic of norms are fatally opposed to insight into the spiritual reality of life that the state is all about.

It is common and essential to all formal processes of integration that they are, as such, without a goal, that they are technical in the sense of pursuing a particular, substantive social goal, but rather resemble the exercises and maneuvers of an army in peacetime that make it into a unit, or social intercourse,[85] dance, gymnastics. When it was said that there was no possibility of making the masses into a state without taxes and military service,[86] what was meant, quite instructively, was the externally purposeless, integrating effect of these state institutions and the individual's inclusion in them, in contrast to their substantive, technical aspect as means of fiscal and military power.

However, in the end there can be no formal integration without a substantive community of values, just as there can be no integration through substantive values without functional form. But generally one or the other clearly prevails; there are acts of group life, and especially of state life, that intentionally emphasize the formal, integrating function, and others that emphasize the substantive, technical content. In the first case,[87] the integrating form vanquishes, so to speak, the substantive material; here the formal communal values in their own right and the material communal values, state goals, etc., enter with particular clarity into a relationship of contrast and a certain commensurability. Even if both elements are often linked as two sides of one and the same constitutional institution, the theories of state and state law must carefully distinguish between them. As a type, the founding of a community through a community of substantive values contrasts starkly with the types of integration through formal elements (personal and functional) treated so far.

SUBSTANTIVE INTEGRATION

That the state is established to actualize common ends, or (to refine the primitive teleology of social contract theory) at least is justified by such ends, is a central tenet of the modern theory of the state. But this thesis must be made more precise in order to bring its truth to light.

The realization of all ideal content requires community, and, in turn, increases, enriches, strengthens, even justifies this community. One might speak of a "sociality of the experiences of meaning," and especially of a "community of cultural activity."[88] Values have a real life only by dint of the community that experiences and actualizes them. Conversely, however, the community also lives off these values. If the individual himself becomes a spiritual personality, lives in a spiritual sense, exists only through the actualization of values, this is truer still of all collective entities, which lack psycho-physical actuality as a given.[89]

Thus the state, too, is not a real entity in itself, which is then used as a means to actualize external goals. Rather, it has actuality at all only to the extent it is an actualization of meaning; it is identical with this actualization of meaning. Thus it cannot be explained or justified through teleological reference to external goals but in its substance can be understood as actualization of values.

This is clearly apparent for the aspects of state life that are the immediate consequence of its essence as a sovereign union of wills. Powerful domination and effectiveness internally and externally can be most easily accepted as the state's own essence, analogous to the psycho-physical life of the individual. Because the state must dominate its own territory, because the individual's vital drive for power is satisfied by sharing this dominance of the commonwealth, and because, at the same time, only in this way does part of the culture's universe of meaning become actual—for these reasons, the state is actual only if it dominates internally based on law and the factual irresistibility of its power, and if it is capable externally of victorious defense.[90]

But things are no different in regard to the state's so-called legal and cultural goals. Here, too, the state is not a person existent in itself that, with its technique and power, takes on and deals with certain external, objective, substantive tasks. Rather, the state has actuality as a spiritual community in equal measure by dint of all the meanings that constitute this community. In particular, one may not distinguish here between form and substance. One can say of the state not only that it is a form of culture, but equally that state-sponsored areas of culture are a form of life of the state; their connection is not comprehensible through the always dangerous[91] idealist categories of form and substance, but as moments of a uniform appearance.

The entirety of the "goals" or "tasks" of a specific state represents a segment of the entirety of culture, a selection made by dint of the tendency, shared by the state with every other cultural arena, toward the maximum,[92] toward encroachment on the entire area of culture, to the extent it can possibly be projected to the level of the life of the state community; a selection, however, that despite all state pleonexy is based also on a certain affinity of the epoch to state co-optation of precisely these community goals in this way. This affinity exists because state life as a whole is not a sum but an individual unity, a totality, determined by the concretization of an objective inherent logic of values in a particular historical situation. The state dominates only because of this plethora of values,[93] that is, only thus is it a constant, unified, motivating connection of experience for those who are part of it—but it is a unified experience only as a totality of values.

One experiences the state, one is integrated into the state, by dint of the experience of this plethora of values or individual moments thereof, as essential moments of the state itself. Thereby, the moment of leadership and integrating procedures can play a role; in contrast, integration through participation in a substantive content of values is another, third type of integration.[94]

The integrating effect of the substantive content of the state community has its own difficulties. In today's state, it is the richness of this content itself that hinders its integrating effect. It is so enormous that it can no longer be ignored by the individual; at the same time, due to this enormity and its rationality, it is so alien to the individual that he finds its impression alienating and does not experience his own share in it.[95] Despite the integrating effect imperceptibly achieved by the substantive life of the state community, even in its details the totality of this life is not perceptible in its extensiveness and therefore not comprehensible in its extensiveness. In order to be experienced, in order to have an integrating effect, it must somehow be condensed into one moment and be represented by this moment. This occurs institutionally in the representation of the values at each point in history through political symbols such as flags, coats of arms, heads of state (especially the monarch), political ceremonies, and national festivals.[96] It occurs in the course of history through representative events that illustrate the meaning of a country's politics—as Salisbury replied to Herbert Bismarck, the only way to influence the masses in international politics in the age of democracy.[97] Above all, it is the contrast with other states that allows one suddenly to experience the values and dignity of one's own state and one's personal inclusion in it. In certain circumstances, the representative moment of the richness of the state's essence can be improvised: The state can "place its boundlessness and honor in each of its details,"[98] and find itself hurt in each of these details, with the effect that its members also share this experience as their own.

However, the increased integrating force of a symbolized substantive content is based not only on the fact that it is experienced with particular intensity as an irrational and individual richness but also on the fact that in this form it is more elastic than in the form of an extensive, rational, legal formulation. As formulated content expressed in a fixed law, it is heteronomous and rigid, and reveals as much the tension between individual and community as it does the inclusion of the individual in the whole.[99] On the other hand, symbolization, grounded historically in the deficit of expression perceived in a more primitive period with a less differentiated universe of values, has turned this deficit into the virtue of a particularly effective, while at the same time particularly elastic, representation of a value. A symbolized value can be experienced by anyone, "as I understand it," without the tension and contradiction inevitably brought forth by formulation and fixed law.[100] At the same time, everyone experiences the value in a totality that cannot be achieved any other way.

Primarily in this way, that is, as an intensive rather than extensive totality,[101] can a state's plethora of values be experienced in its entirety, with an intense and conscious integrating effect. The significance of these states of integration—mostly, in essence, temporary—lies, among other things, in their linkage to the state's ability to make the greatest demand on the individual, for example, in time of war; only under such special circumstances is this demand actually possible, and perhaps only then ethically tolerable.[102] Thus it has been rightly said that the rationalization of political thought, which rules out an understanding of political content as a religious content, at the same time casts doubt upon every binding political form.[103]

Of course, we must not overlook the ongoing, silent integrating effect of the state's substantive content through "mediations" of all kinds, as indicated above,[104] and above all through the boundless interlinkage of all areas of life with one another, and especially with the state.

The substantive contents that comprise the integrating substantive aggregate of a union of wills are as much in flux, as a moment of its life, as it is as a whole. Not only in the sense of their ongoing transformation through the life-progress of the whole, but apart from that, also to the extent that they are never a static property but a goal of willed realization given as an ongoing task. With this in mind, [Rudolf] Kjellén once accurately expressed the essence of the nation in the words of the Rütli oath: "We *want* to be a

united people* of brothers."[105] For this reason, for example, the expansion
of federal powers in a federal state does not necessarily have a practical unifying, that is, integrating effect, because the legal possibility of a state action
does not yet mean the actuality of an integrating unified will in the same direction; if a segment of the nation opposes such action, its legal possibility
can also have a disintegrating, burdensome effect on the whole—a possibility that was obviously overlooked when, in Weimar, basic extensions of federal power were equated with a strengthening of the central government.

This insight into the nature of state "goals" and "tasks" as substantive moments in the state's process of integration, in contrast to a perception of them
as true "goals" for which the state is to serve as a means and the teleology of
which justifies the state—this insight is an essential prerequisite for doing
any justice at all to the meaning of state life. If one sees the state as an organization serving its supposed ends, any assessment of it can only be unfavorable; it serves them extremely inadequately, like a badly constructed machine, "by the skin of its teeth."[106] But it is no different here than for the
individual: his goals, ideals, professional tasks, wishes are just as incapable
of complete fulfillment; but fulfillment in life that is his given task is still
possible. It is this fulfillment in life that demands such resignation; human
beings, like states, would not be the spiritual realities they are if they did not
become hardened in constant battle with so many partial successes and fail-
ures, if they did not have repeatedly to form themselves anew as spiritual
essences. In this renewed formation and fulfillment of essence lies the meaning of their lives, which makes them comprehensible, and not in teleological
efficiency, from which perspective comprehension and justification of human life and the life of the state become equally impossible.

All teleological theories of the state are based in those rationalist linguistic theories that explain language as a rational, that is, a technical discovery
for the purpose of communication, as an ur-Esperanto [Urvolapük], a technical artifact rather than an elementary, inherently necessary form of human
spiritual life—corresponding to the religious philosophy of priestly fraud
and other rationalizations that came to a deserved end earlier than the rationalist influences on modern state theory.[107]

This substantive content is an object of legal theory to the extent that the
legitimacy of the state and its order are largely, if not entirely, based in it.
The concrete values, which require and sustain the validity of a certain state
legal order, establish legitimacy. Because these values can be of many different types, there are also various types, and especially various degrees, of

*Smend quotes the Rütli oath differently than does Anschütz. Anschütz's version (see above,
page 149) is the correct one. We translate Volk as "people" here, though elsewhere in Smend
we translate it as "nation" in order to reflect the fact that the Rütli oath preceded the popular
idea of the nation.—EDS.

legitimacy. Formalists have, of course, given up on this problem, as the question of the positivity of law can be answered only with yes or no, and for them there are no legal questions beyond that. Essentially technical legal disciplines, like civil law, can circumvent the problem; but the problem imposes itself in criminal law, and is unavoidable in the law of the state.[108]

In this context, two further problems have a systematic place: the problem of history and that of the state's territory.

The intrinsic meaning of the life of the state is historical reality. This means that, like the spiritual reality of individual human existence, this meaning is not merely the dividing point between past and future, not mere presence. Spiritual reality differs from meaning in the realm of ideas, in that the latter is timeless or unique, whereas the content of reality is to be understood not through its immanent cohesion but through the fact that a stream of life led up to it and is contained in it as something past but not submerged; and that this stream continues to flow through it, lending it, as an essential element, a movement toward future changes. Therefore, meaning in the realm of reality, in contrast to meaning in the realm of ideas, is only comprehensible and significant if it is historically justified and future oriented meaning—its totality is historically in flux and real, not a product of unique systematization. History and future orientations are contained as dialectical elements in the meaning of present reality, and therefore act as very strong integrating forces—not on their own, however, as superficial party ideologies would have it, but in their capacity as constituent elements of reality, and only to the extent they possess this capacity.

Acknowledgment of history as the causal basis of the present, or as the object of constant reference, at the same time underestimates the significance and limits of its efficacy, and above all of its integrating power.[109]

The problem of the state's territory fits in this context from two points of view.[110]

First of all, from the point of view of an integrating content, possibly the most important substantive content for the state community. One of the major achievements of more recent geography and "geopolitics" has been to demonstrate forcibly the extent to which the life of the state is determined by living space [Lebensraum], the state's territory, its characteristics, borders, and spatial relations, so that we tend to speak of the each state's "particular idea of the state" as its attempt to conform to its particular geographic factors.[111] Here we can only touch upon this area of research, with the wealth of facts and viewpoints it elaborates.

Here we need only reflect critically on the fact that all these geographical considerations, in accordance with their scientific starting point and the apparently spatial, physical nature of their object, tend to treat the state's territory as a causal factor of the life of the state, to see the political sphere as a natural, life-conditioning human living space, just as the geographical living space of animals and plants is a condition of the existence of organic life, the subject of natural science.[112]

As fundamentally wrong as the popular analogy between the state's territory and the human body generally is, here it is instructive. Just as the linkage of all spiritual life to human physical existence and physical, physiological processes does not bind this spiritual life and its insights to the (mechanical and organic) laws of space-filling bodies, but instead allows it to retain its inherent spiritual autonomy, because its physicality is only a dialectic element, not as a causal factor—in the same way, the life of the state, notwithstanding its geographic tie, and unlike the organic life of the natural sciences, cannot be explained by its geographic tie, but can be fully understood only by including them as an essential element in spiritual reality. That is, the theory of the state always deals with this area as an object of spiritual experiences, as an integrating element in the political community, to the extent it is an element of common political destiny, and especially to the extent it is a responsibility, as an object of defense, acquisition, settlement, exploitation, etc.

While the naturalist, mechanist errors of political geography are excusable, and often fruitful as working hypotheses, there is no excuse for the massive territorial naturalism of more recent German state law theory. It expressly places the state in its territory as a spatial reality, as though on a spatial platform, on a saucer.[113] The usual doctrine roughly juxtaposes the three elements, placing the citizenry on this platform, and then placing over both (in the oft-used imagery) the dome of state authority; or the two are held together by state authority, as marionettes in a puppet theater are held by the strings of the puppeteer. This inglorious chapter in the German history of failed ideas [*Ungeistesgeschichte*] is, of course, a rewarding field for the criticism of the Vienna school, to which therefore we can refer.[114] But to their criticism must be added the simple explanation of these errors: The crudeness of this naive realism by necessity supplements the emptiness that would otherwise exist in the formalism of the law of the state and of its theory.

The second integrating function of territory lies in the fact that it symbolizes the accomplishment of the tasks that territory sets the state; it undergoes constant transformation, becomes a cultural product, not only as the bearer of all kinds of particular economic and cultural values, but as a vivid synopsis of the totality of the values of a state and a people. To this extent, it is generally called "fatherland" or "homeland," and more than anything else represents, for example in the language and sentiment of wartime, a living and valuing political community—sometimes in turn represented by its parts, its *sacri termini,* its historic landscape—for example, the Rhine. With this function, territory joins the ranks of integrating symbols of an unformulable plethora of values, of a totality of values; in fact, it moves to the head of these ranks. Just as the statute of an association formulates the association's goal in the first paragraph, constitutions signify the unformulable content of the state's life they regulate by starting with the symbols of this content: territory, colors and coats of arms, state form, and state character.

In this sense, it is true that the state experiences its most essential concretization through its territory,[115] and that changes in this territory are not quantitative, but qualitative changes in the essence of the state. Territory is first on the list of the state's substantive integrating factors, and from this point of view it is a subject of state theory—but not from the point of view of the absurd and impossible doctrine of state elements.

THE UNITY OF THE SYSTEM OF INTEGRATION— TYPES OF INTEGRATION IN RELATION TO ONE ANOTHER— FOREIGN AND DOMESTIC POLICY

. . .

The relationship among various types of integration, especially the two poles of every system of integration, the substantive on the one hand and the functional on the other, is an important problem of theory and politics. However, it is neither explicitly defined in this way nor even understood as such. For it is not fundamentally interpreted and treated as a systematic problem but rather observed as an historical one. Treatment as an historical problem involves, in particular, two possible historical sequences: the replacement of substantive by functional integration, on the one hand, and of functional by substantive, on the other.

The first possibility accords with the course of the modern history of ideas in general. The disintegration of the medieval value-system meant at the same time the disintegration of the developed, natural, unproblematic community of values—a "community" in the sense used by [Ferdinand] Tönnies; that is, the end of the era of primarily substantive integration. The spiritually atomized, desubstantialized, functionalized modern person is not a person lacking in values and substance but a person without community-forming values, especially traditional values, which are at the same time necessary for a stable cultural and social order. Including the modern person in community formation is more dependent than it used to be on functional integrating techniques. As the person of the stable order was integrated through inclusion in the established hierarchy of the state and the estates, the citizen of the nineteenth century was integrated through the formal play of the parliamentary state and the citizen of the democratic era through the plebiscitary forms of life in the mass state. To this extent, despite the insufficiencies of their psychological skepticism, the inroads of mass psychology into modern theories of the state contain some truth. To this extent, too, it is not incorrect to contrast the process-prone modern political groups, as in communism, with the more structure-oriented older parties.[116]

Such changes can sometimes also be observed in miniature, quite independently of these world-historical developments. Karl Bilfinger has impressively shown that it is typical for single German states, in contrast to nation-states, to be held together not so much by substantive elements—economics, culture, ethnicity, and related substantive competencies—but above all by the "principle of state authority"; that is, by the interplay of the forms and functions through which state authority is exercised; that is, functional integration by dint of the public's share in experiencing this functional life, completely separate from its substantive content.[117]

More important for state theory than the number, type, and truth of such singular cases is the fundamental fact that the opposite sequence of events also occurs, also in singular cases, and that it occurs here especially as a practical political program, thus giving it major practical significance.

On the one hand, the disintegration of the more traditional community into modern, rationalized "society" in the sense used by Tönnies means the transformation of the irrational content of community into a content of rationalized, conscious, formulated meanings and values, developed in the theories of social contract, human rights, and the modern state, as well as party programs. Thus the attempt has been made to see the essence of the modern community, as opposed to the older one, in the fact that in the original community, the leader was the determinative and essential integrating factor, while in the modern community, the leader is replaced by ideas and abstractions.[118]

A corresponding trend can be observed in various concrete individual phenomena. Here I will mention only the most significant description, provided by Karl Loewenstein, of the climax from a person-oriented to an issue-oriented plebiscitary constitutional type in England.[119]

It is here, as far as I can tell, that the key to the riddles of the socialist theory of the state can be found. This becomes clearer the more Engels's formulation of the "transition from political rule over people to an administration of things and direction of the processes of production—that is, the elimination of the state"[120] becomes the *leitmotiv* of socialist discussions of the state. Creation of solidarity, which is the prerequisite for eliminating "domination," is based on the creation of the true economic and social order. If this exists, then unity of will—in particular, the unity of political will—is no longer created through domination, through overpowering, through any act of will at all, but instead through insight into the truth of this order.[121] That is why Marxism puts so much emphasis on education; because the people in this new order must necessarily be different and better than those who came before.[122] In any case, however, once implemented, socialism requires no further systems of integration; it already has them, in the substantive new order it has implemented. That is why for Max Adler, for example, the problem of dissenting minorities no longer exists at all in the socialist order.[123]

Here "bourgeois" state theory begins to have its doubts—in the elimination of our familiar reality of political life, a world of lively and therefore battling wills, wills that build the state through this battle and make history possible—quite apart from all other objections to Marxism.

Political integration exclusively through a single integrating content can be the subject only of a theory of the nonstate, as Marxism aims to be, or of a utopia. It is a lost or a future paradise that is so characterized—hence the tendency of all chiliastic utopias toward romanticism. This is not contradicted by the fact that a historical case is realized in the form of the Roman Church. On the one hand, here too the system of substantive integration did not remain pure; on the other hand, it is telling that its own legal system, and the political systems modeled on it, are all hierarchies of authorities deriving their legitimacy from the bearer of the central substantive value. Carl Schmitt's is the most important modern attempt to conceive the state's reality systematically along the lines of this scheme. It is instructive on the right and possibility of any attempt of this kind to develop a theory of the state. It becomes not a theory of the state but one of law, and given its prerequisites it can become nothing else. Thus it is telling that Max Adler finds something of an ally in this theory of value-legitimized legal relations.[124]

All the more attention is warranted by the transformation that, as a general retreat of humane human values before civilizing material values within our cultural universe, brings with it a corresponding shift in the relative significance of states' integrating factors, largely explaining, in particular, the decline of parliamentarism.[125]

We will refrain from further examples of actual or imagined stages of integrating types, which may easily be sifted out of many theories involving evolutionary stages.[126] Despite the relative truth of such observations, we must remain aware that the state is a unified association thanks to all its integrating factors—that is, thanks to its substantive content and volitional life, just as the personal life of the individual experiences its unifying fulfillment in the interplay of its functions and in the substance of its memory, responsibility, and tendency toward the future. Here too, the inherent spiritual logic of values proves itself in the ongoing harmonization of these constantly self-transforming single factors.

One of the most powerful aspects of fascism, however one may judge it otherwise, lies in the fact that it recognized this necessity for all-around integration with great clarity, that it handles the techniques of functional integration masterfully, despite its rejection of liberalism and parliamentarism, and that it consciously replaces the socialist substantive integration that it rejects with another (the myth of the nation, the corporate state, etc.).

Finally, we must be reminded again that, as a rule, none of the integrating types appears in pure form; only one type or another predominates in each individual case. At times, they appear as an inseparable unity; thus the integrating effect of political success[127] is owed equally to the substantive content acquired as a common property and to the experience of this acquisition by the state community, or at least by its organs in its name.[128]

The types of integration and their systematic interplay in creating the unity of the life of the state have thus far been treated essentially from the point of view of domestic politics and illustrated through its most important manifestations. But this view would leave a painful gap if it considered the state, politics, and integration only from the domestic perspective, neglecting the question of the relationship between the developed system of the life of the state and the sphere of external politics, which seem at first glance to be so different in substance and logic. In one sphere, we apparently have the state as a power, that is, a compact unity; in the other, it is broken down into single factors and functions and their ever-changing interplay. In the one sphere, there is the heteronomy of the power game of foreign policy; in the other, the autonomy of the state's creation of its own character. In the one sphere, therefore, there is a necessity that limits the freedom in the other, in the spirit of the oft-mentioned "primacy of foreign policy."

In another context, I attempted to demonstrate that political life is the unity of domestic and foreign politics and that this unity is based in the fact that both tendencies are the state's creation of its own individuality—that is, integration.[129] I have little to add to this discussion.

The conventional view of the essential contradiction between domestic and foreign politics, and of the problematic relationship between these two mutually alien worlds and fields of political force—that it must be a relationship in which the one influences the other, that is, a relationship of the primacy of the one over the other—is usually based on certain historical and practical, but also deeper theoretical, presuppositions.

Theoretically, the alternative of the primacy of domestic or foreign politics is the alternative of, on the one hand, the substantialization (and isolation) of the state's power, and, on the other hand, of the individual as the ultimate bearer of political goals and thus the ultimate engine of political life. The ultimate cause of political events is either the states and their power relationships, which determines domestic politics and the form of the state through foreign politics (the well-known thesis of German historians, repeated ad nauseam and especially employed to justify the German monarchy); or the individuals and the domestic political arrangements they initiate (as is often maintained, for example, in pacifist ideology).

Both ways of thinking are equally untenable from an idealist point of view. The second is that of the prevailing sociology of relationships and interactions having individuals as their inflexible, substantial subjects; in earlier discussions, it was rejected again and again from the idealist point of view. The first is just as incorrect where it is applied; it too hardens the political bodies into inflexible substances, thus removing them from idealist understanding—although their relationships are also ones of spiritual exchange and life, that is, of mutual creation and above all of the self-creation that occurs within mutual creation, but not causal, mechanistic relations between substantial and isolated bodies.[130]

Even though the essential primacy of foreign or domestic politics can thus be justified using arguments based solely on theoretically untenable presuppositions, in practical historical discussion (where the question is generally treated in German historical and political literature), one or the other answer will still be well founded in certain situations. In a country without heavy pressure on its borders, such as the United States, domestic politics is more likely to dominate than in Germany before and after the world war. It is taken more for granted in the Anglo-Saxon context that "*the national life precedes international relations*" [English in the original],[131] than in the German context, with its passive, contemplative, and slightly aestheticizing approach to foreign politics.[132] In revolutionary countries and those with turbulent domestic politics, foreign politics more easily become dependent on domestic politics than in stable constitutional systems.[133] In regard to all these possibilities, it is important here to establish only that foreign politics determines the essence and integration of the entirety of a state as much as domestic politics. To remain within the bounds of the conventional discussion, this fact will be illustrated through several examples. The most obvious is that foreign politics is not about physical objects, which has often been discussed, particularly in the theory of imperialism.[134] The Rhine issue is less a question of the Rhine border than of the overall worth of the German and French peoples.[135] The overall character of a foreign policy, once taken, regularly outlives its actual cause, because it becomes an essential quality of the state, which "cannot escape its shadow."[136] According to Richelieu, larger states honor treaties to a greater degree than small ones, because they have to care more about their reputations;[137] that is because they, as stronger entities, are more identified with their policies, more marked by them. In particular, political treaties and constellations are known to be more difficult to change than, for example, economic ones, because the former determine the essence of those involved to a greater degree than the latter.[138] As an essential attribute of the state, its standing in foreign politics is a point of honor, an integrating element;[139] a diktat such as that of Versailles, for example, is so immoral not only because it demands sacrifice, but because it forces a change in the essence of those affected without their consent. Bismarck's idea of grounding the Austro-German alliance in the constitution would have meant only a quantitative increase in and emphasis on this alliance, which, as is always true of foreign politics, was already an integral element of the essence of the states involved. Thus in practice, healthy foreign politics is not only a condition, but in fact even an element of a nation's domestic health,[140] and theory correctly rejects tearing the political essence apart into a foreign and a do-mestic aspect.[141] Domestic political content and a state's international rela-tions are not two separate parts but only two elements of its reality and in-dividuality. Failure to appreciate this truth leads one astray both theoretically and practically—as when Meinecke sees the problem of ethics and politics only in foreign politics rather than in the unity of the political, and substi-tutes the rigid image of battling powers, to which ethics finds itself in hope-less antithesis, for the actual object of the problem: the fluid life of political integration in its substantive abundance and with its whole richness of per-sonal participation.[142] . . .

Part Two
Consequences for Constitutional Theory

THE ESSENCE OF THE CONSTITUTION

The foundations of a state theory outlined so far provide a very specific basis for the resolution of each and every problem of state theory and, in particu-lar, for a very specific constitutional theory. . . .

The . . . problem [of the essence of the constitution] was treated in detail for the first time by Georg Jellinek.[143] He saw the heart of the question in the fact that "legal precepts are incapable of actually mastering the distribution of power within the state," that "actual political forces move *according to their own laws,* which operate independent of any legal form."[144] To the extent these forces are capable of "transforming the constitution," they make law, and belong to the particular doctrine concerning the sources of constitu-tional law, since the conventional doctrine of the sources of law does not cover them.[145]

Thus there is either the questionable "normative force of fact," which is particularly effective in the constitutional arena [146]—or an unclear juxta-position of and opposition between the written constitution and "actual" "so-ciological" forces.

This problem, here correctly perceived but incorrectly conceived, is the core problem of constitutional theory. It is not an instance of the applica-bility of the general idealist problem of the tension between the "ought" and the "is," meaning and the reality of life. Nor is it an instance of the the-ory of the sources of law. Instead, it is a question of the particular substance of the state as the object of legal regulation by its constitution. . . .

The constitution is the legal order of the state, or more precisely, of the life through which the state has its reality[147]—namely, of its process of inte-gration. The meaning of this process is the constantly renewed production of the totality of the life of the state, and the constitution provides the legal norms for various aspects of this process.

Of course, the state does not live merely through those elements of its life regulated by its constitution; in order to be carried out at all in political life, the constitution must have its supplement in reliance on the basic drives of this life and a wealth of social motivations. But it cannot even entirely master those functions of state life that it does regulate; like all political life, these functions too arise out of the totality of the individual personality and continuously grow together into the super-personal totality of the state. Such a wealth of life cannot be fully comprehended and governed by a few schematic constitutional articles usually based upon constantly new prescriptions at third- and fourth-hand; it can only be hinted at and, to the extent these articles demonstrate integrating strength, be stimulated by them. Whether, and how, the goal of successful, satisfactory integration emerges from these articles depends upon the way in which all the forces of the political life of the entire people come into play. In the process, the stream of political life may often achieve this goal by taking paths that are not exactly constitutional; in that case, fulfillment of the goal of integration set by the inherent logic of spiritual values and the articles of the constitution would, despite these isolated deviations, accord more with the spirit of the constitution than a constitutional life that, though more faithful to the letter of the law, is less successful.

Thus it is the spirit of the constitution itself, its focus not on the details but on the totality of the state and the totality of its process of integration, that not only permits but even requires such elastic, supplementary constitutional interpretation deviating greatly from every other kind of legal interpretation.

Constitutions do not need to provide any special authority for this. Constitutional legislators need be as little aware of the inherent spiritual logic of a constitution as the individual need be aware of the larger meaning of his spiritual life—in particular, of the meaning of his political life as a component of the process of state integration. As a rule, a constitutional document grows out of a different, more doctrinaire view of its tasks. The only modern constitution, to my knowledge, that was drafted with complete, if unreflective, clarity about these tasks is that of the North German Union [*Norddeutscher Bund*] and the Empire [*Kaiserriech*]. But this does not rule out a similar use of other constitutions. Not only do systems of integration governed by norms expand on their own by dint of the inherent logic of spiritual values and its effect on the national creative will, and by way of spontaneous formations (parties, conventions, etc.) that depend on the greater or lesser political talent of the people, but also the institutions governed by norms themselves enter the universe of meaning, which sets them their task with or without the awareness and intent of the legislature; they operate, expand, or modify themselves according to this task, without this being a special legal problem. It is simply the immanent, self-evident point of a formulated constitution that it has this elasticity, that its system can, if necessary, expand and change on its own. Thus a coherent understanding of the object the constitution desires and regulates—that is, the actual system of integration—as well as of the constitution's own objective intentions, is possible only if this elasticity is taken into account, this ability to change and expand with its consequent changes in and expansions of the constitutional system, in spirit as well as in norms.

Thus it should come as no surprise, and is neither a shortcoming nor a reproach, that constitutions are able to grasp their objects only schematically and at certain specific points.[148] The objective intent of constitutions is and can only be to provide hints; they generally do this in traditional ways, in the form of receptions;[149] however, they do not thereby make the same claim to rigidly heteronomous authority as the law of subordinate associations, which must provide abstract and schematic legal norms for many individual cases. They give free rein to the general, occasionally positivized tendency of constitutional life toward integration and its inclination toward self-formation— apart from those occasions on which the constitutions strictly determine this life, attempting to rule in the manner of rigidly heteronomous norms that can only be eliminated by genuine prescriptive law.[150]

This means that constitutions claim their own substantive area of life as their object and task, just as other complexes of legal norms have theirs in regard to other substantive areas of life. It means a rejection of the jurisprudence that attempts to raise the constitution to an essential element of every legal order as such—to a, in fact, to *the* condition of its validity.[151] This does the constitution, and even more the dignity and the idea of law, a great injustice. This type of "constitutional theory" has often been refuted successfully—but this refutation is complete only once positive evidence has been provided of the constitution's own substantive task. . . .

This reality is constantly reproduced not by a constitution that is the "dormant, persistent element in state life"[152] but by a constantly renewed constitutional life. This is no different from the "constituting" of other groups, such as assemblies. Legally formalist, static thinking sees in this the act through which an assembly gives itself a chair, or at most rules of procedure, and declares itself in session—all of which, apart from its technical significance, has a more important actual meaning: It not only establishes the duties of the chair and the speakers but also completes the transition from the previous state of each individual's being in himself to the social state of being assembled. This transition is perceived by all those assembled, without exception, as a real experience, as a synchronized procedure permeating all, as integration into a group whose formation and action was the point of the meeting. But every chair of an assembly knows that the assembly is not set in motion once and for all when it is constituted, like a wound-up clock; rather, the constituting act must, so to speak, be renewed each moment; the integrating force must be newly developed and must play at every moment; and this occurs above all through the orderly procedure of the organs and speakers. Thus the norm, the constitution of the assembled group and its organization, is not the rule of a given, permanent existence and its effects on the environment; it is rather the form of the founding and constant renewal and production of this existence. . . .

The criterion that distinguishes the state from other associations will not be discussed here in full. In any case, the state's special position has two consequences. First of all, its existence is not, as with most other associations, guaranteed by a power outside itself; it is not kept in motion by a motor or referee located outside its own structure; it is not carried by a heteronomous cause or guarantee, but integrates itself, merely by dint of an inherent logic of values, into an integrating system gravitating toward itself. In this sense, state constructions based in mechanistic autonomy, like those of Montesquieu, *The Federalist,* and [Robert] Redslob, are a fortunate parable of reality, although Wilson correctly characterized them as those of the Newtonian age.[153] Thus, in a very different sense than an association's constitution, a state's written constitution can be only a stimulus and barrier to this constitutional life gravitating toward itself, which cannot be guaranteed heteronomously. Further, from this system of integration there constantly develops anew the sovereign decision of the state as a "unity through decision universal in a territory,"[154] and this decision is necessary by virtue of its immanent logic, as granting formal authority and ordering power of final appeal; while those associations are generally optional means of achieving specific, individual, substantive goals. That is the basis of the special status of the state's constitution: first, the categorical necessity of the task of integration assigned it, as opposed to the optional character of other associations; and second, its limitation to its own immanent forces and guaranties in completing this task. . . .

. . . The establishment of the state's goal or sphere of activity and of the status of its members are not essential requirements of a constitution—after all, the state's formal existence and life, and the assurance of this existence and life, are first of all ends in themselves, and thus the only essential tasks of the constitution.

Thus the so-called elements of the state and their constitutive delimitation are not regular objects of constitutional regulation. However, territory is its most basic, substantive concretization and is thus often spoken of in an introductory article of a constitution, just as the goal of an association is spoken of in its charter. While under the law of associations, however, this establishment of a goal is constitutive, mention of the territory that has been established in international law in relation to neighboring states does not, as a rule, bear this significance; thus it is typically missing from the majority of constitutions.

It is the same with the personal "element of the state."[155] The territory essentially determines who is part of the state; the details of obtaining and losing citizenship are essentially technical, specialized questions of legislation that do not involve the essence of the state. Nor is the constitution concerned with the membership status of citizens. The state is not there because of this status, because of these rights, but as an end in itself; regulation of this legal status—for example, through catalogues of basic rights—constitutes the state through substantive elements, through a specific character of its rule of law and its culture, and it is not the equivalent of an association's rules of membership.

In contrast, organs, formal functions, and substantive tasks are essential elements of the constitution. In the creation of its organs, in their existence and constitutional activity, the state lives and is personally integrated; in its formal functions may be found its life as a process, its functional integration; in the substantive content lent by its territory, its constitutional character, and its constitutional tasks lies the third element upon which the community is based. All the same, the third element diminishes in importance; while the territory is essential, the remaining manifestations are far less so in contrast to the two other systems of personal and functional integration. But together, the three form the material content, the material law of the constitution. . . .

Part Three
Consequences for Positive Law

INTERPRETATION OF THE CONSTITUTION AS A WHOLE

The attempt made here is intended not merely as a contribution to the establishment of a idealist theory of state and constitution as a spiritual reality, but also as a contribution to state law theory. For it is from the consideration of positive state law that these views in fact developed,[156] so that they must, in turn, stand the test of positive law. . . .

. . . I begin with questions concerning the constitution as a whole; in particular, the problem of demarcating its content and establishing basic methods of interpretation.

The first, systematic issue of demarcation is that of distinguishing the law of the state from administrative law. The traditional definition that assigns the law of the state the static existence of the state, and administrative law its active functioning, has already been rejected in an earlier context.[157] Like administrative law, the law of the state regulates public life, to some extent even the same public life; for example, where both are responsible for administration, in the latter case as part of the separation of powers, as the executive power, and in the former as an isolated system of purposeful state activity in itself. From this arises the difference in their questions and objects: the law of the state is the law of integration; administrative law is technical law. The guiding thought behind the one group of norms is the integrating interplay of state institutions and functions into a wholeness of state life; that behind the other is the existence of the administration in itself, the technical accomplishment of its specific goals vis-à-vis the public welfare.

The question is not merely one of apportioning the material in this or that course or textbook, but of finding the universe of meaning relevant to the interpretation and evaluation of the material. A legal precept is misunderstood, is done an injustice, if it is seen and acknowledged as a component in a universe of meaning other than the one in which it belongs. It is an illusion, rare even with formalists, that a legal precept will be given the same interpretation and application everywhere, regardless of whether it is placed in the context of public or private, procedural or substantive, political or technical law. . . .

A second, closely related problem is that of distinguishing the formal from the substantive sense of the constitution. It is formalist agnosticism that despairs of creating a system independent of the accidental phrasing of written constitutional clauses—a system of norms that are fundamental elements in an attempt by the citizenry to positivize the integrating order through law.[158] However, creating such a system is not simple[159] and cannot in any case be found in varying lists.[160] It can be achieved only by energetically relating and tracing back the stuff of state law to the simple principle of meaning to which it is oriented. Calling this problem insoluble would mean the abdication of state law theory as a systematic discipline.

The criterion that distinguishes the constitution from the rest of the legal order, again and again, is the "political" character of its object. The distinction was obviously expressed and generally understood during the German revolution, when workers and soldiers councils were declared the repositories of "political power,"[161] while "administrative powers" were reserved to the Bundesrat.[162] Thus the concept of the political is indispensable to the theory of the law of the state. But especially for the demarcation and distinction with which we are concerned, nothing can be defined as political simply through "relation to a state purpose"[163] or in the manner newly established by Carl Schmitt,[164] but only in the sense grounding this treatise.

Even more important, fundamental consequences emerge for the interpretation of constitutional law.

The formalist method here refrains from consciously taking the idealist theory of the state, a theory of the essential quality of its object, as the starting point of its juridical work. It applies to this object its familiar "general" juridical concepts, largely those of a highly authoritarian law of associations. Thus this method breaks constitutional law down into an aggregate of individual norms and complexes of norms [*Institute*] that it subsumes under familiar general schemata by studying the formal legal power of the will and formal duties contained in them. It thereby ignores from the start, among other things, the way in which the constitution differs from all other legal material: that in regulating other legal relationships, the issue is one of establishing abstract norms for an endless number of cases aiming at best for an average suitability; here, on the other hand, the issue is the concrete, individual law of a single reality of life. Every interpreter of the constitution should take at least this from its beginning—from the preamble, definitions of territory, form of state, colors, etc.—even if he finds clear "demarcations of spheres of will" missing: it is about the vital law of something real and concrete, and since this something is not a statue, but a life-process constantly recreating this reality; it is about the law of its integration. This has, to name only several very general rules, at least three consequences.

First of all, all details of state law are to be understood not as isolated, by themselves, but only as elements in a universe of meaning they are to realize in the functional totality of integration. Future discussions will provide examples; here only a few will be sketched in advance.

The Reich's supervisory power over the Länder practically demands treatment by analogy with the Länder's supervisory power over local authorities; here, as there, a superior and an inferior association under public law, with the inferior responsible to the superior for fulfilling certain tasks and subject to the superior's special "supervisory power" to ensure that this responsibility is carried out properly. But while the Länder's supervisory power is exercised in regard to the local authorities when necessary to uphold the law and further the state interest, naturally not without sensitivity to local political conditions but without this sensitivity being legally required, the Reich's supervisory power cannot be isolated this way and must not be under the constitution. The Reich's supervisory power is an element in the fluid coordination of Reich with Länder and must always be seen in conjunction with the converse constitutional influence of the Länder on the Reich. The Reich's supervisory power is acceptable to the Länder only in this context, if the Länder are to retain their political self-respect. The Reich's supervisory power is held together with the Länders' constitutional right of influence by the higher law governing the relationship between Reich and Länder, the law of federal comity, the duty of all those involved to incline constantly toward agreement and consensus. Therefore, the phrasing of the Reich's law of supervision in the Weimar Constitution is not simply a diplomatic statement of what is in fact a relationship between "ruler and subject,"[165] but rather the appropriate expression of a profound difference from the seemingly analogous legal situation of local authorities.

In the same way, constitutional court jurisdiction cannot be seen as analogous to civil or administrative jurisdiction. Constitutional court protection of parliamentary minorities is different from civil court protection of groups of stockholders with their individual interests, for it must serve to integrate and coordinate the parties; court protection of the Länder against the Reich is different from administrative court protection of local authorities against supervision by the Länder, because the former is one possibility among others of reaching a consensus. Parties to civil or administrative proceedings can eventually be forced to obey, whether they want to or not, through the *ultima ratio* of judges' decisions and bailiffs. But the fact that there are no such regular means against obstruction, secession, and the like is not merely a difference in the actual chance of success of constitutional law and jurisdiction; it means, rather, that this law and jurisdiction are of a particular nature. In constitutional law it is scarcely possible, and often not possible at all, to compel obedience; the fulfillment of constitutional duties must constantly be left to good will and the duty to reach a consensus and the duty to establish constitutional cooperation. Therefore, constitutional jurisdiction, at least in the most serious of cases, can only be a means to and a stage of consensus between parties whose good will must be assumed, and who should employ this means only in a spirit of consensus. Just as the Reich's supervisory authority should not "order," thus also should parties to a conflict before the constitutional court fight not for legal victory but for consensus. The duty of mandatory mediation under the Law of Revenue Equalization accurately describes the issue here, and the judgment of a constitutional court is a type of arbitration, a substitute for settlement.

A further consequence of the inclusion of specific constitutional norms in the universe of state integration is that these norms have varying relevance for integration and different degrees of importance. This question of importance is a legal question; it is apparent[166] that to be faithful to the truth a textbook on the law of the state must accurately assess the importance of individual norms and complexes of norms. It is an inadequate interpretation of Article 3 of the Weimar Constitution when leading commentators emphasize that establishing the Reich colors results only in certain duties for the administration and the merchant marine but do not recognize that this provision (as can already be inferred from its position at the beginning of the constitution) ranks high in the constitution—a rank not first created by the sanctions imposed by the Law for the Protection of the Republic, but rather is instead presupposed and protected by these sanctions.[167] It is a legal question whether the parliamentary system, under the Reich Constitution, can be ranked a constitutional principle of the first or second order.[168] It is no different in any other legal field, except that the question of ranking individual elements of the state law system of integration, with its particularly strong systematic cohesion, is also, to a very great extent, an element of its scholarly conception. Even positivism would most likely admit this, to the extent that it has not reached its pinnacle in a logic of norms, in whose kingdom all cats are gray even by day.

Finally, the alterability of the constitution, the possibility of "constitutional transformation," is a characteristic of constitutional law that flows from its all-encompassing nature.[169]

As a system of integration, constitutional law is expected to ensure fulfillment of an ever-changing challenge that must constantly be met in an optimal fashion. The factors in meeting this challenge shift as time goes by and situations change. This transformation can occur outside of constitutional law if it lies in the sphere of social spontaneity, of "extra-constitutional"[170] forces, especially of political parties—a spontaneity presupposed, even taken into account, but not regulated, by the constitution. Transformation can concern the constitution itself, by gradually shifting the rank and importance of constitutional factors, complexes of norms, and norms.[171] It can even introduce a new factor in constitutional life; that would be the case if the limitation on the parliamentary system foreseen by [Willi] Hellpach[172] came to pass through a practice of increasingly creative ministerial decrees. The latter two cases involve "constitutional transformation" that changes the content of the constitution in a material sense. It is clear that this change cannot be bound by the requirements of the development of prescriptive law. It follows from the character of the constitution, which normativizes a system of integration that constantly fulfills its task: this integrating task is the regulative principle not only for the constitutional legislator but even for the fluid development of the constitution's meaning and authority. . . .

EIGHT

Hermann Heller

INTRODUCTION

David Dyzenhaus

The initial research for this project was generously funded by the Alexander von Humboldt Foundation and the Social Sciences and Humanities Research Council of Canada. I thank Cheryl Misak for her comments on a draft of this essay.

Hermann Heller (17 July 1891–4 November 1933) came from a Jewish family in the Austro-Hungarian Empire. He interrupted his studies in law by volunteering for service in the Austrian army during the First World War. His experiences as a front-line fighter left him with a heart condition, which contributed to his death at the age of 42. But his poor health did not dampen his deeply combative spirit—a spirit that he put at the service of German social democracy. In March 1920, together with Gustav Radbruch (who had successfully sponsored Heller's *Habilitationsschrift* at Kiel), he participated in the armed resistance to the Kapp Putsch, aimed at the overthrow of the Weimar Republic. In 1932, he appeared as the legal representative for the parliamentary party of the Prussian Social Democrats in the case *Preußen contra Reich,* which tested the constitutional validity of the conservative federal government's coup d'état against the Prussian (socialist-dominated) state government. In oral argument before the court,[1] Heller frequently incurred the wrath of the president of the court by refusing to allow the court to ignore the fact that the complex legal issues at stake were also political issues with profound implications.[2]

Between 1920 and 1932, Heller participated in building socialist youth movements, in adult education, and, despite the customary anti-Semitic barriers, secured academic posts in Berlin (1928) and Frankfurt (1931). In March of 1933, he accepted Harold Laski's invitation to lecture in England. Events in Germany, including the Nazi statute that deprived him and other Jewish academics of their positions, made a return to Germany perilous; Heller accepted a chair at the University of Madrid, intending to go from there to the University of Chicago, which had also made him an offer. Death cut short Heller's attempt to develop a comprehensive exposition of his theory of the state (*Staatslehre*), although the manuscript was sufficiently complete to be published in 1934 in Holland.[3]

This manuscript, together with Heller's other works, which encompass a broad range of topics—political and legal philosophy, political science, practical legal and constitutional issues, the problem of sovereignty in domestic and international law, as well as studies of Hegel, socialism, education, nationalism, and fascism—were published in three volumes in 1971; a revised edition was published in 1992.[4]

The time it took for Heller's works to be made generally accessible in this form attests to the relatively sparse interest in his position within Germany; he is almost unknown to the English-speaking world. His obscurity may have more to do with the novelty of his ideas rather than with the fact that he did not live long enough to elaborate them or that his political involvement in Weimar meant that his ideas were too closely tied to a particular context.

Heller argued (as did Carl Schmitt, *contra* Hans Kelsen) that all conceptions of law are fundamentally political and tied to particular historical and social contexts. Like Schmitt, he sought to ground legal philosophy in society and culture. However, he opposed as dictatorial Schmitt's celebration of the elimination of political conflict through the imposition of the Volk's "substantive homogeneity" on a pluralist society. Rather, Heller shared with Kelsen a commitment to democracy, to the liberty of the individual, and to social equality. Heller also shared Kelsen's respect for the idea that it is important for a decent political society to make sense of the constraints of the rule of law.

The task that Heller set himself in legal and political philosophy was to vindicate a highly political conception of the *Rechtsstaat*—the state based on the rule of law. This conception sought to defend and extend democracy in the face of attack from the fascist right (or the equivalent on the left), a result achievable, Heller argued, only through the transformation of the formal *Rechtsstaat*—the product of liberal thought—into a social *Rechtsstaat*. In the absence of a "social homogeneity" that guarantees social equality, he reasoned, individual liberties for which liberals fought are worse than worthless. For these liberties can be politically and socially divisive when groups of individuals find the law's formal promise of equality and liberty for all to be merely formal—that is, insubstantial. What this level of social homogeneity is, and how it is to be achieved, must be determined by the citizens of the particular society. For Heller contrasts an active conception of citizenship with what he takes to be the bourgeois conception of the citizen as the passive consumer of benefits accorded by the state.[5]

Heller sought to reconstruct legal theory, not to destroy it from within. His principal target in the field of law was Kelsen's positivism—in part because Kelsen had presented the most sustained account of how law works—but Schmitt remained Heller's principal political target. Heller understood Schmitt's philosophy of politics as the one most likely to exploit the problems raised by Kelsen's apolitical Pure Theory of Law—in particular, by the logic of legal norms, which grants legal validity to any political act.

Heller was for that reason committed to demonstrating not only the illogic of Kelsen's positivism but also its danger. In his view, Kelsen paves the way not for the overcoming of Weimar's crisis but for Schmitt's subversion of Weimar. Kelsen's positivism, which indiscriminately grants the title *Rechtsstaat* to any state, is, in Heller's words, the "ideal catalyst for dictatorship."[6]

Schmitt as well sought to show that legal positivism could not help but accede to sovereign decision, and Heller's critique of Kelsen comes very close at times to Schmitt's. Indeed, Heller derived from Schmitt a sense of the importance of decision and of sovereignty in politics. But there is a crucial difference between Heller's and Schmitt's attacks on Kelsen, so much so that Heller seems at times quite close to Kelsen, at least to those passages in the Pure Theory where Kelsen seeks to substantiate the principle of legality.[7]

Heller, like Schmitt, sought to discern the politics of the *Rechtsstaat,* but his ultimate intent was entirely different. Schmitt posits that the *Rechtsstaat* is in fact a normative nothingness; Heller wants to show that while there is nothing at the end of the positivist trail, this does not mean that there is no valuable conception of politics to be found within the theory and practice of the *Rechtsstaat.* Under his view, one can make sense of the enterprise of governance through law only by nesting law within a highly political democratic theory. One of the two hallmarks of his project was that it sought to resurrect the natural law idea of the *Rechtsstaat* as something substantive and material that sets genuine boundaries to the exercise of power.

Such a theory was to some degree essential for making sense of existing law. Heller did not deny the importance of positive law to any constructive legal theory, but rather the proposition that any theory of positive law can itself be positive in Kelsen's sense—that is, informed solely by some scientific value, where science is understood by contrast with politics, ethics, and sociology. He maintained that such a theory of positive law must end in eliminating the very characteristic of law onto which it exclusively fastens: Positivism cannot explain even the positivity of law.

Heller argued that positivism is plagued by this problem because a theory of law, like any social and political theory, cannot merely reflect reality without risking self-destruction; legal theory, in seeking to understand what is, is prescriptive as well. But the theorist has, in Heller's view, a different task than the politician, for whom ideas are simply weapons in a political battle: The theorist must subordinate political practice to the aim of constructing a theory of such practice, with a view to showing which particular tendencies within the practice should be developed. Moreover, in accordance with his general anti-relativist stance, Heller maintains that there are standards of correctness that can be used to discriminate between political theories. His understanding of the importance of theory is thus deeply pragmatic at the same time that it sets high theoretical goals for inquiry.[8]

The key distinction in Heller's work is between positive law and fundamental principles of law. The idea of law must be established by "relativizing positive law to supra-positive, logical and ethical, fundamental principles of law [*Rechtsgrundsätze*]."[9] Heller's attempt to show an inherent connection between legality and legitimacy rests on precisely this distinction. But Heller also seeks to avoid equating legality and legitimacy in a way that would forfeit the critical ethical and legal conscience that he considers crucial to a healthy political culture. He argues that the modern tendency to strip law entirely of moral elements leads to the glorification of the contingencies of power—that is, to anarchy. At the same time, however, Heller maintains that one should resist tendencies that end in the total moralization of law.[10]

Nevertheless, he puts himself at risk of collapsing the distinction between positive legality and principles of legitimacy. For the second hallmark of Heller's project is his insistence that the content of any *Rechtsstaat* concept be appropriate to the circumstances of the times. Above all, this means that the supra-positive fundamental legal principles of which Heller speaks are not principles that come from outside of our general social practices. In his view, it is a condition of any modern attempt to justify the state or law that its justification be immanent—that is, internal to the practice. It must not appeal to anything that transcends our practice altogether, although it may appeal to, say, principles embedded in our ethical practices. Such principles will be legal principles that transcend positive law in the sense that we need to resort to them in order to understand the force of positive law and to give it appropriate content. But that does not make our recourse to them itself transcendent, since it stops at a practice, that is, in our ethical practices. These practices are but part of the array of practices that compose a particular culture or social reality, but for Heller they are a crucial part, not least because of the constitutive role they play in legal practice and, as a result, in the constitution of the power of the state.

Kelsen and Schmitt would both hold that Heller's appeal to ethics cannot help but be transcendental. Kelsen's relativism requires him to say that one should eschew such appeals; Schmitt, by contrast holds that appeals to ethical principles are both inevitable and determined by the play of power. Indeed, there is very little in common between Kelsen and Schmitt on this point, as is dramatically illustrated by Kelsen's assertion that behind the positive law one always finds the "Gorgon head of power."[11]

Heller argues that Schmitt and Kelsen both make the mistake of supposing that ethical practices are fruitless because they do not afford us an absolutely certain or secure foundation, and that they should therefore play no role in our understanding of law. Such a mistake, in his view, amounts to declaring that the roof of a house whose foundations are insecure must simply do without foundations and stand by itself.[12] While Kelsen and Schmitt attempt to ground their theories—Kelsen in science and Schmitt in "concrete order" thought[13]—Heller argues that their attempts fail; only ethical and political principles, based in social and cultural practices, can serve as a foundation for a *Rechtstaat*.

As the most recent philosophical debates on such issues attest, Heller's argument is at the very least difficult, and, according to many, impossible. He wants ethical foundations for law and the state that will provide a theory of legitimacy, but a theory that remains immanent. For some, the insight that all we have is our practices, so that justification is always immanent, is evidence that it is high time to abandon the search for foundations or justifications. Others argue that our ultimate values cannot be made dependent on what is internal to our practices: These values must be found beyond, whether in some divine source or in principles of rationality that transcend practice.

Heller begins his argument by attempting to demonstrate how both alternatives to his approach are unacceptable. The attempt to find standards of rationality that transcend practice ends in Kelsen's substanceless and thus defenseless theory of norms; Kelsen's theory of law cannot take into account the fact that power is constitutive of law and thus makes law prey to power. By contrast, Schmitt's complete relativization of law to power (and to the contingencies of the particular situation of power) leads to the irrational deification of power and decision. Unlike Schmitt (who places his hopes for purifying society of its contradictions and tensions on the advent of a new prophet) and unlike Kelsen (who similarly seeks to purify *law*) Heller argues for a normative, social basis for law that maintains its inherent contradictions and tensions.

Of course, that the alternatives are unacceptable does not of itself prove Heller correct. The positive step in Heller's project is his argument that just as power must be understood in terms of norms, norms cannot be understood outside of their relationship with the power that is required to positivize them.

In contrast to the positivist tradition, Heller argues that obedience to law is not merely something that has to be secured for a legal order to be effective; obedience is constitutive of such order. Law must secure obedience by appearing to those subject to it not just as an order, but as a norm—as a prescription with a justified claim to be legitimate. This imposes fundamental principles, both logical and ethical, on those who would make law. The principles are logical in that law must contain a content that is communicable to (that is, understandable by) its subjects. But law will not be communicable unless it also seeks to comply with ethical principles that justify its claim to legitimacy. One of the most important among these principles is that of the equality of all individuals before the law.[14]

In short, in order to exercise political power, a ruler needs to secure a framework of order in which he can exercise power; since positive law is essential to securing order, law and political power are mutually constitutive. But they cannot be constitutive in this manner unless law—that is, the legal order or legality—has an inherent claim to legitimacy or justification.

The basis of Heller's argument in this respect is a concept of human nature that is necessarily socially and culturally constructed. Human nature is culturally determined but also determinative of culture. Culture comes about because human nature is utopian in the sense of setting goals and then trying attain them. But these goals necessarily operate within the context of a culture that is not directly of our making and which thus forms a relatively objective and constitutive basis for our individual efforts.

In accordance with this concept of human nature, the social and the individual, norm and power, as well as other pairings that recur in our attempt to understand the world around us, must be understood as components of a dialectical unit. They are not reducible to each other nor to any common element; rather, the existence of the one presupposes the other. Such a dialectical concept is necessary to capture, for purposes of theory, the necessarily contradictory nature of the legal order, which is but a part (albeit a relatively autonomous one), of the political sphere, which is similarly merely a component of the social sphere, itself—by nature—contradictory.

Much work needs to be done to elaborate this position. Besides its inherent difficulties, the argument's exposition in the *Staatslehre* is plagued by ambiguities, the result not only of the book's incompleteness but also, undoubtedly, of the effect on Heller's state of mind of the total collapse of the democracy that he had made his life's work. But there can be no doubt about the power of his project.

Wolfgang Schluchter, in his outstanding exposition of that project, identifies Heller's intent as to "make comprehensible the structure of law, morality, and power, without tearing one of these limbs loose from the others or identifying one with another."[15] The power of Heller's argument is perhaps best demonstrated by the fact that it is only recently that similar ideas have received proper attention—and in a form not much more elaborate than the *Staatslehre*.[16]

MAIN WORKS

Heller's collected works are published in a three-volume edition edited by Christoph Müller: Hermann Heller, *Gesammelte Schriften,* 2nd ed. (Tübingen: Mohr, 1992). What follows is a list of his most significant works in legal philosophy, which are published in volume 2 of the *Gesammelte Schriften—Recht, Staat, Macht [Law, State, Power]* and volume 3, *Staatslehre als politische Wissenschaft [The Theory of the State as Political Science].*

Gesammelte Schriften, II: *Recht, Staat, Macht*

Grundrechte und Grundpflichten. 1924. Pp. 281–317.
Die Krisis der Staatslehre. 1926. Pp. 3–30.
Die Souveränität: Ein Beitrag zur Theorie des Staats- und Völkerrechts. 1927. Pp. 31–202.
Der Begriff des Gesetzes in der Reichsverfassung. 1928. Pp. 203–47.
Bemerkungen zur staats- und rechtstheoretischen Problematik der Gegenwart. 1929. Pp. 249–78.
Die Gleichheit in der Verhältniswahl nach der Weimarer Verfassung. 1929. Pp. 319–69.
Politische Demokratie und soziale Homogenität. 1928. Pp. 421–33.
Rechtsstaat oder Diktatur? 1929. Pp. 443–62.
Freiheit und Form in der Reichsverfassung. 1929/30. Pp. 371–91.
Ziele und Grenzen einer Deutschen Verfassungsreform. 1931. Pp. 411–17.
Europa und der Faschismus. 1931. Pp. 463–609.
Bürger und Bourgeois. 1932. Pp. 625–41.
Autoritärer Liberalismus? 1933. Pp. 643–53.

Gesammelte Schriften, III: *Staatslehre als politische Wissenschaft*

Staat. 1931. Pp. 3–23.
Political Power. 1934. Pp. 35–44.
Political Science. 1934. Pp. 45–75.
Staatslehre. 1934. Pp. 79–395.

LITERATURE

Albrecht, Stephan. *Hermann Hellers Staats- und Demokratieauffassung.* Frankfurt am Main: Campus, 1983.
Blau, Joachim. *Sozialdemokratische Staatslehre in der Weimarer Republik.* Marburg: Verlag Arbeiterbewegung und Gesellschaftswissenschaft, 1980.
Caldwell, Peter. *The Theory and Practice of Weimar Constitutionalism.* Durham, N.C.: Duke University Press, 1997.
Dyzenhaus, David. *Legality and Legitimacy: Carl Schmitt, Hans Kelsen, and Hermann Heller in Weimar.* Oxford: Clarendon Press, 1997.

Müller, Christoph, and Ilse Staff, eds. *Der soziale Rechtsstaat: Gedächtnisschrift für Hermann Heller, 1891–1933*. Baden-Baden: Nomos Verlagsgesellschaft, 1984. [Selections from these essays appear in *Staatslehre in der Weimarer Republik: Hermann Heller zu Ehren*, ed. Christoph Müller and Ilse Staff (Frankfurt am Main: Suhrkamp, 1985)].

Robbers, Gerhard. *Hermann Heller: Staat und Kultur*. Baden-Baden: Nomos Verlagsgesellschaft, 1983.

Schluchter, Wolfgang. *Entscheidung für den sozialen Rechtsstaat: Hermann Heller und die staatstheoretische Diskussion in der Weimarer Republik*. 2nd ed. Baden-Baden: Nomos Verlagsgesellschaft, 1983.

POLITICAL DEMOCRACY AND
SOCIAL HOMOGENEITY

Hermann Heller

Originally appeared as "Politische Demokratie und Soziale Homogenität," in Hermann Heller, *Probleme der Demokratie*, I. Reihe, Politische Wissenschaft: Schriftenreihe der deutschen Hochschule für Politik in Berlin und des Instituts für auswärtige Politik in Hamburg 5 (Berlin: Walter Rothschild, 1928), 35–47. Reprinted in Hermann Heller, *Gesammelte Schriften*, II: *Recht, Staat, Macht*, 2nd ed., edited by Christoph Müller (Tübingen: Mohr, 1992), 421–33. Translated by David Dyzenhaus.

The question of what significance social homogeneity has for political democracy is inexhaustible. Here this question will be explored mainly by a clarification of basic concepts from a political (and thus not social, economic, or ethical) standpoint.

Like any other system of political domination, the democratic is also in essence a territorial decision of potentially universal extent. One rules politically when one makes the final decisions in regard to those acts that pertain to the unity of cooperation or when one engages significantly in the unity of territorial decision. The universality of the territorial decision is of course only a potential one. But if the unitary cooperation—the unity in the plurality that since Machiavelli has been called the state—is to be established, any question that pertains to the order uniting the social life of that territory is potentially subject to political decision. The judgment about the relevance of this or that social act for the unity of cooperation changes with the historical and social situation and location.

The unity of territorial decision makes the essence of the political comprehensible to us. It is the process of dialectical adjustment whereby the unending plurality and perplexity of diverse social acts are brought into an ordering and ordered unity. The politically decisive acts establish and maintain a legal order, whose existence, positivity, or validity remains permanently dependent on the existence of that unity of acts, which must therefore assert itself when necessary even against the positive law itself. The fact of an active common interchange within a determinate territory requires that the ordering unity of acts also make its person-related decisions in principle as universal decisions and thus imposes its order not only on members of the state but on all inhabitants of the territory. Any domination, whether motivated or grounded religiously, pedagogically, economically, erotically, or in any other way, becomes political as soon as it demands for itself as its ultimate goal the unity of decision in a determinate territory.

We call the state the unity of those acts that constitute the institution of territorial decision. Hence, the basic problem of all politics is the following: how this unity of territorial decision is established and maintained, on the one hand, amid the plurality of those acts of will that constitute it, and, on the other hand, amid the plurality of surrounding territories with their domination. This universal unity of territorial decision is of necessity grounded in the "social-unsocial nature" of human beings—in both their essential characteristics of diversity and sociality. It is only in society that the human being, positioned between god and animal, becomes human; only in his unmistakable uniqueness does he come to and remain in spiritual-intellectual and physical existence. The universal, operative unity of a territorial decision, however it comes into existence, is thus the *conditio sine qua non* of the metaphysical, as well as the physical, survival of the human being.

Sociability, which is a fundamental presupposition of the earthly human condition, manifests itself above all as a natural fact that extends down to the animal world. In human society, individual diversity and particularization necessarily correlate, not solely with a community of a natural kind but also with an intellectual decision. While the incomprehensible orders of natural drives play a part, it is also (and above all) the hierarchical "superstructure" of the intellectual orders that gives coherence to the eternally antagonistic structure of human society. The common life of human beings is always a common life that is given order by the concrete human decisions of the will, whereby communities that grow on a naturalistic basis in no way prove themselves as the most stable. An example of an ideal power is that which for thousands of years has joined and divided human beings in the Catholic Church.

These decisions become political as soon as they concern the unity of territorial interchange and cooperation. Increasing civilization and division of labor in combination with an increasing range and complexity of social relationships heighten the necessity for willingly established orders and multiply the number of political decisions made from the center. It also widens therewith the activities of the political unity of decision working with a growing administrative staff, as it increases this unity for the social condition.

All politics consists in the formation and maintenance of this unity. In an emergency situation, all politics must eventually answer an attack on this unity with the physical annihilation of the attacker.

Therein lies the correct core of Carl Schmitt's claim that the specific political distinction is the distinction between friend and enemy. Politics is fundamentally negated when there is no longer the readiness in an emergency situation to annihilate the one who mounts an internal or external attack on the political unity. A state abolishes itself if it forbids the use of deadly force in all circumstances, or fails to shoot when its representatives are under fire from within or without.

But one must contest Carl Schmitt's view that the friend-enemy distinction is specifically political, a distinction to which all political acts and motives can be reduced. Besides the fact that it is epistemologically inadmissible to arrange this distinction among the categorical value-distinctions of good and bad, beautiful and ugly, useful and harmful, Schmitt's friend-enemy distinction is circular. For, without the adjective "political," the distinction indicates nothing essentially political. "My friends are your friends, and your enemies should be my enemies," can apply just as well to the political friend as to any other friend who shares convictions—childhood friend, business friend, and bosom friend. Carl Schmitt is blind to the sphere of unity-formation within the state as politics. Suppose that in fact all political activity could be reduced to the friend-enemy distinction, where the enemy means the one who "in some specially intensive sense is existentially something alien and strange,"[17] one who must be fended off and fought, if need be annihilated, for the protection of the form of life appropriate to its essence. It would follow that the establishment and existence of political unity would be something altogether unpolitical. Schmitt sees only the accomplished political status; but this is not something static; on the contrary it is something that daily has to be formed anew, *un plébescite de tous les jours* [a daily plebiscite].[18]

The dynamic process whereby the state becomes and maintains itself as the unity in the plurality of its limbs is politics in at least as meaningful a sense as the way in which the state maintains itself in external affairs. The word "politics" derives from *polis,* not from *polemos* [war], even though the common root of these terms remains significant. Equally, whether or not one regards it as possible or desirable, the *civitas maxima* [a supreme or world state] is at the least a theoretically unobjectionable supposition that does not contradict the human condition. In our case it serves to show that the political friend-enemy distinction is a category that is not required in all circumstances. By contrast, the unity of territorial decision would adequately characterize even the essence of the world-state. Hence, Schmitt's friend-enemy antithesis is unsuitable for giving the state an ethical purpose just because, according to him, it must be understood as alien to ethical purpose, as a purely vital entity in antithesis to another strange, vital entity, which is as it has to be.

Democracy means rule by the people. If the *demos* [people] is supposed to *kratein* [rule] it must under all circumstances form a unity through action and decision [*Wirkungs- und Entscheidungseinheit*]. That is, like any form of domination, democracy must exhibit a system for unifying wills for which the law of the small number is always valid. The specific nature of the democratic form of domination consists in the fact that its representatives are appointed collegially and have a magisterial and thus not sovereign position. Each democratic representative is directly or indirectly both to be summoned and dismissed by the people, directly or indirectly. Despite his power as representative to make autonomous decisions, he remains legally bound to the will of the people by means of a rationally posited order. The bond that characteristically links democratic representatives to the people is not a sociological or perhaps social-ethical one. Such a bond exists even for autocratic representatives. Indeed, there is no form of domination for which Spinoza's saying is not valid: *oboedientia facit imperantem* [obedience makes the ruler].[19] It is only in democracy that this bond is additionally a legal one and equipped with effective legal sanctions. In democracy, the methods of appointing representatives can be very different. The direct election of central organs developed in liberal democracies is not the only way of selecting democratic representatives. An election mediated by a council system also counts, when it is not merely the appointment of representatives of purely economic interests, bound by an imperative mandate. There are countless possibilities for the status of democratic representatives. Besides parliamentarism and a democratic council system, one can also call democratic the experimental forms of representation in American cities that do without parliament and councils and simply summon one or two representatives with the widest powers of decision, subject to *recall* [English in the original] at any time.

The appointment of representatives is the most important phase in the dynamic of the formation of political unity. The whole problematic of contemporary democracy resides in the fact that the democratic appointment of representatives is supposed to take place in a legal process from bottom to top. The contingencies of history determine how far down the bottom reaches, who should be part of the ruling people, and who is to be excluded by reason of age, sex, or differences in education and property.

It is the insight into the significance of the democratic appointment of representatives that first permits an understanding of the great, though much misunderstood and much maligned, significance of political parties in democracy. They are indispensable even in the council system as the essential factors in that system for unifying wills that we call the democratic

state. Without such a system of mediations, it is impossible to conceive democratically of the unity in the plurality of unmediated opposites.

The significance of social homogeneity for democracy is also comprehended in the problem just outlined. Democracy is supposed to be a conscious process of the formation of political unity from bottom to top; all
representation is supposed to remain legally dependent on the community's
will. The people as a plurality is supposed consciously to form itself into the
people as a unity. For the formation of political unity to be possible at all,
there must exist a certain degree of social homogeneity. So long as there is
belief in such homogeneity and the assumption that the possibility of arriving through discussion at political agreement with one's opponent exists and
so long as can one debate with one's opponent and renounce suppression by
physical force. Carl Schmitt is therefore very wide of the mark when he thinks
he has hit the "spiritual center" of parliamentarism. For he, taken as he is by
the irrational allure of the myth of force, defines the *ratio* of parliament as the
belief in the public nature of discussion and in the discovery of truth through
an unconstrained marketplace of ideas.[20] Such a justification may formerly
have been welcomed by some rationalist apologists and even more by contemporary opponents of parliamentarism. In fact, intellectual history shows
as the basis of parliamentarism the belief, not in public discussion as such,
but in the existence of a common foundation for discussion and thus in the
possibility of *fair play* [English in the original] for one's internal political opponent, in the relationship with whom one thinks one can exclude naked
force and come to agreements. Only when this consciousness of homogeneity disappears does a party, which has until that time been one that debates,
becomes a party that dictates.

It is thus the case that the degree to which it is possible to form a political unity depends on the extent of social homogeneity; likewise the degree to
which it is possible to put in place a system of representation, and stabilizing
the representatives' position. There is a certain degree of social homogeneity without which the democratic formation of unity is impossible. The democratic formation of unity ceases to exist when all politically relevant sections
of the people no longer recognize themselves in any way in the political unity,
when they are not able to identify themselves in any way with the symbols and
representatives of state. In that moment the unity is cleaved, and civil war,
dictatorship, and alien domination are in the cards. The difficult birth of the
continental coalition governments, their short duration, as well as their lack
of any far-reaching operative effect, are the most obvious symptoms of an insufficient social homogeneity and, therefore, most dangerous signs of the
crisis of our democracies.

A correct understanding of this situation (let alone an appreciation of it
or change in it) is today made endlessly difficult by the twin-brothers of a
substanceless form of thought: the utopian idealism that rests simply on

abstractions and the naturalism that has the same foundation. The first constructs as its political ideal a heaven on earth that contradicts life; the second wishes to reduce all social homogeneity to something like the drive for nourishment, a community of blood, or a psychoanalytic *libido*.

But social homogeneity can never mean the abolition of the necessarily antagonistic social structure. The peaceful community free of conflict and the society without domination can be meaningful as prophetic promises. But as a political aim this way of bringing a community of saints to earth, shared by Ernst Michel, denatures the religious as well as the political sphere. Social homogeneity is always a social-psychological state in which the inevitably present oppositions and conflicts of interest appear constrained by a consciousness and sense of the "we," by a community will that actualizes itself. This relative equalization of the social consciousness has the resources to work through huge antithetical tensions, and to digest huge religious, political, economic, and other antagonisms. One cannot say definitively how this "we-consciousness" is produced and destroyed. All attempts to find the impulse for this consciousness in a single sphere of life have failed and must fail. All that we can rightly know is that in each epoch a correspondence between social being and consciousness—in other words, a societal form—emerges. It is always the sphere in which the consciousness of the epoch is most at home that is also decisive for social homogeneity.

In modern Europe, where since the Renaissance ontology has been this-worldly, the most important factors of social psychological equalization have been common speech and a common culture and political history. The contemporary zeitgeist, whether it assumes an idealist or materialist air, knows in truth nothing but the naturalistic sphere of reality. The intellectual "superstructure" dissipates into a derivative, into a powerless ideology and fiction above the economic, sexual, or racial—modes of being that have to an increasing extent been decisive for social homogeneity. In so far as it exposes the positivistic and historicist superstitions, this ideological lesson is quite healthy for human hubris.

However, in politics an awful question is raising its Medusa's head—the question of how one can affirm today's democracy in the midst of these huge class and racial conflicts. Democracy's existence is dependent to a much greater degree than any other political form on the success of social equalization. One can understand why today both the left and the right maintain that it is impossible to take a democratic path in forming political unity. The neo-Machiavellism of a disillusioned bourgeoisie wants, in the spirit of Vilfredo Pareto, to use democratic, nationalist, and socialist, in short all "ideologies" only as *arcana imperii* [mysteries of power] in order dictatorially to maintain itself in power amid the eternal "cycle of elites." In Germany, too, monarchism is, at least for the younger generation, exclusively a disguise for the yearning for the "strong man" who acts and does not transact, who forces into existence both social-psychological homogeneity and the formation of political unity, of course while preserving the position of the bourgeoisie. Meanwhile the proletariat likewise despairs of democratic forms because of the existing economic disparity and, for the present and near future, places its hope of freedom and equality in an enlightened dictatorship. Despite the momentary tranquillity (more accurately, fatigue), the state of social homogeneity, which is the presupposition of political democracy, is lacking to an extent unmatched in previous eras.

To be sure, the last centuries have brought about civil homogeneity. There no longer exist slaves in the legal sense, people who enjoy no freedom under the law and no liberty of action and whose exclusion from the state was taken for granted in the ancient democracies. Every individual, and not just every citizen, enjoys the formally equal protection of person, family, and property. And this is also how formal-legal political homogeneity is brought about: Each citizen is guaranteed the formally equal right of participation in forming political unity and the formally equal right of qualification for official positions. But even this "step forward in the consciousness of freedom," as we might say with Hegel, is one that today threatens the formation of democratic unity.

For this consciousness of freedom is, on the one hand, consciousness of social inequality, and consciousness of political power, on the other. The latter cannot be permanently suppressed by force, but so far has by no means the resources to independently direct culture and form political unity. The social-psychological equalization of consciousness cannot be had without a fundamental change in the economy and a profound revolution in consciousness. Is the democratic political form capable of enduring until then, given the facts of the social class struggle? In and of itself, the class struggle, which grows out of an economic basis, must in no way break democracy apart. But once the proletariat believes that the democratic equality of its over-powerful opponent condemns the democratic form of class struggle to hopelessness, it resorts to dictatorship.

The insight of the ruling classes, or rather of the intellectuals in these classes, is decisive for whether that belief takes hold among the proletariat. It is pointless to find comfort for oneself or for others in the ethic of the democratic form. To be sure, political democracy wants to preserve the equal opportunity of each member of the state to influence the formation of political unity by summoning representatives. But social disparity can make *summum jus* [supreme right] into *summa injuria* [supreme wrong]. Without social homogeneity, the most radical formal equality becomes the most radical inequality, and formal democracy becomes the dictatorship of the ruling class.

In virtue of their superiority in the economy and in everything that concerns civilization, the rulers have adequate means in hand to change political democracy into its exact opposite by means of their direct and indirect influence on public opinion. Through financial domination of party, press, film, and literature, through social influence over schools and universities, they are able, without using direct corruption, to influence the bureaucratic and electoral apparatus in such a consummate fashion that they preserve every democratic form while achieving a dictatorship of content. Their superiority is the more dangerous for the simple reasons that it is anonymous and lacking in responsibility. It turns political democracy into a fiction, preserving the form of the system of representation while falsifying its content.

Should the proletariat become aware of this discrepancy, then it realizes also that not only all the wheels of industry but also the wheels of state will stand still once its strong arm wills it. In that case, it will respect the democratic form of the class struggle only on two conditions. First, the democratic form ensures the proletariat any prospect for success and, second, the proletariat can discern an intellectual and ethical foundation as well as a historical necessity for the contemporary condition of domination. Of course, this also depends on the degree of insight of the proletariat. But it depends incomparably more on the extent of the intellectual and ethical abilities of the rulers and their constituency. The statesman who does not honestly try to make his political decisions transcend class prejudices, the judge who does not constantly attempt to balance the value judgments of all classes in order to avoid a justice tied to one of them—they and all other authorities of the state will represent to the proletarian the naked class-state that has no power to obligate him, but, as a mere instrument of repression, is worthy only of being fought. In such a situation not only the economic condition of both classes but also their intellectual and ethical consciousness will confront each other heterogeneously as entities without any means of mediation. The bourgeois will no longer appear to the proletarian as the same kind of being. The proletarian will confront the dictatorship of the bourgeois class-state with his ideal of the proletarian class dictatorship.

The danger in which the economic disparity between the classes places political democracy can for a time, but in no way permanently, be weakened by a homogeneity of common conventions, something that has been brought about to a certain degree in Switzerland and the United States. Equality of conventions can somewhat reduce the awareness of economic inequalities. Conversely, the more strongly economic differences are emphasized in the ordinary modes of greeting and clothing, the greater the number of social circles and groups who publicly underline their caste distinction by means of their presentability at court, their capacity to become officers, to be members of a corps, and so on; the more closely the conventional steps in upbringing and education are linked with title, rank, and name, the more strictly public accommodations are allocated on distinct lines—whether in the street car or in church—the greater will be the consciousness of the inequality of the classes, the lesser the readiness to secure the *fair play* of equal political opportunities to one's political class opponent.

Finally, that even anthropological homogeneity can be a presupposition of political democracy is demonstrated by the American Negro question. The right to take part in the full electoral process, which was ensured for the Negro after the Civil War, was again taken away. And the altogether honest solemnity that the citizen of the United States lends to universal human rights does not hinder him in the slightest from excluding the Negro from democracy with the same sense of self-evidence as it seemed to Plato that slaves self-evidently are excluded from democracy. To be sure, the Negro question is not just an anthropological one. But it would be wrong to regard it as exclusively economic. In contrast, the European worker question is and will remain, so long as the question is one of our conscious conduct, in the first place an economic one. And nothing is more characteristic of the social disparity that threatens our democracy, nor of the readiness of the ruling class to engage in class struggle, than the attempt to recast the economic disparity into an anthropological one, and to separate the proletariat as inferior in blood from the ones who possess—the aim of which is to justify on the basis of blood the demand that those who possess are to be those who rule. It seems in fact to be the case: *Quos deos perdere vult, dementat prius* [whom the gods will destroy, they first drive mad]. Suppose the proletariat were not only economically heterogeneous with the ruling class and distinguished from it not only by mutable relationships of property and education but also by immutable blood. Then what kind of solidarity should make the proletariat concede to the ruling class's democratic equality?!

For a hundred years bourgeois circles were used to conceiving the national cultural community as an adequate factor for integration into the state. I will not be suspected of underestimating the national cultural community's power in forming a state.[21] But I must just as forcefully emphasize that it is impossible to have a cultural community without a certain degree of social homogeneity. The bourgeois hope that the proletariat's share in the national culture would prove sufficient to keep the propertyless classes within the process of forming democratic unity is in great part a naive self-deception. There is some truth to what Othmar Spann says: "Only insofar as participation in the spiritual community reaches, can the true national distinction, and also the true . . . belonging to a nation, go; beyond that it is just a community of interests."[22]

But if the political conscience is satisfied with Spann and refers to the given cultural incompetence of the "masses,"[23] it confuses mass with class, and desires to maintain that its own class is superior to the other on account of its spiritual nature. In principle, this kind of legitimation of the class-state has the same political effect as the above-mentioned theory of the racial distinction of classes. It must also end by dissolving ultimate ties and starting the drive toward proletarian dictatorship. Let us in this context neglect the fact that the idea of the nation-state has lost much of its persuasive power for all classes in postwar Europe. Even the ruling class has started to take seriously the question whether the contemporary nation-state serves national self-preservation better than a European federal state. For this reason, it will not take long for the national idea to prove itself inadequate for legitimating the formation of democratic unity.

Finally, one should say something about the following crucial issue. Today's deficiency of economic, cultural, and conventional homogeneity cannot be remedied by using a religious we-consciousness to integrate with the class opponent as children of one and the same God. However, this religious homogeneity, as little as it can be influenced by our will, is of the greatest significance for political democracy. For there exist today large circles among the bourgeoisie who recommend the use of religion as the medium by which one can achieve the aim of forming political unity. Not only in France does there exist an atheistic Catholicism that would like to provide a religion for the people while maintaining for itself a theory of domination empty of belief. In Germany we know the type of scholar who now does penance for his prerevolutionary academic socialism by praising the good Lord as a social sedative. Besides the fact that the exploitation of religion as an instrument of politics is blasphemous, its recommendation in itself signifies as well a grandiose political stupidity: one notes and is annoyed.

In Dostoevski's *The Devils,* Schatoff makes this pregnant remark: "Who has no people, also has no god." Even though one can rationally construct out of the "myth of the nation" a religious "myth," one cannot thereby create either a real people or a real God.

THE ESSENCE AND STRUCTURE OF THE STATE

Hermann Heller

Originally appeared as *Wesen und Aufbau des Staates,* part 3 of the *Staatslehre* (Leiden: A. W. Sifthoff's Uigeversmaatschappij, 1934). Reprinted in Hermann Heller, *Gesammelte Schriften,* II: *Staatslehre als Politische Wissenschaft,* 2nd ed., edited by Christoph Müller (Tübingen: Mohr, 1992), 327, 331–39, 354–56, 358–59, 359–61, 390–95. Translated by David Dyzenhaus.

THE JUSTIFICATION OF THE STATE: STATE FUNCTION AND LEGAL FUNCTION

No justification of the state is possible without separating just from unjust. This separation can be accomplished only on the basis of a standard of law that must be accepted as standing above the state. . . . That the most common form today of understanding legitimacy is a belief in legality, the readiness to conform to "*formally* correct precepts that have come into being in compliance with the conventional form,"[24] is simply false insofar as it does not merely unintentionally detect a degeneration in contemporary legal consciousness. A connection between legality and legitimacy is found above all only in the state based on the rule of law with a division of powers [*gewaltenteilenden Rechtsstaat*]. Here this connection is a substantive as well as a formal one following organizational techniques. In the struggle against absolutist arbitrary power, one thought that one could secure legitimacy through legality by having the people themselves decide on the statutes to which they are subject and by bringing the remaining activity of the state into compliance with these statutes. A guarantee of the legality of the statutes decided by the people's legislature had to be deemed to be a given only insofar as one saw an act of self-determining ethical reason in democratic legislation. The organizational division of powers, however, has simply the purpose of guaranteeing legal certainty and is thus simply a technical instrument that has nothing to say about the rightness of law.[25] No one today believes that everything the people's legislature puts into norms to be the right law due to some metaphysical predestination. Hence, the legality of the state based on the rule of law is not in a position to replace legitimacy.

The theory of the state therefore finds itself confronted with the fact that neither the harmonizing of law and power, nor legality, nor a democratic, nationalist, or Bolshevik legitimating ideology, is capable of a generally valid sanctioning of the state as such. But every political exercise of power now asserts of itself that it stands in the service of justice. It is not only the state based on the rule of law that makes this claim, as a propagandist of dictatorship maintains. There is no form of state or government in which an order in itself already exhibits a positive "legal value"; and the formulation, "an order is the best thing in the world,"[26] while it might bring joy to the aesthetes of power in their cultural languor, is a proposition that is false of any form of political power. For it is known that power is established only on the basis of obedience to orders, but obedience essentially lives always and in all forms of rule on the believed justification of the order.

Does the theory of the state resign itself to a relativistic agnosticism in view of this state of affairs? Is nothing left for the theory but the belief that every power stands in service of justice, or is the theory not able to demonstrate principles for a generally valid justification of the state?

It is not difficult to establish a positive answer to this question insofar as one is concerned with the justification of the state as an institution. The state is justified insofar as it exhibits, at a particular evolutionary level, the organization necessary to secure the law. By law we understand in the first place the ethical principles that are foundational for positive law. In all of these principles of law, whose ideal validity has to be presupposed, the demand for social validity is immanent. The obligatory nature of these legal principles has meaning only as an existent obligation. They aim to be valid not merely in ideal absoluteness but also, as far as possible, as positive laws. Hence it is necessary that the universal principles of law, like those, for example, contained in the Decalogue, be promulgated, applied, and executed as positive laws by an authoritarian power. The precept receives all ethical obligation only from the superior, ethical, principle of law. The principle is distinguished from the precept by its lack of legal certainty or legal determinacy, which consists, on the one hand, in determinacy of meaning (in the decidedness of the content of the norm), and, on the other hand, in certainty as to its execution.[27] Principles of law indicate only general directions on the basis of which legality should be established among the members of the legal community. They do not give a decision in the concrete case. They lack decisiveness to do so, that is, one first always needs a decision about what should correspond with those principles in the particular situation in which interests are determined by time, place, and personality. On the basis of the same fundamental principles of law, there can and must even be possible different legal decisions, as well as different legal orders and constitutions, as well as different statutes, judgments, and administrative acts. However, both determinacy of meaning and determinacy of execution require the existence of an authoritarian power, which pronounces upon and implements that which is supposed to be right in a concrete situation. The mere legal conviction does not suffice for either one or the other. . . .

The state institution is thus justified in that a certain level of division of labor and social intercourse requires the determinacy of law in meaning and execution. As only a certain intensity of traffic makes necessary first a special traffic ordinance and then even specialized traffic police, so growing civilization generally makes necessary a growing self-differentiating state organization for the promulgation, application, and implementation of the law.

The state institution is thus sanctioned as an organization that secures the law and only as such. This thesis should not be misunderstood in a liberal or technical manner. Neither does it aim to say that the state has to confine its activity to legislation and the organization of the judiciary, nor does it maintain that securing the law consists merely in policelike activity. That the state can be sanctioned only by its characteristic as an organization for securing the law is meant much more to express that it can be justified only in that it serves the application and implementation of ethical principles of law. The state's securing the law also has nothing to do with the positivist distinction between a purpose of the law and a cultural purpose. Legal principles are most certainly the ones that may require the state's economic, educational, and other cultural activity. It is obvious that our concept of legal certainty includes much more than the usual. The organization of the state is made legally indispensable not just by the indispensability of the certainty of execution secured by state-organized coercion, but, historically and conceptually prior, by the certainty of the law as something with meaning.

However, the ethical principles of law sanction directly only the norms regulating action and not the norms allocating authority. It is the socially valid ideologies of legitimation in a legal community that decide the authority to be called upon to promulgate, apply, and execute positive laws. Such an authority must be both empowered and entitled to secure the law. It must have power to pronounce on the law, to apply it, and also to execute it if possible, and it has this power only insofar as at least the decisive groups believe that it is prepared to secure the just and not the unjust. However, this social legitimation of the law-securing authority has to be distinguished clearly from the ideal justification of the state by ethical principles of law. It is only by dint of a judgment as to the justness of the secured law that one can decide whether the socially legitimate authority is not serving normal legal certainty alone and maintaining an unjust order for order's sake. Legal certainty and lawfulness can conflict with each other, and this tension, which necessarily obtains between both, reveals to us the deep problem of justifying the concrete state.

The theory of the state has abandoned to legal philosophy the question whether the ethical principles of law can simply be reduced to an unmediatedly assured sense of justice or whether they are deducible with an objective epistemological certainty from a rationally formulable supreme law. It has similarly abandoned the difficult questions whether and in what sense there are a priori principles of law, which principles are universal and which bound to particular cultures. However, it must be taken as settled for a realist theory of the state that there are such ethical principles of law that make up the justifying basis of the state and its positive law. Among those ideologies of social legitimation, of which several always exist, one can clearly distinguish by their generality those that make demands on all members of the state. Their claim to validity is, when not absolutely universal, still one that always extends beyond the particular state. . . .

The state can provide the ethical principles of law with such a determination as well as the corresponding determinacy of execution only within its area of efficacy. That the territory of a state and the sphere of a legal tradition coincide is much less plausible than a coincidence between the territory of state and an economic sphere. For the principles of law form not only the normative foundation of the law of the state, but also of the law between states. . . .

The social, legal situation in the modern state reaches the highest degree possible of legal certainty in regard to the determinacy of both meaning and execution, because it has at its disposal a hierarchical organization with a

technically differentiated corps of organs for the promulgation, application, and execution of the positive law. A presupposition of the guarantee of
such a high degree of legal certainty is the sovereignty of the state. Only in
virtue of its characteristic as the superior unity through action and decision
[*Wirkungs- und Entscheidungseinheit*] is the state capable of securing the unity
of the law and its execution and to maintain a uniformly organized procedure for claiming rights and prosecuting complaints. The efficacy of such a
legal system of control is determined by the state's monopoly over legal physical coercion, and thus by the exclusion of a legal right of resistance against
the directives of state power.[28] The state was capable of securing legal certainty as it is available today only in that it excludes every kind of self-help,
but the insignificant remainder of cases of self-defense that can never be
comprehended by technical, organizational means.

All the organizational institutions of the state, however carefully they
may be conceived, are capable only of guaranteeing legal form and legal certainty, but never compliance with law or legality, and never the ethical legitimacy of state acts. For all eternity it is the case that only the individual legal
conscience will be in a position to secure justice. Thus there is established
in the modern state a necessary and unsolvable conflict between compliance
with the law and legal certainty. This conflict is necessary because, within a
vital citizenry, complete agreement over the content and application of valid
fundamental legal principles can never rule. It is unsolvable because both
the state and the individual have life only in the tension in which positive law
and the legal conscience find themselves.

Reason of state has the "right" to maintain that—but only in the modern state!—the legalization of a right of resistance against a state ordinance judged to be ethically repugnant means nothing other than a self-
contradictory legalization of anarchy. The destruction of all legal certainty
must destroy the individual as well as the state.

But reason of law has even more "right" to assume that if the legal conscience capitulates to state power without resistance, it will lead to the destruction of the human being as an ethical personality and thereby finally
also to the disintegration of his state-forming power.[29]

It is a question of the greatest relevance what conclusions should be drawn
in case of a collision between duties arising from ethical principles of law and
from positive laws. It was already Kant who absolutized the validity of positive law and denied any right of resistance, which, by the way, contradicted
his own rationalist presuppositions about the law of reason.[30] Since that time,
the positivism of the continental theory of the state has not in any way recognized a right of resistance and ultimately made a complete sacrifice of
legality to legal certainty. One believes that one opens the door wide to anarchy just by conceding an ethical right of resistance. This axiom became all

the more self-evident and therefore required even less demonstration, the more strongly the ground was prepared in the mid-nineteenth century for the turn to the total state.

In truth, however, clear-sighted reason of state does not at all require a complete capitulation of the legal conscience and the recognition of an ethical right of resistance in no way has anarchy as a consequence. Certainly, it must be established once and for all that the exclusive concern here is the problem of ethical justification and not just any question of legality. One cannot dispute that the recognition of a legal right of resistance is impossible in contemporary states, nor likewise that resistance against acts of state should in no way be allowed when these are, though defective in a legal sense, ethically indifferent. To be sure, it is a necessary requirement of legal certainty in many cases that such acts should also be attributed to the state as do not in form or content correspond to the positive legal order's established conditions for attribution. Generally one is concerned in these cases with infringements of provisions regulating forms of procedure and norms allocating jurisdiction that are almost without exception ethically indifferent. Only the Pure Theory of Law, which concedes without distinction the quality of absolute norms to all positive law, is capable of introducing a seriousness to the positivist theory of legal power, which gives only legality and never legal certainty its due.[31] That state acts enjoy the presumption of legality, by which a mere lack of positive legal validity is cured, is altogether justified by the requirement of legal certainty. It would, however, lead to the dissolution of the legal order if one desired to leave every single case to the *man in the street* [English in the original], and make his obedience dependent on whether, in his estimation, the organ of state is acting in agreement with all norms allocating jurisdiction and regulating legal formalities that are local, relevant, and current. In the state based on the rule of law, a right of resistance against legally defective state acts is for the most part superfluous, because the subordinates and subjects who are thereby burdened are generally capable of protecting themselves against the state by legal means. It also happens, not rarely, that the state, in order to protect a higher legal good, allows acts contrary to positive law to remain as valid legal acts.

But the problem of a right of resistance is different when it concerns a state act repugnant to ethics. Whether the relevant norm is legally unobjectionable or not then plays no decisive role. To take the crudest example: Whoever conscientiously refuses wartime service is threatened with the most serious punishment. Reason of state and the positive law must, for the sake of legal certainty, take such a prescription as indispensable. But a legal conscience is not worthy of the name when in this case first it fails to recognize a tragic conflict of duties, but then deprives the conscientious objector of his ethical right of resistance. To be sure, there are many who even call such an interpretation of state and law heroic. But the exact opposite is the case! That interpretation is heroic which does not one-sidedly resolve the conflict of duties, but rather affirms its tragic insolubility and therewith the ethical right of resistance. It is tragic that all actualization of law remains imprisoned by the demonic element of power. But what is repugnant is the ethicization of that demonic element that is today so widespread. The recognition of an ethical right of resistance should not in any way take the tragedy out of the eternal struggle of the legal conscience against positive law. But by no means should the right be sentimentalized. Hence it is not a consequence of the ethical right of resistance that it provides a basis for excluding guilt or punishment.

It is good and right that the power of the state be challenged by the ethical right of resistance. And it is the opposite of an ethical justification of the state when one metaphysizes the state once and forever into the "actuality of the ethical idea" and thereby irrevocably deprives the only empirical bearer of the legal conscience of the right of resistance against unethical state acts. In this instance, the specter of anarchy is unjustly conjured up. In view of the state's enormously heightened techniques of law and power, the unlegalized resistance of the legal conscience is ultimately possible only at the risk of one's life. Given our character as humans, such a risk is seldom taken. But when it happens, it is all the more a valuable model because the contemporary state's techniques of dealing with the masses and using its power carry the awful danger of a complete deadening of the legal conscience. Those who happen to rule must always have an interest in justifying the state they rule as the objective expression of ethical reason. "The conception of societal institutions as objective reason annuls the function of reason in human society."[32] The justification of the state can never consist in harmonizing law with power at any price. For each state power owes its establishment and structure to human—all-too-human—will. One always finds the highest ethical forces, a frightful mass of stupidity and evil, of baseness and arbitrariness, at work.

. . .

THE STATE POWER AS POLITICAL UNITY THROUGH DECISION

The most significant and most misunderstood relationship between state power and law can generally be characterized by the fact that every political power essentially aspires to the legal form posited and secured by the organs of the state. It must have this tendency, because in the modern state, law as a rule represents the technically as well as intellectually and ethically necessary manifestation of every lasting political power that proves itself. It is the technically (not always politically) most perfect form of political domination. For it makes possible, on average and in the long run, the most precise and practical orientation and ordering of political activity, that is, the most certain calculation and attribution of the actions that constitute and activate state power. Its precision and practicability are based precisely on the transfer of the positing and execution of law (by contrast with ethics, conventions, and international law) to the state power that for these purposes maintains a special apparatus, which proves itself as a rule to be the most powerful unity through action and decision in the territory of the state. This unity of power expressly decides who will "pass" for power-holder and who as subject of power, on what and whose performances one "ought" to count, and which acts of state power "ought" to be attributed to whom. And, in addition, it sets up the organizational arrangements that ensure that this "ought" in general corresponds with an "is." In so doing, the unity of power makes possible orientation and organization within the permanent flux of power situations, and thereby a consolidation of the unstable into a stable situation of domination. Take, for example, the often unanswerable question: Who really exercises the decisive power of the state, the autocrat or his minister, his banker, his valet, or his mistress? On the basis of these "precepts" that are obligatory but not always in accord with political reality, the question can be precisely and practically put and, hence, answered: Who is by law entitled to the power of the state?

On these technical grounds alone, state power is always legal, that is, legally organized, political power. A complex of social relationships, systematically organized into a unity of power, becomes a complex of legal relationships, systematically ordered into a unity of order, derived from the positive constitution. However, on account of its social function, each state power must strive not only for legality in the legal technical sense, but also, for the sake of its self-preservation, for an ethical justification of its positive legal or conventional norms, i.e., for legitimacy. A state power is all the more stable the greater the voluntary recognition that the pillars of its power show for its ethical principles of law and the positive laws that it legitimates. A state power has authority only when the justification of its power enjoys recognition. Its authority is based in legality only insofar as the legality is founded by legitimacy. The legitimation of the state power either can be traced back to tradition, so that its standing is consecrated by its origins, or rests on the belief in the particular gift or genius, and thus on the highly personal authority of the power-holder, or it is based in the recognition of the power-holder as the representative of particular religious, ethical-political, or other values. Only that state power is secure which has authority in this sense with the politically relevant pillars of power.

All the ideologists of force fail to recognize this power formation by law, while conversely all the pacifist ideologists do not want to recognize law formation by power. There cannot be an absolutely homogeneous legal community in a class-divided society, nor even in a society based on economic solidarity; for this would mean the abolition of all and not only the economic differences between individuals. Hence, human common-life constantly requires a state power that enacts positive law and implements it against those who oppose it. However, everyday history shows us examples of the "normative power of the factual," by means of which a power that, while for a time existing merely as a fact and though experienced as unjust, succeeds in winning, bit by bit, recognition of its justification.

STATE POWER AND STATE FORMS

The manner in which state power is divided determines the state form. This is certainly valid for the two basic forms of state. Democracy is a bottom-to-top power structure; autocracy organizes the state from top to bottom. In democracy, the principle of people's sovereignty holds: all power of the state comes from the people; in autocracy, the principle of the sovereignty of the ruler holds: the head of state unites in himself all state power. So far as this localization of sovereignty in the people or the ruler is concerned, one can and must distinguish between law and reality—but not where sovereignty of the state's unity through action is concerned, which comprehends both people and ruler. For these principles of localization are only in part statements of what is; for the rest, they are judgments of what ought to be, with which the actual division of state power does not always agree. In accordance with its function as a rule of orientation and calculation, the law of democracy attributes the formation of state power to the "people." This is so even when the people that votes makes up only a small part of the actual population and individuals outweigh the greater part of the electoral power, for example, because of their superior economic power. But even in a democracy where there is equality of social opportunities, the people can rule only through a ruling organization. But each organization needs an authority, and all exercise of power is subordinate to the law of the small number; those who actualize the organizationally unified outputs of power must always have a certain degree of freedom of decision and thus of democratically unconstrained power. This is as true for the state organization as it is for the power structure of the political parties, which in democracy organize the manifestations of will. In the parties, the larger and more developed the organization, and the narrower the voter's political knowledge and interest, the more easily a very narrow circle of leaders in conjunction with the party bureaucracy concentrates power in its hands. The state administration, which constantly expands and becomes more complex, especially requires a professionally trained and experienced civil service in all its branches. Its expert knowledge and routine absorb a substantial part of the state power that is legally localized in the people, particularly when the bureaucracy is confronted by changing parliamentary majorities and a changing political leadership.

Despite all these limitations and falsifications, the legal localization of sovereignty in the people does not amount at all to a mere fiction, but to a political reality. Indeed, its political significance is grasped only when one correctly understands the people's sovereignty as a polemical principle for the distribution of political power antithetical to the principle of sovereignty of a ruler. That there is no pure realization of this principle in political life disappoints only the doctrinaire. Conversely, only ignorance or demagogy can contest that people's sovereignty expresses a structural principle of the actual distribution of political power. For it is always a fact that, in contrast to autocracy, a greater or smaller circle of the democratic citizenry has effective political power, which becomes practical above all in the appointment, recall, and control of the political leader. It is a political reality of the greatest practical significance that the democratic organization of the state based on the rule of law, with its division of powers and guarantee of basic rights, limits the leadership's political power through constitutional precepts. It secures for all members of the citizenry without exception a certain measure of "freedoms" (that is, of social and political power) that differ according to the particular circumstance.

In contrast, the distribution of state power in autocracy is in principle and in reality altogether different. Here all state power is supposed to come from the autocrat; he alone is supposed to take all politically relevant decisions. It is obvious that this legal principle of attribution must depart from political reality not less but rather more than the principle of the people's sovereignty. For only an omniscient and omnipotent autocrat could direct the entangled mammoth organization of the contemporary state with its entangled international dependencies with full freedom of decision. In practice, even the absolute monarch, and even more the modern dictator, must share his power widely, above all with his bureaucracy and other organs of domination, with national and international church, economic, and other power groups, and first of all with the privileged class, hence, in a dictatorship, with the leadership circle of the dictating party, which organizes the pillar of power that supports him. Yet, one may not deny that the localization principle of ruler sovereignty exhibits a concentration of state power in the hands of the autocrat that is completely unknown to democracy and the state based on the rule of law. That all the legal boundaries of dictatorial state power are removed does not, of course, mean that the dictator possesses total power, still less that all power is actually united in his person. But it does clearly mean that his power finds its boundaries only in the actual constellation of power in the society. However, the apparatus of dictatorship can be perfected with the help of the technique, developed enormously in the last century, of physical and psychological domination of the mass through tank, airplane and gas, press, cinema, radio, and school, as well above all through the compulsion of hunger. Hence the leader of the dictatorial apparatus is able to accomplish to an unprecedented degree the monopolization of state power.

. . .

THE WRITTEN CONSTITUTION

To begin with, we must distinguish four concepts of the constitution: two sociological and two legal. The constitutional concept that is richest in substance considers the characteristic power structure, the concrete form of existence and activity of the state. The extent of this concept renders it scientifically as good as useless; for it covers the "*total situation* of political unity and order,"[33] the "totality of life," and the "reality of the state's life"[34] and thus includes all the natural and cultural conditions of the state unit without any worthwhile differentiation.

Much more fruitful, simply in that it is narrower, is the second realist constitutional concept. It comes about in that, within the totality of the state, a basic structure of the state is valued as fundamental from a particular historical-political standpoint and is singled out as the relatively permanent structure of the unity of the state.

Two idealist and even legal concepts of the constitution correspond to the two sociological concepts. The comprehensive legal concept would have the entire legal existence of the state as its content. At the least, however, it includes all the legal norms contained in the constitutional document together with all other laws of the order of the state that comply with the constitution. Here one has in mind not the actual total situation, but only the situation of political unity and order, which is valid in legal terms, to be sure, without regard to which of the countless precepts are valid because they are "foundational" and which because they are derived. One can speak in this case of a substantive constitution in a wider sense.

More useful is the concept of the substantive constitution in a narrower sense. The basic order that it stresses within the total legal order of the state is a substantive part that is judged to be foundational, but not just as a hypothetical, logical "basic norm."[35] The idea of a substantive constitution in the narrow sense, written or unwritten, posed no difficulty for the natural law of the Enlightenment, because it started in the belief that its postulates, while in truth historically and politically determined, possessed an absolute, suprapositive legal bindingness, and permitted a logical-systematic deduction of all positive precepts. Even Kant[36] wants to understand the legal statute as an abstract, general premise by a deliberate analogy with the logical deductive scheme. Ultimately, only from this belief can one understand the requirement that the constitutional document should include "all the country's institutions and principles of government."[37]

This requirement must be described as incapable of fulfillment because a concrete historic constitution has never exhibited a closed logical system, resting on supra-historical axioms. No written constitutional instrument contains all fundamental norms, and every constitution also contains precepts that cannot count as fundamental from the standpoint of a systematic political analysis. Hence, the substantive constitution in the narrow sense is always composed of a plurality of constitutional provisions, among which a document is designated as the "formal" constitution because of its supreme significance.

The concept of the formal constitution, the fifth constitutional concept in our sequence, considers the totality of the laws fixed in writing in the constitutional document. The legislator alone decides which laws should count as important enough to be accepted into the constitutional document and which, if need be, should participate in its enhanced guarantee of durability. The tendency to bring the written constitution into the greatest possible agreement with the substantive constitution in the narrow sense is clearly visible in the written constitutions, all of which display a typical content, namely, the fundamental structure of organs and functions. The concept of the formal constitution is theoretically necessary because there can never be a complete correspondence between the substantive and the formal constitution. Although constitutional documents contain a typical content, there are no theoretical principles for deciding which provisions must be reserved to the constitution. Tradition, political expediency, the constellation of power, and legal consciousness decide on what the constitutional document rules just as they decide on which provisions must generally be reserved to statute.[38]

This settles Carl Schmitt's attacks on the concept of the formal constitution, the results of which amount in general to a relativization of the constitution based on the rule of law. Certainly, interpretative constitutional scholarship is not merely entitled, but even required, to construct from within the totality of law a concept of the substantive constitution in the narrow sense alongside the formal concept. However, the content of this positive concept of the constitution, as Schmitt has misleadingly termed it, is, just like the content of all formal constitutions, never independent from "demands along party lines."[39] Thus, for example, one could easily dispute whether it is the case, as Schmitt maintains, that the federal structure actually belongs to the fundamental laws of the "positive" German Constitution of 1919.[40] On the other hand, one cannot grasp on what basis Schmitt wants to prevent the German constitutional legislator from, for example, regarding as just as fundamental as the federal structure the principle of separation of church and state, as well as the corresponding secular supervision of schools.[41] Finally, it is not just these but all the provisions of a substantive as well as of a formal constitution that have to be explained "in terms of the political and historical situation"[42] of their creation.

The claim is utterly false that the "positive" constitution—that is, the substantive constitution in the narrow sense—is not a norm and not a statute but a "solitary decision," [43] or, as Schmitt says elsewhere, a plurality of "concrete political decisions," and that the constitutional statutes "were valid" only on the basis of such a decision or decisions. The constitution is not at all comprehensible as "valid" if it is understood as a nonnormative, merely factually existing decision or plurality of such decisions.

At present, two equally one-sided understandings irreconcilably confront each other on the question of the basis of the validity of a state constitution. According to "pure" normativism, represented by Kelsen and his school, the basis is supposed to be the basic norm representing the "logical origin" of the constitution, which as a legal hypothesis puts in place "the constitution-giving authority"; the constitution therefore is supposed to get its "legally"- and not as one might suppose its logically-relevant validity from this norm of origin, and its content "from the empirical act of will of the constituting authority." Schmitt confronts this powerless, merely logical norm, which is not legally valid, with the norm-less power that is not valid at all. For him, the "positive" constitution is not at all normative, but is "valid by force of the existing political will of the one who gives it." [44]

Every theory beginning with the alternatives, law or power, norm or will, objectivity or subjectivity, fails to recognize the dialectical construction of the reality of the state and goes wrong in its very starting point. The power-forming quality of law forbids us to understand the constitution as the "decision" of a norm-less power. A factual power situation becomes a relatively durable constellation of power and thereby a constitution in any wider or narrower sense only if the following obtains: The "decisions" of the power-holder are complied with by at least one, (i.e., one decisive) section of those subject to the power; and this compliance is motivated not just by interest, habituation, and the like, but because the section sees the norms as valid, exemplary, or binding. On the other hand, however, the law-forming quality of power must reject the interpretation which holds that the (content-less) constitution gets its legal validity by means of a powerless norm whose validity is merely logical, but gets its content from the act of a will of the constituting authority (which is first put in place by the basic norm). Efficacy and validity, the "is" and "ought" of the constitution, must indeed be logically distinguished, but they nevertheless apply to the same constitutional reality, in which the statement of one always at the same time asserts the other.

Not every political constitution, but clearly all constitution-giving presupposes a constitution-giving subject, which can be only a unity of will capable of action and decision. In the world of the Middle Ages, in which the construction of political power had over generations grown by tradition, the acceptance of a constitution-giving subject would have been redundant and purely fictitious. However, once the basic order of the modern state is planned and put in norms, it presupposes the existence of a *pouvoir consti-tuant* that is truly capable of action. As such a *pouvoir constituant,* the imma-nent approach, which no longer shares the belief in the politically consti-tuting power of a transcendent God, but could, as early as Marsilius of Padua, conceive only the *populus,* the *universitas civium.*[45] During the French Revolution, the bourgeois section of the people which had awakened to po-litical self-consciousness the nation in the French sense, succeeded in seiz-ing for itself the conscious decision over the state's form of existence and therewith the constitution-giving power. It was only as a feudal monarchic reaction against this democratic revolutionary principle that the Restora-tion formulated the monarchic principle of the hereditary head of state as *pouvoir constituant.* That this principle remained unsuccessful in the history of ideas[46] is due to the insurmountable difficulty in an immanent approach of awarding the constitution-giving power by divine grace to a family.

However, one can consider the prince as well as the people as the subject of the constitution-giving power only if they as well have acquired this qual-ity normatively. The prince possesses constitution-giving power, not because he has it "existentially," but only on the basis of the normative order of hered-itary succession and, hence, as a legal power. The people as a "formless form-ing" cannot have a *pouvoir constituant* because it "[must] be existent and pre-supposed as a political unity if it is to be the subject of a constitution-giving power."[47] One might deny that a people grows both substantively and tech-nically from an amorphous mass into a unity of wills capable of decision only by compliance with a normative order. One might answer the question of its presupposed unity by saying that "in a certain sense"[48] the unitary people constitutes itself and "in its conscious *identity* with itself"[49] is even a political unity capable of action. This may be political ideology, but certainly not a theory of the state. One may designate as the constitution-giving power the political will whose "power and authority" are able to determine the exis-tence of the political unit as a whole. But without a normative act, a mass of human beings has neither a will capable of decision, nor power capable of action, and at the very least it has no authority whatsoever. The normative element cannot be excluded in any way from the concept of authority by the description of authority as a phenomenon resting essentially on continuity, tradition, and duration;[50] for there are indeed revolutionary authorities whose "social validity" rests in particular on the break in continuity.

The question of the legitimacy of a constitution cannot, of course, be an-swered by referring to its coming into existence in accordance with some previously valid positive provisions. But to be a constitution, i.e., more than a highly unstable factual situation of superior power, to be valid as lawful or-der, a constitution needs justification from ethical principles of law. Schmitt contradicts his own assumptions when he declares that one has to award legitimacy to every existing constitution, but that a constitution is only legitimate "that is, recognized not as a mere factual condition, but as a lawful order, when the power and (!) authority of the constitution-giving power, on whose decision it rests, is recognized."[51] The existentiality and normativity of the constitution-giving power do not contradict each other; rather, they depend on each other. A constitution-giving power that is not linked by common principles of law to the groups decisive for the power structure has neither power nor authority, and hence no existence.

NINE

Carl Schmitt

INTRODUCTION

Volker Neumann

I

Carl Schmitt was born on 11 July 1888 in Plettenberg. After studying law and receiving his doctorate, Schmitt wrote his *Habilitationsschrift* at the University of Strasbourg in 1916 on political philosophy (*Der Wert des Staates und die Bedeutung des Einzelnen* [*The Value of the State and the Significance of the Individual*]). Found unfit for the military because of his health, he served instead in the military administration in Munich until 1919. His friendship with expressionist writers and Catholic intellectuals dates from those years; under their influence, he tried his hand as a writer and cultural critic.[1] His first positions as a professor of public law were at the universities of Greifswald (1921–22) and Bonn (1922–28). In 1928, he accepted the chair at the *Handelshochschule* in Berlin that had been held by Hugo Preuss, father of the Weimar Constitution.

During the subsequent crisis-years of the Weimar Republic, Schmitt developed the theory of a state that is "total through its strength."[2] He held the pluralism of parties and associations responsible for what he considered the state's destruction and placed his hopes for the restoration of unity on a presidential dictatorship. That dictatorship, Schmitt hoped, would be led by President von Hindenburg—as guardian of the constitution, supported by the army, the bureaucracy, and a healthy economy in a strong state— who would defend the "substantive contents" of the constitution against the "value-neutral" legality of the political system—that is, against the parties represented in the Reichstag. In this spirit, Schmitt supported Hindenburg's 20 July 1932 coup against the Social Democrat Prussian government and represented the Reich government of Chancellor Papen in proceedings before the State Court in Leipzig. The coup against Prussia—the *Preußenschlag* —was justified, so the argument went, by the actions of the Prussian government against the National Socialist German Workers Party [NSDAP]: The coup sought to end a policy that equated the NSDAP with the Communist Party and to implement one that was "fair and objective" towards the NSDAP.[3] Whatever the Reich government's motivation, the coup against Prussia opened the chancellery to Adolf Hitler.

Schmitt joined the NSDAP on 1 May 1933, published energetically on behalf of the new regime, and was appointed to influential government positions. A high point of his activity was the article "The Führer Protects the Law" [*Der Führer schützt das Recht*], in which he justified the murders ordered by Hitler in connection with the so-called Röhm Putsch.[4] He rose so quickly that he became entangled in the regime's internal power struggles. In 1936, the SS took steps against the convert and managed to end his rising career within the party in a dispute that reached all the way into the top levels of the Nazi hierarchy. Schmitt's writings prior to 1933 and his Jewish friends and mentors served as grist for the attacks.

The reasons for Schmitt's conversion to Nazism have occasioned much debate. To interpret his publishing and political activity as self-protection in a difficult situation is factually untenable;[5] Schmitt was never in danger, and his downfall in 1936 was merely a career setback. One important motivation was his belief that a movement inexperienced in dealing with state power would need political theorists and lawyers expert in the law of the state. Above all, it must be remembered that for Schmitt, as for many other conservative critics of Weimar, Geneva, and Versailles, Nazism had many seductive features.

No anti-Semitic statements can be found in Schmitt's works prior to 1933. This changed. The height of his anti-Semitic effusions came at a conference titled "Jewry in Legal Scholarship" [*Das Judentum in der Rechtswissenschaft*] on 3 and 4 October 1936. Schmitt opened the conference with a defense of "the magnificent battle by Gauleiter Julius Streicher" against "Jewish emigrants."[6] In his closing remarks, he explained that it was quite wrong to depict Friedrich Julius Stahl (a conservative Prussian political philosopher) as

an exemplary conservative Jew in comparison with later Jews, who unfortunately were that no longer. This dangerously overlooks the essential insight that, with every change in the overall situation, a change also occurs in overall Jewish behavior, a demonically enigmatic change of masks, in face of which the question of the subjective good faith of the particular Jewish individual involved is completely unimportant. The Jews' great adaptability has been enormously increased through their history of many thousands of years, due to a specific racial predisposition, and, on top of this, the virtuosity of their mimicry has been fostered by long practice.[7]

Several American accounts have advanced the claim that Schmitt's anti-Semitism paid "lip service to Nazi views by inserting the odd anti-Semitic remark into his publications." These "early references to race" are said to be "irrelevant to the content of his work and artificially placed within the text."[8] This is as erroneous as the even more extreme interpretation that "Schmitt, a Catholic, by paying some lip service to the new vogue, had hoped to steer the rampant anti-Semitism into a more traditional Christian channel."[9] First, Schmitt was not simply parroting anti-Semitic phrases: "proving" Stahl's Jewish background (Schmitt called him "Stahl-Jolson") was Schmitt's own very personal "research contribution" to anti-Semitism. Second, as early as 1933 Schmitt cited Stahl (who had converted to Protestantism) as evidence of the destructive influence of Jews on the Prussian state—a position incompatible with religiously based anti-Semitism. Third, Schmitt's anti-Semitism had a very precise connection to the "content of his work": He denounced as "Jewish" liberalism and legal positivism, "abstract normativism," and the "Vienna School of the Jew Kelsen." Finally, his diary entries for the years 1947 to 1951 trace an unbroken continuity with his anti-Semitic statements from the 1930s and reveal Schmitt as a hard-core anti-Semite long after the defeat of the Third Reich: "The assimilated Jew in particular is the true enemy. There is no point in proving the Protocols of the Elders of Zion to be false."[10]

Following his fall from grace in 1936, Schmitt shifted to international politics and international law. However, he was unable to regain any political influence. After Berlin was conquered by the Red Army, he was arrested by Soviet troops but released following interrogation. In September 1945, his apartment was searched by U. S. soldiers and his library confiscated. He was taken into custody and brought to Nuremberg; there, he was interrogated by Robert M. W. Kempner[11] and released again in May 1947. Schmitt returned to his birthplace, Plettenberg, where he gathered a circle of the like-minded around him and exercised a not-inconsiderable influence on the intellectual history of the young Federal Republic. He died on 7 April 1985, at the advanced age of 97.

II

In the context of twentieth-century German state law theory, Schmitt takes the position opposite to that of state law positivism in general and to Hans Kelsen's theory of legal norms in particular. His criticism of the unity of the epistemological position of the Pure Theory of Law can be boiled down to one sentence: "Unity and purity are . . . easy to achieve if one emphatically ignores the true difficulties and, for formal reasons, eliminates as impure anything that resists systematization." The "true difficulties," and thus his theoretical interests, begin where Kelsen considers the responsibilities of the lawyer to leave off. Kelsen ridiculed the concept of the state as a sovereign power not identical to the legal order, calling it a "legal belief in miracles" borrowed from theology. Schmitt took up the challenge and responded with *Political Theology* [*Politische Theologie* (1922)], which he introduced with the blunt sentence "Sovereign is he who decides on the exception." The progression sovereignty-exception-decision takes aim at the doctrine of the hierarchical ordering of norms [*Stufenbau der Rechtsordnung*], under which the problem of sovereignty is an illusion, the exception to the rule does not exist, and a decision is valid only if the legally responsible authorities have taken it. For Schmitt, the normal and the rule prove nothing; the exception, everything. And the "independent problem of law-creation"—that is, the question of the legal character of a decision not issued on the basis of the existing legal order—is answered by the analogy of political theology. Just as God intervenes in the world through miracles, the decision of the sovereign breaks through the crust of normality and creates law. Opposition, even hostility, to Hans Kelsen is key to all of Schmitt's works.

Schmitt's interest focused on the irregular and pathological characteristics of law and reality. No other Weimar state law theory so deserves the label "jurisprudence of crisis." Schmitt's theory takes the exception as its starting point. Every concept has in view a political enemy and, without this concrete opposition, is a pointless abstraction. Law and politics cannot be neatly separated, state law concepts are based in political principles, and political theory is always a theory of conflict. The supposedly pure legal methodology of positivism is, in reality, quite political: it is an expression of bourgeois security—though in fact outdated, because the bourgeois, liberal rule of law, like bourgeois society itself, was in crisis. "The Liberal Rule of Law " [*Der bürgerliche Rechtsstaat* (1928)], published below, offers insight on the causes of this crisis, to which, in Schmitt's view, the liberal bourgeoisie had shut its eyes: The institutions and procedures of the liberal rule of law had proved unable to integrate the class-conscious working class into the political unity of the state. This anti-Marxist motif dominates Schmitt's Weimar writings and is evident even in his later work.[12]

Schmitt's political stance against Marxism and his simultaneous intellectual affinity with Marxist political philosophy become especially clear in *The Concept of the Political* [*Der Begriff des Politischen* (1928)]. A contemporary called this work the "bourgeois answer to the Marxist theory of class struggle."[13] To Schmitt, a decision is political if it has the power to distinguish between friend and enemy. This concept of politics explains Schmitt's unique position in Weimar state law theory—unique because his cognitive interests mainly involve the social processes that determine and accelerate the dissolution of a political unity into friend and enemy. His merciless analysis also reads like a diagnosis of the weaknesses in the constitutional and social order that led to the failure of the Weimar Republic. Acknowledgment of the diagnostic power of his analysis is one thing; the interpretation of his concept of politics simply as a warning against the outbreak of social conflicts into irreconcilable friend-enemy relations is quite another. Such an interpretation, which moves the concept of the political toward Smend's theory of integration, can be attained only at the cost of significant "interpolative retouching" of the conceptual system and shortening of the text.[14]

Thinking in concrete oppositions still does not explain the inflation of these oppositions to the extreme—that is, into irreconcilable conflicts and enmities that admit of no compromise. This inflation is caused by his political theology. The analogy between concepts of politics and state law, on the one hand, and theological concepts, on the other, has little in common with theology. The analogy is interested in theological content only where it can be used to turn political ideas into absolutes—into ultimate truths. Political theology functionalizes transcendence for secular purposes; more precisely, it is an associative schema that can articulate both dissatisfaction with the merely relative truths of parliamentary democracy and a diffuse, but all the more determined, quest for absolutes. This is the basis of Schmitt's excessive polemic against discussion, compromise, and mediation, the exuberance of determinateness, and the apocalyptic metaphors of the state of exception (taken from the Spanish counter-revolutionary Donoso Cortes). A 1948 diary entry is instructive: "This is the secret key to my entire intellectual and published existence: a struggle for intrinsically Catholic intensification (against the neutralizers, the aesthetic idlers, against abortionists, cremators, and pacifists)."[15]

Schmitt thinks from above—from power. Law and the state are no more based on human autonomy "than the sun is defined as a fire kindled by freezing primitives to warm themselves."[16] This anti-individualism forms the basis of his democratic theory. Democracy is the identity of rulers and ruled. A criterion of this identity is a "specific and substantial concept of equality," as are similarity, homogeneity, and after 1933, "species equality," but not the empirical agreement of expressed wills. This break with all traditions of the Enlightenment is radical: For Schmitt, the ultimate basis of democracy in the philosophy of the state is not self-determination of the individual.

This anti-individualism is supplemented by anti-pluralism, which—as shown by the essay "State Ethics and the Pluralist State" [*Staatsethik und pluralistischer Staat*], published below—is developed through a critique of the Anglo-Saxon authors, G.D.H. Cole and Harold I. Laski. Because social differentiation and the organization of interests in associations desubstantialize substantive similarity, pluralism threatens the state's political unity.

This concept of state theory is rounded off with anti-liberalism and anti-parliamentarism. The state based on the liberal rule of law, with its parliamentarism, is not a political form of state—that is, one that distinguishes between friend and enemy—but a system of restrictions and checks on the state. This system is historically outdated because it is not able to integrate the proletariat, "as a class without property or education,"[17] into the political unity of the state. Therefore, Schmitt recommends rescuing democracy "from its concealment by liberal elements,"[18] which are the parts of the constitution dealing with the rule of law. The secret ballot and parliamentary decision making procedures are replaced by the "original democratic phenomenon" of acclamation, through the "accepting or rejecting shouts of the assembled crowd."[19]

Schmitt's theory of the state culminated in his theory of the compatibility of democracy with dictatorship, developed in the course of a stroll through the history of political ideas, beginning with Rousseau and ending with Mussolini. This argument, based as it is on intellectual history, confirms that Schmitt's thinking was marked by the fundamental conviction that ideas control life; for as long as "ideas survive, the notion prevails that something preexists the given reality of the material, something transcendent, and this always means an authority from above." Human dignity and autonomy are the casualties of vertical thinking.

Schmitt found himself not only in a struggle with Weimar but also with Geneva and Versailles. His essay "The Status Quo and the Peace" [*Der Status quo und der Friede* (1925)] gives some insight into the motivation and purposes of this struggle. In his sharp criticism of the Versailles Treaty, Schmitt was in agreement with almost all his German and professional colleagues. What is problematic is his understanding of the Charter of the League of Nations as a perpetuation of the status quo created by the treaty. His method of conceptual exaggeration led to a restrictive interpretation of Article 19 of the charter, which provided for the possibility of revising treaties that endangered world peace, and could have been applied to the Versailles Treaty —something other German international law scholars in fact recognized. But this would have meant accepting the legality of the League of Nations. Instead, Schmitt extended his critique of constitutional positivism, and soon also of domestic pluralism, to international politics, turning political principles of legitimacy against legality in international law as well. His nationalism explains why he saw in National Socialism a way out of what he considered the "unbearable" (for Germany) "intermediate state between war and peace."[20] His works on international law published after 1933 justify Nazi Germany's foreign policy and military expansion. Nevertheless, here too, certain analyses—such as that of the significance of technology in the order established in a sphere of influence [*Großraumordnung*] or of the instruments of economic imperialism—go beyond propaganda and achieve quite accurate insights.

III

Few German authors have been written about as much or engendered as much controversy as Schmitt. It is no longer possible to keep track of the literature, and it continues to grow. This is not only true of German-speaking countries and countries like Italy[21] or Spain,[22] in which he has long been read and critiqued.[23] In the United States, interest in his work is documented by several translations[24] and a growing number of secondary works, mainly in political science.[25] Increasingly, the conflicts dealt with in the German debate about Schmitt's theory of law are being taken up in the United States. Ellen Kennedy can be credited for courageously kicking off a lively controversy in recent years over the influence of his work.[26] What are the reasons for his (almost) worldwide currency?

Schmitt's position in his disciplines, the law of the state and international law, does not sufficiently explain his currency today. The significance of his contribution to legal doctrine lags far behind the influence of his work. Certainly he developed concepts that remain present in the scholarship of public law and are often used to explain problems situated in the overlap between the law of the state and politics. However, there has been little systematic reception of his theories, in the sense of their integration and further development within constitutional doctrine. This is not surprising, as the reference of state law solutions to the problems of a specific time and Schmitt's development of legal concepts from political principles limit the possibility of processing them into doctrine.

Schmitt's effect on the emergence of the Basic Law of the Federal Republic of Germany [*Grundesetz für die Bundesrepublik Deutschland* (1949)] is a subject of controversy. The constructive vote of no-confidence in Article 67 of the Basic Law (permitting a vote of no-confidence only when there is a replacement, as opposed to a destructive vote of no-confidence, which permits one without a replacement), of which Schmitt is considered the guiding spirit, had many fathers; it was not he, but Ernst Fraenkel, who first called for including this provision in the Reich constitution.[27] It is an exaggeration to assess the guarantee against changing certain eternal constitutional principles in Article 79(3) as an "expression in positive law" of Schmitt's doctrine of the substantive limits of constitutional revision. This provision can plausibly be traced back to Richard Thoma, who participated as an adviser in drawing up the Basic Law and in 1948 proposed such a "norm of inviolability."[28] In 1932, however, Thoma had dismissed Schmitt's doctrine as "wishful legal thinking," so that his position in 1948 can be considered a revision of his Weimar critique. Thus Schmitt was present in the emergence of Article 79(3) at least indirectly. More evident is the influence of his critique of the "value neutrality of a merely functionalist system of legality," a supposed "neutrality to the point of suicide," on Article 21(2) governing bans on parties, even if his name is not mentioned in its formative documents.[29]

All in all, Schmitt's contribution to his discipline was significant but far from outstanding. However, it must be noted that his influence on German state law theory cannot be measured by the visible reception of his work but is also felt in the form of covert influence on attitudes. When in doubt, a Schmittian—and here too, the exception proves the rule—will opt for state order and against democratic freedom.

So why Carl Schmitt? The answer follows from the time in which he lived, the themes about which he thought and wrote, and the method he used. His life and work included four epochs of the German state: the Empire, the Weimar Republic, the National Socialist Third Reich, and, following the interim of occupation, the Federal Republic of Germany. German history in this century was an experimental field for political ideas and forms of state, a laboratory in which the durability of state structures and human associations was tested. Schmitt observed and analyzed these experiments. He did not do this from the distanced perspective of the scholar; instead, he threw his positions and concepts on the "scales of the times."[30] He was aided by a seismographic feel for political processes and intellectual developments that always kept him a bit ahead of his time. His answers to the challenges of the times may be contestable, biased, or even reprehensible; however, in the very problems they pose they reflect the virulence of the times. His work is a guide to this century's political history and history of ideas, and that makes it interesting.

In addition, Schmitt never allowed himself to be confined to the limits of his discipline. His theoretical interests reached far beyond legal scholarship and included philosophy, sociology, political science, theology, and literary criticism. The wealth of issues he discussed, the number of books produced, and the names of the authors he knew and with whom he corresponded are impressive. The response to his works is correspondingly rich. There are probably only a few authors who have become as much the subject of interdisciplinary discussion as he. All this makes his work an "Ariadne's thread"[31] for German and European intellectual history in this century. A separate literary genre, called "Carl Schmitt and . . . ," exists to examine his relationships with contemporary authors. With no claim to completeness, these include Hugo Ball, Karl Barth, Walter Benjamin, Hugo Fischer, Ernst Fraenkel, Hermann Heller, Karl Jaspers, Ernst Jünger, Otto Kirchheimer, Franz Neumann, Helmut Plessner, Johannes Popitz, Rolf Schroers, Leo Strauss, Max Weber, and—we gratefully note that this unacceptable gap in the research has been closed—René Girard![32]

It is not only the subjects dealt with that lead so many authors to take up

"Ariadne's thread" and enter Carl Schmitt's world. Even more, it is his way of working and his style. Schmitt cites unconventionally or not at all, weaving disguised information, hints, and messages into his texts. He is a master of puzzles, and his texts promise to decipher secrets. The reader encounters what he or she believes to be conceptual clarity and evidence, but at the same time things that are inexact and hazy. Upon reading a text a second time, one realizes that what seemed to be the firm center is not nearly as exact as it appeared on first reading. His work and biography invite lifelong dissertation.

In answer to the question, "Why Carl Schmitt?" Bernhard Schlink referred to a need to integrate the Third Reich into German history. This integration becomes easier if more can be seen in National Socialism than the banality of evil. Unfortunately, Schlink defuses the explosiveness of his thesis by generalizing and speaking of "the need of all of us to de-banalize evil."[33] It is no accident that it is Schmitt's person and work through which the attempt is made to lend continuity to German history beyond 1933. Schmitt rejected de-Nazification and uttered not a single self-critical word on his activities between 1933 and 1945. This defiance distinguishes him from others among the defeated, who quickly learned to make a place for themselves in and to adapt to the democracy they had been made a present of. Those who wanted could see in Schmitt's refusal to atone an unbroken biography, entitling him to authentic interpretation of the nation's history. Those who saw it this way joined the Plettenberg group. For them, Schmitt was the guardian of a national tradition, harmed neither by National Socialism nor by the victors. That is how they interpret his role in the Third Reich: For them, Schmitt gave meaning to National Socialism and in seeking to do so was doomed to failure because Hitler, "the executor without presuppositions,"[34] exploited Schmitt's correct ideas with fraudulent intentions. And his anti-Semitism could not be Hitler's anti-Semitism, but something more sublime, perhaps Catholic "anti-Judaism,"[35] whatever that is supposed to be; in any case, something which mysteriously "holds the historical core of the problem."[36] With this, the reinterpretation from theorist of counterrevolution to Catholic thinker has been smoothly completed.

However, not even the most faithful pupil can close his eyes to the fact that the Master was fascinated by National Socialism and readily participated in it. But could not one then conclude that not everything about Nazism could have been evil and banal, if even an intellect as great as Schmitt was impressed by it? This conclusion has not yet been voiced openly. In any case, the prognosis seems correct that the question "whether the C. S. of 1933–1945 should be seen as a mere traffic accident, or as something more" will lead to a "major battle among his heirs."[37] With publication of the *Glossarium,* the fight began. The message to the "Schmitt establishment" is that anyone wishing to belong to the school of Carl Schmitt must accept the entire

Master—including his anti-Semitism and National Socialism. This battle of the heirs will not leave German state law theory unscathed. Thus Helmut Ridder's prognosis[38] must be corrected to read: No end to Carl Schmitt!

MAIN WORKS

Der Wert des Staates und die Bedeutung des Einzelnen. Tübingen: Mohr, 1914.

Politische Romantik. Munich and Leipzig: Duncker & Humblot, 1919.

Die Diktatur. Munich and Leipzig: Duncker & Humblot, 1921.

Politische Theologie. Munich and Leipzig: Duncker & Humblot, 1922.

Die geistesgeschichtliche Lage des heutigen Parlamentarismus. Munich and Leipzig: Duncker & Humblot, 1923.

Römischer Katholizismus und politische Form. Hellerau: Jakob Hegener, 1923.

Die Kernfrage des Völkerbundes. Berlin: Ferdinand Dümmler, 1926.

Der Begriff des Politischen. Berlin: Walther Rothschild, 1928.

Verfassungslehre. Munich and Leipzig: Duncker & Humblot, 1928.

Hugo Preuss. Tübingen: Mohr, 1930.

Der Hüter der Verfassung. Tübingen: Mohr, 1931.

Legalität und Legitimität. Munich and Leipzig: Duncker & Humblot, 1932.

Staat, Bewegung, Volk. Hamburg: Hanseatische Verlagsanstalt, 1933.

Über die drei Arten des rechtswissenschaftlichen Denkens. Hamburg: Hanseatische Verlagsanstalt, 1934.

Der Leviathan in der Staatslehre des Thomas Hobbes. Hamburg: Hanseatische Verlagsanstalt, 1938.

Völkerrechtliche Großraumordnung mit Interventionsverbot für raumfremde Mächte. Berlin, Leipzig, and Vienna: Deutscher Rechtsverlag, 1939.

Positionen und Begriffe im Kampf mit Weimar-Genf-Versailles 1923–1939. Hamburg: Hanseatische Verlagsanstalt, 1940.

Der Nomos der Erde im Völkerrecht des Jus Publicum Europaeum. Cologne: Greven, 1950.

Verfassungsrechtliche Aufsätze aus den Jahren 1924–1954. Berlin: Duncker & Humblot, 1958.

Theorie des Partisanen. Berlin: Duncker & Humblot, 1963.

Politische Theologie II. Berlin: Duncker & Humblot, 1970.

LITERATURE

Biographies

Bendersky, Joseph W. *Carl Schmitt: Theorist for the Reich.* Princeton: Princeton University Press, 1983.

van Laak, Dirk. *Gespräche in der Sicherheit des Schweigens.* Berlin: Akademie, 1993.

Noack, Paul. *Carl Schmitt: Eine Biographie.* Frankfurt am Main: Propyläen, 1993.

On his work

Hofmann, Hasso. *Legitimität gegen Legalität.* 2nd ed. Berlin: Duncker & Humblot, 1992 (1st ed., 1964).

Maus, Ingeborg. *Bürgerliche Rechtstheorie und Faschismus*. Munich: Wilhelm Fink, 1976.

Neumann, Volker. *Der Staat im Bürgerkrieg*. Frankfurt and New York: Campus, 1980.

Quaritsch, Helmut. *Positionen und Begriffe Carl Schmitts*. Berlin: Duncker & Humblot, 1989.

———, ed. *Complexio Oppositorum Über Carl Schmitt*. Berlin: Duncker & Humblot, 1988.

Schneider, Peter. *Ausnahmezustand und Norm*. Stuttgart: Deutsche Verlags-Anstalt, 1957.

Schwab, George. *The Challenge of the Exception*. Berlin: Duncker & Humblot, 1970.

THE STATUS QUO AND THE PEACE

Carl Schmitt

Originally appeared as "Der Status quo und der Friede," in *Hochland* 23, no. 1 (Kempten and Munich: Jos. Kösel'sche Buchhandlung, October 1925), 1–9.

The word of the hour in political discussion today is "status quo." All turns of phrase used to characterize mutual demands, all political proposals and counter-proposals, ideas such as security, guarantee, inviolability of treaties, sanctity of borders, circle about this concept. Three procedures have been proposed to organize peace with the hope that their implementation will bring peace on earth, but with disagreement over their sequence, particularly so in discussions at the League of Nations assembly of September 1924: security, court of arbitration, and disarmament. This sequence seems to have been agreed upon for now; whether it will endure, whether it might not be better to begin with "disarmament" or with a general "court of arbitration," each of these terms ultimately means status quo. In its Memorandum of 9 February 1925, the German government expressly proposed a guarantee of the present status quo on the Rhine and thus opened a series of negotiations and consultations in the course of which the status quo is spoken of again and again.

Characteristically, one speaks today of the status quo and not the status quo ante, which was a favorite formulation in the era of traditional diplomacy. Thus one means the state of affairs as it stands. How it stands is apparently easy to recognize, for it is right in front of us. As to the status quo on the Rhine (which is most often mentioned), it is obviously distinguished primarily by the fact that the Rhineland is *occupied territory*. The Versailles Treaty, the Rhineland Agreement with all its consequences and its practical application, the Inter-Allied Rhineland Commission's right of decree, quartering of soldiers and confiscation of housing, expulsion of Germans, etc.—all this is part of the state of affairs as it stands today. . . .

The status quo on the Rhine continues to be defined by the fact that the Rhineland remains *demilitarized territory,* even beyond the borders of the occupied territory. Germany is prohibited from establishing fortifications on the left bank of the Rhine, or on the right bank within a line running fifty kilometers east of the river; in this zone, permanent or temporary stationing or gathering of forces is prohibited; any military exercise, any measure that could be considered preparation for mobilization, is forbidden. Through such a provision, the Rhineland is distinguished in international law from the rest of Germany. It is not yet neutralized, which would separate its fate in foreign policy from that of the rest of Germany; but we must not mistake the consequences of the existing distinction. No German soldier may ever again set foot on the soil of the Rhineland—not even for the purpose of putting down insurrection and unrest; any rail construction, any road construction, any possible transport or industrial facilities could, under a unilateral interpretation, fall under the limitless heading "preparation for mobilization". . . .

This status quo on the Rhine—occupation and demilitarization—is only one part of the great system of burdens and limitations on the authority of the German state arising out of the Versailles Treaty and its implementation. They include the League of Nations Council's right of investigation under Article 213 of the treaty, territorial rupture of the German borders in the East, separating German tribes from the German Reich, the weight of reparations, foreign control of the German Reichsbank and of German railroads, over which the foreign railroad commissioner can exercise powers that, even though expressly defined as "exceptional," by that very fact prove their link to the issue of sovereignty; further, they include limits on the construction of aircraft, and all the hundreds of treaty provisions that press Germany today. In this regard, the Rhineland is but an especially burdened part of the German Reich.

So this is the status quo on the Rhine and the status quo in Germany. In whose interest is it to guarantee it? In particular, who is interested in the Rhineland? . . .

Generally speaking, international political interest in the Rhineland as an occupied, demilitarized territory is based on its location, at the intersection of English, French, and German interests. What the status quo on the Rhine means can be recognized only from this aspect. The different powers regard the situation from very different points of view. Thus the word "status quo" has a different meaning for each of them. The *English* interest, for the time being, most likely tends toward preferring no disruption of peace on the European continent; preservation of peace accords with the economic interests of English commerce and English industry, as well as the political interest of preserving England's empire. The dangers that could threaten this empire today apparently are found not on the European continent but in

Russia and Asia, and are based on an alliance of the proletarian socialism of the Soviet Republic with the national feelings of the oppressed peoples of Asia and Africa. For Germany, a union of nationalism and communism seems out of the question, although it has occasionally been called for. Still we must not ignore the possibility, especially since the parties that in Germany have so far claimed nationalism for themselves are faced with completely new problems that arise from the increasingly difficult economic and political situation, and have an influence under which traditional bonds between ideas can easily dissolve.

Only this one opponent, the alliance between Bolshevism and nationalism, could produce an English policy aimed at battle and war, allowing the world to experience another crusade following the crusade against Germany. Otherwise, England's political interest is aimed entirely at peace and preservation of the present status quo in the world; that is, the preservation of England's world hegemony. Thus for England, the word "status quo" has a great and simple meaning. In the negotiations on the so-called guarantee pact, England is most concerned with avoiding new obligations, and pointing out that the Charter of the League of Nations already contains the maximum of English obligations.

French interest in the status quo is aimed at not surrendering any of the rights granted France and its allies in the Versailles Treaty. After all, this treaty has the essential quality of a treaty of intervention, in the specific sense of the word; that is, to allow, through purposely vague terms, the political and military treaty opponent to intervene constantly. The famous right to sanctions is only one case of the application of this systematic technique of intervention. For France, the issue is creating additional "security" for the very far-reaching, existing possibilities; here that is especially a commitment from the English government. . . .

For France, therefore, the status quo = Versailles Treaty. Politically, this means preservation of France's military and political hegemony on the European continent; preservation of the military and political dominance of an armed nation of forty million over an unarmed people of sixty million; an armed people with a falling birth rate over an unarmed, sharply growing people whose industry is vainly seeking an outlet.

In comparison with the English and French, the *German* interest in the status quo is more modest, even pitiful. It is an interest in at least preventing the imposition of new obligations, or the emergence of more and more burdens and disruptions through unilateral interpretation of the Versailles Treaty. It is an interest in keeping at least the currency stable and defending it against new sanctions, reprisals, and other pressures. It is an interest that does not command a view of the entire world, as does the English, or at least of Europe, like the French; it is the interest of a people interested primarily in its industry, focused on the next moment, the next breath.

Germany, and especially the Rhineland, stands at the intersection of England's worldwide and France's continental interests. In this situation, all of Germany, and especially the Rhineland, could sink to the level of a mere object counterbalancing these English and French interests. That is Germany's political status quo and the status quo on the Rhine. Any legalization of this situation would perpetuate this object character. . . .

It is quite remarkable that the status quo is to be guaranteed precisely at a point of rapid change and technical progress. It is strange that the age whose thinking is dominated by the idea of eternal becoming, eternal flow, and substanceless functioning would like to stabilize an existing state of affairs within the political domain. This in itself is inconsistent, but the actual inconsistency lies still deeper. From where, to ask again, does the need for a guarantee of the status quo arise? From the fact that the wish for calm, peace, and justice is linked with an inability to find a legal principle, a principle of legitimacy. One can guarantee only a legal state of affairs, not something merely factual; and even a legal state of affairs can be guaranteed only if it is perceived as normal. This being so, as we cannot reasonably deny, then the internal inconsistency in the moral condition of today's Europe seems horrifying. The situation as it actually exists is so unsatisfactory, so abnormal, and thus so unstable that the yearning for stability becomes stronger each day. From the yearning for peace and stability emerges the demand for a guarantee of the status quo—that is, a stabilization. But stabilization of the present situation would stabilize precisely this unsatisfactory, wholly unstable situation; and the result would be that, through artificial perpetuation and legalization, one achieves not calm and peace, but new conflicts, a new sharpening of contradictions, and perpetuation of the lack of stability. A dangerous, perhaps deadly cycle for entire peoples! That is the fateful aspect of this entire system of legalization and juridification of the status quo. We are told that a guarantee of the status quo is peace. Certainly, peace, even *the* peace, the peace of Versailles. A status quo stabilized on this basis is as problematic as the peace itself. Here, too, one sees the wealth of internal inconsistencies that today dominate Europe's political and moral condition. If the status quo is not peace, how can its guarantee produce peace? After all, the yearning for peace arises from the lack of peace in existing circumstances. The exhausted, tormented people who seek above all calm and peace are promised a guarantee that guarantees nothing but the causes of all disturbance and lack of peace.

In the course of the last century, the European peoples have heard many things described as "peace": the Holy Alliance was peace; the French Empire under Napoleon III was peace; then, during the war, we were told that democracy is peace; we were told that the League of Nations is peace, and now we are told that the guarantee of the status quo is peace. But if the status quo itself is not peace, its guarantee is even worse than war—that is, the legalization of an unbearable intermediate state between war and peace, in which the politically powerful deprive the politically weak not only of his life but also of his right and his honor.

THE LIBERAL RULE OF LAW

Carl Schmitt

Originally appeared as "Der bürgerliche Rechtsstaat," in *Abendland* 3, no. 7 (Cologne: Gilde-Verlag, April 1928), 201–03.*

I

The new German Reich is a constitutional democracy. It has a constitution, just as it had a constitution under the monarchy; here, in the "constitutional," lies an essential continuity linking today's Reich with the old Reich of 1871. This means that both forms in which the German Reich has existed as a state—monarchy and democracy—were modified and relativized through the prism of the state based on the liberal rule of law. There is no break, no revolution in the strict legal sense between the old and the new form of state. A constitutional democracy replaced a constitutional monarchy. The German Reich is not simply a democracy but a *constitutional* democracy.

The constitution of the German Reich, the element in the new democracy of a state based on the liberal rule of law, is the Weimar Constitution.

It has become apparent that the Weimar Constitution, contrary to the expectations of its authors and the claims of its defenders, is not a terribly vivid presence in the mind of the German citizen. Why is it something that, in the general view, is empty and unsatisfying? This is so for a number of reasons.

For one, the German Reich has at present been altogether deprived of a

---

*We have generally translated *bürgerlicher Rechtsstaat* throughout Schmitt's essay as "state based on the liberal rule of law." To preserve the pithiness of the German title, we have shortened "state based on the liberal rule of law" to "liberal rule of law" in the English title, as well as in the essay itself. We translate "bürgerlich" as "liberal" rather than "bourgeois," because "bourgeois" has very different connotations in English than does "bürgerlich" in German: "Bürgerlich" combines the ideas conveyed by the two French words, "bourgeois" and "citoyen" ("private man" and "citizen"), and refers to the liberal state in which a person can be both simultaneously—actively pursuing economic interests while enjoying constitutionally guaranteed rights and freedoms. "Bourgeois" in English refers generally to the middle class rather than to a particular structure of state and economic life, and reference to the middle class in this sense is never a compliment; no English-speaker proudly claims the title "bourgeois." The particular *Rechtsstaat* that is the subject of Schmitt's essay is thus the "state based on the liberal rule of law."—EDS.

large part of its political substance, because crucial political issues are being dealt with from the outside. Through the Versailles Treaty and its implementation, through the Dawes Plan, and through more-or-less voluntary treaties, the foreign and even some of the domestic policies of the German Reich have been determined for years to come. The Reich has not yet regained complete sovereignty, and this lack of political substance would relativize the importance of any constitution.

There is also another historical element; in a certain sense, the Weimar Constitution is posthumous. It realizes demands, ideals, and programs that were already current in 1848. At the reestablishment of the Reich in 1870, liberalism and the rule of law—the ideas of this period—entered into Bismarck's constitution only to a small extent. Otherwise, they were stifled for two generations. They did not achieve fulfillment until the monarchy, the opponent of 1848, had disappeared in the collapse of 1918, not because it had been defeated internally, but because an external, military defeat automatically eliminated it. After two generations, the ideas of 1848 won without a struggle. It is as if a young man of twenty who had courted a girl of the same age, but was rejected in favor of a rival, should win the widow decades later. Thus the achievement of the liberal program, which would have been a brilliant victory had it been fought for and won in 1848, came too late in 1919, when it fell without a struggle into the laps of the heirs of the collapse. This is another reason for that feeling of emptiness, that lack of enthusiasm one feels toward the constitution today.

But the Weimar Constitution bears within itself the essential explanation for that sentiment. We must attempt to deal with its structure in two sentences. This constitution is modeled following the type of constitutional scheme inaugurated in 1789. The ideological consciousness that times today are completely different may somehow have been present in certain protagonists of the so-called revolution of 1918, but not even a hint of this is actually expressed in the constitution.

For what was the decision that Germany faced at the end of the war? All at once it had become clear how things stood between West and East. It became apparent that Russia had in reality joined the liberal crusade against Germany only temporarily. The Bolshevik Revolution had proved how little Russia could ever embody the rule of law in the Western sense. A German constitution would have had to include a choice between East and West or a decision emanating from the full strength of German particularity. Awareness of this necessity explains the sociopolitical program in the second part of the Weimar Constitution. The political decision, the substance of the constitution, was made in favor of the West, the tradition of the liberal rule of law of 1789.

This state based on the liberal rule of law is generally characterized by its foundation on the basic rights of the individual and the principle of separation of powers. In this context, the freedom of the individual is essentially unlimited, the state and its powers limited. What the state is permitted to do is assigned exactly. Supervision by specific organs is provided for and legally guaranteed everywhere. In contrast, the personal freedom of the individual is unlimited. It is not fixed by law, and unavoidable exceptions must be determined by previously defined norms. The starting points are a sphere of unlimited opportunity for the individual and comprehensive checks on the state. This liberal principle of allocation [*liberales Verteilungsprinzip*] runs through the entire organization of the state. The state's powers are arranged and the ways of governing balanced against one another in an exceedingly precise manner.

What is interesting here is the essentially political question of the relationship between the liberal rule of law and the form of the state. This question is avoided by reference to "separation of powers." It is no longer the form of state that is discussed, but instead the organization of the legislature, the executive, etc. Nor is democracy any longer the form of a state but rather the form in which legislating is organized. In this way, of course, all the consequences of the democratic in its political sense are prevented. The executive, on the other hand, is organized monarchically, because one cannot "separate powers" without organizing them according to different contrary formative principles. Thus the state based on the liberal rule of law is a *status mixtus* that purposely balances contrary principles in the interest not of political unity but of individual freedom. An absolute democracy destroys freedom no less than an absolute monarchy. This is always the consequence when the monarchic or the aristocratic or the democratic formative element is accomplished in its purity. Even if the state based on the liberal rule of law balances all three elements without accomplishing one consistently, its basic principle—that the individual cannot be controlled—remains intact but the substance of the political is destroyed.

Both principles of the state based on the liberal rule of law—freedom of the individual and separation of powers—are apolitical. They comprise not forms of the state but rather methods of organizing restraints on the state. Here we see the direct influence of liberal thought, hostile to all formative elements: "Freedom constitutes nothing" (Mazzini). It must be emphasized above all that the state based on the liberal rule of law is not a form of the state or a constitution in itself, but only a system of checks on the state.

The typical form in which rule-of-law liberalism appears is the parliamentary system. It contains aristocratic and monarchic elements and is in every respect a mixture of forms arising out of the liberal interest aimed at restricting the essentially political wherever it shows itself. It is the form created by the bourgeoisie to protect itself from the state—that is, an anti-political form, just as the liberal bourgeoisie is itself something apolitical.

It has always been striking how inconsistent the attitude of the liberal bourgeoisie has constantly been toward political matters. It played the monarchy off against the democracy, and vice-versa, without ever deciding in favor of a particular form of state. The bourgeoisie finally found the scheme of the state based on the liberal rule of law, the very point of which is to avoid a political form, in the French constitution of 1875 in force today. It culminates in the parliamentary system. A parliament independent of the people is the high point of the state based on the liberal rule of law. Parliamentarism presents itself as a complicated system of a mixture of political forms. The democratic principle of parliament's dependence on the people is retained, but with sufficient effective counter-elements. The government is simultaneously dependent upon and independent of parliament; most important is its implicit power to dissolve parliament. The position of president of the Reich is constructed completely like that of a temporary monarch, but here, too, the monarchic political form fuses aristocratic and democratic elements. Nowhere are the consequences of a political form drawn.

But what is the point of the whole thing? The task of a parliament consists in integrating political unity—that is, constantly renewing the political unity of a mass of people heterogeneous in class, interests, culture, and religion. A certain uniformity—a homogeneity—is necessary for a people to achieve its political existence in a state. A state's institutions have the function of making this uniformity possible and reproducing it anew every day. In the state based on the liberal rule of law, with its parliamentarism, this involves a particular duty: integrating the bourgeoisie—that is, a segment of the population characterized by the two traits of property and education—into the then-existing monarchic state. It is now necessary to recognize the relativity of the attempt to achieve political unity of the people via the parliament. When the attempt was first made, the new bourgeois classes stood opposite the monarchic state and had to be integrated into it. In the meantime, however, the opponent—the monarchy—which drew its strength from another era, fell away. For this reason alone, the entire system had to run on idle.

The point of the system was to integrate the bourgeoisie into the monarchic state. This task it has fulfilled. Today, however, the situation is completely different. Today the issue is to integrate the proletariat, a propertyless and uneducated mass, into a political unity. For this task, which has scarcely yet been envisaged, only the apparatuses and machines serving the old task of integrating the educated bourgeoisie remain available, even today. The constitution is one such apparatus. Hence everything to us seems so artificial; thus this feeling of emptiness that one so easily has in face of the Weimar Constitution.

In Spengler's famous words, the Weimar Constitution is an English suit put on by the German Reich in 1919. In 1919 no more suitable form could be found. The Weimar Constitution has value only as a makeshift.

The democratic is emphasized sufficiently strongly in this constitution that the people has the opportunity to find a political form at all times—despite all restraints and safety valves and behind the barrier erected by the idea of the state under the liberal rule of law. The issue for constitutional development in the period to come will be saving democracy from being veiled by liberal elements. Only in this way, and not through liberal detachment on the issues of the form of the state and constitution, can the new situation created by the new significance of the proletariat be mastered politically and the political unity of the German citizenry recreated.

II

The fact that even in today's German democracy there is everywhere a refusal to accept the consequences of the democratic can be shown through many examples. Democracy today is democracy without a *demos,* without a people. The democratic principle demands that the people in its entirety decides and governs responsibly. But the methods with which today's democracy attempts to put the people's sovereignty into practice are not democratic, but liberal, methods. Today, the people's political decision comes into being through the *individual secret ballot.* This means that individuals are isolated during the only moment in which they bear public responsibility. In plebiscites and referenda, as well as in elections to parliament, the individual is locked in a voting booth and thus casts his vote. The people, however, is only the people assembled. Public opinion is not the sum of the private opinions of each individual. If the individual sits at home and listens to the radio, his opinion, even if it agrees word-for-word with the opinion of all, is not yet public opinion. The amazing thing is that nowhere in our democratic constitution does the assembled people appear; there are always only assembled representatives, the individual taken out of the mass. Where, in the text of the constitution and in the reality of the state based on the liberal rule of law does the people appear at all? Where is there room for an acclamation that can occur only if a public is created by the people assembled and present? There is no public without the people, and there is no people without a public. Where today, in the method of the secret ballot, is there a public, and where is the people?

Further: democracy is majority decision. Its point is that political issues are regulated according to the politically responsible beliefs of the majority of the people. Liberalism, however, aims specifically to destroy this political decision—to make it impossible. This is the purpose of the individual secret ballot. For the result of such a vote will always be the predominance of the politically uninterested over those who consciously shoulder political responsibility. Majority decision through the individual secret ballot necessarily tends to *minimize* political decision.

All Napoleonic plebiscites gained an overwhelming majority of yes votes. This was true in 1799, 1804, and 1814, but also in 1851 and 1852; following each coup, the people acclaimed the power thus created through their "yes." Conversely, it has been found in Switzerland that new statutes generally are voted down. The reason for this is the same as in France—no one wants to vote against the status quo. The best known case is that of Swiss social insurance, which took decades to win approval. The people always says "no" when anything new is demanded. The majority of those voting in secret always tend to avoid making a political decision, or at least limit it to a minimum. In the case of the Napoleonic plebiscites, this did not constitute responsible assumption of a creative decision. The people was faced with a fait accompli; a decision had long since been made. There the "yes" meant only endorsement of what had already occurred. The Swiss citizens' "no" meant exactly the same thing: We don't want to be bothered with the decision, and prefer to leave things as they are. Something similar is evident in the way the German people are "deciding" today in the matter of the flag. Here the preference for neutral colors, for the colors of states, cities, etc., is striking. People avoid taking a position; they do not want to be burdened with these political issues. Secret ballots lead to a situation in which political issues are decided by all of these politically uninterested, politically irresponsible people. One could say that under the current method, the more a sector of the population tries to avoid political decision and responsibility, the greater becomes its political influence. It is not mere chance that a party emphasizing the economy holds the balance in parliament, and on the most crucial issues it happens that the decisive majority is made up of those who stay home and do not vote. This defect is fostered rather than curbed by the Weimar Constitution. On the issue of expropriation of the princes, for example, it would have been possible to produce great general popular endorsement for or against the princes. But Article 75 of the Weimar Constitution provides that a majority of those eligible to vote must take part in such a plebiscite.* The slogans circulated by various parties, as well as the final outcome of the campaign, remain fresh in our memories. Those who stayed home, who did not decide, determined the result. Today, that is the reality of the phrase "majority decides."

Every democracy requires complete homogeneity of its people. Only such a unity can assume political responsibility. If, as in the case of the state today, we are dealing with a people pieced together heterogeneously, the task becomes the integration of this mass into a unified whole. The true democratic method is not a method for integrating heterogeneous masses. The citizenry today, however, is divided in many ways—culturally, socially, by class, race, and religion. Thus a solution must be sought outside this democratic

*A 1926 plebiscite on expropriation failed as a result.—EDS.

political method, or parliament itself will become the tribune that under-scores the contradictions.

Today this necessary political unity in Germany is being produced more improvisationally from without. The German Reich is primarily a unity for paying reparations; it appears as such from the outside. However, politically nothing is more necessary than to envision the task of integrating the German people into political unity from the inside. Theoretical reflection is necessary to achieve this, as well as a clear recognition of the dangers and contradictions of the current situation. It is the central task of integrating the proletariat into the new state that reveals the inadequacy of the methods of the state based on the liberal rule of law.

STATE ETHICS AND THE PLURALIST STATE

Carl Schmitt

Originally appeared as "Staatsethik und pluralistischer Staat," in *Kant-Studien*, vol. 35 (Berlin: Pan-Verlag Kurt Metzner, 1930), 28–42.

I

The most widespread and thoroughly prevalent assessment of the state is best characterized today by the title of a much-quoted American essay (written in 1915 by Ernest Barker): "The Discredited State" [English in the original]. Even in very strong states whose strength in foreign policy and domestic order are not threatened—in the United States of America and England—the traditional concepts of the state have been strongly criticized since the War; the state's old claim to be the sovereign unity and whole has been shaken. In France, syndicalist theoreticians proclaimed as far back as 1907, "The state is dead." For more than twenty years, there has been a body of legal and sociological literature that challenges the primacy of the state as well as the law, subordinating both to "society." We can refer to Léon Duguit and Maxime Leroy as important and interesting modern legal scholars who weigh in on this issue. In Germany, the crisis only became apparent with the collapse of Bismarck's Reich, when concepts of state and government that had been considered unshakable vanished; since 1919, a broad literature of crisis has emerged here, for which it is enough to recall the title of a book by Alfred Weber: *The Crisis of the European Idea of the State* [*Die Krisis des europäischen Staatsgedankens*]. In addition, there is an extensive body of theoretical literature on the law of the state and international law that attempts to destroy the concept of sovereignty, and with it the traditional idea of the state as a unity transcending all social groups.

A blow to the state is always also a blow to state ethics. For all traditional ideas of state ethics share the fate of the concrete state, which they always presuppose, and fall into discredit with it. When "God on earth" falls from his throne and the empire of objective reason and morality becomes a *magnum latrocinium* [large band of robbers], the parties slaughter the mighty Leviathan and each cuts its bit of flesh from the body. What does "state ethics" mean then? The blow does not affect merely the state ethics of Hegel (which makes the state the bearer and creator of an ethic of its own), nor merely the idea of the *stato etico* (as fascist doctrine employs it); it is also a blow to the state ethics of Kant and liberal individualism. Although the state ethics of Kant and liberal individualism does not see the state as the subject and bearer of an autonomous ethics, but rather as bound to ethical norms, it has so far— with the exception of certain radical anarchists—always proceeded on the assumption that the state is a highest body and the decisive judge of external "mine and thine," through which a merely normative and thus judgeless state of nature—a *status justitia* (more precisely, *judice*) *vacuus* in which each is his own judge—is overcome. Without the concept of the state as a *transcendent* unity and quantity, all practical outcomes of Kant's state ethics become contradictory and invalid. This is most clearly true for the doctrine of the right of resistance. Despite all his relativizing of the state using the laws of reason, Kant rejected a right of resistance against the state on the basis of the very thought of state unity.

II

More recent Anglo-Saxon theories of the state (of interest here are those of G.D.H. Cole and Harold I. Laski) call themselves "pluralist." In this way, they aim not only to negate the state as the highest comprehensive unity, but above all to negate its ethical claim to be a different and higher sort of social relation than any of the many other associations in which people live. The state becomes a social group or association existing at best side-by-side with, but on no account above, the other associations. The ethical consequence and result of this is that the individual lives in unorganized simultaneity of numerous social duties and loyalties: in a religious community, economic associations such as unions, combines or other organizations, a political party, a club, cultural or social societies, the family and various other social groups. Everywhere he has a duty of loyalty and fidelity; everywhere ethics emerge: church ethics, professional ethics, union ethics, family ethics, association ethics, office and business ethics, etc. For all these complexes of duties—for the "plurality of loyalties"—there is no "hierarchy of duties," no unconditionally decisive principle of superiority and inferiority. Specifically, the ethical attachment to the state, the duty of fidelity and loyalty, appears as merely one among many other ties, besides loyalty to the church, union, or family; loyalty to the state takes no precedence, and state ethics is a special ethics among many other special ethics. Whether there is any total social ethics whatsoever is unclear in both Cole and Laski; the former speaks vaguely of an apparently all-encompassing "*society*" [English in the original], Laski of "humanity."

III

There are many good reasons, also of philosophical interest, for the strong impression this theory must make today. If pluralist social theorists such as Cole and Laski adhere mainly to the empirical, they do so as pragmatists and thereby remain consistent with their pragmatic philosophy, to which Laski expressly refers. He especially is philosophically interesting because— at least in intent and seemingly also in result—he transposes the pluralist world view of the philosophy of William James to the state; from the dissolution of the monist unity of the universe into a multiverse, he infers an argument for dissolving the political unity of the state pluralistically. To this extent, his view of the state can be added to the ranks of phenomena in intellectual history that I have termed "political theology." The correspondence of theological and metaphysical world pictures [*Weltbilder*] with images of the state can be discerned everywhere in the history of human thought; the simplest example is the conceptual relationship between monarchy and monotheism, constitutionalism and deism. This relationship can be explained neither materialistically as mere "ideological superstructure," reflex, or "reflection," nor, on the other hand, idealistically or spiritually as "material substructure."

A further element of interest to intellectual history is the fact that pluralist arguments are hardly absolutely new; rather, they are related to old theories of the philosophy of the state and thus part of a great tradition. However, Cole's social ethics justifies a state based on very modern union or guild socialism, and Laski's pluralist doctrine is also linked to the political goals and ideals of the trade union movement; French critics of state sovereignty likewise have a syndicalist federalism in mind. Thus at first glance, one has the impression one is encountering quite new, highly modern theories. Yet what is actually surprising about the theoretical situation—seen from the point of view of intellectual history—is the fact that arguments and viewpoints that otherwise served the social philosophers of the Roman Catholic or other churches or religious sects to relativize the state in regard to the church are now advanced in the interest of trade union or syndicalist socialism. One of Laski's favorite arguments is a reference to Bismarck's

Kulturkampf, in which the then-powerful German Empire was unable to defeat the Roman Church. One of the most important books on which Anglo-Saxon pluralist theory is based (besides those of Gierke and Maitland) is John Neville Figgis's *Churches in the Modern State* (1913). Laski even refers to a name—Saint Athanasius—that, through the well-known writings of Görres, has become for us in Germany a symbol of the struggle of the universal church against the state; he invokes the shadow of this most militant of church fathers for his socialism of the Second International.

But above all, the pluralist view corresponds to the actual empirical situation as it can be observed today in most industrialized countries. To this degree, pluralist theory is very modern and current. The state really does appear to be largely dependent on various social groups, sometimes as a victim, sometimes as the outcome of their agreements, an object of compromise between social and economic power groups, a conglomerate of heterogeneous factors, parties, interest groups, combines, unions, churches, etc. reaching understandings with one another. In the compromise of social powers, the state is weakened and relativized, and even becomes problematic, as it is difficult to determine what independent significance it retains. It seems to have become, if not practically the servant or instrument of a ruling class or party, then a mere product of the balance between various fighting groups—at best a *pouvoir neutre et intermédiaire,* a neutral mediator, a balancer of groups fighting one another, a sort of *clearing office* [English in the original], an arbitrator that refrains from any authoritative decision making, abstains entirely from keeping the social, economic, and religious conflicts under control, even ignores them and is not allowed to take official notice of them. It becomes an "agnostic state," the *stato agnostico* ridiculed by fascist critique. Vis-à-vis such a construct, the ethical questions of fidelity and loyalty must be answered differently than for an unmistakable, overarching, and comprehensive unity. Thus today, in many states, the single individual feels himself to be, in fact, part of a plurality of ethical ties and is bound by religious communities, economic associations, cultural groups, and parties, without a recognized decision on the hierarchy of the many ties in case of conflict.

Such a condition of empirical reality of social life may not be ignored by philosophical discourse. For with a subject like the state, reference to empirical reality is undoubtedly a philosophical and moral argument. For any philosophical reflection on the state—whether individualist or collectivist—the value of the state certainly lies in its concrete reality, and a state that is not real cannot be the bearer or addressee of concrete ethical claims, duties, or feelings. Ethical relationships like fidelity and loyalty are, in the reality of concrete life, possible only in relation to concrete, existing people or structures, not in relation to constructions or fictions. Therefore, it cannot be a matter of indifference in the philosophy and ethics of the state whether the earlier claims of the state to superiority over all other social groups in case of conflict now cease. For an individualist theory of the state as well, the state's accomplishment lies in the fact that it determines the *concrete situation* without which moral and legal norms cannot gain validity. For every norm presupposes a *normal* situation. No norm applies in a vacuum nor in an (in regard to the norm) *abnormal* situation. If the state determines the "external conditions of morality," it means that it determines the normal situation. For this reason alone (according to Locke as well as Kant) is it the supreme judge. If it is no longer the state but one or another social group that in and of itself determines this concrete normality of the individual's situation—the concrete order in which the individual lives—then the state's ethical demand for fidelity and loyalty also ceases.

IV

Despite its accord with empirical perceptions and despite its great philosophical notability, such pluralism cannot be the last word on today's problem of state ethics. Seen from the point of view of intellectual history, such pluralist arguments, aimed at the state as an intrinsic unity, are hardly as new and modern as they at first appear if, under the strong impression of the rapid reordering of today's social life, we summarily recall that philosophers of the state from Plato to Hegel have for centuries seen the unity of the state as the highest value. In truth, there are many gradations among these philosophers, very strong criticism of monist extravagances, and many reservations in favor of independent social groups of the most varied kind. Aristotle's objections to Plato's exaggeration of political monism are familiar: The πόλις, he says, must be a unity, μίαν εἶναι, as well as the οἰχία, but not entirely, ἀλλ' οὐ πάντως (*Politics* II.2.19 and in many other places in book II). Thomas Aquinas, whose monism is very pronounced if only because of his monotheism, and who sees the value of the state in its unity, and equates unity and peace (et ideo id ad quod tendit intentio multitudinem gubernantis est unitas sive pax, *Summa Theol.* Ia. Q. 103 Art. 3), says, following Aristotle, that unity driven to extremes destroys the state (*maxima unitas destruit civitatem*). In addition, for him, as for all philosophers of Catholicism, the church is an independent *societas perfecta* next to the state, which is also supposed to be a *societas perfecta*. This is a dualism that, like any abandonment of simple unity, offers many arguments for an expansion to pluralism. This peculiar attitude toward the state explains the intellectual alliance, at first sight rather odd, between the Roman Catholic Church and trade union federalism that appears in Laski. But at the same time, it proves that Laski's pluralist theory of the state requires greater philosophical depth if it is not to be affected by the obvious objection that the arguments he uses from the Catholic philosophy of the state originate in a particularly determined universalism. The Roman Catholic Church is not a pluralist structure, and in its battle against the state, pluralism has been on the side of the national state since at least the sixteenth century. A pluralist social theory contradicts itself if it plays off against the state the monism and universalism of the Roman Catholic Church, secularized to the universalism of the Second or Third International, while still trying to remain pluralist.

The very ambiguity of such an intellectual coalition shows that the pluralism of this modern social theory is unclear and in itself problematic. It is aimed polemically at existing state unity, which it attempts to relativize. At the same time, pluralist theorists generally speak an extremely individualistic language at decisive points in their argument. In particular, the response to the obvious and crucial question of who settles the unavoidable *conflict* between the various relationships of fidelity and loyalty is that the single individual himself settles it. This is a dual contradiction. First of all, it is a question of a *social* situation that involves the individual but cannot be changed by him at will; it is a matter of social ethics and not of the inner autonomy of the individual. It is true that it accords with an Anglo-Saxon mentality to respond so individualistically, entrusting the final decision to the individual, but by so doing a pluralist social ethics gives up the very thing that was interesting and valuable about it—namely, taking account of the concrete, empirical power of social groups and the empirical situation as determined by the individual's membership in many such social groups. Further, it is empirically incorrect that the individual, rather than a social group, decides. Perhaps there are some skillful and mobile individuals who achieve the trick of remaining free among the many powerful social groups, the way one jumps from one ice floe to the next. But this equilibrated sort of freedom cannot be required as the normal ethical duty of the mass of normal citizens. It is also the opposite of a decision of social conflicts. Empirically, when the unity of the state ceases, the various social groups as such would most likely make such decisions themselves, that is, based on their group interests. For the empirical individual, however, experience shows there is no other space for enjoying his freedom besides that which a strong state is able to guarantee him. Social pluralism, in contrast to state unity, means nothing more than leaving the conflict of social duties to decision by single groups. This thus means sovereignty of the social groups but not freedom and autonomy for the single individual. The second inconsistency lies in ethical individualism having its correlate in the concept of humanity. The empirical individual cannot be for himself enough, and he cannot decide the ethical conflicts of social life based on his singularity. For an individualist ethic the individual is valuable only as a *human being;* the crucial concept is thus *humanity.* In Laski, humanity really does appear as the highest authority—humanity as a whole; and by the word "society" Cole probably means, though it is not entirely clear, something similar to humanity. But that is the broadest, greatest universalism and monism imaginable and anything but a pluralist theory.

As unclear as its pluralism is the theory's opponent, namely, the state as a unity that is supposed to be seized by the pluralism. From the above intimations from the history of philosophy, it can be gathered that political unity can never be understood as absolutely monistic and destructive of all other social groups, just as the "pluralists" sometimes present it for polemical purposes and as might at times be assumed according to the simplifying forms used by lawyers. When constitutional lawyers speak of the "omnipotence" of the sovereign—the king or the parliament—their baroquely exaggerated formulas should be understood as owing to the fact that in the state of the sixteenth to eighteenth centuries the issue was overcoming the pluralist chaos of the churches and estates. One makes one's task too easy if one adheres to such idioms. Even the absolutist prince of the seventeenth and eighteenth centuries was forced to respect divine and natural law and ensure the widest respect for traditional institutions and vested rights. State unity was always a unity from social pluralities. At various times and in various countries it was very different but always complex and, in a certain sense, intrinsically pluralist. A reference to this self-evident complexity can perhaps refute an extravagant monism but does not solve the problem of political unity. In addition, however, apart from these complexities, there exists a wide variety of possibilities for shaping political unity. There is unity from *above* (through command and power) and unity from *below* (out of the substantial homogeneity of a nation); unity through continuing agreements and compromises between social groups or through a *balancing* of these groups achieved in some other way; a unity from *within* and one based only on pressure from *without;* a more *static* and a *dynamic* unity that constantly functionally integrates itself; there is, finally, unity by power and unity by *consensus.* This last, simple contrast dominates the state ethics of pluralism, the ethical meaning of which is apparently to ethically accept only *unity through consensus.* Rightly so. But here the present problem begins. For every consensus, including a "free" one, is somehow motivated and produced. Power creates consensus, often a reasonable and ethically justified consensus; and conversely, consensus creates power, often an unreasonable and—despite the consensus—ethically reprehensible power. Viewed pragmatically and empirically, the question then is, Who has at his disposal the means for producing the "free" consensus of the masses—the economic, pedagogical, psychotechnical means of the most various sorts with the help of which, experience shows, a consensus can be produced. If the means are in the hands of social groups or single human beings and out of the state's control, then what is still officially called the "state" is at an end; the political power has become invisible and irresponsible, but the socio-ethical problem has not been solved with this statement.

The last and most fundamental reason for such unclarities and even in-consistencies lies in the fact that the notion of the *state* among pluralist the-orists of the state is unclear. For the most part they think, purely polemically, of the remains of the old "absolutist" state of the seventeenth and eighteenth centuries. State thus means government apparatus, administrative machin-ery—in short, things that can, of course, be judged only instrumentally, that are in any case not objects of fidelity and loyalty and are rightly usurped by the various social groups in dividing the remainder among themselves. At the same time, however, even for those pluralists, the state is a political unity—constantly reintegrating itself out of these compromises among various so-cial groups that can, as such, make specific ethical demands, even if merely the demand that these agreements and compromises be adhered to. That would be an ethics of *pacta sunt servanda* [agreements must be observed] even though a very problematic one. It is of course possible to limit the word "state" historically to the absolutist state of the seventeenth and eighteenth centuries. It is then easy today to combat it ethically. However, the problem is not the word, which has its own history and can go out of fashion, but the issue itself, the problem of a *people's political unity.* Here now, among pluralist theorists of the state as nearly everywhere, an error prevails that generally persists in uncritical unconsciousness—that the political signifies a specific substance, next to the substance of other "social associations"; that it repre-sents a specific content besides religion, economy, language, culture, and law; and that, therefore, the political group can be understood as standing coordinately next to the other groups—to church, combine, union, nation, cultural and legal communities of all sorts. Political unity thus becomes a special, new substantial unity, joining other unities. Any debates and dis-cussions on the nature of the state and the political will become confused as long as the widespread idea prevails that a political sphere with its own content exists side by side with other spheres. It then becomes easy to take the state as a political unity *ad absurdam* and thoroughly refute it. For what remains of the state as a political unity if we remove all other contents—re-ligious, economic, cultural, etc.? If the political is nothing but the result of such subtraction then it is, in fact, exactly nil. But that is precisely the mis-understanding. *The political more accurately describes the degree of intensity of a unity.* Thus political unity can have and encompass various types of con-tent. But it always describes the most intensive degree of unity, from which, therefore, the most intensive differentiation, grouping into friend and enemy, is determined. Political unity is the supreme unity, not because it all-powerfully dictates or levels all other unities, but because it decides and can, within itself, prevent all other opposing groups from dissociating to the point of extreme hostility (i.e., to the point of civil war). Where it exists, so-cial conflict between individuals and social groups can be decided so that an order, that is, a normal situation, exists. The most intensive unity is either present or not; it can dissolve, and then the normal order disappears. But it is always, inescapably, a unity; for there is no plurality of normal situations, and decisions unavoidably emanate from it as long as it exists at all. Every social group, no matter what its type or substance, is political to the degree to which it participates in the decision, or, even more, to which the decision is concentrated within it. Because the political has no specific substance, the point of the political can be derived from any terrain, and any social group, church, union, business, or nation becomes political, and thus related to the state, when it nears this point of highest intensity. With its substance and values, it nourishes the political unity, which lives off the various domains of human life and thought and gains its energy from science, culture, religion, law, and language. All human life, even that of the highest intellectual spheres, has in its historical realization, at least potentially, a state over it that becomes strong and powerful from such contents and substance, like the mythical *eagle of Zeus* that fed on Prometheus's entrails.

V

The uncertainties and inconsistencies that can be demonstrated in the pluralist theory of state have their basis not in pluralism as such, but only in an incorrectly applied pluralism that is intrinsically correct and unavoidable in all problems of objective spirit. For the world of objective spirit is a pluralist world—pluralism of races and peoples, religions and cultures, languages and legal systems. It is not a question of denying this existing pluralism and violating it with universalism and monism, but rather of *correctly placing pluralism.*

The political world is also essentially pluralist. But the bearers of this pluralism are the political entities as such, that is, the states. In particular, the modern European states in the sixteenth and seventeenth centuries emerged from the dissolution of a universalism, and their concept of sovereignty was aimed polemically against both the universal claim of an imperial world-monarchy and the equally universal political claims of the papacy. It is an astonishing misunderstanding in intellectual history to wish to dissolve these plural political entities on the basis of a universal and monistic view, and to present this as pluralism—even, as Laski does, with reference to William James. In the system of "political theology" the pluralism of James's world view corresponds to the age of today's democratic national states, with their pluralism of peoples who are disposed towards the state on the basis of their nationhood. The monarchy, in its ideal tendency and argumentation, is rather universalist, because it must be *from God* if not justified democratically by the will of the people. Democracy, on the other hand, leads to recognition of each of the many peoples as a political unity. A philosopher of pluralism thus states, correctly, "Just as, in social life, the δῆμος has now and forever come to the fore, and therefore the civilized world cannot endure kings who are not servants of the people, thus in the domain of philosophy that which is being itself, in its entirety and all its variety—that is, the βάθος of experience—emerges as law giving, and the period of its varied schematization and leveling is irredeemably past" (Boris Jakowenko, *On the Essence of Pluralism* [*Vom Wesen des Pluralismus*], Bonn, 1928).

The plurality of states—that is, the political entities of various peoples—is thus the genuine expression of pluralism, correctly understood. Universalist, monist concepts such as *God, world,* and *humanity* are supreme concepts and are enthroned far, far above that plurality of concrete reality. They retain their dignity as supreme concepts only so long as they stay in their supreme position. They immediately change their essence and mistake their meaning and task if they become involved in the brawl of political life and gain a false power and a false propinquity. I do not wish to go so far as to draw a parallel with Max Scheler's conception of spirit and to say of them that they are as powerless in regard to the concrete life of peoples and social groups as is the spirit in Scheler's metaphysics in regard to life and drives. But they are only *regulative ideas* with no direct or indirect power. Therein lies their value and their indispensability. There is certainly nothing human, nor any political life, without the idea of humanity. But this idea *constitutes nothing*—in any event, no distinguishable community. All peoples, all classes, all members of all religions, Christians and Saracens, capitalists and proletarians, the good and the evil, the just and the unjust, delinquents and judges, are human beings, and with the help of such a universal concept, any distinction can be negated and any concrete community ruptured. Such supreme ideas can and should temper and modify. But as soon as certain peoples and social groups, or even single individuals, use them in order to identify with them, the regulative idea is transformed into a terrible instrument of human lust for power. Even in the narrow frame of a state, which fellow citizens can survey, at least for a longer period of time, it is a dangerous deception for individual social groups to pursue their own interests in the name of the whole and to identify without justification with the state. In that case, the name of the state serves only political repression and legal deprivation. However, when the supreme and universal concepts, such as humanity, are exploited politically so that a single nation or a specific social organization identifies with them, the possibility of the most terrible expansion and murderous imperialism emerges. For this the name of humanity can be misused no less than the name of God, and a feeling could be spreading among many peoples and great masses, the authentic expression of which is contained in a modification of Proudhon's awful words: "Who says humanity wishes to deceive?"

In contrast to the political exploitation of such expansive totalities, it is less ambitious to accept and acknowledge the plurality of peoples united in states. In comparison with every such universalism encompassing the world and humanity, this is modest, yet justified *by the immanent dimension* of the social powers. It is true that each of the many political entities are, in the whole of the world and humanity, merely a *bit of order,* merely a fragment. Yet it is the bit accessible to human action and community. Even though deception and lies are still possible in the state, as in all that is human, the fantastic dimensions of a universal deception encompassing the world and humanity are impossible here. In a spiritual world dominated by the law of pluralism, a bit of concrete order is more valuable than the empty generalities of a false totality. For it is an actual order, not a constructed and fictitious abstraction—a general situation of normal life in which concrete human beings and social groups can have concrete existence. It would be a false pluralism to play off world-encompassing entireties against the concrete reality of such plural orders; it is rational and sensible to permit peoples and states to exist after and next to each other, which represents the substance of human history.

States and peoples arise and disappear, and there are strong and weak peoples, healthy and sick, impressive and pitiful states. By reference to the weak, sick, and miserable, the strong and powerful are not refuted. Aristotle's sentence, which Rousseau used as a motto to introduce his treatise on human inequality, applies here: "Non in depravatis sed in his quae bene secundum naturam se habent considerandum est quid sit naturale."* But this also makes clear to what degree political unity is a human deed and task, because it is the definitive unity to be accomplished within the framework of general pluralism, the bit of concrete order, the normal situation. Greater effort and spiritual achievement is necessary for this than for other common enterprises and social entities. In particular, it is easier to realize an economic "association" than a political entity, and it is understandable, even obvious, that in periods of exhaustion and distress people should lose interest in such struggles. The higher and more intensive the community, the higher the awareness and action by which it actualizes itself. All the greater the risk of failure. Thus the successful, consummate state is as magnificent as the state that has failed—morally and aesthetically—is offensive and wretched. One can easily point to the many failed attempts and the miserable caricatures of states that exist today. But obviously this is neither theoretically,

---

*Schmitt quotes the motto at the head of Rousseau's *Discourse on the Origins and Foundations of Inequality among Men:* "Not in corrupt things, but in those that are well ordered in accordance with nature, should one consider that which is natural." Jean-Jacques Rousseau, *The First and Second Discourses,* ed. Roger D. Masters (New York: St. Martin's Press, 1964), 77. The motto is a Latin translation of a sentence from Aristotle's *Politics* 125ª 36–38 (Book 1, chap. V).—EDS.

nor ethically, nor even empirically an argument, nor is it a solution to the task at hand.

This lecture was to provide only a brief glance at a moment in intellectual history. I would like to close with a brief summary, in the form of several theses.

State ethics exists in various different and even contradictory senses. State ethics can mean the *subordination* of the state to ethical norms and thus grounds above all the *state's obligations*. As is discernible especially in Kant's explanation of state ethics, this presupposes an existing state, the "presently existing legislature," as Kant puts it, the existence of which is unproblematically taken for granted. In a concrete sociological sense, the subordination of the state to ethical norms naturally means nothing other than the control and mastery of those human beings and social groups that in concrete reality confront and challenge the concrete state in the name of those ethical norms. Further, state ethics can mean an ethics established by a state as an autonomous ethical subject, *emanating from it,* by which specific *duties towards the state,* going beyond *non-resistance* [English in the original], are created. This, too, presupposes an existing state. If the state now becomes a pluralist party state, the unity of the state can last only so long as the two or more parties agree in acknowledging common premises. Then, unity is grounded primarily in a *constitution* recognized by all parties, which must be absolutely respected as a common foundation. State ethics then becomes *constitutional ethics*. Depending on the substantiality, clarity, and authority of the constitution, a very effective unity may lie within it. But it is also possible that the constitution may dissipate into mere rules of the game and its ethics into a mere ethic of *fair play* [English in the original], and that finally, through the pluralist dissolution of the unity of the political whole, a point is reached where unity becomes nothing more than an agglomerate of changing agreements between heterogeneous groups. Constitutional ethics would then dissipate even further to the ethics of the principle *pacta sunt servanda* [agreements should be observed]. In every case of state ethics mentioned, the state is still a unity, as in the case of either the state's *subordination* to ethics or the state's designation as a *superordinate* ethical subject—a unity presupposed as concretely existing or an equally presupposed unity embodied in the common recognition of a constitutional foundation or of the rules of the game. But no state unity can be based solely on the principle *pacta sunt servanda,* for the single social groups, as contract-forming subjects, are then as such the decisive powers that make use of the contract and are bound to each other only through a contractual bond. They face each other as independent political powers, and what unity there is, is merely the result of an alliance that (like all alliances and contracts) is terminable. The contract then has only the meaning of a conclusion of peace between the groups making the contract, and a conclusion of peace, whether the parties wish it or not, always makes reference to the possibility, if perhaps distant, of war. Thus the backdrop to this sort of contract ethics is always an ethics of civil war; in the foreground is the obvious inadequacy of the principle *pacta sunt servanda,* which, speaking concretely, can be little more than a legitimation of the momentary *status quo,* similar to the way in which it can, in private life, supply a superb ethics for usury. If state unity becomes problematic in the reality of social life, this leads to a condition unbearable for every citizen, for because of this the normal situation vanishes and with it the presumption of every ethical and legal norm. The concept of state ethics then gains a new content, and a new task emerges: consciously bringing about that unity—the duty to collaborate on realizing a bit of concrete, real order and returning the situation to normal. Then besides the *state's duty,* that lies in subordination to ethical norms, and besides the *duties towards the state,* another, very different duty of state ethics emerges: that is, the *duty for a state.*

The Decline of Theory

INTRODUCTION

Reinhard Mehring

Under National Socialism, the theory of the state and its law generally languished. This is evident not only among those scholars who largely clung to their pre-1933 methods and positions and attempted to stay out of politics and matters of state, or those National Socialist authors in the narrower ideological sense who sought a genuinely racist, theoretically unassuming new approach to the theory of the state and its law.[1] Above all, it is evident in the state law scholars directly involved with National Socialism who continued working on the problems and theoretical efforts of the Weimar period. They —and thus also the acceptance and rejection of the Weimar jurisprudence of crisis under National Socialism—are the subject of what follows.

The main participants in the Weimar struggle over methods and aims held very different attitudes toward, and suffered various fates under, National Socialism. Positivists and liberal advocates of the Weimar Constitution either resigned their professorships in 1933 (Georg Anschütz, 1867–1948), were dismissed and retreated into internal exile (Gustav Radbruch, 1878–1949), or were forced to emigrate (Hans Kelsen, 1881–1973). But even the critics of positivism and theorists of a new basis for the theory of the state and its law who pointed out the cultural, social, and political prerequisites and foundations of positive constitutional provisions held quite varying attitudes toward National Socialism. Hermann Heller (1891–1933) emigrated and died abroad in November 1933, before he could complete his *Theory of the State* [*Staatslehre*]. Erich Kaufmann (1880–1972) lost his Berlin professorship in 1934 and emigrated in 1938.[2] Heinrich Triepel (1868–1946) was pensioned off in 1935. Rudolf Smend (1882–1973) had to give up his Berlin chair in 1935 to the rising SS lawyer Reinhard Höhn (born 1904) and moved to Göttingen, where he devoted himself to the history of jurisprudence. Only Carl Schmitt (1888–1985) brought his Weimar constitutional thinking regarding the state and its law into National Socialism, quickly rising to become "crown jurist."

The student generation also followed various paths. Triepel's pupil Gerhard Leibholz (1901–82) was dismissed from a professorship in 1935 and emigrated to England in 1938. Schmitt's student Ernst Friesenhahn (1901–84), who, like Leibholz, later served as judge on the Federal Constitutional Court, withdrew his application for membership in the National Socialist German Workers Party (NSDAP) after June 1934, but received a professorship in 1938 nevertheless. Social Democratic lawyers and scholars such as Ernst Fraenkel (1898–75), Franz Neumann (1900–54), and Otto Kirchheimer (1905–65) held no academic positions in 1933, so we cannot speak of a formal end to their academic careers. Neumann and Kirchheimer emigrated immediately; Fraenkel continued to practice law in Berlin until 1938 and wrote the *Dual State* [*Der Doppelstaat*], the first sustained critical analysis of National Socialism.

Besides Schmitt, the National Socialist theorists of the state and its law who continued the theoretical efforts of Weimar included Schmitt's young conservative students Ernst Rudolf Huber (1903–90) and Ernst Forsthoff (1902–74), as well as Theodor Maunz (1901–93) and Reinhard Höhn.

At the seizure of power in 1933, not a single professor of the law of the state was a member of the National Socialist Party; thus we cannot say that legal scholars had a particular predisposition toward National Socialism. Their motivations for later affirmation were complex and diverse. The systematic conservatism of lawyers in supporting the rulers on the basis of legality does not suffice to explain the motivations behind their sometimes enthusiastic advocacy.[3] Hope for an end to the permanent crisis of the Weimar system was coupled with relief at the demise of an unpopular republic. Often, National Socialism was misunderstood to be a conservative movement. On top of everything else, the coming generation expected it to provide career opportunities and soon filled the positions of the numerous professionals driven out by the Law to Restore the Professional Civil Service [*Gesetz zur Wiederherstellung des Berufsbeamtentum*].[4] In 1933, Schmitt moved to Berlin via Cologne. Huber (Kiel), Forsthoff (Frankfurt), and Scheuner (Jena) received their professorships in 1933, Höhn (Berlin) and Maunz (Freiburg) in 1935.

The revolutionary transformation of Germany's political and constitutional systems was an intellectual challenge taken up enthusiastically by many. The internal development of the Third Reich, in which we may distinguish[5] a formative phase that lasted until 1934, consolidation until 1938, and finally radicalization, presented legal scholarship with various tasks. This can be seen even in the form of publication issued over the course of the 1930s. An initial flood of polemical, programmatic, and laudatory literature gave way, in the consolidation phase, to a series of textbooks, notably Huber's *Verfassung* in 1937 and Arnold Köttgen's *Deutsche Verwaltung* in 1936. After 1938, a "verbal muteness" (Michael Stolleis's term) ensued, along with veiled distancing and prognoses of decline.[6]

The radicalization of National Socialism met with a certain onset of sobriety in legal circles, reflected in their recollection of legal forms and pragmatic attempts to implement legal procedures. Thus in the law of the state, emphasis was placed on the planning aspect of the Führer's will as law; in administrative law, the law's binding authority on the administration and the role of administrative courts were hotly debated. The more disillusioned awareness of the change from the reestablishment of statehood to the dissolution of any residue of statehood was reflected in a debate—rekindled under altered circumstances—on the "total state." By the end of the consolidation phase, it was possible to present an overall view of the "constitution" of National Socialism only by strongly idealizing it. Critical observers already recognized the structure of a "dual state" in its tendency to dissolve all the legal forms through which the functions of the state operate into a "behemoth."[7] Even the leading National Socialist theorists of the state and its law gradually recognized the impossibility of legally describing this abnormal development. However, even after 1945 they were unwilling to admit that legal scholarship had any special responsibility or shared any guilt for the development of National Socialism.

In 1933 National Socialism had elaborated no theory of the state on which legal scholarship could have been based. This explains National Socialism's dependence on the cooperation of the old elites and transitional figures such as Schmitt, as well as the hopes of some scholars of the law of the state that they could persuade National Socialism of their ideas and moderate or tame the movement. The details of the attitude and affinities of these scholars with National Socialist politics are disputed. A study[8] on the rise and fall of Carl Schmitt attempts to show that Schmitt, like Huber and Forsthoff, operated strategically as a group of so-called conservative revolutionaries, their beliefs falling somewhere between Weimar parliamentarism and National Socialist totalitarianism and their hopes directed toward institutionalization of a Christian concept of the "authoritarian state." Despite their Christian self-image, however, these authors must, because of their formal membership and active support, be considered National Socialists.

Among them, Schmitt was the only one who carried his constitutional theory from the Weimar period over to National Socialism. He advocated National Socialist rule during its formative stage through polemical and programmatic writings on the structure of the National Socialist state, its position in constitutional history and international law, and the particular "species" of National Socialist legal thinking.[9] He published numerous articles and essays on the political coordination [*Gleichschaltung*] of legal scholarship and the judiciary,[10] but he was pushed out in 1936 by SS lawyers Richard Höhn and Carl August Eckhardt as well as Otto Koellreutter. Nonetheless, in 1938 he published a study on the problem of constructing a "total state,"[11] and with the outbreak of the war he hoped that, under the leadership of National Socialism, a new international order would be established in "Middle Europe."[12]

His apotheoses of *Führertum* and "homogeneity within species" [*Artgleichheit*] contain no visible pragmatic alternative to the dismantled "liberal rule of law." His diagnosis of the dissolution of the nation-state, though, based on constitutional law and the history of international law, flowing into a theory of the "end of the epoch of statehood," also implied a departure from his own "constitutional theory" and was a theoretical effort that transcended his Weimar works. However, he failed to reach the level of his earlier seminal writings.[13] Thus, during the National Socialist period Schmitt was characterized by his strategic influence on the *Gleichschaltung* of legal scholarship and the judiciary, as well as his aggressive rhetorical occupation of the position of "crown jurist."

The heterogeneity of the National Socialist theory of the state can be seen in the fact that even Schmitt's closest students, Forsthoff and Huber, pursued their own constitutional theoretical concepts. Michael Stolleis, the most knowledgeable writer on the history of public law in Germany, characterizes this tradition primarily by its tendency to "conceive the state with a focus on administration" and give it a "metaphysical foundation."[14] This was especially true of Ernst Forsthoff. Forsthoff took as his starting point Schmitt's diagnosis of the transformation of the modern constitutional state into a "total state" and formulated the new tasks of administrative theory during the National Socialist period. After 1945, he set out the consequences in his *Textbook of Administrative Law* [*Lehrbuch des Verwaltungsrechts*]. In 1933, he commended himself to the authorities with a programmatic work, *The Total State* [*Der Totale Staat*].[15] It conceived the total state as a dual state of "authoritative order" [*Herrschaftsordnung*] and "popular order" [*Volksordnung*] that would overcome the liberal rule of law of the nineteenth century. It justified anti-Semitism by requiring the establishment of the "homogeneity" of a "total" popular order and spiritual community. Forsthoff legitimized the "authority" of this rule through the "transcendence" of a "*Weltanschauung*" such as Christianity or Hegelianism. Unlike many other National Socialists, he viewed political leadership in 1933 as a provisional phenomenon to adapt the state structure to the "administrative needs" of "mass welfare."

In recognition of the transformed tasks of the state, Forsthoff focused primarily on the development of a new administrative theory that would serve as a "sort of substitute" for politically negated basic rights.[16] His changeover to the theory of administrative law was a response not only to National Socialist politics, but above all to a more general trend in constitutional evolution; he thus developed Schmitt's early diagnosis[17] that the liberal state based on the rule of law would be replaced by the "economic" state of industrial society.[18] Forsthoff viewed any political system functionally, as a system of "responsibility for subsistence" [*Daseinsverantwortung*] and "provision for subsistence" [*Daseinsvorsorge*]. Liberalism, too, appeared to him an instrument with which the "bourgeois type" maintained its subsistence, to be replaced, as the tasks of the state grew, with a system of "partaking." This emphasis on the problem of maintaining subsistence—simultaneously elaborated in philosophy by Arnold Gehlen[19]—formed the backdrop to his establishment of administrative law on the basis of the concepts of responsibility for and provision of subsistence. After 1945, he undertook pathbreaking research to develop his theory of administrative law further.

While Forsthoff started with a change in the transformed tasks of the state, Theodor Maunz derived from the revolution in political relationships the necessity for laying "new" foundations for administrative law;[20] thus he did not start socio-historically, with the development of industrial society, but instead with the political fact of the National Socialist revolution. His political view of administration as a ruling "system of offices in the hands of the Führer" was elaborated in 1937 in his textbook *Administration* [*Verwaltung*]. This led him to take a closer look at the police.[21] He saw the destruction of the liberal administrative law inherited from the nineteenth century as the return of administrative theory to its origins as "police science."[22] This view of National Socialism's practice of rule, despite its ideologizing—for example, in distinguishing police from SS and Wehrmacht—had something revelatory about it, but it was no longer fruitful for administrative theory after 1945. Maunz would later become a leading scholar of the law of the state and commentator on the Basic Law of 1949. In 1964 he lost his office as Bavarian minister of culture and education because of his National Socialist background. Only after his death in 1993, however, did it come to light that Maunz had written for years under a pseudonym for the right-wing extremist newspaper, *German National News* [*Deutsche National-Zeitung*] and had provided legal advice to the right-wing party, the German People's Union [*Deutsche Volks-Union*].

Before 1933, Reinhard Höhn was involved in the German Youth Order [*Jungdeutschen Orden*], engaged with the "state system of youth" in its "struggle against the state of bourgeois man."[23] He attempted in 1934 to bring about a "change in state law thinking" with a scholarly critique of the "legal concept of the state" involving the "invisible state personality," which he traced back in doctrinal history to the "concept of the sovereign princely state." Höhn thus demystified statism. In this way, with political engagement and not without scholarly merit, he went beyond Kelsen in developing the deconstruction of "state theology" (Kelsen).[24] In contrast with, and as an alternative to, Otto von Gierke's "organic" theory of the state and its effects, Höhn sought to develop the "people's community" [*Volksgemeinschaft*] as a legal concept.[25] However, his program remained mired in the critique that contemporaneous National Socialist attempts to describe the idea of the "people's community" in traditional legal terms remained unsuccessful. Thus Höhn's critique unintentionally revealed the impossibility of translating evolving National Socialism into legal concepts. Höhn's destruction of the concept of the state and of legal methods in general left only a mere claim of the legal character of National Socialist policies. Thus Höhn explained the legal character of wartime activity in 1942 in terms of the "attractive force" of National Socialism as the "leading and enduring force in the sphere of influence [*Großraum*]."[26] This was no longer a legal view but a cynical justification of the force used in the war.

Höhn's critique of statism marked a stage of internal debate on the legal structure of National Socialism in its consolidating phase. In his formulation of state law theory, Ernst Rudolf Huber went into greater detail, ascribing a constitution to National Socialism. Like Forsthoff, Huber had been influenced by the experience of economic crises in the Weimar Republic. This led him into the new field of the law of economic regulation and finally to the *Structure of German Socialism* [*Gestalt des deutschen Sozialismus* (1934)]. From the start, Huber sought to formulate a national-popular [*national-völkisch*] concept of the constitution in critical contrast to Schmitt. His idea of a dynamic of integration and totality associated itself with Hegel and the tradition of "the collective sciences of the state" [*gesammelte Staatswissenschaften*] and sought to describe the "constitution"[27] of National Socialism with dialectic constitutive logic. According to him, the "Führer" made the "state" by bringing the "movement" into the "people," thus lifting the people into political existence, while bringing the individual into the "service" of the commonwealth, as Huber, with his Protestant ethos, emphatically stated.

Huber's constitutional theory was probably the most ambitious and elaborate attempt at furthering Weimar constitutional theory. His Hegelization of the idea of integration, however, harmonized and idealized the development. Particularly questionable is the crude way in which Huber distinguishes systematically between nationalism, liberalism, and democracy. It led him to identify nationalism, understood as anti-liberal and anti-democratic, with the National Socialist "Führer" state—while clearly distancing himself from the anti-Semitism, racism, and imperialism of the wartime powers of the Reich.

Huber's nationalist ideal of the constitution becomes even clearer in his monograph on the constitutional history of the army, *Army and State* [*Heer und Staat*].[28] In it, he portrayed the "military order" as the "strongest of the constitution-building forces" in history and saw the interrupted Prussian constitutional project of establishing the "people's state" [*Volksstaat*] from the "people's army" [*Volksheer*] completed by National Socialism. Of the National Socialist theorists of the state and its law, Huber was probably the one who most thoroughly idealized and legitimized National Socialism but who also more clearly engaged in a conscientious critique and self-criticism of the "excessiveness of the idea of national power"[29] after 1945. The conclusion of his accounting of the "German catastrophe" (Friedrich Meinecke's term) is a soft monarchism that runs through his monumental postwar work, *German Constitutional History* [*Deutsche Verfassungsgeschichte*].[30]

Michael Stolleis frankly posed the question of the "progress" of legal scholarship under National Socialism. He found it, above all, in the study of Roman legal history (Paul Koschaker, Georg Dahm, Franz Wieacker), where the "reception of Roman law" was defended against National Socialist denunciations. The law of the state, which was particularly political, saw no such progress, according to Stolleis, except in administrative law and theory. Here progress concerned mainly methods; the National Socialist critique of the "bourgeois" nineteenth century led to progress when it did not merely negate and destroy but also supplemented the "legal method" inherited from the nineteenth century with a "topical" view of the purposes of the state and the administration. In the theory of the state and its constitution this had already been achieved during the struggles over methods and aims of the Weimar period; during National Socialism it was integrated into the theory of administrative law.

However, legal scholarship under National Socialism not only experienced a certain amount of methodological progress; it had other experiences and drew other conclusions as well. The risk of political involvement became clear, as did the failure of simple alternatives and solutions. The possibility of revolutionary change had been overestimated and the functional value of the crisis-torn republic underestimated. Not until they had experienced the disappointing evolution of National Socialism did scholars realize what they had had in the "state based on the liberal rule of law" [*bürgerliche Rechtsstaat*]. The experience of crisis had overemphasized the necessity of a radical alternative and failed to recognize the level of modernity and the functional achievements of Weimar; therefore, it was also unable to turn these achievements into its challenges for a National Socialist theory of the state. The negation of Weimar resulted only in the stage set of a "total state." The same theorists who had played off "constitutional reality" against the Weimar Constitution were insensitive and blind to the social and political reality of National Socialism. The ideology of a radical, easy alternative discredited the idea of Weimar even after National Socialism was gone. Weimar theory had introduced social scientific and political perspectives into "legal method," raising the theory of the state and its law to a new theoretical level;

its discrediting by National Socialism left postwar legal scholarship in the Federal Republic theoretically and politically deficient. Certainly it would not have been possible simply to resume the Weimar approaches, given the new order and tasks. But a recollection of the Weimar approaches could have led to a discussion of legal scholarship's theoretical claims and its new orientation toward problems and goals, methods and concepts.

The texts provide examples of the intellectually most significant National Socialist theorists of state law at different stages in the scholarly debate. Many assessments of that period were more-or-less unanimous commonplaces, such as rejection of the Weimar Republic and advocacy of the Führer principle. This was not the case with anti-Semitism. The attempts at founding a new theory of the state were even more diverse but never came together into a "system."

THE TOTAL STATE

Ernst Forsthoff

Originally appeared in Ernst Forsthoff, *Der Totale Staat*
(Hamburg: Hanseatische Verlagsanstalt, 1933), 30–32, 37–39.

Every order of domination [*Herrschaftsordnung*] is based on the distinction between leadership and being led, ruler and ruled. Every order of domination is therefore necessarily undemocratic, for democracy is the form of state essentially determined by making rulers and ruled identical. This identity must necessarily eliminate the authority of the government that can only be an authority vis-à-vis the ruled. Authority cannot develop out of the immanence of democratic functionalism. A government that rules only because it has a mandate from the people is not an authoritarian government. Authority is possible only from transcendence. Authority assumes a rank that takes hold against the people because the people does not grant it, but respects it.

During the final years of the demise of the Weimar Constitution, the governments attempted with increasing distinctness to claim an authoritarian character for themselves. This occurred, in general, through reference to the fact that the president had appointed the government and that the government had largely detached itself from the interplay of parliamentary forces; the claim of authority occurred mainly for the purpose of establishing the government's independence of parliament. The government had only minor real authority among the people. The people proved keenly sensitive to the fact that simple detachment from an ineffective parliament does not ground authority, because it does not prove rank.

Every order of domination is an order of rank; because rank is not a visible fact but a spiritual and political phenomenon, this assumes an intellectual constitution that is receptive to the nature of rank. The distinction between the leader and the led as a principle of state order can only be accomplished metaphysically. A *Freikorps* leader, the leader of a youth group, can gather a flock of devoted people around him and hold them together through the force of his superior will. Such a community is based purely on the dynamic of a personal leader-follower relationship, and fails because of personal failure, a crucial disruption of this dynamic. Here the claim to leadership can exist and maintain itself non-metaphysically, based purely on personal qualities. In the sphere of history, this does not apply to the state. For an authoritarian government with an historical mandate, such a claim to leadership, legitimized by the purely personal, is not a sufficient foundation. Certainly, Adolf Hitler owes his position as Führer to incomparable personal qualities, and his leadership of the National Socialist movement is justified by these qualities. Undoubtedly it is enormously significant that the immense power concentrated in the hands of the Führer of such a movement has now become state power. But through this, through Adolf Hitler's becoming the Führer of the Reich, he became subject to a new law. State and movement cannot be identified with each other. The movement can be consumed by the person of its leader; the state cannot. As strong as the element of personal leadership may be, the state is more than a context for personal leadership. The community of personal leadership [*Führungsgemeinschaft*] dies with the person of the Führer and is thus temporally limited. The state must not die; it is the form of the political existence of the people, and the people must not perish politically. The state is linked to tradition, law, and order.

Authoritarian government requires a justification that goes beyond the personal. This justification must be metaphysical; it must legitimate authority in addition to leadership. Therefore the state, in its current form, needs a coordinate *Weltanschauung,* with *Weltanschauung* understood here in a broad sense to encompass religion. History teaches us that *Weltanschauung*s of various kinds have served as foundations of rank and authority. Christian faith was able to found and establish the rank of Christian government [*christliche Obrigkeit*]; but a secular *Weltanschauung*—such as historical metaphysics of a Hegelian stamp—can also make clear the special dignity of statehood and government. And because *Weltanschauung*s cannot be bred but must grow, it is also impossible to describe which particular *Weltanschauung* matches today's state. . . .

The future structure of the state will be determined by the following requirements. Mass social welfare [*Massenfürsorge*], the necessity of maintaining an orderly social life in an overpopulated country, and satisfaction of the administrative needs of cities of millions make a professional civil service—a predictable and precisely functioning bureaucracy—indispensable. Authority and totality, however, require personal, imperative command. Bureaucratic and imperative administration therefore must—in accordance with the tasks of the state—be formed, balanced, and kept in rational connection so that the unity of the entire administration is assured.

This also clarifies at which places, and in which form, the new leadership class is to participate in responsible political guidance. It is to be entrusted with those tasks that require provisional execution. For what counts here is the decisive and firm political will, which must also show the ability to act in moderation; here the ability to command is indispensable and must be complemented by a readiness to subject oneself to the will of the Führer. Here the statute on the Reich's governors in the states [*Reichstatthalter-Gesetz*] can serve as a model, and it is thoroughly consistent and in accord with the inherent laws of life of the new state that the *Reichsstatthalter* is appointed from the new ranks of the most trustworthy leader of the movement. Other commissary practices are also a clear confirmation of the general developmental tendencies shown here. A decree recently issued in Prussia points in the same direction; it instructs the administrative chiefs of the provinces to maintain a constant working relationship with the National Socialist leaders within the provinces [*Gauleiters*] and to solicit their opinions on more general and important questions of administrative leadership.

The order of domination of the total state must thus have a dual structure. It will remain predictable and bureaucratic in some important areas, but the rest will have to be organized hierarchically, imperatively, in the forms of personal rule. For only a state in which even the lower levels have personal rule, tamed by unlimited responsibility and carried by an initiative that is in principle free but obligated to the will of the Führer, is truly authoritarian and conceivable as a total state. Only such a state can extend its claim to rule to areas that resist all schematization and calculable regimentation. But such a state may legitimately claim to be a state of art, science, and culture in general.

The Weimar state was a state without a people. It was at most a state of those eligible to vote. But the sum of those eligible to vote in elections and referendums is as little the people as the sum of votes cast in isolated, secret ballots can be equated with the will of the people.

Volk is a community based on a homogeneity within life and species [*seinsmäßigen, artmäßigen Gleichartigkeit*]. The homogeneity arises from the sameness of race and national destiny [*volkliches Schicksal*]. The *political people* forms in the final unity of will that grows from the awareness of homogeneity within life. The awareness of homogeneity within species and national identity [*volkliche Zusammengehörigkeit*] becomes actual in the ability to recognize the difference of species and distinguish friend from enemy. The issue is recognizing difference of species when it is not automatically visible

through membership in a foreign nation, for example in the Jew, who successfully attempted to create the illusion of homogeneity within species and
of national solidarity by participating in the cultural and economic life. The
rebirth of a politically German people had to end this illusion and to take
away the Jew's last hope of living in Germany other than in the consciousness of being a Jew.

LEGAL COMMUNITY AS NATIONAL COMMUNITY

Reinhard Höhn

Originally appeared in Reinhard Höhn, *Rechtsgemeinschaft als
Volksgemeinschaft* (Hamburg: Hanseatische Verlagsanstalt, 1935), 20–21.

To reconstruct our doctrine, it is first necessary to establish our starting-point
clearly. It can lie only in the principle that governs the *Weltanschauung* of National Socialism—the principle of community—that opposes the principle
of individualism. It must become a legal principle; only on its basis can all
the processes of our life today be legally conceived. *In the field of the law of the
state the state as a legal person is replaced by the legal concept of the national community.* To grasp and structure the principle of the national community legally is so difficult because this concept has so far been completely unknown
in its current meaning, and also because it is constantly confused, and sometimes lumped together, with similar concepts. *The decisive confusion is caused
by the idea of the legal community.* Today many still believe that the legal community is the only community suited to law. In addition, many still believe
that they can retain traditional values upon which the concept of legal community was always based. But because the legal personality of the state has
fallen, the concept of the legal community upon which the legal personality
of the state is based and upon which its emergence depended must also fall.

THE CONSTITUTION OF FREEDOM

Carl Schmitt

Originally appeared as Carl Schmitt, "Die Verfassung der Freiheit,"
Deutsche Juristen-Zeitung 40 (1935): 1133–35.

On 15 September 1935, when the party met under the motto of freedom
[*Reichsparteitag der Freiheit*], the German Reichstag passed the statute on

the Reich's flag [*Reichsflaggengesetz*], the statute on Reich citizenship [*Reichsbürgergesetz*], and the Statute to Protect German Blood and German Honor [*Gesetz zum Schutz des deutschen Blutes und der deutschen Ehre*].

This Reichstag was something different and more than the parliament of a constitutional compromise, and thus its laws are also something different and more than the products of the discussions and coalitions of a multiparty system. The Reichstag assembled at the party conference was the German people itself, led by the National Socialist movement and following the Führer Adolf Hitler; its laws embody the first German constitution of freedom in centuries.

For centuries, instead of freedom the German people had only liberties [*Libertäten*] or liberalism. The liberties of the German constitution of the seventeenth and eighteenth centuries guaranteed the national disunity of our people to beneficiaries of this sad state in domestic and foreign politics. The liberal freedoms of the constitutions of the nineteenth century were used by the international powers to elevate the religious and class disruptions of the German people to a basic right. Thus constitutional freedom became a weapon and motto for all Germany's enemies and parasites. But we have seen through this deception. We have realized that liberal constitutions become typical camouflages for foreign domination. A people can have the most liberal constitution in the world and still be but a herd of rent and wage slaves. And a constitution can, as is our experience today, be notorious and ridiculed as medieval by all of international liberalism and Marxism, and in that very way give evidence that a people has found its own way and freed itself from foreign spiritual domination.

For the first time in many centuries, the concepts in our constitution are once again German. We do not wish to disparage our liberal ancestors. They were German and belong to us. Even through the errors of their liberal views, their German substance is recognizable, and the voice of German blood can often be heard. Which German lawyer today could not distinguish a Lorenz Stein from a Stahl-Jolson, a Rudolf Gneist from a Lasker, a Rudolph Sohm from a Friedberg? With reverence we carry on the black-white-red, the colors of the Second Reich consecrated in the war. But we cannot carry on the legal and constitutional thinking of our liberal fathers and grandfathers. It was completely entangled in the conceptual net of un-German systems. What they saw as constitutional law was a reception of Anglo-French law. They confused German freedom with the program of a progressive party, and concealed the compromise between the bourgeoisie and the monarchic legitimists with neutral general concepts. Their constitutions were merely constituted; their *Reichtag*s and *Landtag*s were parliaments. Their citizen was an unsuccessful copy of the *citoyen*. Their constitutions did not speak of German blood and German honor. The word "German" appeared only in order to emphasize that "all Germans are equal before the law." But this sentence, which would have found its correct meaning in a concept of "German" that aims at substance and recognizes the people, instead served to treat aliens in species and Germans equally and to view anyone who was equal before the law as German. Thus the nation became the sum of its citizens, and the state an invisible legal person. Is it any wonder that the flag of national-liberal Germany was a juxtaposition of colors, corresponding to the pattern of the tricolor, lacking the power of a true symbol?

Today the German people has—in the legal sense as well—become the German people again. Under the law of 15 September, German blood and German honor are the main concepts of our law. The state is now a tool of the people's strength and unity. The German Reich now has a single flag— the flag of the National Socialist movement—and this flag is not only composed of colors, but also has a large, true symbol: the symbol of the swastika that conjures up the people.

A further constitutional decision was made at the party conference: Should the current regulation of the situation of the Jews not lead to its goal, the Führer has mentioned the possibility of fresh scrutiny and suggested that resolution of the question would then be transferred by law to the party. This is a serious warning. It declares the National Socialist German Workers Party the guardian of the sanctuary of the people, the guardian of the constitution.

The foundations of our national order have now been established: the German people, with its Führer as head of state and supreme judge of the nation; the order of the National Socialist movement as guardian of our constitution; the German *Wehrmacht,* with the Führer as supreme commander. Thus great tasks are at hand for German lawyers. As the German legal profession [*Rechtstand*], we must protect the right of the German people established in those statutes. The warning of the Führer is addressed to us as well. Our law must not fall victim to the heartless demon of degeneracy. Those statutes must not become merely the preambles of future implementing provisions. Nor are they merely three individual important statutes among other important statutes. They encompass and pervade our entire law. They determine what we may call morality and public order, decency and good practice [*gute Sitten*]. They are the constitution of freedom, the core of our German law today. Everything that we German lawyers do gains its meaning and honor from them.

THE ADMINISTRATION AS
PROVIDER OF SERVICES

Ernst Forsthoff

Originally appeared as Ernst Forsthoff, "Die Verwaltung als Leistungsträger,"
in *Königsberger rechtswissenschaftliche Studien,* vol. 2 (Stuttgart and Berlin:
Kohlhammer, 1938); reprinted as Ernst Forsthoff, *Rechtsfragen der leistenden
Verwaltung,* in *Beiträge zum öffentlichen Recht,* vol. 1 (Stuttgart: Kohlhammer,
1959), 26–27, 42.

Undoubtedly, to individual freedoms, under the sign of which technical and
industrial development began, there corresponds an individual responsibility for one's subsistence [*Daseinsverantwortung*]. But a presupposition of individual responsibility for one's subsistence is that a security of subsistence
[*Daseinssicherung*] is either given in a sphere of life [*Lebensraum*] one controls
or at least potentially guaranteed by the smoothly functioning appropriation
of goods necessary for life. The political and economic orientation of the
epoch of high capitalism was obviously defined by this premise. The second
phase of development began with the emergence of the great social tensions
of the mid-nineteenth century; the struggle of workers for a reasonable wage
was a struggle for the opportunities of appropriation contained in wages, for
self-maintenance in a life-space one does not control. In this phase of development, we can no longer speak of individual responsibility for subsistence.
The individual sees his subsistence ensured only in the solidarity of social
groups. This constitution of society reached its greatest height during the
Weimar period. National Socialism has overcome this collective security of
subsistence through the solidarity of social groups, in which no clear responsibility for subsistence developed, by making the holders of political
power (state and party) responsible for subsistence. Thus the development
moved from the individual to the collective to political security of and responsibility for subsistence. . . .

In the modern state, man asserts himself not through guaranteed individual freedoms, but through partaking. Because the extension of the sovereign
sphere no longer permits maintenance outside itself, the question of maintenance becomes one of partaking, one of maintenance within the Reich's
structured sovereign sphere in the form of partaking.

The same development took place in the provision of subsistence
[*Daseinsvorsorge*]. The extent to which the individual is today dependent
on provision for subsistence can be inferred from the remarks made. At
this point, it becomes clear that legally ensured partaking in the provision
for subsistence, considered functionally, offers a sort of substitute for the

outdated securities contained in basic rights. With regard to this, the inclusion of the provision for subsistence in administrative law doctrine may take place.

NEW FOUNDATIONS OF ADMINISTRATIVE LAW

Theodor Maunz

Originally appeared in Theodor Maunz, *Neue Grundlagen des Verwaltungsrechts* (Hamburg: Hanseatische Verlagsanstalt, 1934), 32–34.

Within the administration the principle of legality based on statute [*Gesetzmäßigkeit*] has been replaced by the principle of legality based on law in general [*Rechtmäßigkeit*]. What does this mean for individual public rights?

The loosening of the administration's rigid ties to mere norms, which incidentally can by no means have the effect that subsisting state norms no longer need be applied, means a much more extensive and intensive bond to the law rooted in the people.

This law of the people consists not of norms, but—this is the crucial point in changing administrative law thinking—*of legal patterns [Rechtsgebilden] that bear their order in themselves*. The task of administrative law will consist of revealing and assessing the order of these legal patterns.

ADMINISTRATION

Theodor Maunz

Originally appeared in Theodor Maunz, *Verwaltung* (Hamburg: Hanseatische Verlagsanstalt, 1937), 10–11.

In every community in which the leader of the community cannot carry out the tasks of the community in his own person, there exists a system of offices in the hands of the leader. Thus there is a system of party offices, of labor service offices, of *Wehrmacht* offices. Within this system of authorities and offices, administration takes place. Thus we speak of a party administration, a labor service administration, a *Wehrmacht* administration. The administrative element within a community can generally play only a secondary role. Thus the district leader is the leader of the party organization in his district, rather than an administrative official. But the administration (party offices, district managers, etc.) is subordinate to him. This is also the case in other communities. The community served by this system of offices is not administered; a community is led, not administered. But in the system of offices belonging to the community, administration is undertaken for the community in order to implement the leader's plans. *Administration as an activity means structuring community life through the work of authorities and offices specially appointed to do so, according to a plan set by the leader of the community in a given situation; administration as organization means this structure of offices in a concrete community.*

CONSTITUTION

Ernst Rudolf Huber

Originally appeared in Ernst Rudolf Huber, *Verfassung* (Hamburg: Hanseatische Verlagsanstalt, 1937), 48–49, 50, 127–28, 215.

That a constitution is valid means, above all, that fundamental political precepts are legally binding. Every constitution consists essentially of such principles, which determine the totality of the constitutional order and make up the "spirit of the constitution." There is no equality of rank among the numerous provisions of a written constitutional document. The main principles of the common order have clear priority; the remaining legal precepts are derived from them. In interpreting the constitution, all individual provisions must be referred back to these fundamental precepts. One can say of a constitution that it is valid only so long as this core of the constitution maintains its existence. If the core of the constitution is destroyed, then the entire constitution is wiped out, even if individual constitutional precepts of inferior rank continue to be legally valid.

The core of the constitution in the Weimar system consisted of the principles of democracy, liberalism, parliamentarism, party state, federalism, separation of powers, liberal rule of law. These pillars of the Weimar Republic have been destroyed by the National Socialist revolution. The revolution was aimed against these very principles, in which the Weimar system embodied the people's strife and helplessness. These old principles were immediately replaced by the revolution with the new principles of the people's constitution [*völkische Verfassung*]—the principles of the people's unity and wholeness, of the movement and of leadership. With the fact of the revolution, this new constitutional core easily succeeded. The revolution not only destroyed, but at the same time also founded, a new constitutional order in place of the old. The constitution of the liberal democratic, federalist party state was replaced by the constitution of the people's state of the movement and of leadership [*völkischer Bewegungs- und Führerstaat*]. . . .

The new constitution that replaced the Weimar Constitution is not a constitution in the formal sense, as was typical of the nineteenth century. It provides no written constitutional document for the new Reich. But this new constitution exists as the unwritten fundamental political order of the Reich. It must be recognized by the spiritual powers that inspire our people, by the actual form in which our political life moves, by the basic statutes of the state's structure that have so far been adopted. The advantage of such an unwritten constitution in comparison with a formal constitution consists in the fact that the fundamental order does not grow rigid, but instead remains in lively motion. Not dead institutions, but living fundamental forms make up the essence of the new constitutional order.

. . .

In the people's Reich under the leader [*völkisches Führerreich*], law is neither a parliamentary compromise nor a super-legal regulative norm; it is not a means of equalization in social and political power struggles. Law is rather the immediate expression of the people's life [*völkisches Leben*] and the people's order [*völkische Ordnung*]. It is not a normative balance hovering over the free, unregulated struggle of opinions and interests, but instead the order contained in the reality of the people's life itself. It does not approach life from without, as a "barrier" [*Schranke*], but instead grows out of the communal life of the people itself. In the leader's will, this law achieves its external form; the will of the leader, emerging in statutes, can be nothing else but the conscious, molded form of the people's justice [*völkische Gerechtigkeit*]. Thus statute is only the form in which the given order of the people's life appears. But this does not mean that it is advisable or even admissible for the leader's statute [*Führergesetz*] to be measured against the unwritten law and denied applicability if a supposed discrepancy between statute and law appears. For the leader is called upon above all, as protector and executor [*Wahrer und Vollstrecker*] of the people's order, to recognize the people's law and pour it into the mold of statute. Where he has spoken, the content of the people's law has been determined with unconditional binding force. It is not possible to appeal this statute to law.

. . .

Rights of freedom, guarantees of [civil law] institutions [such as property, marriage, and the right of testamentary succession] and of [public law] institutions [such as municipal autonomy and the civil service] disappear from the people's constitution. The deeper reason for this is that in a people's constitution the principle of "guarantees" has been overcome in general. The essence of the liberal constitution was found in "guarantees"; it was a system of securities and guarantees against the power of the state. The people's constitution does not have this guaranteeing function; on the contrary, it aims to increase the effectiveness and striking power of political authority. It does not protect individuals and groups against the whole, but serves the unity and wholeness of the people against individualist and group subversion.

FORM AND STRUCTURE OF THE REICH

Ernst Rudolf Huber

Originally appeared in Ernst Rudolf Huber, *Bau und Gefüge des Reiches* (Hamburg: Hanseatische Verlagsanstalt, 1941), 30–31.

If we look once again at the current overall situation, the following categories and legal positions emerge:

1. The main group is the bearers of German blood, who are at the same time members of the people [*Volkszugehörige*], subjects of the state [*Staatsangehörige*], and citizens of the Reich [*Reichsbürger*].

2. There are bearers of species-related blood [*artverwandtes Blut*] who pledge allegiance to Germandom and have been accepted into the German national community [*Volksgemeinschaft*]; they too are members of the people, subjects of the state, and citizens of the Reich (Wends, Masurians, etc.).

3. There are bearers of species-related blood who cling to their particular nationality [*Volkstum*] and do not integrate themselves into the German national community; thus they are not members of the German people, but are subjects of the German state and citizens of the Reich (Polish and Danish national groups [*Volksgruppen*] in the old Reich territory).

4. There are bearers of species-related blood who have not been accepted into the German national community and who are subjects of the German state, but not citizens of the Reich (Walloons in Eupen and Malmedy).

5. There are bearers of species-related blood who are neither members of the German national community, nor subjects of the German state, nor citizens of the Reich, but merely subjects of the German Reich (Poles in the Eastern territories).

6. There are bearers of species-related blood who have not been accepted into the German national community and who are subjects of a "state

subordinate to the Reich," but neither subjects of the German state nor citizens of the Reich (Czechs in the protectorate).

7. There are bearers of German blood who are subjects of a foreign state and thus not citizens of the Reich (German national groups abroad).

8. There are members of alien racial groups who are subjects of the German state but not citizens of the Reich (Jews in the old Reich territory).

9. There are members of alien racial groups who are neither subjects of the German state nor citizens of the Reich (Jews in the eastern territories and in Eupen and Malmedy).

"POSITIONS AND CONCEPTS":
A DEBATE WITH CARL SCHMITT

Ernst Rudolf Huber

Originally appeared as Ernst Rudolf Huber, "'Positionen und Begriffe': Eine Auseinandersetzung mit Carl Schmitt," *Zeitschrift für die gesamten Staatswissenschaften* 101 (1941): 42–44.

Not possession of power, but the exercise of power decides whether the order it has created is a morally justified and just order. Whether the evolving order of a sphere of influence [*Großraumordnung*] whose economic, strategic, and geopolitical prerequisites have been described by Schmitt will lead to a new international law will depend on whether it will be an imperialism in the sense of mere expansion of power or whether the leading peoples in the midst of such large spheres of influence live up to the responsibility placed upon them by the possession of power even over the coordinated peoples. The just exercise of power will be the criterion of the contrast between the old imperialism and a true international legal order of spheres of influence.

From yet another of Schmitt's "positions," a decisive objection arises against the legal quality of previous imperialism and at the same time an additional criterion for the contrast between imperialism and the future order of spheres of influence. Modern imperialism . . . is based on the extension of invisible domination over seemingly independent areas. Protective treaties and mutual assistance pacts, economic and financial bonds, concealed rights of control and intervention are the methods typical of the structure of modern empires. With good reason, the concept "indirect domination" has been used for these methods of modern imperialism. . . .

The future order of spheres of influence—in contrast to previous imperialism—would be a system of direct, open domination. But does that not essentially mean expansion of state sovereignty, extension of state borders, creation of a "superstate"—and thus no longer an "order of a sphere of influence" in the elastic sense in which this phrase was originally employed? Can there be an order of a sphere of influence without indirect force and invisible domination?

The answer to this question is closely connected with the problem of the legal quality of the order of a sphere of influence. For true law is possible only as a public, visible order; indirect domination can be a very effective phenomenon of facticity, but it is no basis for law, as law cannot exist without publicity and open responsibility. . . . A direct, open and responsible order of a sphere of influence must go beyond prohibitions on and rights to intervention and lay claim to "sphere sovereignty" [*Raumhoheit*]; and Schmitt came to this conclusion in his latest essay, "Reich and Sphere" [*Reich und Raum*]. The question remains whether there is a real difference between territorial sovereignty and sphere sovereignty, and whether the sphere of influence equipped with sphere sovereignty still differs from a large state or superstate. These questions are not posed here with the intent of polemicizing against a new and fruitful concept of political and legal theory; they have the positive aim of indicating a problem facing German international law theorists because of revolutionary political developments.

REICH, SPHERE OF INFLUENCE, GREAT POWER

Reinhard Höhn

Originally appeared in Reinhard Höhn, *Reich, Großraum, Großmacht*
(Darmstadt: Wittig-Verlag, 1942), 110–11.

Through constant reference to Europe's great common goals, the Reich has managed to dissolve divisions. Already they seem secondary. Today, Europe is like a ship crossing a great river, where everyone is standing in one place. The Reich is able, through its superior inner position, to reconcile the rivalries among the peoples and to assign peoples the space to which they are entitled on the basis of their position under the immanent laws of life [*lebensgesetzlichen Stellung*] and which they could not fill because of artificially erected barriers and inhibitions.

To this extent, the Reich is simultaneously the sustaining force in the sphere of influence. It represents the synthesis of all forces in the sphere of influence; it appears as a sort of guide of the life forces, by winning for the peoples a position in the sphere of influence under the immanent laws of life and in immediate harmony with a new order of common life in Europe.

This leading and sustaining force of the Reich is closely tied to its position as an attracting factor. The Reich did not confront the peoples with a missionary idea, but brought its own house in order and thus concomitantly set all of Europe's and the world's forces of order in motion. The ultimate success and achievement of a new order in Europe will be based largely on the extent to which forces that have hitherto worked against each other draw closer and unite in orientation towards great, unifying tasks in the common sphere of life [*Lebensraum*].

NOTES

INTRODUCTION

1. Abolitionists in the 1840s and 1850s, and communists in the 1930s did not, of course, claim fidelity to the Constitution, but neither group had significant influence over anyone in the United States who was, or could claim to be, in charge of an army.

2. Woodrow Wilson, *Constitutional Government in the United States* (New York: Columbia University Press, 1908), 2.

3. The conversion of Judge Richard Posner of the Court of Appeals for the Seventh Circuit from law and economics theorist (when he was a professor at the University of Chicago Law School) to cornhusking pragmatist is a case in point.

4. Gerhard Anschütz, *Veröffentlichungen der Vereinigung der Deutschen Staatsrechtslehrer,* vol. 3 (Berlin and Leipzig: de Gruyter, 1927), 47.

5. Erich Kaufmann, *Veröffentlichungen der Vereinigung der Deutschen Staatsrechtslehrer,* vol. 3 (Berlin and Leipzig: de Gruyter, 1927), 3.

6. Laband succinctly and profoundly outlined his program in the famous foreword to his *Das Staatsrecht des Deutschen Reiches,* 3 vols., 2nd ed. (Tübingen and Leipzig: Mohr, 1888), 1:x ff.

7. Compare especially his review of the first edition of Laband's *Das Staatsrecht des Deutschen Reiches,* in *Literarisches Centralblatt für Deutschland* (Leipzig: Avenarius, 1876), cols. 241 ff.

8. Hanns Mayer, "Die Krisis der deutschen Staatsrechtslehre und die Staatsauffassung Rudolf Smends" (Dissertation, University of Cologne, 1933), 27.

9. On the constitutional history of the Weimar Republic, see especially Willibald Apelt, *Geschichte der Weimarer Verfassung,* 2nd ed. (Munich and Berlin: Beck, 1964); Ernst Rudolf Huber, *Deutsche Verfassungsgeschichte* (Berlin, Stuttgart, and Cologne: Kohlhammer, 1978–84), vols. 5–7; Hans Boldt, *Deutsche Verfassungsgeschichte* (Munich: Deutsche Taschenbuchverlag, 1990), 2:221 ff.; Gerald D. Feldman, "The Weimar Republic: A Problem of Modernization?" *Archiv für Sozialgeschichte* 26 (1986): 1.

10. For a contemporaneous overview of developments in constitutional law after 9 November 1918, see Walter Jellinek, "Revolution und Reichsverfassung. Bericht über die Zeit vom 9. November 1918–31. Dezember 1919," *Jahrbuch des öffentlichen Rechts der Gegenwart* 9 (1920): 1.

11. The origin of the Weimar Constitution is documented in detail, along with all relevant discussions in the National Assembly, in *Die Deutsche Nationalversammlung im Jahre 1919 in ihrer Arbeit für den Aufbau des neuen deutschen Volksstaates,* ed. Eduard Helfrohn, 9 vols. (1919–20).

12. On the problem of Prussia and the Reich, see Dietrich Orlow, *Weimar Prussia 1918–1925: The Unlikely Rock of Democracy* (Pittsburgh: University of Pittsburgh Press, 1986), 89 ff.

13. See also the constitutional chronicles of the 1920s in Fritz Poetzsch-Heffter, "Vom Staatsleben unter der Weimarer Verfassung," *Jahrbuch des öffentlichen Rechts der Gegenwart* 13 (1925): 1; 17 (1929): 1.

14. See Mario Rainer Lepsius, "Parteiensystem und Sozialstruktur: Zum Problem der Demokratisierung der deutschen Gesellschaft," in Mario Rainer Lepsius, *Demokratie in Deutschland* (Göttingen: Vandenhoeck & Ruprecht, 1993), 25 ff.; Karl Rohe, *Wahlen und Wählertradition in Deutschland: Kulturelle Grundlagen deutscher Parteien und Parteiensysteme im 19. und 20. Jahrhundert* (Frankfurt am Main: Suhrkamp, 1992), 121 ff.; on the problem of continuity in the Empire, see especially Stanley Suval, *Electoral Politics in Wilhelmine Germany* (Chapel Hill: University of North Carolina Press, 1985), 242 ff.

15. Ernst Fraenkel, "Historische Vorbelastungen des deutschen Parlamentarismus," in Ernst Fraenkel, *Deutschland und die westlichen Demokratien,* new enlarged ed. (Frankfurt am Main: Suhrkamp, 1991), 23 ff.; see also Peter-Christian Witt, "Kontinuität und Diskontinuität im politischen System der Weimarer Republik: Das Verhältnis von Regierung, Bürokratie und Reichstag," in *Regierung, Bürokratie und Parlament in Preußen und Deutschland von 1848 bis zur Gegenwart,* ed. Gerhard A. Ritter (Düsseldorf: Droste, 1983), 117 ff.

16. See Achim Kurz, *Demokratische Diktatur? Auslegung und Handhabung des Artikels 48 der Weimarer Verfassung 1919–1925* (Berlin: Duncker & Humblot, 1992).

17. See Larry Eugene Jones, *German Liberalism and the Dissolution of the Weimar Party System, 1918–1933* (Chapel Hill: University of North Carolina Press, 1988), 225 ff.

18. See Michael Stürmer, *Koalition und Opposition in der Weimarer Republik 1924–1928* (Düsseldorf: Droste, 1967).

19. On the final phase of the Weimar Republic, 1930–33, see Karl Dietrich Bracher, *Die Auflösung der Weimarer Republik: Eine Studie zum Problem des Machtverfalls in der Demokratie* (Stuttgart and Düsseldorf: Droste, 1955); Gerhard Schulz, *Von Brüning zu Hitler: Der Wandel des politischen Systems in Deutschland 1930–1933* (Berlin: de Gruyter, 1992).

20. See Dietrich Orlow, *Weimar Prussia, 1925–1933: The Illusion of Strength* (Pittsburgh: University of Pittsburgh Press, 1991), 225 ff.

21. Otto Kirchheimer, *Weimar—und was dann?* (Berlin: Laub [Jungsozialistische Schriftenreihe], 1930), 46.

22. Dating the inception of the American state turns out to be a surprisingly contentious enterprise, since it requires deciding what constitutes a sovereign state,

which was at the time—and to this day in muted tones continues to be—the central struggle of American political theory and politics. One can date the inception from 1774 when the Continental Congress began acting for all practical purposes like a sovereign state but without the formal attributes of what theorists at the time would have considered sovereignty. Gordon S. Wood, *The Creation of the American Republic, 1776–1787* (New York: W. W. Norton & Co., 1972) [1969], 344–54, 356. Or one can date the inception from the resolutions of May and July 1777 by which Congress called on the colonies to form independent governments and declared the "United Colonies" to be "free and independent States." One can date it from 1781, when Congress first assembled under the Articles of Confederation; from 1783, when England recognized the independence of the colonies; or from March 1789, when conventions in eleven of the thirteen states had ratified the Constitution (Article VII required at least nine).

Similarly, one can view the history of the German democratic state, beginning in 1919, as an unfolding crisis, running through the Weimar period, the Third Reich, the division of Germany into the Federal Republic and the German Democratic Republic, and concluding, after seventy years, in reunification.

23. This series of questions roughly tracks the structure of argument in *The Federalist*. After an introduction, Numbers 2 through 14 are devoted to the argument for union. Numbers 15 through 22 discuss the defects of confederation as a device for union, and Numbers 23 through 46 detail the powers a national government must have for union and the powers that may be reserved to the states. Numbers 45 to the end defend the exact structures of government proposed by the Framers to instantiate national power.

24. The Continental Congress, among other actions, adopted commercial codes, established and maintained the army that fought against England, issued a continental currency, set up a military code of law, defined crimes against the Union, and negotiated on behalf of the colonies with foreign powers. Wood, *The Creation of the American Republic*, 355. Also, since most of the delegates were chosen by popular assembly rather than by colonial legislatures, Congress could stake a greater claim than even the colonies to popular sovereignty. Richard B. Morris, *The Forging of the Union, 1781–1789* (New York: Harper & Row, 1987), 55–56.

25. Wood, *The Creation of the American Republic*, 133.

26. The Articles provided for the equality of the citizens of all states in the enjoyment of the privileges and immunities of every state, for universal extradition of criminal suspects and enforcement of judgments (Article IV). They eliminated restrictions on travel and discriminatory trade restrictions (Article IV). They granted the assembled United States Congress a vast array of powers unknown in historical models of confederation (the exclusive power to engage in war except when a state is actually attacked, of sending and receiving ambassadors, of entering into treaties and alliances, and so forth).

27. Morris, *The Forging of the Union*, 245–47. National sentiment was not confined to those, such as Hamilton, whose aim was to forge a unified national market. It was also especially high among the officer corps of the Continental Army, who saw first hand the "deficiencies of the operation of the government under the Articles of Confederation." Morris, *The Forging of the Union*, 33.

28. The Confederation had to rely on the states to enforce confederation law, lacked the power to tax, the power to regulate interstate commerce, and, of course, did not have an army.

29. Morris, *The Forging of the Union*, 92–93; Wood, *The Creation of the American Republic*, 359. Ironically Congress's most significant piece of legislation, the Northwest Ordinance, was enacted in July 1787, the month during which the Philadelphia Convention was reaching the Great Compromise. Morris, *The Forging of the Union*, 229.

30. Wood, *The Creation of the American Republic*, 359.

31. Unlike the Articles of Confederation, the Constitution prudently never mentions sovereignty. Nevertheless, Hamilton is quite explicit about dual sovereignty in Number 9 of *The Federalist*, as is Madison in Numbers 14 and 39.

32. Wood, *The Creation of the American Republic*, 403–09, 467.

33. This is Madison's argument in Number 10 of *The Federalist*.

34. Morris, *The Forging of the Union*, 134; Wood, *The Creation of the American Republic*, 394 and n. 2. Historians who deny the reality of the crisis generally fall in line with the Anti-federalist position on the Philadelphia Convention, that it was a conspiracy of economic or political interests—take your choice—against other economic interests or the liberties of Americans.

35. Morris, *The Forging of the Union*, 130.

36. Morris, *The Forging of the Union*, 17, 136.

37. Morris, *The Forging of the Union*, 264; Wood, *The Creation of the American Republic*, 325–26. The states perhaps set an example, by resisting the "requisitions" requested by the central government—another "deficiency" of the Articles. Max Farrand, *The Framing of the Constitution of the United States* (New Haven: Yale University Press, 1913), 4–5.

38. Charles Warren, writing at a time when economic interpretations of the origins of the Constitution were in the forefront, argues that historians have overemphasized Shays' Rebellion as a moving cause of the Philadelphia Convention and the Constitution. He points out that the rebellion did not become really serious before December 1786, "but long before that time, the leading statesmen of the country had determined that a change in the framework of the National Government was absolutely necessary, and they had agreed upon the general lines on which such a change must be made." Charles Warren, *The Making of the Constitution* (Boston: Little, Brown & Co., 1937), 32.

39. Morris, *The Forging of the Union*, 36–39; Wood, *The Creation of the American Republic*, 323–24.

40. Morris, *The Forging of the Union*, 247–51.

41. Morris, *The Forging of the Union*, 257. Though nine states had appointed commissioners, commissioners from only five states attended the meeting. So the call from Annapolis, though unanimous, did not have overwhelming formal backing. Yet the inability to get business done at Annapolis did provide a goad for the call. Farrand, *The Framing of the Constitution of the United States*, 8–9. Morris, *The Forging of the Union*, 254–55.

42. Morris, *The Forging of the Union*, 268.

43. Morris, *The Forging of the Union*, 299.

44. The Philadelphia Convention also violated Article XIII (and the congres-

sional resolution) in that the Constitution became operative, by its own terms, upon ratification by conventions in nine states, not upon unanimous vote. Bruce Ackerman has exalted the illegality of the method of ratification proposed by the Philadelphia Convention into a virtue: Had the Framers complied with the amendment method required by the Articles, they would have failed to signal the complete break with the past that the new regime sought to establish. Bruce Ackerman, *We The People*, 1: *Foundations* (Cambridge, Mass. : Harvard University Press, Belknap Press, 1991), 173–75. Madison admits that the Convention "departed from the tenor of their commission" these two ways but argues "the absurdity of subjecting the fate of twelve States to the perverseness or corruption of a thirteenth." Madison says that because this objection "has been the least urged in the publications which have swarmed against the convention," the opponents of ratification have "in a manner waived" it! *The Federalist*, ed. Benjamin F. Wright (Cambridge, Mass.: Harvard University Press, 1961) (J. Madison, No. 40), 290. He makes no argument defending the failure to submit the plan to the state legislatures for ratification. Nor does he defend the rather desultory post-ratification dissolution of the Confederation, which directly violated Article XIII ("the union shall be perpetual"): Within two months of the end of the Philadelphia Convention, and one month before the first state ratified the Constitution, only five states were sending delegates to the Confederation Congress. Morris, *The Forging of the Union*, 94, 300.

45. *Gibbons v. Ogden*, 9 Wheat. (22 U. S.)1, 6 L. Ed. 23 (1824).

46. *Dobbins v. Erie Co.*, 16 Pet. (41 U. S.) 435, 10 L. Ed. 1022 (1842).

47. *McCulloch v. Maryland*, 4 Wheat. (17 U. S.) 316, 4 L. Ed. 579 (1819).

48. *Collector v. Day*, 11 Wall. (80 U. S.) 13, 20 L. Ed. 579 (1871).

49. 1 Wheat. (14 U. S.) 304, 4 L. Ed. 97 (1816).

50. More specifically, Section 25 of the Judiciary Act of 1789 provided, in part, that a final judgment or decree in any suit in the highest court of a state, where is drawn in question the validity of a treaty or statute of the United States, and the decision is against its validity, or where is drawn in question the validity of a statute of a state on the ground of its being repugnant to the constitution, treaties, or laws of the United States, and the decision is in favor of its validity, may be reexamined in the Supreme Court of the United States. The idea was that interpretation of the laws and Constitution of the United States ought to be the ultimate responsibility of a single court, in order to avoid conflicting interpretations, and that the single court ought to be the Supreme Court of the United States.

51. Charles Warren, *The Supreme Court in United States History*, 2 vols. (Boston: Little, Brown & Co., 1922), 1:450. Warren records only two other cases in the nineteenth century—*Tyler v. Magwire*, 17 Wall. (84 U. S.) 253, 21 L. Ed. 576 (1873), and *Williams v. Bruffy*, 102 U. S. 248, 26 L. Ed. 135 (1880)—in which defiance of its mandate by the highest court of a state forced the Supreme Court to issue a mandate to the trial court instead.

52. The first half century of the Republic bristled with attempts at nullification. South Carolina's 1832 Ordinance of Nullification was not the first. The Virginia-Kentucky Resolutions of 1798–99 branded the Alien and Sedition Acts unconstitutional but did not block enforcement. In 1807 the Massachusetts legislature declared the Embargo of 1807 "not legally binding on the citizens of this state." For Calhoun's view, see the South Carolina *Exposition and Protest*, in Richard K. Crallé,

ed., *The Works of John C. Calhoun,* vol. 6: *Reports and Public Letters* (New York: D. Appleton & Co., 1854–57), 1–59.

53. Even the Wisconsin legislature's nullification of the Supreme Court's process against a violator of the Fugitive Slave Laws on the eve of the Civil War in 1859 did not deny the legitimacy of constitutional government. It followed the classic pattern of nullification by insisting that the Supreme Court was not the sole authoritative interpreter of the Constitution, and that each state was to be the judge of the constitutionality of federal statutes within its own borders. The Supreme Court affirmed its supremacy in the face of Wisconsin's attack in *Ableman v. Booth,* 21 How. (62 U. S.) 506, 16 L. Ed. 169 (1859) (Taney, C. J.). Harold M. Hyman and William M. Wiecek, *Equal Justice Under Law: Constitutional Development, 1836–1875* (New York: Harper & Row, 1982), 198–201; Samuel Tyler, *Memoir of Roger Brooke Taney* (Baltimore: John Murphy & Co., 1872), 392–400.

54. Dissenting in the *Slaughter-House Cases,* Justice Field says that before enactment of the Fourteenth Amendment, "there was much diversity of opinion among jurists and statesmen whether there was any such citizenship independent of that of the state, and, if any existed, as to the manner in which it originated. With a great number the opinion prevailed that there was no such citizenship independent of the citizenship of the state." *Slaughter-House Cases,* 16 Wall. (83 U. S.) 36, 94; 21 L. Ed. 394, 414 (1873).

55. In Number 39 of *The Federalist* Madison assumes that division of ratification into separate state conventions rather than a single convention representing the nation as a whole adequately respects the sovereignty of the states. "[T]he Constitution," he says, "is to be founded on the assent and ratification of the people of America, given by deputies elected for the special purpose; but . . . this assent and ratification is to be given by the people, not as individuals composing one entire nation, but as composing the distinct and independent States to which they respectively belong. It is to be the assent and ratification of the several States, derived from the supreme authority in each State,—the authority of the people themselves. . . . Each State, in ratifying the Constitution is considered as a sovereign body, independent of all others, and only to be bound by its own voluntary act." *The Federalist* (J. Madison, No. 39), 283. But that is precisely the question: whether the state governments operating according to constitutions long predating the Philadelphia Convention or the people assembled in convention—even state conventions—are the source of the Constitution's authority.

56. 19 How. (60 U. S.) 393, 15 L. Ed. 691 (1857).

57. Nine justices wrote opinions in *Dred Scott,* and the case simply swarms with tough issues. Figuring out exactly what the case stands for has stumped commentators for 150 years. Nevertheless, the clerk of the court, Benjamin Howard, did label Chief Justice Taney's opinion "the opinion of the court, and a recent close reading of the case has concluded that "the Taney opinion *is,* for all practical purposes, *the* Dred Scott decision." Don E. Fehrenbacher, *The Dred Scott Case: Its Significance in American Law and Politics* (New York: Oxford University Press, 1978), 337.

58. 19 How. (60 U. S.) 405, 15 L. Ed. 700–701.

59. There are at least four reasons deducible from the case itself for so thinking:

(1) Scott's claim against John F. A. Sanford (misspelled in the Supreme Court Reports), his master at the time of the federal litigation, had already been litigated to a final conclusion against Scott in Missouri state courts. See *Scott v. Emerson,* 15 Mo. 576 (1852) (the defendant in the Missouri proceedings, Irene Emerson, was the widow of the master who had taken Scott to free Illinois and the free part of the Louisiana Territory, by dint of which Scott claimed emancipation; she later sold Scott to her brother, Sanford). According to the doctrine of *res judicata,* Missouri's decision should have been final, precluding any further litigation by Scott or his master in any court—state or federal. But *res judicata* was looser in those days, and it is possible that relitigation of Scott's claim in federal court was considered proper.

(2) The Court's exact decision was that federal courts lacked the power to hear Scott's claim. Having held that, the Court could have dismissed the claim without deciding any other issue, and today a federal court certainly would. Nevertheless, Hyman and Wiecek argue, without massing evidence, that unlike now, courts then considered it proper to decide other issues once a jurisdictional defect had been shown. Hyman and Wiecek, *Equal Justice Under Law,* 184. But certainly the Court was not compelled to decide other issues.

(3) Perhaps the most persuasive argument is that by relitigating his claim in federal court and appealing to the Supreme Court of the United States, Scott was attempting to do indirectly what he could not do directly: appeal to the Supreme Court of the United States from the decision of the Supreme Court of Missouri. The law was clear that Scott could not appeal Missouri's decision to the Supreme Court of the United States unless the Missouri decision implicated the constitutionality of a law of the United States or a state law, which it did not. See *Scott v. Emerson,* 15 Mo. 576 (1852).

(4) One of the Court's holdings was that pursuant to its decision in *Strader v. Graham,* 10 How. (51 U. S.) 82, 13 L. Ed. 337 (1851), the law of Missouri—the state from which Scott's master departed to Illinois and the Louisiana Territories and to which he returned before litigation started—applied to Scott's claim, not the Missouri Compromise or the law of Illinois. Under Missouri law as stated in *Scott v. Emerson,* Scott's claim would fail. This had been the decision of the trial court, the Circuit Court for the District of Missouri, which had not dismissed for lack of jurisdiction. The Supreme Court could have followed the trial court's decision and avoided deciding the constitutionality of the Missouri Compromise.

There is also substantial evidence that Taney, along with a majority of the Court, believed that a decision about Congress's power to enact the Missouri Compromise would "settle the agitation" that had swept the nation since its repeal in the Kansas-Nebraska Act. Letter of 19 February 1857 from Justice John Catron to President-Elect James Buchanan, quoted in Bernard C. Steiner, *Life of Roger Brooke Taney* (Baltimore: Williams & Wilkins, 1922) [Holmes Beach: Gaunt, 1997], 338. See also Carl Bent Swisher, *Roger B. Taney* (New York: Macmillan, 1935) [Hamden: Archon Books, 1961], 497–98; Warren, *The Supreme Court,* 2:291–92.

60. For reactions to the decision, see Hyman and Wiecek, *Equal Justice Under Law,* 190–201; Warren, *The Supreme Court,* 2:302–17.

61. Hyman and Wiecek, *Equal Justice Under Law,* 335–36.

62. Hyman and Wiecek, *Equal Justice Under Law,* 337. The phrase "constitutional faith" belongs to Sanford Levinson, *Constitutional Faith* (Princeton: Princeton University Press, 1988).

63. Harold M. Hyman, *A More Perfect Union* (New York: Knopf, 1973), 65 ("Civil War America remained an astonishingly free and open society.").

64. Hyman and Wiecek, *Equal Justice Under Law,* 336–38.

65. Hyman and Wiecek, *Equal Justice Under Law,* 253, 305.

66. Thus, the editor of *The Nation,* E. L. Godkin. See Hyman, *A More Perfect Union,* 285.

67. Hyman and Wiecek, *Equal Justice Under Law,* 317.

68. Hyman and Wiecek, *Equal Justice Under Law,* 389–90.

69. The Civil Rights Act of 1866, 14 Stat. 27, provides, in part:

> [C]itizens, of every race and color, . . . shall have the same right, in every State
> and Territory in the United States, to make and enforce contracts, to sue, be par-
> ties, and give evidence, to inherit, purchase, lease, sell, hold and convey real and
> personal property, and to full and equal benefit of all laws and proceedings for
> the security of person and property, as is enjoyed by white citizens, and shall
> be subject to like punishment, pains, and penalties, and to none other, any
> law, statute, ordinance, regulation, or custom, to the contrary notwithstanding.

70. President Johnson's veto message took this position, 6 Richardson, *Messages and Papers of the Presidents* 405 (1897), and the supreme court of one state, Kentucky, actually held one section of the act unconstitutional—upholding the validity of a Kentucky state law prohibiting testimony by blacks against whites. *Bowlin v. Kentucky,* 2 Bush (Ky.) 5, 15–29 (1867). The issue of testimonial capacity, for whites as for blacks, was an important one in those days. Few states permitted parties to civil suits to testify, on the ground that their testimony was self-interested, and none permitted defendants in criminal trials to testify until Maine in 1864. The issue had surfaced originally in fugitive slave suits, where the question was whether the alleged slave would be allowed to testify. See Hyman and Wiecek, *Equal Justice Under Law,* 328–30.

71. "[T]here is a citizenship of the United States and a citizenship of a state, which are distinct from each other and which depend upon different characteristics or circumstances of the individual." *Slaughter-House Cases,* 16 Wall. (83 U. S.) at 75, 21 L. Ed. at 408.

72. Hyman and Wiecek trace this dynamism to the Thirteenth Amendment. Hyman and Wiecek, *Equal Justice Under Law,* 389–99. The Fourteenth Amendment, from this perspective, serves only to draw out what was inchoate in the Thirteenth. Their position is, as they acknowledge, controversial. What is not controversial is that the Fourteenth Amendment explicitly incorporates the dynamic approach to elimi-nating the vestiges of slavery.

73. 16 Wall. (83 U. S.) at 81, 21 L. Ed. at 410. The issue in the *Slaughter-House Cases* involved a Louisiana statute giving a monopoly of the slaughterhouse business in New Orleans to the Crescent City Live-Stock Landing & Slaughter-House Company. Besides the equal protection challenge, plaintiffs also claimed that the statute was

unconstitutional on the ground that it creates an involuntary servitude forbidden by the Thirteenth Amendment, that it abridges the privileges and immunities of citizens of the United States, and that it deprives them of their property without due process of law. The Court rejected all of these arguments.

74. 16 Wall (83 U. S.) at 100–101, 21 L. Ed. at 416.

75. *Yick Wo v. Hopkins,* 118 U. S. 356, 6 S. Ct. 1064, 30 L. Ed. 220 (1886).

76. 118 U. S. at 369, 30 L. Ed. at 226.

77. 163 U. S. 537, 16 S. Ct. 1138, 41 L. Ed. 256 (1896).

78. The Texas "white primary" cases were the first. See *Nixon v. Herndon,* 273 U. S. 536, 47 S. Ct. 446, 71 L. Ed. 759 (1927); *Nixon v. Condon,* 286 U. S. 73, 52 S. Ct. 484, 76 L. Ed. 984 (1932).

79. 4 Otto (94 U. S.) 113, 24 L. Ed. 77 (1877).

80. *Minnesota Rate Case* [*Chicago, Milwaukee and St. Paul Ry. v. Minnesota*], 134 U. S. 418, 10 S. Ct. 462, 33 L. Ed. 970 (1890).

81. *Allgeyer v. Louisiana,* 165 U. S. 578, 17 S. Ct. 427, 41 L. Ed. 832 (1897).

82. 198 U. S. 45, 25 S. Ct. 539, 49 L. Ed. 937 (1905).

83. The relevant cases are *Munn* (see note 79 above) and *Holden v. Hardy,* 169 U. S. 366, 18 S. Ct. 383, 42 L. Ed. 780 (1898). The *Munn* Court certainly would have accepted the judgment of the New York State legislature that the bakery business is "affected with a public interest," but neither the opinion of the Court nor the dissents cite *Munn. Holden* upheld a Utah statute setting a maximum day of eight hours for workers in underground mines and smelters, "except in cases of emergency where life or property is in imminent danger." Following the regime dictated in *Munn,* the Court accepted the legislative judgment as a valid exercise of the police power. The *Lochner* Court distinguished *Holden* on the ground that the Utah statute provided for cases of emergency where the provisions of the statute would not apply. From the perspective of *Munn* this distinction is specious. Presumably the New York statute would be construed by New York courts to provide exceptions for emergencies, such as fires, and bakery work is not as hazardous as mine work in the first place, obviating the need for reference to emergencies in the statute.

84. 208 U. S. 412, 28 S. Ct. 324, 52 L. Ed. 551 (1908).

85. 243 U. S. 426, 37 S. Ct. 435, 61 L. Ed. 830 (1917).

86. *Coppage v. Kansas,* 236 U. S. 1, 35 S. Ct. 240, 59 L. Ed. 441 (1915).

87. 261 U. S. 525, 43 S. Ct. 394, 67 L. Ed. 785 (1923).

88. *German Alliance Insurance Co. v. Lewis,* 233 U. S. 389, 34 S. Ct. 612, 58 L. Ed. 1011 (1914).

89. *Block v. Hirsh,* 256 U. S. 135, 41 S. Ct. 458, 65 L. Ed. 865 (1921).

90. 262 U. S. 522, 43 S. Ct. 630, 67 L. Ed. 1103 (1923) (meat packing).

91. See, for example, *Ribnik v. McBride,* 277 U. S. 350, 48 S. Ct. 545, 72 L. Ed. 913 (1928) (employment agencies); *Williams v. Standard Oil Co.,* 278 U. S. 235, 49 S. Ct. 115, 73 L. Ed. 287 (1929) (gasoline prices); *New State Ice Co. v. Liebmann,* 285 U. S. 262, 52 S. Ct. 371, 76 L. Ed. 747 (1932) (ice business).

92. *Panama Refining Co. v. Ryan,* 293 U. S. 388, 55 S. Ct. 241, 79 L. Ed. 446 (1935) (section 9(c) of the National Industrial Recovery Act of 1933, authorizing the president to prohibit the interstate shipment of oil produced in excess of state-fixed quotas, violates the non-delegation doctrine); *Louisville Joint Stock Land Bank v. Radford,* 295 U. S. 555, 55 S. Ct. 854, 79 L. Ed. 1593 (Frazier-Lemke Act of 1934

violates the Takings Clause of the Fifth Amendment); *Schechter Poultry Corp. v. United States,* 295 U. S. 495, 55 S. Ct. 837, 79 L. Ed. 1570 (1935) (National Industrial Recovery Act delegates excessive power to the president and exceeded Congress's power under the Commerce Clause); *United States v. Butler,* 297 U. S. 1, 56 S. Ct. 312, 80 L. Ed. 477 (1936) (Agricultural Adjustment Act of 1933 regulates and controls agricultural production, which is local and not commerce, hence a matter beyond the powers delegated to the federal government in the Commerce Clause); *Carter v. Carter Coal Co.,* 298 U. S. 238, 56 S. Ct. 855, 80 L. Ed. 1160 (1936) (Bituminous Coal Conservation Act of 1935 not within the power to regulate interstate commerce and a delegation of regulatory authority to a private group); *Ashton v. Cameron County District,* 298 U. S. 513, 56 S. Ct. 892, 80 L Ed. 1309 (1936) (extension in the Municipal Bankruptcy Act of 1934 of the benefits of bankruptcy to subdivisions of the state was an unconstitutional encroachment upon the states' sovereign powers).

93. Changes in the non-delegation doctrine and the Court's Commerce Clause jurisprudence took longer than changes in the Court's Due Process Clause jurisprudence. Commerce Clause jurisprudence was evolving well into the period after the Second World War.

94. 290 U. S. 398, 54 S. Ct. 231, 78 L. Ed. 413 (1934).

95. 290 U. S. at 444, 54 S. Ct. at 242.

96. 290 U. S. at 441, 54 S. Ct. at 241.

97. 290 U. S. at 448, 54 S. Ct. at 243.

98. 291 U. S. 502, 54 S. Ct. 505, 78 L. Ed. 940 (1934).

99. 291 U. S. at 517, 54 S. Ct. 507.

100. 291 U. S. at 525, 54 S. Ct. 511.

101. Two cases seem to step back from *Nebbia,* but in fact do not. *Morehead v. Tipaldo,* 298 U. S. 587, 56 S. Ct. 918, 80 L. Ed. 1347 (1936), struck down the New York minimum wage law for women on the technical ground that the petitioners for certiorari had neglected to ask that *Adkins* be overruled. It does not stand for the continued vitality of *Adkins. Railroad Retirement Board v. Alton R. R.,* 295 U. S. 330, 55 S. Ct. 758, 79 L. Ed. 1468 (1935), held that the Railroad Retirement Act of 1934, forcing carriers to give employees pensions calculated in part on the basis of services rendered prior to passage of the act, constitutes an unreasonable regulation of interstate commerce and denies due process to the carriers by arbitrarily imposing on them liability to pay twice for the services. *Alton* could just as well been a Fifth Amendment takings case, but uses the *Nebbia* standard for due process instead. It would be found unconstitutional today.

102. 300 U. S. 379, 57 S. Ct. 578, 81 L. Ed. 703 (1937).

103. See, for example, Barry Cushman, *Rethinking the New Deal Court: The Structure of a Constitutional Revolution,* Part 1 (Oxford: Oxford University Press, 1998). Cushman's critical evaluation of the evidence includes, among much else, the fact that *Parrish* was decided on 19 December 1936, six weeks before the Court-packing plan, a closely guarded secret, was made public by the Roosevelt administration. Chief Justice Hughes delayed announcement of the decision to await Justice Harlan Fiske Stone's return to the Court after a bout of amoebic dysentery in order to convert a 4–4 affirmance of the lower court's decision to a 5–4 affirmance. Stone returned at the beginning of February, and the Chief Justice further delayed to avoid creating the impression that the Court was reacting to the Court-packing plan. Cushman, *Re-*

thinking the New Deal Court, 18. He needn't have bothered. Legal scholars, at least, persist in the myth. See, for example, Bruce Ackerman, *We The People*, 2: *Transformations* (Cambridge, Mass.: Harvard University Press, Belknap Press, 1998).

104. See, for example, *Roe v. Wade*, 410 U. S. 113, 93 S. Ct. 705, 35 L. Ed. 2d 147 (1973) (right of privacy "founded in the Fourteenth Amendment's concept of personal liberty and restrictions upon state action"). The vitality of *Lochner* in clauses of the Constitution other than the Due Process Clause is reviewed in Cass R. Sunstein, *Lochner's Legacy*, 87 Columbia Law Review 873 (1987).

105. There were exceptions, of course: the struggle over free speech (engendered by the war and the Red Scare), Prohibition, and state enactment of "blue sky" laws regulating the sale of securities.

PROLOGUE

1. Carl Friedrich von Gerber, *Über öffentliche Rechte* (Tübingen: Laupp'sche Buchhandlung, 1852), 23. On Gerber, see especially Peter von Oertzen, *Die soziale Funktion des staatsrechtlichen Positivismus* (Frankfurt am Main: Suhrkamp, 1974).

2. Gerber, *Über öffentliche Rechte*, 23; see also 18.

3. Carl Friedrich von Gerber, *Grundzüge eines Systems des deutschen Staatsrechts*, 2nd ed. (Leipzig: B. Tauchnitz, 1869), vii (preface to 1st edition, 1865).

4. Gerber, *Über öffentliche Rechte*, 30.

5. Gerber, *Grundzüge eines Systems des deutschen Staatsrechts*, viii.

6. In retrospect, Triepel remarked, "Laband's law of the state completely dominated more than one generation of German public law scholars," Heinrich Triepel, *Staatsrecht und Politik* (Berlin and Leipzig: de Gruyter, 1927), 9. Even earlier on Laband's significance, see Philipp Zorn, "Die Entwicklung der Staatsrechtswissenschaft seit 1866," *Jahrbuch des öffentlichen Rechts*, vol. 1 (Tübingen: Mohr, 1907), 47.

7. Paul Laband, *Das Staatsrecht des deutschen Reiches*, vol. 1, 5th ed. (Tübingen: Mohr, 1911), ix (foreword to 2nd edition).

8. Paul Laband, *Das Budgetrecht nach den Bestimmungen der preußischen Verfassungsurkunde* (Berlin: Guttentag, 1871; reprint Berlin: de Gruyter, 1971), 75.

9. Paul Laband, *Das Staatsrecht des deutschen Reiches*, vol. 1, 2nd ed. (Freiburg im Breisgau: Mohr, 1888), v (foreword to 1st ed.) ("The constitution of the Empire is no longer the subject of party struggle but has become the common basis for all parties and their battles.").

10. See the major criticism of Laband in Otto von Gierke, *Labands Staatsrecht und die deutsche Rechtswissenschaft* (1883) (2nd ed., Darmstadt: Wissenschaftliche Buchgesellschaft, 1961); also Felix Stoerk, *Zur Methodik des öffentlichen Rechts* (Vienna: Hölder, 1885).

11. This concept of validity is closely linked to Weber's sociological concept of domination [*Herrschaft*]. See Guenther Roth, Introduction to Max Weber, *Economy and Society*, vol. 1 (New York: Bedminster Press, 1968), lxxxiii–lxxxiv.

12. Max Weber, *Wirtschaft und Gesellschaft*, 5th ed. (Tübingen: Mohr, 1972), 181.

13. Georg Jellinek, in *Gesetz und Verordnung* (Freiburg im Breisgau: Mohr, 1887), vii, ascribes to state law positivism [*staatsrechtlichen Positivismus*] the merit of having transformed state law from being "the fluid element of knowledge of the state difficult to circumscribe" to the "solid state of a legal discipline."

14. See Hans Kelsen, *Hauptprobleme der Staatsrechtslehre ent wiekelt aus der Lehre vom Rechtssätze*, 2nd edition supplemented with a foreword (Tübingen: Mohr, 1923), 4 ff., 23. On neo-Kantian legal theory, Horst Dreier, *Rechtslehre, Staatssoziologie und Demokratietheorie bei Hans Kelsen* (Baden-Baden: Nomos Verlagsgesellschaft, 1986), 70 ff.

15. Kelsen occasionally stressed this himself. See, for example, Hans Kelsen, *Reine Rechtslehre*, 1st ed. (Leipzig and Vienna: Deuticke, 1934), iv (foreword).

16. For more on this and the following, see Stefan Korioth, "Erschütterungen des staatsrechtlichen Positivismus im ausgehenden Kaiserreich," *Archiv des öffentlichen Rechts*, vol. 117 (1992): 212 ff.

17. "Life" here does not refer to biological facts, and does not claim to provide an answer to the meaning of life. "Life" is a polemical cultural concept, targeting a "civilization that has become intellectualist and anti-life," against which it sets the power of "true experience" in all its irrationality. See Herbert Schnädelbach, *Philosophie in Deutschland, 1831–1933* (Frankfurt am Main: Suhrkamp Taschenbuch Verlag, 1983), 172 ff.

18. Rudolf Smend, "Maßstäbe des parlamentarischen Wahlrechts in der deutschen Staatstheorie des 19. Jahrhunderts" (1911), reprinted in Rudolf Smend, *Staatsrechtliche Abhandlungen und andere Aufsätze*, 2nd ed. (Berlin: Duncker & Humblot, 1968), 19 ff., 35.

19. Paul Laband, *Das Staatsrecht des deutschen Reiches*, vol. 2, 5th ed. (Tübingen: Mohr, 1911), 176, 178.

20. See, for example, Gnaeus Flavius (Hermann Kantorowicz), *Der Kampf um die Rechtswissenschaft* (Heidelberg: Winter, 1906); Eugen Ehrlich, *Freie Rechtsfindung und freie Rechtswissenschaft* (Leipzig: C. L. Hirschfeld, 1903).

21. Michael Stolleis, "Die Entstehung des Interventionsstaates und das öffentliche Recht," in *Zeitschrift für neuere Rechtsgeschichte* 11 (1989): 129 ff., 136.

22. This basic attitude is accurately described in Fritz K. Ringer, *Die Gelehrten* (1969) (2nd ed., Stuttgart: Klett-Cotta, 1987), 47 ff., 78 ff., 186 ff.

23. Erich Kaufmann, "Bismarcks Erbe in der Reichsverfassung" (1917), in Erich Kaufmann, *Gesammelte Schriften*, vol. 1, ed. Albert Hilger van Scherpenberg et al. (Göttingen: Otto Schwartz, 1960), 143 ff., 153.

24. See Paul Laband, *Wandlungen der deutschen Reichsverfassung* (Dresden: von Zahn & Jaensch, 1895), 2 ff.

25. See Georg Jellinek, *Allgemeine Staatslehre* (Berlin: Springer, 1922), 520.

26. The doctrine of the law-creating power of the judge, established by Oskar Bülow, *Gesetz und Richteramt* (Leipzig: Duncker & Humblot, 1885), is gaining more and more supporters. Of the most recent literature, see, for example, Joseph Unger, "Über die Haftung des Staates für Verzugs- und Vergütungszinsen," *Grünhuts Zeitschrift* 31 (1904): 108 ff.; Eugen Ehrlich, *Freie Rechtsfindung und freie Rechtswissenschaft* (Leipzig: C. L. Hirschfeld, 1903), and Gustav Radbruch, "Rechtswissenschaft und Rechtsschöpfung," *Archiv für Sozialpolitik* 22 (1906): 355, in the latter, p. 369, a list of the supporters of this current, whose writings, however, are of varied value.

27. See Brinton Coxe, *An Essay of Judicial Power and Institutional Legislation* (Philadelphia: Kay & Bros., 1893), 8 ff., 22. These statistics are not entirely reliable, since, as Coxe emphasizes, in the official figures only twenty cases of congressional statutes declared invalid are listed, among which, however, the famous *Dred Scott* case is not

included. There are no summary statistics on the judges' decisions in the individual states.

28. On constitutional gaps, see my *Allgemeine Staatslehre* (Berlin: Springer, 1922), 347 ff., and in the most recent literature, Gerhard Anschütz, "Lücken in Verfassungs- und Verwaltungsgesetzen," in *Verwaltungsarchiv* 14 (1906), 315 ff., whose findings agree with mine, but who erroneously polemicizes against a claim I never made (p. 335). I said neither in the place quoted by Anschütz nor anywhere else that, in conflicts between government and the popular representative, there is no judge to be found. Quite the contrary; I already pointed, in *Gesetz und Verordnung* (Freiburg im Breisgau: Mohr, 1887), 309, to courts of state law [*Staatsgerichtshöfe*] for the decision of conflicts involving budget laws and also expressly mentioned several tribunals existing for such cases in the German states.

29. See Wilhelm Wundt, *Ethik*, 3rd ed. (Stuttgart: Enke, 1903), 1 ff.

30. See Hans Kelsen, *Hauptprobleme der Staatsrechtslehre* (Tübingen: Mohr, 1923), 6 ff.

31. For details, see Kelsen, *Hauptprobleme der Staatsrechtslehre ent wickelt aus der Lehre vom Rechtssätze*, 47 ff., and 346 ff.

32. Ernst Rudolf Bierling, *Zur Kritik der juristischen Grundbegriffe*, 1st ed. (Gotha: Perthes, 1877), 136. Bierling may be viewed as the most prominent supporter of recognition theory. See also Ernst Rudolf Bierling, *Juristische Prinzipienlehre*, 4th ed. (Freiburg im Breitag: Mohr, 1894).

33. Kelsen, *Hauptprobleme der Staatsrechtslehre*, 172 ff., provides a critique of the concept of the state and the will in inorganic state theory.

34. Wilhelm Wundt, *Grundriß der Psychologie*, 7th ed. (Leipzig: W. Engelmann, 1905), 384.

35. This should be obvious, but as things stand today, such obviousness still needs emphasis in order to be noticed.

36. Oskar Bülow (*Gesetz und Richteramt* [Leipzig: Duncker & Humblot, 1885], 45), says accurately that what is called "judge-made law" is not abstract legal norms, but that "judge-made law" exists nonetheless, and to deny it is self-denial. Bülow's view can only be explained without contradiction if one sees in "judge-made law" a recognition of the methodological autonomy of the criterion of legal practice.

37. When Kohler draws attention in numerous places to the phenomenon of *duplex interpretatio* and to the fact that, while retaining the words of a statute, a changed perception of the law is able to secure recognition by playing the letter of the statute against its spirit (like Portia in *The Merchant of Venice*), then one can follow him to the extent that this general and conscious self-deception in practice contains the thought of respecting as long as possible the most important pillar of legal certainty: the words of the statute.

38. Fear of legal insecurity, of judges' arbitrariness, is always the decisive argument in the vividly emphasized rejection of *contra legem* adjudication; for example, Lorenz Brütt, *Die Kunst der Rechtsanwendung* (Berlin: Guttentag, 1907), 184 ff.; Max Rumpf, *Gesetz und Richter: Versuch einer Methodik der Rechtsanwendung* (Berlin: Liebmann, 1906), 77–78 (he says that disregarding the words of the statutes leads to legal insecurity; that there is no certain criterion for when decisions may nevertheless be made against it; and that everything depends here on the "personality" of the judge); Siegfried Brie, "Billigkeit und Recht, mit besonderer Berücksichti-

gung der Freiheitsbewebung," *Archiv für Rechts- und Wirtschaftsphilosophie,* vol. 3 (1909/1910), 532. Johann Georg Gmelin, *Quosque? Beiträge zur soziologischen Rechtsfindung* (Hannover: Hellwing, 1910). The sentence in Josef von Schein, *Unsere Jurisprudenz und Rechtsphilosophie* (Berlin: Heymann, 1889), 208–209, is remarkable; civil servants should, in the interests of legal security, be more like slaves to the statute than representatives of the state; "an exception can only be made in those extremely rare cases in which the consequences of the statute are so harmful at the moment that they outweigh the interest of legal security, and are so obvious that any organ of state would have to notice them, and thus unreliability does not come into play." The difficulty resulting from the introduction of superpositive norms has an interesting historical parallel in the questions posed for supporters of natural law on the relationship of natural to positive law. In contrast, the solution suggested in the text offers a theoretically unambiguous answer, which is certainly desirable in the study of legal methodology—*though I say it* [English in the original].

1. HANS KELSEN

1. In Geneva, Kelsen had taught in French. Now, at almost sixty years of age, he was forced, in a very short time, to learn to lecture in English.

2. The Pure Theory of Law is a broadly structured theory that cannot be described within this framework. Thus, it seems reasonable to concentrate on those characteristics through which the Pure Theory of Law differs markedly from other legal theories.

3. To avoid misunderstandings, it should be pointed out that Kelsen did not at all dispute the possibility of legal sociology. On the contrary, he made a considerable contribution to it, specifically his *Society and Nature* (Chicago: University of Chicago Press, 1943). However, the Pure Theory of Law opposes those trends in legal sociology that dispute the possibility of normative jurisprudence. See *Hans Kelsen und die Rechtssoziologie,* ed. Stanley Paulson (Aalen: Scientia Verlag, 1992) and, on the debate with "legal realism," Hans Kelsen, *Reine Rechtslehre,* 2nd ed. (Vienna: Deuticke, 1960), 213.

4. On the following, see *Veröffentlichungen der Vereinigung der deutschen Staatsrechtslehrer,* vol. 4 (Berlin, Leipzig: de Gruyter, 1928).

5. To understand the background in intellectual history of the devaluation of the formal, we should recall the following: All "modern" scientific and artistic efforts of this period were stereotypically accused of two things—decomposing traditional values and overestimating the intellectual and analytical (a reactionary work by the philosopher Ludwig Klages, popular in its time, was characteristically titled *Der Geist als Widersacher der Seele* [*The Intellect as Adversary of the Soul*]). Romantic categories such as soul, totality, essence, people [*Volk*], feeling, etc., were mustered—often with anti-Semitic accents—against modern currents. Kelsen's legal theory shared the fate of psychoanalysis, twelve-tone music, and neopositivism, to name just a few examples from Vienna. The fact that such critiques are difficult in a discipline as formal as legal doctrine explains the rigid nature of some constructions by Kelsen's opponents, and perhaps also their often truly hostile attitudes.

6. This is no different from the situation in the natural sciences, where analogous

distinctions must be made. See Edgar Zilsel, *Die sozialen Ursprünge der neuzeitlichen Wissenschaft* (Frankfurt am Main: Suhrkamp, 1976).

7. This attitude does not flow from critical legal positivism, which, as explained above, has no answer to the question of the attitude a person should take in relation to positive law. Thus the option of resistance to positive law remains and is seen that much more clearly when the positive law is worthless. However, one who opposes creating law along democratic paths is, according to Kelsen, no longer a democrat. On the continuing discussion of this position, and especially the further development of Kelsen's concept of democracy during his American years, see Horst Dreier, *Rechtslehre, Staatssoziologie und Demokratietheorie bei Hans Kelsen,* 2nd ed. (Baden-Baden: Nomos Verlagsgesellschaft, 1990), 249.

8. The occasional claim that the Pure Theory of Law holds the content of legal norms to be irrelevant is such an ignorant accusation that I will not even begin to deal with it. A glance at my *General Theory of the State* [*Allgemeine Rechtslehre*] or Merkl's *General Administrative Law* [*Allgemeines Verwaltungsrecht*] will easily convince the reader of the contrary. The Pure Theory of Law works not only with concepts of legal *essence* but also with concepts of legal *content.*

9. See Fritz Schreier, *Die Interpretation der Gesetze und Rechtsgeschäfte* (Leipzig and Vienna: Deuticke, 1927).

10. David Koigen, *Die Kultur der Demokratie* (Jena: Diederichs, 1912), 4.

11. This is, to be sure, not an unprejudiced presentation of the problem. When we ask about the *essence* of democracy, we may not assume from the beginning that it is the best form of state. This seems to be the problem with the otherwise excellent presentation by Gustav Fredrik Steffen in his *Das Problem der Demokratie,* 3rd ed. (Jena: Diederichs, 1917), who, in his efforts to prove democracy to be the best form of state, denies some of its essential characteristics merely because he finds them unfavorable, perhaps with very good reason. Of course, the reverse is just as questionable. One may not consider constitutional monarchy the best form of state if one is to provide an objective "political description" of democracy, as is the case with Wilhelm Hasbach in his *Die moderne Demokratie* (Jena: Fischer, 1912).

12. *Du contrat social,* bk. I, chap. 6.

13. *Du contrat social,* bk. III, chap. 15.

14. Neither does *customary law* resolve the contrast between social "ought" and individual "is," though it might seem to; but it reduces it to a minimum by commanding: Behave as your fellows usually tend to behave. Wrongs, violations of the order are thus a priori mere exceptions to the rule of "is." Thus, customary law proves its democratic character, in contrast to statutes, especially when these—as in ancient times—appear as the commands of a divinity, a priest representing the divine, or a heroic king descended from the gods. As the theory and practice of customary law assert themselves, especially in times of political absolutism, they operate—as a contrary principle and counterbalance—in the direction of a balance of power.

15. For the extent to which the change in ideology characterized here, from *liberalism* or *anarchism* to an étatist idea of democracy, is connected with the position in the state of the social groups that support this ideology, especially with the relationship of the bourgeoisie and the proletariat to state power, see my *Allgemeine Staatslehre* (Berlin: Springer, 1925), 32 ff.

16. Rousseau's *volonté générale*—the anthropomorphic expression of the *objective* state order that is valid independently of the will of the individuals, the *volonté des tous*—is completely irreconcilable with the theory of the social contract, which is a function of the subjective *volonté des tous*. But this contradiction between subjective and objective constructions, or, if you will, this movement from a subjective starting point to an objective end result is no less characteristic of Rousseau than of Kant and Fichte.

17. According to Rousseau, *Du contrat social,* bk. IV, chap. 2.

18. On the *dualism of ideology and reality* typical of all social entities, see my paper in the *Verhandlungen des Fünften deutschen Soziologentages* (Tübingen: Mohr, 1926), 38 ff.

19. See my *Der soziologische und der juristische Staatsbegriff,* 2nd ed. (Tübingen: Mohr, 1928), 4 ff.

20. "From a democratic point of view, there is no people's will as something whole and comprehensible. The people is composed of the expressions of the will of the many. When the many come together in legal, regulated relationships and administer justice, the majority of their wills becomes a people's will. The ideologists of democracy do not realize that a special people's will, in addition to the will to protect the autonomy of each individual, is inherent in the creative legal force." David Koigen, *Die Kultur der Demokratie* (Jena: Diederichs, 1912), 142. The thought seems to arise here that the unity of the people is only possible as an organization, that is, as a legal order. That is why Koigen occasionally asks, "Maybe the concepts of people and law are even identical?" Koigen, *Die Kultur der Demokratie,* 7.

21. See my *Allgemeine Staatslehre,* 149 ff.

22. *Also sprach Zarathustra,* pt. I.

23. See my *Allgemeine Staatslehre,* 159 ff.

24. See Boris Mirkine-Guetzévich, "Die Rationalisierung der Macht im neuen Verfassungsrecht," *Zeitschrift für öffentliches Recht* 8, no. 2 (1920): 259 ff.

25. Given this thoroughly *collectivizing* tendency of *parties,* in which the individual disappears even more than within the *state* as a whole, whose order grants him subjective rights and thus a position as a *legal subject,* it must be considered a misjudgment of the essence of parties to see them as the result of an "atomistic-individualistic conception of the state," as does Heinrich Triepel, in his *Die Staatsverfassung und die politischen Parteien* (Berlin: Liebmann, 1927), 31. *Individualism* is of course *against* parties. So, for example, Rousseau, as Triepel himself is forced to admit. Triepel, *Die Staatsverfassung,* 10.

26. A typical representative of this dogma is Triepel, whose work, cited above, essentially presents this view. "How," he says, "could the legal order make formation of the will of the state formally dependent upon the will of organizations in society which, in their existence, extent, and character, represent the most unpredictable of all mass contexts, which suddenly emerge and disappear, or change their principles, which sometimes after a few decades retain none of their basic elements but their names, which in certain states are formed according to completely incommensurable, at times politically entirely peripheral principles. . . ." Even with the best will in the world, we cannot claim that this characterization of political parties corresponds with actual conditions in the great democracies, such as, for example, the United States and England, with their relatively solid entities—there the Dem-

ocratic and Republican parties, here the Conservative, Liberal, and Labour parties. Triepel himself says that here "the party system has *become rigid* in a two-party system." But neither does the picture Triepel paints match the realities in Germany and Austria, nor even in France. His description of the parties continues: "which are based by nature on self-interest and thus naturally resist inclusion in an organic state community, which do not even always accept the state as such, whose main activity consists in fighting one another." We will return to "self-interest" as the basis of parties in another context. Here let us remark only that if the parties' "self-interest" makes them unsuited for inclusion in a state community, it is not so much the existence of the party as that of the state that appears problematic; for the nature of the *human being* whose community this state wishes to be is most likely not less, and in fact apparently far more, "self-interested." But the self-interest of the parties can arise only from the human beings who form them. There are hardly likely to be "parties" that negate the state as such. *Organized in a party,* anarchism aims *in reality,* like all non-conservative parties, if one leaves aside its *ideology,* to alter the state order. Triepel concludes: "[I]n general, the idea of the party state contains a contradiction that is difficult to resolve." He describes as the predominant opinion in Europe— and one may take this as the form in which Triepel expresses his *own*—that the modern party is "the symptom of a sickness," a "decline" (p. 29). This is thus essentially the same view that, in Triepel's own words, was held by the "German citizen of the Biedermeier period." They "viewed the parties as a threat to peace in the state; they were not averse to seeing the parties as a moral aberration" (p. 10). This was not so much a result of the fact that the citizens of the time—as Triepel believes—were "not democrats, but liberal men" (the liberals of that period were also democrats) but because the ideology of the monarchy, created not least by state law scholarship, had had an effect upon these "citizens of the Biedermeier period"!

27. If one, to defend a political postulate, wishes to deduce *from the essence* of the state or the legal order of the state that the political parties are incompatible with them, one must of course come to a contradiction with reality—not only with the social process, but with positive law and the given state. Triepel poses himself the question—which he calls a "fateful question"—"whether the modern state, and especially the German, has taken on the nature of a *party* state . . . , that is, a state which has built the political parties so firmly into its organization that the state's will and actions in important matters are always based upon the wills and actions of party communities" (p. 7). The question is aimed at *reality*—whether in a sociological or a legal sense; but the answer is aimed at a *value,* a political value that does not correspond with reality. For when Triepel shows that state and party are in essential contrast, he hopes to prove that the modern state is *not* a party state, because such a state, according to Triepel's doctrine of the essences of the state and the party, *cannot exist at all!* "In the sphere of legislation and government, in the area of state 'integration,' which is in the end what we are interested in, the party is an extra-constitutional phenomenon; its decisions, seen from the standpoint of law, are nonbinding and irrelevant expressions of a *social body alien* to the state organism. Thus, when it is said that the modern state is 'based upon' the parties, this is a legally untenable statement" (pp. 24, 25). But Triepel himself is forced to admit that, "under the pressure of circumstance," the initial anti-party attitude of the legal order of the state—the legal order of the monarchic state—has changed (pp. 15–16), and he himself lists

an impressive wealth of provisions of positive law in which the political parties are constituted as factors in forming the will of the state—particularly in the electoral process. It cannot seriously be maintained that this development could not go further. That some of its manifestations are "peculiar" and "grotesque" (p. 22) is a subjective value judgment. It cannot change the reality of positive law. So what might be the sense of Triepel's categorical statement that the parties are an "extra-constitutional phenomenon"? Especially since he admits that, with regard to the efficacy of the party system, actual conditions have progressed much more than the legal order expresses, that these manifestations are "not arbitrary or accidental," but the result of an "entirely natural process" (p. 27)—which, however, does not prevent him later from calling them again "symptoms of illness" and "degenerations." He even says, "we would be hiding our heads in the sand if we were to deny that the reality of political life does in all ways *not* conform to the picture painted by positive law. In truth and deed, it is after all the political parties at whose mercy the government of the state is" (p. 26). And he finally admits "that here (in Germany) too, the party state has become a fact" (p. 27). The party state, which is, according to Triepel, a "contradiction" in terms? In regard to which he says that it is a "legally untenable statement" to declare that the state is based on the parties, which he dismisses as "extra-constitutional" phenomena, as legally nonexistent (pp. 24, 25)? Has Germany perhaps ceased to be a "state," have the parties ceased to be parties, because Germany *is* a party state?

Triepel has at times accused my Pure Theory of Law of formalism, and has offered instead a theory of the law of the state that is "directed more toward real life," that attempts to "relate the norms of constitutional law as closely as possible to the political forces that create and develop them, and which are in turn mastered by state law" (Heinrich Triepel, "Staatsrecht und Politik: Rede beim Antritte des Rektorats der Friedrich-Wilhelms-Universität zu Berlin am 15. Oktober 1926," in Heinrich Triepel, ed., *Beiträge zum ausländischen öffentlichen Recht und Völkerrecht,* vol. 1 [Berlin and Leipzig: de Gruyter, 1926], 17, 18). I fear that Triepel's theory of the law of the state—at least with regard to the problem of political parties—is stuck far more deeply in a formalism detached from real life than the Pure Theory of Law. For the latter tries only to be a theory of *positive law,* and would certainly continue to accept its validity if it took on a content that the theorist considered harmful. This is precisely the reason the Pure Theory of Law is careful with its "purity"; it would rather be accused of formalism—incidentally, an accusation entirely undeserved and *not justified by Triepel*—than of directing itself only toward a "real life" it finds politically sympathetic, and relating the norms of the law of the state as closely as possible only to those "political forces" that it finds subjectively valuable.

But that is the typical method of traditional scholarship on the law of the state! It deduces from the essence or concept of the state that which it finds politically desirable, and proves that those things it politically rejects contradict the essence or concept of the state. Is *that* the true meaning of "conceptual jurisprudence" [*Begriffsjurisprudenz*]? Those employing such methods must understandably oppose the separation of constitutional law and politics; but they should not be surprised if political opponents use them to prove exactly the opposite.

28. Triepel, who rejects political parties as a constitutive element of the state because they are based on "self-interest," says that "state-instituted, self-administered professional bodies" could be considered as a fundament of the state on condition

that "they rest on such great simplicity and such complete *equality of interests* of their members that there were no conflicts in their ranks that could be used by the political parties to invade them" (p. 30). That the parties rest upon "self-interest" means only that they are communities of *interest*. The corporative groups thus represent nothing *different* from the political parties; for they are also merely communities of interest. They will be equal to face the political parties—that is the point of Triepel's depiction—only if the *community of interest* that they represent becomes more rigid.

If one rejects the party state—and this means, in reality, *modern democracy*—so fundamentally, one has a duty, as a scholar of the law of the state of Triepel's stature, to say what one wishes to place in its stead. And he does. "The atomistic-individualistic conception of the state" that Triepel erroneously takes for the root of the party system, must be "given up, and replaced by an organic one." What should the essence of this "organic one" consist of? The change is said to occur only slowly. But the party state's days are numbered. Other community-forming forces are already at work. "These will gradually, in a natural development"—but according to Triepel, the party state also arose through an "entirely natural process"—"lead to a new organization of the people, forming a lively 'unity in diversity' out of a soulless mass." The idea that the people in a democracy—Triepel speaks only of a party state—represents a "soulless mass" does nothing to explain how we should imagine the "organic" in the state of the future; "unity in diversity" is most likely only another word that means just as little. Triepel says, "Many will call such predictions a romantic illusion." That need not be feared, for this "prediction" contains absolutely nothing. Thus, based on what he has revealed so far of the new state-to-be, with which his sympathies obviously lie, it is difficult to understand his assurance that the forces at work are "not phantoms or figures from a fairy tale, but very corporeal beings about to grow out of the mechanized society of the present into organic forms." That the democratic society is "mechanized" is still not a response to the question of how the "organic" state will look. We learn no more than that it will be an "organism": "If we succeed in harnessing the forces of a personally and territorially richly organized new self-government of an economic and intellectual type"—"self-government" is quite a democratic institution—"struggling with elementary power from the bosom of the people, and press it into serving the state, which will not be destroyed, but held together by them, that is, the state will not be dismantled, but on the contrary built up from below; then it will become a true organism, 'where everything weaves together into a whole, each acting and living in the other'." At the end, Triepel expresses the wish that "a happy race may see with its own eyes what we today can only imagine in our spirit as a beautiful image of the future" (p. 31). May he excuse me, but behind his words there is—aside from his aversion to democracy—*nothing* to be seen. But the document is entirely characteristic of the "organic" view of the state that opposes the democratic conception.

29. This was demonstrated by Robert Michels in his *Zur Soziologie des Parteiwesens*, 2nd ed. (Leipzig: Klinkhardt, 1911).

30. Michels, *Zur Soziologie des Parteiwesens*, bk. III, chap. 4.

31. On the following, see my *Das Problem des Parlamentarismus* (Vienna and Leipzig: Braunmüller, 1926) and the literature cited therein.

32. On the fiction of representation, see my *Allgemeine Staatslehre*, 310 ff.

33. See my *Hauptprobleme der Staatsrechtslehre,* 2nd ed. (Tübingen: Mohr, 1923), 97 ff., and *Allgemeine Staatslehre,* 65 ff.

34. See Adolf Merkl, *Allgemeines Verwaltungsrecht* (Vienna and Berlin: Springer, 1927), 85, 157 ff.

35. Ultimately, all efforts aiming at an organization of the state by estates, or at a dictatorship, amount merely to such a *reform of parliamentarism,* however much their programs may postulate its destruction. In connection with a remark by Karl Marx— that the Paris Commune of 1871 was supposed to be not a parliamentary but rather a working body, and that the universal right to vote, instead of deciding once every three or six years which member of the ruling class would reprimand or *trample* [*ver- oder zertreten*] the people in parliament, should rather enable the people in inter- vening directly in the administration (Karl Marx, *Bürgerkrieg in Frankreich,* 3rd ed. [Berlin: Expedition des "Vorwärts," 1891], 47)—Lenin demanded the *elimination of parliamentarism* in his writings that are fundamental to neocommunist theory (Vladimir Ilyich Lenin, *Staat und Revolution: Die Lehre des Marxismus vom Staat und die Aufgaben des Proletariats in der Revolution* [Berlin and Wilmersdorf: Verlag die Aktion, 1918], 40 ff.). He believed that with this he had hit upon true democracy, yet he had not even hit upon parliamentarism. The system of representation established by the Bolsheviks in the constitution of Soviet Russia—for practical reasons they neither could nor would eliminate representation entirely—not only did not overcome de- mocracy, but returned to it instead. The short duration of mandates, the possibility of recalling at any time those deputized by the people to the various soviets, the com- plete dependency on the voters, the intimate contact with the primary material of the people's will—this is the most genuine democracy. The demand for constant and vi- tal connection between the representatives and their voters assumes that the latter will stay together to exercise effective control over their delegates. Periodic assem- blies of voters cannot achieve this goal. Here, however, the single economic enter- prise, the factory, the workshop, the regiment, become electoral bodies in which the voters assemble daily in closest community because they assemble in work units, when every single enterprise votes for the local soviet, the local soviets for the pro- vincial soviets, and these for the highest parliament—the all-Russian Congress of Workers', Peasants', and Soldiers' Councils—which then assigns its legislative and executive functions to a central executive committee consisting of two hundred members. This not only presents the possibility of a *permanent* people's will but also provides the best possible guarantee that the people's will is formed not accord- ing to the coincidences happening within an assembly of voters, but through an in- trinsic principle that becomes evident—if at all—in the ongoing, intimate contact that the community formed within an enterprise inculcates. The fact that in the single enterprise the workers participate in management, or take over the manage- ment themselves, signifies nothing other than the *democratization of the economy.* Its feasibility or expediency is not dealt with here. It should simply be emphasized that with this demand socialism is merely bringing to bear a democratic principle of organization.

The democratic thrust of the organization of voters in enterprises, so characteris- tic of the Soviet constitution, may not, as the history of the Soviet constitution teaches, have been intentional from the start. But most social institutions attain a meaning in the course of their development other than that originally connected with them.

Furthermore, this principle of organization is in no way consistently realized, nor can it be. Even if only active workers are eligible to vote—as is the case in the Soviet constitution—there are, after all, numerous workers who are not employed in enterprises: intellectual workers, artisans, and especially small farmers. Thus the constitution of soviets must, on the one hand, bring into play other organizations, such as unions, as a supplement, and abandon enterprises as the organizational unit for voters in agriculture. Here, a purely territorial unit—the village—is the basis of the electoral process. Manifold disadvantages naturally arise from this mixing of systems of organization, which will not be considered further here. Nor the more important question whether the politicization of economic production connected with use of the enterprise as a permanent electoral body might not pose a danger to production. The experience of Russia confirms this fear only too well. Yet, this very shortcoming is especially characteristic of direct democracy, which was indeed only possible in ancient city-states because the classes of those eligible to participate in politics and of those actually doing economic work, namely, the slaves, were fundamentally separate.

Given the practical unfeasibility of direct democracy in economically and culturally advanced large states, efforts to bring the people's will into the closest, most constant relationship possible with the inevitable popular representatives, and to get at least an approximation of immediacy, lead not to the elimination or even reduction, but rather to the reverse: to an unsuspected *hypertrophy of parliamentarism.* Russia's soviet constitution, set in conscious, intentional opposition to the representative democracy of the bourgeoisie, demonstrates this clearly. In place of a single parliament arising from general popular election, there emerges a whole pyramid of countless parliaments, which are called "soviets" or councils but are simply representative bodies. Hand in hand with this extension of parliamentarism goes its intensification. From mere "gossip mills" the parliaments ought, in the spirit of neocommunism, to become actual working bodies. This means, however, that they ought not to be limited to passing laws or establishing general norms and universal principles but should take on the tasks of the executive and bring the process of making law to the final stage of concretization, to the individual act of state, to the particular contract. To this tendency can also be traced the fact that more narrowly defined local and special parliaments radiate out from the supreme central parliament into its territorially and substantively detailed spheres of action, down into the single enterprise. This is nothing other than an attempt to *democratize administration* as well as legislation. The bureaucratically—that is, autocratically—appointed civil servant, empowered to impose his will with binding force upon the subject within the occasionally quite broad scope of the law, is replaced by the subject he formerly administered. The object of administration becomes its subject—not directly, but through elected representatives. Democratization of the executive starts with parliamentarization. Compare my *Sozialismus und Staat: Eine Untersuchung der politischen Theorie des Marxismus,* 2nd ed. (Leipzig: Hirschfeld, 1923).

Fascism, too, began with a passionate struggle against democracy and parliamentarism. Today, it refers to its *plebiscitary,* that is, apparently, direct and radical—*democratic*—character and has so far by no means eliminated parliament, but has changed the electoral process to ensure the fascist party a majority in parliament. On this, see Robert Michels, *Sozialismus und Faszismus in Italien* (Leipzig: Buske,

1925), 298 ff. On p. 301, he points out that fascism's anti-parliamentary current is based in Vilfredo Pareto, whose "political testament" ("Testamento politico: Pochi punti d'un futuro ordinamento costituzionale," in *Giornale Economico* 1, no. 18 [1940]), states that "for government, the *concurrence* of the masses is necessary, but not their *participation*. The base in a parliamentary majority is insufficient, as every majority is vulnerable to the danger of fragmentation and defection. Nor is it advisable to govern with naked force. The basis of government must be rooted not only in power but in the approval of public opinion; for this purpose, parliament and referendum generally serve a quite useful function. Therefore, even Pareto is not entirely of a mind to support the elimination of parliament. Because the institution of the popular representative body happens to exist, he believes it should be retained. The task of the statesman is entirely limited to finding ways and means of preventing the dangers of parliamentarism to the best of his ability." What, however, are the means that Pareto suggests? *Referendum* and *freedom of the press*. These are radical democratic elements; thus, this anti-democratic, anti-parliamentary theory, with its aristocratic bearing, ends up, once it must make practical political suggestions, at precisely the same point as the theory it opposes. And when Pareto—in Michels's characterization, p. 302—states, "popular rule is not worth much, but it is always worth more than the rule of the popular *representative body;* the issue must therefore be one of leaving parliamentarism as a decorative element in order to spare the democratic ideologies that are alive among the people, but at the same time of rendering it harmless," this is not Machiavellian—as Michels believes—but simply disingenuous, for this political theory knows no better form of state than parliamentarism limited by referendum. That this form of state is felt to be an *evil*, though relatively the lesser, apparently corresponds to the thoroughly *liberal* basic attitude typical of Pareto.

36. See my *Allgemeine Staatslehre*, 154 ff.

37. See Max Adler, *Die Staatsauffassung des Marxismus* (Vienna: Brand, 1922), 116 ff., and my *Sozialismus und Staat*, 123 ff.

38. Otto Bauer, *Die österreichische Revolution* (Vienna: Wiener Volksbuchhandlung, 1923), 16. See also my review of this work in *Kampf* (1924): 50, and Otto Bauer's response titled "Das Gleichgewicht der Klassenkräfte," 57 ff.; also Max Adler, *Politische oder soziale Demokratie* (Berlin: E. Laub'sche Verlagsbuchhandlung, 1926), 112 ff.

39. See above, note 38.

40. The connection between a *metaphysical* world view and a belief in *autocracy* can be traced easily in the history of ideas. In his excellent work "Demokratie und Weltanschauung," *Zeitschrift für öffentliches Recht* 2 (1920): 701 ff., Adolf Menzel has already shown how, in ancient philosophy, all renowned metaphysicians advocated autocratic policies—for example, Heraclitus and Plato (who in this regard must be considered not so much the idealist as the metaphysicist, which need not coincide); while the Sophists linked the struggle for democracy with their natural-philosophy empiricism and relativism. Aristotle maintained a middle ground between the two in both epistemological and ethical directions. Medieval scholasticism's colossal system of metaphysical doctrine cannot be systemically separated from its autocratic politics. For if the organization of human society is conceived as a *universal monarchy,* with the emperor or the pope at its head, this happens entirely because this organization is constructed as an analogy to *divine* world rule. See my *Die Staatslehre des*

Dante Alighieri (Vienna and Leipzig: Deuticke, 1905). *Spinoza,* whose pantheism must be seen as a turn from metaphysics to empirical cognition of nature, is a democrat; the metaphysician Leibniz, with his preestablished, God-given harmony, is, consistently, in favor of autocracy.

Kant takes a unique position. His system is usually termed "idealism," and *opposed* to positivism. But this is certainly incorrect. Precisely Kant's idealism is, by virtue of its thoroughly *critical* character, itself positivist. Transcendental philosophy can be understood correctly only as an epistemology. Thought through to its logical conclusion, it must lead, also in the field of values, to a rejection of all metaphysical absolutes, to a relativist position. As much as the anti-metaphysical, and thus *positivist,* character of Kant's natural philosophy is emphasized, it is traditional to place Kant's ethics and political reasoning in sharpest contrast to a relativist-skeptical philosophy; and this view can undoubtedly be supported by Kant's own words. Kant's ethical-political system is entirely metaphysically oriented, and his practical philosophy, with its conservative-monarchic theory of law and the state, is thus directed entirely to absolute values. (On this, see my "Die philosophischen Grundlagen der Naturrechtslehre und des Rechtspositivismus," *Vorträge der Kant-Gesellschaft,* no. 31 (Berlin-Charlottenburg: Heise, 1928): 75 f.)

His critical system of pure reason, however, makes cognition an eternal, never-completed process, relegating truth to infinity, and thus declaring it essentially as unreachable, as does skepticism. As cognition can never entirely seize hold of its *object,* in Kantian philosophy the question of the object of cognition is replaced by the question of the *method* of cognition; the two questions are in fact made practically identical. Kantianism has been attacked for this *methodologism,* this preference for questions regarding method. Are there not obvious parallels to a political conception that, instead of asking for the right content of the social order, poses the question about the *way,* the *method* of creating this order?

2. HUGO PREUSS

1. Hugo Preuss, "Volkstaat oder verkehrter Obrigkeitsstaat?" *Berliner Tageblatt* (14 November 1918), in Hugo Preuss, *Staat, Recht und Freiheit* (Tübingen: Mohr, 1926), 365 ff.

2. Hartmut Pogge von Strandmann, "The Liberal Power Monopoly in the Cities of Imperial Germany," in Larry E. Jones and James Retallack, eds., *Elections, Mass Politics and Social Change in Modern Germany* (Cambridge: Cambridge University Press, 1992), 93 ff.; on Preuss in particular, Celia Applegate, "Democracy or Reaction? The Political Implications of Localist Ideas in Wilhelmine and Weimar Germany," in Jones and Retallack, eds., *Elections, Mass Politics and Social Change,* 253 ff.

3. Sobei Mogi, *Otto von Gierke: His Political Teaching and Jurisprudence* (London: P. F. King & Son, 1932), gives a good English introduction to Gierke's legal thinking.

4. Christoph Schönberger, *Das Parlament im Anstaltsstaat: Zur Theorie parlamentarischer Repräsentation in der Staatsrechtslehre des Kaiserreichs (1871–1918)* (Frankfurt am Main: Klostermann, 1997), 165 ff. On Laband's constitutional thinking in general, see the excellent account by Peter C. Caldwell, *Popular Sovereignty and the Crisis of German Constitutional Law: The Theory and Practice of Weimar Constitutionalism* (Durham, N.C., and London: Duke University Press, 1997), 13 ff.

5. Hugo Preuss, "Verwaltung," in David Sarason, ed., *Das Jahr 1913: Ein Gesamtbild der Kulturentwicklung* (Leipzig and Berlin: Teubner, 1913), 120.

6. See Ernest Hamburger, "Hugo Preuss: Scholar and Statesman," Leo Baeck Institute, *Yearbook* 20 (1975): 193 ff.; Günther Gillessen, "Hugo Preuss: Studien zur Ideen- und Verfassungsgeschichte der Weimarer Republik" (Dissertation, University of Freiburg, 1955), 129 ff.

7. See Dietrich Orlow, *Weimar Prussia 1918–1925: The Unlikely Rock of Democracy* (Pittsburgh: University of Pittsburgh Press, 1986); Dietrich Orlow, *Weimar Prussia 1925–1933: The Illusion of Strength* (Pittsburgh: University of Pittsburgh Press, 1991); Horst Möller,*Parlamentarismus in Preußen 1919–1932* (Düsseldorf: Droste, 1985).

8. Hugo Preuss, "Denkschrift zum Entwurf des allgemeinen Teils der Reichsverfassung vom 3. Januar 1919," in Preuss, *Staat, Recht und Freiheit*, 387 ff.

9. Edmond Vermeil, *La Constitution de Weimar et le principe de la democratie allemande* (Paris: Librairie Istra, 1923), 303 ff., 347 f.; Horst Möller, "Parlamentarismus-Diskussion in der Weimarer Republik: Die Frage des 'besonderen' Weges zum parlamentarischen Regierungssystem," in Manfred Funke et al., eds., *Demokratie und Diktatur: Geist und Gestalt politischer Herrschaft in Deutschland und Europa. Festschrift Karl Dietrich Bracher* (Düsseldorf: Droste, 1987), 140 ff.

10. See especially Ernst Fraenkel, "Die repräsentative und die plebiszitäre Komponente im demokratischen Verfassungsstaat" (1958), in Ernst Fraenkel, *Deutschland und die westlichen Demokratien,* enlarged ed. (Frankfurt am Main: Suhrkamp, 1991), 194 ff.

11. Hugo Preuss, "Die 'undeutsche' Reichsverfassung," in Preuss, *Staat, Recht und Freiheit,* 473 ff. On the anti-Semitic attacks on Preuss, see Hamburger, *Hugo Preuss. Scholar and Statesman,* 202 ff.; Kurt Töpner, *Gelehrte Politiker und politisierende Gelehrte: Die Revolution von 1918 im Urteil deutscher Hochschullehrer* (Göttingen: Huster-Schmidt, 1970), 212.

12. Hugo Preuss, *Das deutsche Volk und die Politik* (Jena: Diederichs, 1915), 196.

3. GERHARD ANSCHÜTZ

1. Richard Thoma, "Besprechungen," *Zeitschrift für Politik* 7 (1914): 280–86.

2. Georg Meyer and Gerhard Anschütz, *Lehrbuch des deutschen Staatsrechts,* 6th ed. (Leipzig: Duncker & Humblot 1905), 906.

3. Gerhard Anschütz, "Redebeitrag," in *Veröffentlichungen der Vereinigung der Deutschen Staatsrechtslehrer,* vol. 4 (Berlin and Leipzig: de Gruyter, 1928), 74 ff.

4. Gerhard Anschütz, "Redebeitrag," in *Veröffentlichungen der Vereinigung der Deutschen Staatsrechtslehrer,* vol. 3 (Berlin and Leipzig: de Gruyter, 1927), 47 ff.

5. Gerhard Anschütz, "Redebeitrag," in *Veröffentlichungen der Vereinigung der Deutschen Staatsrechtslehrer,* vol. 6 (Berlin and Leipzig: de Gruyter, 1929), 57.

6. Gerhard Anschütz, *Die Verfassung des Deutschen Reichs* (Berlin: Stilke, 1926), 405.

7. On this category and its limited value, see Peter Gay, "The Community of Reason: Conciliators and Critics," in his *Weimar Culture: The Outsider as Insider* (New York and Evanston: Harper & Row, 1968), 23 ff.

8. Thomas Mann, *Von deutscher Republik: Gerhard Hauptmann zum sechzigsten Geburtstag* (Berlin: Fischer, 1923), 1.

4. RICHARD THOMA

1. Biographical information is derived from the single most important secondary work on Thoma, Hans-Dieter Rath, *Positivismus und Demokratie: Richard Thoma, 1874–1957* (Berlin: Duncker & Humblot, 1981), 19–31.

2. See the recollections of Ottmar Bühler in "Finanzgewalt im Wandel der Verfassungen," in *Festschrift für Richard Thoma zum 75. Geburtstag am 19. Dezember 1949* (Tübingen: Mohr, 1950), 2.

3. *Jahrbuch des öffentlichen Rechts der Gegenwart* 4, ed. Robert Piloty (Tübingen: Mohr, 1910), 196–218.

4. Thoma, "Rechtsstaatsidee und Verwaltungsrechtswissenschaft," 199.

5. Long before National Socialism ("Nazism") as a movement came into being, the leading German progressive Friedrich Naumann had formed the "National Social" reform party. Similarly, the reformist Social Democrat Hermann Heller proclaimed the need to combine "nationalism" and "socialism" as part of an anti-fascist republicanism in the Weimar Republic. Thoma in no way relied on racial thinking in his formulations, concentrating instead on the "Emanzipation des vierten Standes" and the achievement of "social equality." See Thoma, "Rechtsstaatsidee und Verwaltungsrechtswissenschaft," 201.

6. Thoma, "Rechtsstaatsidee und Verwaltungsrechtswissenschaft," 204; summary of entire position, 214. See also the formalist critique of the Labandian tradition in state law, Richard Thoma, "Der Vorbehalt des Gesetzes im preußischen Verfassungsrecht," in *Festschrift für Otto Mayer* (Tübingen: Mohr, 1916), 167–221.

7. Thoma, "Der Vorbehalt des Gesetzes," 205–206.

8. Thoma, "Der Vorbehalt des Gesetzes," 206.

9. Herbert Döring, *Der Weimarer Kreis: Studien zum politischen Bewußtsein verfassungstreuer Hochschullehrer in der Weimarer Republik* (Meisenheim am Glan: Anton Hain, 1975), esp. 158–61, 187, 222–23.

10. Hermann Mosler, "Richard Thoma zum Gedächtnis," *Die öffentliche Verwaltung* 10 (1957): 826.

11. See especially Carl Schmitt, *The Crisis of Parliamentary Democracy* (Munich: Duncker & Humblot, 1926), trans. Ellen Kennedy (Cambridge, Mass.: MIT Press, 1985), 26. Thoma criticized Schmitt's notions on more than one occasion. See especially "The Ideology of Parliamentarianism," in Schmitt, *The Crisis of Parliamentary Democracy*, 77–83, and Richard Thoma, *Das Reich als Demokratie*, in *Handbuch des deutschen Staatsrechts*, 2 vols., ed. Richard Thoma and Gerhard Anschütz (Tübingen: Mohr, 1930–32), 1:186–200 (above, pages 157–70).

12. By the mid-1920s, Thoma had already proposed reforms to the system of proportional representation, including the two-ballot system allowing for both party and local candidate to receive separate votes: Richard Thoma, "Die Reform des Reichstags," *Germania* (morning edition), 30 April and 1 May 1925, cited in Mosler, "Richard Thoma zum Gedächtnis," 828.

13. The positivist position on Article 76 occasioned a long-running debate

on the limits to constitutional change that continues up to the present day. For a summary of the Weimar debate with the most important literature, see Ernst Rudolf Huber, *Deutsche Verfassungsgeschichte seit 1789,* vol. 8, *Die Weimarer Verfassung* (Stuttgart: Kohlhammer, 1981), 418–21.

14. Richard Thoma, "Das richterliche Prüfungsrecht," *Archiv des öffentlichen Rechts* 43 (1922): 270.

15. Thoma, "Das richterliche Prüfungsrecht," 274. "Constitutions" referred to those of the Länder as well as the Reich Constitution.

16. "Grundbegriffe und Grundsätze," *Handbuch des deutschen Staatsrechts* (Tübingen: Mohr, 1932), 2:153; see also Rath, *Positivismus und Demokratie,* 147 ff. Review by ordinary courts is different from review by a constitutional court, of course. Thoma came to favor the latter, within the strictly formal limits of the Constitutional Court designed by Kelsen for the Austrian constitutional system. See Richard Thoma, "Grundrechte und Polizeigewalt," in *Festgabe zur Feier des fünfzigjährigen Bestehens des Preußischen Oberverwaltungsgerichts 1875—20. November 1925,* ed. Heinrich Triepel (Berlin: Heymann, 1925), 222–23.

17. See Dieter Grimm's critique "Verfassungserfüllung-Verfassungsbewahrung-Verfassungsauflösung. Positionen der Staatsrechtslehre in der Krise der Weimarer Republik," in *Die deutsche Staatskrise, 1930–1933,* ed. Heinrich A. Winkler (Munich: Oldenbourg, 1993), 183–99.

18. Richard Thoma, *Die Staatsfinanzen in der Volksgemeinwirtschaft: Ein Beitrag zur Gestaltung des deutschen Sozialismus* (Tübingen: Mohr, 1937).

19. See, for example, Thoma, *Die Staatsfinanzen in der Volksgemeinwirtschaft,* 2 (*"rettende Tat"*), 6 (*"mit intuitiver Klarheit"*).

20. See, for example, the pessimistic formulations in Richard Thoma, *Über Wesen und Erscheinungsformen der modernen Demokratie* (Bonn: Dümmler, 1948), 29–30.

21. Richard Thoma, "Über die Grundrechte im Grundgesetz für die Bundesrepublik Deutschland," in *Recht, Staat, Wirtschaft,* vol. 3, ed. Hermann Wandersleb (Düsseldorf: Schwann, 1951), 9–19.

22. See esp. Richard Thoma, "Ungleichheit und Gleichheit im Bonner Grundgesetze," *Deutsches Verwaltungsblatt* 66 (1 Aug. 1951): 457–59, which repeats virtually verbatim the arguments surrounding Article 109 in the Weimar Constitution.

23. As a consequence, Reich and Länder legislation were, and are, *obligated*—according to Article 1, paragraph 2, with its concept of the "people" that reappears in Articles 21, 41, and 73—to grant equal, direct and secret suffrage to *"all* men and women of the German Reich" (Art. 17) in cases not specifically regulated in the Constitution (presidential election, popular referendum and popular initiative in the Reich, the Länder, and, through Article 17, paragraph 2, municipalities). The same holds for the structure of the Prussian provincial constitution, since otherwise an element would be inserted into the frame of the Reich (Art. 63) and Prussian state (through the rights of the State Council) whose part in "state power" would not emanate from the "people," i.e., in the sense of Article 1, paragraph 2.

24. Hermann Heller, *Die Souveränität* (Berlin: de Gruyter, 1927), reprinted in *Gesammelte Schriften,* ed. Martin Drath et al. (Leiden: A. W. Sijthoff, 1971), 2:95–96. As soon as one abandons the strict—and only then correct—terminology that applies the word sovereignty only to states, one sinks into the caprice and confusion of linguistic usage. In this case, one could, according to one's point of view, designate

as sovereign the "people" just as well as the Reichstag ("parliamentary sovereignty" is a concept familiar to the English theory of the law of the state) or, with Carl Schmitt, the organ that has jurisdiction over the state of emergency. Carl Schmitt, *Die Diktatur,* 2nd ed. (Berlin: Duncker & Humblot, 1928). Gerhard Leibholz asserts that the concepts of state sovereignty and people's sovereignty are synonymous. (Gerhard Leibholz, *Das Wesen der Repräsentation unter besonderer Berücksichtigung des Repräsentativsystems: Ein Beitrag zur allgemeinen Staats- und Verfassungslehre* [Berlin and Leipzig: de Gruyter, 1929], 131.) However, since he has previously explained that by "people" one must understand a "politically ideal unity" that is identical with the state, that is a mere tautology. Naturally, it is always linguistically permissible to name the people of a sovereign democracy a sovereign people, the legislator of a sovereign state a sovereign legislator, the National Assembly a "highest sovereign."

25. "Statistik der Vermögensteuer-Veranlagung," published by the Reich Office of Statistics, 1929. On what follows, see Walther Kamm, *Abgeordnetenberufe und Parlament: Die berufliche Gliederung der Abgeordneten in den deutschen Parlamenten im 20. Jahrhundert* (Karlsruhe: G. Braun, 1927).

26. "When two people say 'democracy,' it is most likely that they mean something quite different." Thomas Mann, *Betrachungen eines Unpolitischen* (Berlin: S. Fischer, 1918) [trans. by Walter D. Morris as *Reflections of a Nonpolitical Man* (New York: Ungar, 1987), 205—EDS.]. Widespread usage, following Aristotle, designates as democratic only the institutions of a radical and direct democracy. Thus, Wilhelm Hasbach, in his two richly detailed works, *Der moderne Demokratie: Eine politische Betrachtung* (Jena: Fischer, 1921), and *Die parlamentarische Kabinettsregierung. Eine politische Beschreibung* (Stuttgart: Deutsche Verlags-Anstalt, 1919), tends to qualify as truly democratic only foolish institutions (election of judges, imperative mandate, filling all offices with the supporters of the victorious party, and so on). On this, see my extensive critique in *Archiv des öffentliches Rechts* 40 (1921): 228–42. There are identical tendencies in, for example, Carl Schmitt, and similar terminology in Kelsen and others. See the following note.

27. On the following see my inquiry: "Der Begriff der modernen Demokratie in seinem Verhältnis zum Staatsbegriff: Prolegomena zu einer Analyse des demokratischen Staates der Gegenwart," in *Hauptprobleme der Soziologie: Erinnerungsgabe für Max Weber,* ed. Melchior Palyi (Munich and Leipzig: Duncker & Humblot, 1923), 37–64. (Also notable: Karl Landauer, "Die Wege zur Eroberung des demokratischen Staates durch die Wirtschaftsleiter," in ibid., 111 ff.) Further, see my essay, "Zur Ideologie des Parlamentarismus und der Diktatur," *Archiv für Sozialwissenschaft und Sozialpolitik* 53 (Tübingen: Mohr, 1924), 212 ff. [and in Carl Schmitt, *The Crisis of Parliamentary Democracy,* trans. Ellen Kennedy (Cambridge, Mass., and London: MIT Press, 1985), 77–83—EDS.]; and my article "Staat," in *Handwörterbuch der Staatswissenschaften,* 4th ed., vol. 7 (Jena: Fischer, 1926), 724–56. Carl Schmitt, who allows only a specific, radical ideology as democratic, does not give a true portrait of the meaning and content of my conceptual and investigative approach in his remarks directed against me in the foreword to the second edition of his clever but one-sided essay, *Die geistesgeschichtliche Lage des heutigen Parlamentarismus* (Munich: Duncker & Humblot, 1926) [*The Crisis of Parliamentary Democracy,* trans. Ellen Kennedy—EDS.]. See also, based on Schmitt, Werner Becker, "Demokratie und moderner Massenstaat," *Die Schildgenossen* 5 (1925): 459 ff. In Carl Schmitt's *Verfassungslehre*

(Berlin: Duncker & Humblot, 1928), esp. 221–82, the interesting remarks on democracy keep emphasizing that there is only *one* democracy, diametrically opposed to all liberalism, whose essence lies in a series of "identities" (by which is doubtless meant: fictive identifications). A conceptually critical engagement with Schmitt over the history of ideas and politics is as little possible and appropriate here as with the following authors, whose investigations of the concept and essence of democracy I cite without commentary: Friedrich Naumann, *Demokratie und Kaisertum: Ein Handbuch für innere Politik,* 2nd ed. (Berlin: Buchverlag der "Hilfe," 1900), and *Der deutsche Volksstaat: Schriften zur inneren Politik* (Berlin: Fortschritt, 1917); Gustav F. Steffen, *Das Problem der Demokratie* (Jena: Diederichs, 1912); Hugo Preuss, in several of the articles included in *Staat, Recht und Freiheit: Aus 40 Jahren deutscher Politik und Geschichte* (Tübingen: Mohr, 1926); as well as the literature cited therein (ibid., 583–88), and, summarizing, *Reich und Länder: Bruchstücke eines Kommentars zur Verfassung des Deutschen Reiches,* ed. Georg Anschütz (Berlin: Heymann, 1926), 39 ff.; Theodor Heuss, *Die neue Demokratie* (Berlin: Siegesmund, 1919); James Bryce, *Modern Democracies* (London: Macmillan, 1921), 1:23 ff.; Leo Wittmayer, *Die Weimarer Reichsverfassung* (Tübingen: Mohr, 1922), 44 ff.; Hans Kelsen, "Vom Wesen und Wert der Demokratie," *Archiv für Sozialwissenschaft und Sozialpolitik* 47 (1920): 50–85, so-called second edition (greatly changed), *Vom Wesen und Wert der Demokratie* (Tübingen: Mohr, 1929) [above, pages 84–109—EDS.]; Moritz Julius Bonn, *Die Krisis der europäischen Demokratie* (Munich: Meyer & Jensen, 1925) [*The Crisis of European Democracy* (New Haven: Yale University Press, 1925—EDS.]; Reinhold Horneffer, *Hans Kelsens Lehre von der Demokratie: Ein Beitrag zur Kritik der Demokratie* (Erfurt: Stenger, 1926); Max Adler, *Politische oder soziale Demokratie: Ein Beitrag zur sozialistischen Erziehung* (Berlin: Laub, 1926); Edgar Tatarin-Tarnheyden, "Kopfzahldemokratie, organische Demokratie und Oberhausproblem," *Zeitschrift für Politik* 15 (1926): 97–122; Adolf Grabowsky, "Formal- und Realdemokratie," *Zeitschrift für Politik* 15 (1926): 123–25; Ferdinand Tönnies, "Demokratie," in *Verhandlungen des fünften Deutschen Soziologentages* (Tübingen: Mohr, 1927), 12–36; Hans Kelsen, "Demokratie," in ibid., 37–68; Otto Koellreutter, "Demokratie," in *Handwörterbuch der Rechtswissenschaft* (Berlin: de Gruyter, 1927), vol. 2; Heinrich Triepel, *Die Staatsverfassung und die politischen Parteien* (Berlin: Otto Liebmann, 1927); Leo Wittmayer, *Demokratie und Parlamentarismus* (Breslau: Hirt, 1928); Wilhelm Stapel, *Die Fiktionen der Weimarer Verfassung: Versuch einer Unterscheidung der formalen und der funktionalen Demokratie* (Hamburg: Hanseatische Verlagsanstalt, 1928); Arnold Wolfers, "Vorwort," in *Probleme der Demokratie. Erste Reihe: Schriftenreihe der Hochschule für Politik in Berlin und des Instituts für Auswärtige Politik Hamburg* (Berlin-Grunewald: W. Rothschild, 1928), v–ix; Carl Schmitt, "Der Begriff des Politischen," in ibid., 1–34; Hermann Heller, "Politische Demokratie und soziale Homogenität," in ibid., 35–47 [above, pages 256–65—EDS.]; Max Hildebert Boehm, "Volkstum und Demokratie," in ibid., 48–66; Ernst Michel, "Die Demokratie zwischen Gesellschaft und Volksordnung," in ibid., 67–87; Fritz Berber, "Die Dezentralisierung des Britischen Reiches als Problem der demokratischen Selbstverwaltung," in ibid., 88–97; Gertrud Bäumer, *Grundlagen demokratischer Politik* (Karlsruhe: Braun, 1928); Abbott Lawrence Lowell, *La Crise des gouvernements représatifs et parlementaires dans les démocraties modernes* (Paris: Giard, 1928); Ferdinand Tönnies, "Demokratie und Parlamentarismus," in *Soziologische Studien und Kritiken,* vol. 3 (Jena: Fischer, 1929), 40–84; Otto

NOTES TO PAGES 159–164   363

Pfeffer, "Mensch, Volk, Staat," in Arthur Krause, ed., *Wissen ist Macht: Ein Handbuch des Wissens unserer Zeit und der Kulturfortschriffte der Menschheit*, vol. 3: *Technik, Staat, Volkswirtschaft* (Nordhausen: Volkshochschul-Verlag, 1930), 577–610, 604 ff.; and on anti-democratic ideologies, Hermann Heller, *Europe und der Fascismus* (Berlin: de Gruyter, 1929).

28. See Hermann Heller, "Politische Demokratie und soziale Homogenität," in *Probleme der Demokratie*, 1. Reihe, Politische Wissenschaft. Schriftenreihe der Deutschen Hochschule für Politik in Berlin und des Instituts für auswärtige Politik in Hamburg, H. 5 (Berlin: Walter Rothschild, 1928), 35–47, reprinted in Hermann Heller, *Gesammelte Schriften, zweiter Band: Recht, Staat, Macht*, 2nd ed., ed. Christoph Müller (Tübingen: Mohr, 1992), 421–33 [above, pages 256–65—EDS.], on the conditions under which the proletariat, despite the economically based class struggle, can fit into the democracy.

29. Namely, for "the democratic self-organization of the German people as a political unity" (Hugo Preuss). [Hugo Preuss, "Denkschrift zum Entwurf des allgemeinen Teils der Reichsverfassung" (3 January 1919), in Hugo Preuss, *Staat, Recht und Freiheit: Aus 40 Jahren deutscher Politik und Geschichte*, ed. Theodor Heuss (Tübingen: Mohr, 1926), 370—TRANS.].

30. Richard Thoma, "Der Begriff der modernen Demokratie in seinem Verhältnis zum Staatsbegriff," in *Hauptprobleme der Soziologie: Erinnerungsgabe für Max Weber*, ed. Melchior Palyi (Munich and Leipzig: Duncker & Humblot, 1923), 39–41.

31. Gustav Fredrik Steffen, *Das Problem der Demokratie* (Jena: Diederichs, 1919), 101—TRANS.

32. Friedrich Meinecke, "Die Revolution. Ursachen und Tatsachen," *Handbuch des deutschen Staatsrechts* 1 (1930): 95–119—TRANS.

33. Cf. Carl Bilfinger, *Nationale Demokratie als Grundlage der Weimarer Verfassung: Rede bei der Feier der zehnjährigen Wiederkehr des Verfassungstags, gehalten am 24. Juli 1929* (Halle a. d. Saale: Max Niemeyer, 1929), 18.

34. In principle, statutes accepted or confirmed by popular referendum have no heightened validity and can be either superseded or amended by the Reichstag: thus Gerhard Anschütz, *Die Verfassung des Deutschen Reichs vom 11. August 1919*, 14th ed. (Berlin: Stilke, 1933), 385–87, and, agreeing with him, Carl Schmitt, *Verfassungslehre* (Munich and Leipzig: Duncker & Humblot, 1928), 98, and others. The question remains, however, whether the same holds in an unrestricted way for constitutional amendments launched by popular initiative and approved by popular referendum. For a full account, see Erwin Jacobi, "Reichsverfassungsänderung," in *Die Reichsgerichtspraxis im deutschen Rechtsleben: Festgabe der juristischen Fakultäten zum 50. jährigen Bestehen des Reichsgerichts* (Berlin: de Gruyter, 1929), 233–77. Following careful consideration of the discussions in the National Assembly and its committee, Jacobi comes to the conclusion that popular referenda have priority over decisions of the existing Reichstag but that any future Reichstag, following a new election, can amend or supersede statutes approved by the people. I withhold final judgment on this theory, which would interpret the express rule of Article 8 of the Bremen Constitution into the Reich Constitution.

35. See on the following my lecture, "Sinn und Gestaltung des Deutschen Parlamentarismus," in *Recht und Staat im neuen Deutschland*, vol. 1, ed. Bernhard Harms (Berlin: Reimar Hobbing, 1929), 98–126; Graf zu Dohna, "Das Werk von Weimar,"

364 NOTES TO PAGES 167-173

ibid., 68 ff. See also my essay on the legal significance of the basic law in *Die Grundrechte und Grundpflichten der Reichsverfassung*, vol. 1: *Kommentar zum zweiten Teil der Reichsverfassung*, ed. Hans-Carl Nipperdey (Berlin: Reimar Hobbing, 1929), 1 ff.

36. See Rudolf Smend, *Verfassung und Verfassungsrecht* (Munich and Leipzig: Duncker & Humblot, 1928), 108, 158 ff.; Richard Thoma, "Die juristische Bedeutung der grundrechtlichen Sätze der Deutschen Reichsverfassung im allgemeinen," in *Die Grundrechte und Grundpflichten der Reichsverfassung*, vol. 1: *Kommentar zum zweiten Teil der Reichsverfassung*, ed. Hans-Carl Nipperdey (Berlin: Reimar Hobbing, 1929), 9–11. Comprehensive categories of basic rights and rights of freedom are essential not only for the beginnings of modern democracy but also for their contemporary evolutionary level, as follows from the valuable collection of all declarations of basic rights in today's states, edited by Alphons Aulard and Boris Mirkine-Guetzévitch under the title *Les Déclarations des droits de l'homme* (Paris: Payot, 1929).

37. See Thoma, "Begriff der modernen Demokratie," 58 ff.

5. HEINRICH TRIEPEL

1. Heinrich Triepel, "Empfelt es sich, in die Reichsverfassung neue Vorschriften über die Grenzen zwischen Gesetz und Rechtsverordnung Aufzunehmen" [Is it advisable to include new provisions on the boundary between statute and regulation in the Reich Constitution?], in *Verhandlungen des 32. Deutschen Juristentages* (Berlin and Leipzig: Jansen, 1922), 11–35.

2. Heinrich Triepel, "Die Vereinigung der Deutschen Staatsrechtslehrer," *Archiv des öffentlichen Rechts* 43 (Tübingen: Mohr, 1922): 349–53 (349).

3. Ulrich Scheuner, "Die Vereinigung der Deutschen Staatsrechtslehrer in der Weimarer Republik," *Archiv des öffentlichen Rechts* 97 (Tübingen: Mohr, 1972): 349–74.

4. Scheuner, "Die Vereinigung der Deutschen Staatsrechtslehrer," 355.

5. Alexander Hollerbach, "Zu Leben und Werk Heinrich Triepels," *Archiv des öffentlichen Rechts* 91 (Tübingen: Mohr, 1966): 417–41 (424).

6. Heinrich Triepel, "Zweierlei Föderalismus," *Süddeutsche Juristenzeitung Heidelberg* (1947): cols. 150–52.

7. Heinrich Triepel, *Die Reichsaufsicht: Untersuchungen zum Staatsrecht des Deutschen Reiches* (Berlin: Springer, 1917), 169. See also Heinrich Triepel, "Die Kompetenzen des Bundesstaats und die geschriebene Verfassung," in *Staatsrechtliche Abhandlungen: Festgabe für Paul Laband zum 50. Jahrestage der Doktor-Promotion*, ed. Wilhelm von Calker and Fritz Fleiner, vol. 2 (Tübingen: Mohr, 1908), 326 f.

8. Triepel, *Die Reichsaufsicht*, 173.

9. Klaus Rennert, *Die "geisteswissenschaftliche Richtung" in die Staatsrechtslehre der Weimarer Republik: Untersuchungen zu Erich Kaufmann, Günther Holstein und Rudolf Smend*, Schriften zum Öffentlichen Recht 518 (Berlin: Duncker & Humblot, 1987), 57; Hollerbach, "Zu Leben und Werk Heinrich Triepels," 432.

10. Manfred Friedrich, "Der Methoden- und Richtungsstreit," *Archiv des öffentlichen Rechts* 102 (Tübingen: Mohr, 1977): 161–209 (196).

11. Gerhard Anschütz and Richard Thoma, *Handbuch des deutschen Staatsrechts*, vol. 1 (Tübingen: Mohr, 1930), 4; see also Rennert, *Die "geisteswissenschaftliche Richtung" in die Staatsrechtslehre der Weimarer Republik*, 52.

12. Friedrich, "Der Methoden- und Richtungsstreit," 195.

13. Günther Holstein, "Von den Aufgaben und Zielen heutiger Staatsrechtswissenschaft," *Archiv des öffentlichen Rechts* 47 (Tübingen: Mohr, 1926): 1–40 (31).

14. Heinrich Triepel, *Unitarismus und Föderalismus im deutschen Reiche: Eine staatsrechtliche und politische Studie* (Tübingen: Mohr, 1907), 119; see also Heinrich Triepel, "Die Entwürfe zur neuen Reichsverfassung," *Schmollers Jahrbuch für Gesetzgebung, Verwaltung und Volkswirtschaft,* vol. 43 (Munich and Leipzig: Duncker & Humblot, 1919), 64.

15. For example, Heinrich Triepel, *Die Entstehung der konstitutionellen Monarchie* (Leipzig: Seele, 1899), 35; Triepel, *Unitarismus und Föderalismus im Deutschen Reiche,* 125.

16. Heinrich Triepel, "Wesen und Entwicklung der Staatsgerichtsbarkeit," in *Veröffentlichungen der Vereinigung der deutschen Staatsrechtslehrer* 5 (Berlin and Leipzig: de Gruyter, 1929), 2–29 (28).

17. See Triepel, "Die Entwürfe zur neuen Reichsverfassung," 102–105.

18. Heinrich Triepel, *Staatsrecht und Politik: Rede beim Antritte des Rektorats der Friedrich-Wilhelms-Universität zu Berlin am 15. Oktober 1926* (Berlin and Leipzig: de Gruyter, 1927), 40; Triepel made a similar comment on the draft of the Weimar Constitution: see Triepel, "Die Entwürfe zur neuen Reichsverfassung," 55–106 (65).

19. Heinrich Triepel, *Goldbilanzen-Verordnung und Vorzugsaktien: Zur Frage der Rechtsgültigkeit der über sogenannte schuldverschreibungsähnliche Aktien in der Durchführungsbestimmung zur Goldbilanzen-Verordnung enthaltenen Vorschriften. Ein Rechtsgutachten* (Berlin: de Gruyter, 1924), 28.

20. Triepel, "Wesen und Entwicklung der Staatsgerichtsbarkeit," 28.

21. Heinrich Triepel, *Die Staatsverfassung und die politischen Parteien* (Berlin: Liebmann, 1927), 33 ff.

22. Triepel, *Die Staatsverfassung und die politischen Parteien,* 30.

23. Heinrich Triepel, "Nationale Revolution und deutsche Verfassung," *Deutsche Allgemeine Zeitung,* no. 155–56 (2 April 1933).

24. Triepel, "Nationale Revolution und deutsche Verfassung." Triepel expressed similar sentiments in his *Die Staatsverfassung und die politischen Parteien,* 35 ff.

25. Triepel, *Die Staatsverfassung und die politischen Parteien,* 30.

26. Heinrich Triepel, *Die Hegemonie: Ein Buch von führenden Staaten* (Stuttgart: Kohlhammer, 1938).

27. Heinrich Triepel, *Delegation und Mandat im öffentlichen Recht: Eine kritische Studie* (Stuttgart and Berlin: Kohlhammer, 1942).

28. Triepel, *Die Hegemonie,* 14–31.

29. Heinrich Triepel, *Vom Stil des Rechts: Beiträge zu einer Ästhetik des Rechts* (Heidelberg: Schneider, 1947), 123.

6. ERICH KAUFMANN

1. See Helge Wendenburg, *Die Debatte um die Verfassungsgerichtsbarkeit und der Methodenstreit der Staatsrechtslehre in der Weimarer Republik,* Göttinger Rechtswissenschaftliche Studien, vol. 128 (Göttingen: Otto Schwartz, 1984), 146–51; Klaus Rennert, *Die "geisteswissenschaftliche Richtung" in der Staatsrechtslehre der Weimarer Republik: Untersuchungen zu Erich Kaufmann, Günther Holstein und Rudolf Smend,*

Schriften zum Öffentlichen Recht 518 (Berlin: Duncker & Humblot, 1987), passim; D. Stephen Cloyd, "Weimar Republicanism: Political Sociology and Constitutional Law in Weimar Germany" (Ph.D. diss., University of Rochester, 1991), 24–43.

2. Rennert, Die "geisteswissenschaftliche Richtung" in die Staatsrechtslehre der Weimarer Republik, 29–35.

3. Hermann Heller, Hegel und der nationale Machtstaatsgedanke in Deutschland: Ein Beitrag zur politischen Geistesgeschichte (Tübingen: Mohr, 1921), in Gesammelte Schriften, 2nd ed., ed. Christoph Müller (Tübingen: Mohr, 1992), 235–37, quoting Kaufmann. Heller suggested here that Kaufmann was "the only recent writer who [had] truly felt his way into Hegel's thought."

4. Erich Kaufmann, Kritik der neukantischen Rechtsphilosophie (Tübingen: Mohr, 1921), in Erich Kaufmann, Gesammelte Schriften, vol. 3 (Göttingen: Schwarz, 1960), 81.

5. Kaufmann, Kritik der neukantischen Rechtsphilosophie, 240 (Kaufmann's emphasis).

6. Cloyd, Weimar Republicanism, 25, 73–81.

7. Kaufmann, Kritik der neukantischen Rechtsphilosophie, 244.

8. Kaufmann, Kritik der neukantischen Rechtsphilosophie, 244–45.

9. Erich Kaufmann, "Über die konservative Partei und ihre Geschichte," in Schriften der Deutschen Gesellschaft für Politik an der Universität Halle-Wittenberg, no. 2, ed. Heinrich Waentig (Bonn and Leipzig: Deutsche Gesellschaft für Politik an der Universität Halle-Wittenberg, 1922); Kaufmann, Gesammelte Schriften, 3:133–75.

10. Erich Kaufmann, "Vorwort zum Bande 'Rechtsidee und Recht'," in Kaufmann, Gesammelte Schriften, 3:xxviii–xxix.

11. Erich Kaufmann, Die Gleichheit vor dem Gesetz im Sinne des Art. 109 der Reichsverfassung (Berlin and Leipzig: de Gruyter, 1927), in Kaufmann, Gesammelte Schriften, 3:246–65.

12. In his own view, Kaufmann remained within that tendency, Kaufmann, "Vorwort," Gesammelte Schriften, 3:xxxi. Klaus Rennert suggests he moved outside it, in Rennert, Die "geisteswissenschaftliche Richtung" in die Staatsrechtslehre der Weimarer Republik, 64.

13. Kaufmann, Gesammelte Schriften 3:xxxvii, xliii. See also Wendenberg, Die Debatte um die Verfassungsgerichtsbarkeit und der Methodenstreit, 147.

14. Kaufmann, "Vorwort," Gesammelte Schriften, 3:xxix. He and Rudolf Smend made common cause in arguing for such an institutional understanding.

15. Erich Kaufmann, "Vorwort zu Autorität und Freiheit," Gesammelte Schriften, 1:xxiv.

16. Rudolf Smend, "Zu Erich Kaufmanns wissenschaftlichem Werk," in Um Recht und Gerechtigkeit. Festgabe für Erich Kaufmann zu seinem 70. Geburtstage -21. September 1950, ed. Hermann Jahrreiss et al. (Stuttgart and Cologne: Kohlhammer, 1950), 397. Erich Kaufmann, "Was will Oberst Beck?" in Deutsche Zukunft—Wochenzeitung für Politik, Wirtschaft und Kultur (11 March 1934) (unpaginated).

7. RUDOLF SMEND

1. Rudolf Smend, "Integrationslehre," in Evangelisches Staatslexikon, 2nd ed., ed. Hermann Kunst, Roman Herzog, and Wilhelm Schneemelcher (Berlin: Kreuz-Verlag, 1975), 1075, col. 1026.

2. Hans Kelsen, *Der Staat als Integration: Eine prinzipielle Auseinandersetzung* (Vienna: Springer, 1930, reprint Aalen: Scientia Verlag, 1974), 2.

3. Rudolf Smend, *Verfassung und Verfassungsrecht,* in Rudolf Smend, *Staatsrechtliche Abhandlungen und andere Aufsätze,* 2nd ed. (Berlin: Duncker & Humblot, 1968), 125.

4. Smend, *Verfassung und Verfassungsrecht,* 134.

5. Smend, *Verfassung und Verfassungsrecht,* 136.

6. Rudolf Smend, "Integrationslehre," in *Handwörterbuch der Sozialwissenschaften,* vol. 5 (Stuttgart: G. Fischer, 1956), 299–302, reprinted in Smend, *Staatsrechtliche Abhandlungen,* 481.

7. Smend, *Verfassung und Verfassungsrecht,* 189.

8. Smend, *Verfassung und Verfassungsrecht,* 190.

9. Huber criticized the integration doctrine's dynamization of the state and constitution as inconsistent with the necessity of firm structures of command in the new system. Ernst Rudolf Huber, *Wesen und Inhalt der politischen Verfassung* (Hamburg: Hanseatische Verlaganstalt, 1935), 23 ff. He further criticized Smend's individualistic approach and his representation of integration as a purely spiritual phenomenon.

10. See Günther Holstein's report on the meeting of the *Vereinigung der deutschen Staatsrechtslehrer* [Association of German Teachers of the Law of the State] of March 1926, *Von Aufgaben und Zielen heutiger Staatsrechtswissenschaft: Zur Tagung der Vereinigung der deutschen Staatsrechtslehrer, Archiv des öffentlichen Rechts,* n.s., vol. 11 (Tübingen: Mohr, 1896), 1 ff.

11. Jellinek's own question of "types" (Georg Jellinek, *Staatslehre,* vol. 1, 3rd ed. [Berlin: O. Häring, 1914], 34 ff.), lacks both strict epistemological justification and fruitful results.

12. Erich Kaufmann, *Kritik der neukantischen Rechtsphilosophie* (Tübingen: Mohr, 1921); this is still, despite unavoidable limitations, the most impressive presentation of this context.

13. Recall the mutually exclusive alternatives of scholarship on causality and scholarship on norms, which can be explained only historically "as a desperate attempt to rescue the world of values from theoretical naturalism and mechanism," Erich R. Jaensch, *Über den Aufbau der Wahrnehmungswelt* (Leipzig: J. A. Barth, 1923), 411 f. Heller rightly protests the Vienna School's ignoring the present state of scholarship, Hermann Heller, *Die Souveränität: Ein Beitrag zur Theorie des Staats- und Völkerrechts* (Berlin: de Gruyter, 1927), 78. See also Alexander Hold-Ferneck, *Der Staat als Übermensch* (Jena: G. Fischer, 1927), 19; Hans Oppenheimer, *Logik der soziologischen Begriffsbildung* (Tübingen: Mohr, 1925), 33.

14. As in Hermann Heller, "Die Crisis der Staatslehre," *Archiv für Sozial-Wissenschaft und Sozial-Politik,* vol. 55 (Tübingen: Mohr, 1926): 310 ff.

15. At another level is the problem of individuality and norm, which Heller, in *Die Souveränität,* quite correctly brings to the fore.

16. See Theodor Litt, *Individuum und Gemeinschaft,* 2nd ed. (Leipzig: Teubner, 1924), 54 ff., 85; 3rd ed. (Leipzig: Teubner, 1926), 46 ff., 142 ff., 174 ff., 187 ff., and passim.

17. Litt, *Individuum und Gemeinschaft,* 3rd ed., passim, especially 246 ff., 258 ff., 292 ff., 360 ff.

18. Litt, passim. See, e.g., Litt, *Individuum und Gemeinschaft,* 3rd ed., 71 ff., 376 f. To this extent, Kelsen is right to see nothing leading from the "windowless monad"

of psychology to the social. Hans Kelsen, *Soziologischer und juristischer Staatsbegriff. Kritische Untersuchung des Verhältnisses von Staat und Recht* (Tübingen: Mohr, 1922), 15.

19. Litt, *Individuum und Gemeinschaft,* 3rd ed., 312 ff., 373 ff. On the intentional limitation in meaning that does not change the structure of reality described, see 214 f., 338 ff.

20. See Litt, *Individuum und Gemeinschaft,* 3rd ed., 10 ff. Particularly important applications: Litt, *Individuum und Gemeinschaft,* 2nd ed., 164 f.; Litt, *Individuum und Gemeinschaft,* 3rd ed., 248 f., 284, 292 ff., 361 ff.

21. See Litt, *Individuum und Gemeinschaft,* 3rd ed., 25 ff., 6. See, in its entirety, the brief summary in Siegfried Marck, *Substanz- und Funktionsbegriff in der Rechtsphilosophie* (Tübingen: Mohr, 1925), 96 ff. The program outlining his theory of the state, 148 ff., is unfortunate.

22. Holstein, *Von Aufgaben und Zielen heutiger Staatsrechtswissenschaft: Zur Tagung der Vereinigung der deutschen Staatsrechtslehrer,* 31.

23. On this, see Marck, *Substanz- und Funktionsbegriff,* 89 ff.

24. Thus to the point, Litt, *Individuum und Gemeinschaft,* 1st ed., 210.

25. Litt, *Individuum und Gemeinschaft,* 3rd ed., 222, 281 ff., 285 ff., 290 ff., 327 ff. Against [Alfred] Vierkandt's "psychophysical construction," see 249 n. 2.

26. Litt, *Individuum und Gemeinschaft,* 3rd ed., 204 f., 227 ff.

27. See also Heller, *Die Souveränität,* 82.

28. Rudolf Smend, "Die politische Gewalt im Verfassungsstaat und das Problem der Staatsform," in *Festgabe der Berliner Juristischen Fakultät für Wilhelm Kahl,* ed. Universität (Berlin Ost) Juristische Falkultät, vol. 3 (Tübingen: Mohr, 1923), 16. The word has not yet become precisely the "fashionable word" Leo Wittmayer accuses it of being in "Schwächen der neuen deutschen Bundesstaatslehre," *Zeitschrift für öffentliches Recht* 3 (Vienna: Deuticke, 1922/23), 530 n. 4, but it is no longer uncommon even in Germany. See, e.g., Hans Kelsen, *Vom Wesen und Wert der Demokratie* (Tübingen: Mohr, 1920), 28 (= *Archiv für Sozial- Wissenschaft und Sozial-Politik,* vol. 47, p. 75); Richard Thoma, *Handwörterbuch der Staatswissenschaften,* 4th ed., vol. 7, ed. Ludwig Elster and Johannes Conrad (Jena: G. Fischer, 1929), 725; Smend, *Individuum und Staat,* 18; and at least occasionally, also Friedrich von Gottl-Ottlilienfeld, *Wirtschaft als Leben* (Jena: G. Fischer, 1925), 522.

Meanwhile, Wittmayer himself has expressly raised the concept of integration to a central concept in his own discussions. Leo Wittmayer, "Die Staatlichkeit des Reichs als logische und als nationale Integrationsform," in Walter von Schelcher, ed., *Fischers Zeitschrift für Verwaltungsrecht* (Leipzig: Freiberg, 1925), 57, 145 ff. Integration is defined here (145 n. 1) as "the epitome of all political notions and forces of standardization." I will return at a later point to the substantive content of this essay.

The word has gained currency in sociology because of Herbert Spencer, who used it, however, in another sense. He sees the order of the state's life as thoroughly mechanical and static and calls it political organization (Herbert Spencer, *Principles of Sociology* [London: Macmillan, 1882], p. v, §§ 440 ff., pp. 244 ff.), while political integration (§ 448, pp. 265 ff.) describes mechanical growth through inclusion and amalgamation, with reflection (§ 451) on the starkly mechanical discussions of first principles (§ 169, pp. 480 ff.) in the third edition of 1870. Through Spencer it has passed into English and American sociology.

In any case, a direct line leads from there, if one takes an idealist turn, to the linguistic usage suggested here and apparently increasingly accepted. A suitable word would be desirable, but is not easy to find. "Organization" sometimes describes the same thing (for example, in Otto von der Pfordten, *Organisation* [Heidelberg: Winter, 1917], especially 11), but it is generally too burdened with mechanistic (as in Plenge's *Organisationslehre*), naturalist, and legal senses to be clearly useful in the context described in the text.

Undoubted similarities of some of the views developed in the text with certain concepts of the vitalists, for example, that of regulation (see especially Hans Driesch, *Die organischen Regulationen* [Leipzig: Engelmann, 1901], 95: "regulations or organization and adaptation"), brought to my attention by Walther Fischer-Rostock, cannot be used as nomenclature.

29. Against the one, individualist approach, here once again, as a summary refutation, Litt, *Individuum und Gemeinschaft*, 3rd ed., 226 ff.; against the other, 178 ff. (first of all against Spengler, whose static concept of the state Heller disconcertingly approves of: see Heller, *Die Souveränität*, 315 n. 75).

As the source of the worst errors in our social sciences in the broadest sense, static thinking deserves a comprehensive critique along the lines of Kelsen's. Its natural, most obvious root is the uncritical tendency of naive thinking in spatial terms (examples of typical errors of this sort in Litt, *Individuum und Gemeinschaft*, 3rd ed., passim, e.g., 10 f., 42, 47, 58, 62 ff., 92, 175, 222 f., 228 f., 286 note. In the legal literature, see those cited in James Goldschmidt, *Der Prozeß als Rechtslage* [Berlin: Springer, 1926], 177 n. 966; and Konrad Hellwig, *Zivilprozeßrecht*, vol. 1 [Leipzig: A. Deichert, 1903], 255; Ernst von Hippel, *Untersuchungen zum Problem des fehlerhaften Staatsakts* [Berlin: Springer, 1924], 132; Carl Schmitt, "Zu Gerhard Anschütz: Die Verfassung des deutschen Reichs vom 11. August 1919," *Juristische Wochenschrift* [Leipzig: Moefer, 1926], 2271, upper left). In the history of ideas, it can be traced back primarily, and in its individualist transformation, to natural science and the individualist thought related to it (Ernst Troeltsch, *Historismus* [Tübingen: Mohr, 1922], 258), and only secondarily, and in its tendency to a naive ontology of the communities, to particular prerequisites of the German history of ideas. Kaufmann, *Kritik der neukantischen Rechtsphilosophie*, 94.

30. Thus the irredescent concept of the "genuine life idea" or the "true *Staatsräson*" of a state in Friedrich Meinecke, *Die Idee der Staatsräson* (Munich: Oldenbourg, 1924 and ff.), 1 f. Largely similar to this critique, Carl Schmitt, "Zu Friedrich Meineckes 'Idee der Staatsräson'," *Archiv für Sozial-Wissenschaft und Sozial-Politik*, vol. 56 (Tübingen: Mohr, 1926), 226 ff.

31. Litt, *Individuum und Gemeinschaft*, 3rd ed., 333 f., 312 f.

32. Fascist corporativism thus expressly describes itself as "integral," that is, as integrating, not in the sense of the familiar, older cases of political use of the word, where it means "complete," that is, radical. See, e.g., Ludwig Bernhard, *Das System Mussolini* (Berlin: Schere, 1924), 93 f., 97 ff.

33. Eduard Spranger, *Lebensformen*, 5th ed. (Halle: Niemeyer, 1925), 432 ff., 413 f.; Eduard Spranger, *Psychologie des Jugendalters*, 4th ed. (Leipzig: Quelle & Meyer, 1926), 3 ff.

34. Spranger, *Jugendalter*, 8 f.; Litt, *Individuum und Gemeinschaft*, 3rd ed., 323; Hans Oppenheimer, *Logik der soziologischen Begriffsbildung* (Tübingen: Mohr, 1925), 74 ff.

370 NOTES TO PAGES 219-221

35. From the scholarly literature, we mention only Max Weber's sociology of domination. See also Friedrich von Wieser, *Gesetz der Macht* (Vienna: Springer, 1926), 47 ff. Particularly rich in valuable observations are Friedrich W. Förster's (older) writings on political ethics, to the extent they justify the morally imperative behavior of a statesman, leader, superior, etc., by the integrating force of the required method of leadership—in his well-known working method, here as contestable from the standpoint of theoretical ethics as it is stimulating and fruitful for practical morality.

36. Quite correctly, e.g., Curt Geyer, *Führer und Masse in der Demokratie* (Berlin: Dietz, 1926), 10 ff.

37. Especially typical is Wieser, *Gesetz der Macht.*

38. Perhaps meaning something similar, see Meinecke's observation—in an otherwise quite opposite context (*Die Idee der Staatsräson,* 1st ed., 12)—that the people "with its own latent drives for power and life, also nourishes that of the rulers."

A correct observation in this context, in a theoretically unfortunate, mechanistic setting, is Vierkandt's doctrine of the "spectator." Alfred Vierkandt, *Gesellschaftslehre* (Stuttgart: F. Enke, 1923), 31.

39. Wieser, *Gesetz der Macht,* 127 f.

40. From the need to integrate changing trends and senses of identity through leadership emerges the democratic tendency to change leadership, not from the tendency towards responsibility and towards preventing a monopolized leadership (false, liberal-individualist explanation in Hans Kelsen, "Demokratie," *Verhandlungen des 5. deutschen Soziologentages* [Tübingen: Mohr, 1927], 60).

41. A list of respective images for the functioning of the king appears in Carl Schmitt, *Geistesgeschichtliche Lage des heutigen Parlamentarismus* (Munich: Duncker & Humblot, 1923), 2nd ed. (Munich: Duncker & Humblot, 1926), 50.

A particularly instructive case, belonging to some extent in this context, is the enormous integrating effect of the fact of Hindenburg's remaining at the head of the headquarters of the returning army; cf. Gustav Noske in the *Festnummer* of *"Heimatdienst"* of 2 October 1927, *Heimatdienst* 19 (Berlin: Zentralverlag, 1927): 320 ff.

42. Briefly developed in *Festgabe der Berliner Juristischen Fakultät für Wilhelm Kahl,* vol. 3, 23 f.

43. See Wieser, *Gesetz der Macht,* 364. The personalities of the founders of nations who become and remain heads of state, such as Bismarck or Masaryk, tend to serve integration as both historic and current figures.

44. Hugo Preuss, *Wandlungen des Kaisergedankens: Zur Geier des Geburtstages Seiner Majestät des Kaisers am 27. Januar 1917 in der Aula der Handels-Hochschule* (Berlin: Reimer, 1917), 20.

45. Thomas Mann, *Königliche Hoheit,* 13th ed. (Berlin: Fischer, 1910), 163, 25, 52.

46. Thus Max Weber apparently saw it as impossible that the *Ostjuden* might be leaders of the life of Germany's state, even in the revolution. Marianne Weber, *Max Weber* (Tübingen: Mohr, 1926), 672. Fine observations in Mann, *Königliche Hoheit.*

47. Thus Eulenburg reproaches the Kaiser with the unfavorable impression made by unnecessary imperial journeys during the most tense domestic political

situations (1893): Johannes Haller, *Aus dem Leben des Fürsten E.* (Berlin: Paetl, 1924), 120 f.

48. Letter of 19 August 1790, in Leopold von Schlözer, *Dorothea von Schlözer* (Göttingen: Deuerlich, 1937), 242.

Classically, Leopold von Ranke, *Sämtliche Werke,* vol. 30, *Zur Geschichte von Österreich und Preußen zwischen dem Friedensschluß zu Aachen und Hubertusburg* (Leipzig: Duncker & Humblot, 1886), 55 f., on the integrating function of the government, "which in the end represents its [the state's] spiritual unity, on which depend its development, its progress, its fate, which first shows it what it is, and which tears it from the sterile ideal into the midst of vital interests."

49. Max Weber, passim, especially strongly in *Gesammelte Politische Schriften* (Munich: Drei Masken Verlag, 1921), 134. Correctly, Richard Thoma, *Max-Weber-Erinnerungsgabe,* vol. 2 (Frankfurt am Main: Keip, 1889), 58 f.

Even less plausibly can one say that in a democracy the leaders "are limited in their specific functions to executing laws." Kelsen, *Verhandlungen der 5. deutschen Soziologentages,* 55.

50. Expression from Hans Freyer, *Theorie des objektiven Geistes* (Leipzig: Teubner, 1923), 81.

51. Freyer, *Theorie des objektiven Geistes,* 23.

52. On this sociological side of the theory of natural law, Kaufmann, *Kritik der neukantischen Rechtsphilosophie,* 88 ff.; Heller, *Die Souveränität,* 290 f.

53. As Kaufmann says, *Kritik der neukantischen Rechtsphilosophie,* 90.

54. See *Festgabe der Berliner Juristischen Fakultät für Wilhelm Kahl,* vol. 3, 23 ff.

55. Which is not to say that they are more typical of more genuine forms of state—the form of state depends on the overall constellation of values, which was less differentiated and more static in the beginning than later on, and therefore favored forms of state based on domination.

56. On the phenomenology of the battle in the aspect essential here, the works of Karl Groos are still fundamental, cf. especially Karl Groos, *Der Lebenswert des Spiels* (Jena: Fischer, 1910). Also Georg Simmel, *Soziologie* (Leipzig: Duncker & Humblot, 1908), 247 ff.; Litt, *Individuum und Gemeinschaft,* 2nd ed., 83, 152.

57. On the developmental history of both, Wladymyr Starosolskyi, *Das Majoritätsprinzip,* Wiener staatswissenschaftliche Studien XIII 2 (Vienna: Deuticke, 1916), 6 ff.

58. Thus Litt, *Individuum und Gemeinschaft,* 1st ed., 121 ff., especially 125 f.

59. Entirely incorrect is the undifferentiated equal treatment of the technical majority principle in offices and courts and of the political, integrating principle in elections and parliaments, as in Ruth Haymann, "Die Mehrheitsentscheidung," in Edgar Tatarin-Tarnhey, ed., *Festgabe für Stammler* (Berlin: de Gruyter, 1926), 395 ff., e.g., 451.

60. As one can still observe today, as the basis of the old-German unanimity principle, in some rural Swiss municipalities.

61. All political theories that, following the example of Max Weber and Meinecke, fail to go beyond the "tensions" are insufficient, as they miss this element of political psychology and are also incapable of ethical solutions.

62. This effect can, incidentally, even come from a battle that has none of this institutional spirit, for example, a civil war; I am reminded of the formulation of this fact

by a great poet, in Gottfried Keller's "Landessammlung zur Tilgung der Sonder-bundskriegsschuld 1852," stanzas 3, 5, and 7.

63. Schmitt, *Die geistesgeschichtliche Lage des heutigen Parlamentarismus;* Richard Thoma, "Zur Ideologie des Parlamentarismus und der Diktatur," *Archiv für Sozial-Wissenschaft und Sozial-Politik,* vol. 53 (Tübingen: Mohr, 1924), 212 ff.; Carl Schmitt, "Der Gegensatz von Parlamentarismus und moderner Massendemokratie," *Hochland,* vol. 23 (Munich: Kempten, 1926), 257 ff., reprinted in its essence as the preface to the second edition of his aforementioned book.

64. Schmitt, *Die geistesgeschichtliche Lage des heutigen Parlamentarismus,* 61, 63.

65. Schmitt, *Die geistesgeschichtliche Lage des heutigen Parlamentarismus,* 22 f.

66. In regard to the parliamentary ideology of the eighteenth and nineteenth centuries I investigated earlier in similar fashion, see *Maßstäbe des parlamentarischen Wahlrechts in der deutschen Staatstheorie des 19. Jahrhunderts* (Stuttgart: Enke, 1912), 4 ff.; "Die Verschiebung der konstitutionellen Ordnung durch die Verhältniswahl," in Universität Bonn, Juristische Fakultät, ed., *Festgabe der Bonner Juristischen Fakultät für Karl Bergbohm* (Bonn: Marcus Weber, 1919), 280 ff. I expressed it so that here only the light rationalist exterior must be shed in order to get from this ideology to the actual meaning—described in the text—of the institution.

67. Suggested in *Festgabe der Berliner Juristischen Fakultät für Wilhelm Kahl,* vol. 3, 23.

68. Carl Schmitt still has a correct notion; see his excellent discussion of secret, isolated voting, through which no people's will or opinion (which only exists in the sphere of publicity) can be expressed with vital strength. Schmitt, *Die geistes-geschichtliche Lage des heutigen Parlamentarismus,* 22. The secret voter is the individual of liberal thinking, alien to the state, who is neither integrated nor needs integration. Of course, Schmitt also sees that what counts is no longer the "idea" or "principle" of a form of state, but the gaining of and ruling with a majority. Schmitt, *Die geistesgeschichtliche Lage des heutigen Parlamentarismus,* 11. But that was no different a hundred years ago; only the ideology and technique of integrating a small bour-geoisie in the age of liberalism were different from those of integrating the demo-cratic masses.

69. Schmitt, *Die geistesgeschichtliche Lage des heutigen Parlamentarismus,* 216.

70. Schmitt, *Die geistesgeschichtliche Lage des heutigen Parlamentarismus,* 7, 12 f.

71. Thoma, "Zur Ideologie des Parlamentarismus and der Diktatur," 214.

72. Only express rejection of any idealist thinking has the right to such confusion, such as Hans Kelsen, *Allgemeine Staatslehre* (Berlin: Springer, 1925), 327, who radically equates the discussions of a council of ministers with those of a parliament. Similarly incorrect is Haymann, "Die Mehrheitsentscheidung."

73. We can disregard here the fact that representation and relations among or-gans are not entirely congruent with deputation as conventionally understood.

74. Of course, its decisions, like all acts of will in the name of society that qualify as legal, belong retroactively to the integrating functions—just as the individual hu-man personality creates itself while carrying out and experiencing its functions.

75. On the actual "leadership function of the parliament," see, e.g., Curt Geyer, *Führer und Masse in der Demokratie* (Berlin: Dietz, 1926), 80 ff., 88 ff.

76. See, e.g., Leo Wittmayer, *Die organisierende Kraft des Wahlsystems* (Vienna: Fromme, 1903). See generally Hugo Preuss, *Um die Reichsverfassung von Weimar*

(Berlin: Rudolf Mosse, 1924), 139: "Through the principle of democratic self-organization the masses had to be regained for the national self-assurance from which they were estranged under the rule of the old powers."

77. Bismarck accused the parties "rejecting the state," in contrast to the parties "accepting" it, of a lack of a community of political values and thus, at the same time, of the will to political integration—a distinction justified in principle, and not at all the same as the dualism between good and evil, despite Friedrich Meinecke, *Preußen und Deutschland im 19. und 20. Jahrhundert* (Munich and Berlin: Oldenbourg, 1918), 516.

What is stated in the text is often expressed in terms of party programs being only supplementing parts of a cosmos of values, or that they should be seen as such, or as various techniques for an identical goal. Jonas Cohn, "Die Erkenntnis der Welt and das Worrecht der Bejahung," *Logos: Zeitschrift für systematische Philosophie,* vol. 10 (Tübingen: Mohr, 1921/22): 225 (against Radbruch); Haymann, "Die Mehrheitsentscheidung," 467; Rudolf Stammler, *Rechtsphilosophie* (Berlin: de Gruyter, 1922), § 174.

78. Rudolf Hübner, *Die Staatsform der Republik* (Bonn: Schroeder, 1920), 36 f.; Heinrich Triepel, *Unitarismus und Föderalismus* (Tübingen: Mohr, 1907), 27 f.

79. Vierkandt, *Gesellschaftslehre,* 392 ff.—not entirely in the sense of the text.

80. In this sense only superficially suggested here, even the "cranks and dreamers" not taken into account by Triepel, *Unitarismus und Föderalismus,* 27 f., in the end tend to be not only deniers, but at the same time supporters of law and the state.

81. See above, pages 220–21.

82. Because of this relationship to the values, domination itself is often strongly emphasized as a value—for example, as authoritarian decision by Carl Schmitt or, with reverse premises, as a disqualifying element of bourgeois order by socialists, for example, Max Adler, "Staatsauffassung des Marxismus," in Max Adler and Rudolf Hilferding, eds., *Marx-Studien* IV, vol. 1 (Vienna: Wiener Volksbuchhandlung, 1922), 209 ff., 214 f., 223, 198 f.; Paul Tillich, *Die religiöse Lage der Gegenwart* (Berlin: Ullstein, 1926), 43, 54, 64, 65, 81, 95, 125, where the science, technology, economy, constitution, education, and church of the bourgeois age appear as authoritarian and thus compromised.

Closely related to the differences between domination and representation suggested in the text is the fact that rulers and leaders can be considered, at the same time, factors of personal integration in a very different sense from representatives. See Aloys Fischer, "Herrschaft, Führung, Vertretung," in Gustav Kafka, ed., *Handbuch der vergleichenden Psychologie,* vol. 2 (Munich: Reinhardt, 1922), 387 ff.

83. Kelsen, *Allgemeine Staatslehre,* 38 f.

84. Max Weber, *Wirtschaft und Gesellschaft* (Tübingen: Mohr, 1922), 122.

85. For example, in the spirit of Simmel's famous essay, "Vortrag am Begrüßungsabend, Mittwoch 19. Oktober, zu welchem die Frankfurter Akademie für Social- und Handelswissenschaften eingeladen hat," in *Verhandlungen des ersten deutschen Soziologentages von 1910,* ed. Friedrich Heckmann (Opladen: Westdeutscher Verlag, 1911), 1–16; especially on the integrating significance of games, p. 9.

86. Yorck to Dilthey, 7 May 1879, in Wilhelm Dilthey and Paul Yorck von Wartenburg, eds., *Briefwechsel zwischen Wilhelm Dilthey und dem Grafen Yorck v. Wartenburg 1877–1897* (Halle: Niemeyer, 1923), 13.

87. For example, the constitutional as opposed to the statutory regulation of taxes and finance, etc. I will return later to this example and others.

Such examples make it particularly clear that an integrating effect does not depend on awareness of an integrating intention on the part of the legislator or the parts of the state that are to be integrated.

88. Litt, *Individuum und Gemeinschaft,* 3rd ed., 323 ff., 320 ff.

89. Litt, *Individuum und Gemeinschaft,* 333 f., 375 ff.

90. Therefore, every state suitably expresses its essence when it links its state, and especially military, symbols with symbols of victory; and Anatole France is only half correct in joking about the tendency of every army to call itself the first in the world (*L'Ile des Pingouins* 1,V, chap. IV). For its task, its point is to be invincible, and thus the first, and at the same time the state, not unsuitably, expresses its essential "invincibility as a nation of culture." Wieser, *Gesetz der Macht,* 280, 393.

One of the gaps in criticism of the Versailles Treaty is that Germany's demilitarization is generally combated only from the point of view of its impairment of technical means, rather than of the vital functions and quality of a great nation-state. It is understandable that this distinction is incomprehensible to Americans—but painful that it is so to many Germans as well. This also includes the thoughtlessness with which German pacifists before the world war hoped for the military defeat of Prussian militarism, not the German people (testimony of Hans Wehberg, *Als Pazifist im Weltkrieg* [Leipzig: Neue-Geist Verlag, 1919], 21). The army is not merely an organization or tool, but above all a form of life of the citizenry.

Details on this question follow.

91. Litt, *Individuum und Gemeinschaft,* 3rd ed., 360 f.

92. Expression from Wieser, *Gesetz der Macht,* 104 ff.

93. See, e.g., the observations on the psychology of power in Spranger, *Lebensformen,* 5th ed., 230.

94. There is almost nothing on precisely this aspect of the issue in Siegfried Kracauer, "Die Gruppe als Ideenträger," *Archiv für Sozial-Wissenschaft und Sozial-Politik,* vol. 49, 594 ff.

There is much, on the other hand, in Karl Rothenbücher, *Über das Wesen des Geschichtlichen* (Tübingen: Mohr, 1926), e.g., 15 f.

95. An excellent presentation of this situation in Litt, *Individuum und Gemeinschaft,* 1st ed., 174 ff., 179 ff.

Here lies the special paradox of the problem of substantive integration, which consists in the fact that participation in a more comprehensive and substantively more important group is more difficult to experience, or at least consciously to experience, than one that is lesser in number, content, and duration.

96. Integration through symbols, however, can never be anything other than integration through their symbolized content. Therefore, one cannot "invent" symbols for a nonexistent content, as Robert Coester, *Die Loslösung Posens* (Berlin: Stilke, 1921), 62 f., demands in retrospect. The difficulties experienced by the [republican] black-red-gold Reich colors due to the unclarity of the positive content they symbolize, in contrast to [the imperial] black-white-red, are partially of this nature.

There is a great deal on the theory and practice of political symbols in the literature on fascism—including the link between myth and symbol, of which Kierkegaard is also thinking when he tries through nonrational symbolization to withdraw from the discussion the unformulated basic principle, the roots of the state (like the church): in German, Søren Kierkegaard and Theodor Haecker, *Der Begriff des Auserwählten* (Helterau: Hegner, 1917), 41.

The concept of the symbol is defined here considerably more narrowly than in Litt, *Individuum und Gemeinschaft,* 3rd ed., 153, or that of the "sign" [*Zeichen*] in Freyer's *Theorie des objektiven Geistes.*

97. *This generation can only be taught by events* [English in the original], 22 March 1889, *Die große Politik der europäischen Kabinette 1871–1914,* vol. IV, ed. Johannes Lepsius, Albrecht Mendelssohn Bartholdy, and Friedrich Thimme (Berlin: Deutsche Verlagsgesellschaft für Politik und Geschichte, 1927), 405.

On symbolized events, see especially Rothenbücher, *Über das Wesen des Geschichtlichen,* 38 ff. A good example (the battle of Morgarten, 1315, which made the Swiss aware of the historical significance of their struggle and thus of their political unity) in Andreas Heusler, *Schweizer Verfassungsgeschichte* (Basel: Frobenius, 1920), 85.

Here, in part, lies the significance of the constant emphasis on the revolutionary character of the march on Rome of Mussolini and fascism; only if interpreted in this way is it the symbolic event in the break with the old world and the inauguration of a completely new state content, and precisely for this reason does its unique integrating effect, the justification of specific fascist legitimacy, lie in this revolutionary character.

98. Georg Wilhelm Friedrich Hegel, *Grundlinien der Philosophie des Rechts* (1821), § 334.

99. See the excellent discussion in Litt, *Individuum und Gemeinschaft,* 1st ed., 117 ff., 129 ff.

100. I recall the familiar liturgical experience that a doctrinal content in the form of religious poetry never encounters the problem that blocks its integrating effect on the community when the same content appears as the theologumenon of a formulated, settled article of faith [*Bekenntnis*].

101. The contrast is not quite in the spirit of, for example, Georg von Lukacs, *Theorie des Romans* (Neuwied: Luchterhand, 1962), 31.

102. At least to some extent, the relationship between the integrating bond to the state and the religious bond to a god can be explained through contexts like the one developed here; it has been observed, for example, in Simmel's sociology of religion (*Die Religion,* vol. 2 of *Gesellschaft,* ed. Martin Buber, 1906, 22 ff.), and is in a deeper sense one of the basic ideas in Emanuel Hirsch, *Reich-Gottes-Begriffe des neueren europäischen Denkens* (Göttingen: Vandenhoeck & Ruprecht, 1921), but is also employed practically in the policy of the political myth by [Georges] Sorel and the fascists. See, e.g., Johannes Mannhardt, *Faschismus* (Munich: Beck, 1925), 125, 219, 262, 278 f., 327 ff. In the usage suggested here, the political myth means integration through a symbolically formulated totality of political values that is thus made capable of being experienced as an intensive totality.

Of course, Kelsen's parallel between god and state, most recently in his *Allgemeine Staatslehre,* 76 ff., has nothing to do with this.

103. Yorck to Dilthey, 13 January 1887, in *Briefwechsel zwischen Wilhelm Dilthey und dem Grafen Paul Yorck v. Wartenburg 1877–1897,* 66.

104. See above, pages 226–27.

105. Rudolf Kjellén, *Der Staat als Lebensform* (Leipzig: S. Hirzel, 1917), 110. In a

different, more narrow sense, the static nature of largely substantively integrated forms of state contrasts with the dynamism of the liberal-parliamentary system; I have dealt with this in the context of preliminary remarks on a theory of state forms, *Festgabe der Berliner Juristischen Fakultät für Wilhelm Kahl*, vol. 3, 22 ff.

106. Friedrich Curtius, *Hindernisse und Möglichkeit einer ethischen Politik* (Leipzig: Verlag Naturwissenschaften, 1918), 6, is excellent. However, it is incorrect in providing an explanation "from this confusion of nature and reason," rather than from the nature of spiritual life itself.

107. The most important case of this type in contemporary state doctrine is Kelsen's "mask" theory; see Hans Kelsen, "Gott und Staat," *Logos*, vol. 11 (Tübingen: Mohr, 1923): 267 f.

108. I will return to this issue in individual applied cases, cf. Schmitt, *Geistesgeschichtliche Lage des Parlamentarismus*, 39 ff.; Heller, *Souveränität*, 19; Fritz Marschall von Bieberstein, *Vom Kampf des Rechtes gegen die Gesetze* (Stuttgart: Kohlhammer, 1927), 128 ff., note 381 f.

109. See, e.g., the literature in Litt, *Individuum und Gemeinschaft*, 3rd ed., 80, note 1, and in Max Scheler, *Versuche zu einer Soziologie des Wissens* (Munich: Duncker & Humblot, 1924), 115 f., note.

The rich book by Rothenbücher falls victim to an incorrect alternative of criticism—see in particular Rothenbücher, *Über das Wesen des Geschichtlichen*, 59, 74 ff.—and thus fails to place its wealth of excellently observed details in the idealist context they deserve.

110. This duality is unclear in Ludwig Waldecker, *Allgemeine Staatslehre* (Berlin-Grunewald: Rothschild, 1927), 481 f.

111. E.g., Robert Sieger, *Staatsgebiet und Staatsgedanke*, Mitteilungen der Geographischen Gesellschaft in Wien 62 (Vienna: Östereichische Geographische Gesellschaft, 1919), 1 ff., especially 8.

112. As representative of many, Friedrich Ratzel, *Der Lebensraum* (Tübingen: Laupp, 1901). Only within the limits of what is stated in the text can one justify the rejection of "geopolitics" for the theory of the state in Heller, *Die Souveränität*, 83 and n. 2. It is a big step even from the excesses of geopolitics to the pure subordination of political to physical geography in contemporary Italian literature (on the Napoleonic model); in comparison, even the famous passage in Johann G. Fichte, "Grundzüge des gegenwärtigen Zeitalters," *Werke*, vol. 7, ed. Immanuel Fichte (Berlin: de Gruyter, 1871), 212, is correct in refusing to see the Fatherland in clods of earth, rivers, and mountains.

113. Particularly characteristic passages, to which many others could be added, in Hans Kelsen, *Das Problem der Souveränität und die Theorie des Völkerrecht* (Tübingen: Mohr, 1928), 73; Hans Kelsen, *Allgemeine Staatslehre* (Berlin: Springer, 1925), 294.

114. Kelsen, *Das Problem der Souveränität und die Theorie des Völkerrecht*, 73, and at many other places; Walter Henrich, *Kritik der Gebietstheorien* (Breslau: J. U. Kerns Verlag [Max Müller], 1926).

115. Bernhard Braubach, "Zum Einfluß der Stoa auf die französische Staatslehre," *Schmollers Jahrbuch für Gesetzgebung, Verwaltung und Volkswirtschaft*, vol. 48 (Munich and Leipzig: Duncker & Humblot, 1924), 232.

This integrating effect of the territory and its borders is particularly apparent when it spreads to the free, extra-state "society," as in the adaptation of many

NOTES TO PAGES 235-238

German dialect borders to the border changes at the beginning of the nineteenth century.

For a view that deviates in many respects, see Max Scheler, *Der Formalismus in der Ethik und die materiale Werteethik* (Halle: Niemeyer, 1921), 580 f.

116. Georg von Lukacs, *Geschichte und Klassenbewußtsein* (Neuwied: Luchterhand, 1968), 319 ff.

117. Karl Bilfinger, *Der Einfluß der Einzelstaaten auf die Bildung des Reichswillens* (Tübingen: Mohr, 1922), 85.

118. Thus Freud's mass psychology, here cited without further ado from Kelsen, *Soziologischer und juristischer Staatsbegriff*, 31 f.—an especially representative statement, including the confusion, unavoidable today, of crude naturalism with the romanticism of leadership [*Führerromantik*].

119. Karl Loewenstein, "Zur Soziologie der parlamentarischen Repräsentation in England nach der großen Reform. Das Zeitalter der Parlamentsouveränität (1823–1867)," *Archiv für Sozialwissenschaft und Sozialpolitik*, vol. 51 (Tübingen: Mohr, 1924), 671, 683.

120. E.g., Friedrich Engels, *Herrn Eugen Dühring's Umwälzung der Wissenschaft*, 11th ed. (Stuttgart: Dietz, 1921), 277.

121. Quite typical is Max Adler at the Third Reich Conference of Young Socialists (Berlin: Arbeiterjugend-Verlag, 1925), 12: "There has never been another means of making people's minds unanimous and bringing their wishes into a common line in which they can first achieve lasting strength, than science [*Wissenschaft*] . . . Only in one area must all ways meet, only one force can be avoided by no one, and that is the power of logical thinking," etc.

That is, scientific truth, and its realization as the single integrating factor. No dialectic can deny that the "state" is abolished [*aufgehoben*] in this intellectualist theorem: Max Adler, "Staatsauffassung des Marxismus," in *Marx-Studien*, 4th ed., vol. 2 (Glashütten im Taunus: Avermann, 1918), especially 209 ff., also 129, 146, 223, and passim.

122. Therefore, the focus of all future democracies will lie not in politics, but in education. Adler, "Staatsauffassung des Marxismus," 185.

123. Adler, "Staatsauffassung des Marxismus," 197 note.

A socialism that accuses bourgeois society of reinforcing its values and sets the new education the goal of a "formal, universally functional educational product," Anna Siemsen, *Erziehung im Gemeinschaftsgeist* (Stuttgart: Moritz, 1921), especially 13 f., is to this extent not grounded in socialism.

124. Adler, "Staatsauffassung des Marxismus," 193 ff.

125. Hellpach-Graf Dohna, *Die Krisis des deutschen Parlamentarismus* (Karlsruhe: Braun, 1927), 8.

126. As a more recent example, we may mention here Max Scheler, *Versuche zu einer Soziologie des Wissens* (Munich: Duncker & Humblot, 1924), 99, 109, n. 99 (against Engels), 28, 30, 31 ff., 37 f. Methodologically questionable is the conventional contrast between "ideal and real factors," 9.

127. Hardly to be considered, Norbert Einstein, *Der Erfolg* (Frankfurt am Main: Ruetten & Loening, 1919), especially 50 f.

On the relationship between types of integration, see also above, page 228.

128. Not only are the constitutional theories of the main political tendencies to

be characterized, as suggested above, as varied programs for integration, differing in the employment and combination of individual integrating factors; so too the forms of state (more on this later) and types of national state, whose differences, however (apart from certain simple ones that are valid throughout, such as the greater role of certain sensory, optical, and rhythmical integrating elements among the Roman peoples) are quite intricate and cannot be reduced to simple formulas. Nevertheless, this problem deserves closer study in view of the ambiguities that must arise from the popular reduction to variants of the individualist-collectivist dichotomy. This dichotomy describes necessary elements of all spiritual life and every political particularity. Karl Vossler has classically shown how strongly French culture is social and sociable; and yet the French sense of the state is at the same time starkly individualist, according to the peasant-petty bourgeois experience of law focusing on the tangible object that one can obtain and secure—for example, in the interpretation of the Versailles Peace. Conversely, the French see as an Anglo-Saxon characteristic, despite all individualism, the tendency from a political point of view toward goodwill and cooperation, in contrast to the politically atomist French. André Tardieu, *Devant l'obstacle: l'Amérique et nous* (Paris: Émile-Paul, 1927), 53 f.

129. *Festgabe der Berliner Juristischen Fakultät für Wilhelm Kahl*, vol. 3, pp. 17 f. I interpret Albrecht Mendelssohn-Bartholdy, *Europäische Gespräche*, vol. 1 (Berlin: Deutsche Verlaganstalt, 1923), 168, as the agreement of an authority.

130. See, especially, the excellent discussion of the "interconnection of areas of life" in Litt, *Individuum und Gemeinschaft*, 3rd ed., 379 ff., especially 381.

131. W. R. Seeley, "The Morality of Nations," *International Journal of Ethics*, vol. 1, no. 4 (London: T. Fischer Unwin, 1891): 444 f. I cannot explain how to make consistent the same writer's better-known and apparently contradictory thesis on the connection between external pressure and internal constitution.

132. J. J. Ruedorffer's *Grundzüge der Weltpolitik in der Gegenwart* (Stuttgart: Deutsche Verlagsgesellschaft, 1914) can be mentioned as an example representative of many.

133. For Bismarck's numerous statements on the monarchic constitution as a prerequisite for a lasting politics of federation and alliance, see, e.g., the compilation in Heinrich Ritter von Srbik, *Metternich- der Staatsmann und der Mensch*, vol. 2 (Munich: Bruckmann, 1925), 662 [endnotes] to 551, also 553 below [another work in the *Staatrechtliche Abhandlungen und andere Aufsätze*; Smend cites Bismarck's book, *Die Grosse Politik*—EDS.]. In addition, for the fact that only control over internal forces makes it possible to take advantage of conditions in foreign policy insofar as domestic policy determines foreign policy, see Helmut Göring in "Die neue Front," 397.

134. On this, see *Festgabe der Berliner Juristischen Fakultät für Wilhelm Kahl*, vol. 3, p. 18. If, for example, one state from a group of states achieves an advantage, the remaining states demand compensation, not because each wants the same amount, but because the nature of them all, determined through foreign-policy power relations, would otherwise be impaired. As an example of the nuances possible here of a foreign policy without object and one that stresses an object, see Detlev Vagts, *Europäische Gespräche*, vol. 1 (Berlin: Deutsche Verlaganstalt, 1923), 261.

135. Helmut Göring, *Die Großmächte und die Rheinfrage in den letzten Jahrhunderten* (Berlin: Hobbing, 1926), 72.

136. Göring, *Die Großmächte und die Rheinfrage*, 80.

137. Meinecke, *Die Idee der Staatsräson*, 1st ed., 516.

138. One is reminded of the famous words of Bismarck's Reichstag speech on 11 January 1887, in Horst Kohl, *Politische Reden* (Stuttgart: Cotta, 1892), 12, 217.

This does not exclude the possibility that for this very reason, political negotiations are more elastic than simply technical ones; see Kiderlen's well-known discussion of the fleet treaty of 1909, in Ernst Jäckh, *Kiderlen-Wachter, der Staatsmann und Mensch,* vol. 2 (Stuttgart: Deutsche Verlags-Anstalt, 1925), 50, 57.

I need only recall the honorary clause [*Ehrenclausel*] and other phenomena in international law belonging in the same category.

139. See the quotation from Hegel's *Grundlinien der Philosophie des Rechts,* above page 231, note 98.

140. See, e.g., Kurt Riezler, "Die Agonie des deutschen Parlamentarismus," in *Die deutsche Nation: Eine Zeitschrift für Politik* (Berlin: de Gruyter, 1922), 991, and especially Mannhardt, *Faschismus,* 88, 128, 39, 121, 119, 274 f., 142 f.

141. Carl Schmitt, "Die Kernfrage des Völkerbundes," in *Schmollers Jahrbuch,* vol. 48, fasc. 2 (Munich and Leipzig: Duncker & Humblot, 1924), 774 ff.; Heller, *Die Souveränität,* 118; Maurice Hauriou, *Précis de droit constitutionnel* (Paris: Sirey, 1923), 446, 397; Sieger, *Staatsgebiet und Staatsgedanke,* 11. Very certain, in contrast to the majority of historians, Max von Szczepanski, "Rankes Anschauungen über den Zusammenhang zwischen der äußeren und der inneren Politik der Staaten," *Zeitschrift für Politik,* vol. 7 (Berlin: Heymann, 1920), 489 ff., especially 620. This is generally more obvious to those outside the country than to ourselves. Article 1, sec. 2 of the Charter of the League of Nations, with its requirement that member states "*se gouvernent librement,*" probably means internal and external freedom in equal measure.

142. Introduction and conclusion of the *Idee der Staatsräson.*

143. Georg Jellinek, *Verfassungsänderung und Verfassungswandlung: Eine staatsrechtlich-politische Abhandlung* (Berlin: Häring, 1906).

144. Jellinek, *Verfassungsänderung und Verfassungswandlung,* 72.

145. Nearly thus, Jellinek, *Verfassungsänderung und Verfassungswandlung,* 2.

146. It is telling that Jellinek in *Verfassungsänderung und Verfassungswandlung* gives only an empirical description of important cases and types, not a theory, and especially not a legal one.

147. See above, pages 235 f.

148. Thus the harsh criticism by Erich Kaufmann (*Kritik der neukantischen Rechtsphilosophie,* 207 f.) of the "edifice of paragraphs" of the written constitutional document, especially that of Weimar, is not entirely justified.

149. On the importance of receptions in intellectual life in general, see Litt, *Individuum und Gemeinschaft,* 3rd ed., 181 f.

150. The cases enumerated by Jellinek are clearly not of this type, but are found in the self-structuring of the integration process stimulated or at least permitted by the constitution.

151. In this sense also the concept of the constitution in Gerhart Husserl, *Rechtskraft und Rechtsgeltung* (Berlin: Springer, 1925), 73.

152. Thus the popular comparison with state functions, Montesquieu, *Ésprit sprit des lois,* III.1, translated into the juridical sphere, e.g., by Fritz Fleiner, *Institutionen des deutschen Verwaltungsrechts,* 3rd ed. (Tübingen: Mohr, 1913), 3. The date of its abandonment in German thought is instructive: the analogy is still found in the

young Hegel, *System der Sittlichkeit: Schriften zur Politik und Rechtsphilosophie,* ed. Georg von Lasson, Philosophische Bibliothek 144 (Hamburg 1913), 467, but no longer in the *Enzyklopädie* (§ 536: "its internal structure as a development referring to itself") and *Rechtsphilosophie* (§ 271: "the organization of the state and the self-referential process of its organic life, in which it differentiates its elements within itself and unfolds them into existence").

153. It is probably meant this way in Heller, *Die Souveränität,* 81, when he finds the state's distinction from other organizations in the fact that "the acts implementing it represent a guarantee of the overall cooperation in this area," thus are themselves without such heteronomous guarantees, or in Marck, *Substanz- und Funktionsbegriff,* 123, where, somewhat too generally, the autonomy of associations of public law is contrasted with the character of those in private law, as "artificial products of the legal order."

154. Heller, *Die Souveränität,* 102.

155. The trivial fact that the state does not "consist" of people must unfortunately still be emphasized: thus, correctly, in Heller, *Die Souveränität,* 81.

156. See Felix Stoerk, "Das Ausfuhrverbot und die partielle Suspension völkerrechtlicher Verträge," *Archiv des öffentlichen Rechts,* n.s. 9 (Freiburg im Breisgau and Leipzig: Mohr, 1894), 38.

157. See above, pages 242–43.

158. Examples of such skepticism in Hans Nawiasky, "Die Auslegung des Art. 48 der Reichsverfassung," *Archiv des öffentlichen Rechts,* n.s. 9 (Tübingen: Mohr, 1925), 13 f.; "Zu den Begriffen Versammlungen und Umzüge unter freiem Himmel," *Lammers Juristische Wochenschrift* (Leipzig: Moefer, 1925), 986, note r. The resolution is thus left to the delimitation in criminal law of the "essential principles of the constitution" as an object of high treason, e.g., *Entscheiden des Reichsgerichts* [*Decisions of the Federal Supreme Court*], in *Strafsachen* [*Criminal Cases*], vol. 56, pp. 173 ff., 259 ff. The literature on this issue shows that here, constitutional theory has left unanswered a pressing question of positive law.

See, on this question, in particular Karl Bilfinger, "Verfassungsumgehung. Betrachtungen zur Auslegung der Weimarer Verfassung," *Archiv des öffentlichen Rechts,* n.s. 11 (Tübingen: Mohr, 1926): 181 ff.

Ernst Wolgast draws my attention to a particularly characteristic application in Article 112 of the Norwegian Constitution (unalterability of the "principles" of the constitution).

159. At any rate, not as simple as Carl Schmitt's formula: organization = normal order. Carl Schmitt, "Die Diktatur des Reichspräsidenten nach Art. 48 der Reichsverfassung," *Veröffentlichung der Vereinigung der deutschen Staatsrechtslehrer,* vol. 1 (Berlin and Leipzig: de Gruyter, 1924): 91 f.

160. As in Georg Jellinek, *Staatslehre,* vol. 1, 3rd ed., 505.

161. Declaration of 10 November by the Board of the Independent Social Democratic Party, in Ferdinand Runkel, *Die deutsche Revolution* (Leipzig: Grunow, 1919), 118; Treaty of 22 November between People's Commissioners [*Volksbeauftragter*] and the Berlin Executive Council [*Vollzugsrat*], in Gerhard Anschütz, *Verfassung des Deutschen Reichs,* 3rd and 4th eds. (Berlin: Stilke, 1926), 14 n. 12.

162. Decree of 14 November 1918, *Reichsgesetzblatt,* no. 1311.

163. Heinrich Triepel, "Streitigkeiten zwischen Reich und Ländern," in *Festgabe*

der Berliner Juristischen Fakultät für Wilhelm Kahl, ed. Berliner Juristische Fakultät, vol. 2 (Tübingen: Mohr, 1923), 17.

164. Carl Schmitt, "Der Begriff des Politischen," *Archiv für Sozial-Wissenschaft und Sozial-Politik,* vol. 58 (Tübingen: Mohr, 1927), 1 ff., reprinted as Carl Schmitt, *Der Begriff des Politischen* (Berlin: Walther Rothschild, 1928).

165. Anschütz, *Verfassung des Deutschen Reichs,* note 6 on Article 15 of the Weimar Constitution.

166. Ernst von Hippel, "Über Objektivität im Öffentlichen Recht, *Archiv des öffentlichen Rechts,* n.s. 12 (Tübingen: Mohr, 1927): 417.

167. See Rudolf Smend, "Das Recht der freien Meinungsäußerung," *Veröffentlichung der Vereinigung der deutschen Staatsrechtslehrer,* vol. 4 (Berlin and Leipzig: de Gruyter, 1928), 48 f.

168. Leo Wittmayer, *Die Weimarer Reichsverfassung* (Tübingen: Mohr, 1928), 38.

169. On the following, see also Bilfinger, "Verfassungsumgehung. Betrachtungen zur Auslegung der Weimarer Verfassung," 175 ff.

170. Heinrich Triepel, *Die Staatsverfassung und die politischen Parteien* (Berlin: Liebmann, 1928), 24.

171. For example, Otto Koellreutter, *Der deutsche Staat als Bundesstaat und als Parteienstaat* (Tübingen: Mohr, 1927), 29.

172. Willi Hellpach, "Parlaments-Zukunft," *Neue Rundschau,* no. 7 (Berlin and Leipzig: Fischer, 1927): 3 ff.

8. HERMANN HELLER

1. The Court was the *Staatsgerichtshof,* which claimed jurisdiction under Article 19 of the Weimar Constitution.

2. The Court gave its sanction to the substance of the federal government's action and thus provided an important constitutional precedent for Nazi abuse of legal form. A complete transcript of the oral proceedings was published in 1933 and reprinted in 1976. See *Preußen contra Reich vor dem Staatsgerichtshof* (Glashüte im Taunus: Detlev Auvermann KG, 1976). See pp. 35–37, 63–65, 250, 410–11, and 470 for examples of the exchanges between Heller and the president of the Court.

3. The *Staatslehre* was edited by Gerhard Niemeyer and published in 1934 by A. W. Sijthoff's Uitgeversmaatschappij, Leiden. Heller's wife Gertrud and their three children made their way to England after a brief return to Germany. I am grateful to Ruth Ingram and Jane Winikus, Heller's daughters, and to Elaine Robson-Scott for this information.

4. Herman Heller, *Gesammelte Schriften,* 2nd ed., ed. Christoph Müller (Tübingen: Mohr, 1992) (*"Gesammelte Schriften"*).

5. See Hermann Heller, "Bürger und Bourgeois," in *Gesammelte Schriften,* 2:625.

6. See Hermann Heller, "Europa und der Fascismus," in *Gesammelte Schriften,* 2:463, 529.

7. Kelsen once accused Heller of plagiarizing all but the name of the Pure Theory of Law; see his remarks in *Veröffentlichungen der Vereinigung der Deutschen Staatsrechtslehrer,* vol. 4 (Berlin and Leipzig: de Gruyter, 1928), 176–80.

8. See Hermann Heller, "Bemerkungen zur Staats- und Rechtstheoretsichen Problematik der Gegenwart," in *Gesammelte Schriften,* 2:249, 251. Heller derived his

idea of social theory from the conservative social theorist Hans Freyer. As did Freyer, Heller referred to social theory as *Wirklichkeitswissenschaft,* which may be inadequately translated as "realist theory." For a summary of what Freyer meant to convey by this term, see Jerry Z. Muller, *The Other God That Failed: Hans Freyer and the Deradicalization of German Conservatism* (Princeton: Princeton University Press, 1987), 167–71. However, Heller's view that ideas are not mere weapons in a political battle distinguishes his view from Freyer's.

9. Heller, "Bemerkungen," 275.

10. Hermann Heller, *Staatslehre,* in *Gesammelte Schriften,* 3:79, 302–303.

11. *Veröffentlichungen der Vereinigung der Deutschen Staatsrechtslehrer,* vol. 3 (Berlin and Leipzig: de Gruyter, 1926), 55, quoted in Horst Dreier, *Rechtslehre. Staatssoziologie und Demokratietheorie bei Hans Kelsen,* 2nd ed. (Baden-Baden: Nomos Verlagsgesellschaft, 1990), 246.

12. Heller, "Bemerkungen," 269.

13. Carl Schmitt, *Über die drei Arten des Rechtswissenschaftlichen Denkens* (Hamburg: Hanseatische Verlagsanstalt, 1934).

14. See Heller, *Staatslehre,* 370–71. I borrow the term "publicizable" from Onora O'Neill "The Public Use of Reason," in her *Constructions of Reason: Explorations of Kant's Practical Philosophy* (Cambridge: Cambridge University Press, 1989), 28 ff., at 33–34. Compare the development of the idea (derived from Lon L. Fuller) of a threshold of "general interpretability" in David Sciulli, *Theory of Societal Constitutionalism: Foundations of a Non-Marxist Critical Theory* (Cambridge: Cambridge University Press, 1992), 120–22.

15. Wolfgang Schluchter, *Entscheidung für den sozialen Rechtsstaat: Hermann Heller und die staatstheoretische Diskussion in der Weimarer Republik,* 2nd ed. (Baden-Baden: Nomos Verlagsgesellschaft, 1983), 116. For Schluchter's account of the ambiguities in the *Staatslehre* and his own sketch of a resolution, see pp. 195–216, and see David Dyzenhaus, "Hermann Heller and the Legitimacy of Legality," *Oxford Journal of Legal Studies* 16 (1996): 641.

16. Heller's argument that the link between legality and legitimacy is created by the necessity for a sovereign to communicate with his subjects gives his work obvious affinities with Lon L. Fuller's suggestion that there is an "inner morality of law" that binds sovereign lawmaking power. See Lon L. Fuller, *The Morality of Law,* rev. ed. (New Haven: Yale University Press, 1969). Fuller was aware of Heller's work. See Lon L. Fuller, *The Law in Quest of Itself* (Boston: Beacon Press, 1966), 72 n. 29. Heller also anticipates many of Jürgen Habermas's arguments in his recent architectonic attempt to reconstruct legal theory along democratic lines: see Jürgen Habermas, *Faktizität und Geltung: Beiträge zur Diskurstheorie des Rechts und des demokratischen Rechtsstaats* (Frankfurt am Main: Surhkamp Verlag, 1992), translated by William Rehg as *Between Facts and Norms: Contributions to a Discourse Theory of Law and Democracy* (Cambridge, Mass.: MIT Press, 1996). I discuss these issues in a review of Habermas's book, "The Legitimacy of Legality," in *Archiv für Rechts- und Sozialphilosophie* 82 (1996): 324, *University of Toronto Law Journal* 46 (1996): 129, and in *Legality and Legitimacy: Carl Schmitt, Hans Kelsen, and Hermann Heller in Weimar* (Oxford: Clarendon Press, 1997).

Notes by Gerhard Niemeyer, the editor of the reprinted edition, are indicated by angle brackets, "< . . . >."

17. <Carl Schmitt, *Der Begriff des Politischen* (Berlin: Walther Rothschild, 1928), 4.>

For the same thoughts, see Schmitt's text of 1932, *Der Begriff des Politischen* (Berlin: Duncker & Humblot, 1987), 26–27.—TRANS.

18. A quotation from Ernest Renan, *Qu'est-ce qu'une nation?* 2nd ed. (Paris: Lévy, 1882) (Conférence faite en Sorbonne le 11 mars 1882), 26 f.—TRANS.

19. <See Hermann Heller, *Die Souveränität: Ein Beitrag zur Theorie des Staats- und Völkerrechts*, in *Gesammelte Schriften*, vol. 2, 31, 57 n. 123.>

20. Heller is referring to Schmitt's *Die geistesgeschichtliche Lage des heutigen Parlamentarismus* (first published by Duncker & Humblot, Berlin, 1923), translated by Ellen Kennedy as *The Crisis of Parliamentary Democracy* (Cambridge, Mass.: MIT Press, 1988).—TRANS.

21. See Hermann Heller, *Sozialismus und Nation*, in *Gesammelte Schriften*, vol. 1, sec. 2, pt. 5.

22. Othmar Spann, *Gesellschaftslehre*, 2nd ed. (Leipzig: Quelle Meyer, 1923), 483.

23. Spann, *Gesellschaftslehre*, 483.

24. Max Weber, *Wirtschaft und Gesellschaft*, 2nd ed., vol. 1 (Tübingen: Mohr, 1925), 19.

25. Hermann Heller, "Der Begriff des Gesetzes in der Reichsverfassung," in *Gesammelte Schriften*, 2:210 ff.

26. Carl Schmitt, *Legalität und Legitimität* (Munich and Leipzig: Duncker & Humblot, 1932), 13.

27. Heller, *Die Souveränität*, 69 ff.

28. Kurt Wolzendorff, *Staatsrecht und Naturrecht in der Lehre vom Widerstandsrecht des Volkes gegen rechtswidrige Ausübung der Staatsgewalt: Zugleich ein Beitrag zur Entwicklungsgeschichte des modernen Staatsgedankens* (Breslau: Marcus, 1916).

29. Harold J. Laski, *A Grammar of Politics* (London: Allen & Unwin, 1925), 96.

30. Werner Haensel, *Kants Lehre vom Widerstandsrecht*, Kant-Studien 60 (Berlin: Heise, 1926), 58 ff.

31. Heller, *Die Souveränität*, 123 f., 129 ff.

32. Leonard Trelawney Hobhouse, *Die Metaphysische Staatsidee: Eine Kritik* [*The Metaphysical Theory of the State*, London: Allen & Unwin, 1918—TRANS.] (Leipzig: Meiner, 1924), 91.

33. Carl Schmitt, *Verfassungslehre* (Munich and Leipzig: Duncker & Humblot, 1928), 3.

34. Smend, *Verfassung und Verfassungsrecht*, 78.

35. Hans Kelsen, *Allgemeine Staatslehre*, in Enzyklopädie der Rechts- und Staatswissenschaft 23 (Berlin: Julius Springer, 1925) 249 ff.

36. Immanuel Kant, *Metaphysik der Sitten*, in *Gesammelte Schriften*, ed. Kgl. Preußische Akademie, vol. 6 (Berlin: de Gruyter, 1907), §§ 45 f., p. 312.

37. Heller quotes Ferdinand Lassalle's observation that the written constitution of the modern state collects and determines "in *one* instrument, on *one* piece of paper, all the country's institutions and principles of government": Ferdinand Lassalle, *Über Verfassungswesen* (1862), in *Gesammelte Reden und Schriften*, ed. Eduard Bernstein, vol. 2 (Berlin: Cassirer, 1919), 46.—TRANS.

38. See Heller, "Der Begriff des Gesetzes," 232 f.

39. Schmitt, *Verfassungslehre*, 15.

40. Schmitt, *Verfassungslehre*, 20 ff.

41. Article 144 of the Weimar Constitution.

42. Schmitt, *Verfassungslehre*, 21.

43. Schmitt, *Verfassungslehre*, 21.

44. Schmitt, *Verfassungslehre*, 22.

45. Richard Schmidt, "Die Vorgeschichte der geschriebenen Verfassung," in Richard Schmidt and Erwin Jacobi, *Zwei öffentlich-rechtliche Abhandlungen als Festgabe für Otto Meyer* (Leipzig: Meiner, 1916), 137 ff.

For the term *universitas civium*, see Walter Ullmann's essay, "Personality and Territoriality in the 'Defensor Pacis': The Problem of Political Humanism," in his *Law and Jurisdiction in the Middle Ages* (London: Variorum Reprints, 1988), 397–98.—TRANS.

46. Hermann Heller, *Die politischen Ideenkreise der Gegenwart* (1926), in *Gesammelte Schriften*, 1:294.

47. Heller, *Die politischen Ideenkreise der Gegenwart*, 61.

48. Heller, *Die politischen Ideenkreise der Gegenwart*, 50.

49. Heller, *Die politischen Ideenkreise der Gegenwart*, 63.

50. Heller, *Die politischen Ideenkreise der Gegenwart*, 75.

51. Heller, *Die politischen Ideenkreise der Gegenwart*, 87.

9. CARL SCHMITT

1. See Ellen Kennedy, "Politischer Expressionismus," in *Complexio Oppositorum: Über Carl Schmitt*, ed. Helmut Quaritsch (Berlin: Duncker & Humblot, 1988), 233–51; and Ellen Kennedy, "Carl Schmitt und Hugo Ball," *Zeitschrift für Politik* 35 (1988): 143–61.

2. Carl Schmitt, "Starker Staat und gesunde Wirtschaft" (Keynote Address), in *Mitteilungen des Vereins zur Wahrung der gemeinsamen wirtschaftlichen Interessen in Rheinland und Westfalen*, no. 1 (Düsseldorf: Mathias Strucken, 1932), 13–32 (17).

3. Carl Schmitt, in *Preußen contra Reich vor dem Staatsgerichtshof. Stenogrammbericht der Verhandlungen vor dem Staatsgerichtshof in Leipzig vom 10. bis 14. und vom 17. Oktober 1932* (Berlin: J. H. Dietz Nachf., 1933), 39. See, on the one hand, the statement by Ernst Rudolf Huber in Quaritsch, ed., *Complexio Oppositorum*, 60, and, on the other hand, Ernst Rudolf Huber, *Reichsgewalt und Staatsgerichtshof* (Oldenburg: Gerhard Stalling, 1932), 32, 37, 49, 50.

4. Carl Schmitt, "Der Führer schützt das Recht: Zur Reichstagsrede Adolf Hitlers vom 13. Juli 1934," *Deutsche Juristen-Zeitung* 39 (1934): cols. 954–50.

5. Joseph W. Bendersky, *Carl Schmitt, Theorist for the Reich* (Princeton: Princeton University Press, 1983), 202, 204, 207, 212, 213, 214; George Schwab, "Carl Schmitt Hysteria in the U.S.: The Case of Bill Scheuerman," in *Telos* 91 (spring 1992): 99–107 (103 f.).

6. "Eröffnung der wissenschaftlichen Vorträge durch den Reichsgruppenwalter Staatsrat Professor Dr. Carl Schmitt," in *Das Judentum in der Rechtswissenschaft. Ansprachen, Vorträge und Ergebnisse der Tagung der Reichsgruppe Hochschullehrer des NSRB am 3. und 4. Oktober 1936* (Berlin: Deutscher Rechts Verlag, 1936), 14–17 (15).

7. "Schlußwort des Reichsgruppenwalters Prof. Dr. Carl Schmitt," in *Das Judentum in der Rechtswissenschaft*, 28–34 (33). Schmitt's closing remarks were published in Carl Schmitt, "Die deutsche Rechtswissenschaft im Kampf gegen den jüdischen

Geist: Schlußwort auf der Tagung der Reichsgruppe Hochschullehrer des NSRB vom 3. und 4. Oktober 1936," *Deutsche Juristen-Zeitung* 41 (1936): cols. 1193–99.

8. Bendersky, *Carl Schmitt,* 207. This thesis can be traced back to George Schwab, *The Challenge of the Exception* (Berlin: Duncker & Humblot, 1970), 101.

9. George Schwab, "Carl Schmitt: Political Opportunist?," *Intellect* 103, no. 2363 (February 1975): 334–37 (337); Schwab, *The Challenge of the Exception,* 101 f.

10. Carl Schmitt, *Glossarium: Aufzeichungen der Jahre 1947–1951* (Berlin: Duncker & Humblot, 1991), 18.

11. The transcripts of the interrogations are published in Joseph W. Bendersky, "Carl Schmitt at Nuremberg," in *Telos* 72 (summer 1987): 97–107.

12. See Volker Neumann, *Der Staat im Bürgerkrieg* (Frankfurt and New York: Campus, 1980).

13. Ernst Niekisch, "Zum Begriff des Politischen," *Widerstand* 8 (Berlin: Widerstands Verlag, 1933): 365–71.

14. Hasso Hofmann, *Legitimität gegen Legalität,* 2nd ed. (Berlin: Duncker & Humblot, 1992), xxiiii.

15. Schmitt, *Glossarium,* 165.

16. Carl Schmitt, *Der Wert des Staates und die Bedeutung des Einzelnen* (Tübingen: Mohr, 1914), 93.

17. Carl Schmitt, "Der Bürgerliche Rechtsstaat," in *Abendland* 3 (Cologne, Berlin, and Vienna: Gilde, 1927/28), 201–203 (202).

18. Schmitt, "Der Bürgerliche Rechtsstaat," 202.

19. Carl Schmitt, *Volksentscheid und Volksbegehren. Ein Beitrag zur Auslegung der Weimarer Verfassung und zur Lehre von der unmittelbaren Demokratie* (Berlin and Leipzig: de Gruyter, 1927), 34.

20. Carl Schmitt, "Der Status quo und der Friede," in *Hochland* 23, no. 1 (Kempten and Munich: Jos. Kösel'sche Buchhandlung, October 1925), 1–9 (9).

21. Ilse Staff, *Staatsdenken im Italien des 20. Jahrhunderts* (Baden-Baden: Nomos Verlagsgesellschaft, 1991); Alessandro Campi, "Sulla fortuna italiana di Carl Schmitt: Una Bibliografia 1924–1984," in *La Nottola,* anno III, no. 3 (Roma: Libreria Herder, 1984), 55–78; *Carl Schmitt nella Stampa Periodica Italiana* (1973–1986), ed. Centro Documentazione (Naples, 1986); see discussion by Michele Nicoletti in *Telos* 72 (summer 1987): 217–24.

22. Jose Maria Beneyto, *Politische Theologie als politische Theorie* (Berlin: Duncker & Humblot, 1983); Günter Maschke, *Der Tod des Carl Schmitt* (Vienna: Karolinger Verlag, 1987), 79–82.

23. On France: Manfred Baldus, "Carl Schmitt im Hexagon," in *Der Staat* 26 (1987): 566–86. On Japan: Masanori Shiyake, "Zur Lage der Carl Schmitt-Forschung in Japan," in Quaritsch, ed., *Complexio Oppositorum,* 491–502. On Korea: Bongkun Kal, "Carl Schmitts Einfluß auf das koreanische Verfassungsleben," in Quaritsch, ed., *Complexio Oppositorum,* 503–507.

24. Carl Schmitt, *The Concept of the Political,* trans. George Schwab (New Brunswick, N.J.: Rutgers University Press, 1976); Carl Schmitt, *Political Theology,* trans. George Schwab (Cambridge, Mass.: MIT Press, 1985); Carl Schmitt, *The Crisis of Parliamentary Democracy,* trans. Ellen Kennedy (Cambridge, Mass.: MIT Press, 1985); Carl Schmitt, *Political Romanticism,* trans. Guy Oakes (Cambridge, Mass.: MIT Press, 1986). On the translations that appeared in 1985 and 1986, see the discussion by

John Samples and Henry Grosshans in *Telos* 72 (summer 1987): 205–14 and 214–17. See also Carl Schmitt, "The Legal World Revolution," trans. Gary L. Ulmen, *Telos* 72 (summer 1987): 73–89; Carl Schmitt, "The Plight of European Jurisprudence," trans. Gary L. Ulmen, *Telos* 83 (spring 1990): 35–70; on this last work, see Paul Piccone and Gary L. Ulmen, "Schmitt's 'Testament' and the Future of Europe," *Telos* 83 (spring 1990): 3–34.

25. On the history of its reception, see Joseph W. Bendersky, "Carl Schmitt Confronts the English-Speaking World," *Canadian Journal of Political and Social Theory* 2, no. 3 (fall 1978): 125–35; Helmut Rumpf, "Neues westliches Echo auf Carl Schmitt," *Der Staat* 22 (1983): 281–393; George Schwab, "Progress of Schmitt Studies in the English-Speaking World," in Quaritsch, ed., *Complexio Oppositorum,* 447–59. A pointed critique of this reception ("It is difficult to discern the outlines of an independent reception of Schmitt") can be found in Dieter Haselbach, "Die Wandlung zum Liberalen," in *Carl Schmitt und die Liberalismuskritik,* ed. Klaus Hansen and Hans Lietzmann (Opladen: Leske & Budrich, 1988), 119–40. Bill Scheuerman is clearer in "Carl Schmitt and the Nazis," *German Politics and Society* 23 (summer 1991): 71–79. The dispute over Schmitt's reception is also documented in *Telos:* Jeffrey Hart, Paul Piccone, and G. L. Ulmen, "Reading and Misreading Schmitt," in *Telos* 74 (winter 1987–88): 133–40, and "Schmitt's Testament and the Future of Europe," *Telos* 85 (fall 1990): 93–148. Most recently: Manfred H. Wiegandt, "The Alleged Unaccountability of the Academic: A Biographical Sketch of Carl Schmitt," *Cardozo Law Review* 16 (1995): 1569–98.

26. The subject of the Kennedy-Habermas debate was Schmitt's influence on the authors of the Frankfurt School: Ellen Kennedy, "Carl Schmitt and the Frankfurt School," *Telos* 71 (spring 1987): 37–66, and the response: Martin Jay, "Reconciling the Irreconcilable?" *Telos* 71 (spring 1987): 67–80; Alfons Söllner, "Beyond Carl Schmitt," *Telos* 71 (spring 1987): 81–96; Ulrich K. Preuss, "The Critique of German Liberalism," *Telos* 71 (spring 1987): 97–109; Ellen Kennedy, "Carl Schmitt and the Frankfurt School," *Telos* 73 (fall 1987): 101–16. These pieces were published simultaneously in German in *Geschichte und Gesellschaft* 12 (Göttingen: Vandenhoek & Ruprecht, 1987) and 13 (1988)—with the exception of Kennedy's informed rejoinder! On this debate, see also Jürgen Habermas, "Der Schrecken der Autonomie," in Jürgen Habermas, *Eine Art Schadensabwicklung* (Frankfurt am Main: Suhrkamp, 1987), 103–14; Peter Haungs, "Diesseits oder jenseits von Carl Schmitt?" in *Festschrift für Wilhelm Hennis,* ed. Hans Meier (Stuttgart: Klett-Cotta, 1988), 526–44; William E. Scheuerman, *Between the Norm and the Exception* (Cambridge, Mass.: MIT Press, 1994).

27. Ernst Fraenkel, "Verfassungsreform und Sozialdemokratie," in *Die Gesellschaft* 2 (1932), 486–500, reprinted in Ernst Fraenkel, *Zur Soziologie der Klassenjustiz und Aufsätze zur Verfassungskrise 1931–32* (Darmstadt: Wissenschaftliche Buchgesellschaft, 1968), 89–103 (97). Requiring a vote of no-confidence to be constructive is different from ignoring votes of no-confidence that are merely destructive. See Carl Schmitt, *Verfassungslehre* (Munich and Leipzig: Duncker & Humblot, 1928), 345. Unclear on this point: Lutz Berthold, "Das konstruktive Mißtrauensvotum und seine Ursprünge in der Weimarer Staatsrechtslehre," *Der Staat* 35 (Berlin: Duncker & Humblot, 1997), 81–94 (86).

28. Richard Thoma, *Über Wesen und Erscheinungsformen der modernen Demokratie* (Bonn: Ferdinand Dümmlers Verlag, 1948), 40.

29. Horst Meier, *Parteiverbote und demokratische Republik* (Baden-Baden: Nomos Verlagsgesellschaft, 1993), with extremely interesting remarks at pp. 375–84 on the work of Schmitt's student Johanna Kendziora, *Der Begriff der politischen Partei im System des politischen Liberalismus* (Berlin: Handelshochschule, 1935).

30. Carl Schmitt, *Verfassungsrechtliche Aufsätze aus den Jahren 1924–1954* (Berlin: Duncker & Humblot, 1958), 8 (foreword).

31. The concept comes from Bernhard Willms, "Carl Schmitt–Jüngster Klassiker des politischen Denkens?" in Quaritsch, ed., *Complexio Oppositorum,* 577–97. The question whether it has the characteristics of a classic may be answered in the century after next.

32. Wolfgang Palaver, "A Girardian Reading of Schmitt's Political Theology," *Telos* 93 (fall 1992): 43–68.

33. Bernhard Schlink, "Why Carl Schmitt?" in *Rechtshistorisches Journal* 10 (Frankfurt am Main: Löwenklau Gesellschaft, 1991), 160–76, reprinted in *Constellations* 2 (1996): 429.

34. Schmitt, *Glossarium,* 151.

35. Günter Maschke, "Zum 'Leviathan' Carl Schmitts," in Carl Schmitt, *Der Leviathan in der Staatslehre des Thomas Hobbes: Sinn und Fehlschlag eines politischen Symbols* (Cologne: Hohenhein, 1982), 179–244 (209). On Schmitt's alleged "anti-Judaism," see also Andreas Koenen, *Der Fall Carl Schmitt: Sein Aufstieg zum "Kronjuristen des Dritten Reiches"* (Darmstadt: Wissenschaftliche Buchgesellschaft, 1995), 313–18, 710–13.

36. Maschke, "Zum 'Leviathan' Carl Schmitts," 208.

37. Armin Mohler, "Links-Schmittisten, Rechts-Schmittisten und Establishment-Schmittisten," *Criticon* 98 (1986): 265 ff. (266).

38. Helmut Ridder, "Eppirrhosis? Carl Schmitt und ein Ende," in *Neue Politische Literatur* 16 (1971): 317.

EPILOGUE

1. A rudimentary typology of scholars is provided in Diemut Mayer, *Grundlagen des nationalsozialistischen Rechtssystems* (Stuttgart: Kohlhammer, 1987).

2. See the essays in Helmut Heinrichs et al., eds., *Deutsche Juristen jüdischer Herkunft* (Munich: Beck, 1993); data also in Michael Stolleis, ed., *Juristen: Ein biographisches Lexikon* (Munich: Beck, 1995); brief portraits in *Streitbare Juristen: Eine andere Tradition, Festschrift für Jürgen Seifert zum 60. Geburtstag,* ed. Kritische Justiz (Baden-Baden: Nomos Verlagsgesellschaft, 1988).

3. In addition to those mentioned, see Erik Wolf, *Richtiges Recht im nationalsozialistischen Staat* (Freiburg: Wagner, 1934); Ulrich Scheuner, "Die nationale Revolution: Eine staatsrechtliche Untersuchung," in *Archiv des öffentlichen Rechts,* vol. 24 (Tübingen: Mohr, 1934), 166–220, 261–344; for his later distinction between Italian fascism and National Socialism, see Ulrich Scheuner, "Staatstheorie und Verfassungsrecht des Faschismus," *Zeitschrift für die gesamten Staatswissenschaften* 101 (1941): 252–86.

4. For an unannotated collection of law texts, see Ernst Forsthoff, ed., *Öffentliches Recht* (Hamburg: Hanseatische Verlagsanstalt, 1935), 17 ff.

5. See Norbert Frei, *Der Führerstaat. Nationalsozialistische Herrschaft von 1933 bis 1945* (Munich: Beck, 1987).

6. Ernst Forsthoff, *Recht und Sprache. Prolegomena zu einer richterlichen Hermaneutik* (Halle: M. Niemeyer, 1940); Carl Schmitt, *Land und Meer: Eine weltgeschichtliche Betrachtung* (Leipzig: Reclam, 1942); Theodor Maunz, *Das Reich der spanischen Großmachtzeit* (Hamburg: Hanseatische Verlagsanstalt, 1944).

7. Ernst Fraenkel, *The Dual State* (New York: Oxford University Press, 1941); Franz Neumann, *Behemoth: The Structure and Practice of National Socialism* (New York: Oxford University Press, 1942).

8. Andreas Koenen, *Der Fall Carl Schmitts: Sein Aufstieg zum Kronjuristen des "Dritten Reiches"* (Darmstadt: Wissenschaftliche Buchgesellschaft, 1995); see also Reinhard Mehring, *Carl Schmitt zur Einführung* (Hamburg: Junius, 1992).

9. Carl Schmitt, *Staat, Bewegung, Volk* (Hamburg: Hanseatische Verlagsanstalt, 1933); Carl Schmitt, *Staatsgefüge und Zusammenbruch des Zweiten Reiches* (Hamburg: Hanseatische Verlagsanstalt, 1934); Carl Schmitt, *Nationalsozialismus und Völkerrecht* (Berlin: Junker & Dünnhaupt, 1934); Carl Schmitt, *Über die drei Arten des rechtswissenschaftlichen Denkens* (Hamburg: Hanseatische Verlagsanstalt, 1934).

10. The great importance of methodology for the *Gleichschaltung* of legal scholarship and the judiciary is shown in Bernd Rüthers, *Die unbegrenzte Auslegung: Zum Wandel der Privatrechtsordnung im Nationalsozialismus,* 3rd ed. (Münster: Juristischer Verlag, 1988); Bernd Rüthers, *Entartetes Recht: Rechtslehren und Kronjuristen im Dritten Reich* (Munich: Beck, 1988).

11. Carl Schmitt, *Der Leviathan in der Staatslehre des Thomas Hobbes* (Hamburg: Hanseatische Verlagsanstalt, 1938).

12. Carl Schmitt, *Völkerrechtliche Großraumordnung* (Berlin: Deutscher Rechtsverlag, 1st ed.1939, 2nd ed. 1940, 3rd ed. 1941 [*Um ein Kapitel über Reich und Raum und mehrere Zusätz erweiterte Ausgabe*], 4th ed. 1941 [*Um ein Kapitel über den Raumbegriff in der Rechtswissenschaft erweiterte Ausgabe*]); on this book, see Lothar Gruchmann, *Nationalsozialistische Großraumordnung* (Stuttgart: Deutsche Verlagsanstalt, 1962).

13. Carl Schmitt, *Politische Theologie* (Munich and Leipzig: Duncker & Humblot, 1922); Carl Schmitt, *Die geistesgeschichtliche Lage des heutigen Parlamentarismus* (Munich and Leipzig: Duncker & Humblot, 1923); Carl Schmitt, *Der Begriff des Politischen* (Berlin: Walther Rothschild, 1928).

14. Michael Stolleis, *Recht im Unrecht. Studien zur Rechtsgeschichte des Nationalsozialismus* (Frankfurt: Suhrkamp, 1994), 136; see also Michael Stolleis, *Geschichte des öffentlichen Rechts in Deutschland,* vols. 1 and 2 (Munich: Beck, 1988–92).

15. Ernst Forsthoff, *Der Totale Staat* (Hamburg: Hanseatische Verlagsanstalt, 1933).

16. Ernst Forsthoff, *Die Verwaltung als Leistungsträger* (Stuttgart: Kohlhammer, 1938); see also Ernst Forsthoff, "Das neue Gesicht der Verwaltung und Verwaltungsrechtswissenschaft," *Deutsches Recht* 5 (1935): 331–33; Ernst Forsthoff, "Von den Aufgaben der Verwaltungsrechtswissenschaft," *Deutsches Recht* 5 (1935): 398–400.

17. Carl Schmitt, *Der Hüter der Verfassung* (Tübingen: Mohr, 1931).

18. Ernst Forsthoff, *Lehrbuch des Verwaltungsrechts* (Munich: Beck, 1950); Ernst Forsthoff, *Der Staat der Industriegesellschaft: Dargestellt am Beispiel der Bundesrepublik*

(Munich: Beck, 1971); Ernst Forsthoff, *Rechtsstaat im Wandel: Verfassungsrechtliche Abhandlungen 1954–1973,* 2nd ed. (Munich: Beck, 1976).

19. Arnold Gehlen, *Der Mensch: Seine Natur und seine Stellung in der Welt* (Bonn: Athenäum, 1940); Arnold Gehlen, *Urmensch und Spätkultur* (Bonn: Athenäum, 1956).

20. Theodor Maunz, *Neue Grundlagen des Verwaltungsrechts* (Hamburg: Hanseatische Verlagsanstalt, 1934); Theodor Maunz, *Verwaltung* (Hamburg: Hanseatische Verlagsanstalt, 1937).

21. Theodor Maunz, *Gestalt und Recht der Polizei* (Hamburg: Hanseatische Verlagsanstalt, 1943).

22. See Hans Maier, *Die ältere deutsche Staats- und Verwaltungslehre* (Neuwied: Luchterhand, 1966).

23. Reinhard Höhn, *Der bürgerliche Rechtsstaat und die neue Front* (Berlin: de Gruyter, 1929).

24. Reinhard Höhn, *Die Wandlung im staatsrechtlichen Denken* (Hamburg: Hanseatische Verlagsanstalt, 1934); Reinhard Höhn, *Der individualistische Staatsbegriff und die juristische Staatsperson* (Berlin: Heymann, 1935); Reinhard Höhn, *Otto von Gierke's Staatslehre und unsere Zeit* (Hamburg: Hanseatische Verlagsanstalt, 1936).

25. Reinhard Höhn, *Rechtsgemeinschaft und Volksgemeinschaft* (Hamburg: Hanseatische Verlagsanstalt, 1935); see also Reinhard Höhn, "Gemeinschaft als Rechtsprinzip," *Deutsches Recht* 4 (1934): 301–302; Reinhard Höhn, "Volk, Staat und Recht," in Reinhard Höhn, ed., *Grundfragen der Rechtsauffassung* (Munich: Duncker & Humblot, 1938), 3–27.

26. Reinhard Höhn, *Reich, Großraum, Großmacht* (Darmstadt: Wittich, 1942); see also Ulrich Herbert Best, *Biographische Stiudien über Radikalismus, Weltanschauung und Vernunft 1903–1989* (Bonn: Dietz, 1996), 271.

27. Ernst Rudolf Huber, *Verfassung* (Hamburg: Hanseatische Verlagsanstalt, 1938); see Ernst Rudolf Huber, *Vom Sinn der Verfassung* (Hamburg: Hanseatische Verlagsanstalt, 1935); Ernst Rudolf Huber, *Wesen und Inhalt der politischen Verfassung* (Hamburg: Hanseatische Verlagsanstalt, 1935); Ernst Rudolf Huber, "Die deutsche Staatswissenschaft," *Zeitschrift für die gesamten Staatswissenschaften* 95 (1935): 1–65.

28. Ernst Rudolf Huber, *Heer und Staat in der deutschen Geschichte* (Hamburg: Hanseatische Verlagsanstalt, 1938); see also Carl Schmitt, *Staatsgefüge und Zusammenbruch des Zweiten Reiches* (Hamburg: Hanseatische Verlagsanstalt, 1934); Reinhard Höhn, *Verfassungskampf und Heereseid: Der Kampf des Bürgertums um das Heer (1815–1850)* (Leipzig: Hirzel, 1938).

29. Ernst Rudolf Huber, *Nationalstaat und Verfassungsstaat* (Stuttgart: Kohlhammer, 1965), 274.

30. Ernst Rudolf Huber, *Deutsche Verfassungsgeschichte seit 1789,* 8 vols. (Stuttgart: Kohlhammer, 1958–90).

EDITORS AND CONTRIBUTORS

EDITORS

ARTHUR J. JACOBSON is the Max Freund Professor of Litigation and Advocacy at the Benjamin N. Cardozo School of Law, Yeshiva University, New York. His work in legal theory focuses on the dynamic aspects of jurisprudence. He has edited and written *Justice and the Legal System: A Coursebook* with Anthony D'Amato, and is Supplement Editor for *Corbin on Contracts* with Lawrence A. Cunningham. He edits *State Limited Partnership Laws* and *State Limited Liability Company and Partnership Laws* with Michael Bamberger.

BERNHARD SCHLINK is professor of public law and legal philosophy at the Humboldt University in Berlin. He is the author of *Abwägung im Verfassungsrecht* and *Die Amtshilfe. Ein Beitrag zu einer Lehre von der Gewaltenteilung in der Verwaltung.* Together with Bodo Piroth, he is the author of the *Grundrechte. Staatsrecht II.* He is a justice of the Constitutional Court for the State of North-Rhine-Westphalia, in Münster.

CONTRIBUTORS

PETER C. CALDWELL is assistant professor of history at Rice University, Houston. He is the author of *Theory and Practice of the Weimar Constitution* and has edited *From Liberal Democracy to Fascism: Political and Legal Thought in the Weimar Republic,* with William Scheuerman.

STEPHEN CLOYD holds a Ph.D. in history from the University of Rochester. His dissertation is titled *Weimar Republicanism: Political Sociology and Constitutional Law in Weimar Germany 1919–1933.*

BELINDA COOPER is senior fellow at the World Policy Institute of the New School for Social Research. She has edited *War Crimes: The Legacy of Nuremberg* and an issue of the *Cardozo Women's Law Journal* devoted to *Women and Law in Germany Since Unification.*

DAVID DYZENHAUS is associate professor of law and philosophy at the University of Toronto. His *Hard Cases in Wicked Legal Systems* is a study of the Apartheid legal system in South Africa. He has also published *Truth's Revenge: Carl Schmitt, Hans Kelsen, and Hermann Heller in Weimar.* He has edited and written, with Arthur Ripstein, *Morality and the Law: Readings in the Philosophy of Law.*

STEPHAN HEMETSBERGER is assistant professor of public law at the University of Vienna and Secretary at the Austrian Administrative Court.

CLEMENS JABLONER is president of the Austrian Administrative Court and director of the Hans-Kelsen Institute.

STEFAN KORIOTH is professor of constitutional law, history of the constitution, and general theory of the state at Ernst-Moritz-Arndt-University in Greifswald.

REINHARD MEHRING is a research associate [*wissenschaftlicher Mitarbeiter*] at the Institut für Philosophie at Humboldt University in Berlin. He is the author of *Pathetisches Denken: Carl Schmitts Denkweg* and *Carl Schmitt zur Einführung.* He has also written *Heideggers Überlieferungsgeschick* and *Aufsätze zu Carl Schmitt und zum neueren politischen Denken in Deutschland.*

VOLKER NEUMANN is professor of public and social law at the University of Rostock. He is the author of *Der Staat im Bürgerkrieg: Kontinuität und Wandlung des Staatsbegriffs in der politischen Theorie Carl Schmitts* and *Freiheitsgefährdung im kooperativen Sozialstaat.*

WALTER PAULY is professor of public law, legal and constitutional history, and philosophy of law at the Friedrich-Schiller University in Jena. He is the author of *Anfechtbarkeit und Verbindlichkeit von Weisungen in der Bundesauftragsverwaltung* and *Der Methodenwandel im deutschen Spätkonstitutionalismus.*

RALF POSCHER is a research associate in the Institute for Public Law and National Law at Humboldt University in Berlin.

CHRISTOPH SCHOENBERGER was visiting professor at the Benjamin N. Cardozo School of Law, Yeshiva University, New York, in 1992–93, and has taught law at Humboldt University since. He is the author of *Das Parlament im Anstaltsstaat: Zur Theorie parlamentarischer Repräsentation in der Staatsrechtslehre des Kaiserreichs (1871–1918).*

COPYRIGHT ACKNOWLEDGMENTS

393

Designer:	Nicole Hayward
Compositor:	G&S Typesetters
Text:	10/12 New Baskerville
Display:	New Baskerville
Printer and Binder:	Thomson-Shore, Inc.